Lecture Notes in Computer Science 9254

Commenced Publication in 1973
Founding and Former Series Editors:
Gerhard Goos, Juris Hartmanis, and Jan van Leeuwen

More information about this series at http://www.springer.com/series/7412

Lucio Tommaso De Paolis · Antonio Mongelli (Eds.)

Augmented and Virtual Reality

Second International Conference, AVR 2015
Lecce, Italy, August 31 – September 3, 2015
Proceedings

Springer

Editors
Lucio Tommaso De Paolis
Department of Engineering for Innovation
University of Salento
Lecce
Italy

Antonio Mongelli
Department of Engineering for Innovation
University of Salento
Lecce
Italy

ISSN 0302-9743 ISSN 1611-3349 (electronic)
Lecture Notes in Computer Science
ISBN 978-3-319-22887-7 ISBN 978-3-319-22888-4 (eBook)
DOI 10.1007/978-3-319-22888-4

Library of Congress Control Number: 2015946104

LNCS Sublibrary: SL6 – Image Processing, Computer Vision, Pattern Recognition, and Graphics

Springer Cham Heidelberg New York Dordrecht London

Printed on acid-free paper

Springer International Publishing AG Switzerland is part of Springer Science+Business Media
(www.springer.com)

Preface

This book contains the contributions to the Second International Conference on Augmented and Virtual Reality (SALENTO AVR 2015) that has held in Lecce (Italy) from August 31 to September 3, 2015. We cordially invite you to visit the SALENTO AVR website http://www.salentoavr.it where you can find all relevant information about this event.

The aim of SALENTO AVR 2015 was to bring a community of researchers from academia and industry, computer scientists, engineers, and physicians together in order to share points of views, knowledge, experiences, and scientific and technical results related to state-of-the-art solutions and technologies on virtual and augmented reality applications for medicine, cultural heritage, education, industrial sectors, as well as the demonstration of advanced products and technologies.

This edition of SALENTO AVR ranged over topics from virtual/augmented/mixed reality to 3D user interfaces and the technologies needed to develop applications in many areas such as medicine, entertainment, arts and cultural heritage, the military field, industry, and maintenance. These topics were addressed in paper sessions, demos, and poster sessions.

In this edition of SALENTO AVR, we were honored to have the following invited speakers:

- Monica Bordegoni, full Professor at the Department of Mechanical Engineering, School of Design of the Politecnico di Milano, Italy
- Patrick Bourdot, Research Director at the CNRS/LIMSI, Paris-Sud University, France
- Stéphane Cotin, Research Director at the Inria, France
- Fabrizio Funtò, Hyperreality Partner, Los Angeles, CA, USA
- Luigi Gallo, Research Scientist at the National Research Council of Italy (CNR), Institute for High-Performance Computing and Networking (ICAR), Italy
- Sofia Pescarin, Researcher at the Institute of Technologies applied to Cultural Heritage, National Research Council (CNR ITABC), Italy

We are very grateful to the Program Committee and local Organizing Committee members for their support and for the time spent to review and discuss the submitted papers and doing so in a timely and professional manner.

We would like to sincerely thank the keynote and tutorial speakers who willingly accepted our invitation and shared their expertise through illuminating talks, helping us to fully meet the conference objectives.

We extend our thanks to the University of Salento for the enthusiastic acceptance to host the conference and the sponsors for providing support in the organization of the event.

Last but not least, we would like to thank all authors for submitting their papers and presenting their works at the conference and all the conference attendees for making

SALENTO AVR an excellent forum on virtual and augmented reality, facilitating the exchange of ideas, fostering new collaborations, and shaping the future of this exciting research field.

For greater readability of the volume, the presented paper are classified into seven main parts that include contributions on:

- Applications in Cultural Heritage
- Augmented and Mixed Reality
- Applications in Medicine
- Applications in Industry
- Interfaces
- Short Papers

We hope the readers will find in these pages interesting material and fruitful ideas for their future work.

September 2015
Lucio Tommaso De Paolis
Antonio Mongelli

Organization

Conference Chair

Lucio Tommaso De Paolis   University of Salento, Italy

Conference Co-chair

Patrick Bourdot   CNRS/LIMSI, Paris-Sud University, France

Honorary Chair

Giovanni Aloisio   University of Salento, Italy

Scientific Program Committee

Andrea Abate   University of Salerno, Italy
Fernando Arambula Cosio   Universidad Nacional Autónoma de México, Mexico
Carlo Alberto Avizzano   Scuola Superiore Sant'Anna, Italy
Roland Blach   Fraunhofer IAO, Germany
Selim Balcisoy   Sabancı University, Turkey
Monica Bordegoni   Politecnico di Milano, Italy
Davide Borra   NoReal.it, Turin, Italy
Pierre Boulanger   University of Alberta, Canada
Massimo Cafaro   University of Salento, Italy
Sergio Casciaro   IFC-CNR, Italy
Bruno Carpentieri   University of Salento, Italy
Marcello Carrozzino   Scuola Superiore Sant'Anna, Italy
Mario Ciampi   ICAR/CNR, Italy
Pietro Cipresso   IRCCS Istituto Auxologico Italiano, Italy
Lucio Colizzi   CETMA, Italy
Jean-Marc Cieutat   ESTIA Recherche, France
Mirabelle D'Cruz   University of Nottingham, UK
Yuri Dekhtyar   Riga Technical University, Latvia
Alessandro De Mauro   KU Leuven, Belgium
Giorgio De Nunzio   University of Salento, Italy
Aldo Franco Dragoni   Università Politecnica delle Marche, Italy
Themis Exarchos   University of Ioannina, Greece
Dimitrios Fotiadis   University of Ioannina, Greece
Francesco Gabellone   IBAM ITLab, CNR, Italy
Jaume Segura Garcia   Universitat de València, Spain
Osvaldo Gervasi   University of Perugia, Italy

Luigi Gallo	ICAR/CNR, Italy
Viktors Gopejenko	Information Systems Management Institute (ISMA), Latvia
Mirko Grimaldi	CRIL, University of Salento, Italy
Heiko Herrmann	Tallinn University of Technology, Estonia
Tomas Krilavičius	Vytautas Magnus University, Kaunas, Lithuania
Torsten Kuhlen	Aachen University, Germany
Salvatore Livatino	University of Hertfordshire, UK
Luca Mainetti	University of Salento, Italy
Andrea Martini	CETMA, Italy
Daniel R. Mestre	Aix-Marseille University/CNRS, France
Andrés Navarro	VICOMTech, Spain
Roberto Paiano	University of Salento, Italy
Giorgos Papadourakis	Technological Educational Institute (TEI) of Crete, Greece
Sofia Pescarin	CNR ITABC, Italy
Paolo Proietti	MIMOS, Italy
James Ritchie	Heriot-Watt University, Edinburgh, UK
Robert Stone	University of Birmingham, UK
Franco Tecchia	Scuola Superiore Sant'Anna, Italy
Carlos M. Travieso–González	Universidad de Las Palmas de Gran Canaria, Spain
Manolis Tsiknaki	Technological Educational Institute of Crete (TEI), Greece
Krzysztof Walczak	Poznan University, Poland

Local Organizing Committee

Antonio Mongelli	University of Salento, Italy
Ilenia Paladini	University of Salento, Italy

Tutorials

Research, Prototyping, and Product Development of Medical Simulation Applications Using the SOFA Framework

Stéphane Cotin

Inria, France

Stephane Cotin joined Inria in 2007 as Research Director. Since January 2010, he has lead the SHACRA group, a multidisciplinary team of scientists involved in the field on medical simulation. Stephane also manages the development of a large-scale initiative on medical simulation.

Stephane is a senior research scientist with experience in biomechanical modeling, real-time simulation, and physics-based modeling. He is specialized in medical applications, from training to planning of complex medical procedures, and manages several projects and teams.

Stephane is currently responsible for the development of a national initiative on medical simulation using the SOFA framework as a common platform for research, integration, and validation of new algorithms.

From 1999 to 2007, Stephane was the research lead for the Sim Group at CIMIT in Boston where he was responsible for defining research directions and technical infrastructures for several simulation projects, including a chest trauma training system, a computer-enhanced laparoscopic training system, and an interventional radiology training system.

Cultural Heritage Innovation Design:
What Caught My Eye

Fabrizio Funtò

Hyperreality Partner, Los Angeles, CA, USA

Fabrizio Funtò received the Italian "Laurea" in Philosophy of Language in 1984. After some collaborations with Enidata as teacher of Network Technologies and C Language programming, he joined Infobyte Spa as Programmers Team Leader, and after a couple of year as Managing Director. During his appointment, Infobyte has produced 30+ interactive CD-ROM titles and probably the most famous virtual reality attractions ever published in that pioneer age.

Fabrizio won the Perseo d'Oro (Mediartech, Florence, 1996) in the category of Best Interactive CD ("Galleria Giulia") and, together with Silicon Graphic, the TiLE Award 1997 with "In Searching for the Holy Grail" – first ever multiplayer real-time virtual reality game. He then created the first virtual set for the Italian State Broadcast company (RAI) for two programs, Mixer and SuperQuark.

In 1998 he teamed up with ACS Studio, continuing to produce worldwide level virtual reality titles like The Nero's Domus Aurea, The Mistery City, The Rollercoaster for "The Tech Museum" in San Jose (CA), and some experiences for ESA (EU Space Agency).

In the 2000 he founded a new company, Softdesign, in partnership with Harold Production, and followed two different production directions: real-time attractions for videogames and virtual reality immersive experiences and 3D off-line animations and visual effects.

He was also involved in the launch of the Virtuality Conference (2000–2004, now View Conference) as Artistic Director, and he was asked by the most famous Italian encyclopedia, the "*Treccani*" to edit the entries for visual effects.

After some productions for the Rome Film Fest and participation in an international project for distributing digital movies through satellites (ISIDE for the European Space Agency) as Digital Pictures, he became R&D consultant for Advanced Projects in Activision Blizzard, the USA giant videogames corporate of Vivendi/Universal Group.

He is now involved in the design of large cultural heritage attractions.

Keynote Speakers

Virtual Museums Interacting and Augmenting Cultural Heritage: a European Perspective

Sofia Pescarin

CNR ITABC, Italy

Sofia Pescarin, Archaeologist, Degree in Topography of Ancient Italy, PhD in History and Computing, Master in "Technology of Museums," is a specialist in 3D survey, GIS, landscape reconstruction, virtual museums, as well as Open Source applied to cultural heritage and virtual archaeology.

She works as a researcher at the Institute of Technologies Applied to Cultural Heritage of the National Council of Researches in Rome (CNR ITABC), in the Virtual Heritage Lab. Here she coordinates a research project dedicated to "Virtual Heritage" and was the project coordinator of V-MUST.NET, FP7 ICT Network of Excellence, focused on virtual museums (2011–2015).

She is the chair of the Italian School of Virtual Archaeology (www.archeologiavirtuale.it) and the scientific director of Archeovirtual (www.archeovirtual.it). She was the co-chair of the Digital Heritage 2013 international congress (Marseille, October 28 to November 1, 2013) and of the international school "drones in archaeology and cultural heritage" (Certosa di Pontignano, September 17–27, 2013).

Within V-MUST, she has recently coordinated the exhibition "Keys to Rome" in four museums and co-directed the Italian chapter of the exhibition: "Le chiavi di Roma. La città di Augusto" (Museo dei Fori Imperiali, September 23, 2014, to May 10, 2015).

How Touch and Smell Enhance the Realism of Our Virtual Experiences

Monica Bordegoni

Politecnico di Milano, Italy

Virtual reality experiences are based on an integration of immersion, interaction, and imagination. Users experience the virtual world through their senses, which in most applications are vision and hearing. Technological developments are proposing new devices that can also simulate signals eliciting the sense of touch and smell, which can be integrated with vision and sounds. Specifically, haptics and olfactory displays can be integrated with head-mounted displays and headsets to allow users to live more engaging multisensory experiences, where immersion, interaction, and imagination reach higher levels and are more engaging.

Monica Bordegoni is Full Professor at the Department of Mechanical Engineering, School of Design, at Politecnico di Milano. She teaches Virtual Prototyping at the School of Design and at the School of Industrial Engineering, and is coordinator of the Virtual Prototyping Lab.

Her research interest includes interactive virtual prototyping, virtual/augmented technology for industrial applications, haptic technology and haptic interaction, product experience, and emotional engineering. She is a member of the executive committee board of ASME Society – Computers and Information in Engineering, and co-chair of the Design Society SIG on Emotional Engineering.

Touchless Interaction in Surgery: The Medical Imaging Toolkit Experience

Luigi Gallo

Institute for High Performance Computing and Networking (ICAR-CNR), Italy

During the last few years, we have been witnessing a widespread interest on touchless technologies in the context of surgical procedures. The main reason is that surgeons often need to visualize medical images in operating rooms, but checking a computer through keyboard or mouse would result in bacterial contamination. Touchless interfaces that exploit sensor technologies and machine learning techniques for tracking and analyzing body movements are advantageous in that they can preserve a sterile environment around the patient. In fact, they allow surgeons to visualize medical images without having to physically touch any control or to rely on a proxy, who may not share the same level of professional vision. This talk aims to explore the main issues involved with the design of touchless user interfaces for intraoperative image control. It will overview state-of-the-art solutions, open challenges, and research agendas in this area. Moreover, the talk will present the results of the Medical Imaging Toolkit (MITO) project, which is focused on the design and implementation of a Kinect-based touchless user interface for pre- and intraoperative visualization of DICOM images.

Luigi Gallo received an MEng in Computer Engineering from the University of Naples "Federico II" in July 2006 and a PhD degree in Information Technology Engineering at the University of Naples "Parthenope" in April 2010. He is a research scientist at the National Research Council of Italy (CNR) – Institute for High-Performance Computing and Networking (ICAR), and a lecturer of informatics at the University of Naples "Federico II".

Since January 2011, he has been a member of the iHealthLab – Intelligent Healthcare Laboratory. Since June 2007, he has been a member of the Advanced Medical Imaging and Computing Laboratory (AMICO), developed from a cooperation agreement between the IBB and ICAR institutes of the National Research Council of Italy.

His fields of interest include natural user interfaces and human interface aspects of virtual/augmented reality, specifically considering medical application scenarios.

Collaborative Interactions Within Immersive Environments: Advantages, Drawbacks and Current Research Issues on Multi-Stereoscopic CAVE-Like Setups

Patrick Bourdot

CNRS/LIMSI, Paris-Sud University, France

Collaborative immersive interactions are possible through many technological systems. CAVE-like systems, even if they generally do not provide stereoscopy for several users, are a powerful type of virtual environment with which to address collaborative tasks, because collaborators are not virtualized and thus collective interactions are more natural. Conversely, interconnected HMDs or interconnected one-user CAVEs can provide an exact 3D perception for each user, at the expense of physical coexistence and rich social interactions. In the last ten years, multi-stereoscopic technology has achieved significant progress, enabling a new generation of CAVE-like systems where collaborators may share the same physical space while each having exact 3D perception on the virtual world. Thus it is now possible to preserve a natural dialogue with other collaborators inside a CAVE, while providing at the same time a better immersive experience for each of them. However, some perceptive and cognitive issues remain regarding such collaborative immersive systems. This talk will demonstrate when they occur, and will present some research in progress to analyze and overcome these issues.

Patrick Bourdot is Research Director at CNRS and head of VENISE team (http://www.limsi.fr/venise), the virtual & augmented reality (V&AR) research group he has created in 2001 at CNRS/LIMSI Lab.

Patrick graduated as an architect in 1986, he received his PhD in Computer Sciences at the University of Aix-Marseille in 1992, and joined the CNRS/LIMSI lab in 1993. His main research focus includes multi-sensorimotor, multimodal, and collaborative V&AR interactions, and the related issues for users' perception and cognition.

He coordinated the scientific partnership of his lab and led a number of research projects that have been or are currently funded by the French government or by national and regional research institutes. He was the founding secretary of AFRV, the French association of V&AR.

At the international level, one of his actions has been to manage the CNRS Labs involved in INTUITION, the NoE of the 6th IST framework focused on V&AR, where he was member of the Core Group. He is founding member of EuroVR (www.eurovr-association.org), and was re-elected last year to its executive board.

Contents

Applications in Cultural Heritage

Integrated Technologies for Museum Communication and Interactive Apps
in the PON DiCet Project. 3
  Francesco Gabellone

"Social Heritage" Augmented Reality Application to Heritage Education 17
  Raynel Mendoza Garrido, Danilo Vargas Jiménez, Silvia Baldiris,
  and Ramon Fabregat

Making Visible the Invisible. Augmented Reality Visualization for 3D
Reconstructions of Archaeological Sites 25
  Roberto Pierdicca, Emanuele Frontoni, Primo Zingaretti,
  Eva Savina Malinverni, Francesca Colosi, and Roberto Orazi

Advanced Interaction with Paintings by Augmented Reality and High
Resolution Visualization: A Real Case Exhibition 38
  Roberto Pierdicca, Emanuele Frontoni, Primo Zingaretti, Mirco Sturari,
  Paolo Clini, and Ramona Quattrini

Cloud Computing and Augmented Reality for Cultural Heritage 51
  Pietro Vecchio, Francesca Mele, Lucio Tommaso De Paolis,
  Italo Epicoco, Marco Mancini, and Giovanni Aloisio

Augmented and Mixed Reality

Accurate OnSite Georeferenced Subsurface Utility Model Visualisation 63
  Stéphane Côté and Antoine Girard-Vallée

The Augmented Reality Story Book Project: A Collection of Balinese
Miths and Legends 71
  I. Gede Mahendra Darmawiguna, I. Made Gede Sunarya,
  Made Windu Antara Kesiman, Ketut Resika Arthana,
  and Padma Nyoman Crisnapati

ARBS: An Interactive and Collaborative System for Augmented Reality
Books 89
  Nicolás Gazcón and Silvia Castro

Robust Model Based Tracking Using Edge Mapping and Refinement 109
  Anna Katharina Hebborn, Marius Erdt, and Stefan Müller

Augmented Reality, Embodied Cognition and Learning   125
 Sara Invitto, Italo Spada, and Lucio Tommaso De Paolis

OscARsWelt: A Collaborative Augmented Reality Game   135
 Anna Katharina Hebborn, Milan Dilberovic, Adrian Derstroff,
 Andre Franke, Nils Höhner, Patrick Krechel, Lisa Prinz, Astrid Szirmai,
 Fabian Weigend, and Stefan Müller

Device Registration for 3D Geometry-Based User-Perspective Rendering
in Hand-Held Video See-Through Augmented Reality   151
 Ali Samini and Karljohan Lundin Palmerius

Creativity Support in Projection-Based Augmented Environments   168
 Bruno Simões, Federico Prandi, and Raffaele De Amicis

IMU Drift Reduction for Augmented Reality Applications   188
 Lakshmi Prabha Nattamai Sekar, Alexander Santos,
 and Olga Beltramello

Applications in Medicine

Serious Games for Rehabilitation Using Head-Mounted Display
and Haptic Devices   199
 Stéphane Claude Gobron, Nicolas Zannini, Nicolas Wenk, Carl Schmitt,
 Yannick Charrotton, Aurélien Fauquex, Michel Lauria,
 Francis Degache, and Rolf Frischknecht

VR-Based Serious Game Designed for Medical Ethics Training   220
 Cristian Lorenzini, Claudia Faita, Marcello Carrozzino,
 Franco Tecchia, and Massimo Bergamasco

Scalable Medical Viewer for Virtual Reality Environments   233
 Francesco Ricciardi, Emiliano Pastorelli, Lucio Tommaso De Paolis,
 and Heiko Herrmann

A Pre-operative Planning Module for an Augmented Reality Application
in Maxillo-Facial Surgery   244
 Francesco Ricciardi, Chiara Copelli, and Lucio Tommaso De Paolis

Augmented Reality Assisted Brain Tumor Extraction in Mice   255
 Adrian Schneider, Peter Thalmann, Simon Pezold, Simone E. Hieber,
 and Philippe C. Cattin

Applications in Industry and Robotics

A Virtual Prototyping Platform to Improve CAE Analysis Workflow   267
  Francesco Argese, Andrea Martini, Lucio Colizzi, Marco Fina,
  Giovanni Reo, Fiorenzo Ambrosino, Pasquale Bene,
  and Leonardo Cosma

A Proposed Hardware-Software Architecture for Virtual Reality
in Industrial Applications   287
  Francesco Chionna, Piero Cirillo, Vito Palmieri, and Mauro Bellone

Using Haptic Forces Feedback for Immersive and Interactive Simulation
in Industrial Context   301
  Marwene Kechiche, Mohamed-Amine Abidi, Patrick Baert,
  and Rosario Toscano

A Flexible AR-based Training System for Industrial Maintenance   314
  Andrea Sanna, Federico Manuri, Giovanni Piumatti, Gianluca Paravati,
  Fabrizio Lamberti, and Pietro Pezzolla

Training in VR: A Preliminary Study on Learning Assembly/Disassembly
Sequences   332
  Daniele Sportillo, Giovanni Avveduto, Franco Tecchia,
  and Marcello Carrozzino

Applying Aesthetic Rules in Virtual Environments by Means of Semantic
Web Technologies.   344
  Konstantinos Kontakis, Malvina Steiakaki, Michael Kalochrsitianakis,
  Kostas Kapetanakis, and Athanasios G. Malamos

Bilateral Control of a Robotic Arm Through Brain Signals.   355
  Víctor H. Andaluz, Jessica S. Ortiz, and Jorge S. Sanchéz

Interfaces

Natural User Interfaces for Virtual Character Full Body and Facial
Animation in Immersive Virtual Worlds.   371
  Konstantinos Cornelis Apostolakis and Petros Daras

ARTworks: An Augmented Reality Interface as an Aid for Restoration
Professionals   384
  Raffaello Brondi and Marcello Carrozzino

Design and Preliminary Evaluation of Free-Hand Travel Techniques for
Wearable Immersive Virtual Reality Systems with Egocentric Sensing.   399
  Giuseppe Caggianese, Luigi Gallo, and Pietro Neroni

Perception of Basic Emotions from Facial Expressions of Dynamic Virtual
Avatars   409
  Claudia Faita, Federico Vanni, Cristian Lorenzini,
  Marcello Carrozzino, Camilla Tanca, and Massimo Bergamasco

Bridging Offline and Online World Through Augmentable Smart Glass
Interfaces   420
  Zulqarnain Rashid, Joan Melià-Seguí, and Rafael Pous

Touchless Interaction for Command and Control in Military Operations   432
  Alessandro Zocco, Matteo D. Zocco, Antonella Greco,
  Salvatore Livatino, and Lucio Tommaso De Paolis

Short Papers

Development of a Framework to Support Virtual Review Within
Complex-Product Lifecycle Management   449
  Giorgio Bernabei, Angelo Corallo, Roberto Lombardo, Simone Maci,
  Valerio Galli, Danilo Cannoletta, and Antonio Notaro

3D Physics Virtual Laboratory as a Teaching Platform   458
  Yevgeniya Daineko, Madina Ipalakova, Viktor Dmitriyev,
  Andrey Giyenko, and Nazgul Rakhimzhanova

Experiences in the Development of an Augmented Reality Dressing Room . . .   467
  Ugo Erra and Valerio Colonnese

Development of a Virtual Laboratory for Investigating the Interaction
of Materials with Plasma   475
  Anuar M. Zhukeshov, Asylgul T. Gabdullina, Assem Amrenova,
  Zhandos M. Moldabekov, Anar Kusyman, Mira Amirkozhanova,
  Tannur Bakytkazy, Kuantay Fermakhan, Argynbek Kaibar,
  and Kaster Serik

Aspects Concerning Algorithms of VRML Surfaces' Generation   482
  Lucian Ilea, Catalin Boanta, Cornel Brisan, and Veturia Chiroiu

Towards a Framework for Information Presentation in Augmented Reality
for the Support of Procedural Tasks   490
  Tobias Müller

A Dynamic-Oriented Decision Support System for Group Interview
Knapsack Problem   498
    Sihem Ben Jouida and Saoussen Krichen

Virtual Reality as a Cross-Domain Language in Collaborative
Environments   507
    Carlo Vizzi

Author Index   515

Applications in Cultural Heritage

Integrated Technologies for Museum Communication and Interactive Apps in the PON DiCet Project

Francesco Gabellone(✉)

IBAM CNR, Istituto per i Beni Archeologici e Monumentali, Lecce, Italy
f.gabellone@ibam.cnr.it
http://www.itlab.ibam.cnr.it

Abstract. This paper illustrates some results obtained by the IBAM ITLab in the Cultura e Turismo: DiCet project financed with National Operational Program (Programmi Operativi Nazionali – PON) funds. In this project procedures were developed to produce technical models for an efficient management of 3D and 2D resources, and to define best practices and methical protocols for quality certification and process standardization, capable of increase cross-sector dialogue. The sites were identified as a function of a supply-and-demand analysis with regard to a placement on the market of innovative models and services based on the creation of hyper-realistic digital models and virtual scenarios. Particular attention was given to those uses that permit greater visibility, protection, and conservation of cultural assets characterized by difficult access, vulnerability, seismic risk, hydro-geological risk, etc. In view of this, innovative models and tools were designed and developed for capitalizing on and exploiting cultural heritage, understood as an integrated and complex system conceived as a holistic model strongly based on the use of ICT technologies. Virtual enjoyment is understood here as a form of representing reality that accelerates and strengthens cognitive capacities, which is to say it becomes capable of generating extremely sensitive, "virtuous" learning processes based on metaphors of the real world, and thus easy to use and understand. Operationally, our working group has made some Augmented Reality solutions available; these enable the interactive display – directly in situ and especially on mobile devices – of archaeological monuments integrated within the urban fabric. A simple solution allows the user to display an interactive 3D reconstruction directly on the real site, using the latest-generation gyroscope function. In addition to this, certain inaccessible monuments of the cities of Lecce and Catania have been virtualized, mainly using image-based technologies and ultra-realistic laser scanning, to allow them to be visited remotely both via smartphone and on large virtual theatres. In any case the virtual reconstruction of the ancient monuments is the starting point of communication process and represent the point of interest around which every technological solution is proposed.

Keywords: 3D reconstruction · Virtual heritage · Palmieri · Lecce · Image-based · Laser scanning

© Springer International Publishing Switzerland 2015
L.T. De Paolis and A. Mongelli (Eds.): AVR 2015, LNCS 9254, pp. 3–16, 2015.
DOI: 10.1007/978-3-319-22888-4_1

1 Introduction

The DiCet project purses the objective of creating a platform enabling the processes of sustainable development for a smart city, based on the spread of knowledge and on an innovative model for the correct use and enhancement of the cultural heritage. The project supplies, through an open platform, smart services of cultural asset-capitalization, capable of strengthening social inclusion and encouraging the formation of virtuous places, either real or digital, where you can create, develop and share information in order to improve the life of citizens and companies within a desirable framework of social and economic growth. DiCeT is based on an social innovation approach, where the services are co-created involving all actors of an ecosystem oriented towards smart culture and tourism (companies, research, public authorities, final users). The project analyses and builds innovative solutions for the elements that constitute the cultural offer: namely the knowledge of cultural heritage to offer to the users (tourists, citizens, curators, researchers, etc.); its use; its conservation and preservation. With regard to the use, we want to implement (by extending and improving open source technologies already built in the past) a smart system capable of enabling the concept of exploration (increased usage) of cultural heritage. Information, narratives, relevant and pertinent stories that enrich its vision, tracing the life of cultural assets, manipulating and/or moving virtually within them, documenting and sharing their use. The digital exploration is carried out using mobile services and applications that integrate automated reasoning systems, user interfaces that are multimodal, multimedia, proactive, captivating, immersive, participatory and based on new interaction metaphors that integrate Smartphone, large fixed displays and devices directly in the environment. This can be done by means of virtual and augmented reality tools and new forms of interaction (adaptive storytelling: personalized multimedia narratives constructed on-the-fly).

This article discusses some of the achieved results concerning the 3D reconstruction of some monuments of Lecce, their reconstructive study and the digital solutions adopted for their on-site use, but also for communication purposes in the Living Lab space. This is conceived as a living museum, that allows to prepare for the visit, but also to improve the knowledge of monuments already visited.

2 Integrated Techniques for the Virtual Visit

The first case study we intend to explain, regards the 3D survey of the Hypogeum Palmieri, a monumental chamber tomb located in the center of Lecce (south Italy), which currently can't be opened to tourists visit. This monument is located in a private residence and is therefore part of a larger research objective of the IBAM ITLab, aimed to use 3D-based digital technologies to allow the virtual tour of inaccessible places. In the survey of the Palmieri hypogeum the technique of "Camera Mapping" was used in order to obtain a realistic and metrically accurate 3D model. The survey was executed by an indirect active method, with the use of a laser scanner Leica ScanStation 2 (Fig. 1).

Fig. 1. 3D survey of Palmieri hypogeum. Texture mapping after the baking process

The 3D survey involved both the entrance corridor, characterized by an illustrated frieze running on the right and left hand side of the entrance stairs, plus four spaces that are radially distributed downstairs. During the same survey campaign, all the photographic shots required for a documentation of the conditions of the spaces and for further texture mapping tasks of 3D models have been taken. Each picture has been conveniently treated with PTLens software of Tom Niemann. In this way, the distortions induced by the lenses have been filtered out. The 3D model has been subsequently optimized in order to achieve an advanced texture mapping, adopting some camera projection methodologies on multiple patches experimented on purpose and documented by our laboratory in recent years. The correct mapping of the three-dimensional model acquired through laser scanning is usually one of the most problematic issues in order to process the data and offer a verisimilar restitution of the artifact under test. The results of this method[1] are visible in the attached images, but the real utility of this technique in this project is related to the possibility of obtaining a unique mesh with only three large textures applied in UVW mode. This has allowed an easy porting of the 3D model and an efficient management of high resolution textures (10000 × 10000 pixels) with classical LOD systems. Thanks to the availability of this model, and with the fundamental contribution of the ISTI CNR of Pisa, one of the components has been tested for the creation of interactive multimedia presentations, aimed at allowing the use of the monument on the web. The 3DHOP application is available at the URL: http://vcg.isti.cnr.it/palmieri/. The central component of the 3DHOP allows the navigation of the 3D model with the movement restricted on a path: in practice we can imagine the camera fixed on a rail. Navigation's hotspots have been added moving the camera operated by the user within the 3D model of the hypogeum,

---

[1] See: http://cipa.icomos.org/fileadmin/template/doc/PRAGUE/056.pdf.

with the result of an optimal real time navigation of the 3D data. In addition to the web application, a native application for iOS has been implemented. This application displays in real time the Palmieri hypogeum, using an interface based on the mobile iPad Air sensors. Considered the remarkable difficulty of the process of texturing based on "Camera Mapping", that we had to use for mapping meshes obtained from laser scanner, the ability to get so expeditious and excellent model in a complete automatic way, with texture, is a great benefits for everyone, not negligible even for those using scanners with integrated camera. The particular nature of automatic generation of 3D models from photos are now widely discussed and widely used by non-specialists. The presence of two figured friezes in the entrance *dromos* of the Palmieri hypogeum, we suggested to use image-based techniques in order to obtain the highest possible verisimilitude of the relief elements. It seems certainly unusual to replace the laser scanning technique with the latter. However, the examples below demonstrate that the texture accuracy, in these cases, is the most important element of the whole acquisition process. In our experience it has been used a Canon 5DMKII, with 24 MP. The 3D models of the two friezes are very similar in terms of geometric resolution and associated textures. Both are calculated with Agisoft PhotoScan, using medium parameters of accuracy and moderate depth filter. It was not possible to calculate these models with higher parameters due to long waiting times, not compatible with the delivery of the work. However, it took a full coverage of the parts to be detected with photos taken in a way of moving a dolly camera, i.e. with large overlap between contiguous frames, to get a 3D model virtually indistinguishable from the real. How often it happens to ascertain, any deficit in the sub-millimetric definition of these models is compensated by the wealth of high-resolution textures. Thanks to UVW mapping, even the smallest details, such as surface scratches, small efflorescence, small holes, are well represented. About the management of native UVW, should be highlighted considerable management software for parts undercut and sides characterized by a complex plastic. As it is well known, the management of the mapping of these subjects involves a considerable engagement with software sometimes expensive and not always equally effective. Both models, with the actual length of about 3 m by 2 m high, were restituted with about 300 images from 24 MP each, at a resolution of 2 mm and 3 million of polygons in total. A resolution certainly not very high, but it is adequate to describe in detail the studied friezes. Moreover, the prerogative of each survey must be the final purpose and his effectiveness. As no survey can be perfect, we need a compromise and a purpose for the survey itself. This survey could go up the mesh definition, but for the purposes of a tourist use and a study of the figurative style would give redundant and superfluous data. Unnecessary and difficult to manage.

The Fig. 2 shows the 3D model of the figured frieze in phong shading mode. In this image you can appreciate both the level of detail of meshes and the amount of noise. In particular, as often happens for this type of restitution, the noise level increases with the level of uncertainty of measurement. This is related to many factors, some internal, depending for example by the algorithm itself used by the software for the generation of 3D points. Among the external causes of noise generation, that are attributable to the operator or to the settings of shoots, we can certainly report three parameters at least. The first is related to ISO, this should be set to the lowest value, and otherwise high ISO values will induce additional noise to images. The second is linked to the quantity

Fig. 2. Image-base model of the figured frieze in phong shading. The low amount of noise is generally an indicator of good quality of 3D model.

of images, and then the photo coverage. The third is, in our experience, due to the correct lighting of real scene. Good lighting produces, of course, best shooting conditions, taking the possibility of very low uncertainty in the identification of the individual pixels, the movement of which must be tracked in space, in accordance with the algorithm of structure-from-motion. In this work only LED lamps (6500 K) were used for lighting.

I would like to remark in this example (Fig. 3) the low visible differences between the 3D model in high resolution (three million of polygons) and the low resolution model with 250 K polygons. As you can see, the huge difference in the mesh resolution not produce important differences, because the richness of texture, as mentioned above, allows you to maintain a high level of photographic detail. Of course, this result brings clear advantages in terms of portability of files, especially on mobile device and for all those augmented reality applications that require light 3D models.

3   Semi-Augmented Reality for the on-Site Visit

As previously mentioned, these 3D models were used for a virtual tour with different types of hardware, but all the proposed solutions make use of real time 3D systmoreems. Furthermore, it has been experienced other forms of use of it, more simple use modes possibility, which do not require special hardware equipments. In these applications, that could be called "semi augmented reality" and that are based on observable panoramas, the innovative element is the ability to connect the virtual reconstruction on the real context with an immediate dimensional and spatial feedback. These simple solutions allow to create an overlap between the real experience and the virtual information (multimedia information, geo-located data, analytical data, and so on) in an environment

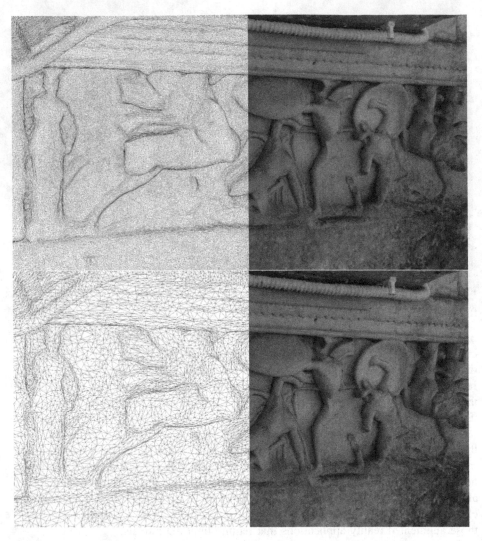

Fig. 3 a, b The figured frieze. On the top the 3D model with 3 Millions of polygons, the lower image shows a model with 250 K polygons. The differences on the textured areas are really very low.

wherein the multimedia elements "increasing" information on reality can be progressively added, superimposed and displayed through a "direct vision" approach. There are several ways to view in AR mode. The most classic form presents a simple superimposition of information directly displayed on the framed object. Texts, images and other information appear directly on the framed object, but in some implementations of graphics libraries it is possible to overlap simplified three-dimensional models that help to understand the archaeological structures within the urban fabric. The idea of linking 3D models in the real environment has been experienced for a long time now, even in the manufacturing industry, in automotive, in fashion. Moreover, many research groups have developed solutions that allow to contextualize 3D objects directly on a smart-phone. The use of these libraries, however, is strongly affected by the limitations of the various computational device, compromising, as a matter of fact, the fruition on many poorly performing equipment. One solution to this limitation is given by a hybrid mode of AR, in which ultra-realistic three-dimensional reconstructions are mixed with high-resolution spherical VR panoramas. Many sceptics and lovers of performing technologies lose sight of these old solutions, well supported in HTML5, where the aspiration to technicality generates a communicative effectiveness, easiness of use and quality of yield.

The basic idea of this solution is very simple. The three-dimensional model of the old building is placed in the center of the spherical panorama, taking care of finalizing this process to the linking of the attachment points to the points detected on the ground and reported in the 3D scene. These attachment points must exactly match those in the landscape. Therefore, they have to rotate accordingly to the camera when this one focuses on the centre of gravity of the VR panorama. In this way, we can show the 3D object perfectly anchored to the real scene. Within this process, special attention has been devoted to the lighting of the scene and to the implementation of a set-up that recreates the same environmental conditions present in the actual scenario, in order to provide a convincing result, that can be perfectly superimposed to the site. This solution allows to view the various monuments in their original context, in an "optimized" and efficient management, even in particularly complex scenarios. Specifically, this happens to old buildings stacked in urbanized environments, where the adoption of a simplified 3D model, without shadows, without radiosity and with low texture resolution would provide a poor integration. An unacceptable quality of the final result, not to say about the meaningful problem of the items located at various depths, which partially obliterate the reconstruction and are partially obliterated by the reconstruction in turn. In one AR scene, a 3D object should solve all these problems, plus the problems related to the real time restitution. In the solution shown in these pages, the reconstructed three-dimensional model is integrated into the urban fabric by means of a simple masking that considers various objects placed in depth, the global illumination and, last but not least, the point of view of the observer (Fig. 4).

The use of spherical panoramas or javascript enabled us to create simple applications in which visitors interact with the view in front of him, having finally as result an overlap with the reconstruction. A similar approach was also used in the graphic reconstruction of a few years ago: for example the onion skin or the rotoscoping techniques used in animated films. A simple approach based on GPS allows to recognize the points on which there is a semi-augmented reality view.

4   A Simple Interactive JavaScript to Reveal 3D Reconstruction

Of course the possibilities to interactively reveal an image over another one are infinite, there is only a problem of creativity linked to this. Despite this we must consider the importance of various problems, for example the porting on different browsers, on different smartphones, on different platforms. One last question, may the heaviest of all, is

Fig. 4a and 4b. Semi AR application. The virtual reconstruction of the amphitheatre of Lecce superimposed to the real site.

the ability to create complex scripts with cross-platform languages, such as JavaScript. Unfortunately my architectural studies does not allow me great programming options, but as always in these cases, the creativity and the ability to respond to concrete problems suggest some interesting answers. My goal in this project is to create an interactive transition between the current state of a monument and its reconstruction perfectly superimposed on it. I would like to create a simple slide that would allow to do this in a very simple and intuitive way. So I would like to share my experience presenting this robust solution, which does not require a specialized preparation in programming.

The solution I found is based on some free library of jQuery Foundation, non-profit trade association for web developers. jQuery is a fast, small, and feature-rich JavaScript library. It makes things like HTML document traversal and manipulation, event handling, animation, and Ajax much simpler with an easy-to-use API that works across a multitude of browsers. With a combination of versatility and extensibility, jQuery has changed the way that millions of people write JavaScript.

To start you download from the jQuery web-site "before-after" libraries[2]. First, your before and after images must be the same size. Both images must exist within a containing div which must have an ID. See this example.

```
<div id="container">
<div><img alt="before" src="before.jpg" width="600" height="366" /></div>
<div><img alt="after" src="after.jpg" width="600" height="366" /></div>
</div>
```

All images must have the width and height declared otherwise the plugin won't work in Safari, Chrome, and any other webkit-based browsers. The plugin requires jQuery (of course) and the draggable component of jQueryUI. Both files are bundled with the plugin however you can point to other copies if you prefer (e.g. jquery on Google and jqueryui on Google). Upload the plugin files on your site and link to them:

```
<script type="text/javascript" src="jquery.min.js"></script>
<script type="text/javascript" src="jquery-ui.min.js"></script>
<script type="text/javascript" src="jquery.beforeafter.js"></script>
<script type="text/javascript">
$(function(){
$('#container').beforeAfter();
});
</script>
```

The approach is really simple. The most problematic element is instead the creation of two overlapping images, which requires severe procedures to find the exact camera location in the real photo, which must be used to calculate the rendering to be superimposed over it. There are several solutions to calculate the position of a camera in real photos. The first way is to use the perspective lines, it's necessary to find the center of vision which is the geometric center of the frame. This is done by drawing diagonal lines. The center of vision is where those lines cross in the exact center of the frame. Next find the left and right vanishing points as per the principles of two point perspective. The procedure continues with the search for the principal point and the camera field of view in according with principles of descriptive geometry.

The second way, today thankfully easier than the previous, is to use specialized software for digital photogrammetry, like EOS Systems Photomodeler or PhotoMatch for Maxon Cinema4D eases the integration of 3D elements in loaded background photos by calibrating the camera and by offering specialized modeling tools. An example of this simple technique is shown in Fig. 5.

The same visualization technique has been used in another PON project (IN-CULTURE Project) to show the results of digital restoration applied to the frescoes of the Church of Santo Stefano at Soleto (Lecce, Italy South). The immediate and interactive approach allows to reveal the pictorial additions over the real image, consenting an optimal reading of lost or partially damaged pictorial elements (Fig. 6).

---

[2] http://www.catchmyfame.com/catchmyfame-jquery-plugins/jquery-beforeafter-plugin/.

Fig. 5. Virtual reconstruction of roman theatre of Lecce. The interactive approach based on jQuery library.

5   Narratives and Passive Communication Methods

The interesting innovations proposed by the current technological scenario, some of them just described and other extremely interesting, that make use of immersive environments, haptic interfaces, collaborative environments, require a direct and active participation of the public, which will require some preparation in the use of interactive systems. Despite these applications are quickly spreading in modern museums, in our opinion the medium that offers the greatest chance of diffusion of cultural message is given by CG animation and the emotional narrative. In an age of horizontal diffusion of culture, to communicate means to use the language of the new media in the belief that the border between elite culture and mass culture is no longer as clear as it was. With this in mind, the role of virtual heritage also consists in transmitting information using the language of modern mass media and cognitive metaphors of serious games, considering these as cultural paradigms for a form of communication that is freed from the classic rules of elite culture. These new perspectives have determined an increase in the demand of digital technologies able to transmit historical-cultural contents, naturally with greatest scientific rigor. Where communication has become an important component of the museum presentation and organisation, the museums have become home to a new way of conceiving cultural communication, and looking for new dynamics of social communication. The introduction of communication forms based on emotional narration are the most successful examples of the new methods available to contemporary museum studies. There is no doubt that everything that gravitates around virtual heritage can no longer avoid confronting the themes used by those who would raise

Fig. 6. Santo Stefano a Soleto. San Nicola. An example of virtual restoration interactively revealed

Fig. 7. The amphitheatre of Lecce. A frame of narrative approach for the DiCet project.

awareness in the wider public, nor the new epistemological challenges that result from them. The historical competence of the average citizen is now formed largely by information that comes from the new media, thus creating a great increase in the demand for products with a high technological content, with the aim of popularising historical re-evocations and reconstructions of the past (Fig. 7).

Conscious of this, we have created for the DiCet project some movies where the archaeological monuments of Lecce in the roman age are the focus of a narrative. In about six minutes made entirely in 3D Computer Animation and stereoscopic mode, we tried to tell at a glance the main features of the three monuments under study, the

Fig. 8a and 8b. The Palmieri hypogeum of Lecce, virtual reconstruction. Two frames of narrative approach for the DiCet project (Color figure online).

Palmieri hypogeum, the Theater and the Amphitheater. The visitor has the opportunity to understand in a synthetic way and with an emotional narrative, historical data, planimetric and architectural info, preparing for a more detailed visit that can take on site or on the extras interactive application. But perhaps the most interesting aspect is the ability to re-contextualize the fragments of the statues in the Theater scene, the friezes and the *porticus* of the Amphitheater, the original appearance of the Palmieri hypogeum.

For the Palmieri hypogeum, in particular, analysis based on the integrated survey has allowed us to formulate a reconstructive proposal of the monument, which gives a partially original reading of the monumental tombs in Messapian age. The study of the monument was started with the search for any traces of painting on the walls. A very important aspect, as recent discoveries testify to the widespread use of color also on grave goods and not just on architectural surfaces. The analysis carried out by means of video microscope and on samples taken from relevant areas, allowed us to identify only a few traces of red colour on the boundary lines of the wall decoration in false ashlar-work (Fig. 8).

A different treatment of the surface of the plaster, partly smooth and partly worked with an "orange peel": effect, gives to the parietal decorations a shallow plastic movement, with a simple red line of demarcation between the different blocks. The overview shows an unexpected sobriety of polychromies, played only on the effect of chiaroscuro given by the false ashlar-work and the red colour of the walls of the *dromos*. The same colours are found on the figural frieze (red and white) and on the floral frieze (red, green and blue). An example, this, of concrete interdisciplinary approach, carried out to give form and substance to an increasing demand of information and suggestions, that people from every cultural background claim (Fig. 9).

Fig. 9. The theatre of Lecce, virtual reconstruction. A frame of narrative approach for the DiCet project.

6   Conclusions

Virtual enjoyment is understood here as a form of representing reality that accelerates and strengthens cognitive capacities, which is to say it becomes capable of generating extremely sensitive, "virtuous" learning processes based on metaphors of the real world, and thus easy to use and understand. Operationally, our working group has made some Augmented Reality solutions available; these enable the interactive display – directly in situ and especially on mobile devices – of archaeological monuments integrated within the urban fabric. A simple solution allows the user to display an interactive 3D reconstruction directly on the real site, using the latest-generation gyroscope function. In addition to this, certain inaccessible monuments have been virtualized, chiefly using image-based technologies and ultra-realistic laser scanning, to allow them to be visited remotely both via smartphone and on large virtual theatres.

We used many digital techniques and the most expedient possible to provide an efficient product to communicate the archaeology and associated contents. We have so many technologies available today, but the central point is always the quality factor, which summarizes itself all the capacity of humans to manage them to produce something that has a value over time. Because the promising technologies of today will be obsolete tomorrow, the technological aspect can never equal the human's ability to produce emotional products, also with traditional means.

Acknowledgements. Special thanks to Ivan Ferrari and Francesco Giuri (IBAM - ITLab team) for the great contribute in every 3d work process. Maria Teresa Giannotta, Francesco D'Andria and Maria Chiffi for the reconstruction of Palmieri hypogeum. The Guarini family for great support during the survey campaigns of Palmieri hypogeum.

References

1. D'Andria, F.: La Puglia romana, in La Puglia dal Paleolitico al Tardoromano, Milano, pp. 329–330J (1979)
2. D'Andria, F.: Enciclopedia Treccani, s.v. Lecce, vol. IX, p. 522
3. Bendinelli, G.: Un ipogeo sepolcrale a Lecce, in Ausonia, 8, pp. 9–26 (1913)
4. L'Arab Gilda, L'ipogeo Palmieri di Lecce. In: Mélanges de L'Ecole française de Rome. Antiquité T. 103, N°2, pp. 457–497 (1991)
5. Micalella, M.: Un antico ipogeo a Lecce, in Apulia, 4, pp. 93–112 (1912)
6. Tiné Bertocchi, F.: La pittura funeraria apula, Napoli, Macchiaroli Editore (1964)
7. Gabellone, F., Giannotta, M.T.: Marta Racconta: a project for the virtual enjoyment of inaccessible monuments. In: CHNT 18, International Conference on Cultural Heritage and New Technologies, Stadt Archäologie, Wien, 11–13 November 2013
8. Gabellone, F., Giannotta, M.T., Ferrari, I., Dell'Aglio, A.: From museum to original site: 3d environment for the virtual visit of finds re-contextualized in their original provenance. In: 2013 Digital Heritage International Congress, 28 October–1 November 2013, Marseille 2013, France (DigitalHeritage), vol. 2, pp. 215–222 (2013)
9. Gabellone, F., Ferrari, I., Giuri, F.: A quick method for the texture mapping of meshes acquired by laser scanner. In: Cepek, A. (ed.) Journal of Geoinformatics FCE CTU, Faculty of Civil Engineering, Czech Technical University in Prague, vol. 9, Prague, pp. 107–115 (2012)

"Social Heritage" Augmented Reality Application to Heritage Education

Raynel Mendoza Garrido[1](✉), Danilo Vargas Jiménez[2], Silvia Baldiris[1],
and Ramon Fabregat[1]

[1] University of Girona, Girona, Spain
rmendoza@tecnologicocomfenalco.edu.co,baldiris@eia.udg.edu,
ramon.fabregat@udg.edu
[2] Fundación Universitaria Tecnológico Comfenalco, Cartagena, Colombia
dvargasj@tecnocomfenalco.edu.co,dvargasj@gmail.com

Abstract. Heritage education can be conceived as a pedagogical and didactical process focusing on knowledge, perceptions and values of Heritage being part of a society and interpreted and known by people. This process can be offered to a society by any educational institution in formal contexts, but also by specialized organizations or persons in informal contexts. For instance, it is common to see citizens learning about heritage in their own cities, but also learning about heritage as tourists in other cities. Nowadays, the processes of heritage education in informal contexts have been supported by those technologies such as tourist guides, audio guides, and tactile televisions, among others. However, technologies such as augmented reality, contribute to the knowledge of heritage in a contextualized, situated, and enriched learning process.

The purpose of this paper is to present Social Heritage, and a solution aiming to develop heritage education processes based on augmented reality. Social Heritage runs in mobile devices; it is based on the collaborative construction of heritage content and can be used in both, formal and informal learning contexts.

Keywords: Heritage education · Informal learning · Augmented reality

1 Introduction

Heritage education as a process is based on learning theories and specific didactic methodologies, with the purpose of achieving genuine appropriation and participation among citizens. This as a consequence, conserves heritage using it properly [1–3].

Heritage education has been carried out traditionally in formal learning contexts where the main actors are students and teachers who using a standardized curriculum, interact to achieve a basic understanding of heritage. Frequently, this learning process is not situated in heritage itself due to different reasons: actors could not be located in the cities that were considered in the learning process or perhaps it was easier due to economic and logistic limitations.

© Springer International Publishing Switzerland 2015
L.T. De Paolis and A. Mongelli (Eds.): AVR 2015, LNCS 9254, pp. 17–24, 2015.
DOI: 10.1007/978-3-319-22888-4_2

Technology has been used in order to facilitate heritage education, tourist guides, audio guides, and interactive screens; mobile applications and web sites, are examples of technologies which facilitate approaching among citizens or visitors to their heritage.

However, emerging technologies offer outstanding opportunities to contextualize and enrich the heritage learning process [4]. Augmented reality particularly allows users to interact in heritage scenarios through the enlargement of different kind of information that helps citizens or visitors having a better understanding of their heritage [5].

This paper proposes a mobile augmented reality application, allowing heritage appropriation based on collaborative content construction that can be used in both formal and informal learning contexts.

2   Technologies to Heritage Education

As mentioned before, technologies such as tourist guides, audio guides, and interactive displays have been used in order to facilitate heritage education. These technologies have been really useful but not allowing user interaction to enrich or improve the content they offer, is one of their limitations; furthermore, they reduce decision making among users on where to go or what to do.

Applications for heritage education based on augmented reality can be identified from the ones shown below.

2.1   Ayuntamiento Arjona

Ayuntamiento Arjona application aims to encourage tourism in Arjona. Using today's technologies, Mythical Technology company has developed this application with augmented reality where tourist sites and areas can be seen by visitors and citizens in this Spanish town located in the province of Jaén. Application functions include marking recognition labels locating places related to heritage content and information on Arjona tourist site routes [6].

2.2   Guimarães

Guimarães is an application that offers information on heritage and the Guimarães city history, ancient capital of Portugal. With Guimarães, city's official application, medieval historic center exploration in a didactic and interactive way can be done; it was declared World Heritage by UNESCO in 2001. This heritage route application includes functions such as theme tours, treasure hunt for children, knowledge test, augmented reality vision, accommodation in the city search engine and content sharing [7].

2.3   Valladolid Tu Corazón

It is a technological solution that extends the current cultural and tourist services for citizens and visitors who come to Valladolid. Application functions include sightseeing tours information, parking, augmented reality vision and hotel booking information [8].

2.4 Artà Travel

Artà Travel application provides augmented reality information on heritage, tradition, modernity, nature and tourism technology. Application functions include language choice, heritage routes selection, audio guide, geo positioning and QR reader [9].

2.5 Camino Mozárabe de Santiago

Camino Mozárabe de Santiago application uses ARPA® Mobile Technology with augmented reality to quickly and easily locate tourist information centers, heritage resources, accommodation, museums, and restaurants. Application functions include heritage category selection, heritage route search engine, content sharing, record of places already visited, visualization of the nearest places with augmented reality and how to get there. It is known as one of the most complete applications, providing information on heritage interests, however as preset cities implemented information is static it lacks scalability [10].

Our contribution to the above mentioned applications is the possibility to create collaborative heritage content as well as integral consideration of heritage educational process.

3 Social Heritage Application

Social Heritage is an application based in augmented reality seeking heritage education process development, based on collaborative construction content and user role definition to support heritage educational process.

Fontal proposes different strategies and models to Heritage Education [2], including: (1) Teacher-centered models (2) Student-centered models (3) Content-centered models and (4) Context-centered models and other variations (Fig. 1).

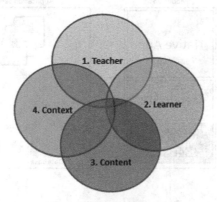

Fig. 1. Heritage teaching model - fontal

This work is based on hybrid models where learner, content and context in a process of formal and informal education are articulated. The learning process takes place in real scenarios where individual needs are customized. In addition, the content is developed collaboratively among the learning process actors (Fig. 2).

Fig. 2. Social heritage logo

Social Heritage, an augmented reality mobile application, has been developed for Android OS devices, allowing users real time experience.

Social Heritage is based on geo positioning for heritage interest places display, through a geographic information system method and screen overlapped radars with augmented reality. This application provides users the ability to interact with heritage, also benefit from provided information to achieve a greater rapprochement and heritage appropriation.

3.1   Process Roles

For heritage education process, the application displays two roles: Users (citizens and visitors) learning about their heritage and Heritage Managers, heritage specialists, supporting the process of education through the validation of content and identifying places of heritage interest.

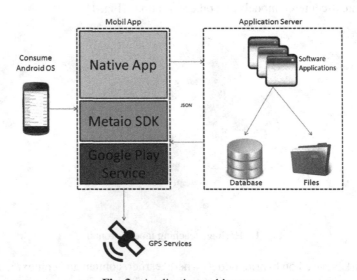

Fig. 3.   Application architecture

3.2   Architecture

In order to provide users enough information and have a reliable, truthful and efficient heritage education process, this application contains two components, a Native Application and a Web component, consuming services from it for proper functioning in order for users to acquire heritage principles. The application architecture can be seen in Fig. 3.

3.2.1   Functions

Social Heritage application offers users the possibility to initially register and login once user has already registered. The registration module is composed of data allowing user preference setting, in order to generate recommendations on interesting heritage content (Fig. 4).

Fig. 4.   Register and login screen view.

In order to offer heritage education process services, information provided is divided into three modules: (1) visualization of places of interest, through geographic information system (GIS), (2) custom search through lists and (3) visitor information centers

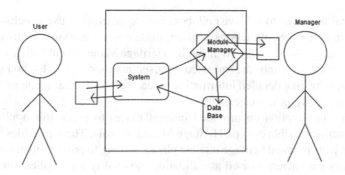

Fig. 5.   Content validation process.

with augmented reality visualization. Offering versatile observation capabilities and extending appropriation experience among users.

Appropriation process should be completed along ability among users working with the construction and dissemination of content, such as images, videos, texts, etc., in order to provide users with accurate and quality information; content is validated by the heritage Manager after loading it. Validation is made in order is verify the relevance and quality of the content. See Fig. 5.

Heritage education modules offer users the possibility to interact with information they are visualising, displaying marking maps, highlighting designated heritage landmarks through a heritage route. Viewing by lists, gives the user all the interesting heritage places, organizing them by initiation points, moreover, it counts with a specific search engine to enhance user-system interaction.

Augmented reality overlaps screen radar views representing heritage interest places displayed through geo positioning, marking heritage interest places. This type of display offers users detailed information on interest places, providing routes to get there and also further information if required. See Fig. 6 for GIS Module and lists.

Fig. 6. Geographic information system modules and list.

Additional functions to achieve collaborative experiences to users include modules allowing system heritage attractions loading, these created marking points are offered but before being published, they go through a Heritage Management validation process.

Heritage interest points are oriented to user appropriation, displaying specific windows and providing detailed information on each place, such as name of the interest place, description, videos, images, etc.

Validating information on provided interest places to users, this application has validated functions visible only on Heritage Manager's role. These provides the administrator a list with assigned heritage interest places, aiming to pre-establish some quality and credibility parameters as well as validating the quality and application of videos, images, sounds, etc. added as heritage interest content.

3.2.2   Developer Tools

As application is initially oriented for users with mobile devices with Android operating system, IDE development is required to support Android SDK, Eclipse software with a specialized version for mobile applications for Android programming was chosen for it [11]; to guarantee information display to users via GPS and Augmented Reality, Google Play Services were used by the Google Maps Android API V2 component, this library can generate map markings, indicating places of interest and displaying signaling routes and Metaio SDK [13] provides libraries to create on screen overlapping radars through augmented reality.

4   Validation

Cartagena was declared a World Heritage and Cultural site by UNESCO being the city with the highest tourism and heritage riches level in Colombia.

For validation development purposes, proceedings to define heritage landmarks in the historic center of the city of Cartagena was set, for each of these places, basic content was built: description, images, and video.

Once having the basic contents, proceedings to perform a validation test with local users and visitors to the city of Cartagena was set, testing the application, users were able to interact with it.

The application was well received by users in general, expressing a good perception through a survey. All participants agreed on the application being able to become a great support for heritage education process development.

5   Conclusions and Future Work

It is important to develop technologies that allow people to achieve heritage appropriation; for this type of development, augmented reality becomes a great opportunity to allow people interacting with heritage and tourist scenarios in real time.

Technology as Social Heritage can be used both formal and informal contexts; it can be used by teachers supporting their classroom work and it can also support visitors or citizen by simply sightseeing and learning about their heritage.

Future work is aimed for the application to recommend heritage content and places of interest to users, based on a user model in order to deliver content according to user needs and interests and also carrying out a larger validation process in the cities of Cartagena (Colombia) and in Girona (Spain).

References

1. Colom, A., et al.: Educación no formal. Ariel, Barcelona (1998)
2. Fontal, O.: Educación Patrimonial: Teoría y Práctica en el Aula, el Museo e Internet. Trea, Asturias (2003)
3. Pastor, M.: Pedagogía museística: Nuevas Perspectivas y tendencias actuales. Ariel, Barcelona (2004)

4. Fernandez, M., Guerra, W., Maisel, A.: Políticas para reducir las desigualdades regionales en Colombia, pp. 342–345. Banco de la Republica - Colección de economía regional Banco de la Republica, Cartagena (2007)
5. Prendes, C.: Realidad Aumentada Y Educación: Análisis De Experiencias Y Prácticas. Revista de Medios y Comunicación **46**, 187–203 (2015)
6. Mítica Technology: App de Realidad Aumentada para el Ayuntamiento de Arjona. Recuperado el 10 de abril de 2015 (2015). de http://www.miticatechnology.com/
7. Monument Tracker: The history of the monuments of Guimaraes with Monument Tracker. Recuperado el 10 de abril de 2015 (2014). de http://www.monument-tracker.com/en/towns/europe/guimaraes/
8. Ayuntamiento de Valladolid: Guías para el móvil. Recuperado el 10 de abril de 2015 (2014). de http://www.info.valladolid.es/turismo/servicios/guias-para-el-movil
9. ArtaMallorca: Rutas Turísticas Arta. Recuperado el 10 de abril de 2015 (2014). de http://audioguias.travel/artamallorca/es/
10. Camino Santiago Andalucia: El Camino Mozárabe de Santiago ya cuenta con una aplicación para móviles. Recuperado el 10 de abril de 2015 (2013). de http://caminosantiagoandalucia.org/wordpress/2013/11/20/el-camino-mozarabe-de-santiago-ya-cuenta-con-una-aplicacion-para-moviles
11. Matos, V., Grasser, R.: Building applications for the android OS mobile platform: a primer and course materials. J. Comput. Sci. Coll. **26**(1), 23–29 (2010)
12. Meier, R.: Professional Android 4 Application Development, p. 817. Wiley, Indianapolis (2012)
13. Renukdas, P., Ghundiyal, R., Gadhil, H., Pathare, V.: Markerless augmented reality android app for interior decoration. Int. J. Next Gener. Comput. Appl. **1**(7), 12–17 (2013)
14. Barros, S.: Cartagena y su denominación como patrimonio en 1985. Tesis (Historia) – Universidad de Cartagena. Facultad de CienciasHumanas. Programa de Historia (2011)

Making Visible the Invisible.
Augmented Reality Visualization
for 3D Reconstructions of Archaeological Sites

Roberto Pierdicca[1](✉), Emanuele Frontoni[1], Primo Zingaretti[1],
Eva Savina Malinverni[1], Francesca Colosi[2], and Roberto Orazi[2]

[1] Universitá Politecnica Delle Marche,
Via Brecce Bianche 12, 60131 Ancona, Italy
{r.pierdicca,e.frontoni,p.zingaretti,e.s.malinverni}@univpm.it
http://www.univpm.it
[2] CNR-ITABC,
Via Salaria Km. 29,300, 00016, Monterotondo Street, Roma, Italy
{francesca.colosi,roberto.orazi}@itabc.cnr.it
http://www.itabc.cnr.it/

Abstract. In archaeology, findings are completely freed from the earth
which had been covering for centuries but in most cases they must be covered again in order to protect them. In this paper we present a augmented
reality (AR) experience for the visualization of 3D models in-situ, giving the possibility to see conceived findings. The experience was carried
out for archaeological purposes in Chan Chan, the America's greatest
pre-Columbian town. From 2001, our mission is operating at Chan Chan
carrying on a wide action of documentation, conservation and exploitation. We propose an interesting workflow: image acquisition, 3D photogrammetric reconstruction, 3D simplification, AR visualization. Also
a knowledge base applied to archaeological sites is here presented.

Keywords: Augmented reality · Archaeology · Knowledge base · 3D
Reconstruction · Survey · Visualization

1 Introduction

Augmented Reality (AR) is a growing technology in the field of Computer Vision.
AR has the capability of adding virtual objects in the physical reality, allowing
users a direct communication with the exhibitions. AR can be summarized as an
enhancement of sensory experience using digital or computer-generated contents,
with the aim to increase knowledge about everything that surrounds us. Thanks
to the cinematography, the 1960 is considered the year of birth of the AR, when
Morton Heilig [14] proposed *Sensorama*, a system able to increase the sensory
perception of the reality. Only thanks to the work of Krueger et al. [13], the first
system of Virtual Reality (VR) that allowed the users to interact with virtual
object has been created, known as *Videoplace*. The passing from the VR to the

© Springer International Publishing Switzerland 2015
L.T. De Paolis and A. Mongelli (Eds.): AVR 2015, LNCS 9254, pp. 25–37, 2015.
DOI: 10.1007/978-3-319-22888-4_3

AR has only occurred in the 1990 [12], when the information came out from the device, due to the overlapping of digital contents.

AR has reached a high degree of development during the year 2000 when it has involved different fields of application [1,2]: medicine, education, navigation, urban planning and architecture, military, entertainment and cultural heritage. Considering the cultural heritage aspect, only in the recent years a large number of works has been proposed [8,18,23]. An important guide for archaeological sites is represented by the work of Vlahakis et al. [21]. *Archeoguide* provides a personalized augmented tour of archaeological sites, using augmented reality methods to reconstruct ruined sites, simulating also the ancient life. The system allows to recreate the archaeological site, maintaining the user in the real world. Another AR system is *Lifeplus* applied to historical and archaeological sites that uses handled devices on site displays [19]. Another most recent work [3] combines historical and archaeological details to improve the experience of the visitors by imaging the relation archaeological ruins with the ancient landscape. ARAC Maps [10] is a very recent AR application for archaeological sites, with the aim to enhance archaeological maps using 3D models together with other interactive approaches.

Nevertheless, the use of AR for archaeological applications is still broadly missing; although, as we have previously said, there are several examples of projects with this aim, there is the necessity to introduce such a technology to drive people towards a new concept of archaeological tourism.

For this purpose, the aim of our project is to cope with the lack of wide-spread interactive solutions to serve archaeologist and tourists. Augmented reality allows to discover, in an alternative way, monuments or ruins by simply scanning the surrounding environment, loading contents from a remote repository and visualizing them as virtual objects. There would be many advantages using AR solutions for both visitors and scientists.

From one hand, additional information can be given at any point of the tour, visitor interests can be closely matched, user interaction supports and increase learning process, Edutaiment (Educational Enterteinment) fascinates children as well as adults. From the other side, scientists and insiders can raise their awareness of cultural heritage, have a useful tool to better conduct their research, verify their archaeological interpretation of findings, improve their documentation activity. The most important feature is the possibility to visualize findings, also when they are covered. It is well known that, due to conservation reasons, once the rests, monuments or graves are discovered, if there is not the possibility to store and save them, they are covered again. AR allows the visualization of rests, also where they are invisible. To exploit AR experience the main components are wearable or handled devices with a series of embedded sensors for tracking systems (e.g. camera, compass, GPS receiver and so on), Network Connectivity card and input devices for user interaction (e.g. display or vocal commands). For the development, many free and open-source software solutions are growing, which allow to integrate sensors with the contents, in order to make the device able to analyze and know the surrounding reality.

Every device able to geo-localize the user and to overlap contents could be used, as well as to inform, also to drive him with a sort of augmented route guidance. This technology is just beginning but combining GIS data, localization and a simple tablet, it is already possible to walk out onto the site and augment it with sights, sounds, 3D reconstructions and virtual models of past people. Linking them is a good solution for way finding and opens up new perspectives and possibilities of exploring the results of spatial modeling, changing chronologies, and different types of building reconstructions. The paper is organized as follow: next session introduces Chan Chan archaeological site, with particular focus over those findings used for our AR experience Sect. 3 describes the acquisition campaign and the techniques of survey, Sect. 4 is an explanation to achieve a good solution of AR visualization, 4 and 5 are focused on the methodology related to, respectively.

2 Case Study: Chan Chan Archaeological Site

The archaeological complex of Chan Chan is located in the northern part of Peru no far from the town of Trujillo and about 550 km. from Lima. The town, that represents the largest mud brick pre-Columbian settlement covers an area of 14 km^2 and is placed on a sedimentary terrace a few hundred meters from the Pacific Ocean. Chan Chan was the capital of the Chimu culture, one of the great civilizations that arose along the coast of northern Peru during the early centuries of our age. The most important architectural typology of the urban area is represented by nine palaces or ciudadelas. Each of them is made of a large enclosure four to seven hundred meters long and two to five hundred meters wide. The nine ciudadelas are characterized by some recurrent architectural features: the main entrance is placed on the north side, everyone of the palaces is divided in three main sectors the first of which is characterized by the presence of a large square for public ceremonies and meeting with the king. The second and the third sectors are reserved for the king and his court and present a great quantity of small yards, warehouses, houses and audiencias (small U shaped rooms with ritual function). Moreover the second sector is characterized by the "plataforma de entierro" or royal grave where the king was going to be buried at the moment of his death ([4,6]). The entire palace was usually decorated with geometrical or natural bass-relieves along the walls of the corridors or of the audiencias representing scenes referred to the activity of fishing and to the marine world. From a strictly geographic point of view, Chan Chan is located in the tropical zone between the Equator and the Tropic of Capricorn, but due to a cold water stream that runs along the coast of Peru, the temperature of the region is quite mild and the rainfall extremely scarce. The climate is therefore ideal for the conservation of earthen architecture, though some heavy factors of decay are present. These last are mainly caused by illegal excavations that have been carried on since the time of the Conquistadores, by marine salt transported by the wind or absorbed by the walls through capillarity and, finally by the sometime devastating phenomenon of the Niño. Unfortunately, due to the precarious state of conservation, many of the friezes have been lost. The few which are still on the site have been documented by simple photographs and protected from the atmospheric agents by covering the original decoration with a new mud brick wall. Due to this situation, to the large dimension of the site and to the fact that the touristic visit is limited to Palacio Tschudi, the only one restored, it is impossible to have a look to the precious decorative aspects of the Chimu civilization if not by mean of old and bi-dimensional pictures. Up to now it was difficult to plan an exposition of the friezes of the town, but thank to new technologies for the diffusion of information this action is not anymore impossible. An occasional opportunity arose last year while the PECACH (Proyecto Especial Complejo Arqueologico Chan Chan), that is the local operative branch of the Ministero de Cultura, was working at the restoration of some parts of Palacio Rivero. The main door introducing into the large square of the first sector is the architectural element that we exploited for the test presented in this paper. The door was completely freed from the earth which had been covering the structure for centuries; at this stage we had the possibility, in just few hours, to take photogrammetric shoots of the original entrance before being covered again in order to protect it. Figure 1 shows the original entrance door before and after its coverage.

Fig. 1. The main door introducing into the first sector. Upper image: before the excavation the door covered by earth. Lower image: the door freed from the earth

The Italian Mission in Peru, which is operating on the site since 2002 ([7]), in accordance with a PECACHs program of documentation and monitoring of all the hidden friezes of Chan Chan, is going to realize the 3D models of the wall decorations in order to show them in a specific immersive room of the new Museum and arrange, in this way, a kind of pre-visit to the wide and still unknown Chimu decorative world.

3   Acquisition and Photogrammetric Reconstruction

Besides the extreme importance of keeping safe such an important monument, the work carried out over the entrance door pioneered several issues in the field of archaeological conservation and dissemination, which for years are object of discussion in the scientific community. It is well known that excavations are generally conducted in emergency conditions, surveys are often unprogrammed and the documentation of findings is a hard task during campaigns. The workflow presented in this paper has the purpose to face these issues and to outline best-practices in the field of archaeology, from the excavation phase until the dissemination and fruition through AR. The introduction of new photogrammetric techniques acquisition and cutting edge solution for the visualization of rests are mandatory for both conservation/documentation and promotion of archaeology. With our approach we provide:

- Free and low cost solutions allowing unplanned data acquisition;
- Rapid and smart techniques to facilitate documentation during excavation work;
- High level of detail for the representation of complex 3D objects;
- Contextualized visualization of archaeological findings.

3.1   Acquisition Campaign

During our campaign in Chan Chan in the past years, to perform the 3D survey we used different types of technologies such as GPS, laser scanner or spherical photogrammetry [5]. However, these techniques require an accurate a priori planning of the survey campaign, as well as a costly and cumbersome equipment. In this case we faced with a condition of emergency, besides the fact that the documentation and acquisition was totally unprogrammed; furthermore, the only available equipment was a calibrated SONY SLT-A77V camera, hence we performed the survey via terrestrial photogrammetry technique. The camera features CMOS Exmor APS-C with 24,3 MP resolution, coupled with an 24–70 mm objective. Approximately 440 images were acquired with the same survey, carried out in November 2013. The images were acquired keeping the camera at the focal length of 40 mm, with the highest resolution (6000 × 4000 pixels), with an overlap of about 30 "%". Pictures were taken from 5 points of view (POV) in order to have a full coverage of the architecture; each set of pictures for each POV has been used to create a panorama (see Fig. 2), using a stitching software. This allows to speed up the process of photogrammetric reconstruction and to simplify the texturing procedure, as explained in the following section.

3.2   Photogrammetric Reconstruction

For the 3D model reconstruction of the findings we adopted Structure from Motion (SfM) techniques. Even if there are many different packages available [11] for this kind of process, the steps to achieve a reality-based model of the object are quite similar. In particular in our case we have:

Fig. 2. Panoramas output from the stitching software. Left and right part of the archaeological finding

- A set of pictures of the door, with a very high resolution;
- Images alignment to fix the camera position;
- Point cloud generation;
- Mesh generation.

For our work we used Agisoft Photoscan, a commercial software able to create 3D content from still images. The final output of this procedure is summarized in Fig. 3, where are visible the images POVs, as well as detailed information over the pictures and the 3D model characteristics.

At this stage, the 3D model is ready to be used for different purposes; for archaeologist the maximum level of detail (LOD) is needful for documentation or restoration aims. However, such a high LOD requires very high computational

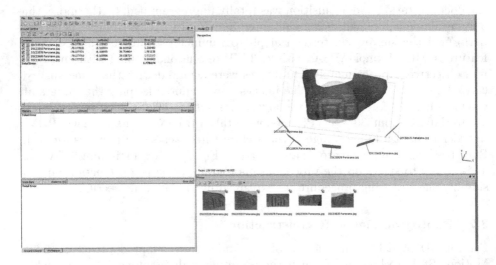

Fig. 3. Images during the SFM process. After the orientation phase, the relative position of the photos is fixed. The final result is a detailed 3D mesh of the door (in this case a single portion)

Fig. 4. 3D models with maximum LOD.

expenses, and the 3D model would be unusable for touristic or public visualization purposes. This is true especially for an Augmented Reality experience; 3D models are visualized into commercially available smart devices, where real time rendering performances are yet low; besides, due to portability issues, applications require strong optimization. 3D models, developed with the aforementioned techniques, are visible in Fig. 4; the high accuracy of reconstruction, as well as the resolution of the textures, would not allow the visualization in AR. A hard task is the model simplification with the higher lossless compression possible. This problem has been addressed and the AR was made possible, as explained in the next section.

4   Augmented Reality

The application developed for this case study performs location-based AR to visualize *in-context* the entrance door rests. As the archaeological findings are conceived, a classical image-based target detection is not possible. Furthermore, a location-based AR allow to simply retrieve contents from the database. There are several key aspects that must be taken into account for this kind of AR experience; terrestrial coordinates are mandatory for a correct positioning of 3D models. This is possible thanks to GPS receiver built-in into smart devices, while the coordinates of the model have been calculated from the images exif file; in fact, the camera is equipped with GPS receiver that register the position of each single shot. Transformation parameters have been stored into the database, while the device orientation is expressed as a 3-D vector thanks to the gyroscope. Managing all these information it is possible to project the 3D model on the screen from the perspective of the camera's view, based on the orientation of the device. The application was developed for iOS devices, and in particular was tested on iPad Air due to its highest performances (i.e. hardware components and display resolution). The development has been conducted using XCode 5 and Metaio SDK framework an Augmented Reality framework which provides advanced development tools[1]

---

[1] http://www.metaio.com.

Fig. 5. On site augmented reality visualization

Table 1. List of parameters and features about 3D models. Max LOD is referred to the photogrammetric process output, while AR LOD is referred to the 3D model after the simplification.

Features	Max LOD	AR LOD
Polygon counting	84697	14029
Faces	199999	20058
Vertexes	99805	10173
3D model dimension	$134{,}33Mb$	$1{,}953Mb$
3D model file format	$.ply$	$.obj$
Texture dimension	$54Mb$	$4{,}5Mb$
Texture file format	$.tiff$	$.png$

The user experience visualization is strictly related to the ability of displaying accurate and detailed 3D models. As said before, the problem is to provide simplified model, without loosing quality. However, polygon counting, textures dimensions and file formats for mobile applications reveal several limitations[2]

To overcome these issues, a tidy process of simplification was carried out in order to achieve the results visible in Fig. 5, while data about 3D model are shown in Table 1.

5   Discussion: Towards a Cultural Object Standardization

In this part we present our proposal of creating a knowledge base applied to archaeological sites, that can be easily extended to cultural objects in general, always in term of augmented reality. In our paper we refer to an archaeological

---

[2] https://dev.metaio.com/content-creation/3d-animation/polygon-count/ general-guidelines/.

site, in this context our idea is to create a standard for the augmented reality applied to archaeological sites with the aim of adding to the real world, a 3D model, together with multimedia objects (such as image, text, audio, video) and/or a description, based on this standard. For the aim of this paper, the idea is to dictate general guidelines valid to build an AR environment for archaeological sites. Where most of the monuments become ruins have the necessity to be restored or rebuilt.

From the standardization point of view, ARCO project [16,17,22] also proposed a novel metadata element set useful to describe cultural objects and their representation for building virtual exhibition. However, this application is for museum as other referring works [9,15,20].

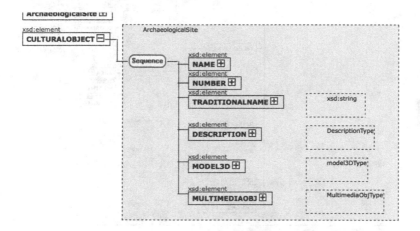

Fig. 6. Graphical representation of XML Schema archaeological site.

Figure 6 shows the graphical representation of XML schema of an archaeological site that is also valid for any cultural object. The scheme shows the attributes characterizing the cultural object class. The cultural object is described both regarding physical, localization, conservation aspects and also from the AR point of view. This last refers to the 3D model of the virtual object and to the multimedia objects that can be superimposed to the real environment.

According to the specifications based on ICCD (Istituto Centrale per il Catalogo e la Documentazione)[3] we have defined the Description class, as Fig. 7 shows. In this class are listed physical, localization, conservation and chronological aspects describing the archaeological site, important for its correct identification and geolocalization.

The attributes of the 3D model and of the multimedia objects overlapping to the site are described together with their features in Figs. 8 and 9. The 3D model of the virtual object superimposed on the real environment is created on the base

---

[3] http://www.iccd.beniculturali.it/index.php?it/473/standard-catalografici.

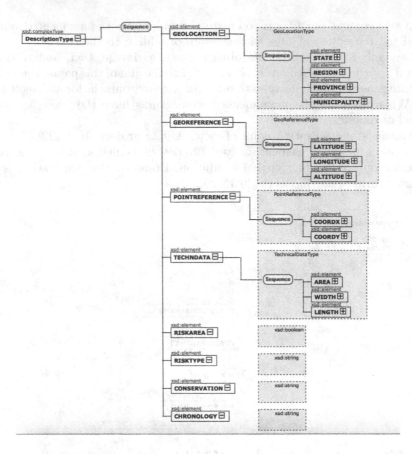

Fig. 7. Graphical representation of Class Description.

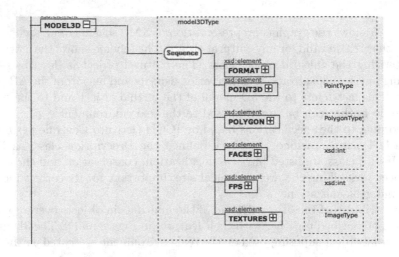

Fig. 8. Graphical representation of Class 3D Model.

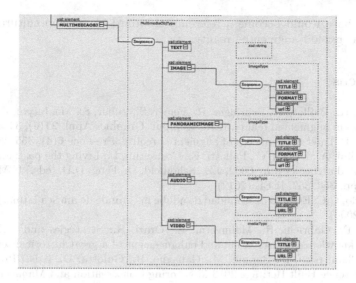

Fig. 9. Graphical representation of Class Multimedia Object.

of the attributes of Model3D. Observing Fig. 8, we listed the attributes of the 3D model, highlighting the key characteristic of being a scalable object. In other words, the 3D model can be adapted to build any different object compatible with whichever resolution or file format, and so on. The purpose is to create a 3D model class more scalable possible in view of the standardization. A scalable structure means making data multipurpose; as explained in Sect. 3.2, the LOD needed by archaeologists or scientist is different from tourist's one.

6 Conclusions

In this paper we outlined best practices for the applicability of Augmented Reality in the archaeological domain, starting from unplanned survey campaign. Chan Chan, as well as many other archaeological sites in the world, hide their priceless rests under earth due to conservation reasons; although this practice allows to preserve cultural heritage, prevents the wider public to see these rests. AR allows the visualization of rests, also where they are invisible. 3D models have been tested and handled to be suitable for AR visualization, for a quick and responsive user experience. Our solution pursue the aim to outline a workflow for archaeologists during their campaigns. The 3D visualization and the distribution of additional information is needful for both insiders or non-expert users.

In the last paragraph, we have also introduced the idea to create a knowledge base applied to cultural object in general and then to archaeological sites, always in term of augmented reality. Even if the approach here presented is still experimental, we retain that it is important to further develop this aspect in order to construct a knowledge base for Cultural Heritage using augmented reality. This knowledge base would become a reference standard to develop cultural object project that exploit augmented reality.

References

1. Azuma, R., Baillot, Y., Behringer, R., Feiner, S., Julier, S., MacIntyre, B.: Recent advances in augmented reality. IEEE Comput. Graphics Appl. **21**(6), 34–47 (2001)
2. Azuma, R.T., et al.: A survey of augmented reality. Presence **6**(4), 355–385 (1997)
3. Bernardini, A., Delogu, C., Pallotti, E., Costantini, L.: Living the past: augmented reality and archeology. In: 0002, J.Z., Schonfeld, D., Feng, D.D. (eds.) ICME Workshops, pp. 354–357. IEEE (2012)
4. Delgrado, C.C: Estudio de la ciudad de adobe ms grande de amrica latina. Editorial Orus (2006)
5. Colosi, F., Gabrielli, R., Malinverni, E., Orazi, R.: Strategies and technologies for the knowledge, conservation and enhancement of a great historical settlement: Chan Chan, peru. In: Boriani, M., Gabaglio, R., Gulotta, D., (eds.) Proceedings of Conference Built Heritage 2013 Monitoring Conservation and Management, pp. 56–64 (2013)
6. Colosi, F., Orazi, R.: Studi e progetti per la creazione del parco archeologico di chan chan. Rivista italiana di studi americanistici **30**(31), 139–172 (2011)
7. Colosi, F., Fangi, G., Gabrielli, R., Orazi, R., Angelini, A., Bozzi, C.A.: Planning the archaeological park of Chan Chan (peru) by means of satellite images, gis and photogrammetry. J. Cult. Herit. **10**, e27–e34 (2009)
8. Damala, A., Marchal, I., Houlier, P.: Merging augmented reality based features in mobile multimedia museum guides. In: Anticipating the Future of the Cultural Past, CIPA Conference 2007, 1–6 October 2007, pp. 259–264 (2007)
9. Doerr, M.: The CIDOC conceptual reference module: an ontological approach to semantic interoperability of metadata. AI Mag. **24**(3), 75 (2003)
10. Eggert, D., Hücker, D., Paelke, V.: Augmented reality visualization of archeological data. In: Buchroithner, M., Prechtel, N., Prechtel, D. (eds.) Cartography from Pole to Pole. LNGC, pp. 203–216. Springer, Heidelberg (2014)
11. Herrmann, H., Pastorelli, E.: Virtual reality visualizationfor photogrammetric 3D reconstructions of cultural heritage. In: De Paolis, L.T., Mongelli, A. (eds.) AVR 2014. LNCS, vol. 8853, pp. 283–295. Springer, Heidelberg (2014)
12. Kato, H., Billinghurst, M.: Marker tracking and hmd calibration for a video-based augmented reality conferencing system. In: Proceedings of the 2nd IEEE and ACM International Workshop on Augmented Reality 1999 (IWAR'99), pp. 85–94. IEEE (1999)
13. Krueger, M.W., Gionfriddo, T., Hinrichsen, K.: Videoplace an artificial reality. ACM SIGCHI Bull. **16**, 35–40 (1985). ACM
14. L, H.M.: Sensorama simulator (28 August 1962) uS Patent 3,050,870. http://www.google.com/patents/US3050870
15. McKenna, G., Association, M.D., et al.: SPECTRUM: The UK museum documentation standard. Museum Documentation Association (2005)
16. Mourkoussis, N., Liarokapis, F., Darcy, J., Pettersson, M., Petridis, P., Lister, P., White, M.: Virtual and augmented reality applied to educational and cultural heritage domains. In: Proceedings of Business Applications of Virtual Reality, Workshop (2002)

17. Mourkoussis, N., White, M., Patel, M., Chmielewski, J., Walczak, K.: Ams-metadata for cultural exhibitions using virtual reality. In: International Conference on Dublin Core and Metadata Applications, pp. 193–202 (2003)
18. Noh, Z., Sunar, M.S., Pan, Z.: A review on augmented reality for virtual heritage system. In: Chang, M., Kuo, R., Kinshuk, Chen, G.-D., Hirose, M. (eds.) Learning by Playing. LNCS, vol. 5670, pp. 50–61. Springer, Heidelberg (2009)
19. Papagiannakis, G., Ponder, M., Molet, T., Kshirsagar, S., Cordier, F., Magnenatthalmann, N., Thalmann, D.: Lifeplus: revival of life in ancient pompeii. In: Proceedings of the 8th International Conference on Virtual Systems and Multimedia (VSMM 02) Gyeongju, Korea, pp. 25–27 (2002)
20. Trant, J., Richmond, K., Bearman, D.: Open concepts: museum digital documentation for education through the amico library. Art Libr. J. **27**(3), 30–42 (2002)
21. Vlahakis, V., Ioannidis, N., Karigiannis, J., Tsotros, M., Gounaris, M., Stricker, D., Gleue, T., Daehne, P., Almeida, L.: Archeoguide: an augmented reality guide for archaeological sites. IEEE Comput. Graphics Appl. **22**(5), 52–60 (2002)
22. White, M., Mourkoussis, N., Darcy, J., Petridis, P., Liarokapis, F., Lister, P., Walczak, K., Wojciechowski, K., Cellary, W., Chmielewski, J., et al.: Arco-an architecture for digitization, management and presentation of virtual exhibitions. In: Proceedings of the Computer Graphics International 2004, pp. 622–625. IEEE (2004)
23. Zollner, M., Keil, J., Wust, H., Pletinckx, D.: An augmented reality presentation system for remote cultural heritage sites. In: Proceedings of the 10th International Symposium on Virtual Reality, Archaeology and Cultural Heritage VAST, pp. 112–116. Citeseer (2009)

Advanced Interaction with Paintings by Augmented Reality and High Resolution Visualization: A Real Case Exhibition

Roberto Pierdicca[1]($\boxtimes$), Emanuele Frontoni[1], Primo Zingaretti[1],
Mirco Sturari[1], Paolo Clini[2], and Ramona Quattrini[2]

[1] DII-Dipartimento di Ingegneria Dell' Informazione,
Università Politecnica Delle Marche, Ancona, Italy
{r.pierdicca,e.frontoni,p.zingaretti,m.sturari}@univpm.it
http://www.univpm.it
[2] DICEA-Dipartimento di Ingegneria Civile Edile E Dell' Architettura,
Università Politecnica Delle Marche, Ancona, Italy
{p.clini,r.quattrini}@univpm.it
http://www.univpm.it

Abstract. In this paper, an interactive installation system for the enjoyment of the cultural heritage in a real case museum environment is presented. By using Augmented Reality technology, mobile application and High Resolution visualization we provide the users with a visual augmentation of their surroundings and a touch interaction technique to display digital contents for cultural heritage promotion, allowing museum visitors to interact with digital contents in an intuitive and exciting manner. The exhibition here presented is the result of previous research over the use of new technologies (e.g. Augmented Reality) for Cultural Heritage promotion. Descriptions of the hardware system component and software development details are presented, with particular focus over the application implementation. Furthermore, we outline a possible Multimedia AR Installation connected with a semantic network.

Keywords: Augmented reality · Cultural heritage · Mobile application · Museum · Visualization

1 Introduction

Nowadays, cultural heritage (CH) exhibitions are becoming ever more interactive. Museums undertake the strategy of offering technological services to its visitors; furthermore, insiders are increasing their awareness about the need to provide visitors innovative solution of experiencing art. The spreading of advanced digital tools (e.g. mobile applications, addictive interaction systems and multimedia contents) made possible a new paradigm for art installations. Despite some art curators still believe that the use of technology will place art in background, new trends in the international panorama demonstrate how such

© Springer International Publishing Switzerland 2015
L.T. De Paolis and A. Mongelli (Eds.): AVR 2015, LNCS 9254, pp. 38–50, 2015.
DOI: 10.1007/978-3-319-22888-4_4

innovative tools are the best (and only) way to enhance the fruition of CH. With this aim, we present our work, experienced into a real exhibition to prove how a personal own approach with the visual arts produces an increasing enjoyment for the users. The installation described in this paper took place in Reggio Emilia within the temporary exhibition titled *"PIERO DELLA FRANCESCA. Il disegno tra arte e scienza"*[1]; more in deep, the facsimile of Urbino's Ideal City, a masterpiece of Renaissance age, was enhanced with two different contents: on a touchscreen, the high definition (HD) picture of the painting enables a 3X zoom visualization while the mobile app allows connecting several notes (textual or info graphics) also over the painting throughout augmented reality (AR) technologies. A schematic clarification about the developed workflow is described in Fig. 1. The inspiration for the concept of such installation is twofold. On the one hand, a goal is to provide visitors with a mobile tool to deepen their knowledge of the painting in an interactive way, also thanks to the AR section, extending the visualization of the real painting with the superimposition of digital contents. On the other, the high resolution allows to visualize several details otherwise invisible with the naked eyes. The combination of the aforementioned contents are the result of a previous work [6], over the use of innovative techniques for the CH promotion; indeed, previous research delivered meaningful results arising from a user test in the AR app usability. Improvements for image matching were made in terms of feature extraction as well as key point detection, both aspect that embrace many other computer vision fields [9,10,23]. Starting from this, we purse the aim to show strong enhancement in terms of usability and tracking system for AR, improvements that led to the real installation here presented. This paper is organized as follows: in the next section we debate over the importance of digitization for CH promotion purposes; Sect. 3 is dedicated to the presentation of the real scenario installation, with the description of digital contents implementation. Finally, in the last part of the paper, we discuss our approach and we also open some new opportunities of developments taking into account our experiences.

2 Mobile Application and Interaction Systems for Museums Exhibitions

Toward the direction of enhancing CH fruition, researchers are conducting their efforts on the development of new digital tools; the main goal of this research field is to provide users - insiders as well as non expert public - with new instruments for the knowledge and dissemination of artistic heritage. The ICT approach also for CH domain is carrying successful influence, for example increasing the interest of young people by means of new tools. Generally, museums installations that do not introduce new technologies, are often boring and do not always have the reputation of being attractive [11]. Furthermore, learning experiences in museums

---

[1] Website: http://www.palazzomagnani.it/2014/11/piero-della-francesca-il-disegno-tra-arte-e-scienza.

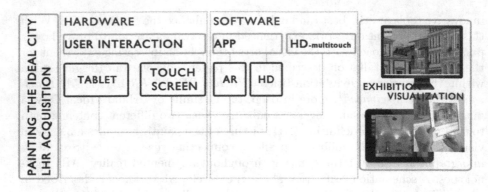

Fig. 1. Phases and connections between elements: the production chain from the LHR acquisition to the exhibition.

have been facilitated only by the use of labels and descriptions, to accompany the exhibits which are informative but not interactive [14]. Nevertheless, during the last years, a great number of art galleries decided to offer multimedia services in order to replace - or better, improve - the existing standard solutions [4]. Moreover, the ICT approach enables new media and storytelling, that represents as a major interest in users experience [18,21]. This is particularly true in terms of mobile development. Since the use of mobile devices is increasing also for cultural and museum sectors, the number of apps available on the main stores (e.g. Google Play, Apple Store) is daily growing; in particular, many Museums Apps are noteworthy. A good survey over this kind of application, as well as over impact of mobile devices in terms of app development can be found in [13]. Also in the Italian National panorama this trend is strengthening, as demonstrated by the increasing number of mobile apps available in the stores[2]. Many aspects have to be taken into account developing a mobile app; planning and production of cultural content for mobile usage should respect the synergy between digital contents and usability. Furthermore, proper planning of the steps development is mandatory. Helpful dissertation over mobile development for CH can be found in [2]. For the development of our solution, as described in Sect. 1, all these issues have been considered.

Also Augmented Reality systems have demonstrated to be valuable solution for Cultural Heritage promotion. AR represents a stimulating solution in order to navigate, interact and discover within museum settings. It can provide a more intuitive interaction technique with the displayed objects, while for the AR scientific community, museums provide contextually rich indoor environments for experimentation with AR applications [7]. More in deep, there are many technical challenges to overcome and museum environments are particularly suitable to manage with different lighting conditions which is the main issue to face with for the development of image-based tracking system [16]. The recent

---

[2] Website: http://www.beniculturali.it/App.

increase of computational capabilities, sensor equipment and the advancement
of 3D accelerated graphics technologies for handheld devices, offer the potential
to make the AR heritage systems more comfortable to carry and wear, facilitating the spread of this kind of AR systems to the mass market [12]. Literature provides many relevant works about using AR mobile application for CH
purposes [1,3,5,8].

Another important aspect that is useful to be introduced is the visualization of art contents through advanced display techniques. Recent advances in
visual display solutions are enabling users to experience digital content in new
ways through multimedia touchscreen [17,22]. The key aspect that make such
techniques particularly suitable for museum application, is the possibility to
visualize paintings with a very high level of detail, with the possibility to dive
into brushstroke-level detail[3]. Conveying all the aforementioned considerations,
in the following our solution is presented, with particular focus on the exhibition
and the preliminary development phases.

3   Overall Exhibition Design

The whole installation system (see Fig. 2) is composed by a faithful (and real-
scale) facsimile of the "Ideal City" painting and a touchscreen. The artwork is
flanked by tablets, which allow visitors to interact with multimedia contents
thanks to the applications, already installed; inside the touchscreen the HR
image of the painting is installed. The different "visions"of the same artwork,
here accessible, form a new way to communicate paintings and to facilitate its
disclosure with *edutainment* practices. The HD makes more evocative looking
at the painting, because it allows to watch it as well as the artist and to enter
the will of representation. The "Città Ideale" app facilitates the link with the
painting thanks to the technology, but the tool still needs the real art work, in its
physical dimension, in a close relationship between art and technology. Details
about development and technical issues are discussed below.

3.1   Multi-touch High Resolution

In the exhibition it is possible to use a browser to navigate the Ideal City
macrophotography trough a touchscreen. The user can perceive an amplifica-
tion of the painted surface that puts in contact to the work of the artist at
a brushstroke-scale. To permit the use of huge imagery for users visualization
purposes, we used a virtual texturing technique, a combination of classical MIP-
mapping and virtual memory usage [15]. The approach consists in storing tiled
images composing a multi-resolution pyramid, and loads only the tiles needed to
perform the texture at user request. For each level of zoom, the set of tiles corresponding to the observed texture lookup (2D+level- of-detail/scale coordinates)
is determined [19]. The implementation was performed by Zoomify[4], a specific

---

[3] Website: https://www.google.com/culturalinstitute/project/art-project.
[4] Website: http://www.zoomify.com.

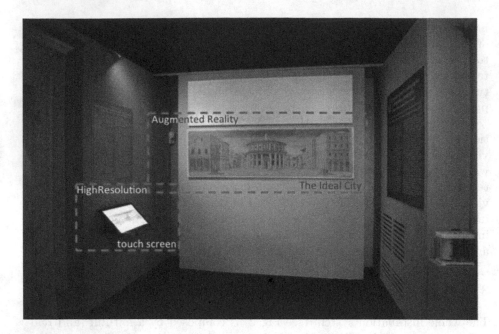

Fig. 2. The exhibition outlook. On the touchscreen the high resolution imagery of the painting. On the center the *facsimile* of the Ideal City artwork for the AR visualization.

tool that makes high-quality images zoom-and-pan for fast, interactive viewing with HTML, JPEGs, and JavaScript. Also multi touch gestures were developed for a more intuitive interaction with the image. This interesting feature has been included also as one section of the mobile application, discussed in the Sect. 3.2.

3.2 Mobile Application

The mobile application (see Fig. 3) has been developed for tablet running both Android and iOS operative systems. The application is available in the stores[5,6,7]; the whole project was implemented using Titanium Appcelerator SDK[8], a powerful tool to build native cross-platform mobile application using JavaScript and the Titanium API, which abstracts the native APIs of the mobile platforms.

The application schema is simple and intuitive. At the bottom of the homepage screen, five buttons enclose static themes:

– Where and when, for a general overview;
– Hidden geometry, to show hidden preparatory lines made by the author during the painting realization;

---

[5] https://itunes.apple.com/it/app/citta-ideale-ar/id897564242?mt=8.
[6] https://itunes.apple.com/it/app/citta-ideale/id897022892?mt=8.
[7] https://play.google.com/store/apps/details?id=com.univpm.it.
[8] http://www.appcelerator.com.

– Restoration, provide details about restorations made among the years;
– Twin tables, to deep analogies with other similar paintings in the world and
– Ideal Cities, to discover some attempts made in the history to realize such cities

   Also a useful toolbar was designed to drive the user toward a dynamic fruition of the painting, enabling for a entertaining interaction. The four sections are:

– High resolution:

   starting from the tools explained in Sect. 3.1, the HR image visualization has been incorporated also into the mobile application. In this case, to support the user in discovering conceived details of the paintings, a scrollbar with hotspot was designed at the bottom of the screen. This section tells some highlights through magnifications in some portion of the paining. In the meanwhile textual contents facilitate the comprehension, HR visualization is a handy instrument.
– 360 virtual tour:
   exploits spherical photogrammetric acquisition to virtually discover and navigate the entire museum collection, switching among different rooms. This function fulfill two aspects: a remote navigation through museum spaces and an improvement in terms of way finding when the user is in the Museum context.
– Sharing:
   also a social network sharing was designed; the possibility to share the art collection and the user experience into the main social network is a best practice in the field of CH promotion.
– Augmented Reality:
   the device recognizes the tracked image and using this image it connects to internet getting associated images, visuals and 3D shapes, then putting them into the view. Details about this feature will be discussed in Sect. 3.3.

3.3   Augmented Reality

"Città Ideale AR" application is available for both iOS e Android platform stores too. For the development, we used Metaio Framework[9] and, to achieve the best user experience, we adopted image-based tracking system (i.e. markerless), using as tracking images ("trackables") small portions of the painting. In this way the user experience is natural and the continuum between real and virtual is achieved. To drive the user in a more intuitive manner of this tool, an audio-guide suggests the position of the Points of Interest (POIs). Once the video stream of the built in camera is on, the device implements a matching with the pre-loaded "trackables", searching for the *keypoints* associated to the images. Then the digital contents are projected on the screen from the perspective of the camera's

---

[9] http://www.metaio.com.

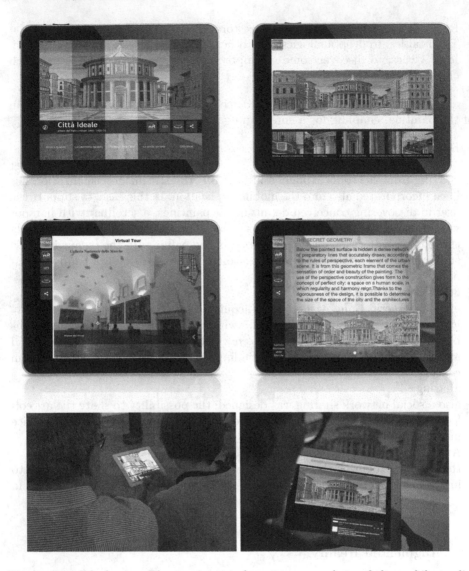

Fig. 3. Città Ideale app. The top images show two screenshots of the mobile application, the home page and the High Resolution sections. The images in the middle represent the virtual tour and one of the static pages for in-depth analysis. The bottom images show visitors using the app in front of the painting

view, based on the orientation of the device (Fig. 4). On the portrait we defined 6 different POIs for AR detection and user content overlapping. In particular we tested image-based contents, videos (with transparent background), shapes with text and interactive buttons to cope with social network activities and share contents from the AR application. The virtual exhibitions, displayed in the end-user interface, are dynamically generated based on parameterized visualization

Fig. 4. Augmented Reality application. Contents like images or videos are superimposed over the tablet screen.

templates and database contents. Highlights have been accurately selected by art curators and then stored on a external cloud-based database. The advantage of storing AR contents on an external repository lies in the possibility to change or update contents without the necessity to replace the app in the web stores. "Città Ideale AR" app, starting from the aforementioned work, proposes an innovative solution of experiencing paintings, allowing to interact with all the available multimedia contents realized for this project. Some key aspects of the application are:

- augmented view of the artwork;
- improvement of knowledge and curiosity about the painting;
- stable POI selection for different lighting conditions.

Furthermore, because of the aforementioned, the application is fully portable. It is possible standardize it, as the national panorama of Cultural Heritage would need a wider adoption of such instruments. In the next section, a possible conceptual model for multimedia interaction and semantic approach for CH application is presented.

4   Discussion and Future Developments

This installation naturally led us to conceive a sort of conceptual model for multimedia interaction. On the real side there are the artwork and the devices (i.e. handheld device and high-resolution touch-panel), on the virtual side there are the POIs while Information Technologies are in the middle like facilitator.

A POI is identified by an UUID (Universally Unique IDentifier), linked to artwork, associated to one or more multimedia content, containing at least one "marker/descriptor" and an optional series of possible interactions. UUID recalls immediately the world of DBMS (DataBase Management System): POIs and artworks are managed by an informatical system. Applications and installations are based upon this system that permits uniform organization of information and better management. This seems to be an obvious part, but this is the base for various developments. For example possibility to analyze visitors interaction with installations or in general with the entire museum collection through sensors network, like in retail field [20], for the improvement of museal stands. Relations, links and associations can go over well-known database and bring to concepts like sematic and ontology. Artworks are described in a semantic manner, POIs are theirselves semantic node connected directly with an artwork for hotpoint interaction and at the same time linked with other artworks and POIs. Figure 5 outlines interactions between user and multimedia installation, and data exchanged by components with a focus on XML schema defition of our POI.

These capabilities in an installation could bring to an improvement in the navigation path of the musuem, an association through visitors experience with other artwork in the same location or in other museums and collections. We do not ask visitors about their museal experience with questionable answers. The

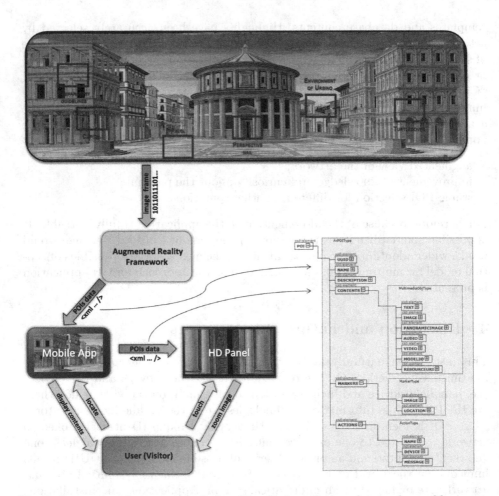

Fig. 5. Interactions between user and multimedia installation, data exchanged by components, compact representation of the POI's XML schema defition.

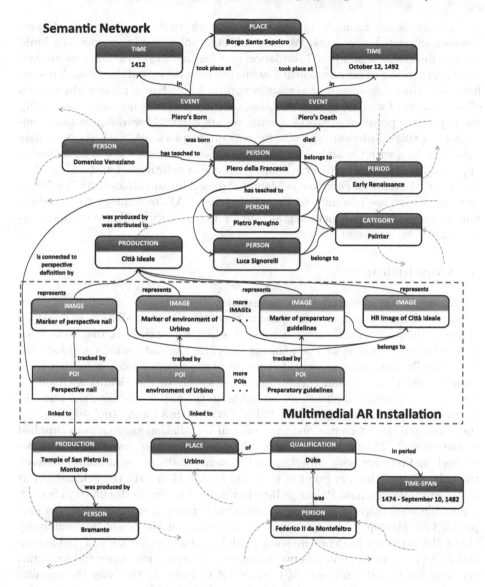

Fig. 6. Multimedia AR Installation connected in a sematic network.

musuem can tells us what visitors want to see or known and how they navigate through it. Multimedia content, markers and interactions should be described in the same semantic way to be an ontology entrypoint to the museal network. Museal experience can be built over multiple pathways for different user level, from curious visitor to expert. All the information are virtually floating over the artwork and visitor can choose those of his interest. In this way halls of the museum are covered by guidelines and a visitor can built his own enriched path.

Figure 6 is an example of semantic network that can describe relations between subjects and objects. We are studying a solution to incrementally build these connections around the installation in a feasible way. In general we are facing with fragmented information at low quality level for actual digital-multimedia handling. Under development semantic approach involves a greater abstraction effort compared with a common database project but it is necessary to amplify the expressive power of artworks. Lastly, we are currently working on the development of this exhibition type also for two masterpieces of "Galleria Nazionale delle Marche", with the ambitious attempt of a serialization schema for a "multi-app" development. The project is about the famous paintings "La Muta" by Raffaello and "Portrait of Federico da Montefeltro and his son Guidobaldo" by Pedro Berruguete; we are planning to extend the use of AR technology to the whole museum collection, also including an Augmented Reality guidance to guide visitors inside the museum.

5   Conclusion

In this paper we presented a new interesting installation to enhance the experience of visitors in a real case museum scenario. Our installation is made up of interactive tools strictly related on each other. An interactive touchscreen for a detailed visualization of the painting provides the user with a brushstroke-level visualization; some conceived elements of the artwork, such as hidden lines, author's afterthoughts and curiosities can be visible to the visitors with simple gestures. The mobile applications, available on the app stores, give the possibility to deepen the knowledge of the "Ideal City" with a handy tool and to reach the wider public. Of course, for the museum installation tablets were supplied to the visitors. Thanks to the Augmented Reality section, users can frame the artwork and interact with superimposed contents that are a continuum between the painting and the user point of view. On Friday 13th 2015 the exhibition was installed inside Magnani Palace in Reggio Emilia. Finally, as discussed in Sect. 4, a possible knowledge base for digital cultural heritage documentation was proposed. Our attempt is to open up the discussion on the scientific community about the necessity to delineate some guidelines to standardize ICT implementations to connect them in a network. Artworks become resources and museums act as cultural hosts in a sort of Internet Of Culture. In this way the installation should not remain a stand-alone object, but should become an interactive component of the semantic network that pervades artworks of the museum.

References

1. Bimber, O., Coriand, F., Kleppe, A., Bruns, E., Zollmann, S., Langlotz, T.: Superimposing pictorial artwork with projected imagery. IEEE Multimedia 12(1), 16–26 (2005)
2. Boiano, S., Bowen, J.P., Gaia, G.: Usability, design and content issues of mobile apps for cultural heritage promotion: the malta culture guide experience (2012). arXiv preprint arXiv:1207.3422

3. Brondi, R., Carrozzino, M., Tecchia, F., Bergamasco, M.: Mobile augmented reality for cultural dissemination. In: Proceedings of 1st International Conference on Information Technologies for Performing Arts, Media Access and Entertainment, Firenze, Italy, pp. 113–117 (2012)
4. Chen, C.Y., Chang, B., Huang, P.S.: Multimedia augmented reality information system for museum guidance. Pers. Ubiquitous Comput. **18**(2), 315–322 (2014)
5. Choudary, O., Charvillat, V., Grigoras, R., Gurdjos, P.: March: mobile augmented reality for cultural heritage. In: Proceedings of the 17th ACM international conference on Multimedia, pp. 1023–1024. ACM (2009)
6. Clini, P., Frontoni, E., Quattrini, R., Pierdicca, R.: Augmented reality experience: From high-resolution acquisition to real time augmented contents. Adv. Multimedia **2014**, 9 (2014)
7. Damala, A., Cubaud, P., Bationo, A., Houlier, P., Marchal, I.: Bridging the gap between the digital and the physical: design and evaluation of a mobile augmented reality guide for the museum visit. In: Proceedings of the 3rd international conference on Digital Interactive Media in Entertainment and Arts, pp. 120–127. ACM (2008)
8. DAmico, G., Del Bimbo, A., Ferracani, A., Landucci, L., Pezzatini, D.: Onna project: a natural interaction installation and mobile solution for cultural heritage. In: Toniolo, L., Boriani, M., Guidi, G. (eds.) Built Heritage: Monitoring Conservation Management, pp. 359–365. Springer, Switzerland (2015)
9. Frontoni, E., Mancini, A., Caponetti, F., Zingaretti, P.: Fast mobile robot localization using low cost sensors, vol. 8 (2006)
10. Frontoni, E., Mancini, A., Zingaretti, P.: Feature group matching: a novel method to filter out incorrect local feature matchings. Int. J. Pattern Recogn. Artif. Intell. **28**(05), 23 (2014)
11. Gerval, J.P., Ru, Y.L.: Fusion of multimedia and mobile technology in audioguides for museums and exhibitions. Intell. Syst. Ref. Libr. **84**, 173–205 (2015)
12. Giovanni, M., Fratarcangeli, M., Empler, T.: Augmented visualization on handheld devices for cultural heritage, pp. 97–103 (2013)
13. Laudazi, A., Boccaccini, R.: Augmented museums through mobile apps, vol. 1336, pp. 12–17 (2014)
14. Lu, W., Nguyen, L., Chuah, T., Do, E.: Effects of mobile ar-enabled interactions on retention and transfer for learning in art museum contexts. In: 2014 IEEE International Symposium on Mixed and Augmented Reality-Media, Art, Social Science, Humanities and Design (IMSAR-MASH'D), pp. 3–11. IEEE (2014)
15. Mayer, I., Scheiblauer, C., Mayer, A.J.: Virtual texturing in the documentation of cultural heritage-the domitilla catacomb in rome. In: Proceedings of XXIIIrd International CIPA Symposium (2011)
16. Miyashita, T., Meier, P., Tachikawa, T., Orlic, S., Eble, T., Scholz, V., Gapel, A., Gerl, O., Arnaudov, S., Lieberknecht, S.: An augmented reality museum guide, pp. 103–106 (2008)
17. Novotnỳ, M., Lacko, J., Samuelčík, M.: Applications of multi-touch augmented reality system in education and presentation of virtual heritage. Procedia Comput. Sci. **25**, 231–235 (2013)
18. Pescarin, S., Wallergird, M., Hupperetz, W., Pagano, A., Ray, C.: Archeovirtual 2011: an evaluation approach to virtual museums. In: 2012 18th International Conference on Virtual Systems and Multimedia (VSMM), pp. 25–32. IEEE (2012)
19. Petrovic, V., Vanoni, D.J., Richter, A., Levy, T.E., Kuester, F.: Visualizing high resolution three-dimensional and two-dimensional data of cultural heritage sites. Mediterr. Archaeol. Archaeometry **14**(4), 93–100 (2014)

20. Pierdicca, R., Liciotti, D., Contigiani, M., Frontoni, M., Zingaretti, P., Mancini, A.: Low cost embedded system for increasing retail environment intelligence (2015)
21. Quattrini, R., Baleani, E.: Theoretical background and historical analysis for 3D reconstruction model. villa thiene at cicogna. J. Cult. Heritage **16**(1), 119–125 (2014)
22. Wojciechowski, R., Walczak, K., White, M., Cellary, W.: Building virtual and augmented reality museum exhibitions. In: Proceedings of the ninth international conference on 3D Web technology, pp. 135–144. ACM (2004)
23. Zingaretti, P., Frontoni, E.: Appearance-based localization in partially explored environments. IEEE Robot. Autom. Mag. **13**, 59–68 (2006)

Cloud Computing and Augmented Reality for Cultural Heritage

Pietro Vecchio[1], Francesca Mele[1], Lucio Tommaso De Paolis[1], Italo Epicoco[1(✉)],
Marco Mancini[2], and Giovanni Aloisio[1,2]

[1] Department of Engineering for Innovation, University of Salento, Lecce, Italy
pvecchio2014@gmail.com,
{francesca.mele,lucio.depaolis,italo.epicoco,
giovanni.aloisio}@unisalento.it
[2] Euro-Mediterranean Center on Climate Change, Lecce, Italy
marco.mancini@cmcc.it, giovanni.aloisio@cmcc.it

Abstract. In this paper the use of augmented reality and cloud computing technology to enrich the scenes of sites with a relevant cultural interest is proposed. The main goal is to develop a mobile application to improve the user's cultural experience during the sightseeing of a city of art through the integration of digital contents related to specific sites or historic monuments. The mobile application has been developed exploiting the Wikitude SDK software library. The huge amount of cultural digital contents (mainly represented by images) justifies the exploitation of a cloud-computing environment to obtain a multi-platform solution. In particular, we have chosen the KVM and OpenNebula as cloud platform technologies to build a private cloud environment, since they exhibit great features like openness, accessibility, simplicity and scalability. The work has been validated through test beds realized both in laboratory, using images captured from PC display, and in a real environment.

Keywords: Cloud computing · Augmented reality · Cultural heritage

1 Introduction

Nowadays many attempts for sharing and maintaining cultural contents by using cloud-computing technology have been made all over the world. ICT services and cloud computing make easier users access to cultural contents by providing application services (such as e-Learning, e-Library, e-Lab, e-Course), data services (such as learning materials, library collections and scientific publications) and infrastructure services (such as virtual storage). So, they can be used to narrowing the gap between different areas, gradually eliminate the digital divide, satisfy the people's cultural needs, improve the construction of a public cultural service system [1, 2].

The European biggest effort to digitize all of Europe's heritage and to make it publicly available for everyone is the Europeana project [3]. By combining databases from over 3,000 Europeana cultural heritage institutions and providing the access to more than 15 million cultural objects (images, texts, sounds, and videos), it gives a

© Springer International Publishing Switzerland 2015
L.T. De Paolis and A. Mongelli (Eds.): AVR 2015, LNCS 9254, pp. 51–60, 2015.
DOI: 10.1007/978-3-319-22888-4_5

unique online perspective on Europe's cultural heritage. An increasing number of projects, built using Europeana API, are contributing with technology solutions, cultural services and contents to Europeana. These projects are run by different cultural heritage institutions, and are co-funded by the European Commission's Content plus programme and the Information and Communications Technologies Policy Support Programme (ICT PSP). Among the others, CARARE is one of the most relevant project [4]. It aims at aggregating contents from the archaeology and architectural heritage making digital contents related to Europe's unique archaeological monuments and historic sites available to Europeana users. Moreover, the project provides tools and services to support its network of partners to make their digital contents interoperable with the Europeana environment and enables the access to 3D and Virtual Reality contents through Europeana cloud [5].

3D contents brought to European via the CARARE project, are complemented by 3DICONS project [6]. It enhances the contents base available to European users focusing on digital contents that include 3D models and reconstructions, enlarged models of important details and related images, texts and videos. It will also include and re-contextualize in 3D, objects belonging to a monument but presently located elsewhere, for example in museums. The project's activities also include the conversion of some existing 3D data into formats that are accessible by European users. The 3DICONS enriched Europeana with an unprecedented quantity of high-quality, 3D, well-organized and attractive information about the masterpieces of European architecture and archaeology [7].

In this context one of the most promising technology for enhancing the users experience, during the navigation through cultural heritage digital contents, is represented by the augmented reality. It can provide the user with an integration of digital contents with real images.

Due to the growing integration of powerful compute capabilities in mobile systems and smart-devices (i.e. oculus [8], google glass [9]), the augmented reality has become one of the research areas with higher demand and interest [10]. Nowadays the augmented reality is becoming even more pervasive in several applications such as in cultural heritage for improving tourism experience with a time navigation or with the integration of historic media [11, 12], in medical application to enhance and support surgical decisions [13, 14], in architectural construction, inspection and renovation [15] or to enhance the gaming experience [16].

This work describes how the augmented reality has been used in the cultural heritage context to enrich the scene of a point of interest (POI) with digital information. The implementation of such system and, in particular, the augmented reality applied in outdoor environment, requires that some challenging issues must be addressed such as the detection of a POI and its tracking when the camera moves. At the beginning, the first augmented reality platforms were implemented with some specific hardware solutions, adapted to different environments (e.g. [17–19]). With the grow of the market, mainly driven by the game consoles (i.e. Kinetic [20] and Nintendo Wii [21]), the devices which integrate cameras and sensors for motion detection, became the first augmented reality systems integrated in mobile systems. In that context, although there were some smart phones with supporting AR technology with marker-based algorithms, the solutions in an outdoor environment remained critical, due to hardware power that was still limited [22]. Many of those mobile platforms were not really user-friendly. The *Archeoguide* platform, that proposed an augmented reality system for the exploration of cultural sites located in the archaeological site of Olympia in Greece, visualizes the missing and artifacts in the damaged areas of site of Olympia overlaying much additional information. The disadvantage of that project was the use of a heavy wearable HDM integrated helmet (Head Mounted Display) that was not quite mobile. Afterwards, the advantages deriving from the increase of computational power embedded in the new generation of mobile systems led to the development of newer and more performing techniques of augmented reality for outdoor environment. In this regard, the image processing algorithms focused to the matching and tracking of the POIs within of the frame set of observation [23–25] represent the most accurate algorithm for detecting POIs. The increase of computational performance in mobile systems and the use of cloud technologies fostered the development of frameworks devoted to easy the implementation of AR applications, such Wikitude [26, 27] and Metaio [28]. These frameworks provide easy tools to build different multimedia applications exploiting the augmented reality techniques.

The main goal of this work concerns the development of a mobile application with augmented reality capabilities, able to enhance the user's experience while she walks through the streets of a city looking at monuments, cathedrals and more in general at sites with cultural interest, having all the digital contents in his hands [29].

The next section describes the requirements analysis and the software architecture; The Sect. 3 reports the details about the implementation; follows the description of a case study. Conclusions and future work are described in the last section.

2   Architecture

The requirements analysis represents the first phase of the development process, immediately followed by the design of the software architecture. The application is meant for users with very low knowledge of computer science that would like to enjoy the digital contents related to the cultural heritage by means of a common mobile device. For this reason the application must be intuitive, easy to use and it must respond in real time to the user interaction. The following main functional requirements have been identified for the application:

- Objects detection: the user must be able to easily use the camera equipped in her own mobile device for the purpose of framing a cultural asset and getting additional related digital contents. The application must hence be able to detect objects within the scene.
- Overlapping of digital contents with the real scene: once an object has been identified, the application retrieves all the related digital contents and provides the user with such information putting the virtual content on top of the real image acquired from the camera.
- Management of huge amount of data: the application must be able to handle a huge amount of data with several formats, such as texts, images, video, sounds associated to a specific cultural asset.
- Offline mode: the application should operate also when the connectivity is reduced or absent.

The application must also meet non-functional requirements:

- Intuitive to use: the user should be able to use the application without reading any user's manual. The GUI must include intuitive icons and tips
- Real Time: the application must respond in real time to the user actions.
- Cross platform: the application should be used on different mobile platform
- Fault tolerant: the application must correctly handle faults coming from external modules i.e. connection lost or noise images from the camera.

The proposed framework can be divided into two principal subsystems. The first subsystem contains the *Mobile* components loaded into a mobile device, while the second subsystem represents the *Cloud Layer* with its support systems. The overall system architecture is shown in Fig. 1. The *Mobile* subsystem is implemented from the *Scene Identifier* and the *Rest Call-Images Collector* modules.

The *Scene Identifier* module acquires the image from the camera in real time and, by means of the algorithms of *Wikitude SDK*, obtains the recognition of a particular Point Of Interest (*POI*) inside the acquired video frame. The recognition is obtained by comparing the *POI* inside the frame with those ones loaded in the *Target Collection File* (*wtc* file) of *Wikitude*. If the comparison finds some images, then the *Scene Identifier* module invokes a *REST CALL* request to the *Data Node* subsystem, which then returns all the images related to the matching POI in the video scene. All the selected images are also placed into a logical structure, called Images Collector, which acts as a cache space for the mobile application.

As shown in Fig. 1, the collection of images used for the POI recognition is placed and, continuously updated, in the database of the Data Node. The Data Node module

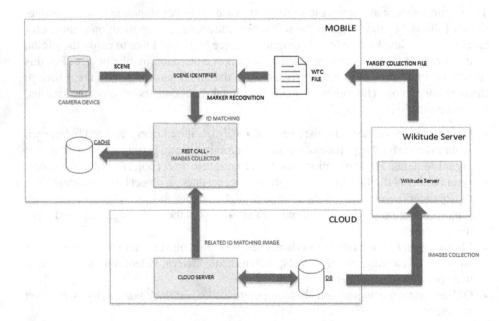

Fig. 1. Ovearall architecture of the system.

can add or remove images from the database; at the same time it interacts with the Wikitude Server to create or update the Target Collection File (wtc file) used by the Mobile subsystem. In this way, the Mobile device is able to use both the images loaded in the Data Node and the images stored locally in the mobile device for the detection of POIs. The local data cache also grants the use of the application in the offline mode.

3 Implementation

The proposed application uses the Wikitude SDK framework [10] and cloud computing technologies for obtaining an innovative, multi-platform and user-friendly augmented reality solution. Wikitude SDK ensures the integration with the main hardware platforms, i.e. Android, iOS, Smartphone, Tablet, Smart Glasses. It can integrate more cross-platform languages like JavaScript with HTML directly, to obtain a prototype portable on different mobile platforms. Wikitude implements the API calls in multi-platform environment with an SDK development toolkit in JAVA language.

All the API calls can be re-configured and customized according to the application environment. The JAVA language improves the implementation of multi-platform applications, like Android, iPhone and other smart-devices. The decision to adopt the JAVA language was also supported by the ability to integrate the java applets within web pages with dynamic content as JavaScript.

Wikitude SDK provides the tools to manage the dynamic interactions between the API calls of Augmented Reality with the HTML contents. At the same time, the use of JAVA language ensures the integration of the application modules of augmented reality with other Client/Server applications, like the cloud services and the database access.

The Wikitude framework includes a kernel for intercepting a particular POI inside the frame set of the mobile system, using particular matching and tracking algorithms. In this context, Wikitude engine continuously reads and compares in real time the captured frameset with a the model file with .wtc extension. The wtc model file contains all the information for all the POIs that the application should detect. According to the user requests and by the global position of the mobile system, the model file could be generated by the cloud or locally load into the mobile systems. When one POI is detected into the frame set, the Wikitude engine will send API calls for loading all the images from the cloud repository. A virtual slider with navigation buttons and various touch-screen interactions is created. According to the Internet services and with the user settings, the proposed application could be used offline, by using images and internet structures saved in the cache memory of the mobile system. The virtual slider is synthesized with the historical images loaded for a particular POI and it is implemented by using only the Wikitude Toolkit. The development has been realized through the Instrument for Development with Eclipse in Android environment.

For the purpose of our research we have chosen KVM (Kernel-based Virtual Machine) and OpenNebula open source cloud platform [30] as private cloud technology, since it exhibits great features like openness, simplicity and scalability. OpenNebula assumes that physical infrastructure adopts a cluster-like architecture with a front-end, and a set of hosts where Virtual Machines (VM) will be executed. In order to meet the storage needs of Wikitude application, the Ceph software storage platform [31] is used. It is a distributed store object and file system designed to provide excellent performance, reliability and scalability. Its distributed storage solution allows the system to scale horizontally with multiple machines/heads instead of the more traditional methodologies which use centralized heads with large amounts of storage attached to them. Like most distributed storage solutions, Ceph really has 3 main components:

- *Ceph OSDs* (Object Storage Devices) i.e. the place where the blocks get stored. A Ceph OSD Daemon stores data, handles data replication, recovery, backfilling, rebalancing, and provides some monitoring information to Ceph Monitors.
- *Ceph MDS* (Meta-Data Server) i.e. the place where the meta-data about files and blocks gets stored, especially used for looking up where the blocks are stored;
- *Ceph MON* (Monitors) i.e. the component keeping track of the state of the clustering. It is responsible for cluster management, configuration and state.

4   Case Study

In this section the cloud hardware infrastructure hosting Wikitude application is described. Our cluster configuration is composed by six nodes equipped with the following hardware specifications:

- 2x Intel Xeon Processor E5-2660 v2 (25 M Cache, 2.20 GHz)
- 256 GB RAM (16 blocks of 16 GB)
- 1x 200GB SSD IBM S3700 Enterprise
- 2x1TB HD in Raid 1 hosting the OS
- 4x3TB HD in JBOD mode (for Ceph Storage Cluster)
- 3x NIC 1 Gb/s
- 2x NIC 10 Gb/s

The cluster is configured as a private cloud with OpenNebula 4.10.2 and Ceph v0.87 Giant release (used as a datastore for Virtual Machine images). Each cluster node, running Linux Cent OS 7.0, acts both as a hypervisor node (Libvirt with QEMU/KVM) for the execution of virtual machines and as a Ceph storage node. Each node is configured with 4 Ceph OSD Daemons, one for each 3TB spinning drive; moreover on 3 of the 6 nodes, there is also the Ceph monitoring daemon. In order to augment storage performance, each node SSD is used for reducing random access time and read latency and accelerating throughput; in particular each SSD is partitioned in the ratio of 1:4 to store the journal data of each Ceph OSD daemon, while the object data are stored on the spinning hard disk drives that are subject to limitations on seek time, access time, read and write times, as well as total throughput. Those physical limitations affect overall system performance–especially during recovery, and can be furthermore reduced by using a dedicated drive (2xHD in raid 1 in our case) for the operating system and software, different from the HDs used for the object storage. Regarding the networking setup, one of the 10 Gb/s NIC is used for the accessing Ceph Storage from the VMs while the other 10 Gb/s NIC is used as an intra-cluster network during the Ceph recovery and rebalancing operations for performance and security reasons. One 1 Gb/s NIC serves to connect to Internet, another 1 Gb/s NIC is used for management, and the third 1 Gb/s NIC is used for connecting to other computing resource.

Ceph stores the client data as objects within storage pools. Using a *crush* algorithm, Ceph calculates which placement group should contain the object, and further calculates which Ceph OSD Daemon should store the placement group. The *crush* algorithm enables the Ceph Storage Cluster to scale, rebalance, and recover dynamically. Since 4.0 version, OpenNebula provides an interface for *Ceph RBDs* (RADOS Block Device), which allows registering images directly in a Ceph pool, and running VMs using that backend. In order to assure the correct use of OpenNebula with Ceph the OpenNebula worker nodes are part of a working Ceph cluster, the Ceph pool is available and the Libvirt/KVM is used as hypervisor.

For the test bed, a tablet Nexus 7 Asus with Android Kit-Kat 4.4.4 has been used. In Fig. 2 the result of the temporal/historical interaction is shown.

Fig. 2. Result shows an added images slider, on the bottom of the display, and a historical image overlapped on the real scene

In the proposed approach all of the historic images of the cathedral are displayed in the slide bar at the bottom of the screen. The user can select the historic image that will be superimposed on the real one. In the first phases, the images captured directly from the display of a PC have been used; afterwards others test beds will be conducted in real environment. When the user selects an historic image, a pop-up window is shown with the detailed information about the selection. The selected image can be seen in the contextual window and eventually in full screen (see Fig. 3).

Fig. 3. The augmented reality shows an image slider and a temporal label related to the object on the right of the display

5   Conclusion

The manuscript treats an innovative system to enhance the edutainment in the cultural heritage with a cloud computing support. The proposed framework implements two principal components: *Mobile* component and the *Data Node* module. The *Data Node* module manages the *Rest Call* request calls from the mobile device and updates the images collection for detecting new *POIs*.

The *Mobile* component detects POIs inside the captured video frame and composes the augmented scene with a virtual image slider. The *Mobile* component implements the augmented services and communicates with the *Data Node* for retrieving the images to synthetize the virtual slider. The overall architecture has been implemented around the *Wikitude Sdk* engine both for the *Mobile* component and for the *Data Node*. The prototype of the *Mobile* component has been implemented through the Instrument for Development with Eclipse in Android environment; while the *Data Node* module has been performed by using Ceph software storage platform.

Future developments will be conducted by improving the interoperability with different data formats, and by introducing cross platforms technologies in order to support a wide variety of mobile devices, i.e. *iPhone* and *Window Phone*.

Acknowledgments. This work was carried out under the DICET - INMOTO - ORganization of Cultural HEritage for Smart Tourism and Real-time Accessibility (OR.C.HE.S.T.R.A.) project with the financial support of the Italian Ministry of Education, Universities and Research. The authors would like to thank the CMCC Supercomputing Center for providing support in the setup of the private cloud infrastructure.

References

1. Li, S., Wang, D.: The study of culture sharing project based on cloud computing. In: 2013 Sixth International Conference on Business Intelligence and Financial Engineering (BIFE), pp. 62–69, Hangzhou, 14–16 November 2013
2. Nan Cenka, B.A., Hasibuan, Z.A.: Enhancing educational services using cloud technology. In: 2013 International Conference of Information and Communication Technology (ICoICT), pp. 155–160, Bandung, 20–22 March 2013
3. Europeana project website. http://www.europeana.eu/portal/
4. CARARE project website. http://www.carare.eu
5. Masci, M.E., De Santis, A., Fernie, K., Pletinckx, D.: 3D in the CARARE project: providing Europeana with 3D content for the archaeological and architectural heritage: the Pompeii case study. In: 2012 18th International Conference on Virtual Systems and Multimedia (VSMM), pp. 227–234. IEEE, Milan (2012)
6. 3D ICONS project website. http://www.3dicons-project.eu/
7. D'Andrea, A., Niccolucci, F., Bassett, S., Fernie, K.: 3D-ICONS: world heritage sites for Europeana: making complex 3D models available to everyone. In: 2012 18th International Conference on Virtual Systems and Multimedia (VSMM), pp. 517–520, Milan, 2–5 September 2012
8. LaValle, S.M., Yershova, A., Katsev, M., Antonov, M.: Head tracking for the Oculus Rift. In: International Conference on Robotics and Automation (ICRA). IEEE, 31 May 2014–7 June 2014
9. Ackerman, E.: Google gets in your face: google glass offers a slightly augmented version of reality. IEEE Spectr. **50**(1), 26–29 (2013)
10. Butchart, B.: Augmented reality for smartphones. Technical report, JISC Observator (2011)
11. Fiore, A., Mainetti, L., Manco, L., Marra, P.: Augmented reality for allowing time navigation in cultural tourism experiences: a case study. In: De Paolis, L.T., Mongelli, A. (eds.) AVR 2014. LNCS, vol. 8853, pp. 296–301. Springer, Heidelberg (2014)
12. Zoellner, M., Keil, J., Drevensek, T., Wuest, H.: Cultural heritage layers: integrating historic media in augmented reality. In: International Conference on Virtual Systems and Multimedia, VSMM 2009, vol. 15, pp. 193–196, 9–12 September 2009
13. De Paolis, L.T., Aloisio, G., Pulimeno, M.: An augmented reality application for the enhancement of surgical decisions. In: ACHI 2011: The Fourth International Conference on Advances in Computer-Human Interactions
14. Kilby, J., Gray, K., Elliott, K., Martin-Sanchez, F., Waycott, J., Dave, B.: Interface, information and interaction: an exploration of mobile augmented reality present and future. IBES The University of Melbourne
15. Webster, A., Feiner, S., MacIntyre, B., Massie, W., Krueger, T.: Augmented reality in architectural construction, inspection and renovation. In: Proceedings of the ASCE Third Congress on Computing in Civil Engineering, pp. 913–919, June 1996
16. Piekarski, W., Thomas, B.: ARQuake: the outdoor augmented reality gaming system. Commun. ACM **45**(1), 36–38 (2002)
17. Hoellerer, T., Feiner, S., Terauchi, T., Rashid, G., Hallaway, D.: Exploring mars: developing indoor and outdoor user interfaces to a mobile augmented reality system. Comput. Graph. **23**, 779–785 (1999)
18. Vlahakis, V., Karigiannis, J., Tsotros, M., Ioannidis, N., Stricker, D.: Personalized augmented reality touring of archaeological sites with wearable and mobile computers. In: Sixth International Symposium on Wearable Computers (ISWC2002), pp. 15–22 (2002)

19. Wither, J., Diverdi, S., Hllerer, T.: Using aerial photographs for improved mobile AR annotation. In: International Symposium on Mixed and Augmented Reality, pp. 159–162 (2006)
20. Zhang, Z.: Microsoft kinect sensor and its effect. Published by the IEEE Computer Society 1070–986X/12/ IEEE Multimedia at Work 2012
21. Pavlik, R.A., Vance, J.M.: A modular implementation of Wii remote head tracking for virtual reality. In: Proceedings of the ASME 2010 World Conference on Innovative Virtual Reality WINVR 2010, Ames, Iowa, USA, 12–14 May 2010
22. Hirzer, M.: Marker detection for augmented reality applications. Institute for Computer Graphics and Vision Graz University of Technology, Austria
23. Lowe, D.G.: Distinctive image features from scale-invariant key-points. Int. J. Comput. Vis. **60**(2), 91–110 (2004)
24. Bay, H., Tuytelaars, T., Van Gool, L.: SURF: speeded up robust features. In: Leonardis, A., Bischof, H., Pinz, A. (eds.) ECCV 2006, Part I. LNCS, vol. 3951, pp. 404–417. Springer, Heidelberg (2006)
25. Viola, P., Jones, M.J.: Robust real-time face detection. Int. J. Comput. Vis. **57**(2), 137–154 (2004)
26. Lechner, M.: A proposed step-by-step guide to an AR standard. Wikitude GmbH (2011)
27. Wikitude API Documentation GmbH. Homepage of Wikitude API. http://www.wikitude.com/doc/alr/index.html
28. Angermann, F., Krushwitz, M.: AR development with the Metaio product suite: demonstration of use cases in industry. In: IEEE International Symposium on Mixed and Augmented Reality (ISMAR) (2014)
29. Keil, J., Zollner, M., Becker, M., Wientapper, F., Engelke, T., Wuest, H.: The house of Olbrich - an augmented reality tour through architectural history. In: Proceedings of the 2011 IEEE International Symposium on Mixed and Augmented Reality - Arts, Media, and Humanities, pp. 15–18. IEEE (2011)
30. Homepage of OpenNebula. http://opennebula.org
31. Homepage of Ceph. http://ceph.com

Augmented and Mixed Reality

Accurate OnSite Georeferenced Subsurface Utility Model Visualisation

Stéphane Côté[1](✉) and Antoine Girard-Vallée[2]

[1] Bentley Systems, Québec City, QC, Canada
Stephane.cote@bentley.com
[2] Sherbrooke University, Sherbrooke, Canada

Abstract. Subsurface utilities, essential to our modern life, must be regularly maintained to ensure continued operation. Subsurface utility engineering would greatly benefit from augmented reality, which would provide workers with direct up to date information about the underground pipes. Unfortunately, while accuracy is very important for engineers, outdoor augmented reality cannot yet guarantee a constant and known level of accuracy. In this paper, we propose a system based on the use of a robotic total station that provides the user's georeferenced position in real time. A tablet displays a 3D rendering of the subsurface utility network at the user's location, enabling him to explore the network without having to carry paper plans and make measurements. The system highlights several potential advantages over classical measuring methods, as well as with augmented reality.

Keywords: Subsurface utilities · Augmented reality · Pipes · 3D model

1 Introduction

Public utilities (electricity, gas, water, sewer, etc.) are essential to our modern life, and like any other type of infrastructure, they must be maintained regularly to ensure proper operation. Since many utilities are buried under the road surface, any maintenance operation has to be preceded by the localization of those assets. This is particularly important when the maintenance work involves excavation, which causes traffic disruption and potential hazards due to the presence of gas pipes, which may affect population and the local economy. To minimize its impact, excavation work must therefore be planned carefully.

The exact location of subsurface utilities (SU) is generally unknown. Therefore, excavation work usually starts with a survey of existing data as well as in situ pipe scanning [1]. Utilities are generally represented in 2D geo databases that indicate the approximate location and average depth for each pipe type with respect to surface features such as buildings, hydrants and street borders. Scanning devices such as ground penetrating radar can complement that data by detecting the presence of pipes, with varying levels of success and accuracy. The presumed location of SU obtained from geo databases and scans is then manually marked with color spray paint on the road surface (Fig. 1), which is used as a guide for excavation work.

© Springer International Publishing Switzerland 2015
L.T. De Paolis and A. Mongelli (Eds.): AVR 2015, LNCS 9254, pp. 63–70, 2015.
DOI: 10.1007/978-3-319-22888-4_6

The use of augmented reality (AR) for planning excavation work was proposed several years ago [2, 3]. Schall et al. [4] introduced the concept of virtual excavation (VE) for subsurface utilities AR. To facilitate interpretation and work in conditions where data is inaccurate, Su et al. [5] proposed the concept of uncertainty for SU AR. Côté et al. [6] proposed the use of AR for live excavation operations. By displaying SU renderings at their presumed location directly within the physical world, AR would likely accelerate the excavation planning task, and facilitate understanding of the underground network.

Fig. 1. Road markings indicating the presumed location of SU (Color figure online).

Augmented reality (AR) has an enormous potential in the Architecture, Engineering and Construction (AEC) world. It could enable a wide range of useful applications including: building site monitoring, asset identification and query, and many potential applications addressing the general problem of sense-making within very complex data. Decisions taken by architects and engineers have a direct impact on public safety, and must therefore be supported by accurate data. Consequently, AR applications for the AEC world would therefore need to be very accurate. Unfortunately, while approximate, low accuracy AR is easy to obtain, robust and accurate AR is still challenging.

For a long time, the main difficulty with augmented reality has been, and still is, registration. Considering the various limitations of portable pose estimation hardware, the problem of image-based tracking has received a lot of attention. Those techniques depend upon tracking identified features that can reliably be recognized on sequential video frames. Unfortunately, in an outdoor city environment, moving vehicles, people and vegetation make the tracking process challenging. In addition, the well-known canyon effect caused by nearby buildings can decrease reliability of GPS position estimation, which accuracy is not sufficient for AR anyway. Consequently, the resulting augmentation of a street environment with SU models is likely to be insufficiently accurate for the needs of city maintenance workers.

In the engineering field, the concept of handheld augmentation may not always be ideal. Although it can be useful to locate objects quickly, sometimes free hands may be required. With handheld augmentation, stability may be affected by hand movements, hands are required to hold the device in the specific direction of the augmented object, and distance to the augmented surface may be limited by the camera's field of view. The use of goggles would free the user's hands, but would not solve the other issues.

To reach a level of accuracy that is compatible with engineer's needs, AR needs very accurate camera position information. We discussed above the limitations of GPS and computer vision to reach such levels of accuracy in an outdoor city environment. On the other hand, other types of equipment are commonly used for high accuracy positioning in outdoor city environments. Survey devices, such as robotic total stations (RTS), can be used to measure the geolocation of an asset within millimeter accuracy. RTS devices have been used in the past to accurately capture buildings for creating AR models [7].

The specific problem we are interested in is the marking of the road to indicate pipe locations. In a typical use case, a user visits the site with a set of drawings, a measuring tape, and a bottle of spray paint. He then measures pipe locations on the drawings, and carries those measurements on the surface of the street, indicating the location of pipes using painted lines and symbols. The process is lengthy and could be error prone. By displaying the location of pipes at their presumed location on a portable electronic device, we believe we could save the user from having to use printed drawings and to measure anything.

In this project, we propose using RTS devices as a basis for an accurate onsite model visualization system for high accuracy geo-localized renderings of SU models, that could be used to facilitate the task of paint marking.

2 Proposed System

To verify our hypothesis, we used a Trimble RTS773 Robotic Total Station, a survey prism mounted on a pole, and a computer tablet attached to the same pole (see Fig. 2). The first step is to survey the station's location using standard surveying methods. Then, the station is used to track the prism location in real time as it is being moved, and accurately calculate its geographical position in real time. However, the station can only measure the position of the prism (and not its orientation), and can only do so at a frequency of about 2 Hz. Consequently, it was not appropriate for the development of first-person view augmented reality applications.

Considering these constraints, we decided to develop a system to facilitate the ground marking process by allowing the user to navigate in the 3D model at 1:1 scale, as he moves in the physical world. The RTS is used as a position tracking system, which saves us from having to rely on inaccurate GPS or unstable optical features for pose calculations.

Let's hypothesize the 3D model is scaled up to 1:1 and aligned with the physical world. Consequently, the size and position of the model elements would be the same as those of the physical world objects they represent. In our application, the user uses the prism as a pointing device into the virtual model. By moving the prism around in the physical world, the user actually navigates the corresponding portion of the model. He can therefore explore parts of the 3D model simply by walking to the corresponding location in the physical world. This is illustrated in Fig. 3, where the picture on the left shows the user holding the prism and tablet, and on the right is the virtual scene displayed by the tablet, roughly centered at the same position, but from a 3rd person perspective.

As the user rotates, the virtual rendering could be rotated accordingly using an orientation sensor (although not implemented in our prototype – rotation was simulated in the paper). A top view, displayed on the top right, rotates at the same rate.

Fig. 2. A Trimble robotic total station, with survey prism and computer tablet.

Fig. 3. Example use of the system, showing user holding the prism and tablet in a specific position and orientation (top), the tablet displaying a 3rd person view of the virtual scene at the same location. As the user rotates (bottom), the scene changes orientation.

A typical use of the system is illustrated in Fig. 4. As the user moves the prism around (A), the tablet display is updated in real time, and shows a 3D virtual excavation near the prism location (B) as well as pipe depth at the prism location. The user wants to explore the model without moving, and defines a remote target (C). The excavation location is moved accordingly by the system (D), this time not following the prism location, showing the pipe layout at the target location. The user starts walking in the direction of the target (E) and the virtual prism location is updated accordingly, following the position of the physical prism (F), distances to target and station being updated live on display. When the user finds the desired pipe, he marks the ground at prism position (G).

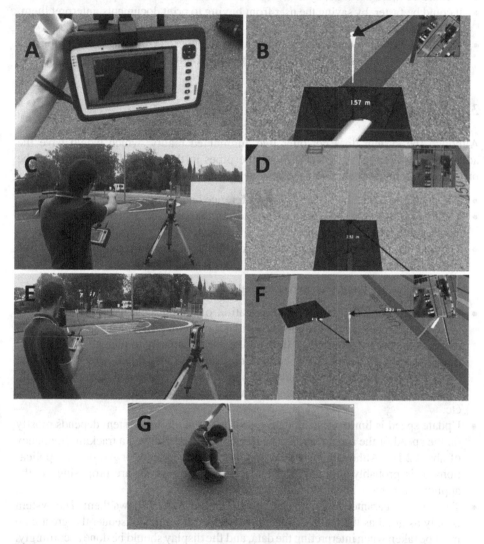

Fig. 4. Example use of the system. User moves prism (A) and tablet updates the model rendering at prism location in real time (B). User sets remote target (C) and moves virtual excavation to that location (D) without moving prism. User starts walking to new location (E), virtual prism position is updated accordingly (F), showing distance to target. When he reaches pipe location, user marks ground (G).

When compared to the typical manual road marking technique, the system we developed has the potential of offering the following advantages:

- It could saves the user from having to interpret drawings contents, as well as his own position and orientation with respect to the drawing.
- It could be more accurate, by avoiding the manual measurement processes.
- It could be faster, by saving the user from having to print documents, interpret them, and make measurements.
- It could lower the mental burden of trying to imagine 2D drawings as 3D pipes, as the system would display them directly in their 3D context.

3   Discussion

Although the system does not offer live augmented reality, which would have the advantage of offering a live 3D view of the pipes in their real 3D environment, the proposed system has several advantages over typical augmented reality applications:

- The display on the tablet is always georeferenced and accurate.
- The display does not show the typical jittering that often characterizes vision-based augmented reality applications.
- The application does not require the user to point at target for augmenting it – the view depends on the prism location only, not on arms orientation.

On the other hand, our system has several limitations:

- It does not represent a faithful representation of the physical world. Although our system has been designed to show the virtual view with the same position and orientation as the user, it still relies a little on the user's capacity to mentally map the 3D rendered view to the physical world. Consequently, any differences between the rendered view and physical reality will make that mental mapping more difficult. Those include terrain topography, natural features (trees, people), street furniture, etc.
- Update speed is limited. The update speed of the rendering system depends mostly on the speed of the robot station. The device we used allowed a tracking frequency of about 2 Hz. Although this would be totally unacceptable for AR or VR applications, it is probably sufficient for model exploration as we are proposing, as the application is more about model understanding.
- There is no guarantee pipes are actually where the system shows them. The system is only as good as the quality of the data we feed it with. Consequently, great care must be taken when interpreting the data, and the display should be done accordingly.

The last point is very important, and deserves a longer discussion. The system could be used to display various types of georeferenced data. Those include: paper drawings, geodatabases, photographs, GPR scans, interviews with utility maintenance workers, etc. Naturally, the quality of that data varies greatly. The American Society of Civil Engineers defined 4 quality levels for subsurface utility data [8]. QL-D utility data is from owner records, verbal recollections, and other sources of data for which no one is willing to take responsibility for the accuracy. QL-C data adds visible surface structures such as fire hydrants and valve box covers that have been surveyed. QL-B confirms existence and shows the infrastructure's horizontal position that has been detected using pipe locators, GPR, seismic devices, etc. Finally, QL-A shows pipes that have been surveyed when exposed. In this case, the exact location of the pipes can be guaranteed at the excavation point. Quality information is extremely important, and data must be interpreted accordingly. Consequently, it appears fundamental that such quality information should be revealed to the user, when displayed on the tablet, otherwise this could lead the user into taking decisions based on unreliable information. The user must know what information he can rely on, depending on the task (marking, excavation) or on the type of pipe (sewer, water, gas). The way this accuracy level should be displayed to the user should be investigated in another study.

4 Future Work

The system could be enhanced several ways. For instance,

- Model and terrain renderings could make use of topography data and aerial photos. This would provide the user with renderings that are closer to the physical world, which would help him understand context more easily.
- Subsurface utility data is generally owned and maintained by each individual utility company. Consequently, the data often needs to be requested from each company and merged. The system we proposed would greatly benefit from having access to all the data at once in a central location, remotely accessible, for easy access on site. The development of such central inter-disciplinary databases, which is partly technical, partly political, would have to be examined.
- The system could also be used to collect data on site, such as hydrant and manholes location, that would be fed directly into the database.
- The technique could also be used in other contexts, for instance for assistance to construction work, building site monitoring, or augmentation of building walls (to see structure hidden behind walls).

References

1. Côté, S.: Augmented reality: x-ray vision for utility professionals. Util. Horiz. Q4 2012 (2012)
2. Roberts, G.W., Evans, A., Dodson, A.H., Denby, B., Cooper, S., Hollands, R.: The use of augmented reality, GPS and INS for subsurface data visualisation. In: FIG XXII International Congress. Washington, D.C., 19–26 April 2002
3. Behzadan, A.H.: ARVISCOPE: georeferenced visualization of dynamic construction processes in three-dimensional outdoor augmented reality. Ph.D. dissertation, Department of Civil and Environmental Engineering, Ann Arbor. University of Michigan, MI (2008)
4. Schall, G., Mendez, E., Kruijff, E., Veas, E., Junghanns, S., Reitinger, B., Schmalstieg, E.: Handheld augmented reality for underground infrastructure visualization. Pers. Ubiquit. Comput. 13(4), 281–291 (2008). Special Issue on Mobile Spatial Interaction. Springer

5. Su, X., Talmaki, S., Cai, H., Kamat, V.R.: Uncertainty-aware visualization and proximity monitoring in urban excavation: a geospatial augmented reality approach. Vis. Eng. **1**(2), 1–13 (2013)
6. Côté, S., Létourneau, I., Marcoux-Ouellet, J.: Augmentation of live excavation work for subsurface utilities engineering. In: 2014 Proceedings of the International Symposium on Mixed and Augmented Reality (ISMAR), Munich, Germany, September 2014
7. Olalde, K., Garcia, B., Seco, A.: The importance of geometry combined with new techniques for augmented reality. In: International Conference on Virtual and Augmented Reality in Education, Puerto de la Cruz, Spain, November 2013
8. American Society of Civil Engineers: Standard Guildine for the Collection and Depiction of Existing Subsurface Utility Data (38-02). American Society of Civil Engineers, p. 32 (2002)

The Augmented Reality Story Book Project: A Collection of Balinese Miths and Legends

I. Gede Mahendra Darmawiguna[(⊠)], I. Made Gede Sunarya,
Made Windu Antara Kesiman, Ketut Resika Arthana,
and Padma Nyoman Crisnapati

Laboratory of Cultural Informatics, Informatic Education Department,
Ganesha University of Education, Buleleng, Indonesia
{mahendra.darmawiguna,sunarya,windu.kesiman,
resika,crisnapati}@undiksha.ac.id

Abstract. The Balinese people often tell their stories through dance, drama, textile designs, puppetry and music. Many stories are important as they teach children ideas about their land, traditions and customs. This project aims at the development of augmented reality story book that focusing on Balinese miths, and legends. Augmented reality is a live direct or indirect view of a physical, real-world environment whose elements are augmented by computer-generated sensory inputs. The application for augmented reality story book is developed in android mobile devices and was developed by using Unity3D with additional Vuforia libraries. The idea of the project is to make a story telling book with augmented reality technology. The book contains the image target as marker to display the objects from augmented reality application. When the application is pointed to the marker of book, the animated 3D scenes will show up combining with the narration of story and music.

Keywords: Balinese folklore · Miths · Legends · Augmented reality story book · Android

1 Introduction

Bali is an island and province of Indonesia. Bali Island is the most famous tourist destination in the world. Not only the beauty of the island itself but also the amazing Balinese culture, folklore, myths and legends that can not be separated in their life style. Balinese myths and legends are retold to each new generation so that their lessons and morals are constantly passed on. They are most commonly passed down by parents or grandparents to children through the oral retelling of stories. Different art forms are also a popular way of expressing many of the island's myths and legends. The Balinese people often tell their stories through dance, drama, textile designs, puppetry and music. Many stories are important as they teach children ideas about their land, traditions and customs. Nowadays, young people in Bali are less interested in miths and legends because they think, that those are not relevant in globalization era that is completely up to date and modern. In Balipost (local newspaper) in 2012 was written that the interest of Balinese miths and legends start worrying (Rizky 2012). It is

© Springer International Publishing Switzerland 2015
L.T. De Paolis and A. Mongelli (Eds.): AVR 2015, LNCS 9254, pp. 71–88, 2015.
DOI: 10.1007/978-3-319-22888-4_7

characterized by a reduced numbers of Balinese miths and legends in book stores and the increasing numbers of story books from abroad where some of those is not in accordance with the culture of Bali. Balinese miths and legends usually contain local wisdoms that very positive for the formation of the character of young generation of Bali, both in terms of attitudes, ethics, mental, and spiritual. Two contributing factors that making folklores becoming obsolete are the presentation of miths and legends that are less attractive and rapid technological developments. One of solutions to solve these problems is to use technology to attract the attention of people to Balinese miths and legends.

At the Ganesha University of Education (UNDIKSHA), Indonesia, a laboratory of research, namely Laboratory of Cultural Informatics (LCI), is working recently on the development of technology-based (especially computer-based) learning material and media. Laboratory of Cultural Informatics (LCI) mainly focused on the finding of some aspects of local wisdom potentials of Balinese (Hindu) people that might be relevant to the development of modern education. The existence of the local wisdom should be taken into account in developing the concepts of a cultural-based technology. After a few years of grand designing of research program, the laboratory of LCI is finally focused on the development of computer-cultural-based education media. One of main focuses of computer-based cultural researches is augmented reality application of collection of artistic and cultural objects which are developed in Android operating system.

Based on the data from Statista (The Statistic Portal), in 2014, the estimation of number of smartphone users in Indonesia are about 38 millions users. They use smartphone technology for several reasons, such as searching various kinds of information, accessing social media, and also doing online transactions. According to data from the StatCounter Global Stats, Android leads the global smartphone market, with 59.91 %.

Based on the above background, this project aims at the development of an augmented reality story book which focusing on Balinese Miths and Legends.

2 Balinese Miths and Legends

A legend is a narrative of human actions that are perceived both by teller and listeners to take place within human history and to possess certain qualities that give the tale verisimilitude. Legend, for its active and passive participants includes no happenings that are outside the realm of "possibility", as that is defined by a highly flexible set of parameters, which may include miracles.

There are many miths and legends in Bali. Many stories are important as they teach people, ideas about the land, traditions and customs. Some of legends that are famous for Balinese people are Balong Landung mith and legend, Jayaprana and Layonsari legend, and Kebo Iwa legend, and Ki Barak Panji Sakti King legend.

2.1 Barong Landung Mith and Legend

Barong landung Legend is began from the historic and legendary 12th century accounts of King Sri Jaya Pangus and his beloved wife Kang Ching Wie, the daughter of a

Chinese merchant. Many years have passed but no sign of a child, the royal couple turn happiness into sadness so the King decides to leave his wife for a journey across the waters to find his taksu. Following the storm at the sea the King is washed ashore into strange and magical island with baby animals surrounded him. He finds his place for meditation not long until he is awaken with the rise of Dewi Danu, the water goddess of the volcanic lake Batur. Accompanied by her forest spirits, Dewi Danu seduces the King. He can not resist (Fig. 1).

Fig. 1. Barong Landung puppets in Balinese Ceremony (Source: http://renungandharma. wordpress.com)

Meanwhile after years of waiting, Kang Ching Wie put her courage to travel far to find her husband, sadly only to find her husband has married Dewi Danu and they have a child. Kang Ching Wie in her disappointment sets her guards against Jaya Pangus. A raging battle ensues, but their strong love keeps them together to face the monster attack and the natural disasters. In her equal anger, Dewi Danu in her spirit power turns The King and his Queen into statues.

The people in the village lost their beloved King and Queen but happy to greet their new young King. With the presence of Dewi Danu, the new Prince is crowned by the spirits of Jaya Pangus and Kang Ching Wie. The villagers are happy. The story ends with the origin of 'Barong Landung' that is presented as the living embodiment of their former King and Queen up to this day. Kang Ching Wie is one of the two supreme deities in Balinese tradition and is considered to be the Goddess of Prosperity. Her shrines are erected at every trading location and merchant's home. Dewi Danu is the other supreme deity and is considered to be the symbol of fertility. Dewi Danu is also the goddess of lake Batur which is the source of the water that irrigates the island abundant farmland.

Barong Landung is a pair giant human puppet almost three meters high, one figure is a man in black face, and the other is a beautiful princess in white face. It effigies of the King and his wife, Kang Ching Wie are paraded only once in every 210 days through the streets of Bali as an ogre-like 'Barong Landung', warding off bad luck and evil spirits (Bali Safari Marine Park 2010).

2.2 Jayaprana and Layonsari Legend

This legend is actually Balinese love story about loyalty, faithfulness, and devotion. Once upon a time there was a small kingdom called Kalianget. At one time the kingdom was plagued by deadly diseases which killed many of its people including most of the king's family members. This made the King very sad so he decided to visit his people to entertain himself and his people. At a crossroad he met a boy child who was crying for the loss of his parents and brothers. The king decided to adopt the boy since he had already lost all his children in the epidemic that swept through the kingdom. He took the boy to his palace and made arrangements for him to become one of the family. This boy was Jayaprana (Fig. 2).

Fig. 2. Jayaprana and Layonsari Temple in Bali (Source: http://bali.panduanwisata.id)

The king loved him as his own child and did everything to keep him happy. Still, as the boy grew to become a handsome adult Jayaprana decided not to interfere with others and approach life in a simple way, even though being the son of a King. Then, the time had finally come and Jayaprana fell in love with a beautiful flower seller at the market. The girl was Layonsari. She also fell in love with Jayaprana and his father, the King, agreed with their good intentions and accepted the notion of marriage.

The kingdom was delighted with the marriage of Jayaprana and Layonsari but shortly after dark clouds of trouble began to hover above the kingdom. The king had fallen in love with Layonsari which was now the wife of his only son, Jayaprana. The king, hypnotized by his feelings for Layonsari, began to plan on ways to get rid of Jayaprana. He ordered Jayaprana to travel to the forest near the sea accompanied by his guards to kill people who were disrupting the peace in his Kingdom. The king's dark plan was to keep Jayaprana away while trying to persuade Layonsari to become his wife instead.

Jayaprana was devastated and felt he had nothing in his life except his dear loving wife, but, to fulfil his promise to his father, the King, he decided to let the head of commander, Patih Sawung Galing kill him. Jayaprana had flowers in his hair and he picked them one by one and placed them in the hands of Patih Sawung Galing. He also gave him his Keris (instinctive & asymmetrical dagger) so that he could use it to kill him. He asked Patih Sawung Galing to tell his wife, Layonsari, that he died in order to fulfil his promise to the King. He could easily kill Jayaprana with one hit and did just that. All of a sudden a fragrant scent from Jayapranas dead body began to spread. It continued to spread and cover the whole forest making all animals scream with sadness. All but one; a white tiger. The white tiger rushed to Jayapranas dead body to find Patih Sawung Galing holding his bloody Keris and killed him in one fierce blow.

The news spread throughout the Kingdom and Layonsari chose to commit suicide after knowing that the king's misdeeds had resulted in the death of her husband, Jayaprana. Not long after her committing suicide a fragrant scent began to spread throughout the palace. The fragrant scent was a sign that they were pure in mind without any sins. As both Jayaprana and Layonsari were dead the king managed to break out from his illusionary state and realized what he had done. The King withdrew himself from reining the Kingdom.

The people of the Kingdom decided to bring the body of Layonsari to the forest where Jayaprana was killed to unite them in death and two graves were built. One grave for Jayaprana and Layonsari and another grave for Patih Sawung Galing who was the man destined to guard the graves forever. After a complete ceremony Jayaprana and Layonsari were stated as holy people (Home In Bali 2015).

2.3 Kebo Iwa Legend

Once upon a time in Bali, a man and his wife were praying. They had been married a long time but did not have any children. They prayed regularly to God to give them a child. Finally their prayers were answered. They had a baby boy. Their house was filled with joy. The baby was very much different from other babies. He ate and drank a lot. Day after day he ate more and more. His body grew bigger and bigger. And by the time he was a teenager, he was as big as a buffalo. People then started to call him Kebo Iwa.

Because of his gluttony, Kebo Iwa's parents spent most of their money to buy him food. They finally went bankrupt. They sought the villagers' help to feed Kebo Iwa.

The good villagers then worked together to cook and build a big house for Kebo Iwa. He was a giant. He could not stay in his parents' house anymore because of his size. Sadly, after a few months, even the villagers could not afford to cook food for him. They then asked Kebo Iwa to cook his own food. The villagers just prepared the raw materials. Kebo Iwa agreed and as an expression of his gratitude to the villagers, he himself built a dam, dug wells, and protected the villagers from animals and people who wanted to attack their village. Meanwhile, the troops of Majapahit Kingdom were planning to attack Bali. They knew about Kebo Iwa. And they also knew that they could not conquer Bali with Kebo Iwa there. Kebo Iwa was more powerful than they were.

Gajah Mada, Chief Minister of Majapahit was suffering from a long dry season and needed much water. Kebo Kingdom then planned something. They were pretending to invite Kebo Iwa to Majapahit to help them dig some wells. They said that Majapahit Iwa, unaware of the plan, went to Majapahit. When Kebo Iwa was busy digging the well, the troops covered the well from above. Kebo Iwa suffocated and died inside the well.

After the death of Kebo Iwa, Bali was conquered by Majapahit. Even now, people remember Kebo Iwa for what he had done for Majapahit and Bali. The stone head of legendary Kebo Iwa can be found in Pura Gaduh temple in Blahbatuh (Setiawan 2011; Fig. 3).

Fig. 3. Gunung Kawi Temple built by Kebo Iwa with his fingers (Source: indonesia-heritage. net)

2.4   Ki Barak Panji Sakti King Legend

Long time ago, in 1300s, there was village called Gelgel in Singaraja Bali. There was a king named Dalem Sagening. He was a wise, clever, brave, and powerful king who mad Gelgel become safe and peaceful.

He had a lot of wives. His last wife was Ni Luh Pasek. She was the most beautiful wife and that made the other wives were jealous. They often told bad things to the king. Sadly, the king was influenced and he finally asked Ni Luh Pasek to leave the palace. Ni Luh Pasek was very sad, but she had no other choice. She became very sad when she knew that she was pregnant. Ni Luh Pasek arrived at a village. An old man felt very sorry with her condition. His name was Jelantik Bogol. He was a holy man and had supernatural power. He married Ni Luh Pasek. And when the baby was born, Jelantik Bogol named him I Gusti Gede. He loved I Gusti Gede just like his own son (Fig. 4).

Fig. 4. Ki Barak Panji Sakti (Source: www.wikipedia.org)

I Gusti Gede grew as a strong man. He also mastered a lot of skills such as martial arts and supernatural power. His step father taught him the skills. One day his step father asked him to go to a jungle in Den Hill. It was the place Ni Luh Pasek was born. Jelantik Bogol asked him to go there to get more supernatural power. Before he left, his step father gave him two weapons, a spear and a keris, it's a traditional wavy double-bladed dagger.

He started his journey. When he arrived at Panombangan Beach, there was an incident. There was a ship from Bugis sinking at the beach. The people had tried to help, but they did not succeed. I Gusti Gede wanted to help. He asked the people to stay away from the ship. He prayed and took out his weapons. Suddenly, two big spirits came out of the spear and the keris. I Gusti Gede asked the spirits to pull the sinking ships back to sea. The people could not see the spirits. They only saw I Gusti Gede moving his hands. The spirits slowly pulled the ship. In just a minute, a ship just back in the sea. The owner was very happy. He gave some of his wealth to I Gusti Gede. People were amazed with his power. they named him as I Gusti Panji Sakti.

I Gusti Panji Sakti went back to Den Hill. He started to build a village. People came one by one. I Gusti panji Sakti protected them from bad people. Slowly the village became a kingdom. I Gusti Panji Sakti became the king and he named the kingdom as Sukasada. Sukasada became a big kingdom, I Gusti Panji Sakti planned to make another kingdom. He opened up a new area. It was full of buleleng trees. Therefore he named the kingdom as Buleleng Kingdom. He also build a great palace. People named it Singaraja. Singa means lion and Raja means king. With his power I Gusti Panji Sakti was like a lion. He always protected his people from bad people. While he became a king, Buleleng Kingdom was safe and prosperous (Setiawan 2011).

3   Augmented Reality Story Book Projects

3.1   The Augmented Reality Story Book

Augmented Reality story book (AR story book) is a combination between a regular book with AR technology. AR story book project has two main components. First, the story book that comes with the Quick Response Code (QRC) marker which is the picture on almost every page. The second one is the application to capture the marker and displays the results. AR story book is designed just like picture storybook. Its combine the art of storytelling with the art of illustration. AR story book can also be regarded as a media because it is printed material that can display information. AR story book project is included in the category of specially designed learning resources, because it was developed as a component that purposed to facilitate users to understand the content of the book by displaying a three-dimensional object on a two dimensional image which is printed on the book (Figs. 5, 6, 7 and 8).

Fig. 5. Barong Landung story book

3.2   The Functional Model of Augmented Reality Story Book Application

In this functional model describes the overview of the software that is developed. Figure 9 describes the flow of the augmented reality book project development.

Fig. 6. Jayaprana and Layonsari story book

Fig. 7. Kebo Iwa story book

Fig. 8. Ki Barak Panji Sakti story book

The project is divided into two parts. The first part is designing the augmented reality book. It is the combination of pictures and texts based on the story. The second part is developing the augmented reality application. It begins from the development of 3-dimensional objects, making of sound files, converting images to become markers library, and combined them to become the augmented reality application.

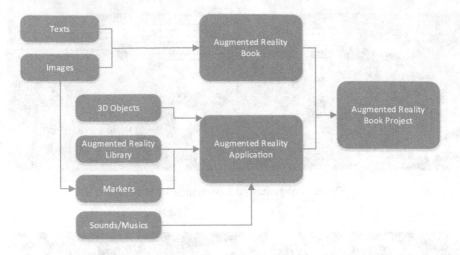

Fig. 9. Flow of augmented reality book project development

The flowchart of augmented reality application is shown in Fig. 10. When the application is started, the camera of smartphone is detected. Then the camera will read the marker from AR Book. If the marker has not been captured, the application will continue to find and read the marker. When the marker is captured, the application will display 3D objects and also the sounds (narration of the story and music background). After that, the application will be point to another marker. If the there is no more marker, then the application is stopped.

3.3   The Implementation of Augmented Reality Story Book Application

The augmented reality application for AR story book is developed for Android operating system. There are five stages in the implementation of augmented reality story book application.

3.3.1   Implementation of 3-Dimensional Objects and Animation

The first stage in development augmented reality story book is creating 3D objects and animation. The tools that is Blender version 2.70. In the development of 3D objects and animation, there several steps that are done.

a. *Modeling*. This is the process of creating 3D mesh (characters and other 3D objects) using some mesh tools such as plane, cube, circle, uv sphere, icosphere, cylinder, cond, grid, and torus. The technique that is used is extrude technique and mirror modification (Fig. 11).
b. *Materials and Texturing*. This process is used to simulate a surface color or property of 3D mesh. This could be based on a photorealistic interpretation of a real material or on some artistic style, like a cartoon, or an impressionistic painting (Fig. 12).
c. *Rigging and Skinning*. For some complex objects which are characters (humanoid mesh), the best way to animate is through the use of Armatures. An armature acts

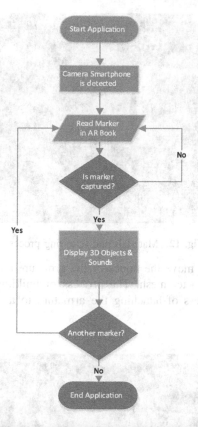

Fig. 10. Flow chart of augmented reality book application

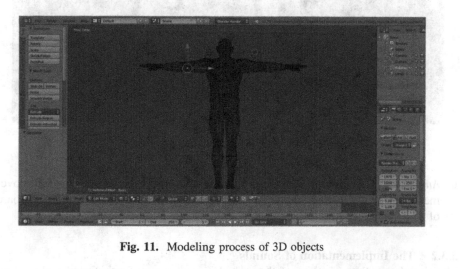

Fig. 11. Modeling process of 3D objects

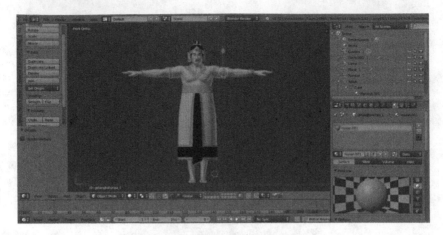

Fig. 12. Materials and texturing process

like a skeleton. It can move the bones of the armature and those bones drive the animation of the character mesh. The process of building an armature is called rigging, and the process of attaching the armature to a mesh is called skinning (Fig. 13).

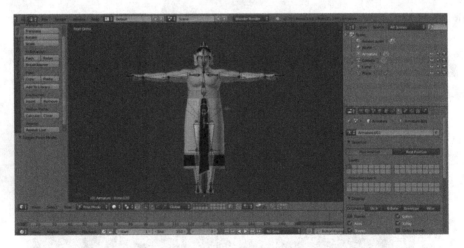

Fig. 13. Rigging and skinning process

d. *Animation.* This process is done to give the movement of 3D objects. The movements are set in every keyframe. The animations are created based on the storyboard of story on every page of augmented reality story book (Fig. 14).

3.3.2   The Implementation of Sounds

The sounds are the narrations of the story in every page of augmented reality story book. The sound is recorded by using audacity software. The recording of narration is

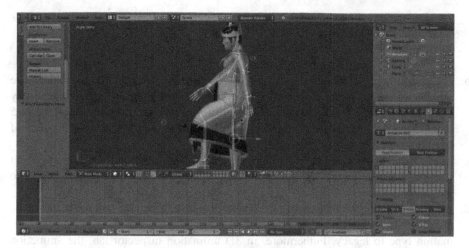

Fig. 14. Animation process

saved in *.mp3* format file. After recording process, the narrations are combined with background musics to suit the story of every page of augmented reality story book. Every augmented reality story book has different numbers of pages. The number of recorded sounds depend on the number of pages in augmented reality story book.

3.3.3   The Implementation of Markers (Image Targets)

Markers (image targets) represent images that the Vuforia SDK can detect and track. Unlike traditional fiducial markers, data matrix codes and QR codes, Image Targets do not need special black and white regions or codes to be recognized. The SDK detects and tracks the features that are naturally found in the image itself by comparing these natural features against a known target resource database. Once the markers is detected, the SDK will track the image as long as it is at least partially in the camera's field of view. In order to make images can be detected and tracked by SDK Vuforia, those images should be uploaded to Target Manager as database that is provided by Vuforia. The target manager can be accessed in https://developer.vuforia.com/target-manager. Once the status of the target changes to active, the download database button for Unity editor can be clicked. This downloads a *.unitypackage*.

3.3.4   The Implementation of Augmented Reality

The implementation of augmented reality is using Unity3D. Before working with Unity3D, sdk extension of Vuforia should be installed in order to be able to use Augmented Reality features. The sdk extension can be downloaded in Vuforia website (https://developer.vuforia.com/resources/sdk/unity). The steps can be seen below:

a. Several files have to be imported into Unity3D. Those files are:

   1. Vuforia-unity-android-ios-2-6-7.unitypackage which is the unity package for working in mobile application.

2. The markers (image targets) that have been downloaded with *.unitypackage* format (See. 4.3.3).
3. 3D objects and its animations with *.blend* format.
4. Narrations sounds with *.mp3* format.

b. Creating a numbers of scenes on Unity3D which are saved in Assets folder. The number of scenes depend on numbers of episodes are there in augmented reality story book. For example, augmented reality story book for Kebo Iwa needs 5 scenes. It means there are 5 episodes. Every episode consists of several pages of augmented reality story book.

c. Every scene in Unity3D consists of AR camera, directional light, and image target (markers). Image targets are set in ImageTarget prefab and change the dataset to database of markers.

d. In order to make the animation of 3D objects move, animator controller has to be created. After that, settings on rig can be done in inspector by changing the animation type to legacy. Futhermore, in 3D animation inspector tab, the animation scene needs to change into default in accordance with the movements that were created earlier in Blender.

e. The last step is building process in Android platform. The setting of Android application can be set in player settings. It also can add icon, splash image, and default orientation. Then, android application ready to be built and run. The result of application will be in *.apk* format (Fig. 15).

Fig. 15. Augmented reality projects in Unity3D

Interaction that occurs between user and the augmented reality application can be seen in Fig. 16. User will interact directly with the android smartphone that is equipped with augmented reality applications. When the camera of the smartphone is directed to the AR book which is equipped with markers, it will display a 3-dimensional object building along with voice narration according to the marker.

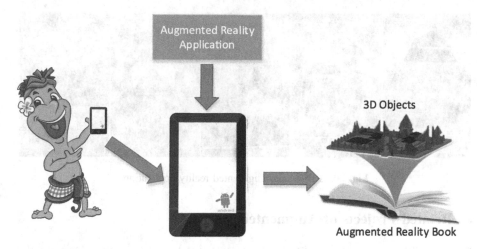

Fig. 16. Interaction diagram between AR application, AR book, and user

The application will use the smartphone camera to point the marker in the book and show the animations. Some of screenshots of the result of the augmented reality application can be seen in Figs. 17, 18, 19 and 20.

Fig. 17. Jayapangus augmented reality application

Fig. 18. Jayaprana and Layonsari augmented reality application

Fig. 19. Kebo Iwa augmented reality application

Fig. 20. Panji Sakti augmented reality application

4   Related Projects of Augmented Reality

There are other augmented reality book projects that have been done since our first projects in 2012. Most of augmented reality book projects are related to Balinese cultures such as Balinese cultural heritages (Darmawiguna et al. 2014) with their landscape, Balinese ornaments, Balinese music instruments, Balinese dances movements, and tourist resorts (Kesiman et al. 2014). All of them are packaged with books. Some of the projects can be seen in Fig. 21.

Fig. 21. Other augmented reality book projects

5   Findings and Conclusion

Based on the responses that are distributed to 30 people of various ages, our findings show that augmented reality story book attracts people of all ages especially youth people and children to get to know closer an learn more about our Balinese miths and legends. They are so excited with augmented reality technology. They showed good responses and feedbacks to improve our applications. The young generation can now learn and know more about their own cultures with the help of technology. This projects also can be tools to promote Bali and its cultures to the world. For future developments, we will focus on markerless augmented reality projects to support easier way of wordwide distribution.

Acknowledgements. We are grateful to Eka Putra Widiantara, Gede Agus Putra Yasa, Putu Putri Aryasih, and Ni Made Desi Arisandi as part of Augmented Reality Story Book Team for their contributions in application development processes.

References

Bali Safari Marine Park: The Legend of Goddess (2010). http://balisafarimarinepark.com/

Widiantara, E.P., Darmawiguna, I.G.M., Sunarya, I.M.G., Crisnapati, P.N.: Augmented reality story book project Legenda Asal Mula Barong Landung (In Indonesian). KARMAPATI (Kumpulan Artikel Mahasiswa Pendidikan Teknik Informatika) **3**(5), 326–333 (2014). ISSN: 2252-9063

Yasa, G.A.P., Sunarya, I.M.G., Kesiman, M.W.A., Crisnapati, P.N.: Augmented reality story book project Legenda Asal Mula Barong Landung (In Indonesian). KARMAPATI (Kumpulan Artikel Mahasiswa Pendidikan Teknik Informatika) **3**(5), 334–342 (2014). ISSN: 2252-9063

Home in Bali: Jayaprana and Layonsari – A Balinese love story about loyalty, faithfulness and devotion.   http://www.homeinbali.com/jayaprana-and-layonsari-a-balinese-love-story-about-loyalty-faithfulness-and-devotion/. Accessed 30 March 2015

Darmawiguna, I.G.M., Kesiman, M.W.A., Crisnapati, P.N., Wiartika, I.M.E., Suparianta, K.D., Susena, I.K., Yudiantara, I.M.: Augmented reality for the documentation of cultural heritage building modelling in Bali, Indonesia. In: Kultur un Informatik: Reality and Virtuality, Proceeding of Culture and Computer Science Conference, Berlin, Germany, pp. 107–117 (2014)

Kesiman, M.W.A., Darmawiguna, I.G.M. Crisnapati, P.Y., Ardipa, G.S., Mariyantoni, I.K.Y., Nugraha, M.L., Prasetya, A.Y.R.A., Dewantara, I.M.A.Y.: The AR Book project: collection of augmented reality application of Balinese Artistic and Cultural Objects. In: Kultur un Informatik: Reality and Virtuality, Proceedings of Culture and Computer Science Conference, Berlin, Germany, pp. 93–105 (2014)

Arisandi, N.M.D., Sunarya, I.M.G., Arthana, I.K.R., Crisnapati, P.N.: Pengembangan Aplikasi augmented reality story book Legenda Kebo Iwa (In Indonesian). KARMAPATI (Kumpulan Artikel Mahasiswa Pendidikan Teknik Informatika) **3**(5), 364–372 (2014). ISSN: 2252-9063

Aryasih, P.P., Kesiman, M.W.A., Arthana, I.K.R., Crisnapati, P.N.: Pengembangan Aplikasi augmented reality story book Panji Sakti (In Indonesian). KARMAPATI (Kumpulan Artikel Mahasiswa Pendidikan Teknik Informatika) **3**(5), 343–352 (2014). ISSN: 2252-9063

Risky: Cerita Rakyat Bali Mencemaskan. http://www.balipost.co.id/. Accessed 30 July 2012

Azuma, R.T.: Augmented reality: approaches and technical challenges. In: Barfield, W., Caudell, T. (eds.) Fundamentals of Wearable Computers and Augmented Reality. Lawrence Erlbaum Associates, Mahwah (2001). ISBN 0-8058-2901-6

Stat Counter Global Stats: Top 8 mobile operating systems in Indonesia from Jan to Dec 2014 (2015). http://gs.statcounter.com/#mobile_os-ID-monthly-201401-201412

Statista: Number of smartphone users in Indonesia from 2011 to 2018 (in millions) (2015). http://www.statista.com/statistics/266729/smartphone-users-in-indonesia/

Setiawan, Y.: Folk stories, April 2011. https://www.scribd.com/doc/53181529/Folk-Stories

ARBS: An Interactive and Collaborative System for Augmented Reality Books

Nicolás Gazcón[1,2](✉) and Silvia Castro[1]

[1] VyGLab, Department of Computer Science and Engineering,
Universidad Nacional del Sur, Bahía Blanca, Argentina
{nfg,smc}@cs.uns.edu.ar
http://vyglab.cs.uns.edu.ar
[2] National Council of Scientific and Technical Research (CONICET),
Ciudad Autónoma de Buenos Aires, Argentina

Abstract. Augmented Reality (AR) has been studied from different application fields since the early 60s. In particular, AR has been usefully applied in the educational field, specially based on a versatile AR application called Augmented Book. We introduce the *Augmented Reality Book System* (ARBS), an interactive and collaborative application for traditional books augmentation. The proposed system allows the incorporation of AR content to any pre-existent traditional book. Once the AR content is incorporated to the book, it can be shared and explored by other users, allowing collaboration among readers. The ARBS does not require special programming or previous technical knowledge from the user. To validate the proposed system, we designed and conducted a novel experimental study with novice AR users. Very positive feedback from participants confirms the usefulness of the ARBS.

Keywords: Augmented book · User evaluation · Augmented reality · Computer graphics

1 Introduction

Augmented Reality (AR) has been studied by the research community for more than fifty years. First contributions to this field can be tracked back to the 60s, with Sutherland's *"ultimate display"* [24]. Nevertheless, due to technological limitations, massive adoption of these features was pushed back. In fact, both widely accepted definitions of AR were introduced in 1994 and 1997, by Milgram and Kishino [18] and Azuma [3] respectively.

AR has been addressed in several different fields [5,6,29,33]. In particular, AR shows a huge potential in educational applications [15,23,30]. Indeed, the research community has focused on the exploration of different approaches to enhance students motivation [13]. AR environments allow students to interact with both the real and the virtual world, exploring objects, performing dedicated tasks, learning concepts, developing skills and carrying out collaborative activities. Moreover, the immersion, interaction and navigation features that enable

L.T. De Paolis and A. Mongelli (Eds.): AVR 2015, LNCS 9254, pp. 89–108, 2015.
DOI: 10.1007/978-3-319-22888-4_8

AR technologies play an important role to raise the students motivation [23], allowing experimental learning [30] or supporting advanced spatial visualization and interaction. These possibilities have been the most important aspects that motivated different types of AR learning environments for regular classroom practices [7].

A very promising AR application for education is the *MagicBook* of Billinghurst et al. [4]. It uses special books with AR fiducials (i.e. special markers that can be recognized by a computer software) as the main interface objects. People can turn pages of the book, look at the pictures and read the text like they are used to. However, if they look at the pages through an AR display (e.g. computer screen) they would be able to appreciate virtual contents appearing over the pages. This approach works over special books shaped as an augmented book from scratch, making impossible the augmentation of a traditional pre-existent book.

Despite the fact that in the last years there was a great increment of e-books and its specific hardware (e.g. e-readers like Kindle, Sony Book Reader, Nook, etc.), as stated by Grasset et al. [9] the physical qualities of traditional books (i.e. transportability, flexibility, annotation capabilities, etc.) are still preferred by readers. Other studies tried to port physical characteristics of books to purely virtual versions of traditional books [14], arguing that capabilities like flipping quickly through pages or annotating pages should resemble a printed book as much as possible. In this way, Park et al [20] stated that besides the advantages and disadvantages, both e-books and paper books will coexist for several years to come.

Many researchers and companies [1,31] explored the experience around AR books, adding new ways of interactions [9,13] or introducing collaborative tasks [16]. However, most of these approaches involved special books conceived as augmented books from scratch and are not applicable to traditional pre-existent books. This limitation has been overcome by research works that proposed authoring tools to generate augmented books [16]. Nevertheless, there are still limitations on sharing the virtual contents incorporated to a given book. For instance, the specific book created with these tools has to be installed manually in other device. Moreover, the AR field already counts with authoring and deployment tools [17,27] that allow users to create augmented contents and share them in a seamlessly way. Although these tools have proved to be effective for commercial or advertising and promotional purposes, they are still a general approach around AR and therefore lack of specific features which are necessary to facilitate the reading experience of books.

In this paper we introduce the *Augmented Reality Book System* (ARBS), an interactive and collaborative application for traditional books augmentation. The proposed system allows the incorporation of AR content to any pre-existent traditional book. Once the AR content is incorporated to the book, it can be shared and explored by other users, allowing collaboration among readers.

To validate the proposed system, we designed and conducted an experimental study with novice AR users. The results obtained not only reflect how novice users interact with the ARBS but also present some interesting findings on how they interact with AR applications in general.

The contributions of this paper can be summarized as:

- The design and implementation of a novel, interactive and collaborative system for augmented books based on the augmentation of any pre-existent book.
- The evaluation of the proposed approach within a novice AR user context and the report of the results and conclusions of the experiment.

The rest of this paper is structured as follows. Section 2 provides the related work concerning to augmented books. In Sect. 3 details of the ARBS approach are presented. The design and procedure of the experimental study is presented in Sect. 4, and the results are provided in Sect. 5. Section 6 presents the discussion of the proposed approach based on the obtained results as well as future research directions. Finally, Sect. 7 states the conclusions of this research work.

2 Related Work

The first augmented book based on Azuma's definition [3] can be tracked back to Rekimoto's research work [22]. However, the first approach that formalized the idea of an augmented book is the *MagicBook* proposed by Billinghurst et al. [4]. This initial version featured a handheld display based interface. The great impact was the immersive virtual environment that the user could explore. The Billinghurst's Augmented Book paradigm was applied in several fields [2,28, 32]. This approach is proven to be still effective, for example for spatial skills development [15] or for learning geometric shapes [13].

Grasset et al. [10] explored the design space of what they called the *Mixed-Reality Book* and discussed different interaction techniques including gaze interactions, finger interactions and tangible interaction.

Many researchers used augmented books to address improvements in what is called *markerless* capability. Although AR based on fiducials has proved its usefulness, some people argue that these markers distract readers or even worse, ruin the book's environment. Thus, several registration methods based on textures (i.e. a distinctive image) were developed and used in augmented books [12,25]. In this way, a more natural usage is achieved because there is no difference between the augmented book and the real book (e.g. there are no markers that expose the registration method used).

Recently, authoring tools that enable non programmers to create their own augmented books are emerging [13,21]. Thus, the process of creation of this kind of books does not require highly qualified skilled professionals of information technologies. Nevertheless, all these approaches are based on books shaped as an augmented book from scratch and the only interaction with the book consisted in observing the virtual content. It means that none of the mentioned approaches can be applied to traditional pre-existent books. In contrast, there are alternative approaches like [11] that allows the update of digital contents of the book and provide other interactions types (e.g. multisensory feedback).

However, its production only can be accomplished by developers or researchers with technical background.

As stated before, the potential of AR books is promising, but there are some limitations. With all these constraints in mind, our work tries to overcome them by introducing an interactive and collaborative system (ARBS) that allows incorporation of AR content to any traditional pre-existent book. Once incorporated to the book, the AR content can be explored, modified and shared. The present work includes an evaluation of the ARBS by a robust statistical experimental study. As far as we know, up to now there are no standardized methodologies to evaluate AR books [8]. This motivated us to design an experimental study to evaluate AR books by different kind of novice AR users. In order to evaluate the books, we propose a two-scenario task-based evaluation to study the ease of use and learnability of the approach under two possible conditions (i.e. creating a new augmented book or starting from an already created one).

3   System Overview

We propose an interactive and collaborative and AR system called ARBS. This novel system allows the integration of augmented contents to any traditional pre-existent book. Since the system was designed to be used by novice AR users, the ARBS provides interactions to easily transform a traditional book into an augmented book. Moreover, the AR contents introduced to the book can be shared with other users, enabling and facilitating collaboration among readers.

The ARBS environment is composed by three main elements, namely: (i) the user, (ii) the computer device and (iii) the physical book. In the ARBS environment, the reader is represented with a user profile, through which the user is able to explore, create and interact with the augmented contents. The system is deployed in a computer with the classical configuration for AR applications (i.e. a camera to capture real world and a display to show the augmented world). It is important to mention that the ARBS implementation does not require any special device (like augmented glasses or sophisticated displays). Finally, when the user incorporates augmented content to a traditional book he/she is creating an Augmented Reality Book (ARB), which is stored in the system, and later shared with other users. Thus, the ARBS allows users to perform the creation of a new ARB, as well as the exploration of an already created one.

The following sections describe these elements in the ARBS environment. We detail the ARB representation and design that supports the incorporation of AR contents to any pre-existent book, the usage of the application to enrich traditional books with augmented contents, and finally the implementation and architecture of the system that allows the collaboration among users.

3.1   Augmented Reality Book

In the ARBS a physical book has its virtual counterpart in the form of an Augmented Reality Book (ARB). An ARB contains some basic information related to the physical book (like title, authors, description and ISBN code), the augmented contents and AR facilities that enhance the traditional book. The ISBN code[1] is used to uniquely identify an ARB. In addition to these basic attributes, an ARB provides a structure to storage the augmented contents. This structure is arranged in containers, and each container is assigned to a page of the physical book. Therefore, each augmented content is located on a specific region of a given page, enhancing the original content of the printed page. It is important to remark that multiple containers can be associated to the same page. In this way, the containers not only serve as a structure to hold augmented contents, but also allows to group contents based on the reader's decision.

Multiple augmented contents can be introduced to an ARB, such as images, 3D-models, sounds and text. In order to show them as virtual contents, a specific *marker* must be attached. As an initial interface for AR contents we propose the black & white markers (i.e. standard fiducials of AR applications). In addition, regarding to content placement we propose a single marker approach called *fixed marker*. We defined different locations to place the markers (see Fig. 1). The

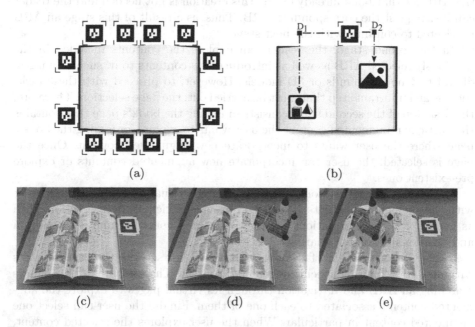

Fig. 1. Possible fixed positions for markers (a) and an example of the contents displacement concept (D_1 and D_2) from a single marker to situate two augmented elements over the book (b). Finally, an example of a book with a fixed marker at its right (c), an augmentation without any displacement (d) and the same augmentation with a transformation applied (e).

---

[1] The International Standard Book Number (ISBN) is a unique numeric commercial book identifier.

reader can place augmented content on a given marker location and apply 3D transformations to move the content to a specific place over the book's page.

Despite this single marker approach, we considered another type of marker defined as *free marker*. This is the classical use of markers from the point of view of a tangible user interface, allowing users to move the marker freely throughout the book. Thus, there is no constrained location for this kind of markers.

Besides these two marker approaches, there is no restriction on the quantity of markers to be used by the readers. Users can add as much markers as they consider necessary.

3.2   ARBS Workflow and Interface Application

In order to enrich pre-existent books with augmented contents, we propose a usage workflow which involves two main stages (see Fig. 2): the creation/request of an augmented book and the incorporation/exploration of digital contents. The first stage consists in the creation of the ARB for a traditional book. However, if the ARB for that book already exists, this creation is not needed and the reader can just request the corresponding ARB. Thus, as a result of this stage an ARB is selected to continue with the next stage.

In the second stage, the reader can explore the contents included in the previously selected ARB as well as introduce new contents to it, such as images, digital text notes, sounds or 3D models. However, to proceed with these tasks there is an important step that must be carried out: the page selection. Therefore, the first step of the second stage consists in issuing the book's page that contains the particular augmented content the user wants to explore, or issuing the book's page where the user wants to incorporate new augmented content. Once the page is selected, the user can incorporate new augmented contents or explore pre-existent ones.

In the last step of this workflow, the reader can visualize, explore and interact with the augmented contents. The ARBS provides a rich set of interactions such as geometrical transformations for the augmented contents, markers selection and positioning, content sharing, etc.

Figure 3 shows the interface of the ARBS. In this session, the user interacts with an ARB exploring specific augmented content. The system interface allows searching an ARB and navigation through its virtual pages to explore the augmented contents associated to each one of them. Finally the user can select one augmented content in particular. When the user explores the selected content, the interface shows the type of marker that must be used, and in the case of a fixed marker it shows its corresponding location.

On the other hand, the user can create a container for a given page of the book in order to introduce a new content to it. Thus, the ARBS provides an interface to introduce a new content (see Fig. 4). The user can select the type of augmented content as well as the desired type of marker. Finally, using the geometric transformations in 3D (i.e. scaling, rotation and translation), the augmented content can be situated at some specific location over the book.

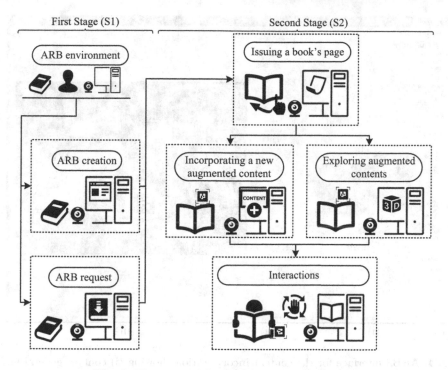

Fig. 2. The proposed workflow using the ARBS.

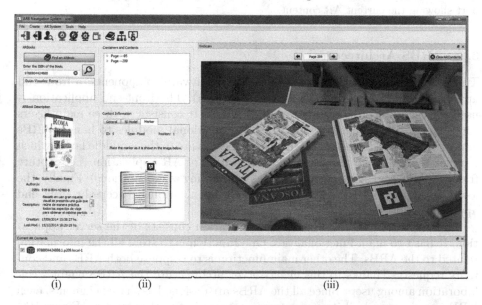

Fig. 3. ARBS interface showing (i) the search section with the loaded books and the information of the selected book; (ii) the corresponding containers and contents of the selected book, with the information of the selected content; and (iii) the viewport showing the frames captured by the camera with the rendered AR content.

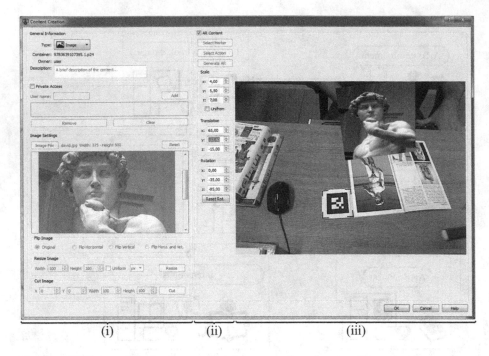

(i)   (ii)   (iii)

Fig. 4. ARBS interface for the content incorporation showing (i) content general and specific attributes; (ii) markers selection and transformations setup; and (iii) the viewport showing the current AR content.

3.3   ARBS Architecture

The ARBS Architecture is composed by two software components: a front-end application and a back-end server (see Fig. 5(a)). The front-end application is used for the creation and exploration of ARBs. It consists in three main layers components. The upper layer provides the functional modules to handle ARBs and its contents. The AR and Rendering modules are in the a middle layer, which handles the real-time requirements of this type of AR application (i.e. capture frames to process them and show the corresponding augmentations). Finally, the lower layer provides the support for the communication between the front-end application and the back-end application.

On the other hand, the back-end application consists of the server application. It has two main functionalities. One function is to store all the information related to the ARBs. The other main function is to response both ARBs and contents requests. Thanks to this client-server architecture the ARBS enables collaboration among users. Since all the ARBs are designed as shared elements, each ARB is unique and all its contents are accessible to other readers. Figure 5(b) shows the collaboration schema offered by the ARBS.

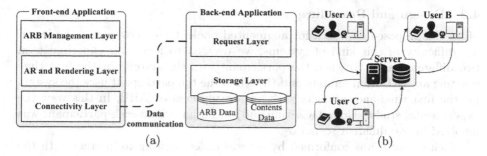

Fig. 5. The ARBS client-server architecture (a) and the collaboration schema among users (b).

The ARBS was implemented in C++ using the Qt Framework[2]. The rendering process was developed using the programmable pipeline of OpenGL[3]. AR features were developed using the ALVAR library1[4]. Finally, we used the OpenCV library[5] to capture frames with the camera. Both front-end and back-end software components were developed using a framework based approach. This allows to easily extend the ARBS with new features, such as more complex interactions or new types of augmented contents. Further customization can be done by adding new modules to the corresponding architecture layer.

4   Experimental Study

The overall goal of the experiment was to study how novice users interact with the proposed application in order to customize traditional books into augmented books. In addition, we intended to observe how different physical properties of books affect the augmented content incorporation.

4.1   Participants

Sixteen participants with ages ranging from 25 to 59 (M = 34.3, SD = 11.1) and comprising of 8 males and 8 females participated in this experiment. Nine participants informed they had used at least one 3D modeling application. Twelve had heard about AR but only ten stated they thought they knew what AR was. Only two participants informed they had used an AR application.

The computer experience of the participants was established from a three category scale, namely: novice, intermediate and advanced. Ten participants considered themselves as users and six as intermediate users. The main activities of the participants were BsC Students (5), PhD Students (5), Professors (3) and other activities (3).

---

[2] http://www.qt.io/.

[3] https://www.opengl.org/.

[4] http://virtual.vtt.fi/virtual/proj2/multimedia/alvar/.

[5] http://opencv.org/.

4.2 Design and Procedure

Since the proposed approach for augmented books tries to overcome the learning difficulty of this kind of systems, we decided to focus our experiment on two different cases: (i) when the participant uses the system for the first time creating an ARB from scratch; and (ii) when the the participant uses the system for the first time and interacts with an already created ARB. In this way, the experimental study followed a within-subject design where each participant was involved in two different scenarios.

Each scenario was conformed by several tasks pointing to interact with the augmented books including creation and visualization of different types of contents (e.g. text, images and 3D models). The evaluation also considered physical properties of books (i.e. how users perceive thickness, size or curvature of pages while positioning augmented contents) as well as how participants handle multiple books concurrently. Moreover, we studied the markers usage by introducing tasks where participants had to choose the type of marker (fixed vs free markers) or deciding how many markers to use.

Participants were evaluated individually performing an experiment composed of five phases (see Table 1). The first phase presented a questionnaire pointing to gather the background and demographic information of the participants. Secondly, the evaluator gave the participant a brief talk (about 10 min) of what AR is and the main uses of the proposed approach for augmented books. In order to avoid any bias, this brief introduction was structured to be explained in a similar fashion to each participant and without using or referring to specific features of the system.

Phase 2 and 3 consisted in the evaluation of the two scenarios. Each scenario was composed of 12 tasks that were provided individually and presented in a printed sheet of paper. Each task was defined as a description of what must be carried out without any explicit reference to the application's interface. We divided the evaluation in two groups of participants randomly assigned. Group A performed Scenario I in phase 2 and Scenario II in phase 3. In an opposite manner, group B performed Scenario II and Scenario I in phase 2 and phase 3 respectively. To evaluate the ease of use and learnability of this approach we measured the completion time [19, 26] and also the success rate of each task. Both scenarios had similar but not identical tasks.

Finally, the purpose of phase 4 and 5 was to collect qualitative information. Phase 4 consisted of a subjective questionnaire, including questions about system's usability and the evaluation (five-level likert scale questions), opinions about AR technology (dichotomy and multiple choice questions) and information and feedback for future directions (open text questions). Lastly, phase 5 conformed a semi-structured interview, in which the evaluator asked open questions to obtain more feedback about the participants opinion.

4.3 Environment Setup

The computer used for the experiment was a machine with AMD Phenom II X4 840 CPU, 4GB DDR3 memory and an ATI Radeon HD 5750 video card

Table 1. Description of the evaluation design. Group A and B consisted of 8 participants each. In Scenario I participants created an ARB from scratch and in Scenario II participants used an already created ARB.

	Group A	Group B
Phase 1a	Background questionnaire	
Phase 1b	Brief introductory phase	
Phase 2	Scenario I evaluation	Scenario II evaluation
Phase 3	Scenario II evaluation	Scenario I evaluation
Phase 4	Subjective questionnaire	
Phase 5	Semi-structured interview	

running Microsoft Windows 7 64-bit operating system. The display was a 22-inch LCD and the camera was a Logitech 9000 pro. We provided four markers and four books with different characteristics such as hardcover/softcover, size and quantity of text/illustrations (see Fig. 6).

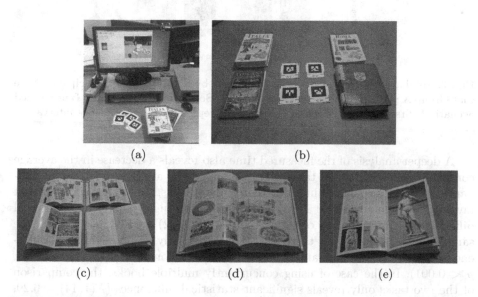

(a)   (b)

(c)   (d)   (e)

Fig. 6. Evaluation environment (a); the four books and markers used in the experiment with different characteristics such as soft/hard cover and different thickness properties (b); different page layout of books used (c); example of curvature of pages (d); and influence of top-most pages of the book (e).

5   Results

5.1   Completion Time

The completion time of each task was measured. The total average time of scenarios from each group is shown graphically in Fig. 7. These results were submitted to an initial analysis which consisted of a paired t-test revealing a significant statistical difference for the scenarios of both groups (Group A $t(8) =$ 6.978, $p = 0.0002$ and Group B $t(8) = 7.749$, $p = 0.0001$). From this prior analysis we can infer that the second scenario performed by each group reveals a faster operation. Thus, we can consider this as a first indication of knowledge transfer between scenarios.

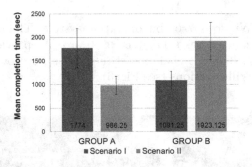

Fig. 7. Total average time of scenarios performed by both groups of participants. Note that Group A performed Scenario I first and then Scenario II, while Group B performed Scenario II first and then Scenario I. Error bars represent 95 % confidence interval.

A deeper analysis of the measured time also reveals a decrease in the average completion time of related tasks. Figure 8 shows the average time that participants of Group A spent on three different types of tasks. Among the six tasks that involved augmented content incorporation there is a highly significant statistical difference as determined by one-way ANOVA ($F(5, 42) = 11.03$, $p < 0.001$). The same analysis showed that there is also a statistically highly significant difference in the three tasks related to visualization of contents ($F(2, 21) = 24.14$, $p < 0.001$). In the case of using concurrently multiple books, the comparison of the two tasks only reveals significant statistical differences ($F(1, 14) = 6.29$, $p < 0.025$).

Participants belonging to Group B, which performed in first instance the Scenario II and secondly Scenario I, also reveal a general decrease in the time spent on the different tasks (see Fig. 8). An one-way ANOVA test determined highly statistical differences on the six tasks related to augmented content incorporation ($F(5, 42) = 14.26$, $p < 0.001$). For the case of tasks that involved augmented content visualization we also found highly statistical differences ($F(2, 21) = 32.29$, $p < 0.001$). Finally, we found significant differences ($F(1, 14) = 5.56$, $p < 0.033$) between the only two tasks based on handling multiple books.

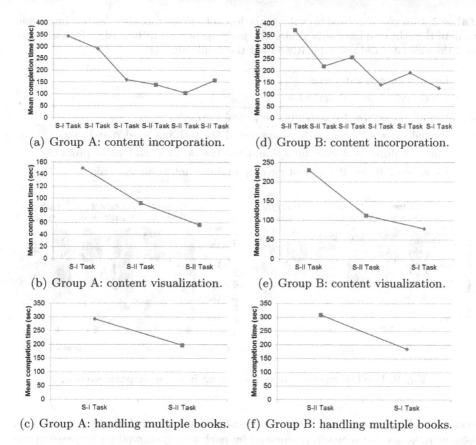

(a) Group A: content incorporation.

(d) Group B: content incorporation.

(b) Group A: content visualization.

(e) Group B: content visualization.

(c) Group A: handling multiple books.

(f) Group B: handling multiple books.

Fig. 8. Average completion time of tasks from both scenarios performed by Group A and B of participants (tasks are shown in performing order).

Based on the exposed statistical results of the two groups of participants we can confirm significant differences in the time spent to perform tasks. On the basis of this analysis, we have concrete evidence supporting both ease of use and learnability of the proposed approach.

5.2   Success Rate

We have measured how effectively participants were able to complete the tasks in both scenarios. We decided to use a level of success model [26] instead of the binary success rate model, in order to capture the learnability of the system. Thus, we defined four levels of success based on the degree of the tasks completion and the assistance needed to complete them (see Table 2).

We analyzed the same group of tasks described in the previous section. The degree of success in each task can be expressed as a percentage, shown graphically in Fig. 9. In neither of both groups participants gave up on any task, being able to

Table 2. Categories utilized to evaluate the level of success rate of tasks. It is important to note that the evaluator only guided the participants when they asked for assistance and the evaluator did not explicitly solved their difficulty.

Level of success categories	
Category	Description
Complete success	Successfully completed the task
Partial success	Successfully completed the task but needed assistance
Partial failure	Successfully completed the task but had major problems
Complete failure	Participant gave up and did not finish the task

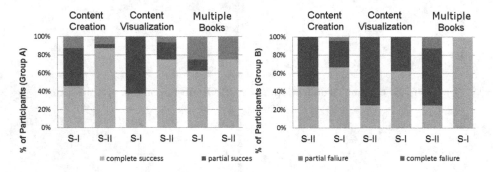

Fig. 9. Level of success rate of tasks from both participants groups.

complete all the tasks. Some degree of assistance was needed in the first scenario, however the second scenario performed by each group showed an increase in the success of the completed tasks. These results also empower the research findings about the learnability and ease of use of the ARBS.

5.3   Subjective Results

Results regarding to the ARBS approach are shown in Fig. 10(a). In general both groups informed similar opinions about the usage of the system. Marker positioning was not perceived as an issue by both groups of participants. They also did not considered a problem to deal with printed markers. The feedback obtained suggests that participants did not noticed books' characteristics as an issue.

Survey about the evaluation showed that both groups of users agreed on the fact that Scenario I and II seemed equivalent and participants got more skilled as they progressed in the evaluation (see Fig. 10(b)). These results were submitted to a two-sample t-test analysis which outcomes are grouped in Table 3. From this analysis emerges that there are no significant statistical differences in the answers of both groups. Therefore, we can conclude that starting to use the system with an already created book or creating it from scratch, was conducted similarly.

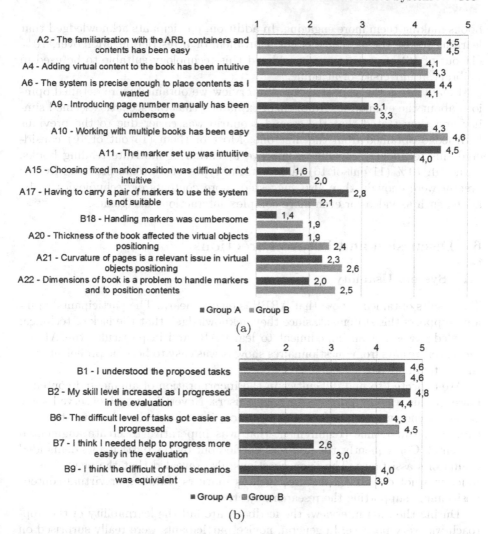

Fig. 10. Subjective questionnaire results from the usability of the ARBS (a) and the evaluation (b). The scale used was *totally disagree(1), disagree(2), neither agree or disagree(3), agree(4)* and *totally agree(5)*.

Table 3. Two-sample t-test of the evaluation questionnaire's results.

Two-sample t-test					
Questions	B1	B2	B6	B7	B9
sig.	−	0.15	0.51	0.52	0.80

Regarding to the subjective opinion about this technology all the participants agreed that AR technology has been really interesting to use with books. They also considered that the ARBS results in a useful complement to traditional books making them more engaging. In addition, participants acknowledged that learning to use the system was not a problem or a restriction. Moreover, 70 % (11 out of 16) of participants considered this technology suitable to be used in a library, a university or at home.

Finally, from the semi-structured interview we obtained more detailed opinions about the evaluation. All of them explained that the scenarios seemed similar and they stated that the second scenario was easier due to the previous knowledge obtained from the first one. Most of them (15 out of 16) considered this technology capable to improve attention or motivate reading books. Although 70 % (11 out of 16) said that the types of contents provided by the system were enough, they also suggested more contents or technologies to be added such as videos or even more complex interactions like games.

6   Discussion and Future Directions

6.1   System Usability

The results obtained expose that ARBS is easy to learn. The participants' opinions supports this statement, since they acknowledged that the lack of technical knowledge was not an impediment to learn AR, and in particular the ARBS. Moreover, results from questionnaires show it was easy to become proficient with the System and AR.

We expected to find difficulties in the incorporation of augmented contents, however this was not an issue for novice users. Nevertheless, we observed some issues on the system interface. For instance, it was not clear how to start the camera the first time (requirement that was imperative to create augmented contents). Consequently, the first task carried out by the participants demanded evaluator's assistance. The open questions also revealed that the needed assistance was not due to AR features such as markers handling or virtual content positioning, supporting the research objective.

During the final interview, the feedback around the learnability of the approach was very positive. In general, novice participants were really surprised on how easy they get used to the technology. Opinions such as *"I though it would be harder"* or *"I did not expected to enjoy the evaluation"* remark the positive aspect of easiness of the approach. However, based on the observed interface difficulties and opinions about the interface, we believe that including automatic guidance in the system would solve most of these issues.

6.2   Book Physical Properties

Observations during the evaluation revealed that the different physical properties of the books did not negatively influenced the usage of the ARBS. We expected to find some negative reactions from participants when they had to incorporate augmented contents in situations were curvature of pages or thickness of the book could affect the task. However, it was really surprising how natural users handle these situations. We can conclude that this behavior is due to the natural interface that offers the book, since every participant used them as they were used to.

Other interesting finding is how participants dealt with multiple books. In general each participant handled multiple books in a particular way. For instance some participants used different markers for each book allowing to use books in parallel. Other users used books concurrently changing them as they needed or even keeping always one book on top of the other. Finally, another case we observed is that some participants did not changed books at all since they worked only with one marker. We conclude that this last situation, although it was not a standard practice, is due to the lack of page recognition (because it is not required to keep visible the issued page).

Finally, we proposed the possibility of implementing an automatic page recognition feature. Opinions were diverse. All of participants agreed that incorporating such automatic system would be a benefit. However, they also agreed that introducing the page number manually on the system was not cumbersome. These mixed opinions need further research to draw a conclusion on which option results more convenient.

6.3 Markers

In general participants were not distracted with the marker location, however they had to be careful not to occlude the marker. We did not notice difficulties on the usage of fixed markers over free markers. Nevertheless, we observed that in tasks where participants were suggested to choose a marker, the preference was even.

Nevertheless, most participants (14 out of 16) agreed on using several markers and not just one. During the interview the general opinion was that only one marker is too restrictive. They did not perceived as a problem carrying a couple of markers either.

We observed that users get used to the markers' positioning quickly. The subjective results confirm this, since participants did not revealed negative remarks on the proposed locations for fixed markers. Moreover, some participants stated they understand the use of fixed markers, however free markers resulted more engaging. We think this is due to the possibility of the direct manipulation of markers, allowing more interaction.

6.4 Future Work

Although promising feedback was obtained, the ARBS system still has other features to be taken into account. The ARBS provides several augmented contents and interactions for them. However, there are still other contents to be considered (e.g. videos) as well as other kind of interactions (e.g. multimodal interactions).

Though the single marker approach is effective, we plan to improve the existent AR features adding *Markerless Registration and Tracking* in order to obtain a more natural interface with the book. Since the ARBS was implemented using a framework approach, these new features can be easily added to the system. We also plan to port our system to mobile devices. A mobile system could be useful in environments where it is difficult to have a desktop computer for each reader (e.g. a library).

There are other research possibilities to explore around the evaluation. To evaluate learnability we conducted the experiment in two scenarios with only 15 min of difference. We would like to study how this is affected with longer trials, such as after a week or even a month. Since ARBS system allows to share contents with other readers, it is interesting to design tasks oriented to study how readers can interact using this feature. This might involve performing the evaluation of more than one participant at the same time. We also would like to evaluate the system with greater number of participants with advanced knowledge in order to make a comparison to novice users.

7   Conclusions

In this paper we presented a novel system for augmented reality books. The ARBS allows readers to incorporate augmented contents to any pre-existent printed book. This novel application facilitates the generation of new augmented books by users without technical background, enhancing their books with information that a conventional book does not provide.

The application has been evaluated by 16 participants who created and edited augmented books under two scenarios. Quantitative and qualitative measures suggest that this technology is easy to learn and use, and opens up great possibilities to enrich the traditional reading experience. Participants were able to enhance four books incorporating different types of augmented contents. We summarized future directions for this approach and we expect to use this technology in different environments such as libraries and classrooms.

Acknowledgments. This research work was partially funded by the project 24/N028 of Secretaría General de Ciencia y Tecnología, Universidad Nacional del Sur, Bahía Blanca, Buenos Aires, Argentina. Our sincere thanks to the participants for their voluntary participation. The authors would like to thank Luján Ganuza and Dana Urribarri for their comments on previous drafts of this manuscript.

References

1. AR-Books: Augmented reality books (2012). http://www.ar-books.com/. Accessed 21 November 2014
2. Asai, K., Kobayashi, H., Kondo, T.: Augmented instructions - a fusion of augmented reality and printed learning materials. In: Fifth IEEE International Conference on Advanced Learning Technologies, ICALT 2005, pp. 213–215 (2005)
3. Azuma, R.: A survey of augmented reality. Presence **6**(4), 355–385 (1997)
4. Billinghurst, M., Kato, H., Poupyrev, I.: The magicbook - moving seamlessly between reality and virtuality. IEEE Comput. Graph. Appl. **21**(3), 6–8 (2001)

5. Buchs, N.C., Volonte, F., Pugin, F., Toso, C., Fusaglia, M., Gavaghan, K., Majno, P.E., Peterhans, M., Weber, S., Morel, P.: Augmented environments for the targeting of hepatic lesions during image-guided robotic liver surgery. J. Surg. Res. **184**(2), 825–831 (2013)
6. El Choubassi, M., Nestares, O., Wu, Y., Kozintsev, I., Haussecker, H.: An augmented reality tourist guide on your mobile devices. In: Boll, S., Tian, Q., Zhang, L., Zhang, Z., Chen, Y.-P.P. (eds.) MMM 2010. LNCS, vol. 5916, pp. 588–602. Springer, Heidelberg (2010)
7. Cuendet, S., Bonnard, Q., Do-Lenh, S., Dillenbourg, P.: Designing augmented reality for the classroom. Comput. Educ. **68**, 557–569 (2013)
8. Dünser, A., Billinghurst, M.: Evaluating augmented reality systems. In: Furht, B. (ed.) Handbook of Augmented Reality, pp. 289–307. Springer, New York (2011)
9. Grasset, R., Dunser, A., Billinghurst, M.: The design of a mixed-reality book: is it still a real book? In: Proceedings of the 7th IEEE/ACM International Symposium on Mixed and Augmented Reality, ISMAR 2008, pp. 99–102. IEEE Computer Society, Washington, D.C., USA (2008)
10. Grasset, R., Dünser, A., Billinghurst, M.: Edutainment with a mixed reality book: a visually augmented illustrative childrens' book. In: Proceedings of the 2008 International Conference on Advances in Computer Entertainment Technology, ACE 2008, pp. 292–295. ACM, New York, NY, USA (2008)
11. Ha, T., Lee, Y., Woo, W.: Digilog book for temple bell tolling experience based on interactive augmented reality. Virtual Reality **15**, 295–309 (2011)
12. Kim, K., Lepetit, V., Woo, W.: Scalable real-time planar targets tracking for digilog books. Vis. Comput. **26**(6–8), 1145–1154 (2010)
13. Kirner, T., Reis, F., Kirner, C.: Development of an interactive book with augmented reality for teaching and learning geometric shapes. In: 2012 7th Iberian Conference on Information Systems and Technologies (CISTI), pp. 1–6 (2012)
14. Liesaputra, V., Witten, I.H.: Realistic electronic books. Int. J. Hum.-Comput. Stud. **70**(9), 588–610 (2012)
15. Martín-Gutiérrez, J., Saorín, J.L., Alcaniz, M., Pérez-López, D.C., Ortega, M.: Design and validation of an augmented book for spatial abilities development in engineering students. Comput. Graph. **34**(1), 77–91 (2010)
16. Matcha, W., Awang Rambli, D.R.: Design consideration for augmented reality book-based application for collaborative learning environment. In: 2012 International Conference on Computer Information Science (ICCIS), vol. 2, pp. 1123–1126 (2012)
17. Metaio: Metaio creator (2014). http://www.metaio.com/creator/. Accessed 21 November 2014
18. Milgram, P., Kishino, F.: A taxonomy of mixed reality visual displays. IEICE Trans. Inf. Syst. **E77–D**, 1321–1329 (1994)
19. Nielsen, J.: Usability Engineering. Morgan Kaufmann Publishers Inc., San Francisco (1993)
20. Park, A., Lee, K.J., Casalegno, F.: The three dimensions of book evolution in ubiquitous computing age: digitalization, augmentation, and hypermediation. In: 2010 IEEE International Conference on Sensor Networks, Ubiquitous, and Trustworthy Computing (SUTC), pp. 374–378 (2010)
21. Park, J., Woo, W.: Multi-layer based authoring tool for digilog book. In: Natkin, S., Dupire, J. (eds.) ICEC 2009. LNCS, vol. 5709, pp. 234–239. Springer, Heidelberg (2009)

22. Rekimoto, J.: Matrix: a realtime object identification and registration method for augmented reality. In: Proceedings of the 3rd Asia Pacific Computer Human Interaction, pp. 63–68 (1998)

23. Di Serio, A., Ibáñez, M.B., Delgado Kloos, C.: Impact of an augmented reality system on students' motivation for a visual art course. Comput. Educ. **68**(0), 586–596 (2013)

24. Sutherland, I.E.: The ultimate display. In: Proceedings of the IFIP Congress, pp. 506–508 (1965)

25. Taketa, N., Hayashi, K., Kato, H., Noshida, S.: Virtual pop-up book based on augmented reality. In: Smith, M.J., Salvendy, G. (eds.) Human Interface, Part II, HCI 2007. LNCS, vol. 4558, pp. 475–484. Springer, Heidelberg (2007)

26. Tullis, T., Albert, W.: Measuring the User Experience: Collecting, Analyzing, and Presenting Usability Metrics, 2nd edn. Morgan Kaufmann Publishers Inc., San Francisco (2013)

27. Vuforia: Unity extension - vuforia v3.0 (2014). https://developer.vuforia.com/resources/sdk/unity. Accessed 21 November 2014

28. Walczak, K., Wojciechowski, R.: Dynamic creation of interactive mixed reality presentations. In: Proceedings of the ACM Symposium on Virtual Reality Software and Technology, VRST 2005. pp. 167–176. ACM, New York, NY, USA (2005)

29. Webel, S., Bockholt, U., Engelke, T., Gavish, N., Olbrich, M., Preusche, C.: An augmented reality training platform for assembly and maintenance skills. Robot. Auton. Syst. **61**(4), 398–403 (2013). (models and Technologies for Multi-modal Skill Training)

30. Wojciechowski, R., Cellary, W.: Evaluation of learners attitude toward learning in aries augmented reality environments. Comput. Educ. **68**, 570–585 (2013)

31. Wonderbook: an augmented reality peripheral for the playstation 3 console (2012). http://wonderbook.eu.playstation.com/. Accessed 21 November 2014

32. Woods, E., Billinghurst, M., Looser, J., Aldridge, G., Brown, D., Garrie, B., Nelles, C.: Augmenting the science centre and museum experience. In: Proceedings of the 2nd International Conference on Computer Graphics and Interactive Techniques in Australasia and South East Asia, GRAPHITE 2004, pp. 230–236. ACM, New York, NY, USA (2004)

33. Zhang, M., Xu, M., Han, L., Liu, Y., Lv, P., He, G.: Virtual network marathon with immersion, scientificalness, competitiveness, adaptability and learning. Comput. Graph. **36**(3), 185–192 (2012). (novel Applications of VR)

Robust Model Based Tracking Using Edge Mapping and Refinement

Anna Katharina Hebborn[1][(✉)], Marius Erdt[2], and Stefan Müller[1]

[1] Institute of Computational Visualistics,
University of Koblenz-Landau, Universitätstr. 1, 56070 Koblenz, Germany
{ahebborn,stefanm}@uni-koblenz.de
[2] Fraunhofer IDM@NTU, Nanyang Technological University,
50 Nanyang Avenue, Singapore, Singapore
marius.erdt@fraunhofer.sg

Abstract. We present a markerless tracking approach for augmented reality in poorly textured environments. The approach enables a robust and accurate camera pose estimation merely on basis of a coarse edge model. The edge model of the object to be tracked is enhanced and refined during the tracking process. New edges are added to the edge model and already existing ones are refined. A collection of reference poses with a set of corresponding edges, called keyposes, enables a selection of good edges to track depending on the current view and makes the tracking process robust and accurate. Keyposes are also used to reinitialize automatically after tracking failures, e.g. the object to be tracked is occluded. Therefore, the proposed method overcomes the limitations of traditionally used edge based tracking approaches in terms of reinitialization and edge model creation. Evaluation on synthetic and real image sequences demonstrates the significant improvement of the proposed method over a standard edge based tracking.

Keywords: Augmented reality · Model based tracking · Edge tracking

1 Introduction

Monocular pose tracking and estimation with respect to an object or an environment is a well-known task in augmented reality. As described in Teichrieb *et al.* [11] markerless tracking approaches can be classified in two main categories: model based and structure from motion based (SfM). In model based methods the environment or the object to be tracked is known. These techniques use a 3D model, such as an edge model which is often created by a manual modeling step or an offline procedure. In contrast to these methods, SfM approaches (such as in Klein *et al.* [7]) do not require any knowledge about the scene. The model to be tracked is created during runtime and extended while the camera is moving in the scene. Therefore, SfM based systems are not limited to the visibility of a known tracking model. However, the significant drawback of SfM systems and their use in augmented reality applications is that they are not capable

© Springer International Publishing Switzerland 2015
L.T. De Paolis and A. Mongelli (Eds.): AVR 2015, LNCS 9254, pp. 109–124, 2015.
DOI: 10.1007/978-3-319-22888-4_9

of providing an absolute reference coordinate system. In model based tracking systems, on the contrary, virtual content can be registered in the coordinate system of the known model. The most popular model based tracking methods use edges instead of textural information like local point features. Edges are easy to detect and highly invariant to illumination and view point changes. Edges are also stable on poorly textured objects which are often found in urban environments. However, in contrast to point features, edges are less differentiable and do not offer a large number of description and matching techniques. That is why common model based tracking methods use information from the prior frames and follow a recursive scheme (frame-to-frame tracking). RAPID[1] developed by Harris *et al.* [5] as one of the first and most known 3D edge trackers, for example, is based on the comparison between projected 3D sample points along the model edges to strong gradients detected in the current frame. This procedure needs a projection close to the real edges which is often realized by the last estimated camera pose. This means if the tracking fails once, the system is unable to reinitialize the tracking procedure. In addition RAPID-like methods and their several improvements are still sensitive to interference such as background clutter or texture on the object itself which often results in wrong correspondences. Furthermore, these techniques require an accurate edge model.

We present a model based tracking method extended by an edge management, mapping and refinement procedure. The next section discusses existing work and highlights the differences to our approach. Section 3 gives an overview of our proposed method. The following Sects. 4, 5, 6 and 7 explain the method in detail and present experimental results. The final Sect. 8 shortly summarizes the content of this paper and discusses future work.

2   Related Work

Many model based tracking approaches rely on edges [6,9] or use edges of an object to initialize the tracking [2]. The traditional edge based approaches, for further reading compare [6,13], require a complete edge model of the object or the scene to be tracked. A complete and precise edge model makes the tracking accurate and stable. The ideal edge model only contains edges which are robust for the tracking procedure. Non-relevant edges often result in wrong correspondencies and reduce the accuracy of the pose estimation. The creation of the model is often done manually in an offline step. In most cases, the edges describing the model are extracted from a mesh representation of the model or they are generated by a rendering step during the tracking process. A manual creation of a well-designed edge model is very time-consuming and the modeler should have knowledge about the tracking algorithm to select suitable edges. The easiest way to create an edge model is to identify sharp edges out of the surface model. Choi *et al.* [3], for example, use the angle between the surface normals of attached faces as an indicator for sharpness. The drawback to this is that the resulting edge model does not contain texture and silhouette edges. Texture edges lie on

---

[1] Real-time Attitude and Position Determination.

planar or smooth curved surfaces of the object and are defined by the texture of the model. Silhouette edges instead, separate the object from the background and are view-dependent.

Another approach is to generate the edges during the tracking process. Wuest *et al.* [12] and Reitmayr *et al.* [9], for example, render the textured or non-textured 3D model with the last camera pose or a pose prediction. They extract 2D edges out of the rendered scene (depth or color buffer) and apply a back-projection to obtain 3D edges to be tracked. With this method a view-dependent edge model is created which contains, according to the selected method, silhouette, geometry and texture edges.

An alternative to deal with an incomplete representation of the scene is to extend the model during the tracking. So called *extensible* model based tracking algorithms [7] make use of a static object in the scene to initialize the tracking process and follow a SfM procedure. Bleser *et al.* [2], for example, use an edge model which represents a part of the scene to initialize the tracking. There is no need for a model during the tracking process. The scene is reconstructed while the camera is exploring the scene. The tracking is realized by a detection and tracking of point features from frame to frame. Thus, these types of approaches enable a tracking if the initial object is not seen by the camera and overcome SfM problems in a AR context (such as unknown scale and coordinate system). Most of these approaches, however, make use of point features and thus are often unsuitable in industrial or urban environments. Instead, point features perform very good in well-textured scenes. Our method, in contrast, makes use of edges to enable tracking in poorly textured scenes. Gee *et al.* [1] present an algorithm which extends the model to be tracked with new line segments. Starting from a reference object, such as a marker, new lines are initialized. These lines are used within a RAPID-like model based tracking.

In this paper an alternative approach is proposed that creates a suitable edge model and works with relatively few 3D edges as well as utilizes a surface model (ideally a surface model of the complete scene) as input. Starting from the coarse edge model new edges are extracted and added. We extend the idea from Gee *et al.* and collect reference poses, called keyposes, during the tracking process. These keyposes store a set of corresponding edges and enable an edge management to select good edges to track depending on a pose prediction. In this way, a level of detail based culling as well as a hidden line removal is automatically performed. Newly added edges are refined during the tracking and completely removed from the edge model if they are constantly detected in the 2D image or their appearance often varies. As a result, non-relevant edges, which could arise from dynamic objects or shadows, will be removed from the model.

3   Method Overview

A concise overview of our method is shown in Fig. 1. Our starting point is the tracking technique of Wuest *et al.* [13]. This tracking method follows a RAPID-like scheme with further improvements in terms of robustness and performance. The camera pose estimation is done by fitting 3D edge points to strong image

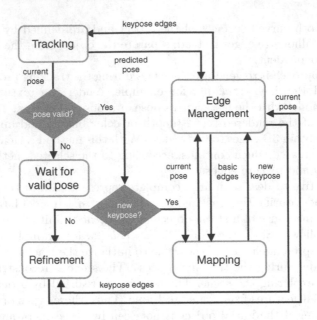

Fig. 1. Schematic overview of our proposed method. The model based tracking
system estimates a camera pose by fitting a selection of robust 3D edges to strong
image gradients. If the quality of the pose is good and it is a new keypose, the mapping
component will add new 3D edges to the model. Otherwise the refinement component
refines the 3D edges for the current keypose. The edge management takes care of the
administration of the edge model and its keyposes.

gradients. The main drawback of this method is the need for a well-designed 3D
model which keeps robust tracking edges as described in the previous sections.
Starting from a coarse edge model which represents, for example, only a small
part of the object, new edges are created and added as the camera moves around
the object. Furthermore, the system makes use of keyposes in order to realize an
intelligent edge management, to perform a drift reduction and a reinitialization if
the tracking fails. Keyposes represent a relatively small area with respect to the
object to be tracked. They are initialized by the basic edges of the input model
and extended through new 3D edges which are refined if the current estimated
camera pose is similar. Not only does the tracking profit from keyposes for the
reinitialization, but also from the selection of good edges to track. The stability
of edges depends on the view position of the camera. So, for example, they are
even more robust if they lie orthogonal to the viewing direction or are so-called
silhouette edges. Besides, the occurrence and appearance of an edge depends on
the distance to the object.

We define a confidence factor as a rough indication for the robustness of an
edge. This factor is derived, among others, from the occurrence of the edge in

subsequent images after its initialization, like in [1,10]. In our work this factor is calculated per keypose and enables a dependent selection of good edges to track by a pose prediction.

4   Edge Model

The edge model is formed by the edges of the input model and a set of keyposes which are generated during the tracking process. These keyposes approximate possible camera poses in the already visited environment around the known 3D object. A keypose keeps information about the 3D camera pose and a collection of 3D edges. These edges are created and refined while the camera pose, estimated by the tracking component, is close to the stored one.

4.1   Keyposes

Depending on the input model the edge model initially contains only edges which describe a relatively small part or the contours of the object. When the tracker is initialized the first keypose will be added. If the current camera pose differs from the initial pose or previous selected keyposes, a new keypose gets created. Each generated keypose stores the following information: a 3D camera rotation and translation with respect to the object and a set of 3D edges extracted from the input images. At first 2D edge segments are extracted from the current frame in order to create a keypose. The 2D segments are then back-projected on basis of the surface model to obtain 3D edges. These observed edges are refined and new 3D edges are mapped and added to the keypose if the estimated camera pose is close to the stored one. The idea of keyposes is shown in Fig. 2.

Keyposes are added whenever the following conditions are true: the tracking quality is good[2]; most of the object is visible; and the camera is a minimum distance away from each keypose already in the edge model. The distance between two camera poses is calculated by the translation distance in combination with the angle difference between the viewing directions (in our system currently set at $10°$). The translation distance between two camera poses depends on the size of the model. We calculate an appropriate threshold by taking the bounding box extent into account. The minimum translation distance is given in percentage of the radius of the bounding sphere (we choose 15%). In most cases the camera moves slowly, so it is sufficient to compare the distance between the current pose and the last active keypose as well as its closest neighbors.

4.2   Edges

Starting from the input edges the model keeps only the basic edges which are simply represented by their two end points. New edges are added to the model

---

[2] The calculation of the tracking quality is based on the covariance matrix and the number of detected edges in the current frame.

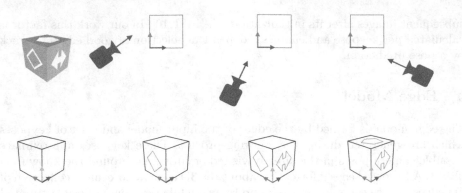

Fig. 2. Schematic view of keyposes. These keyposes are generated from three different camera poses and their corresponding edges (blue). Basic edges (black) are defined
by the coarse input model (Color figure online).

as the camera moves around the object or the first keypose is initialized, and
it is quite likely that some of these edges are incorrect. Some false edges arise
because of different lighting conditions, e.g. shadows. These edges are detected
in the camera image, but are not associated with a physical object edge and
unstable in their observation and thereby not suited to track. Moreover, some
edges are incorrectly initialized in their 3D positions, e.g. wrong back-projected
edges due to uncertainties in algorithms for 2D edge detection.

The first assumption in order to solve these problems is that a 3D edge which
often occurs in a 2D image is a good edge to track. Therefore, new initialized
edges are associated with a confidence factor. This factor increases through each
successful observation and gives an indication about the robustness of this edge
in relation to the corresponding keypose. The second assumption is that an
edge which is frequently changing its appearance or often corresponds to nearby
edges (like parallel edges) is a bad edge to track. These edges are unstable in
their position and thus the confidence should be decreased. To deal with these
types of edges each new initialized edge is updated if the tracking quality is good.
Furthermore, the variance is calculated for the end points of the edge in order
to get a measurement about the uncertainty of the 3D position. The confidence
factor in combination with the variance of the 3D position is helpful to identify
false edges and to select good edges to track. The selection of good edges to
track as well as the elimination of false edge will be explained in detail in the
next section.

5   Edge Management

The edge management component of our system takes care of the administration
of the current edge model and the selection of edges for the tracking, mapping
and refinement step. We use different edge states to determine which edges are
good to track, should be only used during the mapping and refinement process
or should be completely eliminated.

5.1 Edge States

Each edge of the model is assigned to one of the following edge states: *truth*, *robust* or *under control*. All basic edges of the input model are marked as *truth*. These edges are correctly positioned, correspond to a real edge of the scene and are therefore continuously used for tracking. Furthermore, these edges are useful for the initialization of a new keypose and thereby for drift avoidance. New initialized edges are not used for tracking immediately. They are marked as *under control* and only used during the refinement step which is processed in every frame. As described in Sect. 4.2, the end points of these edges are updated and the confidence increases every subsequent frame after the initialization of the edge occurs. If the number of detections reaches a threshold and the variance of the end points is still low, the edge will be assigned to *robust* and used for the tracking procedure for this keypose. If this occurrence counter does not increase within a specified number of frames or the variance gets too high, the edge can be classified as a false edge and gets completely eliminated from the associated keypose.

5.2 Reinitialization

In some cases the tracking step fails, for example because of fast camera movements, the object to be tracked is out of the image or is not visible. For this reason the tracking quality is observed in every frame. If the tracking quality is very low, the tracking continues for some few frames, but the system does not allow any further steps like adding new keyposes or mapping and refinement. If the quality is still low after these frames, the tracking is recognized as lost and a reinitialization process is initiated. The reinitialization is realized on basis of the previous collected keypose information. Starting from the last pose, keyposes with corresponding robust edges are selected and the system tries to reinitialize the tracking process.

Ideally the object should be visible and tracked for a while at the beginning of a tracking phase. In this way new keyposes are initialized and good edges to track can be classified.

6 Edge Mapping and Refinement

This section describes the process by which the edge model is updated if an accurate camera pose, estimated by the tracking component of our system, is available. Already existing edges are refined and new edges are added. This procedure can be summarized by the following steps:

1. **Extracting edges**
   The first step extracts straight edge segments represented by two 3D points in world coordinates out of the current camera image.
2. **Establishing edge correspondence**
   The second step identifies already existing edges and adds non-existing 3D edges to the keypose which is the closest to the estimated one.

3. **Updating edge confidences**

   The last step updates all edges which are identified in the previous step and updates their confidence.

These steps are shown in Fig. 3 and will be explained in detail in the following subsections.

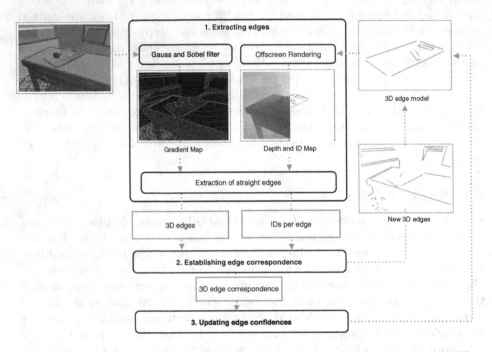

Fig. 3. Schematic pipeline of the edge mapping and refinement step. The image is convolved with a Gauss and a Sobel mask in order to create significant edge points and straight edges (1. step). A depth map is used for a back-projection process and an ID map is used to establish edge correspondence (1. and 2. step). New edges are added to the current edge model and already existing edges are updated (3. step).

6.1   Extracting Edges

First, we follow a canny-like scheme and create a gradient image by applying a simple Gauss and Sobel filter mask. The algorithm then walks along the gradient image, applies a non-maximum suppression and creates a structured representation of significant and connected 3D edge points.

In order to create structured 3D edge points efficiently, we perform an off-screen rendering step. Within this step the surface model with the estimated camera pose and the same image resolution as the input image gets rendered. The resulting output image provides depth information per pixel of the gradient image. The depth values are used to perform a back-projection procedure of 2D gradient points with high values. At this point we discard all of the points which do not lie on the surface of the 3D model or have a large discrepancy in depth to previous connected ones. Large differences in depth values are caused by uncertainties of the 2D edge detection, mostly in case of a silhouette or depth edges. Silhouette edges are located at the border of the object surface and the background, whereas depth edges are located within the object region (e.g. caused by self-occlusion). It may happen that the wrong depth value is selected.

The connected 3D edge points are then subdivided into straight edge segments represented by two points. The resulting 3D edge segments are described in camera space. We transfer them to the coordinate system of the edge model by applying the inverse rotation and translation of the current camera pose for further processing.

6.2   Establishing Edge Correspondence

In our system it is necessary to decide if a 3D edge already exists in the current edge model or if it has to be added. According to the Edge-ID method described in Lima *et al.* [8] we perform a matching between the existing and newly created 3D edge segments. The original method is usually used to perform hidden line removal but can be easily transferred to the matching problem if the camera rotation and translation is known.

Each 3D edge in each keypose is therefore assigned with a unique identifier (ID). In the same manner as we render the depth map, we render each existing edge with their ID encoded as color. This is done in one rendering pass. We use a simple RGB coding scheme, as in [8], to map the IDs to RGB and vice versa. With this coding scheme the maximum number of edges per keypose is $2^{32} - 1$. The edge count per keypose depends on the complexity of the scene or object as well as on the threshold values for the difference of two keyposes. But it will never reach the maximum number of edges.

To identify edges which are already existing in the keypose, the edge extraction algorithm as described in the previous subsection, is extended. Connected points are split to straight segments and the ID image at the corresponding 2D point is evaluated and the occurrence per ID is counted. If one edge ID occurs more often than a threshold (currently set to the half length of the segment) it can be assumed that the edge already exists. The corresponding edge is then identified by decoding the ID and the confidence is updated as shown in the next subsection. If a lot of different IDs occur it is quite likely that there is background clutter in the surrounding of the edge. These types of edges should be ignored. Otherwise, a new 3D edge will be added to the current keypose. Note that edges are only updated or added when a certain number of edges got detected. Otherwise, it is assumed that the quality of the estimated pose is not accurate enough for the mapping and refinement step.

6.3   Updating Edge Confidences

The confidence of an edge per keypose is calculated by taking the occurrence and the appearance into account. If the number of detections in the 2D image n reaches a certain threshold t (with $t > 0$) the variance σ^2 for each end point e will be calculated by:

$$\sigma^2 = (\frac{1}{n} \sum_{i=0}^{n} (p_i - \mu)^2)/l, \tag{1}$$

where μ is the current position of e, $\{p_1, p_2, \ldots, p_n\}$ are the already observed positions and l is the length of the edge in the 3D space. The division by l assures equality of σ^2 for different edge lengths as sketched in Fig. 4. If the variance constantly grows, the edge will be classified as non-robust as discussed in Sect. 5.

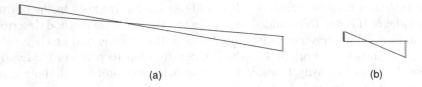

(a)   (b)

Fig. 4. Effectiveness of the division by the edge length. Two observations of two different edges with various edge lengths. The edges in (a) are more equal than in (b). The division of the variance by the length results in a higher value for edge (b) than for edge (a).

7   Experimental Results

In this section, we present the evaluation of our method with several experiments. We performed the experiments with two different objects and scenes in a set of synthetic and real image sequences. Note that these models are different in terms of the complexity and characteristics as shown in the following sections.

7.1   Synthetic Image Sequences

We used a set of synthetic sequences to compare our proposed method with the standard edge tracker without any mapping or refinement step. These image sequences were generated by moving a virtual camera around a static object and store ground truth pose data for each image. The model of the chopping board (object to be tracked shown as in Fig. 5) is placed in a kitchen model, so that the scene is more realistic for example with background clutter. The surface

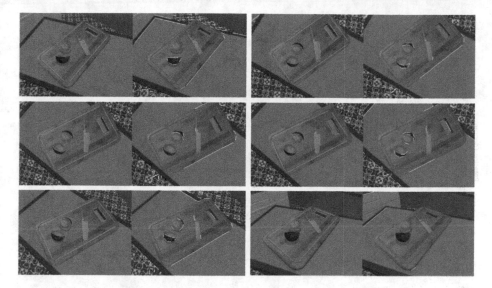

Fig. 5. Tracking results of a synthetic generated scene. Results with the proposed mapping and refinement step (orange edges) and without this step (green edges) are shown in the synthetic sequence of the chopping board. Note that the white edges are only used during the mapping and refinement step. They are currently not used for tracking (Color figure online).

models of the chopping board and the kitchen are taken from 3D Warehouse[3]. The corresponding coarse edge model of the chopping board has been generated manually by using Blender[4].

Figure 5 shows the tracking results and Fig. 6 shows the corresponding 6-DOF camera pose plots for one image sequence. The tested image sequence starts with a slow camera movement, which is fairly easy to track. After some time, around frame 350, tracking gets more complicated, especially the translation velocity increases. Based on the line plots, we can easily see that the proposed method continually shows similar or better results in terms of the robustness and accuracy than the method without any refinement or tracking step. The standard tracking was able to track only 56.4 % of the images, whereas the tracking with the mapping was able to track 92 %. Our method does not lose the camera pose easily and is capable to recover faster if the tracking is lost. The reinitialization is easily done by finding the best matching keypose as described in Sect. 5.2. The camera just has to move near to an already stored keypose. The tracking without our extension needs a camera pose near to the last tracked pose to reinitialize the tracking process.

---

[3] https://3dwarehouse.sketchup.com/.
[4] http://www.blender.org/.

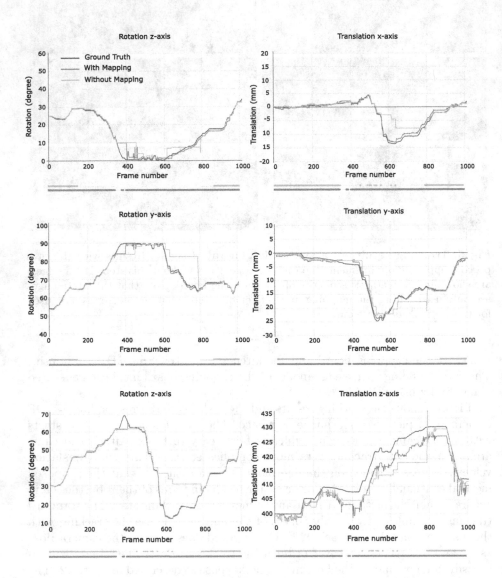

Fig. 6. 6-DOF camera pose plots of the chopping board in a synthetic generated image sequence. The line plots below the diagrams indicate successful tracked frames. In general, our approach (orange) continually achieves better results than the tracking without a mapping and refinement (green) (Color figure online).

Moreover, the tracking without any mapping and refinement step highly depends on the quality of the input edges. There is no general statement about the selection of good edges to track. Increasing the number of input edges, for example, does not necessarily mean that the accuracy or robustness increases. To show this we calculated the root mean square (RMS) errors for the sample sequence with a different number of input edges as shown in Table 1. The generality of our system for different input edges can be seen. It is able to track the scene with different input edges with similar results in terms of accuracy and robustness.

Table 1. RMS (root mean square) error in a synthetic generated sequences. The upper rows show the results of our proposed method and the lower rows show the results of the method without any refinement or mapping procedure. The number of input edges is presented in the second column, the third column shows the percentage of tracked frames.

Method	Edges (#)	Frames (%)	RMS (root mean square) error					
			R_x (degree)	R_y (degree)	R_z (degree)	t_x (mm)	t_y (mm)	t_z (mm)
With	5	90.9	0.59211	0.51526	0.59501	0.56182	1.19744	2.17623
Without		35.7	0.54594	0.43345	0.22434	0.59579	0.64225	3.20885
With	7	100	0.56358	1.30319	0.77255	1.20516	1.39944	5.42438
Without		100	1.10871	1.83799	1.03849	1.78927	1.23728	6.76075
With	8	100	0.94687	1.68201	0.93394	1.66943	1.31145	6.05157
Without		100	1.26483	2.06454	1.23755	2.12224	1.32286	7.64757
With	9	94.6	0.54248	0.84202	0.55344	0.90416	0.294224	5.09546
Without		73.1	1.22008	2.11999	1.03555	2.23612	0.563874	8.63815
With	10	92	0.31508	0.36303	0.45056	0.38775	0.86188	1.74504
Without		56.4	0.34329	0.32387	0.19249	0.24481	0.50929	2.01651

7.2 Real Image Sequences

We tested our method in real image sequences which represent much greater challenge as the synthetic generated scenes. The real image scenes represent noise, motion blur and different lighting conditions. We use a simple model of a house with a lot of planar surfaces and textures. The surface model of this object and the coarse edge model is generated manually using Blender. Note that only the surface model of the object to be tracked is available. Therefore, new edges are only mapped to the edge model if these lie on the object.

Figure 7 shows the tracking results with and without mapping and refinement. We can easily see that the tracking with mapping and refinement profits from already stored keyposes for reinitialization as seen before in the synthetic scenes. The tracking with refinement and mapping achieves 98 % tracked frames. The tracking without this procedure achieves only 83 % tracked frames. In terms of accuracy both methods show almost identical results.

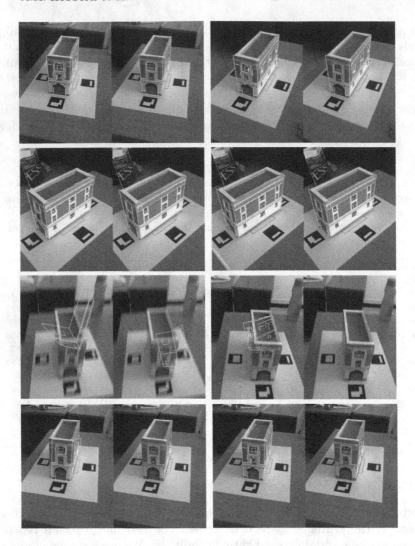

Fig. 7. Tracking results of a real scene. The effectiveness of the keyposes for reinitialization is shown. Results with the proposed mapping and refinement step (orange edges) and without this step (green edges) are shown in the real sequence. The white edges are only used during the mapping and refinement step. They are currently not used for tracking. Also note that the markers were only used to initialize the tracking step (Color figure online).

8   Conclusion and Future Work

We present a method which extents a model based tracking approach for augmented reality. Our algorithm is able to track an object on basis of a coarse edge model and overcomes some well-known limitations of standard edge trackers. As shown in the evaluation, our method performs better in terms of reinitialization speed. Furthermore, a coarse 3D edge model of the object to track is absolutely suitable as new edges will be added during the tracking process. So there is no need of putting a lot of effort in creating suitable edge models manually.

In contrast to well-known SfM approaches, virtual content can be registered in the coordinate system of the model and an accurate collision as well as occlusion handling between virtual and real components can be realized by the surface model. Moreover, our system is able to deal with poorly textured scenes due to the use of edges.

Future work should concentrate on the enhancement of the edge model beyond the surface model to overcome the limitation that tracking solely works if the model is within the visible region. The use of a particle filter approach (as in Choi *et al.* [4]) could additionally improve the reinitialization process.

Acknowledgments. Part of this research was done for Fraunhofer IDM@NTU, which is funded by the National Research Foundation (NRF) and managed through the multi-agency Interactive & Digital Media Programme Office (IDMPO).

References

1. Gee, A.P., Mayol-Cuevas, W.: Real-time model-based SLAM using line segments. In: Bebis, G., et al. (eds.) ISVC 2006. LNCS, vol. 4292, pp. 354–363. Springer, Heidelberg (2006)
2. Bleser, G., Wuest, H., Stricker, D.: Online camera pose estimation in partially known and dynamic scenes. In: Proceedings - ISMAR 2006: Fifth IEEE and ACM International Symposium on Mixed and Augmented Reality, pp. 56–65 (2007)
3. Choi, C., Christensen, H.I.: Real-time 3D model-based tracking using edge and keypoint features for robotic manipulation. In: Proceedings - IEEE International Conference on Robotics and Automation, pp. 4048–4055 (2010)
4. Choi, C., Christensen, H.I.: 3D textureless object detection and tracking an edge based approach. In: IEEE/RSJ International Conference on Intelligent Robots and Systems (IROS) (2012)
5. Harris, C., Stennett, C.: RAPID - a video rate object tracker. In: Procedings of the British Machine Vision Conference 1990, pp. 15.1–15.6 (1990)
6. Klein, G., Murray D.: Full-3D edge tracking with a particle filter. In: British Machine Vision Conference, pp. 1119–1128 (2006)
7. Klein, G., Murray, D.: Parallel tracking and mapping for small AR workspaces. In: 2007 6th IEEE and ACM International Symposium on Mixed and Augmented Reality, ISMAR (2007)
8. Lima, J., Simões, F., Figueiredo, L., Kelner, J.: Model based markerless 3D tracking applied to augmented reality. SBC **1**, 2–15 (2010)
9. Reitmayr, G., Drummond, T.W.: Going out: Robust model-based tracking for outdoor augmented reality. In: Proceedings - ISMAR 2006: Fifth IEEE and ACM International Symposium on Mixed and Augmented Reality, pp. 109–118 (2007)
10. Schumann, M., Hoppenheit, J., Stefan, M.: Feature evaluation and management for camera pose tracking on 3D models. In: VISAPP 2014 - Proceedings of the 9th International Conference on Computer Vision Theory and Applications, vol. 3, pp. 562–569 (2005)

11. Teichrieb, V., Lima, M., Lourenc, E., Bueno, S., Kelner, J., Santos, I.H.F.: A survey of online monocular markerless augmented reality. Int. J. Model. Simul. Petrol. Ind. **1**(1), 1–7 (2007)
12. Wuest, H., Stricker, D., Herder, J.: Tracking of industrial objects by using CAD models. J. Virtual Reality Broadcast. **4**(1), 9 (2007)
13. Wuest, H., Vial, F., Stricker, D.: Adaptive line tracking with multiple hypotheses for augmented reality. In: Proceedings - Fourth IEEE and ACM International Symposium on Mixed and Augmented Reality, ISMAR 2005, pp. 62–69 (2005)

Augmented Reality, Embodied Cognition and Learning

Sara Invitto[1], Italo Spada[2], and Lucio Tommaso De Paolis[3(✉)]

[1] Human Anatomy and Neuroscience Lab, Department of Biological and Environmental Science
and Technology, University of Salento,
Lecce, Italy
sara.invitto@unisalento.it
[2] Virtual, Augmented Reality and Multimedia Area, CETMA Consortium,
Brindisi, Italy
italo.spada@cetma.it
[3] Augmented and Virtual Reality Lab, Department of Engineering for Innovation,
University of Salento, Lecce, Italy
lucio.depaolis@unisalento.it

Abstract. Augmented Reality allows a more detailed understanding of a learning object. Aim of this work was to analyse embodied cognition of the learning object, when it is presented in 2D or in 3D presentation in AR. Our sample was composed by University Students that differed with respect to the knowledge of plankton (naïve and competent condition). The subjects had to manipulate in AR some Application about plankton. After the AR manipulation, the subjects had to perform a recognition task during an EEG recording. We examined Event Related Potential P1, N2 and P3 components. Main result of the study was a significant change in amplitude in the parietal and central left lobe in all components in direction of greater amplitude in naïve condition. We interpret these results like a modulatory effect in the interaction with augmented reality application.

Keywords: Augmented reality · Embodied cognition · Learning object

1 Introduction

Cognitive neuroscience and Virtual and Augmented Reality began to interact through the study of perception and through the implementation of Brain Computer Interfaces (BCIs) [1, 2].

Brain Computer Interface system was initially developed for clinical use, but in recent years these systems have also been used in other areas, such as in the field of virtual reality and games. So, the development of interactive, participatory, and multi-sensory environments that combine the physical with the virtual comes as a natural continuation to the computer game industry's constant race. This is not a trend limited to the entertainment domain; non-formal learning environments for children and student are also following this path.

© Springer International Publishing Switzerland 2015
L.T. De Paolis and A. Mongelli (Eds.): AVR 2015, LNCS 9254, pp. 125–134, 2015.
DOI: 10.1007/978-3-319-22888-4_10

In a recent work Roussou [3] explored a central thread in learning as well as an essential characteristic of virtual reality environments: interactivity. The interactivity is examined in relation to learning, play, narrative, and to characteristics inherent in virtual reality, such as immersion, presence, and the creation of illusion. Virtual and Augmented Reality eases so systemic experimentation of human functions both in healthy and diseased states. Virtual reality scenes can give the human brain a sense of immersion as in the real world, receiving more real-world realistic information.

Thus, using virtual reality technology to construct realistic experimental scenarios, the mechanisms of cognitive processing in the human brain could be better studied then in the real world because in the virtual environment are available some controllable parameters. The use of VR technology in the study of the cognitive process in the human brain has been reported in some Event Related Potentials (ERP) literature. An event-related potential is the measured brain response that is the direct result of a specific sensory, cognitive, or motor event [4]. So, using virtual reality technology to construct realistic experimental scenarios, the mechanism of cognitive processing in the human brain could be better studied.

In [5], through the presentation of traffic signs with correct or incorrect background colours in a virtual reality traffic environment, the authors have studied the cognitive processing in the human brain using event-related potential method. The results showed that simpler contents and larger contrast between the background colours and foreground colours of traffic signs would make the human brain respond faster.

According to this approach, some studies highlight that AR could be a candidate to produce better adherence to correct procedures by virtue of increasing motivation [6, 7].

Today, technology creates a basic multimedia experience for users. Virtual objects in AR will take on more roles, they will be more smoothly integrated into the real-world scene and they will offer greater interactivity. Virtual reality programs for general education and for medical education too, now enable users to interact directly in a 3D environment with internal anatomical structures (or zoological structure, environmental structure and others).

In this regard, the study of Jang et al. [8] examines the facilitative effects of embodiment of a complex internal anatomical structure through three-dimensional interactivity in a virtual reality program.

The aim of this work is considering how greater interactivity, that involves the embodied cognition [9], can be more activating in the stimulus discrimination and learning. In a previous study we examined difference by Marine Biology students and Cultural Heritage students in a presentation of 3D planktonic elements without interactive application [10, 11].

In this situation we found that 3D condition allows a better perception of the stimulus but also that there is a significant left lateralization in students competent in planktonic elements. In this work we used an interactive condition with the same objects and Aurasma app like AR app. Aurasma is a HP augmented reality platform that is available as a SDK or as a free app for iOS and Android mobile devices. Aurasma's image recognition technology uses the smartphone or tablet camera to recognize real world images and then overlays some media in the form of animations, videos, 3D models and web pages. Aurasma permits to create and share the own augmented reality experiences as well as to discover hidden digital content. Teachers are among the most active group using this platform. In this regard, we presented the learning objects through the applications CETMA -DUNE®.ar and AURASMA©2015 [10], interactive images expressly designed for a task of learning about plankton stimuli (Marine Biology learning in the University), and we interfaced it with an EEG task, in order to monitor some cognitive processes of stimulus recognition.

2   Methodology

Our study and experiment consisted in an embodied cognition analysis of the learning object, when it is presented in a 2D presentation or in 3D presentation using the Augmented Reality. This paper analyses how a percept presented through augmented reality can be facilitative in a task of recognition of the stimulus, rather than the object detected after a simple presentation of the 2D stimulus. In this case, the stimuli were presented in 2D visual mode and 3D movie mode with AR condition. Images of task were elements of plankton and the duration of the 3D movie was about about 50 s for every AR application. We had 8 subjects of Planktonic Elements: Acartia (Fig. 1), Ceratium, Chaetoceros (Fig. 2), Coscinodiscus, Globigerina, Pelagia, Pleurosigma, Tintinnide.

Our sample was composed by university students matched by age and sex. The sample of volunteers recruited had normal hearing, normal or corrected to normal vision and had a right manual dominance. Subjects recruited had no previous experience of EEG cognitive task. The sample was composed by two groups: one (7 students) without any knowledge study about plankton, and the second, 4 students with knowledge study about plankton; both samples performed in Baseline Condition study (with a 2D presentation of the plankton images) and in AR condition (3D plankton image with CETMA-DUNE®.ar Application). All participants gave written informed consent according to Helsinki declaration. In this experiment we chose students of bachelor of Optic, Psychology and Marine Biology.

A. Technological Tools

For the experiment described above two kinds of interaction technologies have been used:

- CETMA-DUNE® augmented reality application that has been designed by CETMA and is based on markerless content recognition;
- AURASMA©2015, an open source application based on printed physic marker recognition. Before explaining some technical issues regarding such augmented reality applications, it's worth noting that the stage of the digital content production aimed either at realizing both the dynamic 3D real time models for DUNE® app and AURASMA©2015 customized multimedia objects.

The main goal was to understand how different educational contents could be adapted to two different AR applications.

DUNE® allows to visualize the real-time advanced 3D objects easily, with a mobile device pointing any indoor and outdoor areas of interest. The application recognizes shapes and colours in the framed space and it automatically downloads from a cloud server a 3D content that is characterized by low polygons geometries and mapped with middle resolution textures.

Users are able to visualize the selected digital contents mixed to the physical space; once downloading the digital contents in the virtual scene, they can manage the 3D data by positioning, scaling and tracking it. To make easy this kind of real-time interaction, the application requires a perfect geometry realized by solid shapes with one side normal, connected tangents, plain textures and without construction history. For those reasons a film box extension data (.FBX) has been used for the imported 3D objects.

AURASMA©2015 allows visualizing multimedia educational contents (video, voices and images) based on a marker type recognition. After the 3D reconstruction and the stage of 3D animation, all contents are translated in to movie files (.MOV) with compressed extension for the streaming playing (.FLV). For a proper working, AURASMA©2015 needs to frame a physical paper copy; latter is designed adding and connecting digital information to images or texts by means of a remote editor.

Using a mobile device the user will visualize and interact with digital contents by pointing a book or a magazine page. Such application devices allow understanding educational contents in a new interactive manner.

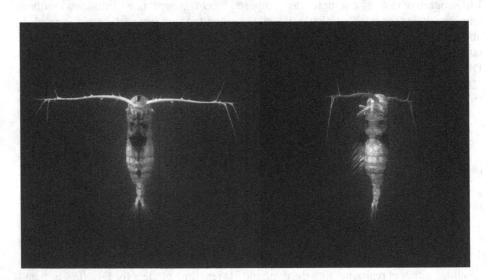

Fig. 1. Acartia in CETMA DUNE®.ar

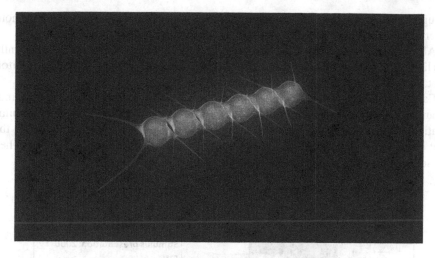

Fig. 2. Chaetoceros in CETMA DUNE®.ar

B. Psychophysiological Tools

During the images presentation task we have recorded data coming from an EEG 16 Channels of Brain AMP-Brain Vision Recorder, and Galvanic Skin Reflex. We considered, in EEG tracks, the Event Related Potentials for averaged waves for planktonic elements, colored screens, objects and animals.

The EEG signal was recorded by 16 surface recording electrodes, obtained by Brain Vision Recorder apparatus (Brain Vision). A further electrode was positioned above the right eyebrow for electro-oculogram recording. The ERP's analysis was obtained using the Brain Vision Analyzer and the time off-line analysis was from 100 pre-stimulus to 500 ms post-stimulus with 1000 ms baseline-correction. Thereafter, trials with blinks and eye movements were rejected on the basis of horizontal electro-oculogram with an ICA component analysis.

An artefact rejection criterion of 60 V was used at all other scalp sites to reject trials with excessive EMG or other noise transients; sampling rate was 256 Hz. After a transformation and a re-segmentation of data with the Brain Vision Analyzer, the artefact-free EEG tracks corresponding to the affordance object, marked by the motor response, were averaged in each case to extract the main waveforms, the N1 in the time range 120–175 ms, the P2 in the time range 175-250 and P3 component in the 260–400 ms time interval, according to literature. We performed a semiautomatic peak detection for the different components of ERP's wave.

C. Experiments

The experiments have been performed using a first group of students of Psychology and Optic without any knowledge about plankton and another group of students with knowledge about plankton. Both the groups performed the task in Baseline Condition (2 min for the 2D presentation of plankton images followed by the recognition task) and in AR condition (2 min for 3D presentation of plankton image using the CETMA-DUNE® application followed by the recognition task). The images have been selected through a repository of neutral images (coloured squares on a light background), non-target images (animals, everyday objects) and target images (plankton 3D).

All stimuli have a dimension of 240 × 210 pixels, and have been displayed centrally on a light grey background and to the same level of brightness on the computer monitor. The task was administered via the E-prime software 2.0.

Each trial, composed of a single type of target alternated randomly background-colour, has lasted 600 s, with a stimulus duration of 2000 ms and 1000 ms interstimulus duration. The participants were instructed to stand upright with ca 75 cm between the front edge of the chair and the floor. The instruction was: 'Please click a button when you see an element which has been previously shown' (Fig. 3).

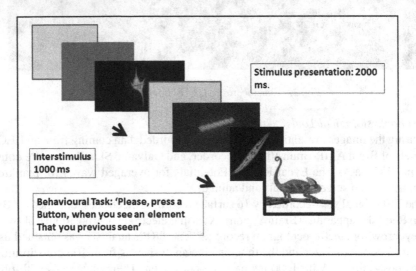

Fig. 3. Recognition task during EEG recording

3   Results

We performed a one-way Anova analysis (3D Augmented Reality without plankton knowledge, and 3D Augmented Reality with plankton knowledge) and with dependent variables the latencies and amplitude of P1, N2 and P3 components of ERP.

In P1 component we found significant results on P7 Amplitude (F = 8,549; p = 0,015 -Group 1 mean amplitude 3,23 microvolt; Group 2 mean amplitude -1,35) and in C3 Latency (F = 7,459; p = 0,021 Group 1 mean Latency 102; Group 2 mean latency 127) in direction of a greater amplitude and faster latency in Group 1. In P2 component we found significant results on P7 amplitude (F = 5,482; p = 0,041 -Group 1 mean amplitude -0,63 microvolt; Group 2 mean amplitude -7,08 microvolt) in direction of a greater N2 in Marine Biology group (Fig. 4).

In P3 component we found significant results on P7 amplitude (F = 6,003; p = 0,034 -Group 1 mean amplitude 6,39 microvolt; Group 2 mean amplitude -0,339 microvolt).

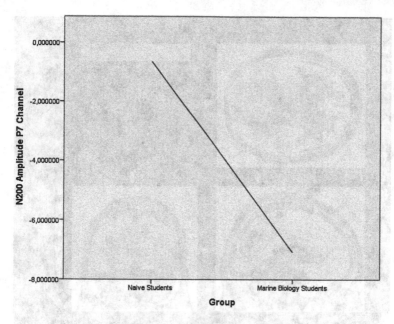

Fig. 4. Amplitude on P7 channel.

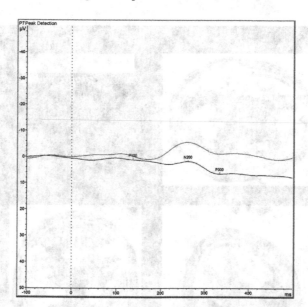

Fig. 5. Matching ERP of grand average: black line –naïve condition; red line – competent condition.

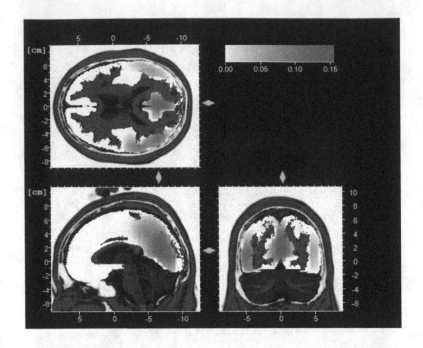

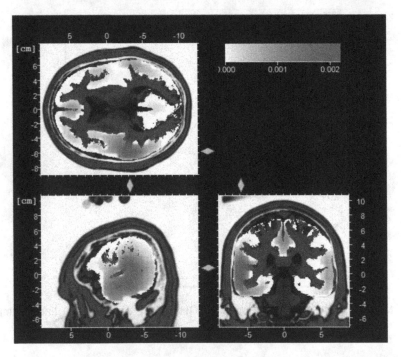

Fig. 6. Loreta of naïve condition and loreta of competent condition.

4   Conclusions and Future Work

According to literature we can consider that a product in Augmented Reality, like a condition linked to the theory of embodied cognition, facilitates the interaction and understanding of the stimulus. From the results of our experiments we can say that the major differences were found in the parietal left lobe, specializing in stimulus recognition (it the way of 'what is and object), in a general attention system (P1, N2) and in higher cognitive functions (P3) (Figs. 5 and 6).

We have specific results for Competent condition; in this condition we found a specific activation due to a very competent knowledge of plankton stimuli (like it could happen in a face recognition task). Still, central left area has a faster latency in Naïve condition. IN P1 and in P3 component we have a greater arousal in Naïve students group, probably because the plankton stimulus is not a familiar object and because the interaction with AR allow a better stimulus understanding enhancing attentional system.

Clearly, the study of this kind of the elements (in this case the plankton, hardly discriminated as a semantic object, unless it is a learning object) mostly active brain areas involved in stimulus's recognition, while the interaction in augmented reality activates areas related to motor involvement, action planning and attentional arousal rather than a not interactive presentation and a simple 2D presentation (like we found in our previous work) or 3D presentation without motor interaction [12]. Our sample is made up of few subjects, but then this protocol will be further developed with a larger sample, with the analysis of further variables of learning and with different interaction through the game-app Dune AR.

So, from these results, we can think that, through the use of interactive AR interface (with augmented reality and virtual reality in this case) educational information can be more effectively convey too. Use of interactivity, like can be an object in augmented reality, allow a 'embodied cognition' and it can be seen in brain activity too.

Further future investigations will be related to the kind of involvement that the interaction modulates in learning.

Acknowledgment.   This work has been supported by the following projects: (a) PON R&C 2007-13 EDOC@Work Project 3.0 - Education and Work in Cloud; (b) "Easy Perception Lab" Living Lab Project, Apulia Region.

The authors wish to thank Dario Turco, manager of Agilex srl, for the contribution at the project "Easy Perception Lab".

References

1. Rose, F.D., Attree, E.A., Brooks, B.M., Johnson, D.H.: Virtual environments in brain damage rehabilitation: a rationale from basic neuroscience. In: Riva, G., Wiederhold, B.K., Molinan, E. (eds.) Virtual Environments in Clinical Psychology and Neuroscience: Methods and Techniques in Advanced Patient-Therapist Interaction, pp. 233–242. IOS Press, Amsterdam (1998)

2. Rose, F.D., Brooks, B.M., Attree, E.A.: An exploratory investigation into the usability and usefulness of training people with learning disabilities in a virtual environment. Disabil. Rehabil. **24**(11–12), 627–633 (2002)
3. Roussou, M.: Learning by doing and learning through play: an exploration of interactivity in virtual environments for children. ACM Comput. Entertainment **2**(1), 1–23 (2004)
4. Luck, S.L.: An Introduction to the Event-Related Potential Technique, 2nd edn. The MIT Press, Cambridge (2014)
5. Baolin, L., Zhongning, W., Guanjun, S., Guagning, W.J.: Cognitive processing of traffic signs in immersive virtual reality environment:an ERP study. Neurosci. Lett. **485**, 43–48 (2010)
6. Neumann, U., Majoros, A.: Cognitive, performance, and systems issues for augmented reality applications in manufacturing and maintenance. In: Proceedings IEEE Virtual Reality (VR 1998), pp. 4–11 (1998)
7. Mania, K., Chalmers, A.: The effects of levels of immersion on memory and presence in virtual environments: a reality centered approach. CyberPsychol. Behav. **4**(2), 247–264 (2001)
8. Jang, S., BlacK, J., Jyung, R.: Embodied cognition and virtual reality in learning to visualize anatomy. In: 32 Annual Conference of the Cognitive Science Society, Portland (2010)
9. Shapiro, L.: The Handbook of Embodied Cognition. Routledge, New York (2014)
10. Invitto, S., Spada, I., De Tommaso, M., Belmonte, G.: Virtual reality and planktonic elements: cognitive preference and 3d perceptions in marine biology students. In: Neuropsychological Trends, LED Editions, Proceedings Abstract, XXII Congress of Italian Society of Psychophysiology, November 2014
11. Banos, R.M., Botella, C., Alcaniz, M., Liano, B.A., Guerrero, B., Rey, B.: Immersion and Emotion: their Impact on the Sense of Presence. Cyberpsychol. Behav. **7**, 734–740 (2004)
12. Dune Suit Area DIM Data Processing and Immersive Environment. http://www.cetma.it/LinkClick.aspx?fileticket=m7lY0e5gjME%3D&tabid=200&language=it-IT

OscARsWelt: A Collaborative Augmented Reality Game

Anna Katharina Hebborn(✉), Milan Dilberovic, Adrian Derstroff,
Andre Franke, Nils Höhner, Patrick Krechel, Lisa Prinz, Astrid Szirmai,
Fabian Weigend, and Stefan Müller

Institute of Computational Visualistics, University of Koblenz-Landau,
Universitätstr. 1, 56070 Koblenz, Germany
ahebborn@uni-koblenz.de

Abstract. Combining physical and virtual objects in a computer game
is becoming more and more popular, not only for players, but also for
developers due to their flexibility in creating the game. We extended the
idea by including a car-like Raspberry Pi robot, called OscAR which can
be maneuvered through a realistic model city via a steering wheel and
pedals, providing immersive gameplay. The gimmick in OscARsWelt is
that the driver does not necessarily need to be personally on site, but
can play our game from all over the world as long as he connects to our
robot. To allow multiplayer gameplay, it is possible to join OscARsWelt
as an additional player by using an Android device. The player has the
choice to either support or to hinder the driver. Required to guarantee
an immersive user experience are low-latency video streaming, a real-
time-capable tracking system that remains stable while the robot is in
motion, a fully remote-controllable car and a sufficient field of view.

Keywords: Augmented reality game · Collaborative game

1 Introduction

Augmented reality (AR) has become increasingly popular in the game industry.
For example recent game consoles, such as the PlayStation 4 and others, support
augmented reality games, indicating that AR is the next step towards future
gaming.

In this paper we introduce an augmented reality application in a model city.
The city is augmented with virtual objects and can be explored by a remote
controlled car equipped with a camera. It is possible to control the robot car
with a steering wheel and pedals. To enhance the gameplay, multiple players
may join the game. The car is controlled by one user, while another user can
help him or her to solve his or her tasks, using an Android application. The
main devices involved are a Raspberry Pi controlling the robot car, a laptop
displaying the camera images overlapped with the AR elements and an Android
device like a smartphone or tablet. Figure 1 shows the interaction between these

L.T. De Paolis and A. Mongelli (Eds.): AVR 2015, LNCS 9254, pp. 135–150, 2015.
DOI: 10.1007/978-3-319-22888-4_11

components. By integrating smartphones and tablets we respond to the fact that in the past few years, they have become increasingly important in our everyday life and are used more frequently as a gaming device. The Android application enables the user to remotely control certain virtual elements.

We faced the problem of a fast data transmission to realise the collaboration between the different devices. An important part of our work is the tracking of the robot's position and orientation. Several tracking strategies were tested to ensure we use the most stable and suitable method for our application. The tracking is well adapted to the specific setting of our model city and is able to determine the accurate pose of the robot car. This is necessary to blend virtual objects into the scenery recorded by the camera and to compute collisions or overlaps.

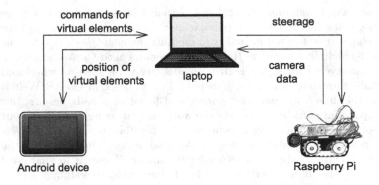

Fig. 1. Interaction between the three main components.

This paper is divided in six parts: In the following section we present related works in augmented reality. In section three we introduce the concept behind our game and its logic. After this a short system overview containing the collaboration between the multiple devices is given. In section five we present our augmented reality components and section six deals with the tracking algorithm we used. In the last part we draw a comprehensive conclusion and give prospects on possible future work built on this research.

2   Related Work

Many collaborative and mobile applications with AR have been developed. Our work was inspired by several of these existing AR games. Human Pacman [2], for example, is an interactive role-playing outdoor game based on the classic arcade game Pacman. The human players are assigned to two opposing teams: The Pacman team and the Ghost team. Every player is provided with a custom-built wearable computer, including a video see-through head-mounted display. In AR mode, the Pacman and Ghost players can see virtual cookies scattered over the real physical world. The goal of the Pacman character is to collect all virtual cookies while avoiding the Ghosts. Additionally, the Pacman players can collect physical ingredients like sugar to make special virtual cookies. If they "eat" them, they achieve immunity from being caught by Ghosts or power to catch Ghosts for a short time. On the other hand, the aim of the Ghosts is to catch all Pacmen by touching the capacitive sensor pad on their shoulders. To promote collaboration, a Helper character is added as an advisor for each Pacman and Ghost player. The Helpers can remotely join with their PCs to watch a virtual reality representation of the action and use text messaging to communicate with the participants.

A collaborative approach of an augmented reality racing game was realized by Oda et al. [7]. The driver wears a video see-through head-mounted display tracked by an attached camera and controls a virtual car with a passive tangible controller. It consists of two marker arrays attached to a pair of bicycle handle-bars. By rotating the controller the car can be turned and by tilting forward or backwards the car is accelerated or decelerated. The game board is formed by a planar array of optical markers and virtual objects are overlaid on the game-board. Additional virtual objects, which act as physical obstacles or waypoints, can be attached to separate movable markers. Therefore, other players can participate by manipulating waypoints that the car has to pass and obstacles the car can collide with. The additional players watch stationary displays associated with cameras which can be positioned and oriented randomly in the environment to have a sufficient view on the gameboard. The driver's goal is to finish three laps as quickly as possible.

The Sunshine Aquarium in Tokyo, Japan launched a marketing campaign called Penguin Navi[1]. In the resulting mobile application virtual penguins direct and lead visitors towards the aquarium. By using motion-capture technology, the Sunshine Aquarium was able to record images and walking patterns of penguins. With augmented reality technology these images are overlaid onto a users phone or tablet. Moreover, GPS is used to figure out paths from various places in Tokyo towards the aquarium.

An example of a mobile application of interactive remote toys with augmented reality is shown in [4]. In this AR game, the player navigates a real remote controlled car through a virtual animation of a traffic light. To control the car they have to use virtual buttons superimposed onto the display of a mobile device which is connected to the car via Bluetooth. A green traffic light is safe to pass, but passing through a red traffic light causes warning. This game has an education purpose as users learn and practice the traffic rules.

3   OscARsWelt

OscARsWelt is an augmented reality application which provides not only a single-player, but also a multiplayer experience. The setting is a realistic model city, augmented with various virtual objects.

---

[1] http://www.penguinnavi.erba-hd.com.

The main player (driver) steers a remote controlled vehicle from a first person point of view. The player tries to reach the game objectives as fast as possible. In addition, he or she has to aim for virtual items that randomly appear on the map to wash away the paint and hence turn back the player's progress.

A side player (non-driver) is actively involved in the game by using an Android application. By manipulating the virtual surroundings, he or she influences the success or failure of the driver. It is possible to use an android capable device to draw on a digital city map, pointing the driver towards important game elements and thus accelerating his flow of play. At the end of a game, the achieved points of the driver are saved in a high-score table, so that he or she can compare his performance with other players.

4   System Overview

The previously outlined project idea requires a fully remote controlled car system that is capable of recording its environment with a camera and simultaneously broadcasting a video stream to a distant host. Furthermore, we try to increase realism by using a steering-wheel and pedals as input devices for the end user. The pedals consist of a gas and a brake pedal, the latter is also used for reversing. This is more intuitive for driving a car-like robot instead of using a bicycle handlebar, such as in the aforementioned racing game. We decided on a Raspberry Pi driven system due to its extensibility and the availability of all needed components. Namely the Raspberry Pi camera module, the support for a Wi-Fi connection and easy to use chassis kits. As an operating system we chose Arch Linux. Figure 2 shows the systems used.

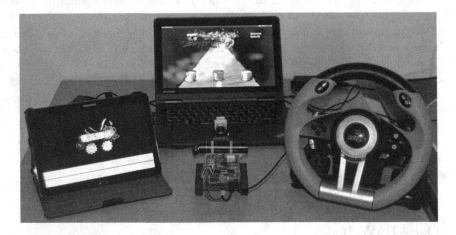

Fig. 2. The tablet as our Android device, the laptop, OscAR and the steering-wheel.

The Android application utilises UDP Sockets to communicate with the host system as shown in Fig. 3. Every Android device with API Level 8 or higher is compatible with our program.

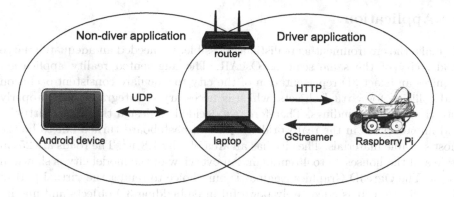

Fig. 3. Network infrastructure with used protocols.

4.1 OscAR

In this section we give a detailed description about the functionality of the remote controlled car system, called OscAR.

Controls. The application takes the input from the USB steering wheel and the pedals and send them via HTTP to the Raspberry Pi if the input signal exceeds a certain threshold. This is useful to prevent unnecessary network traffic, because the motors are not precise enough to translate small velocity variation. On the Raspberry Pi, the incoming signal is processed with a Python script that controls the motors through the GPIO interface. Unfortunately, the horizontal and vertical field of view provided by the Raspberry Pi camera are small and make it rather difficult to control the robot by only looking at the video stream. Therefore, we added a wide-angle lens to improve the user experience.

Video Stream. The fundamental requirements for practical video streaming are a low latency on the one hand and a decent video quality on the other. The former guarantees a better user experience, as it results in quicker feedback, while the latter is important for the introduced tracking methods and results in a more robust and precise pose estimation. An increasing video quality usually leads to a higher latency and vice versa. To cope with this situation we need to find a reasonable compromise which typically involves computationally intensive encoding techniques. The Raspberry Pi camera module supports h.264 hardware encoding, which fulfils our requirements. To utilise this, we make use of the GStreamer framework that allows to stream the generated video output without further de- or encoding. On the host side, we are able to receive the stream directly with OpenCV due to its compatibility with the GStreamer framework (as seen in Fig. 3). With this setup we are able to stream the camera output with 25 frames per second in a 640 × 480 resolution. The latency is appreciably lower in comparison to other streaming techniques like MJPEG-streaming.

5 Application

To make the environment as realistic as possible, we needed an adequately large model city of the same scale as OscAR. The augmented reality application requires an exact 3D representation of the city to calculate consistent occlusion and collision for virtual objects, which is necessary to integrate them properly into the real surroundings. Therefore, we decided to design the model virtually and implement it in the real world. Wood and pasteboard turned out to be the most suitable materials. The city has an area of 2 by $1.8\,m^2$. The roads are 25 cm wide and the houses 40 to 45 cm high. An overview of the model city is shown in Fig. 4. The Ogre3D Graphics Engine[2] is our choice to render the virtual part of the application. It is adequately powerful in embedding 3D objects and manipulating shaders to fulfill our expectations. Additionally, it works together well with the ViSP tracking framework, which is used to determine the position of virtual objects in relation to the real world.

Fig. 4. The complete realistic model city.

As mentioned previously, the application is divided in a driver part and a non-driver part. The driver controls OscAR with a steering wheel and pedals. Every required information, which is needed to play the game, is provided on a single monitor. This includes the first person point of view from OscAR, a graphical user interface, and the virtual components the game consists of. The non-driver participates in the game through an Android application from a top-down perspective on the city and is able to assist the driver. The visibility of the realistic model city is not required for either user, hence the game is playable from a great distance as long as a network connection is available.

---

[2] http://www.ogre3d.org.

5.1   Driver Application

Upon starting the application, the driver is located in the main menu. The randomly generated player name is displayed, in addition, there is access to the current list of high scores, short instructions, and starting a new round. The driver's challenge is to colour the whole city which is virtually cartoonified and dyed black at the start of the game. He or she can generate a virtual colour ray for that purpose, that enables him or her to aim at every individual house and on triggering the spray, colour it as a whole. Grey ghosts act as virtual adversaries and convert the already coloured houses back to black. To prohibit the ghosts from doing so, the driver can target them with the colour ray and turn them into a friendly version of themselves. Subsequently these ghosts will no longer colour the houses black, but help the player to proceed with the quest. However, grey ghosts have the ability to convert close by friendly ghosts back to their own kind. Each ghost, be it grey or friendly, follows a randomly generated path through the city and is only able to spray at houses from relatively close proximity. After every spray event a distinct timer starts and prevents the affected ghost from spraying for 15 s. Additional game elements facilitate or exacerbate the game for the driver. On the one hand, up to three power-ups spawn randomly at one of the possible locations in the city. They can be gathered by driving over them and provide either a bonus on the remaining play time or refill the colour tank. On the other hand, a barricade blocks the path at a random location. This roadblock periodically switches position.

The graphical user interface provides information concerning the game. The city map in the bottom right corner helps the driver to orientate him- or herself and navigate through the city, by displaying the state of each house and the position and attitude of each ghost. The remaining play time, the count of grey and friendly ghosts and the fill level of the colour are shown in a status bar, situated at the top of the screen. The general information area at the bottom left informs the driver about a paused game òr restricted movement abilities.

We use bounding-boxes to realise collisions between virtual objects amongst each other or with OscAR. To enable collisions with the virtual surroundings, OscAR's current position from the real world is translated to his position in the virtual application. In the next step his own bounding-box is calculated. On leaving the city boundaries or colliding with a virtual obstacle, OscAR stops automatically and a message is displayed on the general information area. It is only possible to lift the blockade by driving in the opposite direction of the obstacle. This prevents the driver from leaving the playable area or breaching the rules of the game.

If the driver or a ghost sprays, it is guaranteed that only the first house or ghost hit is coloured. The colour ray consists of a particle system whose sprites move towards the hit object. The whole game is accompanied by music to increase the entertainment and give feedback about certain events and activities, like the activation of a power-up. If the driver manages to colour all houses and ghosts, the game ends immediately. Otherwise, a game round lasts for 3 min.

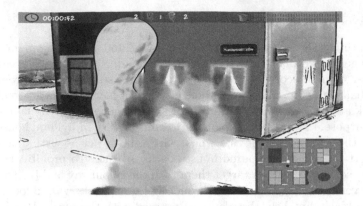

Fig. 5. OscAR converting a ghost with its virtual colour ray.

Thereupon, the attained points are displayed in an end-screen and are saved in the high score table. An example of a running game round is shown in Fig. 5.

Rendering. In general, shaders are used for two effects. The first one is to switch between RGB and grey-scale visualization in defined areas on the screen. Second use is to give OscARsWelt its cartoonified look with black outlines and saturated colours. The toon shading reduces the visual difference between real and virtual objects. It unites the realistic model city, which is seen in the camera picture, with rendered ghosts, items and grey houses. The RGB/Grey-scale effect is used to indicate haunted houses by converting the RGB camera picture to grey-scale values as shown in Fig. 6. This is achieved by two screen-filling quads, stencil and depth buffer. Every screen-filling quad gets the camera picture as a texture. The grey-scale quad covers the RGB quad and stencil buffer decides which areas are rendered. To fill the stencil mask correctly and define which

Fig. 6. Cartoonified view at the town hall building with items and grey houses in background.

object of the in-game environment has to be rendered in colour or grey-scale, the RenderQueueListener class was implemented. It changes the Ogre render queue to our needs. RenderQueueListener contains six steps, each step is made for a certain type of object:

1. *Grey houses:* Fills the stencil mask with a "1" in every place where the object is rendered.
2. *RGB houses:* Writes "2" in the mask where the object is visible. If depth check fails, it keeps the given mask value, so grey houses covering RGB houses are possible.
3. *RGB plane:* This is the RGB screen-filling quad. Now just the RGB camera picture is visible but the houses' depth and stencil values are kept.
4. *Ghosts and items:* Writes "2" in stencil mask if not covered by houses.
5. *Grey houses with slime texture:* In this step the grey houses' front faces are rendered again with a slowly moving slime texture.
6. *Grey plane:* The second screen-filling quad coveres all rendered objects where stencil-mask-values still equal "1". A shader converts the RGB output colour to grey-scale. To make the slime texture translucent, the alpha value is slightly reduced.

Now that coloured and grey areas are separated, the next step is to cartoonify the final image. For this effect an Ogre compositor is used. A compositor creates a third screen-filling quad in front of the scene, showing the rendered image as a texture. This makes image filtering possible by accessing surrounding pixels in the fragment shader via texture coordinates. Our toon shader contains image processing filters and techniques. It uses Laplace and Sobel to calculate an edge strength value. If this value exceeds a given threshold, the pixel is painted black. If not, the pixel gets mixed with surrounding pixels by mean filtering. In addition to that, luminance and contrast are adjusted for the desired saturated cartoon look. The edge strength varies with the environments light situation and does not define all edges clearly due to noise and motion blur. But with the slime texture added in render queue step 5, a characteristic pattern is always visible, providing that users are able to recognise haunted houses at first sight.

5.2   Non-driver Application

As an extension to the PC application, an Android application has been developed to support the player who controls OscAR. The purpose is to create a cooperative game, where both players have to work together to get a better score. Therefore, the two players don't need to be in the same physical location. Every device displays just a part of the information, so they have to exchange it. On PC side, the ghosts are visible and it is possible to see whether the houses are haunted or already coloured by OscAR's ray. On Android, the locations of OscAR, power-ups and obstacles are displayed on a top view of the map. The task of the player using the Android device is to guide the driver past obstacles to the power-ups. This is possible by drawing lines on the top view map, where red lines indicate obstacles and green lines show the way to power-ups. The player can use the red and green coloured fields in the right bottom corner to switch between the colours. The lines are sent to the PC application and are displayed on the ground so that the driver is able to follow the line to the power-ups (refer to Fig. 7). By touching the display with two fingers all strokes will be removed on the Android side and a message is sent to PC side to delete all lines there as well.

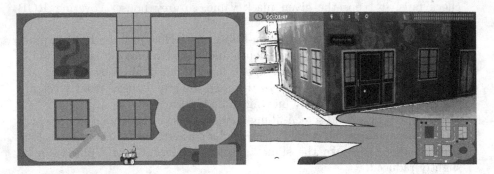

Fig. 7. The Android application of OscARsWelt with two fields to switch between two colours (left) and how a line is displayed on the ground to lead OscAR (right) (Color figure online).

Network Communication. The communication is realised by using the UDP protocol. The received datagram can be interpreted by our parser. In addition, UDP is even faster than the TCP protocol. The disadvantage, namely the possibility of duplicated, lost or reordered data, does not matter in our case, as the data consists of X and Y coordinates painted independently of order. Moreover, some missing coordinates do not distort the result. On PC side SFML UdpSocket[3] is used while Android uses the native DatagramSocket. Input and output on both devices are split into two threads, using two Sockets.

Android Functionality. By starting the Android application, a login screen appears where the IP address of the host PC has to be entered. After that the top view map and the line colours are displayed. Touching the display for the first time will establish connection to the PC side, if it is reachable by the given IP address. After that it is possible to send the line information to the PC. The line actually consists of a set of points with a fixed radius. Every point has a 2D position and a colour, either red or green. Since the detection rate of the Android device's display can be too slow, fast drawn lines might result in just a few points, with huge gaps in between.In order to fill the gaps, new points will

---

[3] http://www.sfml-dev.org/documentation/2.0/classsf_1_1UdpSocket.php.

be inserted between two points that are more than half their radius apart. It is assured that all points are drawn in the right order. All new created points will be send to the PC side. The Android device also receives the position of OscAR, the power-ups and the obstacles, and displays them.

Computer Functionality. At game start the local IP of the PC is being displayed so the player using the Android application is able to log in. After the connection is established the PC starts to send the positions of OscAR, all power-ups and obstacles as soon as they appear in the virtual world of the PC application. The points, received from the Android side, will be saved in a ring buffer. Adding a point to a full buffer results in removing the oldest point at the head of the buffer and adding a new point to the tail. On each frame all points in the list are rendered as circles on top of the ground.

6 Tracking

One fundamental problem in augmented reality is the robust and precise pose estimation of a camera. There are several approaches, like edge or feature based tracking. A simple method is an ID-Marker based tracker. A marker is an individual pattern in the scene, whose position and appearance is already known and can easily be recognised during the tracking process. The pose can then be estimated from the corner points of the detected marker and their corresponding world coordinates. As shown in Fig. 8 the appearance of ID-Markers doesn't blend in with the urban look of our city. Therefore, we decided to use a feature based tracker in combination with image markers. In our case we found that images of graffiti produced great results and suit our proposed game idea. Moreover, the existing house textures can be used as markers.

Fig. 8. Comparison between an image based (left) and ID-Marker (right).

In the city, we have multiple individually placed image markers, whose real-world coordinates are fixed and known. We implemented a tracker that supports multiple markers and is capable of tracking them in real-time. In order to achieve this, we built a state machine that utilises FAST-Keypoints [8,9] and BRIEF-Descriptors [6] to estimate the marker position, respectively its corner points. With this information we initialise the template tracker of the ViSP-Framework [5] that utilises image registration algorithms [1] to track the image marker in the next frames. Subsequently, we rely on the framework's visual servoing approach [3] to compute the current pose from all detected points and their corresponding world coordinates. The application relies on this information to render the 3D-model of the city correctly in proportion to its real world counterpart. Furthermore, the calculated position is used to implement collision detection between OscAR and virtual objects, like road blocks. Additionally, we ensure that the player cannot leave the game area and damage OscAR.

6.1   State Machine

In order to guarantee a flawless user experience, it is crucial that the tracking process is able to deliver robust results in real-time and provides a fast reinitialisation. To achieve this, we took advantage of the fact that the markers can be considered independently from each other which offers great potential for parallelism. Furthermore, we introduced the concept of marker neighbourhood which is explained thoroughly in the next section. Additionally, we split the tracking-pipeline in four different substates that are described in detail in the following subsections. A brief overview is shown in Fig. 9.

Neighbourhood. While a marker is tracked, its neighbours represent all other markers that might be visible from the cameras point of view. The set $M :=$ $\{m_0, m_1, m_2, \ldots, m_k\}$ denotes the image markers, where k is the number of all used markers. We define two sets T and N with $T, N \subseteq M$. The subset T contains the currently tracked markers and N describes all corresponding neighbours. An example is shown in Fig. 10. Note that we take advantage of $|N| \leq |M|$.

BRIEF Tracking. In this state we have no information of our current position in the city. Therefore, all markers have to be considered. In order to prevent the frame rate to drop, we take the current frame and stash it as a key frame. In a separate thread we iterate through all possible markers and try to find them in the key frame. If we are successful, we proceed to the initialisation of the template tracker state, as described in the next section. Otherwise, we take the next key frame and start from the beginning.

Initialisation of the Template Tracker. We assume that the camera has not moved much since the last key frame in which the marker was detected. In the best case this marker is still visible in the current frame and we are able to relocate it. Then we use it to initialise the ViSP template tracker and the result is a template image created out of the area described by the four corner points of the marker. In other respects, if the marker is not visible and cannot be relocated, we have to reinitialise (as shown in Fig. 9).

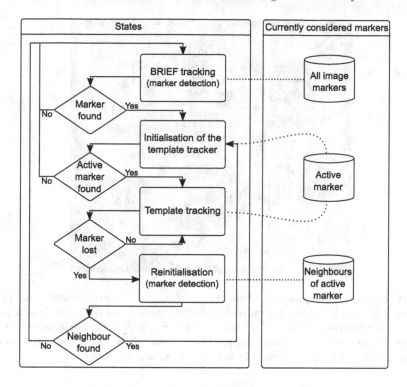

Fig. 9. Overview of our state machine.

Template Tracking. The ViSP template tracking algorithm follows an image registration process and minimises the difference between the template image obtained during the initialisation and the current image. Therefore, the template tracker tries to estimate the marker's displacement in relation to its initial position according to the generated homography matrix H:

$$H = \begin{pmatrix} 1 + p_0 & p_3 & p_6 \\ p_1 & 1 + p_4 & p_7 \\ p_2 & p_5 & 1.0 \end{pmatrix},$$

where the elements $p_0, ..., p_7$ describe the rotation and translation of the image marker that are needed for this transformation. If the estimation fails, we switch to the image marker lost state. Otherwise, the template tracking continues and we use the corner points to update our pose.

Reinitialisation. We take advantage of the fact that contrary to the BRIEF tracking state, we have some information of our position in the city. It is safe to assume that the camera is still near the previously lost marker and that the chances are high to find one of its neighbours. This leads to a significantly smaller number of markers that have to be considered (refer to $|N| \leq |M|$).

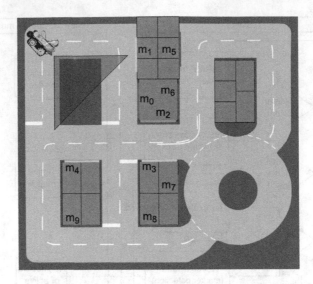

Fig. 10. Example configuration where $M := \{m_0, m_1, \ldots, m_9\}$ contains all placed markers, $T := \{m_0\}$ contains the currently tracked marker and $N := \{m_1, m_2, m_3, m_4\}$ contains all neighbours of m_0. Note that marker $m_2 \in N$ although it is not visible. However, there are possible locations for the camera where m_0 is the active marker and m_2 is visible e.g. if our camera is in front of m_4 and faces m_0.

We iterate through all of them and try to reinitialise the tracker in the image marker detected state. If we fail in the next 120 frames we begin again at the initialisation state.

7   Conclusion

This project could be ground-breaking for future works, concerning Raspberry Pi and its interaction with different devices, especially smartphones and tablets. We showed an efficient tracking method applied to the realistic model city. Moreover, the robot car, which can be controlled with a steering wheel and pedals, enhances the game experience.

Additionally, the application combines virtual and real elements in a dynamic way, by using shaders efficiently. Dark houses seem to belong to the virtual world, while houses with no shader overlay belong to the real world. The city does not look like one single virtual element, instead the separated virtual and real world are blended into one new world. Despite the complexity of virtual elements, the application runs in real time without any lag.

Our image-based tracker allows us to integrate customised markers and delivers robust results. However, our approach, like many other marker based tracking systems, is only able to maintain the pose while at least one marker is partly visible. Furthermore, the tracking suffers from light jittering due to the size difference between the markers, the 3D-model of our city and the noise of the camera images. There are some ways to improve the tracking. Namely the use of odometry, which might help to bridge the time gap while no marker is visible, or the subsequent Kalman filtering of the pose to avoid jitter. You and Neuman [10] for example show great results in the fusion of vision and gyro tracking.

Regarding the Android application we developed, there is still room for improvements and innovations, such as replacing the top view map by the camera frame. When seeing the realistic model city through the camera, virtual information like ghosts or haunted houses are augmenting the camera frame. The player is then able to draw directly on the streets. The image markers used for OscAR could be reused for the tracking, but some image markers should be added on the roofs of the city, since the Android device has more freedom in moving around the city than OscAR. Another idea is to include a third player with another Android device who can take control of the ghosts and obstacles and effectively plays against the first Android player, thus against OscAR.

Future works, based on this paper, may realise an adaptation of this application for a real city, instead of a model city. This adaptation would need a technology to obtain the 3D-model of a real city to solve the overlaps of real and virtual components. Markerless tracking is an option for a further development of this project. While it is not needed for a model city, apart from beauty-related intentions, it is a useful improvement for a real environment, because in the real world it is harder to verify that all markers are unique. The problems that occurred in the model city are likely to not appear in a real city. Overall, our paper lays the foundation for realising an augmented reality game in a real city.

Above all, the presentation of our project showed a good user reaction: We successfully presented OscARsWelt at the night of technology[4] in Koblenz and even won the audience award at the day of computational visualistics[5] at the University of Koblenz-Landau.

Acknowledgments. The authors wish to thank Maximilian Luzius and Sebastian Prusak who also contributed to the development of OscARsWelt. This project initially started as a student project and was funded by the Institute for Computational Visualistics at the University of Koblenz-Landau in Germany.

References

1. Baker, S., Matthews, I.: Lucas-kanade 20 years on: a unifying framework. Int. J. Comput. Vis. **56**(3), 221–255 (2004)
2. Cheok, A.D., Fong, S.W., Goh, K.H., Yang, X., Liu, W., Farzbiz, F., Li, Y.: Human pacman: a mobile entertainment system with ubiquitous computing and tangible interaction over a wide outdoor area. In: Chittaro, L. (ed.) Mobile HCI 2003. LNCS, vol. 2795, pp. 209–223. Springer, Heidelberg (2003)
3. Comport, A., Marchand, E., Pressigout, M., Chaumette, F.: Real-time markerless tracking for augmented reality: the virtual visual servoing framework. IEEE Trans. Visual. Comput. Graph. **12**(4), 615–628 (2006)

---

[4] http://hwk-koblenz.de/presse/nacht-der-technik.html.
[5] http://userpages.uni-koblenz.de/~cvtag/web/.

4. Lin, C.-F., Pa, P.-S., Fuh, C.-S.: Mobile application of interactive remote toys with augmented reality. In: 2013 Asia-Pacific Signal and Information Processing Association Annual Summit and Conference (APSIPA), pp. 1–6. IEEE (2013)
5. Marchand, E., Spindler, F., Chaumette, F.: Visp for visual servoing: a generic software platform with a wide class of robot control skills. IEEE Robot. Autom. Mag. **12**(4), 40–52 (2005)
6. Calonder, M., Lepetit, V., Strecha, C., Fua, P.: BRIEF: binary robust independent elementary features. In: Daniilidis, K., Maragos, P., Paragios, N. (eds.) ECCV 2010, Part IV. LNCS, vol. 6314, pp. 778–792. Springer, Heidelberg (2010)
7. Oda, O., Lister, L.J., White, S., Feiner, S.: Developing an augmented reality racing game. In: Proceedings of the 2nd International Conference on INtelligent TEchnologies for interactive enterTAINment, p. 2. ICST (Institute for Computer Sciences, Social-Informatics and Telecommunications Engineering) (2008)
8. Rosten, E., Drummond, T.: Fusing points and lines for high performance tracking. In: IEEE International Conference on Computer Vision, vol. 2, pp. 1508–1511, October 2005
9. Rosten, E., Drummond, T.: Machine learning for high-speed corner detection. In: Leonardis, A., Bischof, H., Pinz, A. (eds.) ECCV 2006, Part I. LNCS, vol. 3951, pp. 430–443. Springer, Heidelberg (2006)
10. You, S., Neumann, U.: Fusion of vision and gyro tracking for robust augmented reality registration. In: Proceedings of the Virtual Reality 2001 Conference, VR 2001, Yokohama, Japan, 13–17 March, pp. 71–78. IEEE Computer Society (2001)

Device Registration for 3D Geometry-Based User-Perspective Rendering in Hand-Held Video See-Through Augmented Reality

Ali Samini[✉] and Karljohan Lundin Palmerius

Department of Science and Technology, Linkping University,
Norrköping, Sweden
{ali.samini,karljohan.lundin.palmerius}@liu.se

Abstract. *User-perspective rendering* in Video See-through Augmented Reality (V-AR) creates a view that always shows what is behind the screen, from the user's point of view. It is used for better registration between the real and virtual world instead of the traditional *device-perspective rendering* which displays what the camera sees. There is a small number of approaches towards user-perspective rendering that over all improve the registration between the real world, the video captured from real world that is displayed on the screen and the augmentations. There are still some registration errors that cause misalignment in the user-perspective rendering. One source of error is from the device registration which, based on the used tracking method, can be the misalignment between the camera and the screen and also the tracked frame of reference that the screen and the camera are attached to it. In this paper we first describe a method for the user perspective V-AR based on 3D projective geometry. We then address the device registration problem in user perspective rendering by presenting two methods: First, for estimating the misalignment between the camera and the screen. Second, for estimating the misalignment between the camera and the tracked frame.

Keywords: Augmented Reality · Video see-through · Dynamic frustum · User-perspective

1 Introduction

The most commonly used approach for hand-held Video See-through Augmented Reality V-AR is to create the view on the screen completely based on the view of the camera that captures the world, *device-perspective rendering* (DPR). This approach, however, leads to a misalignment between the real view, seen around the screen, and the augmented video feed on the screen. An alternative approach is to create a dynamic view that is based on the relative transformation of the user's view; *user-perspective rendering* (UPR). This makes the V-AR system a window to the real world that is co-registered with the world based on the view of the user. UPR V-AR on a hand-held device requires a continuously tracked

L.T. De Paolis and A. Mongelli (Eds.): AVR 2015, LNCS 9254, pp. 151–167, 2015.
DOI: 10.1007/978-3-319-22888-4_12

pose of both the user's eye and the screen. In our implementation we use external tracking that continuously provides the pose of a tracked frame of reference that the screen and the camera are attached to it and here will be called as the tracked frame. The tracked frame is equipped with tracking markers that based on the needs of tracking method can be infrared reflectors, illuminative LEDs, etc. Using the pose of the tracked frame as the screen pose in UPR calculations will cause registration error that is the effect of the misalignment between the tracked frame and the screen. The camera pose can be assumed to be the same as the screen pose if the screen and the camera are co-registered. However if they are not co-registered the latter assumption will cause registration error between the real world and the video that is displayed on the screen and also the augmentations. In this paper we first present a detailed description of the 3D geometry approach to user-perspective rendering method first introduced in [7]. The method is based on Virtual Reality principles and uses an external camera-based motion tracking system to capture the screen and the user's eye pose. The external tracking provides the method with accurate tracking data and enables the separation of the tracking problems from the user-perspective rendering but also dictates limitations to the system and overall experience.

We then propose a two-part registration method that estimates the misalignments between the parts of the system. The first part estimates the relative pose of the screen and the camera and the second part estimates the relative pose of the tracked frame and the camera. The geometrical nature of this approach makes it easily calibrated by applying transformations to its internal frames of reference. To avoid the confusion between the camera that is used for calibration and, the camera on the back side of the screen that is used to capture the real world, we call the latter one AR-camera in this article.

The main contributions of this paper are:

- An elaborate description of the 3D geometry based UPR method.
- A method to estimate the relative pose of the screen and the AR-camera.
- A method to estimate the relative pose of the tracked frame and the AR-camera.
- Demonstration of the presented method with different external tracking systems.

2   Related Work

There are few approaches towards the video see-through Augmented Reality with user-perspective rendering. Yoshida *et al.* [13] developed an ARScope. They used an opaque hand-held device and a head mounted projector both equipped with a camera. Their method creates a homography based on the matched feature points of the images from both cameras and use it to generate an image from user's point of view. The projector projects created image on the surface of the hand-held device. Their work does not need explicit head tracking but requires user to wear a projector and a camera on his head.

To our knowledge, Hill et al. [5] developed the first hand-held V-AR system with the UPR view. Their method creates the UPR based on homography using a hand-held device equipped with a front and rear camera, however, their work is limited by the assumption that the scene is parallel to the screen with a single depth.

Tomioka et al. [11] presented a hand-held V-AR that generate the UPR view by the homography transformation that approximates the strict perspective projection instead of having one for each 3D measured point. Their method succeeds to generate the UPR view; however, as they state, using homography causes some registration error that is caused by detection errors of both the scene and the face. The results has jitter that is caused by instability in homography and latency that is the result of expensive detection and pose estimation calculations. The camera/screen misalignment is considered to be known and is used in the UPR calculations, although no method is presented for the screen/camera registration.

Presented methods use homography transformation to create the UPR view, therefore, they have registration insurances that is caused by the detection and pose estimation errors. Accurate 3D pose estimation using homography is still an open problem. It is dependent to variables like the camera focus, the geometry, and the light condition of the scene.

We could not find any specific method presented for the registration of the screen and the back-side AR-camera or the tracker. The device registration reduces the registration error in UPR. Our device registration method is straight forward to implement and can be used for different UPR V-AR systems with various tracking methods.

The geometry based method, first introduced in [7], creates the UPR view based on projective geometry using 3D tracked data instead of homography transformation that is provided by an external tracking system. Therefore, it isolates the detection and tracking problem from the UPR view generation. The results doesn't suffer from homography inaccuracies like jitters or the latency that is caused by the expensive homography calculations. Using an external tracking system adds restrictions; such systems are expensive, need set-up and calibration process, work in a limited size environment and need to use markers on tracked devices. However, having an accurate pose tracking enables the focus on the UPR problem while the tracking can easily be replaced by any other method, because it is isolated from the UPR.

3   3D Geometry-Based UPR

The 3D geometry-based method for V-AR UPR applies a virtual reality technique to generate a user-perspective view of both video see-through and virtual augmentation on the screen. This view is described first followed by a description of the virtual image plane in the view.

3.1   Dynamic View and Frustum

It is common in Virtual Reality (VR) to use the screen position and size, and the user's eye position, to create a view that projects virtual objects onto the screen with correct perspective, making it look like the virtual objects are absolutely positioned in the real world. For more details read for example [12]. This principle is applied to provide the UPR view that aligns the real view around the screen, and both the camera video feed on the screen and the virtual objects augmenting this feed. Here we need both a tracked screen and a tracker that provides the user's *eye position*; however since we are not using stereo vision, we use the position between the two eyes as the eye position. The dynamic view and projection of the UPR view are created each frame using the continuously updated eye position and the screen pose, to be used by Graphics APIs, such as OpenGL.

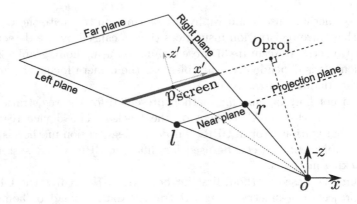

Fig. 1. Top-view of the dynamic frustum. Here, o and p_{screen}, show the eye and the screen position. These are used to calculate the frustum planes.

The view matrix will express the extrinsics of the virtual view that is the user's view towards the screen in the virtual world. The *position* of this virtual view should be the same as the position of the real view, thus the tracked eye position of the user. We define a projection plane (the *near plane* in OpenGL) parallel to the screen, that makes the projection of virtual objects in correct perspective for the viewer, from their angle. The virtual view *orientation* will actually be the same as the orientation of the screen, see Fig. 1. Thus, we create the 4×4 view matrix, M_{view}, as

$$M_{\text{view}} = \left(\begin{array}{c|c} R_{\text{screen}} & t_{\text{eye}} \\ \hline 0 & 1 \end{array} \right) \tag{1}$$

where R_{screen} is a 3×3 rotation matrix for the orientation of the screen and t_{eye} is the position of the user's eye given in homogeneous coordinates.

In graphics APIs the intrinsics of the virtual view are expressed as a truncated pyramid shape called the *frustum*, which is used to calculate the projection matrix. Here the shape of this frustum changes with the movement of the eye and the screen, and needs to be updated for every frame. The complete definition of the frustum is based on six boundary planes. The near and far planes can be placed at arbitrary distances from the eye. The positions of other frustum planes are specified on the near plane and are calculated based on the position of the eye and position/orientation of the screen. Thus we need to do all calculations in the camera's frame of reference, $\hat{x}'\hat{y}'\hat{z}'$, being right, up and back, respectively. Based on triangle similarity we can estimate the left plane position, l as

$$l = \frac{n\left(o_{\text{proj}} + \hat{x}' \cdot (p_{\text{screen}} - o) + \frac{1}{2}W_{\text{screen}}\right)}{|o_{\text{proj}} - o|} \tag{2}$$

where W_{screen} is the width of the screen, n is the distance of the near plane from the eye and o_{proj} is the projection of the eye position, o, onto the plane of the screen

$$o_{\text{proj}} = o - \hat{z}'\frac{\hat{z}' \cdot (o - p_{\text{screen}})}{|\hat{z}' \cdot (o - p_{\text{screen}})|} \tag{3}$$

The position of the right, top, and bottom planes, are estimated similarly. The projection matrix can be created from these frustum planes by using the standard projection matrix definition [10].

3.2   Video See-Through Rendering

In the UPR V-AR the view of the real world is captured by a camera and is then rendered on the screen to make it look like a see-through glass by showing on the screen what is behind it. For this the camera's video feed is rendered on a virtual image plane, placed in the virtual world. Since we already have, from the previous section, a correct projection of the virtual world aligning it with the real world, this should align also the video feed with the real world. We do, however, also need to address the problem that is caused by the eye and camera not being co-located and therefore have different views of the world.

To create a correct alignment between the real world and the rendered video feed on the screen both the *extrinsic* and the *intrinsic* parameters of the camera are needed. We use a tracked camera and thus have the extrinsics. The intrinsics are estimated through camera calibration process using Zhang's calibration plane method [14] that is based on the pinhole model. The estimated intrinsic parameters are: the focal length of the camera in x and y directions described in pixels (α_x and α_y) where, $\alpha_x = fm_x$ and $\alpha_y = fm_y$, f being the focal length of the camera, and m_x, m_y scale factors that relate distance to pixels [3]; and the position of the principal point of the camera (c_x, c_y). The Brown-Conrady model [1,2] is used for image rectification that corrects both radial and tangential distortion.

Having the image undistorted and identified the intrinsics needed, the next step is to render the video feed in a way that aligns it correctly with the virtual environment, which is already aligned with the real world, as described in

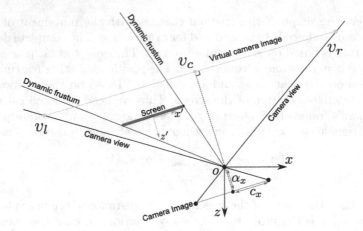

Fig. 2. The virtual camera image is a rectangle created parallel to the camera image plane. The size of the virtual camera image is calculated based on the intrinsic parameters of the camera, placed at the center of the view(o), pointing towards $-z'$(in the local coordinates of the camera). Here α_x is the focal length of the camera in x direction, in pixels and c_x is the x component of the principal point of the camera.

Sect. 3.1. In our approach, the video feed is shown on the screen by rendering it on a textured rectangle. The rectangle represents the camera's virtual image plane inside the 3D virtual world. To align the real and virtual camera, the virtual image plane is created based on the camera's intrinsic parameters, parallel to the image plane of the camera, as shown in Fig. 2. Based on the similarity of triangles we can estimate the distance from the centre to the left of the virtual camera image, v_l as

$$\frac{-v_l}{ov_c} = \frac{c_x}{\alpha_x} \Rightarrow v_l = -ov_c\frac{c_x}{\alpha_x}$$

where ov_c is the arbitrary distance of the virtual plane from the eye. α_x and c_x are x components of camera's focal length and principal point expressed in pixels. The right, top, and bottom boundaries of the virtual camera image can be estimated similarly.

3.3 Reality/Virtuality Alignment

What the camera sees and what the user sees will never be the same, since the camera cannot be co-located with the user's eye. It is, however, important that the virtual view is co-located with the camera view, since they would otherwise misalign real image and virtual augmentation. The most straightforward solution is to simply render the camera's image as if the camera was located at the head position. This will, however, result in a misalignment caused by the introduced offset, see Fig. 3. Here, there are three views of the world: (1) the *real view*, as seen around the screen, (2) the *video feed* shown on the screen, and (3) the *virtual augmentation* that also is rendered on screen. We already have a misalignment

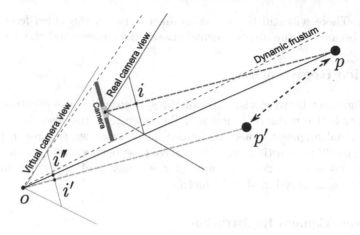

Fig. 3. The misalignment that is caused by having the camera on the hand-held device whereas the virtual view is placed in the eye position (o). Here p is an object in real world and i is its projection on image plane of the camera, i' is rendered object on the virtual image plane that is the projection for real object being at p' and i'' shows the projection of p if the camera was at the eye position. We can see the misalignment, $i'i''$ on the virtual image plane and pp' in the real world.

between the real view and the video feed that is caused by the displacement of the camera and the eyes. The amount of misalignment introduced here, however, will be identical to the displacement of the camera from the eye, which for a hand-held device, will be limited by the length of the user's arm. By rendering the camera image as if the camera is located at the eye position we also introduced a misalignment between the video feed and the augmentation whereas creating an alignment between the real view and the augmentation.

The alignment can be improved by displacing the virtual rendering, instead of displacing the camera rendering. The virtual view is placed in the same place as the real camera as if the head was located at the camera position. Having the virtual camera and the real camera co-located corrects the alignment between the video feed displayed on the screen and the virtual augmentation. The new view matrix, M_{view}, is calculated based on the tracked position and orientation of the camera as

$$M_{\text{view}} = \left(\begin{array}{c|c} R_{\text{screen}} & t_{\text{camera}} \\ \hline 0 & 1 \end{array} \right) \tag{4}$$

where R_{screen} is the orientation of the screen and t_{screen} is the position of the camera that here is assumed to be co-located with the screen.

Here the alignment between the video feed and the augmented virtual world is corrected but the alignment between the real world and the augmentation is lost. The graphical augmentations are merged with the video feed and displayed on the screen so the misalignment between them are visually more apparent than the one between the augmentations and real world that is visible around the screen. There will still be a misalignment between the video feed and the real view, because of the displacement between the camera and the user's eyes.

4   Device Registration

Any misalignment between the parts of the system will cause additional registration error between the real view and the video feed and also the video feed and the virtual augmentations. To reduce latter error we propose a two-part calibration method for estimating the relative pose between the AR-camera and the screen and also the tracked frame of the screen and apply the calculated values to our geometry based UPR method.

4.1   Screen/Camera Registration

In the presented UPR method it was assumed that the AR-camera and the screen are co-located and identically oriented. That means the center of the screen and the camera sensor are on the same plane sharing the same center and having aligned coordinate systems. However, in reality there is often some misalignment between the screen and the camera, Therefore we have to find the relative pose of the screen and the AR-camera.

The first part of the registration method calculates the misalignment between the screen and the AR-camera i.e., the rigid transformation from the center of the screen to the camera center. The method uses a secondary camera that points towards the screen and a printed chessboard marker m_1 that can be seen from both the AR-camera c_1 and the second camera c_2, as is shown in Fig. 4. A second chessboard marker m_2 is displayed on the screen.

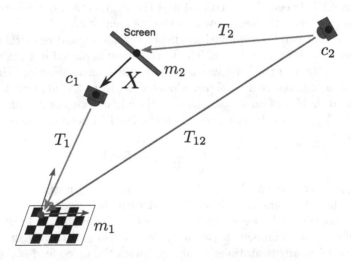

Fig. 4. The transformation X between the AR-camera (c_1) and the screen is calculated by using a secondary camera (c_2), a printed marker m_1 and a marker that is displayed on the screen m_2.

The pose of the camera c_1 in the coordinate system of the marker m_1, is estimated as the rigid transformation T_1 from c_1 to m_1. The pose of the camera c_2 is estimated in the coordinate system of the marker m_2, as the rigid transformation T_2 from c_2 to m_2 and also in the coordinate system of the marker m_1, as the rigid transformation T_{12} from c_2 to m_1. The rigid transformations T_1, T_2, T_{12} are estimated using Perspective-N-Point (PnP) with the real measurement of the marker corner points and the detected marker corner points from the camera images as the set of point correspondences. For details of the method see [4].

The displacement between the centers of the marker m_2 and the screen is calculated using the on-screen pixel distances and metric screen measurements, as a 2D translation and is applied to the transformation T_2 to make it from the camera c_2 to the screen center instead of the origin of the marker m_2.

Considering two trajectories between the screen and the camera c_1 we can estimate the rigid transformation X between the screen and camera c_1 as

$$X = T_2^{-1} T_{12} T_1^{-1} \tag{5}$$

Using fiducial markers to detect point correspondences, we get some noise in the position of the detected corner points that results in an estimated X by the PnP solver. To refine the estimation of X we average over multiple screen/camera poses X_i. Each X_i is estimated with a different position of the device, the printed marker m_1, and the second camera m_2 while the screen/camera pose X is fixed. The transformation part of X_i is averaged separately and for the rotation part we use the re-normalized unit quaternion average.

4.2   Frame/Camera Registration

An external tracking system will provide transformation from its frame of reference to the tracked frame attached to the screen. The center and the orientation of the tracked frame and the screen will typically not be perfectly aligned. The registration method estimates the transformation between the tracked frame and the AR-camera that along with the transformation of the screen and the camera X that we estimated in the last section gives us the screen pose in the coordinates of the tracking system. The method uses two tracked position of the screen/camera to estimate the misalignment Y as is shown in Fig. 5, where the AR-camera, the screen and, the tracked frame are fixed together. A tracked fiducial marker m is placed visible from the camera. The poses of the camera T_{11}, T_{21} are estimated from two different placements of the system, relative to the coordinates of the marker m. T_{12}, T_{22} are the poses of the tracked frame that is attached to the screen, in the reference frame of the tracking system. The position of the center of the tracking o and the marker m is fixed through the registration process.

Considering the trajectory from the origin of the tracking system to the marker m going through the tracked frame and screen-camera for two different placements of the system as is shown in Fig. 5, we have

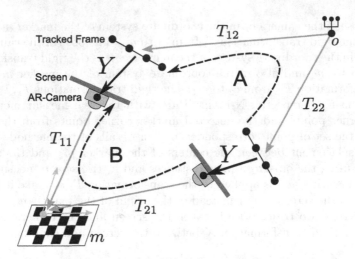

Fig. 5. The transformation Y between the AR-camera and the center of the tracked frame of markers attached to the screen-camera that are tracked by external tracking. We reform the problem into the $AY = YB$ equation by using two different poses of the screen-camera.

$$T_{12} Y T_{11} = T_{22} Y T_{21} \Rightarrow T_{22}^{-1} T_{12} Y = Y T_{21} T_{11}^{-1} \tag{6}$$

$T_{22}^{-1} T_{12}$ can be interpreted as relative motion made by the tracked frame between two system placements and we denote it by A; so

$$A = T_{22}^{-1} T_{12} \tag{7}$$

Similarly we see $T_{21} T_{11}^{-1}$ as the relative motion of the camera and denote it by B as

$$B = T_{21} T_{11}^{-1} \tag{8}$$

Using 6–8 we have

$$AY = YB \tag{9}$$

Which is a well known equation often called the *robot-sensor calibration prob-lem*. It is used to find the transformation between a robot hand and a wrist mounted sensor like a camera on it. There are many approaches towards solv-ing this equation. The solutions can generally be categorized as separable and simultaneous solvers based on if the rotation and translation parts of the Y are calculated separately or simultaneously. Shah *et al.* published an overview of the different methods for the robot-sensor calibration problem [8].

We have implemented and compared two methods to estimate Y with mul-tiple samples. Both solutions separate the equation $AY = YB$ into orientation and translation parameters as

$$R_A R_Y = R_Y R_B$$
$$R_A t_Y + t_A = R_Y t_B + t_Y \tag{10}$$

and solve the orientation part then use the result to calculate the translation part. The first method is based on the work of shiu and Ahmad [9] where they solve the orientation part by reforming the rotation matrix into angle-axis form and solve a linear system of equations. The second method is based on the work of Liang et al. [6] where the Kronecker product is used to create a linear system from orientation part that is then solved to get the rotation part of Y. Both methods calculate the transformation part based on the second part of Eq. 10 after the estimation of the rotation. Both methods suggest using multiple relative transformations A and B to get more accurate estimation of Y.

4.3 Method Application

The registration method estimates the transform Y from the tracked frame to the AR-camera in the coordinate system of the tracked frame, and the transform X from the screen coordinate system to the camera's coordinate system. The transform Z between the tracked frame and the screen can be directly estimated as YX^{-1}. T_{tr} being the pose of the tracked frame, $T_{tr}Y$ and $T_{tr}Z$ gives the camera and screen poses in the coordinates of the external tracking system.

In the geometry-based method estimated camera and screen pose is used to create the dynamic view, frustum, and the virtual image plane as discussed before. The relative pose of the camera and the screen X can also be used with other UPR methods that use homography instead, where the screen pose is estimated from the tracked pose of the camera.

5   Implementation

Our system has been developed as part of a project on Collaborative Unmanned Aircraft Systems (CUAS). The system is executed and tested in the Indoor Micro Unmanned Aerial Vehicle Laboratory at the Department of Computer and Information Systems, Linkping University and at the exhibition area of Visualization Center C in Norrkping.

5.1   Hardware

The live video feed is captured with a Logitech webcam C920 that is able to capture HD video. A Lenovo Twist convertible tablet PC is used as the central processing and video see-through rendering unit. The tablet has 12.5 in. HD display, 3rd generation Intel Core i7-3517U processor, Intel HD Graphics 4000 graphic hardware and 8.0 GiB DDR3 1600 MHz memory. The tablet is mounted on a wooden frame along with the camera, the grabber, and IR reflector markers, as is shown in Fig. 6.

Our test and development environment is equipped with the Vicon tracker. The Vicon system is a fast and accurate 3D tracking system that is able to track multiple objects simultaneously, in six degrees-of-freedom (DOF). Reflective markers are attached to the tablet frame and other tracked objects. A pair

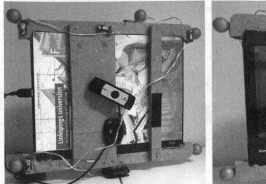

Fig. 6. Front and back side of the system prototype: the wooden frame is holding the tablet computer, the camera, the LED markers, and IR reflector markers.

of safety glasses, also with the reflectors, is used for tracking the eye position. Tracked quadcopters are used as flying augmented objects. In another test we used PhaseSpace tracking system. PhaseSpase is a fast and accurate motion tracking system capable of six DOF tracking with the use of LED illuminative markers.

5.2   Software

The Robot Operating System (ROS) is used to communicate between the Vicon and the AR system and the Virtual-Reality Peripheral Network (VRST) is used to communication with the PhaseSpace motion tracking system. We developed the V-AR system by using C++ programming language, OpenGL (Open Graphics Library) and GLSL (OpenGL Shading Language). OpenCV (Open Source Computer Vision Library) is used for camera capture, calibration, and image undistortion and also for the marker detection and pose estimation in the device registration. SDL (Simple DirectMedia Layer) is used to access input devices and graphic hardware via OpenGL. MATLAB is used for the device registration calculations.

6   Device Registration Statistics

The registration method is used to calibrate our prototype device Fig. 6. To estimate the misalignment between the screen and the camera we used 27 separate estimations of X. Figure 7 shows the translation and rotation discrepancy, of each estimated X and their mean value against a manual measurement of the X in our prototype system. The average error is up to 0.24 mm in translation and up to 0.65° in rotation. We estimate the manual measurement error to be in the order of up to 1° and 2 mm, due to the tools used and the shape of the

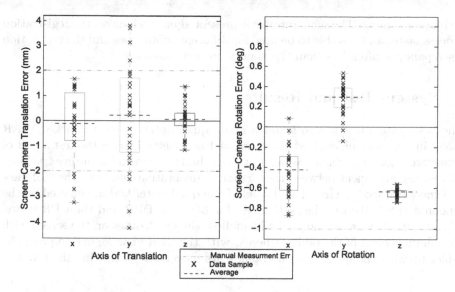

Fig. 7. plot of discrepancy between the estimated screen/camera displacement X and the manual measurements of our prototype system using 27 separately estimated Transformation X. Left: The translation discrepancy along each axis in millimeters, Right: The rotation discrepancy around separate axis in degrees. x shows the error for each individual sample and the dash-line is the mean value.

camera. The results show that the average estimation and most of the separate estimations are within the accuracy of the manual measurements.

The relative pose of the tracked frame and the camera Y is estimated with two methods mentioned in Sect. 4.2. Table 1 shows the discrepancy between manual measurement of the prototype system and the estimated Y using 10 relative A and B transformation sets. The discrepancy values are presented separately for the translation part in millimetres and the rotation part in degrees for both implemented methods. It can be seen that the second method introduces smaller amount of overall discrepancy. The manual measurement of our prototype system has an estimated accuracy in the order of $1°$ and $2\,\mathrm{mm}$.

The device registration should be re-done with the changes in the relative poses of the frame, the screen, or the camera. The manual measurement of the misalignments between the parts of the system often needs special equipment and

Table 1. Frame/Camera Displacement (Y) discrepancy

Estimation	Translation (mm)			Rotation (°)		
	x	y	z	x	y	z
Method 1	7.5	−4.2	1.8	0.92	0.83	−0.89
Method 2	2.4	1.4	0	0.86	0.55	−1.0

is time consuming. The semi-automatic presented method makes the registration process faster and possible to be used for different prototypes and the estimation discrepancy is often less than the manual measurements.

7   System Test and Results

The first system test was to follow a flying quadcopter with our tracked V-AR tablet in our tracking enabled environment Fig. 8 (left). During the test a pair of transparent glasses, which was being tracked, had to be worn for the eye tracking. To test the alignment between the virtual augmentation and both the real view and the video feed, a virtual 3D model of the quadcopter was augmented on the rendered video. We ran the system test for both the DPR and the UPR views. With the DPR view we mostly had to follow the quadcopter on the screen with a small movement of the tablet, whereas with the UPR view we had to point the tablet towards the quadcopter and follow its movement by moving the tablet.

Fig. 8. Left: The system test in our laboratory environment. The dynamic frustum is shown as well as the rectangle that draws the virtual camera image. For illustration purpose we also include computer graphics rendering of the user's head, the tablet, and the quadcopter. Right: The prototype test With the PhaseSpace motion tracking system. The UPR view is used to explore the pipe line within a wall.

In our second test we used the PhaseSpace motion tracking system to verify that our method can work with various tracking methods. We had to change the reflective markers with the illuminative ones that work with the PhaseSpace. There where no need for changes within the V-AR UPR view generating software as a result of the tracking and rendering isolation. During the test we followed an imaginary virtual 3D model of pipes that where used as the augmentation on the video feed Fig. 8 (right).

Our prototype type worked without noticeable lag or latency with a rendering speed of 30 frames per second during both tests. The UPR view creates a similar view on the tablet screen as looking through a window. In the first test, the virtual augmentation of the quadcopter is co-located with its appearance in the video feed on the screen, and its appearance in the real view, as seen around the screen, so that the quadcopter is always visible on the screen when it's behind the screen, regardless of position or orientation of the camera, tablet or the head. Figure 9 shows sequential pictures of our first system test, first row by using the DPR and second row the UPR view. We used a tracked camera to take the pictures for the UPR view. Tracked camera pose is used as eye pose to create a correct perspective in pictures.

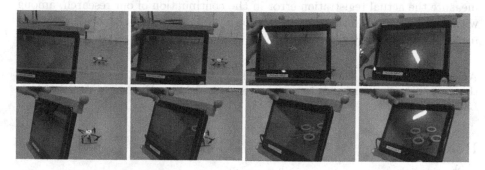

Fig. 9. Sequential pictures of our running system. First row: The traditional DPR view is used. It is visible in all images that the video, the augmentation, and the real world have large amount of misalignment and the screen shows what the rear camera of the tablet sees. Second row: Our UPR method is used. Images are taken by a secondary camera that is tracked as head position. In the left-most image the quadcopter is visible behind the tablet on the floor. We can see that the view changes while moving the tablet in front of the quadcopter. The presented approach creates an alignment between both the virtual augmentation and the video feed, as well as with the real view, as seen around the screen.

Our test results show that there is a small misalignment between the real view and the video feed and also the virtual augmentation. This is mostly because of the displacement of the eyes and the camera as we discussed earlier.

We plan to address the actual measurement of the amount of the registration error in both the UPR system with and without our device registration in the continuation of our research.

8   Conclusions and Future Work

In this paper we have addressed the problem of static view in hand-held video see-through augmented reality with an approach to create the user perspective rendering view with the use of 3D projective geometry based on the *Virtual Reality* principles. In our method, we use dynamic view and frustum that is created based on tracked position and orientation of the user's view and the screen, and is updated in each frame. We use external tracking that enables us to isolate the rendering software from the tracking and having more accurate tracked data that leads to more accurate UPR view. However, external tracking systems are expensive and have limitations like set-up and calibration process and also the markers that have to be attached to tracked objects. We also managed to reduce the UPR misalignment error by using the registered pose of the screen and the AR-camera.

Our prototype system was successful to deliver the UPR view without noticeable jitter or latency through our informal tests. There where misalignments that where caused mostly by the displacement of the eye and the camera. We plan to measure the actual registration error in the continuation of our research, among with the user study using our prototype system to prove the benefits of our method and the UPR view in hand held V-AR.

Acknowledgments. The authors would like to thank Joakim Kilby for his help with the project development and the staff at the Indoor Micro Unmanned Aerial Vehicle Laboratory.

References

1. Brown, D.C.: Decentering distortion of lenses. Photometric Eng. **32**(3), 444–462 (1966)
2. Conrady, A.E.: Decentered lens systems. Mon. Not. R. Astron. Soc. **79**, 384–390 (1919)
3. Hartley, R., Zisserman, A.: Multiple View Geometry in Computer Vision, 2nd edn. Cambridge University Press, New York (2003)
4. Hartley, R.I., Zisserman, A.: Multiple View Geometry in Computer Vision. Cambridge University Press, New York (2004). ISBN: 0521540518
5. Hill, A., Schiefer, J., Wilson, J., Davidson, B., Gandy, M., MacIntyre, B.: Virtual transparency: introducing parallax view into video see-through AR. In: 2013 IEEE International Symposium on Mixed and Augmented Reality (ISMAR), pp. 239–240 (2011)
6. Liang, R.-H., Mao, J.-F.: Hand-eye calibration with a new linear decomposition algorithm. J. Zhejiang Univ. Sci. A **9**(10), 1363–1368 (2008)
7. Samini, A., Palmerius, K.L.: A perspective geometry approach to user-perspective rendering in hand-held video see-through augmented reality. In: Proceedings of the 20th ACM Symposium on Virtual Reality Software and Technology, VRST 2014, pp. 207–208. ACM, New York (2014)
8. Shah, M., Eastman, R.D., Hong, T.: An overview of robot-sensor calibration methods for evaluation of perception systems. In: Proceedings of the Workshop on Performance Metrics for Intelligent Systems, PerMIS 2012, pp. 15–20. ACM, New York (2012)
9. Shiu, Y.C., Ahmad, S.: Calibration of wrist-mounted robotic sensors by solving homogeneous transform equations of the form ax = xb. IEEE Trans. Rob. Autom. **5**(1), 16–29 (1989)
10. Shreiner, D., T. K. O. A. W. Group: OpenGL Programming Guide: The Official Guide to Learning OpenGL, Versions 3.0 and 3.1. Addison-Wesley Professional, 7th edn. (2009)

11. Tomioka, M., Ikeda, S., Sato, K.: Approximated user-perspective rendering in tablet-based augmented reality. In: 2013 IEEE International Symposium on Mixed and Augmented Reality (ISMAR), pp. 21–28, October 2013
12. Ware, C., Arthur, K., Booth, K.S.: Fish tank virtual reality. In: Proceedings of the INTERACT 1993 and CHI 1993 Conference on Human Factors in Computing Systems, CHI 1993, pp. 37–42. ACM, New York (1993)
13. Yoshida, T., Kuroki, S., Nii, H., Kawakami, N., Tachi, S.: Arscope. In: ACM SIGGRAPH 2008 New Tech Demos, SIGGRAPH 2008, pp. 4:1–4:1. ACM, New York (2008)
14. Zhang, Z.: A flexible new technique for camera calibration. IEEE Trans. Pattern Anal. Mach. Intell. **22**(11), 1330–1334 (2000)

Creativity Support in Projection-Based Augmented Environments

Bruno Simões$^{(\boxtimes)}$, Federico Prandi, and Raffaele De Amicis

Via Alla Cascata, 56/C, Trento, Italy
{bruno.simoes,federico.prandi,raffaele.de.amicis}@graphitech.it
http://www.graphitech.it

Abstract. A key theme in ubiquitous computing is to create easy-to-use smart environments in which there is a seamless integration of people, user experience, information, and physical reality. The next generation of ultra-portable handheld projectors is paving the way in this direction, as it develops to its pinnacle. When coupled with appropriate tracking technologies, this technology can extend user experience beyond the confines of the device itself to encompass the physical properties of environment. In this paper, we introduce a projection-based augmented reality framework that aims at facilitating the creation of augmented environments where digital content is snapped to objects around the user. We extend previous literature with a projection-oriented framework that leverages on handheld projectors to seamless combine physical interactions with projection-based content snapped to real objects, while solving inherent issues related to use of projective technology. To evaluate the relevance and impact of this study, we discuss a few application scenarios that are enabling this interaction paradigm.

Keywords: Projection-based augmented environments · Augmented reality · Tangible user interface · Handheld projectors

1 Introduction

Projection-based technology is receiving increasing attention over the last years, in part because it provides effective means to overcome the inherent information-display limitations associated with small screens. The driving idea behind this technology is that we can create interaction displays that go much beyond the confines of the device itself, for example, to encompass virtually any external object present in a given a physical space.

The use of projection-based technology is not completely new. Yet, the level of interactivity with such technology is, at the moment, somewhat pedestrian. The way most applications work is similar to the idea of an ordinary projector connected to a laptop. In many applications, the image that is projected is actually a clone of the image of the device controlling it, and the user interaction is basically limited to the interaction with the device itself. This implies that the display space and the user interaction remain separate; information does

© Springer International Publishing Switzerland 2015
L.T. De Paolis and A. Mongelli (Eds.): AVR 2015, LNCS 9254, pp. 168–187, 2015.
DOI: 10.1007/978-3-319-22888-4_13

not adapt to the shape of physical objects and users cannot interact with the projection itself. In the end the technology is only used to extend the areas on which content is displayed and not to pave the way to new types of collaborative interaction and shared experiences that facilitating the interaction with information that can be visualised directly on the object or subject of interest using real world interaction metaphors as we know them.

Typically, the interaction with the projection device (e.g., proximity, using tilt gestures, etc.) or on the device (e.g., tap, touch, etc.) has direct influence on the display space and not on the projection space. Examples include the use projection to facilitate social interaction on a workplace by displaying photos associated with the person in physical proximity [26], or to function as a community poster board, which shows both content that has been user created or automatically sampled from the workplace intranet [10]. More recently, it has also been used to create new ways of experiencing daily activities. SubliMotion [43] for example, is using projection mapping to provide an unparalleled techno-gastro experience that goes beyond the experience of taste. In most of the cases, the main advantage of using projections is that the projected image can easily be shared among a multiple of users. Hence, the user interaction with the projection itself is somehow limited to translation, rotation and scale, as the situation requires. Yet, there are more exciting ways of using content projections that capitalise on a new wave of projection-based devices like smartphones that have an integrated camera and embedded projector, and digital cameras that can project their photos, which due to their probability can make projection-based interaction more ubiquitous, something that in the past has been limited to fixed project-based systems setups.

In this work, we introduce new a projective augmented reality paradigm that aims mostly at supporting creativity processes. The augmented reality systems that are available today for our smart phones do not provide seamless integration between reality, user experience and information. On the one hand, they lack of a proper communication infrastructure. On the other hand, most applications require users to wear head-mounted displays or to hold up the smart phones or tablets and switch on the camera view to overlay graphical elements into the reality, which are well-suitable for solitary, single user experiences. Hence, in many cases, they are more like display or portal to the reality rather than the immersive reality itself. The interaction techniques consider the case where user have access to handheld projectors, so the interactivity between users and projectors can result in a rich design space for multi-user interaction, and ultimately path a new way in the augmentation of the surrounding environment with new scenarios for collaborative experience.

2   Motivation and Objectives

In the previous section, we described the driving idea behind projection-based technology. In this section we present our motivation and we enumerate open issues and research challenges correlated to our approach. In the next section, we survey the relevant literature, both to see if similar studies have been done, and to define the framework from which to evaluate the relevance and impact of this study. Then, in Sect. 4, we describe the proposed methodology as well as the implementation details. In Sects. 5 and 6 we present several use case scenarios as well as an evaluation of the framework. Lastly, in Sect. 7, we wrap up the results of our work with a few conclusions and future work.

Our motivation to exploit the use of projection-based technology is driven by three factors. First, in our framework called c-Space, we capitalise on the ongoing move of smart phones towards near-ubiquity to create near real-time automatic 3D reconstructions of spatio-temporal events, e.g. concerts, moving objects, etc. Hence, we seek new ways of interaction with replicas of physical objects of events, that are similar to real world interaction metaphors as we know them. Second, it is undeniable that smart phones have, aside from the lack of memory and processor power, the very small display sizes as their major bottleneck. Therefore, we want to investigate if the interactivity between users and Personal Pico Projection (PPP) technology (e.g. smartphones with integrated projectors) can result in a rich design space for multi-user interaction – one of the key side-effect of interacting with small display sizes. Lastly, we want to investigate to which point this new way of interaction can support creativity and collaborative experiences, which include but are not limited to i.e. creation of spatio-temporal annotations, combination of real objects with digital content, and content sharing and reuse. Figure 1 summarises the c-Space framework, which aims at providing a new disruptive technology that unleashes users' creativity to create and user 4D content in a completely new way.

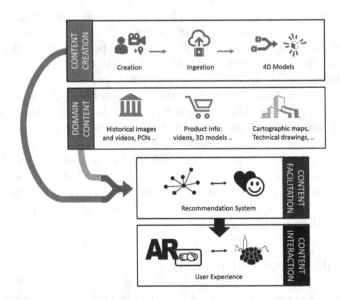

Fig. 1. Overview of the c-Space framework

The list of research challenges that were identified while creating dynamic projections with mobile setups based on time-of-flight camera (ToF camera) and PPP technology are:

RC1 How can we exploit the real world scene depth to create projections that fit in intelligent way different types of surfaces, in order to avoid the image projected to be perceived as distorted?

RC2 How can we seamless compose (i.e. how can we efficiently define projection mappings) and share new interactions that bridge digital content and real word objects, independently of the projector's location and orientation?

RC3 How can affective computing and recommendation systems be integrated into a projective augmented system, so we can adapt the content to the emotional state or needs of the user?

RC4 What mechanisms can be put in place to foster or promote collaboration and content sharing among users?

RC5 The use of projective interfaces exposes the end-user to the risk of projecting sensitive information by mistake, e.g. phone number, contact list, etc., which open up new privacy challenges. Hence, what mechanisms can we implement to tackle the issue of sensitive information disclosure?

RC6 The invasiveness of projected content can lead to "visual pollution" or bring annoyance to other people in the vicinity. Additionally, more powered projecting devices with the potential to project from a long-range distance can be even dangerous for other users. Hence, which is the social impact of PPP technology? How can we create a normative policy that regulates the use and the power of PPP technology in certain scenarios like streets, where drivers or passengers could be temporarily blinded by the projection?

RC7 Manually setting the projection focus raises a critical barrier to mobile content projections because users have to readjust the focus every time they move. Hence, how can we reduce the effect of out-of-focus in projections when using non-laser projectors?

3   Related Work

In this section we review works that relate to our 3D projective augmented environments concept. Afterwards, we discuss in detail how our solution advances the state of the art.

We consider existent literature to be clustered into three major categories: projector-based augmented spaces, multi-user handheld projector systems, and projector tracking.

3.1   Projector-Based Augmented Spaces

Traditional techniques to augment the world with additional information require the use of head-mounted displays [1] or a portable device serving as a "magic lens" [3]. Their weakness resides at the hardware level. Their hardware is not designed for simultaneous multi-user interaction, in contrast to projection metaphors that target multi-individual experiences by augmenting objects in the user environment without hampering any existent collaboration.

In 1999, Underkoffler [42] described for the first time a system that uses projection (I/O bulb co-located projector) and video-capture techniques for distributing digitally-generated graphics throughout a physical space. Later, Hereld et al. [17] described how to build projector-based tiled display systems that incorporates cameras into the environment, to automate the calibration process. Afterwards, the authors of [32] investigated the use of steerable projector to explore content projection on arbitrary indoor surfaces. In 2003, Raskar et al. introduced a system called iLamps that creates distortion free projections on various surfaces [35]. The RFIGLamps [34] extended iLamps with the possibility to create object adaptive projections. One of the use case scenarios proposed consisted in visually identify products with the closest date of expiry.

Prototypes that target mostly interactive tabletop experiences include Play Anywhere [48], the work of Hang et al. [15] that takes advantages of projected displays to explore large-scale information, The Bonfire that uses several handheld projectors mounted on a laptop to extend the desktop experience to the tabletop [20], Map Torchlight that enables paper map content augmentation [38], and Marauder's Light that can be used to project on a paper map locations retrieved from Google Latitude [24].

In 2005, Blasko et al. [4] investigated possible interactions with a wrist-worn projection display. A short-throw projector was used in their lab' experimental setup to simulate the mobile projector. A few years later, Mistry et al. [27] introduces Wear Ur World, an application that relies on a portable projector, a mirror and a camera, to demonstrate that mobile projection can be integrated in daily life interactions. Fiducial markers attached to fingertips were used to improve precision and speed of the computer vision process. More recent works include SecondLight [18] that can be used to interact with projected imagery on top of real life objects and in near time; and OmniTouch [16] for interactive multi-touch applications using arbitrary surfaces by employing a wearable depth-sensing as well as a projection system.

3.2   Multi-user Handheld Projector Systems

Modern handheld projectors can produce relatively large public displays, often considered an important requirement in many multi-user interaction scenarios. The possibilities of multi-user interaction with handheld projectors has been an active research field. In 2005, Sugimoto et. al. described an experimental system that explored the concept of overlapping two projection screens to initialise file transfer between different devices [41]. In 2007, Cao et. al. presented a wide range of multi-user interaction techniques to manage virtual workspaces that relied on motion capture systems for location tracking [6,7], e.g. they designed interaction techniques to visualise content, define content ownership, to perform content docking, and to initiate transfers.

Multi-user games have also received some attention in recent years. Hosoi et. al. introduced a multi-user game where users have the challenge of guiding a small robot by line up projected pieces of track so the robot can move around [19]. The prototype used a fixed camera that was placed above the interaction area to enable the interaction between the handheld projectors. Another example of a game that uses projection metaphors is the multi-user jigsaw game proposed by Cao et. al. where users have to pick up and place pieces of a puzzle together [8]. In this case, the interaction between multiple handheld projectors was enabled by means of a professional motion capture system.

3.3   Projector Tracking and Interaction

2D barcode-style fiducial markers have been used widely in tracking due to their robust and fast performance. A well-known issue with this type of fiducial markers is their unnatural appearance – which is not readable by users. Additionally, the integration of barcode style markers into the design of interactive systems raises also resistance due to some of their properties, e.g. fixed aesthetic and intolerance to changes in shape, material and colour.

There are numerous techniques that were developed to hide or disguise fiducial markers from the user. Park et al. used invisible inks to create markers that are visible with IR cameras [31]. Grundhofer et al. investigated the use of temporal sequencing of markers with high speed cameras and projectors [14]. In 2007, Saio et al. created custom marker patterns that are disguised to look like normal wallpaper [37]. The use of IR lasers to project structured pattern style markers was investigated in [21,45]. Nakazato et al. used retro-reflective markers together with lights and IR cameras [28]. Other works include the projection of IR [9,40,44] or hybrid IR/visible light markers [22].

The use of natural marker was also proposed as a solution to overcome some of the limitations of 2D barcode-style fiducial markers, e.g. fixed aesthetic. For this reason, most work has now been placed in the development of natural marker detection techniques that can use the natural features of the object as a marker, therefore, replacing the need of incorporating structured marker patterns [5,30]. The issue with natural markers is that normally they require a training step for each object that has to be recognised and they are computationally more expensive than structured marker detection techniques.

Sensor-based projection tracking designs were also proposed in many works. Dao et al. proposed the use of fixed positions [12]. A technique presented in [36] works by making assumptions about the user's arm position. In 2011, Willis et al. [47] described a system that used a motion sensor input and an ultrasonic distance sensor for pointing-based games, which was used to study users' pointing behaviour. The different version of the system investigated a camera-based approach, where a customised prototype camera+projector with infrared fiducial markers was used for tracking [46]. Additional visual-based device tracking methods include projector-based pointing interaction [2,33], and shadow pointing to the projected image to interact [11].

Most methods described in the literature either require a pre-calibrated infrastructure to be installed in the physical environment [7] or limit the interaction between participants and the projection [39]. Additionally, most systems were designed to project on flat surfaces, therefore, ignoring the depth of the real scenes which leads to distortions. In our prototype, we use a vision-based approach to track user-defined AR setups – based on natural markers – that enable the user to interact and spontaneously change its location, as the projection automatically adjusts to changes in the projector position.

4 Methodology

In this section, we describe the methodology that was developed to solve the research challenges in Sect. 2. The explanation is provided in parallel to the description of the application workflow.

4.1 Overview

An important consideration that we must bear in mind while projecting images on a surface that is not perpendicular to the projector view is how to acquire information on scene depth – which influences the distance between two projection points. Scene depth can either be extrapolated in automatic with computer vision techniques or, alternatively, by means of hardware that can capture depth, like depth cameras. Many of these techniques either require intensive computing algorithms or the end-user to execute additional calibration steps.

The solution that we propose in this manuscript to RC1: *How can we exploit the real world scene depth to create projections that fit in intelligent way different types of surfaces, in order to avoid the image projected to be perceived as distorted?* is deeply interlinked with the solution that we propose to RC2: *How can we seamless compose (i.e. how can we efficiently define projection mappings) and share new interactions that bridge digital content and real word objects, independently of the projector's location and orientation?*. Our methodology does not require the computation of depth matrix to guarantee that projections will not be distorted by the depth of the scene objects.

Scene depth is extracted automatically from the transformation matrix that is computed for each user movement, as well as any user-defined information on the scene. In the next sections, we describe in detail how our novel optical-flow-based tracking technique can achieve this with the following steps: first we search for distinctive invariant features in the video stream; then we use a user-friendly interface to defined where and how content is projected; afterwards we rely on the use of optical-flow-based techniques to track the user movements; and finally we integrated new ways of interacting with PPP technology.

4.2 Invariant Feature Detection

In this section we explain how to detect distinctive features in images – the first step that has to be performed in order to track the projector' camera position.

In order to detect distinctive features in images, we need to know the role of unknown variables such as lens distortion, illumination, viewing angle, and so forth, in the image formation process [25]. For example, the difference in perspective between two frames constitutes a significant factor especially when the camera baseline is large between the two views. The process of feature matching requires the extracting of key features from images that have invariant properties for large differences in viewing angles and camera translation. Additionally, the features that are used have to be discriminative if we want the process of recognising the scene to be robust.

In this work, we use the scale invariant feature transform BRISK algorithm [23] to detect distinctive features. The BRISK algorithm provides a robustness and performance comparable to the well-know SURF algorithm, but at much less computation time [23]. A strategy to select pairs between frames can be computed according to their spatial distance. The distance between BRISK descriptors can be calculated with the Bruteforce Hamming algorithm. The correspondences between features in different frames can then be used for estimating a camera pose.

4.3 Optical-flow-based Tracking

In this subsection we explain how pairs of BRISK descriptors can be used to track features in the real world without the use of fiducial markers.

There are several actions – given our problem statement – that can be implemented in order to reduce the computation time of the feature matching step. We know a-priori the regions of interest, i.e. around control points that are used to define projection mappings, therefore, we can use that information to reduce the search space for BRISK features. Afterwards, we can compute the list of pairs. The problem of tracking a shape between two consecutive frames is considered in literature as a small-baseline tracking problem because the transformation from the image at time frame t to the image that corresponds to the time frame $t + dt$ can be modelled with a translational model, given a small dt.

The computation of the optical flow for feature points that correspond to the control points of a user-defined shape is the core of the algorithm for a frame-to-frame feature tracking in which the computation of the translational model corresponds to the computation of the homography matrix between two different frames. Homography is a projective transformation that provides the relation between a point on the camera space and a point in the world space.

The use of the homography matrix implies that under special circumstances a point in the reference image frame relates, by a linear relation, to a point that depicts the same information in different image frame. These circumstances are valid in case of pure rotation or if the view is a planar scene. In such case, the 3×4 matrix that represents the projective relation between a 3D point and its image on camera becomes a 3×3 matrix.

In our case each shape is defined to cover only a planar surface. Nevertheless, our system provides support for multiple shapes which can then be used to apply content to non-planar surfaces. Thus, in our case, homography can be used, if we provide the right quantity and quality of matching point. Before we can compute the homography with the OpenCV' function called findHomography, we first need to find the list of feature points of interest, and extract their descriptors in order to find good matches. To find good matches more accurately, we compute the homography after removing the outliers with the RANSAC algorithm [13]. We use RANSAC to remove features that are on nonplanar objects, thus maintaining the planarity condition even for those images that consist of more complex geometry than a single working plane. We can use the RANSAC because we have the constraint that shapes can only be projected on planar structures. We use the RANSAC algorithm also for imposing the epipolar constraint between different images which help us to reject false matches.

The function to compute the homography requires an input of at least four points. Otherwise, we will not be able to map the points in the first image to the corresponding points in the second image. Afterwards, we compute the inverse homography with OpenCV's perspective Transform function to find the matrix that maps points in the reference image to the equivalent points in the destination image. Note that homography works well if the BRISK descriptors are well distributed inside the shape. Otherwise homography might result too unstable for practical applications. To avoid the propagation of errors, we do not compute the tracking between two consecutive frames. We try to use the current frame against the oldest frame possible. For that, our algorithm keeps the oldest frame for which the homography was successfully computed, the current frame.

To make the user experience smoother, we implemented a threshold filter for low quality pairs, and we used the sensors of the smartphone to estimate the new pose. Our system shows a user notification if the homography cannot be computer within a few interactions. Tracking can be unsuccessful for two reasons. First, the initial surface of projection is not suitable for tracking due to the fact that we cannot extraction enough key points. Second, the camera

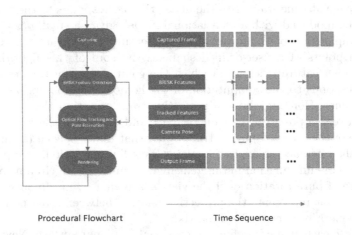

Procedural Flowchart   Time Sequence

Fig. 2. Feature tracking using an invariant feature algorithm

baseline between the two views is too large or the surface is no longer visible. In this case the shape becomes invisible. Once the projection surface is again visible in the image frame the tracking restarts and the shape is drawn again in the right spot. Figure 2 provides an overview of the tracking process.

4.4 Creating and Maintaining a Virtual Scene

In this section, we describe how user-defined projection mappings are created and how they are visualised on top real world objects. User-defined projection mappings, or simply "shapes", have the following properties: they are always defined by four points, they have graphical content associated (e.g. a video, an image, or some interactive 3D content), and they can store a user-defined depth correction.

In our application, users can drag shapes into the virtual reality scene and then map the vertices of the scene to the object they want to map – with simple drag-and-drop gestures (Fig. 3). Afterwards users can defined which content to associate to that shape and the slope of the surface – scene depth.

The physical setup consists of a smartphone that renders the content that will augmented the physical space and then sends it to the projector mapped in the projector's perspective. We decided for this specific setup because our goal is to test the concept of interaction with portable technology that is both ubiquitous and accessible by everyone. The use of smartphones is not fundamental but is extremely useful to facilitate the process of creating and designing new augmented scenes. For example, users can use smartphones as lens during the process of creating a projection mapping, to facilitate the modelling process. An issue in our initial approach was that the field of view of the projection and the field of view of the camera attached to the projector (used to compute the pose of the projector) were not the same. To solve this issue we decided to project in each corner of the projected image an image, which we use as markers to track the field of view of the projector. In this way, we can automatically calibrate the projector and the camera attached to it. This is extremely important in order to be able to convert smartphone views into the projection view.

Another issue that we had to address was RC7: *How can we reduce the effect of out-of-focus in projections when using non-laser projectors?* This limitation raises a critical barrier to mobile content projections, since users have to readjust the focus if the distance to the projected surface changes. Hence, the whole purpose of having a fully automated interaction is lost in the case that the projector does not use a laser to keep the image focus. This problem can be solved by using a rangefinder and a closed-loop motion system consisting of a micro motor like piezoelectric SQUIGGLE and a non-contact position sensor like TRACKER. As an alternative, the out-of-focus projection blur can be reduced with image-based methods like the one proposed by Oyamada [29], which is well-suitable to reduce the image blur in non-perpendicular projections.

Our solution to RC5: *What mechanisms can we implement to tackle the issue of sensitive information disclosure?* is based on the fact that our system does project a clone of the mobile screen. The projector is identified and used as a

Fig. 3. Mobile editor interface

different display. In this display, we do not render any user interface, as they are not needed. Only the shapes defined by the user are projected as well as any other information related to the collaborative task.

In our framework, we have also integrated in-house developed affective computing and recommendation systems - RC3: *How can affective computing and recommendation systems be integrated into a projective augmented system, so we can adapt the content to the emotional state or needs of the user?*. The affective computing system is capable of detecting user emotions, which are then combined with the user preferences to filter content or to change the way the user is interacting. This is especially relevant to us, as our system was originally designed for urban planning and advertising scenarios. In the same way that our mood affects the type of music we listen to, this system helps users to reach the user goals faster. That means, finding relevant/appealing products or suggesting designer's alternatives.

To propose the RC6: *How can we create a normative policy that regulates the use and the power of PPP technology in certain scenarios like streets, where drivers or passengers could be temporarily blinded by the projection?* we propose a system that is based on image analysis. The system analyses the content of a frame in order to understand what kind of elements are present there. Hence, architectural elements or other things like people, and streets can be easily identified. To test our system, we defined a rule that interrupts projection if a street is detected. Figure 4 show the image analysis results, in percentage, for a given image frame.

In the next section, we explain what we did in what concerns the RC4: *What mechanisms can be put in place to foster or promote collaboration and content sharing among users?*.

5   Use Cases

Although our technology is applicable to a wide range of different scenarios, we decided to describe here only three use cases: an architecture and urban planning

Fig. 4. Image context analysis using cloud services

scenario; and augmented mobile advertisement scenario; and cultural heritage tourism scenario.

5.1 Architecture and Urban Planning

It is fundamental in scenarios like architecture and urban planning to have a system for decision-making that provides an overview of information relevant to the analysis (context) together with more detailed information for the various sub-tasks of interest.

Fig. 5. Architecture and urban planning

Interaction with handheld projectors can be designed to effectively support this type of activities. For example, one projector can be held far from the projection area to create the low-resolution coarse-granularity, and another handheld projector can be held close to the focus region to display more detailed information, since the user can archive higher pixel densities as projection area shrinks.

Fig. 6. Snapping multiple objects

Hence, we would get an image resolution gradation interaction-based technique that capitalises on the distance between the projection surface and the projector itself, and a technique that would enable the visualisation of multiple information granularities. The viewing experience would be similar to that of a focus plus context display. Figure 5 shows a multi-granularity city map. The context region shows main streets only, while the focus region shows augmented urban information.

The solution that we propose is more flexible than previous focus plus context solution, where the resolution and position of both focus and context displays is fixed. In the solution that we propose, users can dynamically move in the environment and manipulate the resolution of the projections.

5.2 Cultural Heritage Tourism

In the previous use case, we described an interaction technique based on direct blending of multiple views. However, we can give a step further in terms of interaction with projected content. We can use the intersection of different projections as the trigger to quickly view information that involves multiple objects. For example, we can think of an interaction were multiple objects being projected by different handheld projectors can snap to each other when close enough. When snapped together, either they change their appearance to disclose additional information or they trigger the visualisation of more information. To unsnap them, we need to keep a small distance between objects that can trigger such actions (Fig. 6).

As an example, suppose that there are two users projecting information. The first user is projecting a map and a second user is exploring the 3D model of a monument. Intersecting the projection of these two users results in the visualisation of a map with the 4D model pinpointed. Then a third user projects another an object that has location associate. The intersection with the previous projections draw a route path between the location of the user's object and the position of the monument now snapped to the map. The application supports the projection of multiple objects per projector. Hence, the limit of this technology lays on the creativity of its users. Additionally, the linkage between objects can be used as an authentication mechanism, where data is only disclosed when two objects are projected.

A side effect of using mobile devices to process the visual information that will be projected is that, without projectors, they can work as a traditional AR tools. For example, we use the mobile application to overlap historical pictures. Figure 7 depicts a smartphone overlapping the real world with an historical image.

Fig. 7. Tracking system: Overlap of a historical picture using the smartphone

5.3   Augmented Mobile Advertisement

The advertisement market can also benefit from the use our technology to reach out their audiences. First, our mobile prototype allows simple authoring of "augmented" advertisement content which then can be used to generate interaction with user within the "real" scene (Fig. 8). Below we have a smartphone product on a tabletop. In Fig. 9, the smartphone is the object being tracked by the projector's camera. In this case, we use occlusion of features as an action trigger. For example, if the user puts a hand over the natural features of the button "more info" then our system triggers the action associated with that button.

We have also tested projection-based metaphors as a new way of transferring content to a mobile device without the requirement of having connectivity. This

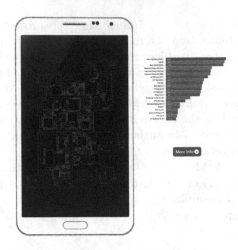

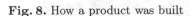

Fig. 8. How a product was built

Fig. 9. Interaction with menus based on feature occlusion

technique is especially relevant for tourists that are often dependent on roaming connectivity, which can be expensive. In our setup, we used a projector to display an animated QR code and a smartphone to read the animation in the form of download. The transfer rate archived is not suitable for general file transfers but works well for small amounts of information like text and small images, for example, information related to a product.

6 Evaluation

In this section, evaluate the relevance and impact of this study. As part of a preliminary user study, we asked 9 individuals to experiment our prototype. First, we demonstrated to each participant the features of the system, and then suggest them to try out the techniques described in the previous section. Each interaction session between participants lasted about 30 min. During the experiment we observed how participants used the system and then we conducted individual post-study interviews.

All participants manage to grasp the basic concepts of the prototype quite fast. Additionally, the participants did not show any difficulty learning the projection-based interaction techniques that were proposed. As we expected, the feature that was reported as the most appealing is the ability to easily exchange and combine information in a shared workspace, in addition to user-friendly approach used to setup a projection mapping.

There are although some technical aspects that can be improved. First the image analysis algorithm that we use to enforce normative policies cannot be executed at a real time frame rate. In our implementation it streams an image frame to an image analysis service that returns a set of tags that describe the image. The projection is automatically blocked if the projector is pointing, for example, to a car, people, or streets. In the future, we want to restrict the projection in such way that it will never hit people in the face, but while keeping the projecting around the person. This can be easily archived with a face tracking algorithms, which are already available in OpenCV.

The computational time required for tracking operations can also be improved. At the moment, the tracking algorithm can process only 17 frames per second. The method implemented for reducing out-of-focus blur helped us to archive better results with projectors that do not support auto-focus. Yet focus and projection size needs to be calibrated manually, because the focus of the projector can only be adjusted manually. This problem can be solved with the use of a laser-based projector.

7 Conclusion

In this paper we explored new perspectives on augmented reality systems that crystallise on new concepts of 3D projective mapping and interaction between multiple co-located users using handheld projectors. Interpersonal communication and collaboration may be supported more intuitively and efficiently compared to current handheld devices. Informal user feedback indicated that our designs were promising. Our work is the first mobile authoring system for 3D projective mapping that uses computer vision tracking techniques to facilitate the design live projections.

The current mobile projection technology has some limitations in terms of the light intensity, in addition to the fact that it can only provide image focus at a particular distance. Current handheld projectors have a luminance between 5 and 100 lumens, which we believe that will increase considerably next few years – some low-cost fixed projectors can nowadays reach 2,500 lumens. This limitation implies that handheld projectors can only be used indoors or outdoors at night. For dynamic mobile projections with variable distance between the projection surface and the projector, we advise the use of laser projectors which seem to be better suited, to the projection of sharp images.

As a future work, we are interested in empirically investigating how interaction between people may evolve with the usage of handheld projectors and how the technology is used for creative purposes. Finally, we plan to extensively explore other was of interacting with handheld projectors, by integrating for example gamification strategies, which may change the way people currently think. We will also investigate improvements in transfering data with QR codes through the visualisation of animated arrays since projected spaces have on their side the advantage of using large surfaces.

Acknowledgements. This research has been supported by the European Commission (EC) under the project c-Space (Grant Agreement N. 611040). The authors are solely responsible for the content of the paper. It does not represent the opinion of the European Community. The European Community is not responsible for any use that might be made of information contained herein. Special thanks should also be given to Ferdinando Cesaria, for his valuable technical support and useful recommendations.

References

1. Azuma, R.T., et al.: A survey of augmented reality. Presence **6**(4), 355–385 (1997)
2. Beardsley, P., Van Baar, J., Raskar, R., Forlines, C.: Interaction using a handheld projector. IEEE Comput. Graph. Appl. **25**(1), 39–43 (2005)
3. Bier, E.A., Stone, M.C., Pier, K., Buxton, W., DeRose, T.D.: Toolglass and magic lenses: the see-through interface. In: Proceedings of the 20th Annual Conference on Computer Graphics and Interactive Techniques, pp. 73–80. ACM (1993)
4. Blasko, G., Coriand, F., Feiner, S.: Exploring interaction with a simulated wrist-worn projection display. In: Proceedings of the Ninth IEEE International Symposium on Wearable Computers, pp. 2–9. IEEE (2005)
5. Cao, X.: Handheld projector interaction. Ph.D. thesis. University of Toronto (2009)
6. Cao, X., Forlines, C., Balakrishnan, R.: Multi-user interaction using handheld projectors. In: Proceedings of the 20th Annual ACM Symposium on User Interface Software and Technology, UIST 2007, pp. 43–52. ACM, New York (2007). http://doi.acm.org/10.1145/1294211.1294220
7. Cao, X., Forlines, C., Balakrishnan, R.: Multi-user interaction using handheld projectors. In: Proceedings of the 20th Annual ACM Symposium on User Interface Software and Technology, pp. 43–52. ACM (2007)
8. Cao, X., Massimi, M., Balakrishnan, R.: Flashlight jigsaw: an exploratory study of an ad-hoc multi-player game on public displays. In: Proceedings of the 2008 ACM Conference on Computer Supported Cooperative Work, pp. 77–86. ACM (2008)
9. Chan, L.W., Wu, H.T., Kao, H.S., Ko, J.C., Lin, H.R., Chen, M.Y., Hsu, J., Hung, Y.P.: Enabling beyond-surface interactions for interactive surface with an invisible projection. In: Proceedings of the 23nd Annual ACM Symposium on User Interface Software and Technology, pp. 263–272. ACM (2010)
10. Churchill, E.F., Nelson, L., Denoue, L., Helfman, J., Murphy, P.: Sharing multimedia content with interactive public displays: a case study. In: Proceedings of the 5th Conference on Designing Interactive Systems: Processes, Practices, Methods, and Techniques, pp. 7–16. ACM (2004)
11. Cowan, L.G., Li, K.A.: Shadowpuppets: supporting collocated interaction with mobile projector phones using hand shadows. In: Proceedings of the SIGCHI Conference on Human Factors in Computing Systems, pp. 2707–2716. ACM (2011)
12. Dao, V.N., Hosoi, K., Sugimoto, M.: A semi-automatic realtime calibration technique for a handheld projector. In: Proceedings of the 2007 ACM Symposium on Virtual Reality Software and Technology, pp. 43–46. ACM (2007)
13. Fischler, M., Bolles, R.: Random sample consensus: a paradigm for model fitting with applications to image analysis and automated cartography. Comm. ACM **24**, 381–395 (1981)
14. Grundhofer, A., Seeger, M., Hantsch, F., Bimber, O.: Dynamic adaptation of projected imperceptible codes. In: 6th IEEE and ACM International Symposium on Mixed and Augmented Reality, ISMAR 2007, pp. 181–190. IEEE (2007)
15. Hang, A., Rukzio, E., Greaves, A.: Projector phone: a study of using mobile phones with integrated projector for interaction with maps. In: Proceedings of the 10th International Conference on Human Computer Interaction with Mobile Devices and Sservices, pp. 207–216. ACM (2008)
16. Harrison, C., Benko, H., Wilson, A.D.: Omnitouch: wearable multitouch interaction everywhere. In: Proceedings of the 24th Annual ACM Symposium on User Interface Software and Technology, pp. 441–450. ACM (2011)

17. Hereld, M., Judson, I., Stevens, R.: Introduction to building projection-based tiled display systems. IEEE Comput. Graph. Appl. **20**(4), 22–28 (2000)
18. Hilliges, O., Izadi, S., Wilson, A.D., Hodges, S., Garcia-Mendoza, A., Butz, A.: Interactions in the air: adding further depth to interactive tabletops. In: Proceedings of the 22nd Annual ACM Symposium on User Interface Software and Technology, pp. 139–148. ACM (2009)
19. Hosoi, K., Dao, V.N., Mori, A., Sugimoto, M.: Cogame: manipulation using a handheld projector. In: ACM SIGGRAPH 2007 Emerging Technologies, p. 2. ACM (2007)
20. Kane, S.K., Avrahami, D., Wobbrock, J.O., Harrison, B., Rea, A.D., Philipose, M., LaMarca, A.: Bonfire: a nomadic system for hybrid laptop-tabletop interaction. In: Proceedings of the 22nd Annual ACM Symposium on User Interface Software and Technology, pp. 129–138. ACM (2009)
21. Köhler, M., Patel, S.N., Summet, J.W., Stuntebeck, E.P., Abowd, G.D.: Track-Sense: infrastructure free precise indoor positioning using projected patterns. In: LaMarca, A., Langheinrich, M., Truong, K.N. (eds.) Pervasive 2007. LNCS, vol. 4480, pp. 334–350. Springer, Heidelberg (2007)
22. Lee, J., Hudson, S., Dietz, P.: Hybrid infrared and visible light projection for location tracking. In: Proceedings of the 20th Annual ACM Symposium on User Interface Software and Technology, pp. 57–60. ACM (2007)
23. Leutenegger, S., Chli, M., Siegwart, R.Y.: Brisk: binary robust invariant scalable keypoints. In: 2011 IEEE International Conference on Computer Vision (ICCV), pp. 2548–2555. IEEE (2011)
24. Löchtefeld, M., Schöning, J., Rohs, M., Krüger, A.: Marauders light: replacing the wand with a mobile camera projector unit. In: Proceedings of the 8th International Conference on Mobile and Ubiquitous Multimedia, MUM 2009, pp. 19:1–19:4. ACM, New York (2009). http://doi.acm.org/10.1145/1658550.1658569
25. Ma, Y., Soatto, S., Kosecka, J., Sastry, S.: An Invitation to 3d Vision: From Images to Models. Springer, New York (2003)
26. McCarthy, J.F., Congleton, B., Harper, F.M.: The context, content & community collage: sharing personal digital media in the physical workplace. In: Proceedings of the 2008 ACM Conference on Computer Supported Cooperative Work, pp. 97–106. ACM (2008)
27. Mistry, P., Maes, P., Chang, L.: Wuw-wear ur world: a wearable gestural interface. In: CHI2009 Extended Abstracts on Human Factors in Computing Systems, pp. 4111–4116. ACM (2009)
28. Nakazato, Y., Kanbara, M., Yokoya, N.: Localization system for large indoor environments using invisible markers. In: Proceedings of the 2008 ACM Symposium on Virtual Reality Software and Technology, pp. 295–296. ACM (2008)
29. Oyamada, Y., Saito, H.: Focal pre-correction of projected image for deblurring screen image. In: IEEE Conference on Computer Vision and Pattern Recognition, CVPR 2007, pp. 1–8, June 2007
30. Ozuysal, M., Calonder, M., Lepetit, V., Fua, P.: Fast keypoint recognition using random ferns. IEEE Trans. Pattern Anal. Mach. Intell. **32**(3), 448–461 (2010)
31. Park, H., Park, J.I.: Invisible marker based augmented reality system. In: Visual Communications and Image Processing 2005, pp. 59601I–59601I. International Society for Optics and Photonics (2005)
32. Pinhanez, C.: The everywhere displays projector: a device to create ubiquitous graphical interfaces. In: Abowd, G.D., Brumitt, B., Shafer, S. (eds.) UbiComp 2001. LNCS, vol. 2201, pp. 315–331. Springer, Heidelberg (2001)

33. Rapp, S., Michelitsch, G., Osen, M., Williams, J., Barbisch, M., Bohan, R., Valsan, Z., Emele, M.: Spotlight navigation: interaction with a handheld projection device (2004)
34. Raskar, R., Beardsley, P., Van Baar, J., Wang, Y., Dietz, P., Lee, J., Leigh, D., Willwacher, T.: Rfig lamps: interacting with a self-describing world via photosensing wireless tags and projectors. In: ACM Transactions on Graphics (TOG), vol. 23, pp. 406–415. ACM (2004)
35. Raskar, R., Van Baar, J., Beardsley, P., Willwacher, T., Rao, S., Forlines, C.: ilamps: geometrically aware and self-configuring projectors. In: ACM SIGGRAPH 2006 Courses, p. 7. ACM (2006)
36. Robinson, S., Jones, M.: Haptiprojection: multimodal mobile information discovery. In: Ubiprojection Workshop at Pervasive 2010 (2010)
37. Saito, S., Hiyama, A., Tanikawa, T., Hirose, M.: Indoor marker-based localization using coded seamless pattern for interior decoration. In: Virtual Reality Conference, VR2007, pp. 67–74. IEEE (2007)
38. Schöning, J., Rohs, M., Kratz, S., Löchtefeld, M., Krüger, A.: Map torchlight: a mobile augmented reality camera projector unit. In: CHI 2009 Extended Abstracts on Human Factors in Computing Systems, CHI EA 2009, pp. 3841–3846. ACM, New York (2009). http://doi.acm.org/10.1145/1520340.1520581
39. Shilkrot, R., Hunter, S., Maes, P.: Pocomo: projected collaboration using mobile devices. In: Proceedings of the 13th International Conference on Human Computer Interaction with Mobile Devices and Services, pp. 333–336. ACM (2011)
40. Shirai, Y., Matsushita, M., Ohguro, T.: Hiei projector: augmenting a real environment with invisible information. In: The 11th Workshop on Interactive Systems and Software (WISS2003), pp. 115–122 (2003)
41. Sugimoto, M., Miyahara, K., Inoue, H., Tsunesada, Y.: *Hotaru*: intuitive manipulation techniques for projected displays of mobile devices. In: Costabile, M.F., Paternó, F. (eds.) INTERACT 2005. LNCS, vol. 3585, pp. 57–68. Springer, Heidelberg (2005)
42. Underkoffler, J., Ullmer, B., Ishii, H.: Emancipated pixels: real-world graphics in the luminous room. In: Proceedings of the 26th Annual Conference on Computer Graphics and Interactive Techniques, SIGGRAPH 1999, pp. 385–392. ACM Press/Addison-Wesley Publishing Co., New York (1999). http://dx.doi.org/10.1145/311535.311593
43. Velasco, S.: 'sublimotion', un viaje a través de los sentidos. Revista Internacional de Protocolo: Ceremonial, Etiqueta, Heráldica, Nobiliaria y Vexilogía **71**, 74–77 (2014)
44. Weng, D., Huang, Y., Liu, Y., Wang, Y.: Study on an indoor tracking system with infrared projected markers for large-area applications. In: Proceedings of the 8th International Conference on Virtual Reality Continuum and its Applications in Industry, pp. 239–245. ACM (2009)
45. Wienss, C., Nikitin, I., Goebbels, G., Troche, K., Göbel, M., Nikitina, L., Müller, S.: Sceptre: an infrared laser tracking system for virtual environments. In: Proceedings of the ACM Symposium on Virtual Reality Software and Technology, pp. 45–50. ACM (2006)
46. Willis, K.D., Poupyrev, I., Hudson, S.E., Mahler, M.: Sidebyside: ad-hoc multi-user interaction with handheld projectors. In: Proceedings of the 24th Annual ACM Symposium on User Interface Software and Technology, pp. 431–440. ACM (2011)

47. Willis, K.D., Poupyrev, I., Shiratori, T.: Motionbeam: a metaphor for character interaction with handheld projectors. In: Proceedings of the SIGCHI Conference on Human Factors in Computing Systems, pp. 1031–1040. ACM (2011)

48. Wilson, A.D.: Playanywhere: a compact interactive tabletop projection-vision system. In: Proceedings of the 18th Annual ACM Symposium on User Interface Software and Technology, pp. 83–92. ACM (2005)

IMU Drift Reduction for Augmented Reality Applications

Lakshmi Prabha Nattamai Sekar[1,2]($\boxtimes$), Alexander Santos[1],
and Olga Beltramello[1]

[1] European Organization for Nuclear Research, CERN, Geneva, Switzerland
{ns.lakshmiprabha,a.alvsantos,olga.beltramello}@cern.ch
[2] University of Rome Tor Vergata, Rome, Italy

Abstract. Pose estimation is a major task in any augmented reality
(AR) application. Sensors like inertial measurement units (IMUs) and
cameras are used for this purpose. IMU provides fast data, from which a
pose can be determined with fewer calculations. In most cases, this data
is influenced by drift. This paper investigates a drift reduction technique
on positions calculated from accelerometer data and the result shows that
this technique significantly reduces drift in fast dynamic movements. Furthermore, this drift reduced IMU pose can be fused with low pose updates
from vision algorithms to improve the accuracy and speed suitable for
AR applications.

Keywords: Augmented reality · Pose estimation · Inertial measurement
unit · Marker tracking · Sensor fusion

1 Introduction

In the past 50 years, the digital computer transformed from a research apparatus
to laptops that are used daily. There is also a huge growth from telephones to
smart phones and to wearable devices. These devices using augmented reality
(AR) technology display the appropriate information in our field of view. The AR
technology enables us to perceive reality in a more informative dimension. One
such useful application is replacing paper manuals with AR for machine maintenance procedures [1]. This work demonstrates an AR maintenance application
in the ATLAS detector[1], a particle physics facility in Large Hadron Collider
(LHC)[2].

One very important task in any AR application is the determination of object
pose for overlapping the correct virtual information. This pose estimation has
to be quite fast to cope up with the user movements. Sensors like vision camera,
Inertial measurement unit (IMU), magnetic field sensors, GPS, Network access
points, beacons are used for this purpose. These sensors provide either the position or orientation (or both together as pose) of an object or about itself in a

---

[1] http://atlas.ch/.
[2] http://home.web.cern.ch/.

© Springer International Publishing Switzerland 2015
L.T. De Paolis and A. Mongelli (Eds.): AVR 2015, LNCS 9254, pp. 188–196, 2015.
DOI: 10.1007/978-3-319-22888-4_14

scene. The selection of sensors greatly depend on an application environment. For example, GPS cannot be used in an indoor application. Among different sensors, vision camera and inertial measurement unit (IMU) are the two sensors that provide a 6D pose for both indoor and outdoor AR applications.

Camera based pose estimation provides position and orientation. However, it is computationally expensive and cannot provide fast pose updates required for an AR application. These algorithms also suffer from motion blurs and landmark occlusions. Alternatively, IMUs are faster (easily gives data at 400 Hz) but the major disadvantage is that they typically suffer from drift. This drift can sometime make the IMU data unreliable and useless. One well known method to overcome this drift is to use other low drift data (for example poses computed from the vision images) and then fuse the two data together. There are ways to reduce drift in position calculation from the accelerometer data as it is adopted for measuring vehicle displacement [9]. These reduction techniques can help to achieve a more reliable position information from the IMU. The level of pose accuracy required for any AR application is quite high since a small change in pose values can result in huge registration error. Hence it is important to fuse pose estimation from a camera and an IMU that can complement each other in terms of accuracy and speed.

This paper investigates firstly the performance requirements in terms of time in an AR application. Camera and IMU calibration to determine the relative pose between them is discussed in Sect. 3. The pose estimation and detailed procedure for reducing the drift in position calculation is elaborated in Sect. 4. Further, this drift reduced position together with the orientation from an IMU fused with the pose data from the vision algorithm for an AR application is detailed in Sects. 5 and 6. The experimental evaluation of the drift reduction procedure is discussed in Sect. 7.

2   Performance Requirements in an AR Application

In any AR application, the virtual object rendering must be synchronized with the update-rate of the displays (30–60 Hz). The exact object pose with respect to the user movement is required for displaying the virtual content in their field of view. Otherwise this will cause motion sickness to the user. Hence fast and accurate pose computation is a must for any augmented reality application. The time taken by different modules in an augmented reality system from image capturing to AR virtual content rendering is shown in Fig. 1. In a first analysis of the plot, the time taken for pose estimation based on a camera is very prominent. For this reason, in most AR applications pose estimation from a camera is fused with other sensor information. Other than the time taken by different modules for computation, there is also latency produced from the camera, display device and the data transmission between different modules.

T_{calc} varies from several milli seconds to seconds based on the vision based algorithm computation. Essentially, the sensor fusion using camera and IMU

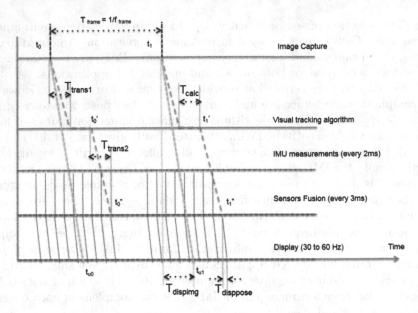

Fig. 1. Time taken by different modules in an augmented reality system. T_{frame} - time duration between two subsequent image frames, f_{frame} - camera frame rate, t_0 - time instance at which image captured, t_0' - time instance at which pose parameters are ready, t_0'' - time instance at which pose parameters reaches the sensor fusion, t_{u0} - time instance at which image is rendered, T_{trans1} - time duration required for transmitting image from camera to the visual tracking algorithm, T_{trans2} - time duration required for transmitting pose parameters from visual tracking algorithm to sensor fusion, T_{calc} - time duration required by the visual tracking algorithm for the pose parameter calculation, $T_{disppose}$ - time duration required for pose to be rendered, $T_{dispimg}$ - time duration required for image to be rendered.

data can deliver pose update rates that are better, faster and more accurate than single sensor measurements. In the following sections, IMU and camera calibration followed by pose estimation methods are discussed.

3   Camera-IMU Calibration

In order to fuse the information from a camera and an IMU, it is important to know the exact temporal offset and spatial displacement between the camera and the IMU for any AR application. Starting from hand-eye calibration by Tsai and Lenz [5], there are many algorithms proposed for this purpose [6–8]. An improvisation and simplification of hand-eye calibration was proposed in [7], but this method requires additional hardware and careful manual movements for calibration. These shortcomings were overcome by Hols et al. in [6] where they determine the calibration parameter by minimizing a weighted quadratic cost function using Extended Kalman Filter (EKF). Recently, [8] proposed a method for determining the spatial and temporal registration of multiple sensors with a simple calibration pattern. In this work, the method proposed in [8] for calibration purposes[3].

4   Pose Estimation Using IMU

An inertial measurement unit works by detecting the current rate of acceleration using one or more accelerometers and angular velocity using one or more gyroscopes. Some also include a magnetometer in the same packaging in order to assist calibration against orientation drift. The cost and size of inertial sensors increases with higher accuracy and lower drift. The Xsens IMU (3 accelerometers, 3 gyroscopes and 3 magnetometers) was used in this work because of its smaller size, weight and low power consumption. Following subsections explain in more detail the orientation and position calculation from angular velocity and acceleration data from an IMU.

4.1   Orientation Calculation

The orientation in terms of quaternions was calculated using explicit complimentary filter (ECF) discussed by M. Euston et al. in [3]. Let $q = \begin{bmatrix} q0 & q1 & q2 & q3 \end{bmatrix}$ be the quaternion to calculate, $g = \begin{bmatrix} gx & gy & gz \end{bmatrix}$ be the angular velocity from gyroscope and $a = \begin{bmatrix} ax & ay & az \end{bmatrix}$ be the acceleration from the accelerometer. Following steps are used to calculate the orientation,

1. Normalize the acceleration data.
   $a_n = \frac{a}{||a||}$
2. Estimated direction of gravity and vector perpendicular to magnetic flux.
   $$v = \begin{bmatrix} vx \\ vy \\ vz \end{bmatrix} = \begin{bmatrix} 2(q1q3 + q0q2) \\ 2(q0q1 + q2q3) \\ q0^2 - q1^2 - q2^2 + q3^2 \end{bmatrix}$$
3. Error is sum of cross product between estimated and measured direction of gravity.
   $$e = \begin{bmatrix} ex \\ ey \\ ez \end{bmatrix} = a_n \times v$$
   where $\times$ is the cross product.
4. Proportional and Integral feedback.
   $g_{out} = g + k_p e + k_i e \, \triangle t$
   where $\triangle t$ is smaple period, k_p and k_i are the proportional and integral gains.
5. Compute rate of change of quaternion.
   $q_{dot} = q_{t-1} \otimes g_{out}$
   where $\otimes$ is the quaternion multiplication.

---

[3] https://github.com/ethz-asl/kalibr.

6. Integrate to yield quaternion.
   $q_t = q_{t-1} + \frac{1}{2}q_{dot} \triangle t$
   Normalize q_t to get the orientation quaternion at time t.

   The position calculation using double integration of the accelerometer data is discussed in the next section.

4.2   Drift Reduction in Position Calculation

The process of integrating acceleration data twice to calculate the position is not so direct, since the accelerometer data contains the body acceleration and the gravity component. In order to calculate the linear acceleration, it is a must to remove the effect of gravity. Since, gravity is a constant vector in earth's frame, it is required to know the orientation of the sensor. The orientation quaternion obtained from ECF is used for this purpose. The accelerometer data is transformed to the earth's frame using rotation quaternions. The linear acceleration can be calculated by subtracting constant gravity and converted to m/s^2. By double integration this linear acceleration will result in the position.

The accuracy of the position from an IMU is influenced by two sources of error: drift and measurement noise. Any small noise or drift in this acceleration values will result in a huge deviation in position values and that makes the data useless in some cases. Thus, it is required to process the linear acceleration to reduce this drift and noise. The drift is of low frequency whereas measurement noise is of high frequency. Hence, the noise can be reduced by a low-pass filter and the drift can be reduced by a high-pass filter. Another problem in double integration is the lack of initial conditions. Initial velocity and position must be known from the direct measurements for proper double integration. The need of initial conditions in a real environment are not possible in many situations. One way to overcome this is to make use of a high-pass filter to eliminate the DC components in the integration results [9].

The linear acceleration is first low-pass filtered to remove the high frequency noise. The resulting data is then high-pass filtered to remove the very low frequency drift and then integrated to calculate the velocity. This velocity is high-pass filtered to remove DC components and that eliminates the need for initial conditions. The resulting data is again integrated to get position values and it is high-pass filtered to remove the DC component similar to velocity. The different steps involved in drift reduction is shown in Fig. 2. The position and orientation quaternions from IMU are combined together to form the 6D pose. The results from the drift reduction detailed above is discussed in the experimental evaluation section.

5   Pose Estimation Using Camera Images

In order to simplify the visual tracking system, a prepared environment with fiducial markers are used. There are several libraries mainly used to resolve the

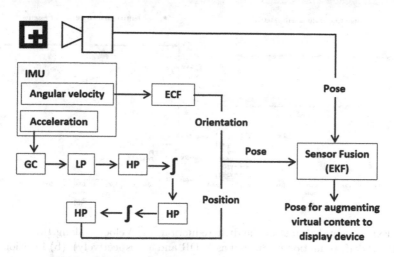

Fig. 2. The overall schematic showing data-flow and different process with the detail on drift reduction in position calculation. GC- Gravity compensation, LP - low-pass, HP - high-pass.

marker tracking issues in the given scene. Most well known marker tracking libraries are ARToolKit [11], osgART [12], DWART [13], ARTag [14], Ubitrack [2] etc. In this work, marker tracking from Ubitrack[4] library is used. The precise marker tracking is possible when it is provided with the camera parameters (intrinsic and extrinsic) calculated using camera calibration[5] [15]. The 6D pose from an IMU and the camera is fused using the method detailed in the sensor fusion section.

6 Sensor Fusion

The fusion of pose data is performed with an Extended Kalman filter (EKF) approach, a technique widely used in state estimation problems such as pose estimation in robotics, aviation and augmented reality [10]. The filter should be able to cope up with unsynchronized pose data coming from an IMU and a camera. The overall schematics of the data flow and process involved is shown in Fig. 2. The drift reduced pose from the IMU is fused with the marker tracking pose from the camera images and the final pose is used for rendering the virtual content for the maintenance application. As stated in Sect. 2, the virtual object rendering in the AR application has to be synchronized with the update-rate of the displays (60 Hz). Thus, this fusion of pose data from the camera and an IMU can deliver faster pose data than single sensor measurements (Refer [10] for more details on EKF).

---

[4] http://campar.in.tum.de/UbiTrack/WebHome.
[5] http://www.vision.caltech.edu/bouguetj/calib_doc/.

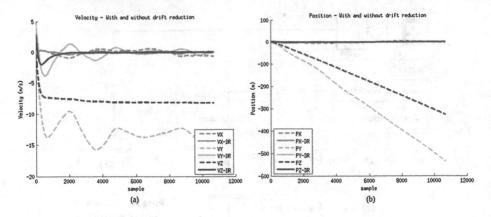

Fig. 3. Experimental results of the drift reduction, (a) Velocity along three axis with and without drift reduction (indicated as V-DR and V respectively), (b) Position along three axis with and without drift reduction (indicated as P-DR and P respectively).

7   Experimental Evaluation

The experiments are carried out using an Xsens IMU and a Logitech C920 camera. Firstly, the results obtained from the drift reduction for position calculation are shown in Fig. 3. The plot clearly shows that the proposed procedure experiences a clear reduction of the drift in both velocity and position calculation after integration. Especially when the IMU is subjected to fast dynamic movements, the velocity after drift reduction stays stable compared to the errors experienced in the velocity without drift reduction. It is obvious that any AR application on wearable devices (head mounted display for example) will always involve fast dynamic movements. Thus, the drift reduction technique improves the reliability of pose calculation from an IMU data.

Both the camera and IMU are firmly attached and they are calibrated to perfection (see Sect. 3). In order to demonstrate the use of an IMU pose and sensor fusion, only a 2 Hz (two pose per second) pose from marker tracking is used. This will help to mimic real computational vision algorithms on mobile devices where it is a tedious job to have a 2 Hz pose estimation. Figure 4(a) and (b) show an AR maintenance application only with 2 Hz marker tracking and sensor fusion. The AR visualization content was developed using a Unity3D game engine[6]. The sensor fusion results are promising whereby less jitter and smooth movement of the virtual object in the scene were observed. The reliable pose calculation from IMU further reduces the dependency on vision algorithms for pose updates.

---

[6] http://unity3d.com/.

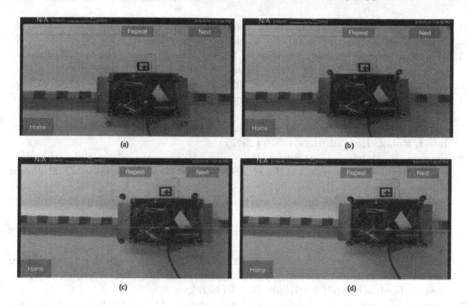

Fig. 4. AR maintenance application, (a) and (c) Camera marker tracking at 2 Hz pose rate, (b) and (d) Sensor fusion results of camera (2 Hz pose) with IMU.

8   Conclusion

This paper presented the drift reduction technique for position calculation from the IMU data. The experimental results illustrated that the technique reduces the drift to a large extent especially during fast dynamic movements. This IMU absolute pose can be further fused with other sensor pose data for increasing the accuracy required for any AR application. One such AR maintenance application using an IMU and a camera pose is shown in this paper with its promising results.

Acknowledgements. The authors wish to thank all other members of the EDUSAFE consortium. This research has been supported by a Marie Curie Initial Training Network Fellowship of the European Commission FP7 Programme under contract number PITN-GA-2012-316919-EDUSAFE.

References

1. Henderson, S., Feiner, S.: Exploring the benefits of augmented reality documentation for maintenance and repair. IEEE Trans. Visual Comput. Graphics **17**(10), 1355–1368 (2011)
2. Newman, J., Wagner, M. et al.: Ubiquitous tracking for augmented reality. In: Third IEEE and ACM International Symposium on Mixed and Augmented Reality, pp. 192–201 (2004)
3. Euston, M., Coote, P. et al.: A complementary filter for attitude estimation of a fixed-wing UAV. In: IEEE/RSJ International Conference on Intelligent Robots and Systems (2008)

4. Hol, J.D., Schon, T.B. et al.: Sensor fusion for augmented reality. In: 9th International Conference on Information Fusion, pp. 1–6 (2006)
5. Tsai, R., Lenz, R.: A new technique for fully autonomous and efficient 3D robotics hand/eye calibration. IEEE Trans. Robot. Autom. **5**(3), 345–358 (1989)
6. Hol, J.D., Schon, T.B., Gustafsson, F.: Relative pose calibration of a spherical camera and an IMU. In: International Symposium on Mixed and Augmented Reality, pp. 21–24 (2008)
7. Lobo, J., Dias, J.: Relative pose calibration between visual and inertial sensors. Int. J. Robot. Res. **26**(6), 561–575 (2007)
8. Furgale, P., Rehder, J., Siegwart, R.: Unified Temporal and Spatial Calibration for Multi-Sensor Systems. In: IEEE/RSJ International Conference on Intelligent Robots and Systems (IROS) (2013)
9. Slifka, L.D.: An accelerometer based approach to measuring displacement of a vehicle body. Master Thesis, University of Michigan, Dearborn (2004)
10. Bishop, G. Welch, G.: An introduction to the Kalman filter. In: Proceedings of SIGGRAPH, Course 8 (2001)
11. Kato, H., Billinghurst, M.: Marker tracking and hmd calibration for a video-based augmented reality conferencing system. In: 2nd International Workshop on Augmented Reality (IWAR 1999), pp. 85–94 (1999)
12. Looser, J., Grasset, R., Seichter, H., Billinghurst, M.: OSGART - a pragmatic approach to MR. In: International Symposium of Mixed and Augmented Reality (2006)
13. Bauer, M., Bruegge, B., Klinker, G., MacWilliams, A., Reicher, T., Riss, S., Sandor, C., Wagner, M.: Design of a component-based augmented reality framework. In: International Symposium on Augmented Reality (ISAR) (2001)
14. Fiala, M.: ARTag Revision 1, A fiducial marker system using digital Techniques. NRC Technical Report (NRC 47419), National Research Council of Canada (2004)
15. Salvi, J., Armangu, X., Batlle, J.: A comparative review of camera calibrating methods with accuracy evaluation. Pattern Recogn. **35**(7), 1617–1635 (2002)

Applications in Medicine

Serious Games for Rehabilitation Using Head-Mounted Display and Haptic Devices

Stéphane Claude Gobron[1]([✉]), Nicolas Zannini[1], Nicolas Wenk[1],
Carl Schmitt[2], Yannick Charrotton[2], Aurélien Fauquex[3,6],
Michel Lauria[4], Francis Degache[5], and Rolf Frischknecht[6]

[1] School of Engineering, HE-Arc, HES-SO, Neuchâtel, Switzerland
stephane.gobron@he-arc.ch
[2] Biomedical Engineering Group, HEIG-VD, HES-SO,
Yverdon-les-Bains, Switzerland
[3] Lambda Health System SA, Yverdon, Switzerland
[4] Robotics Laboratory, Hepia, HES-SO, Geneva, Switzerland
[5] University of Health Sciences, HES-SO, Lausanne, Switzerland
[6] Service of Neuropsychology and Neurorehabilitation, CHUV,
Lausanne, Switzerland

Abstract. In the health domain, the field of rehabilitation suffers from a lack specialized staff while hospital costs only increase. Worse, almost no tools are dedicated to motivate patients or help the personnel to carry out monitoring of therapeutic exercises. This paper demonstrates the high potential that can bring the virtual reality with a platform of serious games for the rehabilitation of the legs involving a head-mounted display and haptic robot devices. We first introduce SG principles, nowadays rehabilitation context, and an original applied haptic device called *Lambda Health System*. The architecture of the model is then detailed, including communication specifications showing that lag is imperceptible for user. Finally, to improve this prototype, four serious games for rehabilitation using haptic robots and/or HMD were tested by 33 health specialists.

Keywords: Serious games · Virtual reality · Rehabilitation · Haptic robot · Head-mounted display · Health application

1 Introduction

This paper presents a project entitled "SG4R" standing for *Serious Games for Rehabilitation* and recent user-tests (see Fig. 1) relative to Virtual Reality (VR) domain applied to health and specialized to lower limbs rehabilitation. Considering the technical needs outlined by Mo *et al.* [MJA14], after introducing the literature Serious Games (SGs) the following paragraph details the medical context and needs for VR applications based on SGs. The rest of the introduction briefly describes original ingredients of our proposal: mixed SGs including haptic robot and HMD which brings up the issue of organization in this strongly interdisciplinary consortium. After illustrating the general methodology pipeline, the next

L.T. De Paolis and A. Mongelli (Eds.): AVR 2015, LNCS 9254, pp. 199–219, 2015.
DOI: 10.1007/978-3-319-22888-4_15

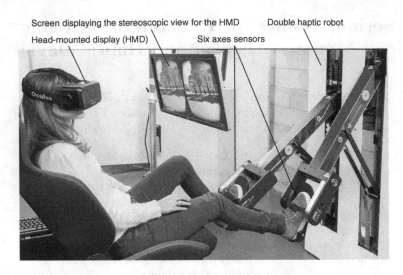

Screen displaying the stereoscopic view for the HMD   Double haptic robot

Head-mounted display (HMD)   Six axes sensors

Fig. 1. Test of the serious games using the virtual reality devices, HMD and haptic robots (*Lambda Health System*). Notice that the screen displays what the 3D screen is rendering at the Occulus Rift level (*i.e.* HMD).

section details the Materials and Methods architecture of the model from force sensors to head-mounted displays (HMD, Occulus Rift 4) via a user interface, and a SGs control platform. That section also introduce the mechanic principles as well as a summary of the communication protocol allowing no perceivable lag from user point of view (see Sect. 3.1).

1.1   Serious Games

This section introduces general concepts relative to SGs: definition and litera-ture related to VR devices (HMD or haptic) and health-care. In 2005, Rizzo *et al.* [RMJ+05] developed a virtual therapeutic environment for post-stroke recovery that includes different levels of haptic sensory feedback and to evaluate the effectiveness of these applications for neurorehabilitation training. This was not a SG, but only a virtual environment (VE) –*i.e.* no scoring or fun attributes. Nevertheless it involved haptic in a context of rehabilitation. From that con-text they also showed the need of a multidisciplinary consortium: Communica-tion, Cell Neurobiology, Computer Science, Psychology, and Physical Therapy. In 2010, Sabri et al. [SCK+10] proposed a SG for training replacing of the knee allowing residents to focus on and develop an understanding of the proce-dure itself *i.e.* steps and the required tools. Recently, Hanning *et al.* [HLS+13] proposed a project called "Skills-O-Mat" as an interactive serious game for training rhythmic and period motor skills that supports dental students being trained in alginate mixing in a blended learning course. Similar to our proposal, their model was tested among a population. Rodriguez *et al.* proposed this year (2015) [RRDV+15] an original SG to study emotional regulation in adolescents.

Their interesting approach based on a simple game was very serious as it can help resolving psychosocial and behavioral issues that this fragile segment of the population often encounters. Directly linked to SG, health and haptic, last year, Tommaso De Paolis *et al.* presented the development of a serious game for training on suturing in laparoscopic surgery that focused on the physical modeling of the VE using two *Novint Falcon* haptic devices, but the potential immersion of an HMD. Even if the above literature depicts only the tip of the iceberg of the large domain of SG, we believe our approach to be relatively original since there is not many works relative to SGs with haptic and HMD for rehabilitation.

1.2 SG and VR for Rehabilitation Interventions

General Medical Context. Worldwide neurological disorders such as stroke, brain injury and spinal cord injury, are important sources of motor disability and loss of quality of life [BW05,NLCZ+]. Stroke is by far the most frequent disabling condition in this field. Over the coming years the countries in the industrialized world will continue to experience an increase of the prevalence of motor disability related to the nervous system. The incidence of stroke increases with age [BW05] and the proportion of elderly people in these countries will increase markedly. Improved lifesaving procedures and treatments also increase the number of survivors of previously fatal health conditions at the price of disability.

Such disabilities can be reduced by appropriate rehabilitation interventions [LCP09]. To cover the increasing demand for rehabilitation and limit the costs associated, it becomes increasingly important to develop efficient and cost effective approaches to restore and maintain motor function. In most of the cases, the patients with motor disabilities need more than just retrain muscle force and endurance. They have to relearn the lost motor skills with appropriate task oriented therapeutic exercises. To be effective these motor relearning approaches require the impaired motor tasks to be retrained very precisely and with a high number of repetitions [BWFB03,WWM+06,LCP09]. In a hospital environment such repetitive task oriented training sessions can become very tedious and patients might get rapidly disinterested in exercising [Dob05]. Decreased tolerance or motivation to exercise often lead to intentionally or unintentionally hampered execution of the suitable exercises or even opposition to carry them out [LCS+11]. In addition most of the brain lesions are also associated with cognitive impairments. These patients often have difficulties to maintain their attention and to concentrate on monotonous exercises. Frequently they are very fatigable mentally and physically.These shortcomings put them at risk to under-perform during repetitive task oriented training and get reduced or delayed results.

Added Value of SGs for Motor Rehabilitation. SGs allow transforming a tedious, repetitive exercise carried out in the real world into a pleasant and motivating activity in a game or a virtual world (VW). To keep the motivation of a patient high the game or the VE should be chosen preferably within one of his domain of interest. While carrying out in the real world the exercises needed for his functional recovery, the patient draws his motivation and pleasure from a transformed projection of his activity into a game or a VW. Therefore SGs or VR are expected to increase the efficiency of the rehabilitation process, the motivation of the patients to perform the rehabilitation exercises as well as their adherence to the treatment.

SGs platforms allow also collecting data about the way the patient works out. The information collected can be integrated in an appropriate way into the game or the VW. The information returned to patient during the rehabilitation intervention can take the form of an immediate feedback or of a virtual system rewarding the workload carried out or the results achieved. Doctors and therapist can use these data to check the patient's daily performance, pilot and document the rehabilitation process and appraise progress. The collected data can also be used to guide home based rehabilitation interventions and devices through online connection within so called "tele-rehabilitation" programs [BB14].

Perspectives for Using SG and VR to Treat Cognitive Dysfunction. As mentioned above, most patients with brain lesions also present neuropsychological dysfunction. SGs or VR platforms allow either to create specific training programs for tackling such impairments or to add appropriate cognitive tasks or exercises to games conceived for the rehabilitation of motor tasks. The current clinical observation is that the addition of motor activities to cognitive exercises enhances the patients arousal and increases his capacity to train cognitive tasks [RL11]. SGs in a VR also allow simplifying the VE so as to reduce distraction during exercises in patients with a reduced ability to concentrate.

Mirror Neurons and Motor Rehabilitation. The recent discovery of mirror-neurons adds another dimension to the use of SGs or VR. The mirror neurons related to a specific task are activated either if the person observes the task or if the person performs the task [RC04, RFDC09]. The activation of the mirror neuron system by observation enhances motor learning [IWB+99, SCD+05, MG05, SF12]. If the task to be trained is integrated visually into a game or a VR scenario driven by an exercise for the same task, the resulting learning effect on the motor skill is expected to be superior [MG05, SCD+05, SCCC08]. This opens a large spectrum of possibilities to assist motor relearning in neurological patients and enhance functional recovery.

1.3   Haptic Device

Haptic is a term derived from the Greek verb "haptesthai" which means "to touch" [AEI+08]. A haptic device is a technology which enables interaction between a person and a machine through touch. Thus, the user's movements could especially define fully or partially the machine behavior and this one could, simultaneously, return a tactile feedback by forces or motion to the users according to the interaction rules defined in the virtual environment [HACH+04].

In this study, we use the haptic interaction for giving a force feedback to the lower limbs and also as a remote control for the serious games.

Designing an haptic interface that faithfully reproduces the haptic phenomena requires a specific design approach. The system has to be mechanically reversible or controllable in active compliant mode [HSV+09]. To achieve this, the most direct mechanical transmission and low inertia parts should be favored. The measurement of the interaction between the machine and the user can be done with a sensor or can be made using kinematics and dynamics models for interpreting actuator's efforts.

More technical details of this original haptic robot are presented in the next section where team organization as well as software and hardware general pipeline are proposed.

2   Materials and Methods

This section presents the architecture model enabling virtual reality devices to communicate and react with user in real-time with no perceivable lag (see Sect. 3.1).

2.1   Global Pipeline Architecture

As illustrated by Fig. 2, this model has required six R&D laboratories regrouped into five teams (computer science, game technologies, HMI, robotics, bio-electronics, and rehabilitation & medical supervision) to work together –as illustrated in the Fig. 2. Similarly, the Fig. 3 shows how haptic robots are

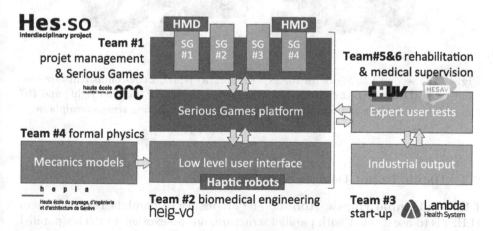

Fig. 2. SG4R: an interdisciplinary project involving seven teams from game technologies, software communication, electro-mechanics, robotic structure, mechanics models, to health.

controlled by an human machine interface (HMI) and mechanical models. Information transfer in real-time from user's legs, to robot sensors, to SG platform, to the selected SG context (i.e. HMD illustrated Fig. 4), and back to the user with visual, sound and haptic feedbacks. Graphics rendering are displayed either on a classical screen or on an HMD (both shown in the Fig. 1).

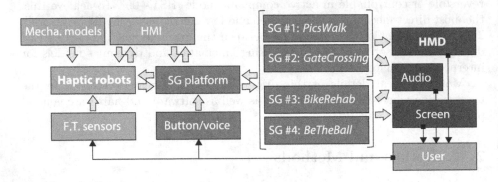

Fig. 3. Global process pipeline: from haptic robots (LHS) to an HMD or a classic screen display.

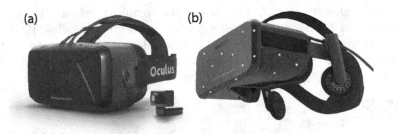

Fig. 4. The second VR device for the experiment: (a) HMD, *i.e.* Occulus Rift development kit II (DK2) with the infrared camera for head tracking (bottom right) and (b) official release that should occur before the end of 2015 including stereo headphone.

2.2   Haptic Robot Devices Specifications

LHS: A Double Haptic Robot. The originality of Lambda Health System (LHS) is to use a robot with parallel structure, not an exoskeleton. This parallel structure allows to separate the mobilization robot from orthoses, which keep the legs in the sagittal plane when necessary. This layout facilitates the transfer of the subject on the device. Moreover, there is no anthropometric adjustment.

An easy use by disabled people becomes possible. This new approach reduces the burden of physiotherapists in hospitals.

LHS is a hybrid robot [Cla94] with three degrees of freedom (DOF) consisting of two linear actuators –see Fig. 1 as well as Fig. 5(a) and (b)–placed in parallel. They control the movement of the foot (point P) in the sagittal plane of the subject (XY axes). These two actuators are used to make straight or curved trajectories in the xy plane. A third actuator (3) placed in series control the rotation of the ankle (around the z-axis). Two LHS robots are set on a mechanical structure, one for each leg.

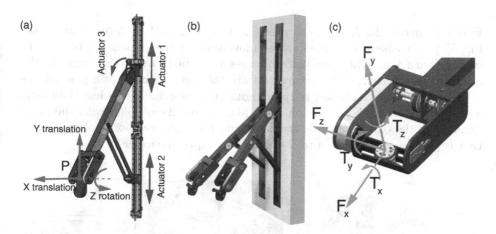

Fig. 5. The first VR device for the experiment: a double haptic robot called "LHS" standing for *Lambda health system*. (a) side view of the draft similar to the shape of the Greek letter λ where the three actuators develop three DOF; (b) picture of the current prototype (v.2): double haptic system with two LHS; (c) six axes sensors placed under each pedal: FT (*i.e.* Force and Torque) sensors in the pedal at the interaction between the subject and the haptic device. Measurement are in six DOF, only F_x and F_y are useful to the SG active control.

2.3   Robots Implementation

User Interface. The robot is controlled by an intuitive User Interface that has been developed by the University Of Applied Sciences (HES-SO), HEIG-VD branch. It allows the therapist to manage its subject database and to directly launch some exercises on the robot. Various exercises are available in a Library of preconfigured movements. The practitioner can easily modify and configure those exercises to adapt them to the patient needs. The serious games described in this paper are of course available in this library. Those exercises are then downloaded in the real-time application described here under to be executed by the robotic structure.

Real-Time Control Software. To guarantee the optimal performance of this low-level application, it is necessary to use a real-time kernel. Scheduling is performed with a 1 ms period in hard real-time. A Master *EtherCAT* is then used to communicate with the different slaves that are drives or sensors. This part of the software manages the position of the robot. The trajectories are calculated in the application and a new position is given to the motor drives each cycle. As explained here above, the communication is also performed with a period of 1 ms. In the event of an error, it would be detected in 1 ms, and the robot will be stopped in a few tens of milliseconds. This real-time system also allows to ensure patient safety in all circumstances.

Force Sensor. Each Lambda robot is equipped with a force sensor –see Fig. 5(c)–to measure the intention of movement of the patient to be able to interact with him. They are placed between the pedals used to maintain the feet, and the mechanical structure and are the base of the haptic possibilities of the LHS. Their resolution is approximately corresponding to less than 50 g, which represents a high precision. This high sensibility coupled with the great dynamic of the parallel robotic structure and the high precision motion control that is performed, leads to a really high-class haptic device (Fig. 6).

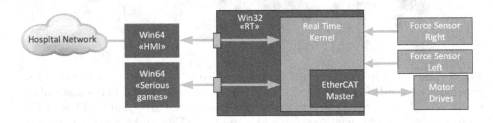

Fig. 6. Haptic device: summary of the low-level architecture.

2.4   Formal Mechanics Model

Most modern robotic systems are fast and repeatable position controlled machines. However, because of their inability to interact safely, robustly and in a versatile manner with humans, they mostly remain confined to controlled areas where they execute specific preprogrammed actions. Providing high performance motion simultaneously with the ability to physically interact significantly remains a challenge. Human-robot interaction theory that was first introduced in [Hog85] three decades ago describes a set of non-conventional control paradigms allowing robots to operate out of controlled and constrained operating conditions of conventional industrial robot manipulators. In such cases, robots must safely manage the intentional physical contact with human, even while performing fast (high bandwidth), high-force, high fidelity and precision tasks.

Such tasks are present in a multitude of human-machine cooperative interactions (*e.g.* sport training, physical therapy, rehabilitation, training assistance, surgery assistance, haptics, orthoses and prostheses motorization, exoskeleton).

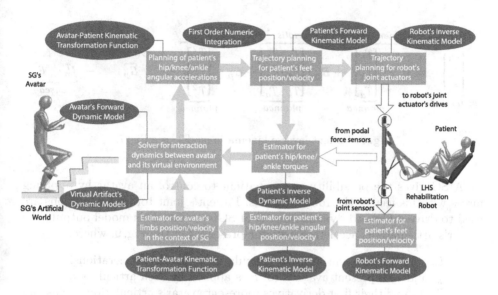

Fig. 7. Admittance control architecture scheme.

The design of the algorithms allowing controlling the human-robot interaction behavior (Fig. 7) is mostly influenced by the hardware implementation of the robot motorization subsystem. Most of the existing commercially available haptic devices –*e.g.* Novint's Falcon–are small low-power safe robotic systems that are based on impedance control schemes (*e.g.* force-out-for-motion-in). However, Lambda Health System uses powerful industrial motors and drives that cannot be directly force controlled without compromising human safety. For this reason, we choose to implement an admittance control scheme–*e.g.* motion-out-for-force-in) that relies on the information provided by a six axis force-torque (FT) podal sensor measuring the human-robot interaction dynamic.

To be able to generate robot's motion trajectories from podal force measurements (thus implement admittance control) we must first estimate patient's torques applied by each articulations (*e.g.* hip, knee, ankle). This can be done using patient's inverse dynamic model shown in the Fig. 8, where:

- τ_h, τ_k, and τ_a represent patient's torques applied by each articulation (h: hip, k: knee, a: ankle);
- T_h, T_k, T_a and their derivatives represent patient's planned articulation angles, angular speed and acceleration;
- M_p, B_p, C_p, and G_p are inertial, coriolis, centrifugal, gravitational matrix from patient's (p) dynamic model;

– J_p^T is the transpose Jacobian matrix from patient's kinematic model;
– F_o is the podal force vector measured by a sensor placed between the robot and patient's foot.

$$
\underbrace{\begin{bmatrix} \tau_h \\ \tau_k \\ \tau_a \end{bmatrix}}_{estimated} = M_p \cdot \overbrace{\underbrace{\begin{bmatrix} \ddot{T}_h \\ \ddot{T}_k \\ \ddot{T}_a \end{bmatrix}}_{planned}}^{inertial} + B_p \cdot \overbrace{\underbrace{\begin{bmatrix} \dot{T}_h \cdot \dot{T}_k \\ \dot{T}_h \cdot \dot{T}_a \\ \dot{T}_k \cdot \dot{T}_a \end{bmatrix}}_{planned}}^{coriolis} + C_p \cdot \overbrace{\underbrace{\begin{bmatrix} \dot{T}_h^2 \\ \dot{T}_k^2 \\ \dot{T}_a^2 \end{bmatrix}}_{planned}}^{centrifugal} + \overbrace{\widehat{G_p}}^{gravitational} - \underbrace{J_p^T \cdot F_o}_{sensed}
$$

Fig. 8. Patient inverse kinematic model –see Fig. 7.

A SG gives the possibility to the patient to control an avatar by applying forces with his feet to the robot's pedals. Patient's joint torque estimations are used to drive a forward dynamic model of SG's avatar. This model outputs the avatar's articulations acceleration vector presented in the Fig. 9, where:

– $\ddot{T}_h$, $\ddot{T}_k$, and $\ddot{T}_a$ represent avatar's articulations angular accelerations;
– τ_h, τ_k, and τ_a represent avatar's torques applied by each articulation;
– T_h, T_k, T_a and their first derivatives represent avatar's articulation angles and angular velocity (estimated states);
– M_A, B_A, C_A, and G_A are inertial, coriolis, centrifugal, gravitational matrix from avatar's ('A') dynamic model;
– $J_i^T F_i^e$ represents i^{th} term of the interaction dynamics between avatar and its virtual environment.

$$
\underbrace{\begin{bmatrix} \ddot{T}_h \\ \ddot{T}_k \\ \ddot{T}_a \end{bmatrix}}_{planned} = M_A^{-1} \cdot \left(\underbrace{\begin{bmatrix} \tau_h \\ \tau_k \\ \tau_a \end{bmatrix}}_{estimated} - B_A \cdot \underbrace{\begin{bmatrix} \dot{T}_h \cdot \dot{T}_k \\ \dot{T}_h \cdot \dot{T}_a \\ \dot{T}_k \cdot \dot{T}_a \end{bmatrix}}_{estimated} - C_A \cdot \underbrace{\begin{bmatrix} \dot{T}_h^2 \\ \dot{T}_k^2 \\ \dot{T}_a^2 \end{bmatrix}}_{estimated} - G_A - \underbrace{\sum_i J_i^T \cdot F_i^e}_{\substack{interaction \\ with\ virtual \\ environment}} \right)
$$

Fig. 9. Avatar's articulations acceleration vector model.

This approach allows us to take into account a wide range of virtual mechanical interactions between the patient and the artificial world of the SG (e.g. walls, guides, frictions, motion helpers or restrainers). A simple first order integration algorithm coupled with patient forward kinematic model and robot's inverse kinematic model is then used to derive robot's path planning in actuators space.

2.5 Communication Protocols

Communication between SGs and LHS is performed in three steps. In the first phase, the "RT" reads sensor values from the robot. This task was realized every 10 ms. The communication is made by using UDP network protocol used by the haptic device. In the second step, the game platform retrieves all necessary information according to the SG context from the RT computer. The communication is also made by using the UDP. This type of communication is relatively fast but unstable (i.e. from 2 to 14 ms). It is the easiest way to transfer data between two computers. In the last phase, the current SG reads the values available on the SG platform. This communication is achieved by shared memory which is fast and relatively stable (around 0.4 ms). To reduce the overall time and improve the stability of communication between SGs and equipment the three phases are realized asynchronously and two buffers were added. During the graphics rendering of the game, the platform retrieves the values from the RT and then the RT reads the sensors.

This communication is achieved by shared memory which is fast and relatively stable (around 0.4 ms). To reduce the overall time and improve the stability of communication between SGs and equipment, a buffer was added between the two protocols of communication. The SG continuously reads values from the device in the buffer via a thread. We found a procedure allowing the SG to receive a reading time less than 2.3 ms (see Results Sect. 3) so that no perceivable lag would occur at user level. In the worst case the information have a delay of 14 ms which is not a problem for the display (*i.e.* 60 Hz) but can contribute to noisy minor lags (*i.e.* system responsiveness). To overcome this issue we have set up directly at the platform level an information gap-free system so that even if no lag occurs an extrapolated information is transmitted (see Fig. 10).

Details and results of this model are presented on the first part of the following section.

3 Results

This section presents first the real-time acquisition results, then the purpose and some graphics from the four SGs, and finally results from a user-test based on 33 health specialists focusing on the rehabilitation using VR topic.

3.1 Guarantying Real-Time

This paragraph describes how information is captured and transferred so that lag (*i.e.* time between user's action on a robot sensor to the corresponding SG's graphics feedback) user's level are almost imperceivable: inferior to 31 ms –*i.e.* screen refreshment rate.

Data Acquisition from Force Sensor. This information acquisition is connected via an Ethernet network directly to the real-time application described
here above and has a constructor guarantying frequency of 1 kHz (*i.e.* 1 ms). In
this case, it is not mandatory to reach such a high frequency because the patient
interaction contains lowest frequencies. The sampling frequency that was chosen in consultation with therapist is 100 Hz. A separated task is responsible of
updating the last measured values and prepare them for the haptic models in
the real-time application.

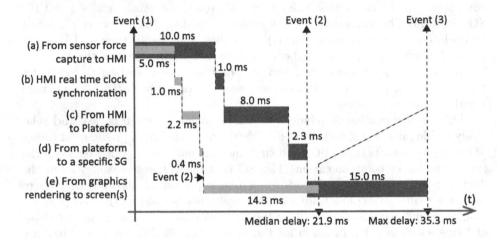

Fig. 10. This figure illustrated the median and maximum delay for the data transfer
from user's action on haptic sensors to its actual effects on screen: these statistics were
obtained with 100'000 samplings. The total delay can be subdivided into five sub-delays
(a–e) and three important events have to be identified: (1) user applies a force on a
sensor; (2) effects of event (1) is computed at HMIs level implying an haptic feedback
for user; (3) effects of event(1) occur at user's visual (and audio) senses.

Global Lag. Communication between an event on sensor and SGs renderings
(graphics or audio) take a maximum of 35 ms and a median time of 21 ms (see
Fig. 10). Considering that the five sub-delays (a)–(e) occurs in parallel we can
guarantee the SG real time loop to be stable at 30 Hz. These measurements
were carried out on a sample of 100 thousands "pings" using the SG called
"BikeRehab" with a bidirectional communication.

3.2   SGs Presentation

How to make a choice of rehabilitation exercise and what type of video game
would be the most appropriate? This question revealed itself to be impossible
to solve at the early stage of our study. Indeed, on the one hand the engineering
research teams are not trained to master rehabilitation issues and on the other
hand, medical staff could not know what capabilities to expect from SGs.

To solve this issue we decided that instead of looking to solve a single pathology with a specialized SG (that could only satisfied a minority) we would make the four SGs covering the maximum number of (1) rehabilitation exercises for legs and (2), categories of games (*e.g.* 1st or 3rd person, 2D or 3D, target for teenagers or elder persons).

The SGs presented in this work have been designed and developed by the HE-Arc (HES-SO) using the game engine called Unity (http://docs.unity3d.com/Manual/index.html). Using this game engine enables to manage not only sound effects and graphics renderings but a convenient physical engine and input/output for a very large variety of devices in an almost plug-and-play environment. For the ones not familiar with these kind of product, an average of 50 C-sharp classes of 30 lines were implemented for each SGs, which is tiny compared to the prototype we implemented using *MOgre* (a C-sharp version of the Ogre engine).

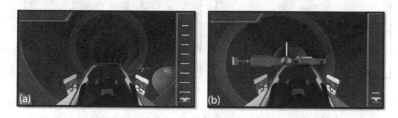

Fig. 11. *GateCrossing*, the first SG of the platform, 3D first person game in space focusing on precision: (a) beginning of the training; (b) arriving at the space station.

SG#1: *GateCrossing.* Figure 11 summarizes the first SG entitled "GateCrossing". Specifications of the game are the following:

- **Scenario:** user is a young space pilot learning how to use a spaceship by going through gates from the training station to the Mir space station;
- **Rehabilitation task:** asynchronous control of the legs (y-axis: based on the feet distance difference) and ankles (x-axis: difference of angles) to make the spaceship turn. To avoid the exercise to be too complex, both rotations are not played simultaneously;
- **Technologies:** proportional resistance of simulation to the angle of rotation;
- **Originality aspects:** precision results in boosts that require more attention;
- **Target:** all ages, all genders.

SG#2: *BikeRehab.* Figure 12 summarizes the second SG entitled "BikeRehab". Specifications of the game are the following:

- **Scenario:** the player is delivering pizza as soon as he can avoid obstacles that decrease his appearance (*e.g.* mud splashes on the clothes if driving on puddles) and jeopardize his potential tip;

- **Rehabilitation task:** cycling;
- **Technologies:** different positive or negative slopes;
- **Originality aspects:** Mario-like game with cartoon-like rendering where player can customize his avatar;
- **Target:** mainly kids or young adults, both genders with some options oriented toward female.

Fig. 12. *BikeRehab*, the second SG of the platform, 2D Mario-like game focusing on endurance: (a) and (b) different types of slopes and environments (*i.e.* soft valley or arid volcano); (c) tuning window; (d) scenario selection window.

SG#3: *BeTheBall*. Figure 13 summarizes the third SG entitled "BeTheBall". Specifications of the game are the following:

- **Scenario:** Perform at a faster path motivated by his own high-score presented in the form of a ghost;
- **Rehabilitation task:** press leg;
- **Technologies:** haptic simulating the inertia of an heavy stone ball;
- **Originality aspects:** maximizing accuracy and velocity;
- **Target:** male teenagers and young adults.

SG#4: *PicsWalk*. Figure 14 summarizes the fourth and last SG of the current platform entitled "PicsWalk". Specifications of the game are the following:

- **Scenario:** take the best pictures that answer a specific theme such as "only wild animals" which doing a walk in a park;
- **Rehabilitation task:** simulating the walking movement approximated with a flat ellipse;
- **Technologies:** feeling the ground with haptic (*work in progress*);
- **Originality aspects:** many animals and plants are hidden in different landscapes;
- **Target:** adults or seniors.

Fig. 13. *BeTheBall*, the third SG of the platform, 3D third person racing game focusing on cardio: (a) and (c) different types of races and environments (*i.e.* tropic and desert): (b) and (d) presentation of the ghost simulating the best race of the player.

3.3   User Tests

As shown by the Fig. 15 the system was tested by 33 health specialists, two third were rehabilitation experts, *i.e.* physiotherapist, occupational therapist, physical medicine and rehabilitation doctors, the other were mainly neuro-psychologists and neuroscience researchers. The original goal was to identify gaming properties and attributes that health specialists recognized to be potentially useful, useless, or inadequate for rehabilitation.

It is not possible to extract absolute conclusions since compared SGs were having different contexts –*e.g.* scenario, user interface, interactive devices. Nevertheless, obtaining opinions, appreciations, and comments from health professionals provide improving future professional SG designs. From this hypothesis, interesting factors directly related to VR were simultaneously demonstrated from this experiment: a clear positive effect for the use for Haptic and HMD with serious games for rehabilitation.

As shown in the Fig. 16, SG *gameplay* receives positive answers in both cases: using haptic linked to HMD or not. Two screen based games (*i.e.* "BikeRehab" and "BeTheBall") even had a median both at "strongly agree" level.

Before comparing potential effects of haptic and HMD devices, the effectiveness of the SGs have to be check: gameplay as well as rehabilitation exercises must be certified. The Fig. 16 shows in blue the strong positive appreciation of the SGs gameplay. In red, current rehabilitation exercises were also considered positively but moderately. This can be explained by the large range of type of

Fig. 14. *PicsWalk*, the fourth SG of the platform, 3D first person game bringing user attention to the surrounding world: (a) and (b) different types of walks (*i.e.* in a forest, around a lake); (c) example of animal to take in picture; (d) final visualization of pictures with corresponding scoring.

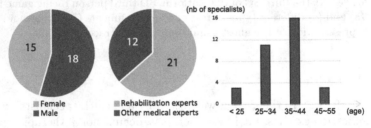

Fig. 15. Users' profiles.

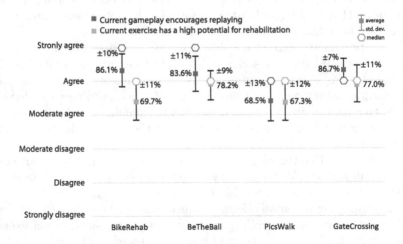

Fig. 16. Gameplay and exercise potentials of each the serious games: (in blue) for replaying, i.e. more rehabilitation; (in red) as a tool for rehabilitation (Color figure online).

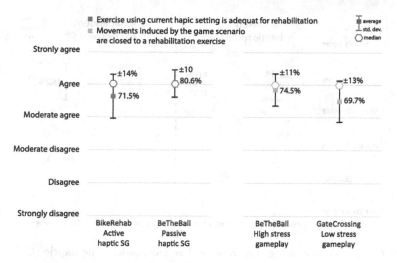

Fig. 17. Comparing SGs using interactive vs. passive haptic (Color figure online).

health specialists. Nevertheless, none of the 33 strongly disliked any of the four SGs exercises.

Haptic Device Effects. The left part of Fig. 17 studies the effect of active or passive haptic game modes. Basically, if the SG context often directly interferes with users such as the slope to climb suddenly increases or user's avatar hits a virtual object, we name this mode to be active; passive is where the SG does not often gives user these haptic feedbacks. This notion of active/passive is not to be mixed with the training mode called "passive-motion". Both game modes seem to receive a moderate positive judgment for correctness of the rehabilitation exercise.

The right part of Fig. 17 shows the effect of game ambiance, loud music and visual effect for "BeTheBall" vs. relaxing futuristic musics and smoothly space motion for "GateCrossing". Similarly to the two previous games, users have moderately positively appreciated the consistency of the game scenario.

Results from the Fig. 18 compare if there is a difference between exercises with different haptic robots use: in blue, both legs had dependent movements (*i.e.* "linked haptic robots"); in red, each leg could interact freely with the corresponding haptic robot (*i.e.* independent haptic robots). Even if the difference is relatively small, the second category was observed to be more appreciated by specialists.

HMD Device Effects. Appreciations of displaying the graphical environment on a classical display or an HMD are illustrated by the Fig. 19. We were surprised to realized that not only HMD was well supported during 10–20 min but it demonstrates to bring strong enthusiasm from heath specialists.

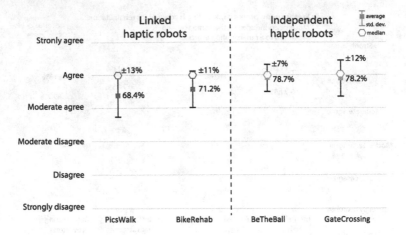

Fig. 18. Comparing SGs using constrain vs. free movement using haptic (Color figure online).

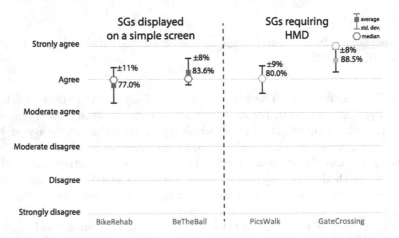

Fig. 19. Comparing appreciation on graphical environment using classic displays or HMD (Color figure online).

Global Results. Based on more than 200 comments and suggestions from health specialists this model has shown a very strong enthusiasm: physiotherapists, occupational therapists, neuro-psychologists, and rehabilitation doctors are willing to start contributing to a professional prototype; specialists not directly concerned by lower locomotor system suggested new tracks for using VR devices with SGs in their own professional contexts.

4   Discussion

This paper has presented a process pipeline using Serious Games for the rehabilitation of legs with a various set of physical exercises (*e.g.* rhythmic, periodic or free motions). The games were designed using haptic and HMD tools for immersion and constant immediate feedback on the players? performance and virtual environment (2D, 3D first and third person views).

This interdisciplinary model has been designed involving four research teams and two medical partner groups. Based on an anonymous survey within 33 specialists, virtual reality devices (*i.e.* HMD and haptic robots) applied to serious games (SGs), have demonstrated not only to be convincing tools for health but has shown to have very strong potential in the field. Probably the most significant conclusion of this work is that it demonstrates that even if the graphics, sounds, and scenarios of the SGs were relatively poor compared to nowadays standard video games, health professional are strongly welcoming VR tools based on SGs.

As introduced in the user test Sect. 3.3, the original objective was to identify within the tested SGs and the VR hardware the properties and patterns that medical experts believe to have a high potential for medical rehabilitation purposes. Guided by these results research and development teams are currently redesigning SGs coupled with adequate VR devices. We believe that related research in the domain should study the use of other VR hardware cannot be restricted to haptic and HMD. Hospitals and health professionals are seeking to speed up functional recovery and to increase patient's functional outcomes and even with limited resources. They are eager to adopt technical means able to enhance motor relearning. The use of rehabilitation haptic robots, SGs or the combination of the two are interesting treatment options in this respect.

We are convinced that beyond the use of advanced VR devices, user interfaces should offer a more human like relationship to patients. In this domain, we are looking for the developing of a SG stimulating mirror-neuron where virtual agent including realistic facial expression (*i.e.* consistent emotion models [GAS+11] based on classified patient to machine conversation) would play a fundamental role for empathic relationship, a crucial issue for the increase of the number of elderly persons, which will undergo motor rehabilitation.

Acknowledgement. This work was supported by the University of Applied Sciences Western Switzerland (HES-SO) interdisciplinary grant (contract no. 13IT25-S37771) as apart of the Serious Games for Rehabilitation project. We would like to thank all the health professionals that participated to the investigation or contributed otherwise to this project; many thanks are also to the CHUV (Lausanne University Hospital, Switzerland) for hosting the investigation team and the equipment for these tests. We also would like to thank Prof. François Birling, Prof. Yassin Rekik, Mr. Gael Boquet, Nicolas Perret, and Mr. François Rémy for there respective contributions.

References

[AEI+08] Alamri, A., Eid, M., Iglesias, R., Shirmohammadi, S., El Saddik, A.: Haptic virtual rehabilitation exercises for poststroke diagnosis. IEEE Trans. Instrum. Meas. **57**(9), 1876–1884 (2008)

[BB14] Brahnam, S., Brooks, A.L.: Two innovative healthcare technologies at the intersection of serious games, alternative realities and play therapy. In: Innovation in Medicine and Healthcare. IOS Press (2014)

[BW05] Barnes, M.P., Ward, A.P.: Oxford University Press (2005)

[BWFB03] Barreca, S., Wolf, S.L., Fasoli, S., Bohannon, R.: Treatment interventions for the paretic upper limb of stroke survivors: a critical review. Neurorehabil. Neural Repair **17**(4), 220–226 (2003)

[Cla94] Clavel, R.: Robots paralleles. Techniques de lIngenieur, traite Informatique industrielle (1994)

[Dob05] Dobkin, B.H.: Rehabilitation after stroke. Engl. J. Med. (Proceedings of NEJM) **16**, 1677–1684 (2005)

[GAS+11] Gobron, S., Ahn, J., Silvestre, Q., Thalmann, D., Rank, S., Skowron, M., Paltoglou, G., Thelwall, M..: An interdisciplinary vr-architecture for 3d chatting with non-verbal communication. In: Coquillart, S., Steed, A., Welch, G. (eds.) EGVE/EuroVR, pp. 87–94. Eurographics Association, 20–21 September 2011

[HACH+04] Hayward, V., Astley, O.R., Cruz-Hernandez, M., Grant, D., Gabriel, R.T.: Haptic interfaces and devices. Sensor Rev. **24**(1), 16–29 (2004)

[HLS+13] Hannig, A., Lemos, M., Spreckelsen, C., Ohnesorge-Radtke, U., Rafai, N.: Skills-o-mat: Computer supported interactive motion- and game-based training in mixing alginate in dental education. J. Educ. Comput. Res. **48**(3), 315–343 (2013)

[Hog85] Hogan, N.: Impedance control: an approach to manipulation. J. Dyn. Syst. Meas. Contr. Trans. ASME **107**(1), 1–24 (1985)

[HSV+09] Ham, R., Sugar, T.G., Vanderborght, B., Hollander, K.W., Lefeber, D.: Compliant actuator designs. IEEE Robot. Autom. Mag. **16**(3), 81–94 (2009)

[IWB+99] Lacoboni, M., Woods, R.P., Brass, M., Bekkering, H., Mazziotta, J.C., Rizzolatti, G.: Cortical mechanisms of human imitation. Science **286**(1), 2526–2528 (1999)

[LCP09] Langhorn, P., Coupar, F., Pollock, A.: Motor recovery after stroke: a systematic review. Lancet Neurol. **8**, 741–754 (2009)

[LCS+11] Lange, B., Chang, C.Y., Suma, E., Newman, B.A., Rizzo, S., Bolas, M.: Development and evaluation of low cost game-based balance rehabilitation tool using the microsoft kinect sensor. In: Annual international conference of the IEEE on Engineering in Medicine and Biology Society, EMBC 2011, pp. 1831–1834. IEEE (2011)

[MG05] Mattar, A.A.G., Gribble, P.L.: Motor learning by observing. Neuron **46**(1), 153–160 (2005)

[MJA14] Ma, M., Jain, L.C., Anderson, P.: VirtuaL, Augmented Reality and Serious Games for Healthcare 1. Springer, Berlin (2014)

[NLCZ+] Nichols-Larsen, D.S., Clark, P.C., Zeringue, A., Greenspan, A., Blanton, S.: Factors influencing stroke survivors quality of life during subacute recovery

[RC04]   Rizzolatti, G., Craighero, L.: The mirror-neuron system. Annu. Rev. Neurosci. **27**, 169–192 (2004)

[RFDC09] Rizzolatti, G., Fabbri-Destro, M., Craighero, L.: Mirror neurons and their clinical relevance. Nat. Clin. Pract. Neurol. **5**(1), 24–34 (2009)

[RL11]   Ratey, J.J., Loehr, J.E.: The positive impact of physical activity on cognition during adulthood: a review of underlying mechanisms, evidence and recommendations. Rev. Neurosci. **22**(2), 171–185 (2011)

[RMJ+05] Rizzo, A., McLaughlin, M., Jung, Y.B., Peng, W., Yeh, S.C., Zhu, W.R.: Virtual therapeutic environments with haptics: an interdisciplinary approach for developing post-stroke rehabilitation systems. In: Arabnia, H.R. (ed.):Proceedings of the 2005 International Conference on Computers for People with Special Needs, CPSN 2005, pp. 70–76, Arabnia, HR, 20 June–23 September 2005

[RRDV+15] Rodriguez, A., Rey, B., Vara, M.D., Wrzesien, M., Alcaniz, M., Banos, R.M., Perez-Lopez, D.: A vr-based serious game for studying emotional regulation in adolescents. IEEE Comput. Graphics Appl. **35**(1), 65–73 (2015)

[SCCC08] Stefan, K., Classen, J., Celnik, P., Cohen, L.G.: Concurrent action observation modulates paractice-induced motor memory formation. Eur. J. Neurosci. **27**(3), 730–738 (2008)

[SCD+05] Stefan, K., Cohen, L.G., Duque, J., Mazzocchio, R., Celnik, P., Sawaki, L., Ungerleider, L., Classen, J.: Formation of a motor memory by action observation. J. Neurosci. **25**(41), 9339–9346 (2005)

[SCK+10] Sabri, H., Cowan, B., Kapralos, B., Porte, M., Backstein, D., Dubrowskie, A.: Serious games for knee replacement surgery procedure education and training. Procedia Soc. Behav. Sci. (Innovation and Creativity in Education) **2**(2), 3483–3488 (2010)

[SF12]   Sale, P., Franceschini, M.: Action observation and mirror neuron network: a tool for motor stroke rehabilitation. Eur. J. Phys. Rehabil. Med. **48**(2), 313–318 (2012)

[WWM+06] Wolf, S.L., Winstein, C.J., Miller, J.P., Taub, E., Uswatte, G., Morris, D., Giuliani, C., Light, K.E., Nichols-Larsen, D.S.: Effect of constraint induced movement therapy on upper extremity function 3 to 9 months after stroke: the exite randomized clinical trial. J. Am. Med. Assoc. **296**(17), 2095–2104 (2006)

VR-Based Serious Game Designed
for Medical Ethics Training

Cristian Lorenzini[✉], Claudia Faita, Marcello Carrozzino, Franco Tecchia, and
Massimo Bergamasco

PercRo, TeCIP Institute, Scuola Superiore Sant'Anna, Via Alamanni 13b,
San Giuliano Terme, 56017 Pisa, Italy
{c.lorenzini,c.faita,carrozzino,f.tecchia,bergamasco}@sssup.it

Abstract. Virtual Reality technology is increasingly used for game based
learning application, i.e. Digital Serious Games. Simulating reality serious games
improve technical skills in different fields and it is often used in medical area. In
this research is described "A Day In The HOspital" (ADITHO), a serious game
aiming at increase the process of decision making in young physicians through a
training that reproduce a realistic clinical situation. In ADITHO the player, from
a first person perspective, has to tackle important ethical issues for facing a clinical
case. After a description of the game architecture, this paper present an evaluation
of the usability of the system and an assessment of the user's sense of presence
and immersion within Virtual Environment during the game experience.

Keywords: Digital serious game · Medical ethics · Medical training · Virtual
reality · Problem based learning · Decision making · Physician-patient relationship

1 Introduction

Virtual Reality (VR), or more formally precise, Virtual Environments (VEs), can be
defined as a complex technology based on low-level technologies (such as 3D graphics,
robotics, etc....) able to recreate an environment in which the user feels completely
immersed and can interact.

VEs are increasingly used as tool of educational, training, teaching and dissemination
because they increase users' knowledge involving users through sensory inputs as
images, sounds, 3d realistic objects etc. VEs can be also used to acquire novel knowledge
by exploring the environment and simulating certain daily life activities in a realistic
way. For this reason the virtual training has been effactually adopted in many different
context [1, 2].

Digital Serious Games (DSGs) are types of VE applications intentionally designed
for "serious" purposes such as corporate training, education, health, public policy, and
strategic communication objective [2]. DSGs represent a well-defined subset of the
reality that can simulate or simplify real life conditions through a coherent scenario. The
first multimedia DSGs were developed for U.S. Army in 2002 (www.america-
sarmy.com), then videogames have been increasingly adopted for training, advertising,
simulation or education. The Woodrow Wilson Center for International Scholar in

© Springer International Publishing Switzerland 2015
L.T. De Paolis and A. Mongelli (Eds.): AVR 2015, LNCS 9254, pp. 220–232, 2015.
DOI: 10.1007/978-3-319-22888-4_16

Washington, D.C. founded the DSG Initiative, and the term "serious games" became widespread (www.seriousgames.org) as "games for purposes other than entertainment". The efficiency of DSGs on training and education are corroborated by a low cost on implementation and a wide usability. The benefits of training based on video game and the ability in transfer the acquired knowledge and skills to the operational environment were evaluated by measuring subjective factors such as immersion and presence [3, 4]. Immersion is a powerful experience in game and it may contribute to the amount of information acquired, skills developed and subsequent transfer of knowledge to real environments [4, 5]. Whereas presence is the subjective feeling to be actually present in the computer-mediated environment even when one is physically situated in another [6–8]. For this reason a strong sense of presence within VE increases motivation and provides a more engaging experience [9].

DSGs use the intrinsic playful aspects of a game to make the learning process more engaging and effective. DSGs are commonly based on the playful metaphor called Problem-Based Learning (PBL). PBL is an education methodology used to orient students to reflect on given problems, and to transfer the skills for facing and solving the problems themselves [10, 11].

DSGs can support the development of a number of different expertise as analytical and spatial skills, strategic skills and insight, learning and recollection capabilities, psychomotor skills, visual selective attention [12, 13]. DSGs can be classified by the type of educational content (i.e., school, military, medical, professional, etc.), the principle of learning (i.e., social problem solving, cognitive problem solving, knowledge acquisition for exploration etc.), the target age group (i.e., school, college, post-graduate etc.) or for the type of games technologies (i.e., Desktop environment, HDMI and Cave immersive environment, etc....).

DSGs based on VE applications are effective training tools because it can simulate countless real-life scenario in an ecological way [14].

This paper presents A Day In The HOspital (ADITHO), a first-person VR-based DSG designed as a Problem Solving game which faces the issue of Medical Ethics.

Since healthcare is considered one of the main decision makers worldwide, serious games in the medical field has been wide used. For this reason a lot of medical games were developed, and they can be classified as follow [15]:

- the main purpose (to gain knowledge or skills, simulate situations to avoid/concern risks, safety, budgets etc.),
- the role of the players (if the player is a patient or not a patient),
- the stage of disease (susceptibility, clinical disease, recovery, disability or death),
- functionality and features (application area, interface, game engine, health objective, etc....).

All this studies do not pay attention to the ethical behavior of the physician in the medical practice. The novelty of our research was to create a games in which the player in the role of a physician and has to address a clinical case taking care to relate ethically with patient, his family and colleagues. In ADITHO players learn to deal with complex relationship and gain new skill on medical ethics, by facing a clinical case in an ecological way.

The importance of ethics in clinical profession is underestimated. It often depends on the building of the medical curriculum. It has been shown, in fact, that most medical students has received a good theoretical knowledge in ethics but a poor training [16]. In order to create a correct "informed choice" based on a correct ethical approach between patient and physician, is fundamental to pursuit a shared decision-making process in which patients are considered an autonomous person [17]. ADITHO focuses on the interaction between the player (medical personnel or medical students) and patients, family and colleagues within a 3D environment representing a virtual hospital. Like in a real clinical case the physician has to adopt the correct behavior to address the situation. The aim of the game is to accumulate the maximum score by adopting an attitude compatible with medical ethics. The game has been developed as a part of SONNA (www.sonna.unisi.it), a larger research regional project aimed at investigating novel technology-enhanced learning methodologies based on the use of social media and 3D Virtual Environments [18].

The goal of ADITHO is to become a useful tool both for training physicians in medical ethics and for evaluating ethical profile of the user. In order to assess this aim the study presents the evaluation of the sense of presence feeling by the user during the game experience and the evaluation on the usability of the system. An experimental session was performed by 12 subjects, who had to face a clinical case and take a decision on the best therapy for the patient, bearing in mind all ethical variables in play. In this paper, first the game storyboard, architecture and mechanics, then the experimental procedure participants, result and discussion are presented.

2   Game Storyboard and Evaluation Methods

In this section we describes the game storyboard, and the criteria of the evaluation of the game.

2.1   The Game Storyboard

The patient in treatment in ADITHO is a young person suffering from cystic fibrosis (CF). This is a genetic disorder higher in young Caucasian populations (1 in 2000 – 1 in 2500 people in medium, but it is variable in base of the country where the data is analyzed). The survival level is influenced by a variety of factors, some of which are modifiable by health services and some of which are not (such as the genotype or other socioeconomics factors). For example, in US the standardized mortality is calculated from 4.4 to 25 per 1000 depending of genotype combination [19]. The commonest clinical presentation of CF remains acute or persistent respiratory symptoms and other complications [20]. When the disease causes crisis the role of the physician is extremely complicated not only in the context of therapy, but also in the relationship with patient and his family.

In the game, the player treats a patient that came back in therapy after some respiratory crisis and have to decide the best way to proceed in order to grand a correct medical ethics behavior. For that he had to interact with the patient and his parents investigating their opinions and take information from several other medical personnel (See Sect. 3). A player can also confront with other players that are playing in the same moment in a shared room of the hospital.

ADITHO starts with the choice of the avatar gender and a help guide screen describing all commands. Users are initially located in the hospital hall and a nurse welcomes and remind them to visit the CF patient in his room, to assess his health. Then the game develops through a series of events connected with the evolution of the clinical case.

2.2 Training and Evaluation of Users' Ethical Profile

In order to evaluate the medical ethics profile of participants, the serious game provide to track player's behaviors during the game session and assign to all of them a combination of score systems based on 2 different criterion that will generate a single user profile. The first criteria is based on the Italian Code of Medical Ethics 2014 (CME) [21]. CME is a system of moral principles democratically chosen by physicians to which they should standardize their behaviors. This code should be based on some ethics principles that are universally shared [22] since ethics looks at the inner attitudes and to the intentionality of the agents [23]. The other criteria is, for that, founded on the four principles of biomedical ethics postulated by Tom Beauchamp and James Childress [24], and in particular:

- Respect for autonomy (A): physicians recognize self-determination and give the opportunity of individuals to make reasoned informed choices;
- Beneficence (B1): physicians have to balance the benefits against the risks and costs of treatment;
- Non-Maleficience (B2): physicians have to consider that although all treatment involves some harm, even if minimal, the harm should not be disproportionate to the benefits of treatment;
- Justice (J): physicians have to take in consideration that health resources are scarce and their distribution depends of the decision of who gets what treatment.

In ADITHO, B1 and B2 were combined because of their similarities in a single principle abbreviated B. In order to evaluate the ethical attitude of the physician it was added another important criteria:

- Communication (C): the capability of the physicians accompanying the patient in his diagnostic-therapeutic path of sharing meaningful information and show cooperative attitudes.

The correlations between the scores assigned to each answer at the experimental questions, in terms of the combination of the four principles (A, B, J, C) and the ethical code (CME), was analyzed using a two-tailed Spearman rank-order test. We found a significant correlation for all the analyzed variable (Spearman's $rho(27) > .66$, $p < .01$ for all the test).

The game allows the users to acquire several information about the clinical case by talking with Non-Player Characters (NPCs) (See Sect. 3) and by accessing to the diary of the patient. Moreover, the player could consult several resources linked to the specificity of clinical case (web resources, videos and relevant written opinions, i.e. the positions of religions about transplantation).

The dialogues with NPCs and the consultation of the patient's diary contribute to the scoring system. Some of the dialogues are forced by the system (as they are needed to proceed to the final decision), while others could not be done by the players to complete the game. Dialogues are composed by a sequence of sentences encoded by the system and a set of sentences with multiple choice answers. Each choice results in a score in the range [0, +4] following CME and/or in the range [−2, +2] following one or more of the principles of ethics tracked (A, B, J and C). Then, players go to the last dialogue in which they communicate to the patient the diagnostic-therapeutic path, and the game shows the user profile generated in the game session (Fig. 1). It is saved on the web server (Table 1).

When a player has completed all the mandatory dialogues he can take a final decision, between intubate the patient before the transplant or give up the transplant and proceed with palliative care. Since ADITHO is focused on ethical issues, neither of these two choices gave a score to the user.

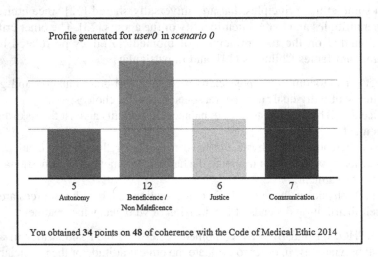

Fig. 1. This picture shows the user's profile. The bars visualized in different colors represent the four principle of biomedical ethics: red – Respect of autonomy; green – Beneficence /Non Maleficence; yellow – Justice and blue – Communication. The sentence declares the score on code of medical Ethics (Colour figure online).

3   Game Architecture and Design

ADITHO is implemented separating the core game engine (CGE) from a set of game information including the resources and the interaction from the users and the resources, as an integrated framework that allow the developing of different games. CGE is realized using XVR technology [25]. This is a framework to realize web-based [26, 27] and/or stand-alone interactive VR applications [28], as in this case.

Table 1. An example of a complete user profile. Each question is associate with a specific score. In the bottom the sum of the score obtained (Profile) and the competition time.

Question	Answer	A	B	J	C	CME
Q1	2	0	−2	−2	1	0
Q2	3	2	1	2	2	4
Q3	2	2	2	2	2	4
Q4	2	2	2	2	2	4
Q5	3	0	0	0	0	4
Q6	3	2	−2	−2	1	0
Q7	2	−2	−1	0	0	0
Q8	2	2	1	2	2	4
Q9	3	2	2	0	2	4
Q10	3	1	1	−1	1	2
Dairy	yes					8
Profile		11	4	3	13	34
Intubation:	yes	Duration: 26 min				

CGE interprets and manages game information, which are described in an XML file that contains the set of the resources to load and the relationship between the resources each other and the users' interactions with them. This file describes the game mechanics in terms of a set of different actions (divided by typology).

CGE activates actions if all their enabling condition are verified based on CGE global states. Actions can be timer, images/video pop-ups, sounds or interaction with or between scene objects. Conditions are verifiable using different states, characterized by an integer value that can change during the game session. When actions terminate their execution, they can generate one or more reactions. These can modify the aspect of the scene and/or modify one of the CGE global state. This can simply disable the current action and trigger the activation of other actions. In this way, more actions can be enabled in the same time, but, otherwise, the actions can be activated in an ordered sequence.

The game provides agents animated by the system as NPCs. NPCs are animated characters realized using Autodesk 3D Studio Max and Motion Builder. At last they are exported to the native geometry format of XVR, using a particular care in producing low-poly versions of the models and low-size animation and texture. This is possible because XVR easily produces a wide range of animations with a reduced set of resources.

Dialogues with NPCs are described in the XML resource file. The base element of a dialogue is a sentence, a single phrase from the user to the NPC (or vice versa) used to compose linear dialogues. The other dialogue element is the question, which can be alternated to other sentences. A question is a request of an answer from a NPC inter-locutor to the user. Depending of user's choice and dialogue description, different answers can generate different dialogues, developing thus a dialogue structured as an oriented graph without loops. Answers can also generate reactions to modify global states. This feature is useful to "remember" different choices in the continuation of the story of the game, and saving them to the server allowing to reconstruct the log of the user for his evaluation (Table 1).

XML file also describes a simple GUI. Enabling conditions can show/hide and acti-vate/deactivate GUI buttons in similar way of the actions. In ADITHO game, buttons allow the user to open some resources and a game help. A fourth button non available at the beginning of the game allow the user to complete the game taking a decision about the clinical case (Fig. 2).

Fig. 2. A question on a dialogue with the patient.

The game has a background chatter effect with a variable volume depending on the room where the player is to increase the immersion on the environment and other sound features corresponding to ambient sounds such as the ring tone of the phone/fax.

The game also provides a shared environment in which players can interact with each other as it happens in real case. We simulate this possibility with the creation of a shared location (a coffee room) in the virtual hospital. When a player is inside this room he can see by the other users as an animated character (similar as NPC) and all the users can speak each other using an integrated text chat. They can also "tag" other users in their messages using the name of the tagger user. For example, if user_A wrote "Hello user_B", all the users in the room will see a black, normal, message except user_B that will see a red, tagged, message.

4   User Experience and Usability Test

The aim of this research was to evaluate if the game experience of ADITHO is charac-terized by both a strong sense of presence and a high level of "playability". The effectiveness of social interaction of the game was also investigated. For this purpose three different kinds of questionnaires were used. In this section the questionnaires, participants and results are presented.

4.1 Questionnaire

In order to evaluate the usability of the system, the System Usability Scale (SUS) [29] was adopted. SUS is a 10 items Likert scale used to investigate the subjective assessment of usability by covering effectiveness, efficiency and satisfaction of the experience. Each statement indicates the degree of agreement or disagreement in a 5 point scale. The measure of usability cover the effectiveness (i.e. the ability of users to complete tasks using the system), the efficiency (i.e. the level of resource consumed in performing tasks) and the satisfaction (i.e. users subjective reaction to using the system). Since usability does not exist in any absolute sense [29], it was adapted to the game nine statements and it was added fours specific questions related to the starting demo, the movement system inside the environment, the understanding of the task during the game and the usefulness of coffee room as social place.

Moreover, four specific questions related to the test session, the movement system in the environment the understanding of the task during the game and the usefulness of the coffee room as social place were added. The level of user immersion and involvement in the virtual game was evaluated by using Presence Questionnaire (PQ) [8]. PQ is composed by 19 items and other 5 for VEs including sound and haptic, rated on a 7 points Likert scale. PQ uses 4 main categories of factors:

- Control (degree, immediacy, anticipation, mode, and physical environment modifiability);
- Sensory (modality, environmental richness, multimodal presentation, consistency of multimodal information, the degree of movement perception, and active search);
- Distraction (isolation, selective attention, and interface awareness);
- Realism (scene realism, information consistent with the objective world, meaningfulness of the experience, separation, and anxiety/disorientation).

These factors that exert their influence on presence by affecting both involvement, immersion [8]. We used 12 items of the questionnaire: Q1–Q5 and Q10–Q11 for Control Factor; Q4, Q6, Q8, Q12 for Sensory Factor; Q9 for Distract Factor, and Q7 for Real Factor.

The third questionnaire was adopted to investigate the sense of presence in a social space [30]. This questionnaire is composed by 5 items on a 7 points rating scale, and is requests to the users if they entered in coffee room and interacted with other players during the game.

The very last section was an open-end question in which we have collected feedback and suggestions of participants in order to improve the game experience in future application.

4.2 Participants

A sample of 12 members of the Perceptual Robotics Laboratory of Scuola Superiore Sant'Anna in Pisa composed by 3 females and 9 males, age between 25–40 (30.58 ± 4.88) was recruited for the experiment. Before starting with the test session they filled a questionnaire in which we rated on a 5 points Likert scale from 1 (no experience) to 5 (frequent use) their experience with computer (average 5 ± 0), video-games (average 3 ± 1.28), VEs (average 3.75 ± 0.97) and DSG (75 % of the users know DSGs and 50 % already played to one or more of them) (Fig. 3).

Fig. 3. Experimental session with some users.

4.3 Procedure

Users played ADITHO in the experimental room of the Perceptual Robotics Laboratory in Pisa. Before starting the experiment they have read and accepted an informed consent for the informal collection of the personal data and in which the experimental procedure was explained. Moreover the experimenters have detailed instructed the participants about the experiment procedure.

A test session was experienced to get familiar with the system. During this phase all players interprets a virtual agent in the same hospital ward of ADITHO and has to talk with a NPC that explains him the functions of the game through the assignment of specific tasks. After this session players had learned how to navigate the environment and procedure to talk with NPCs. When all participants finished with this session the proper game started. All the users have played the game at the same time, using computers connected to a network in order to allow them to communicate each other. A summary screen with the obtained score was shown to participants at the end of the game (Fig. 1).

Finally all participants have completed all the questionnaires previous mentioned.

5 Results and Future Works

In this session the results about the score assigned to each participants and the questionnaires were showed and discussed. Future development and experimentation of the game were presented.

5.1 Results and Discussion

In addition to the questionnaires assessing the subjective experience of ADITHO, also the final score and the ethics profile resulting at the end of the game was collected. In Fig. 4 is shown the correlation of the users results both in CME and in the sum of the four principles as explained in Sect. 2.2.

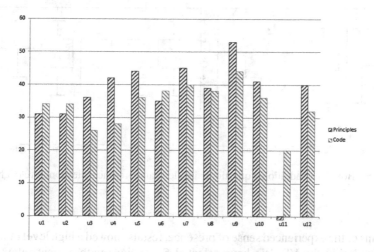

Fig. 4. Comparison of profiles of each user according to the four principles and CME. The left blue barred columns are the profiles generated with the sum of the principles A, B, J and C, the right red barred columns are the CME profiles (Colour figure online).

Having the participants no medical experience, these information are collected to be used as comparative data for a forthcoming wider investigation on the game involving real physicians.

The SUS score was calculated in the range 0–100 based on questionnaire guidelines [29]. Very high results were obtained with the average score of 74.5 ± 15.2 as shown in Fig. 5.

Additional questions showed a good results especially for Q10 "I found the starting demo very useful to use", and Q11 "I found difficult to understand what to do during the game". In question Q12 "I found very easy to use the movement system" a lower score was obtained compared to the others questions (Fig. 6). This is in line with the suggestions collected in the open-end question, where many participants proposed to improve the movement system. They pointed out that the navigation system was not

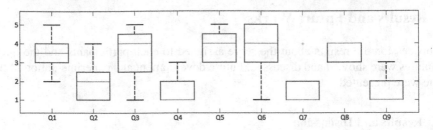

Fig. 5. Boxplots of SUS questionnaire.

optimal, both in terms of keyboard layout and in terms of ease of movement inside the VE, suggesting the use of a wider choice of keyboard/mouse combinations.

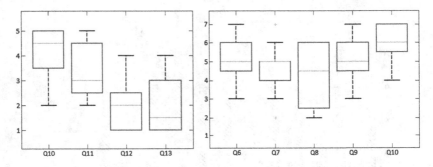

Fig. 6. Boxplot of additional questionnaire (left) and presence questionnaire (right).

In terms of the experienced sense of presence, results showed a high level of involved and immersion in the VE. We have selected 5 questions with a great relevance for ADITHO, from Q6 to Q10, representing all 4 factors [8]. Q7 *"How much did your experience in the VE seem consistent with your real world experience"* obtained a high rate even if no participant had experience in the medical field. This could be explained as a strong level of adjustment to the virtual game by the user. This explanation is in line with the very high rate obtained in questions Q9 *"How involved were you in the VE experience"* and Q10 *"How quickly did you adjust to the VE experience"* (Fig. 6). A strong dispersion in the median was obtained in question Q8 *"How compelling was your sense of moving around inside the VE"*. This result is consistent with the deficiency in the movement system observed by users in the open end question and in line with the rate obtained in the additional question Q12 (Fig. 6).

Only 2 subjects used the coffee room to interact each other. This could can be due to the fact that players had little competencies to share about the clinical case and also because it was not easy to find other people in the common room just by chance.

In conclusion, high results obtained in SUS and PQ questionnaires corroborate the efficiency of the system in terms of usability and user experience and motivate to further experimentations with real subjects involved in medical training.

5.2 Future Works

The results of the experiments showed two main critical issues. Because of their expertise with computers, participants found WASD keys better than arrows keys to move inside the environment, especially using laptop PCs. For the future all the two modality will be enabled. The second one is given by our monitoring of the game session that involved the players. Several users move in collaborative area but they do it in different moments, except for 2 players that have an interactive session each other. For that, in future experiment we add two features:

- a "info" cloud on the bottom left of the scene that advice the player that one or more users are on collaborative area;
- an invitation for a "coffee break" after a given time from the begin of the game: if the player does not go to chat room after this invitation, he cannot take any decision for resolve the clinical case and terminate the game. We estimate empirically 15 min the time required before the invitation, taking into account that the first game test was from 15 to 35 min.

After this experimentation and the resolution of these critical issues, the next step for the validation of the serious game is a wider investigation that involves some physicians or, more generically, a group of medical personnel.

Acknowledgment. We thank to Stefano Miniati and Patrizia Funghi from University of Siena and Professor Francesco Giunta from University of Pisa for their helpful comments in ethical contents of the game and all Perceptual Robotics people that participate to this experiment.

References

1. Seymour, N.E., Gallagher, A.G., Roman, S.A., O'Brien, M.K., Bansal, V.K., Andersen, D.K., Satava, R.M.: Virtual reality training improves operating room performance: results of a randomized, double-blinded study. Ann. Surg. **236**(4), 458 (2002)
2. Zyda, M.: From visual simulation to virtual reality to games. Computer **38**(9), 25–32 (2005)
3. Muchinsky, P.M.: Psychology Applied to Work. Cengage Learning, Boston (2006)
4. Alexander, A.L., et al.: From gaming to training: a review of studies on fidelity, immersion, presence, and buy-in and their effects on transfer in pc-based simulations and games. In: DARWARS Training Impact Group 5, pp. 1–14 (2005)
5. Brown, E., Cairns, P.: A grounded investigation of game immersion. In: CHI 2004 Extended Abstracts on Human Factors in Computing Systems. ACM (2004)
6. Slater, M., Usoh, M., Steed, A.: Depth of presence in virtual Environments. Presence **3**(2), 130–144 (1994)
7. Slater, M., Frisoli, A., Tecchia, F., Guger, C., Lotto, B., Steed, A., Bernardet, U.: Understanding and realizing presence in the Presenccia project. IEEE Comput. Graph. Appl. **27**(4), 90–93 (2007)
8. Witmer, B.G., Singer, M.J.: Measuring presence in virtual environments: a presence questionnaire. Presence: Teleoperators Virtual Environ **7**(3), 225–240 (1998)
9. Lombard, M., Ditton, T.: At the heart of it all: the concept of presence. J. Comput.-Med. Commun. 3(2) (1997)

10. Barrows, H.S.: Problem-Based Learning: An Approach to Medical Education. Springer Publishing Company, New York (1980)
11. Burguillo, J.C.: Using game theory and competition-based learning to stimulate student motivation and performance. Comput. Educ. **55**(2), 566–575 (2010)
12. Susi, T., Johannesson, M., Backlund, P.: Serious games: an overview (2007)
13. Djaouti, D., Alvarez, J., Jessel, J.-P., Rampnoux, O.: Origins of serious games. In: Ma, M., Oikonomou, A., Jain, L.C. (eds.) Serious Games and Edutainment Applications, pp. 25–43. Springer, London (2011)
14. Ratan, R., Ritterfeld, U.: Classifying serious games. In: Ritterfeld, U., Cody, M.J., Vorderer, P. (eds.) Serious Games: Mechanisms and Effects, pp. 10–24. Routledge, New York (2009)
15. Wattanasoontorn, V., Hernández, R.J.G., Sbert, M.: Serious games for e-health care. In: Cai, Y., Goei, S.L. (eds.) Simulations, Serious Games and Their Applications. Gaming Media and Social Effects, pp. 127–146. Springer, Singapore (2014)
16. Campbell, A.V., Chin, J., Voo, T.-C.: How can we know that ethics education produces ethical doctors? Med. Teach. **29**, 431–436 (2007)
17. Charle, C., Gafni, A., Whelan, T.: Shared decision-making in the medical encounter: what does it mean? (or it takes at least two to tango). Soc. Sci. Med. **44**(5), 681–692 (1997)
18. Carrozzino, M., Evangelista, C., Brondi, R., Lorenzini, C., Bergamasco, M.: Social networks and web-based serious games as novel educational tools. Procedia Comput. Sci. **15**, 303–306 (2012)
19. Walters, S.A.R.A.H., Mehta, A.N.I.L.: Epidemiology of cystic fibrosis. Cyst. Fibrosis **3**, 21–45 (2007)
20. FitzSimmons, S.C.: Cystic Fibrosis foundation. Patient registry. In: 1995 Annual data report. Bethesda, MD (1996)
21. Federazione Nazionale degli Ordini dei Medici Chirurghi e degli Odontoiatri: Codice Di Deontologia Medica (2014). www.fnomceo.it
22. Di Pietro, M.L., Pennacchini, M.: La comparsa della bioetica nei codici di deontologia medica italiani: profilo storico e analisi dei contenuti. Medicina e morale **52**(1), 29–62 (2002)
23. Fineschi V., Busnelli F.D.: Il codice di deontologia medica. Giuffrè (1996)
24. Beauchamp, T.L., Childress, J.F.: Principles of Biomedical Ethics. Oxford University Press, Oxford (2001)
25. Carrozzino, M., Tecchia, F., Bacinelli, S., Cappelletti, C., Bergamasco, M.: Lowering the development time of multimodal interactive application: the real-life experience of the XVR project. In: Proceedings of the 2005 ACM SIGCHI International Conference on Advances in Computer Entertainment Technology, pp. 270–273. ACM (2005)
26. Pecchioli, L., Carrozzino, M., Mohamed, F., Bergamasco, M., Kolbe, T.H.: ISEE: information access through the navigation of a 3D interactive environment. J. Cult. Heritage **12**(3), 287–294 (2011)
27. Carrozzino, M., Brogi, A., Tecchia, F., Bergamasco, M.: The 3D interactive visit to Piazza dei Miracoli, Italy. In: Proceedings of the 2005 ACM SIGCHI International Conference on Advances in Computer Entertainment Technology, pp. 192–195. ACM (2005)
28. Carrozzino, M., Evangelista, C., Scucces, A., Tecchia, F., Tennirelli, G., Bergamasco, M.: The virtual museum of sculpture. In: Proceedings of the 3rd International Conference on Digital Interactive Media in Entertainment and Arts, pp. 100–106. ACM (2008)
29. Brooke, J.: SUS-A quick and dirty usability scale. In: Jordan, P.W., Thomas, B., Weerdmeester, B.A., McClelland, A.L. (eds.) Usability Evaluation in Industry, pp. 189–194. Taylor and Francis, London (1996). 4–7
30. Bailenson, J., Blascovich, J., Beall, A., Loomis, J.: Equilibrium theory revisited: mutual gaze and personal space in virtual environments. Presence **10**(6), 583–598 (2001)

Scalable Medical Viewer for Virtual Reality Environments

Francesco Ricciardi[1,2], Emiliano Pastorelli[2], Lucio Tommaso De Paolis[1](✉),
and Heiko Herrmann[2,3]

[1] Department of Engineering for Innovation, Università Del Salento, Lecce, Italy
{francesco.ricciardi,lucio.depaolis}@unisalento.it
[2] Institute of Cybernetics at Tallinn University of Technology, Tallinn, Estonia
{hh,pastorelli}@cens.ioc.ee
[3] Institut Für Physik, Technische Universotät Chemnitz, Chemnitz, Germany

Abstract. This paper presents a scalable virtual reality-based software for medical visualization. Usable on a desktop, on a head-mounted display or on a CAVE-like system, the application allows the full inspection of CT or MRI images superimposed to the 3D models of the organs built from these images. Additionally full volume rendering functionalities and several interaction tools as transparencies, choice of the CT slice to display, hiding and showing of meshes and additional information on the scanning procedure are available. The tool aims at offering an indepth inspection of the body organs for medical, education and surgical preoperative planning.

1 Introduction

Scientific visualization is the branch of science in charge of simplifying complex data analysis by visualizing it through appropriate techniques. Due to the predominance of vision among the human senses and the capabilities of the brain in terms of pattern recognition, an advanced visualization often leads the scientists to a better understanding of the data. As a majority of modern research problems tends to be modeled in more than two dimensions, scientific visualization is often mainly concerned with the three-dimensional visualization of phenomena [4].

Due to its complexity or its three-dimensional nature certain data can be ambiguous or unreadable while displayed on a traditional monitor. For this reason, articulated meshes, wire-like shapes and datasets crowded by an high amount of information often offer almost no 3D depth information in a two-dimensional or pseudo-3D visualization. Immersive visualization is, in the research field, a natural and intuitive extension of scientific visualization. It consists in extending the traditional visualization in terms of immersivity by using systems that enhance the displayed data so to emulate a real-life interaction. In the ideal immersive environment the user should feel like observing real 3D data and interact with it as naturally if it was a real object.

L.T. De Paolis and A. Mongelli (Eds.): AVR 2015, LNCS 9254, pp. 233–243, 2015.
DOI: 10.1007/978-3-319-22888-4_17

By emulating the human eyes behavior, stereoscopic visualization provides the user the perception of a very realistic simulation of the 3D environment observed. Additionally, the six-degrees-of-freedom (6DoF) navigation makes the interaction even more natural. The whole immersive environment allows the user to focus his attention solely on the analysed data and use his senses to more easily detect hidden information and patterns.

The expression "medical imaging" refers to the generic process of creating visual representations of the interior organs of a body. These representations are useful for teaching, research, clinical analysis and medical intervention. Many techniques and principles are used in order to produce medical images. Some imaging techniques produce stacks of two-dimensional images in order to represent three-dimensional structures.

Medical visualization originates from medical imaging techniques and it consists in the use of computers to create 3D medical representations from medical imaging data sets. Displaying the medical data in a realistic three-dimensional way allows physicians to make most effective analyses. König [6] categorizes 3-D medical visualization into three application fields: virtual endoscopy, surgical planning and medical training. Houts et al. [8] highlight that the medical visualization is also useful for the physician to improve the communication with the patients in order to obtain the informed consent. The possibility of showing anatomical structures as they are in the real world is also important for educational purpose [12]. Even though medical visualization techniques began to become popular only recently, they may completely substitute in future the "traditional" medical imaging.

Immersive visualization of medical images is a very important process for many reasons. First of all it grants the user a more realistic visualization of anatomic structures due the use of stereoscopic visualization; the depth enhancement granted by the 3D effect allows a much better perception of the complex internal structures of the human body (organs, vessels, bones, etc.). The direct manipulation of the data through 6DoF wands, additionally, allows a comfortable and familiar interaction that usually tends to be less tiring and more intuitive. Another important advantage of the immersive environments is that the user can display a one to one visualization scale factor of the entire anatomic model despite its size. It increases a lot the realism of the virtual model and is very difficult to obtain on a computer monitor unless the user visualizes only small anatomic parts [11].

In this paper we present the development of a portable and scalable software application for medical visualization on virtual reality environments (VE). The terms portable and scalable are important because they describe the capability of the application to run not only in a CAVE-like VE [3] but also in a a variety of other system, from standard desktops to Head Mounted Displays (HMD). The application is capable of loading and visualizing data from medical images in the standard DICOM format and allows to create a volumetric rendering of the same. The system supports both Computer Tomography (CT) and Magnetic Resonance (MRI) medical images. The user can also load 3D surface models of anatomy after their reconstruction with external specific software. The VE used

Fig. 1. The Kyb3 Virtual Reality Environment

in the development process is the Kyb3 [15], the CAVE-like environment of the
Institute of Cybernetics at Tallinn University of Technology.

2   The Kyb3 Virtual Reality Environment

Operational since 2013 at the Institute of Cybernetics of Tallinn University of
Technology, the Kyb3 (Fig. 1) is the first Virtual Environment (VE) built in
Estonia. Designed to stick to space-occupation and budget constraints, it features
2.7 m^2 of display surface distributed over 3 screens perpendicular to each other
in a corner-like setup. The whole system is enclosed in an area of approximately
1.9 m × 2 m × 1.8 m. The Kyb3 makes use of three pairs of DLP projectors and
circular polarization filters in order to provide full stereoscopic 3D visualization.

The compact size of the system despite the large display surface was only
possible due to the combined use of short-throw projectors and mirrors. This
choice added an additional level of complexity to the configuration of the system
(the short throw projectors use highly deforming lenses in order to generate a
large image with a short throw range, and the mirrors amplify any alignment
error) but allowed to only need approximately 75 cm behind each screen for a
80 cm × 110 cm image.

The whole VE is supported by a custom-designed aluminium frame, built
with fully configurable components in order to facilitate the alignment of projectors and mirrors.

In order to monitor in real time the user position, and therefore to maintain a correct 3D effect and user immersivity [5], the system uses an electromagnetic 6DoF tracking device, the WinTrackerIII.

The user interaction is handled through the Razer Hydra, a 6DoF gaming device consisting of two wands, each with one analogical joystick and 8 configurable buttons. The input infrastructure is completely managed through a VRPN server [17] (VRPN: Virtual Reality Peripheral Network), compatible with the majority of the existing VR-ready software.

The Kyb3 has been initially designed with the specific aim of being a supporting tool in the research on micro-structured materials but has also the flexibility to be much more. It is a prototyping platform for CAVE-oriented [3] improvements and software development. Additionally, we wanted to use it in a variety of visualizations in different application fields. Among those already implemented: cultural heritage, hydro-geological coastal surveys and architectural city planning.

3   Development Platform

Created by Oliver Kreylos at the U.C. Davis California University, VRUI [10] is a cross-platform (Linux and Mac OS X) development kit for Virtual Reality environments. VRUI was created in order to make the development of software as independent as possible from the configurations of the systems it will be used on (display, distribution and input).

It does so by providing a display-independent OpenGL rendering context, by hiding from the user the specific configuration of the Virtual Reality (VR) system (multi-CPU, computer clusters, etc.) and by providing a mechanism to hide the hardware details of the input devices.

Thanks to the above mentioned features, any software developed on VRUI can be easily run with just a change of configuration files on a variety of system, from laptop computer to CAVE-like environments.

4   MedImVR

MedImVR (Medical Imaging for VR), the software presented in this paper, was born from the need of having an open-source portable tool to inspect 3D reconstructions of CT-scans on a variety of different platforms. The main novel aspects of the application reside mainly in its portability and scalability. It is indeed an optimized medical visualization application that can run on a personal computer, but can also express its full VR capabilities in an immersive or semi-immersive environment.

Used on a VE, the application offers the user a unique experience in medical visualization. The reconstructed physical parts are displayed with different techniques as if "floating" in the VE, giving the user the possibility to move around them and manipulate them in a way otherwise denied in a standard computer.

Additionally, the possibility to scale the models to very large sizes, represents another valuable feature for a detailed analysis.

Aimed at both medical and educational uses, the software was designed taking into account the following features:

- visualize multiple meshes representing the internal organs of a human body;
- superpose the original CT or MRI slices to the segmented meshes;
- reconstruct and display a full volumetric visualization of CT or MRI data;
- be scalable, portable and VR-ready but also usable on traditional systems.

The above requirements have brought to the use of VRUI as development platform due to the performances: powerful, flexible and scalable. As already mentioned, the VRUI platform offers direct support for OpenGL library calls and relieves the user from all the problems related to the specific underlying hardware. In addition the VRUI platform has been created by Oliver Kreylos with several sets of classes useful for mesh loading and visualization. These classes offer the support for the most common mesh formats and represent the starting point in the application development.

In order to validate the development results some free sample CT scan datasets available from the Osirix free online library [1] have been used.

4.1 Mesh Generation and Visualization

The first application feature that we have developed is the loading and visualization of the models. The application offers support for meshes in OBJ, PLY, LWO, LWS and ASE format and can load a single file, multiple ones, or all the compatible meshes contained in a folder given as input. These are the most common formats for saving meshes.

The manual process to generate the organs' meshes used in the application development was the following:

- the segmentation of the organs of interest, building the 3D model and exporting them in VTK format;
- the processing of the meshes to obtain compatible and pleasantly looking models;
- the production of the associated materials and textures in OBJ format.

The segmentation and reconstruction of the organs was performed with 3D Slicer [16], an open-source software that supports medical image computing and visualization. The coarse segmentation of the organs of interest was obtained using the thresholding tool, then a manual approach was used in order to improve the results of segmentation. The final processing of the models in order to obtain the final meshes and materials was done with ParaView [7] and Blender [2]. ParaView was used to convert the meshes from the VTK format to the X3D format and Blender was used to associate to the mesh the materials and save it in OBJ format.

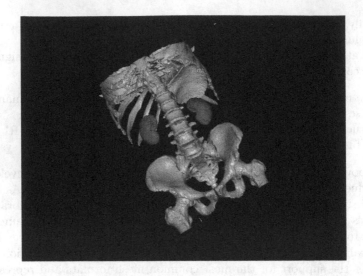

Fig. 2. Anatomical mesh models loaded in the application.

Figure 2 presents an example of the visualization of the obtained meshes. For each model the user can decide to toggle the visualization and modify the opacity to better explore otherwise hidden parts of the dataset for instance. A mesh properties 3D-space menu (fully usable also during the immersive experience) was created for this purpose and can be either accessed from the main menu or more simply on direct selection of the organs. In the latter case, it includes a laser-like selection tool that, connected to a wand, grants the user a very fast interaction with the meshes of interest (Figs. 3(a) and (b)). The mesh visualization and interaction offer obvious possibilities also during the educational process.

4.2   DICOM Integration

One fundamental feature of the developed software is the capability to show medical images together with the models built from these images. This is a very important requirement because physicians are used to work with these medical images and they often require also them in the environment of a medical model visualization. In order to simplify the on-boarding process, it is therefore important to provide them also with types of data they are familiar with. Figure 4 shows the CT slice visualization of a clinical case under study (Fig. 4(a)) and the related interaction panel (Fig. 4(b)).

Tomographic medical images are usually distributed in the DICOM standard format [13]. This standard defines the rules to embed an entire set of informations for each acquired medical image in a single file. These informations are saved as DICOM tags. These tags are used to store information like: patient data, scanning modality name, manufacturer and model of the scanner, image dimensions

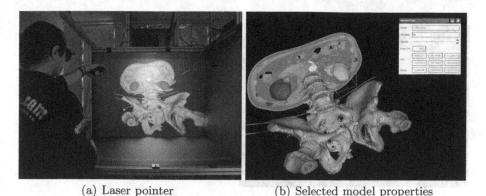

(a) Laser pointer   (b) Selected model properties

Fig. 3. Model selection with laser pointer.

and orientation. Each DICOM file usually contains a two-dimensional image; a full volume is therefore encoded in a set of images.

To load the DICOM data in the application we developed a custom class based on the Insight Toolkit (ITK) library [9]. ITK is used to open the entire DICOM directory and load all the tomographic volume in memory. Our subclass then permits to extract the geometry of the volume, converts a slice of choice from the RAW format to RGB format, specifies the conversion levels and provides other features used inside the software.

To show the images in the 3D space we used an OpenGL plane textured on both sides with the slice of interest. The geometric properties of the plane are extracted from the DICOM tags through our custom class.

To control the visualized slice, its parameters and all the DICOM information, we provide the user with a simple but complete graphical window (Fig. 4(b)). The interface includes information like image resolution, voxel spacing and slice thickness. It also allows the user to change the currently visualized slice and the conversion levels with which the image is converted from RAW data.

4.3   Volumetric Reconstruction and Rendering

Volumetric rendering allows displaying the 2D projection of a 3D discretely sampled data set. Usually this 3D discretized sample data corresponds to a 3D scalar field. In CT scans, for example, this scalar field corresponds to the measure of X-ray absorption of each discretized volume element of the material (e.g. tissue, bones). These 3D volume elements are called voxels.

Having volumetric rendering integrated in the application represents an important visualization feature because such a rendering is obtained directly from voxel data without any additional user elaboration. By contrast, surface rendering techniques for mesh models require a pre-elaboration step of the data to extract the surface meshes. The latter is a faster rendering technique from

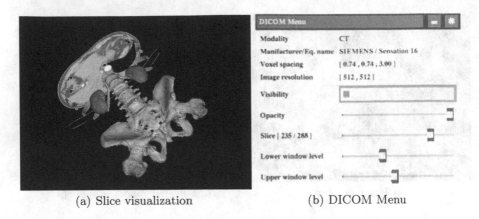

(a) Slice visualization   (b) DICOM Menu

Fig. 4. CT slices and models loaded together.

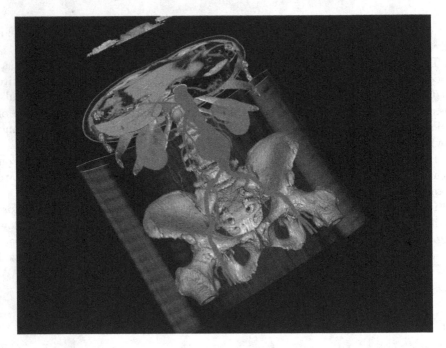

Fig. 5. Volumetric rendering of arteries, together with a DICOM slice and mesh models.

the computer hardware point of view but it requires a lot of work in order to have files ready to be loaded in the application. The mesh models are extracted by a physician from the DICOM volume through manual or semi-assisted image segmentation. This last step usually requires a lot of time and a large experience from the user to obtain valid anatomic models.

To handle the volumetric loading and rendering features we modified a set of pre-existing classes for VRUI. We introduced the possibility to generate the voxel volumes dynamically at runtime from the loaded DICOM images in the standard behaviour, which was originally only designed to pre-load existing raw volume files. We expanded the existing file loader in order to load additional file formats commonly used in medical applications (NRRD and NHDR+RAW formats). Figure 5 shows the combination of DICOM slice, mesh and volumetric rendering. On the back side of the model a red artifact is visible that stems from the scanner bed detected in the images.

5 Conclusion and Future Work

In this paper we presented the development of MedImVR, a portable and scalable software application that allows medical visualization in standard, semi-immersive and immersive environments. Its flexibility and scalability, due to VRUI features, give the possibility to run the software on several different system configurations. The porting to different platforms does not require any modification on the software but only a different configuration file.

The work done on the MedImVR software had a double aim. The first was to endow the Kyb3 VE with software able to expand its available application fields, the second was to begin the process of developing an open-source medical visualization tool for VR systems.

Due to the large beneficial contributions of an immersive visualization to the complex tasks of analysing medical data and the natural interaction granted by a 6DoF-tracked approach, the software is able to simplify the understanding of complex datasets. The possibility to show the images in an immersive environment increases the visualization realism of anatomical structures by enabling the user's depth perception on the models. This is usually hard to obtain in a common desktop system.

Another great advantage of immersive environments is the size of the visualization surfaces and therefore the possibility to reach a one to one scale factor also for models of big dimensions. In the Kyb3 environment we are able to show the chest and abdomen as they are in the real world without a scale factor. This also contributes to further increase the realism in the visualization.

Available on the online repository of the Visualization Group [14] of the Laboratory for Nonlinear Dynamics of the Center of Excellence for Nonlinear studies, the MedImVR software can offer a solid starting platform for further and more advanced developments.

As future work we plan to add the vocal interaction to the immersive environment in order to enable a new way of interaction with the virtual models. With simple voice commands the user should be able to modify the zoom level, rotate the model, reset the view and make other simple interactions.

Acknowledgments. The paper was compiled with the assistance of the Tiger University Program of the Estonian Information Technology Foundation (VisPar system, EITSA/HITSA Tiigriülikool grants 10-03-00-24, 12-03-00-11 and 13030009).

This research was supported by the European Union through the European Regional Development Fund, in particular through funding for the "Centre for Nonlinear Studies" as an Estonian national centre of excellence. This research was also supported by the European Social Fund's Doctoral Studies and Internationalisation Programme DoRa 4 (through a long time stipend for E.P.) and DoRa 5 (for the short term stipend of F.R.). Furthermore, the IDK 2014/2015 grant for E.P.'s studies is gratefully acknowledged.

References

1. OsiriX DICOM sample image sets. http://www.osirix-viewer.com/datasets/
2. Blender Online Community: Blender - a 3D modelling and rendering package. Blender Foundation, Blender Institute, Amsterdam (2015). http://www.blender.org
3. Cruz-Neira, C., Sandin, D.J., DeFanti, T.A.: Surround-screen projection-based virtual reality: The design and implementation of the CAVE. In: Proceedings of the 20th Annual Conference on Computer Graphics and Interactive Techniques, SIGGRAPH 1993, pp. 135–142, ACM, New York, NY, USA (1993)
4. Friendly, M.: Milestones in the history of thematic cartography, statistical graphics, and data visualization, August 2009
5. Gutierrez, M., Vexo, F., Thalmann, D.: Stepping into Virtual Reality, 1st edn. Springer-Verlag TELOS, Santa Clara, CA, USA (2008)
6. König, A.H.: Usability Issues in 3D Medical Visualization. Ph.D. thesis, Technische Universität Wien (2001)
7. Henderson, A.: The ParaView Guide: A Parallel Visualization Application. Kitware, November 2004
8. Houts, P.S., Doak, C.C., Doak, L.G., Loscalzo, M.J.: The role of pictures in improving health communication: a review of research on attention, comprehension, recall, and adherence. Patient Educ. Couns. **61**(2), 173–190 (2006). http://www.sciencedirect.com/science/article/pii/S0738399105001461
9. Johnson, H.J., McCormick, M., Ibáñez, L., Consortium, T.I.S.: The ITK Software Guide. Kitware Inc, 3rd (edn.) (2013). http://www.itk.org/ItkSoftwareGuide.pdf, In press
10. Kreylos, O.: Environment-independent VR development. In: Bebis, G., Boyle, R., Parvin, B., Koracin, D., Remagnino, P., Porikli, F., Peters, J., Klosowski, J., Arns, L., Chun, Y.K., Rhyne, T.-M., Monroe, L. (eds.) ISVC 2008, Part I. LNCS, vol. 5358, pp. 901–912. Springer, Heidelberg (2008)
11. Lin, Q., Xu, Z., Li, B., Baucom, R., Poulose, B., Landman, B.A., Bodenheimer, R.E.: Immersive virtual reality for visualization of abdominal ct. In: Proceedings of SPIE. vol. 8673, March 2013
12. McGhee, J.: 3-D visualization and animation technologies in anatomical imaging. J. Anat. **216**(2), 264–270 (2010)
13. Medical Imaging & Technology Alliance: The dicom standard 2015. http://dicom.nema.org/
14. MedImVR contributors: MedImVR software repository (2015). https://bitbucket.org/VisParGroup/medimvr
15. Pastorelli, E., Herrmann, H.: A small-scale, low-budget semi-immersive virtual environment for scientific visualization and research. Procedia Comput. Sci. **25**(iii–iv), 14–22 (2013)

16. Pieper, S., Halle, M., Kikinis, R.: 3D slicer, pp. 632–635 (04 2004)
17. Taylor, II, R.M., Hudson, T.C., Seeger, A., Weber, H., Juliano, J., Helser, A.T.: VRPN: a device-independent, network-transparent VR peripheral system. In: Proceedings of the ACM Symposium on Virtual Reality Software and Technology, pp. 55–61, VRST 2001. ACM, New York, USA (2001)

A Pre-operative Planning Module for an Augmented Reality Application in Maxillo-Facial Surgery

Francesco Ricciardi[1,2]([✉]), Chiara Copelli[3], and Lucio Tommaso De Paolis[1]

[1] Department of Engineering for Innovation,
University of Salento, Lecce, Italy
{francesco.ricciardi,lucio.depaolis}@unisalento.it
[2] ICT, Innovation and Research Division,
Casa Sollievo Della Sofferenza Hospital, San Giovanni Rotondo, Italy
[3] Operative Unit of Maxillo-Facial Surgery, Head and Neck Department, Casa
Sollievo Della Sofferenza Hospital, San Giovanni Rotondo, Italy
chiaracopelli@hotmail.it

Abstract. Treatment of deformities, diseases or traumas of the facial skeleton is very important for the functional and aesthetic importance of this structure. Craniofacial surgical techniques have had a great development during last decades. However, some problems still remain regarding the accurate repositioning of skeletal components and in defining margins in complex oncological resections. Computer technologies aid surgeons to solve these problems but most of proposed solutions are based on Virtual Reality. Virtual Reality technology provides many advantages but also the disadvantage that the surgeon has to adapt the virtual planning to the real surgical field. Augmented Reality represents the solution to this problem. We are developing an Augmented Reality platform for computer assisted surgery in the field of maxillo-facial surgery. In this paper we present the development of a surgical planning module that is integrated in this platform. The novelty is that this is the first Augmented Reality platform that includes such advanced planning module.

1 Introduction

The treatment of complex congenital and acquired deformities, and of complex traumas, such as ablative and reconstructive tumor surgery are often difficult because of the anatomical complexity of the facial skeleton and the functional and aesthetic importance of the structures involved [3,12,15]. Craniofacial surgical techniques have been developed and refined during the past 30 years. Advances in diagnostic imaging, rigid internal fixation and microvascular free tissue transfer have profoundly affected the predictability in which todays surgeons are able to restore patients to form and function [3]. However, problems remain with regard to reestablishing facial symmetry, accurately repositioning skeletal components into optimal relationships or correctly define the margins of complex oncological resections. There are several factors that contribute to poor

© Springer International Publishing Switzerland 2015
L.T. De Paolis and A. Mongelli (Eds.): AVR 2015, LNCS 9254, pp. 244–254, 2015.
DOI: 10.1007/978-3-319-22888-4_18

outcomes, including surgeons reliance on 2-dimensional imaging for treatment planning on a 3-dimensional problem, difficulty in assessing the intraoperative position, poor visualization of deep skeletal contours and variations in head position and craniofacial development [3,12,15].

Thanks to the technological improvements of the last years, different system are today available to aid cranio-maxillo-facial surgery. They can be divided into three main categories: computer aided pre-surgical planning, intraoperative navigation and intraoperative CT/MRI imaging [3]. Pre-surgical planning allows the surgeon to analyze CT or MRI data and to simulate and plan the surgical procedure, thanks to manipulations or options such as mirroring, segmentation or insertion of anatomic structures. The virtual data can be imported into a navigation system that is used to provide guidance for the accurate and safe placement of the anatomical structures, for movement of bone segment, resection of tumor and/or osteotomy design. Finally, mobile intraoperative CT scanners can be used to confirm the accuracy of the reconstruction before the patient leaves the operating room [3,12,15].

Nevertheless the importance and increasing utility of these innovations, they all are limited to pre-operative virtual planning. That problem results some times in a lack of accuracy and in the difficulty for the surgeon to adapt the virtual planning to the surgical field. The Augmented Reality technology can bypass these problems merging the virtual pre-operative planning on the real operative field. The surgeon has the possibility to visualize in real time the operative scenario with the overlap of virtual 3D models such as the tumor, the anatomical structures, etc. obtained by means of a processing of the patient's medical images (CT or MRI).

The first application of Augmented Reality was described in neurosurgery [12, 15]. Similar systems have been developed independently and applied to general surgery, otolaryngology, orthopaedic surgery, maxillo-facial surgery and thoracic and cardiovascular surgery.

Nijmeh et al. in [11] presented a review of guidance system developed for oral and maxillo-facial surgery with two case reports. In both presented cases the Augmented Reality technology improved the surgeon accuracy in tumor removal. Although the utility and great importance that Augmented Reality can have in surgery, a standard platform has not yet been developed because of the tremendous variability in fundamental elements such as: definition of accuracy, image acquisition, registration techniques, computers and software interfaces, localization devices, integration of real time data, tissue displacement, and, also, judgment and clinical experience.

In this paper we present the development of a surgical planning module that is integrated in an Augmented Reality guidance platform for maxillo-facial surgery. This platform is focused on ablative and reconstructive tumor surgery but it can be used also in other cranio-facial application fields. The novelty is that for the first time many surgical planning tools developed for maxillo-facial surgery are joined together in a surgery aiding platform that is based on the Augmented Reality technology.

2   Previous Works

One of the first Augmented Reality system for maxillo-facial surgery was presented by Wagner et al. in [18]. They used an Augmented Reality guidance system for the osteotomies of the facial skeleton. This system uses an head-mounted display (HMD) to realize the superimposition of the osteotomy guidance line defined on the patient CT scans. To track the patient head position they used a magnetic tracker. The main conclusion of this work is that Augmented Reality is a promising technology but the accuracy obtained with their system is the overriding concern when the reconstruction accuracy is below 1 mm.

Salb et al. in [14] presented an Augmented Reality system for cranio-facial surgery based on the use of a Sony Glasstron display for optical see-through overlay combined with two micro cameras placed on the visor mount. A NDI Polaris optical tracker has been used in order to track the camera and the surgical instruments. The system has been evaluated in a laboratory test and a very low uncertainty value was obtained.

In [9,10] Mischkowski et al. presented an Augmented Reality tool for computer assisted surgery. The system consists of a portable display tracked by an optical tracker that can be used to show the virtual models superimposed on the patient's face. The system was used in orthognathic surgery to check the correct positioning of the maxilla after its translocation; an uncertainty value below 1 mm was measured.

Swiatek-Najwer et al. presented a navigation system to support oncologic surgery in the maxillo-facial area [17]. The proposed system offers only a Virtual Reality based guidance module but it provides an interesting and advanced module for surgical planning.

Badiali et al. in [2] presented an Augmented Reality system for computer aided maxillo-facial bone surgery. This system is composed of a stereoscopic HMD that holds two USB SXGA cameras. Image registration is obtained via a machine vision algorithm that uses small spheres for virtual models alignment. Some tests of maxillary repositioning were conducted on a stereolithographic replica of human skull. In these tests the system exhibits a mean positioning error value that is below 2 mm.

In this paper we describe and present the development and the characteristics of the planning section of an Augmented Reality based platform designed for maxillo-facial surgery. If compared with previous works, the novel aspect of the proposed Augmented Reality guidance platform is that it includes in an unique application an advanced surgical planning module. No one of the previous cited works include a complete surgical planning module and an Augmented Reality guidance system in the same application.

3   Development Technologies

The application core is developed in C++ language and is based on IGSTK framework [6,8]. IGSTK, Image-Guided Surgery Toolkit, is a component based open-source framework developed for image-guided surgery applications. It is a cross-platform library and its most important feature is robustness. The framework robustness is an essential requirement because the IGSTK based applications are usually designed to be used in an operating room. IGSTK is designed to prevent every possible application error when the application is used in surgery room. Another important architectural feature of IGSTK consists in the use of a state machine to ensure an error free behaviour. The state machine paradigm provides the possibility of doing a formal validation of the software. This design pattern is widely accepted in the development of safety-critical applications [5, 7]. With all these characteristics IGSTK could be considered the best framework in the developing of applications that have to be used in the operating room.

The mesh editor and reconstruction planning tools of application are developed using the VTK framework [16]. VTK is an open-source framework written in C++ for 3D computer graphics, scientific visualization, image processing and much more. VTK is also used in many commercial applications. We used VTK to develop a set of tools that are not provided within the IGSTK framework. The main reason of choosing VTK is the simplicity of integration with IGSTK. In addition IGSTK is based on the VTK framework for all tasks related to medical images and 3D models visualizations. This ensures the full cross-compatibility of the two frameworks. Another reason of choosing VTK is that it is a very powerful library and provides a lot of classes that are able to satisfy almost every needs.

The application interface is developed using Qt [1] that is a complete framework for modern user interface development. Qt provides a multi-platform support that permits to have an highly portable application. It is also compatible with IGSTK framework that provides some ready to use widgets usable in Qt environment without additional effort. Qt framework is in its free license form compliant with projects developed with GPL, LGPL v2.1 and LGPL v3 licenses.

4   The Developed Application

We are currently developing a portable Augmented Reality based platform devoted to maxillo-facial surgery. The developed application should supply to maxillo-facial surgeons a guidance tool during cancer resection and face reconstruction. In Fig. 1 is shown the application interface that permits to load the CT scans of the patient and the anatomic models reconstructed from these. These informations can be used in an Augmented Reality view in order to guide surgeons in the operating room. To track the patient and objects positioning we use an optical tracker. The correct use of this application requires a very accurate registration procedure that is based on fiducial points.

The developed surgical planning module has been completely integrated in this complete platform. This module consists of three different parts:

- Anatomy inspector
- Mesh editor
- Reconstruction planner.

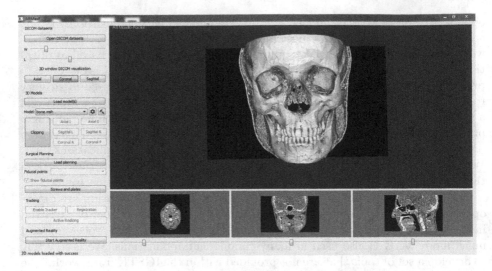

Fig. 1. Application interface after CT and skull model loading.

With these functions provided this module should allow surgeons to make a more detailed planning of the surgery.

There are many reasons to integrate a surgical planning module in the context of an Augmented Reality platform. Having an integrated surgical planning modules permits to have a complete surgery aiding platform. In this way surgeons can have a complete surgical workflow inside an unique application. Surgeon can load, visualize and manipulate the 3D models without using other applications for these purposes. Actually we do not provide any support for models building inside the platform and all models have been obtained using 3D Slicer [13].

Secondly the surgeon can use a simple and ready to use interface to manipulate the meshes. He doesn't need to learn how to use complex mesh editing software to make some basic operations like meshes cutting, mirroring or transform. This aspect lead to a reduction of the costs in terms of time saving. It could be also seen in terms of money saving but nowadays there are some solutions for mesh editing (like Blender [4]) that are powerful and free.

The most important reason for such integration is related to the surgeon's knowledge of the achievable results when using some manipulation commands. Some kind of mesh manipulations like rotation, translations and mirroring in fact could led to dangerous situations for the patients. For example, if the surgeon unintentionally translate a mesh in the virtual space and then he uses this mesh in the operating room as a guidance reference, he could incur in a wrong guidance indication. This could happen because the moved mesh is no longer aligned with the CT scans data and so no longer registered with the patient in the operating room. In fact we have to consider that the registration procedure is based on CT scans data. This could represent an harmful situation for the patient. For this reason we added in the application mesh editor some warning messages associated with the starting of specific commands. These messages inform the user that the editing of meshes using these commands could lead to incorrect guidance.

The details of the developed surgical planning modules are reported in the following.

4.1 Anatomy Inspector

The anatomy inspector tool permits to have a better comprehension of the patient internal anatomy. Using CT images together with anatomy models it offers to surgeons many visualization modalities that can be used in order to have a more detailed view of the area of interest.

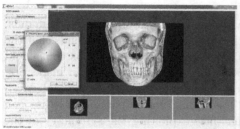 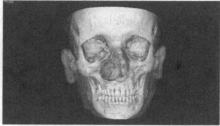

(a) Mesh properties customization   (b) Mesh advanced visualization

Fig. 2. Anatomy inspector tool.

For each model surgeons can customize color and opacity of the mesh using the interface shown in Fig. 2(a). This user interface can also used in order to obtain some advanced visualizations as shown in Fig. 2(b) where the skin is rendered with a lower opacity to permit to see inside and the tumor mass colored in green. This kind of visualization permits to identify in a clear manner the tumor extension and its positioning. Three-dimensional models are aligned with CT slices and can be visualized together in the 3D view allowing a more traditional clinical friendly inspection.

An advanced visualization clipping tool that allows selective mesh cutting is also provided. Figure 3 show an example of use of this tool in order to selectively cut the skin and to see inside it. Clipping planes are coincident with CT slices and the user choose on each direction the clipping planes position. Moreover after the models-patient registration in the operating room the slices visualization can be controlled by the surgical navigation tool taking into account the position of the tip of the surgical tool. This features can also be used to control the mesh clipping during surgery. Mesh clipping can also be combined with transparency effects to obtain a more versatile visualization.

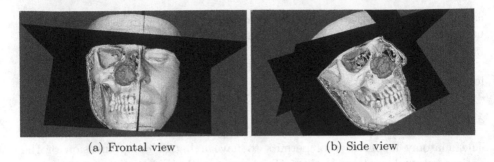

(a) Frontal view   (b) Side view

Fig. 3. Anatomy inspector tool: mesh clipping visualization.

4.2   Mesh Editor

Mesh editor module is developed to provide some basic mesh editing commands. The main reason of the introduction of this tool inside the application is that the surgeon must be informed when makes some meshes manipulations that could result harmful for the patient. The application is not thought as an inspection tool but it is designed to be used in the operating room as a guidance tool. Mesh editing commands are sometimes useful for reconstruction planning as they can extract the building blocks of the patient face exploiting the symmetry of the human body. The edited meshes can also be saved to be loaded in the application afterwards. Four mesh editing tools are provided in the application:

– Mesh clipper
– Cut outliner
– Mesh mirror
– Mesh transform.

Mesh clipper tool permits to cut the mesh along an arbitrary plane. More planes can be combined together to obtain complex cutting patterns and plane normals can be inverted to define two different cutting directions. Each cutting plane can be adjusted in position and dimension but also in orientation by moving its normal vector. In Fig. 4(a) a clipped mesh is shown.

The mesh clipper tool differs from clipping tool provided in the anatomy inspector because it is designed as an editing tool and not as an inspection tool. Indeed here cutting planes are completely free and independent from CT slice planes and clipped meshes can be saved as new models.

The results of the cut outliner tool are shown in Fig. 4(b). It works like the mesh clipper tool but it permits to extract and visualize the clipping outline without clipping the mesh. The cut outline visualization is useful to highlight the cutting points on the bones. It can be used to guide the surgeon resection if it is superimposed to the patient face during the surgery by the means of an Augmented Reality visualization.

The mesh mirror tool allows reflecting mesh with respect to a reflection plane. Reflection planes are aligned with traditional medical body planes. The user can

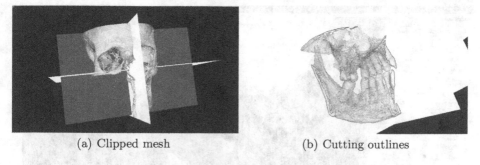

(a) Clipped mesh   (b) Cutting outlines

Fig. 4. Mesh editor tool: mesh clipper tool and cut outliner tool.

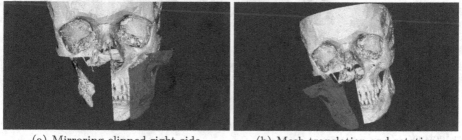

(a) Mirroring clipped right side   (b) Mesh translation and rotation

Fig. 5. Mesh editor tool: mesh mirror tool and mesh transform tool (Colour figure online).

modify the position of the reflection plane along the normal axis of the choosen plane. Figure 5(a) shows in red the results of the reflection of a clipped mandible, maxilla and part of cheekbone. It is reflected from the right side to the left side and can be used in this case for comparison purposes.

Mesh transform tool permits to move and orientate a mesh in an arbitrary manner. Combined with clipping tool and mirror tool can be used to simulate the reconstruction of a face area exploiting the face symmetry. Figure 5(b) show the use of the mesh transform tool to move and rotate a mesh.

4.3   Reconstruction Planner

In maxillo-facial surgery the surgical reconstruction often uses screws and plates to keep together bones, to define the reconstruction shape and favourite the process of osteosynthesis. To have an effective face reconstruction the screws placement should be carefully planned.

The reconstruction planner tool is developed to permit surgeon to plan the best position of these screws. In Fig. 6 the placement of four screws is simulated in a mandible reconstruction. Once completed the placement of a screw the surgeon can select a mesh and ask the application to compute the intersection points with that mesh. These intersection points are shown on the mesh surface

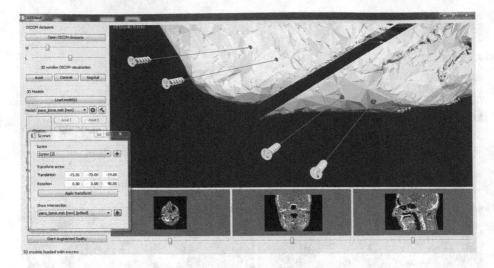

Fig. 6. Screws positioning in reconstruction planner.

as small red spheres. A line segment is also shown to put in evidence the screw trajectory.

These information (intersection point position and trajectory) obtained by means of an augmented visualization, can guide the surgeon during the real surgical procedure. In this way the surgeon is helped to obtain a more precise positioning of the screw on the patient body.

5   Conclusions and Future Works

We are developing an Augmented Reality guidance platform for computer assisted maxillo-facial surgery. This platform can be used as a guidance system in cancer resection and facial reconstruction. It can also be used in other application fields. In this paper we present the development of a set of tools that can help surgeons in surgical pre-operative planning. The novel aspect of the platform is that all these tools are integrated in a common Augmented Reality software application.

The first developed module consists in an anatomy inspector tool that is designed to give the surgeon the possibility to have a better comprehension of the patient anatomy. It uses CT scans images and patient three-dimensional models to offer surgeon many visualization modalities. These modalities can be merged together to create a customizable and powerful visualization.

We developed also a mesh editing tool to offer the surgeon some instruments to manipulate the meshes. This editor permits the surgeon to edit the mesh directly inside the application in an integrated workflow. This module should increase the patient safety by the means of some alert messages during the meshes manipulations. This should avoid, for example, unintended manipulations.

Surgical reconstruction sometimes uses screws and plates to fix the bones positioning and promote osteosynthesis. The last provided module consists in a reconstruction planner with which the surgeon can decide screws positioning. With this module the surgeon can evaluate the screw insertion point and also the screw trajectory in the anatomy models. These informations will be used in a future development to guide the surgeon in operating room using the Augmented Reality technology.

A future development for the reconstruction planner module will be the capability of loading different types of screws. Actually the surgeon has the possibility to load only a fixed type of surgical screw. This feature open the possibility to develop another module that should permit to evaluate how much space we have around the screw and how deeper is the bone in the choosen insertion point. These informations could be also related to the bone density to evaluate how strong is the screw placement in that position.

The reconstruction planner could be also improved by adding the possibility of loading and positioning virtual surgical plates. In this way the surgeon will be able to choose not only the best screw positioning but also which is the best surgical plate for a patient specific anatomy. This could enable also the possibility to develop a module for screw automatic positioning.

Actually our application doesn't support surgical models building. These are reconstructed from the CT scans with a third party software. As a future application development we plan to integrate a module for model building in the mesh editor. In this way the surgeon can complete the entire surgical planning workflow inside our application without needing of external model building tool.

References

1. Qt - cross-platform application & UI development framework. http://www.qt.io
2. Badiali, G., Ferrari, V., Cutolo, F., Freschi, C., Caramella, D., Bianchi, A., Marchetti, C.: Augmented reality as an aid in maxillofacial surgery: validation of a wearable system allowing maxillary repositioning. J. Cranio-Maxillofac. Surg. **42**(8), 1970–1976 (2014)
3. Bell, R.B.: Computer planning and intraoperative navigation in cranio-maxillofacial surgery. Oral Maxillofac. Surg. Clin. North Am. **22**(1), 135–156 (2010)
4. Blender Community: Blender - a 3D modelling and rendering package. Blender Foundation, Blender Institute, Amsterdam. http://www.blender.org
5. Cheng, A.: Real-Time Systems: Scheduling, Analysis, and Verification. Wiley Interscience, New Jersey (2002)
6. Cheng, P., Zhang, H., su Kim, H., Gary, K., Blake, M.B., Gobbi, D., Aylward, S., Jomier, J., Enquobahrie, A., Avila, R., Ibanez, L., Cleary, K.: IGSTK: framework and example application using an open source toolkit for image-guided surgery applications. In: Image-Guided Procedures and Display proceedings, pp. 11–16. San Diego, CA, February 2006. http://www.igstk.org
7. Douglas, B.: Real-Time Design Patterns: Robust Scalable Architecture for Real-Time Systems. Addison-Wesley Professional, Reading (2002)
8. Enquobahrie, A., Cheng, P., Gary, K., Ibanez, L., Gobbi, D., Lindseth, F., Yaniv, Z., Aylward, S., Jomier, J., Cleary, K.: The image-guided surgery toolkit IGSTK: an open source C++ software toolkit. J. Digit. Imaging **20**(Suppl. 1), 21–33 (2007)

9. Mischkowski, R., Zinser, M., Kubler, A., Seifert, U., Zoller, J.: Clinical and experimental evaluation of an augmented reality system in cranio-maxillofacial surgery. In: CARS 2005: Computer Assisted Radiology and Surgery Proceedings of the 19th International Congress and Exhibition, vol. 1281, pp. 565–570 (2005) (International Congress Series)

10. Mischkowski, R.A., Zinser, M.J., Kbler, A.C., Krug, B., Seifert, U., Zller, J.E.: Application of an augmented reality tool for maxillary positioning in orthognathic surgery a feasibility study. J. Cranio-Maxillofac. Surg. **34**(8), 478–483 (2006)

11. Nijmeh, A., Goodger, N., Hawkes, D., Edwards, P., McGurk, M.: Image-guided navigation in oral and maxillofacial surgery. Brit. J. Oral Maxillofac. Surg. **43**(4), 294–302 (2005)

12. Pham, A.M., Rafii, A.A., Metzger, M.C., Jamali, A., Strong, B.E.: Computer modeling and intraoperative navigation in maxillofacial surgery. Otolaryngol. Head Neck Surg. **137**(4), 624–631 (2007)

13. Pieper, S., Halle, M., Kikinis, R.: 3D SLICER, pp. 632–635, April 2004

14. Salb, T., Brief, J., Welzel, T., Giesler, B., Hassfeld, S., Muehling, J., Dillmann, R.: Inpres (intraoperative presentation of surgical planning and simulation results) augmented reality for craniofacial surgery. In: SPIE, Stereoscopic Displays and Virtual Reality Systems X. vol. 5006, May 2003

15. Schramm, A., Schon, R., Rucker, M., Barth, E.L., Zizelmann, C., Gellrich, N.C.: Computer-assisted oral and maxillofacial reconstruction. J. Comput. Inf. Technol. **1**, 71–76 (2006)

16. Schroeder, W.J., Martin, K., Lorensen, W.: The Visualization Toolkit: An Object-Oriented Approach to 3d Graphics, 3rd edn. Prentice-Hall, New York (2003). http://www.vtk.org

17. Swiatek-Najwer, E., Majak, M., Popek, M., Pietruski, P., Szram, D., Jaworowski, J.: The Maxillo-facial surgery system for guided cancer resection and bone reconstruction. In: 2013 36th International Conference on Telecommunications and Signal Processing (TSP), pp. 843–847, July 2013

18. Wagner, A., Rasse, M., Millesi, W., Ewers, R.: Virtual reality for orthognathic surgery: the augmented reality environment concept. J. Oral Maxillofac. Surg. **55**(5), 456–462 (1997)

Augmented Reality Assisted Brain Tumor Extraction in Mice

Adrian Schneider$^{(\boxtimes)}$, Peter Thalmann, Simon Pezold, Simone E. Hieber,
and Philippe C. Cattin

Department of Biomedical Engineering, University of Basel, Basel, Switzerland
adrian.schneider@unibas.ch

Abstract. Computer assisted navigation is a widely adopted technique in neurosurgery and orthopedics. In general, the used tracking systems are applicable to multiple situations. However, these general-purpose devices are costly and in case of unusual laboratory applications, a dedicated solution often shows a better performance. In this paper, we propose a cost-effective 3D navigation system for the augmented reality assisted brain tumor extraction in mice, used for cancer research. Off-the-shelf camera 3D reconstruction algorithms are used to individually track a target and a surgical tool. Relative to its costs, the experiments showed an excellent navigation error of 0.48 mm ± 0.25 mm.

Keywords: Augmented reality · 3D Reconstruction · Single camera · Navigation · Micro computed tomography · Cancer

1 Introduction

According to the *World Health Organization*, cancer is a leading cause of death and its prevalence is increasing [12]. Although state-of-the-art oncology is steadily progressing, one of two patients loses the fight against cancer. Current research is tackling the illness at multiple fronts. The main effort targets the design of new drugs, proliferation, the improvement of radiotherapy methods, and the development of sophisticated surgical interventions. To improve the effectiveness of cancer therapies, a better understanding of cancer is highly important. For example, vessel parameters such as diameter and tortuosity are suspected to play a crucial role in the angiogenesis of cancer and therefore also for anti-angiogenic therapies. For the quantification of these vessel parameters, sophisticated 3D imaging techniques are necessary.

In vivo measurements are highly desired, but do not yet provide sufficient resolution. Furthermore, typical absorption-contrast micro-computed tomography (μCT) is not applicable as the contrast for soft tissues is too small for segmentation, and magnetic resonance tomography (MRT) is not yet able to visualize the smallest capillaries (diameter $\sim 5\,\mu$m) due to lack of resolution.

Simone E. Hieber and Philippe C. Cattin shared last authorship.

© Springer International Publishing Switzerland 2015
L.T. De Paolis and A. Mongelli (Eds.): AVR 2015, LNCS 9254, pp. 255–264, 2015.
DOI: 10.1007/978-3-319-22888-4_19

In the mouse model, one approach to overcome these issues is to use vascular corrosion casting, where the mouse is perfused with Heparin, followed by a polyurethane mixture as described in [6]. The remaining tissue is removed from the polymer specimen with a formic acid solution. Following a standard protocol, synchrotron radiation-based micro-computed tomography (SRμCT) in absorption-contrast mode [8] or, as shown recently, high-resolution laboratory CT [11] is subsequently used for imaging the specimen. However, this approach is only reliable for tumors at early stages.

A second approach is to use in-line phase-contrast SRμCT [10], a technique known for much better discrimination of soft tissues compared to standard absorption-contrast μCT, even without staining. For this technique, however, the spatial resolution of the acquired tomograms highly depends on the specimen size, such that scanning a smaller object enables achieving a higher resolution. The detectors at the synchrotron beamlines typically deliver an image with a fixed size of 2000×2000 pixel. Thus, when scanning the whole mouse brain of about 15 mm size, a spatial resolution of 7.5 μm can be reached. This is not enough to visualize the tumor's capillaries. An obvious solution is to measure only the brain part in which the tumor is located. In laboratory mice, the tumors of interest reach a diameter of approximately 2 mm. Extracting them from the brain into specimen of the size of 3 mm, the spatial resolution is increased by a factor of 5 and reaches 1.5 μm. This enables the visualization of the smallest capillaries, which feature diameters on the level of micrometers.

In this paper, we describe a novel approach to perform such a tumor extraction based on the combination of MRT and computer vision. In particular, a dedicated high resolution MRT device is used to localize the tumor within the mouse brain. Then, a single video camera is used to simultaneously track the brain and a dissection tool. To increase usability and enable a seamless integration into the surgical workflow, an intuitive augmented reality (AR) visualization technique is used. Figure 1 depicts an overview of the whole workflow.

Existing medical 3D navigation systems are highly adaptable and can be used for a multitude of navigation tasks. An accurate and common tracking technology is based on optical stereo frames operating in the infrared spectrum. Such systems achieve submillimeter accuracy in a relatively large measurement volume [2]. Therefore, they are good potential tracking solutions for our application, too. However, these devices are bulky and expensive. By contrast, we are going to present a compact navigation system that achieves comparable results for a fraction of the costs.

2   Materials and Methods

2.1   Specimen Preparation

The tumor samples are gained from mice. At the age of two months, *gliome murine cells* (GL261) are injected into the brain of a mouse. The mouse is sacrificed 12 days after the injection. At this stage, the tumor has reached a

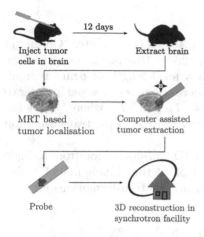

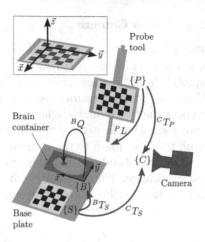

Fig. 1. Workflow from farming the tumor up to 3D reconstruction. This paper is mainly about the tumor localization and extraction. The red dot indicates the tumor (Color figure online).

Fig. 2. Setup of the navigation system. Curved arrows denote affine transformations and the red dot indicates the tumor. In the upper left, a chessboard and its spanned coordinate system are shown (Color figure online).

diameter of approximately 2 mm. The target region – cancerous cells – is then extracted from the brain with our newly developed navigation system.

2.2 Navigation System

The setup of the proposed navigation system is shown in Fig. 2. The base plate carries a container for the whole mouse brain. To trepan the tumor from the mouse brain, the probe tool is used. A third part is a camera, which establishes an accurate spatial relationship between the base plate and the probe tool.

In the following, we are going to describe each part of the navigation pipeline in detail, covering deployed materials and algorithms. To familiarize the reader with our nomenclature, we would like to explain briefly the term *affine transformation*. An affine transformation describes a rotational and translational relationship between two coordinate systems (CS) and can be compactly represented by a 4×4 matrix in the 3D case. The notation $^{X}T_{Y}$ denotes an affine transformation matrix that transforms a point expressed in the $\{Y\}$ CS ^{Y}P into a position relative to the $\{X\}$ CS ^{X}P. The actual transformation from ^{Y}P to ^{X}P is carried out using matrix–vector multiplication:

$$^{X}P = {}^{X}T_{Y} \cdot {}^{Y}P.$$

2.3   Video Camera

The *MQ013CG-E2* digital camera from *XIMEA GmbH* (Münster, Germany) was used, which delivers images of the size of 1280×1024 pixel. As a lens, the *002915* from *Tamron* (Saitama, Japan) with a focal length of 8 mm is used. Using the notation introduced in Fig. 2, the camera image is processed in order to recover the two dynamic affine transformations $^{C}T_P$ and $^{C}T_S$, where $^{C}T_P$ is the transformation from the probe tool to the camera and $^{C}T_S$ is the transformation from the base plate to the camera.

To understand the methods of estimating a 3D transformation from a single camera image, it is necessary to have a closer look at the pinhole model, which is used to describe a projective camera. The projective transformations for $^{C}T_P$ and $^{C}T_S$ are defined as

$$^{P}u \propto K \cdot {}^{C}T_P \cdot {}^{P}X \quad \text{and} \quad {}^{S}u \propto K \cdot {}^{C}T_S \cdot {}^{S}X,$$

where K are the intrinsic camera parameters, ^{P}u is the 2D pixel location of the projected 3D point ^{P}X, and ^{S}u is the respective projection of ^{S}X. Those pairs are called 2D–3D point correspondences and can be robustly created and recovered by using simple and detectable patterns. The $\propto$ sign indicates proportionality, because the projected pixel coordinates are usually normalized to $[u, v, 1]^{T}$.

Initially, K has to be determined. These parameters describe the projective behavior of the camera and are determined only once. A common camera calibration method is based on using multiple 2D–3D point correspondences created from planar calibration patterns [13], e. g. chessboard patterns. In addition to K, this calibration algorithm also estimates non-linear lens distortion parameters, such as *tangential distortion* and *radial distortion*.

Tracking an object with a calibrated camera is very similar to the calibration process itself. The 2D–3D point correspondences are created by extracting the 2D coordinates from the camera image and connecting them with the chosen 3D coordinates of the pattern. Based on these correspondences, an iterative method using Levenberg-Marquardt optimization is applied to estimate the extrinsic camera parameters, in particular the affine transformations $^{C}T_P$ and $^{C}T_S$.

Camera Calibration Error and Tracking Error. The camera calibration [13] and the object tracking algorithm [3] both have residual errors. Several error measures can be applied to quantify the quality of the found solution [4]. A commonly used measure is the *backprojection error* E_B, which represents the average pixel error in the image: The computed solution is used to project the i-th 3D point $^{Y}X_i$ of the 2D–3D point correspondences to the image plane. These projections u_i' are then compared with the recorded 2D pixel coordinates u_i taken from point correspondences. If there are N 2D–3D correspondences, then

$$E_B = \frac{1}{N} \sum_{i=1}^{N} \|u_i - u_i'\| \quad \text{with} \quad u_i' \propto K \cdot {}^{C}T_Y \cdot {}^{Y}X_i.$$

In general, the calibration error and tracking error depend heavily on the applied equipment and the scene itself. For further detail, we refer the reader to [7], where a comprehensive error estimation for single camera tracking systems is described.

2.4 Probe Tool

The probe tool is used to trepan the tumor from the mouse brain. The user brings the tool into the right pose by following the guidance instructions of our navigation system (Sect. 2.6).

In reference to Fig. 2, the missing tool tip position ^{P}L, expressed in the $\{P\}$ CS, can be found by the algorithm described in [9]. However, since the exact orientation of the tool's chessboard CS is known, a better method to determine ^{P}L is simply measuring the translation, e. g. by using a sliding calliper.

2.5 Base Plate and Brain Container

The complete brain of the mouse is surgically removed and put into the brain container. The location of the tumor Q is measured using a dedicated high resolution MRT device (*PharmaScan 47/16, Bruker BioSpin*, Ettlingen, Germany). Using the container shape, the MRT origin can be aligned with the CS $\{B\}$ easily, at the same time providing the tumor location ^{B}Q in $\{B\}$. To enhance the visibility of the container itself on the MRT image, we place it in a water bath during the scan.

The base plate has a slot to plug in the brain container. Since both geometries and the orientation of the base plate's chessboard are known, the rigid transformation $^{B}T_S$ can be measured very precisely. In a more complex situation, e. g. if the construction data of the base plate is not available, one could apply a 3D–3D registration as described in [1].

2.6 Augmented Reality Assisted Navigation

Once all affine transformations of the navigation system are known, the remaining task is to generate the navigation view. Since we use an AR user interface, it makes sense to choose the camera as the common CS. In reference to Fig. 2, the probe tool tip ^{P}L and the tumor location ^{B}Q are transformed to $\{C\}$ by

$$^{C}L = {}^{C}T_P \cdot {}^{P}L \quad \text{and} \quad {}^{C}Q = {}^{C}T_S \cdot {}^{B}T_S{}^{-1} \cdot {}^{B}Q.$$

The tumor location ^{C}Q is visualized on the camera image using the camera calibration. Furthermore, the user gets updated with the current distance from the tool tip to the tumor, $d_T = \left\| {}^{C}L - {}^{C}Q \right\|$, by means of a dynamically scaled vertical bar that we overlay on the camera image. Figures 3 and 4 give an impression of the AR assisted navigation.

Fig. 3. AR visualization I: The base plate with the brain container is on the left; a vertical green bar displays the distance d_T, the augmented green dot indicates a simulated tumor location. The probe tool is on the right (Color figure online).

Fig. 4. AR visualization II: The chessboard coordinate system frames $\{B\}$, $\{S\}$, $\{P\}$, and the probe tool's orientation are overlaid. The distance d_T becomes smaller with the tool tip approaching the tumor location.

3   Experiments and Results

In this section, we determine the precision and accuracy of our method under several aspects. The used hardware is as presented in Sect. 2. For the following experiments, a camera calibration with a backprojection error $E_B = 0.2$ pixel was used. The calibration was performed based on 20 different chessboard poses and setting the tangential distortion to zero.

3.1   Transformation Robustness

In this experiment, our goal is to estimate the robustness of the proposed tracking method. In particular, two chessboards with a known, rigid transformation in between them are simultaneously tracked (Fig. 5). The estimated transformation between both chessboards can be quantitatively compared against the true one. This is done from several different camera poses.

The first chessboard has 4×5 fields and spans the CS $\{X\}$. The second board has 4×3 fields and spans the CS $\{Y\}$. Both have square fields, each with a length of 3 mm. The rigid transformation $^X T_Y$ between the two chessboard CSs was chosen so that there is no rotation, but only a translation of 30.0 mm. The transformations from each chessboard to the camera CS $\{C\}$, $^C T_X$ and $^C T_Y$, are recovered from the camera image. Therefore

$$^X T_Y = {}^C T_X{}^{-1} \cdot {}^C T_Y.$$

In the following, this transformation is estimated from $N_q = 25$ different camera poses. Each transformation $^X T_{Y_q}$ is compared with the true transformation $^X T_{Y_t}$.

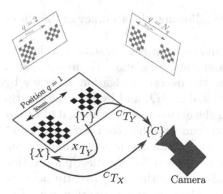

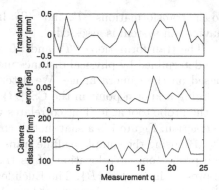

Fig. 5. Transformation robustness experiment setup.

Fig. 6. Transformation robustness experiment results.

The differences can be split into a rotational part $\Delta\Theta_q$ and a translational part Δt_q. We compute $\Delta\Theta_q$ by the *inner product of unit quaternions* [5] and Δt_q by the difference of the CS offsets, as

$$\Delta\Theta_q = \arccos\left(\left|q\left(r\left(^X T_{Yt}\right)\right)\cdot q\left(r\left(^X T_{Yq}\right)\right)\right|\right), \quad \Delta t_q = \left\|t\left(^X T_{Yt}\right)\right\| - \left\|t\left(^X T_{Yq}\right)\right\|.$$

The function $q(.)$ converts a rotation matrix into a 4×1 quaternion, $r(.)$ extracts the 3×3 rotation matrix from the transformation and $t(.)$ returns the 3×1 translation component.

The distance d_q between the camera and the tracked pattern has an influence on the accuracy [7]. In our case, d_q is the average distance from both chessboards to the camera and is computed like

$$d_q = \frac{1}{2}\left(\left\|t\left(^C T_{Xq}\right)\right\| + \left\|t\left(^C T_{Yq}\right)\right\|\right).$$

Results The results can be seen in Fig. 6. The mean translation error is 0.20 mm and has a standard deviation of 0.25 mm. The average rotation error is approximately 0.035 rad (2°). The experiments were performed within a camera distance range of 100 mm to 200 mm. However, the supposed correlation between the camera distance and the corresponding errors is not observed. The model for a theoretical error estimation of a single camera navigation system [7] does not consider an equivalent situation, thus a comparison is difficult. But it shows that the determined rotation errors and translation errors are plausible.

3.2 Navigation System Accuracy

In the above experiment, we determined the precision and robustness of tracking two chessboards. Regarding the proposed system (Fig. 2), this only corresponds to the transformations ^CT_S and ^CT_P. In the following, the accuracy of the whole navigation system is assessed.

The transformations ^BT_S and ^PL are known from the construction data or are determined by physical distance measurements. ^CT_S and ^CT_P are estimated based on the camera image. We determine the overall navigation accuracy by defining a known point in the CS $\{B\}$, denoted as ^BQ, and by pointing the tip of the probe tool at it. This correlates with the actual task of a navigated tumor extraction. Figure 4 is a snapshot of this experiment. The green dot is the point ^BQ. By using the complete affine transformation chain of our navigation system, the probe tool tip's location ^PL is then transformed to ^BL, the tip's position expressed in the CS $\{B\}$. The Euclidean distance of the computed tip position ^BL from its reference location ^BQ can be considered as the navigation error E_N. It is given by

$$E_N = \|^BL - {}^BQ\| \quad \text{with} \quad {}^BL = {}^BT_S \cdot {}^CT_S^{-1} \cdot {}^CT_P \cdot {}^PL.$$

The marker for the base plate is a 4×5 chessboard that spans the CS denoted as $\{S\}$. The probe tool is tracked via a 4×3 chessboard that spans the CS denoted as $\{P\}$. Both chessboards have square fields, each with a length of 3 mm.

Results The experiment was repeated 25 times within a camera distance range of 100 mm to 200 mm. The average navigation error E_N is 0.48 mm with a standard deviation of 0.25 mm. This corresponds to the accuracy observed with commercial medical navigation systems using a pointing tool [2]. However, our measurement volume is much smaller but adequate for the problem at hand.

3.3 Brain Extraction

The navigated tumor extraction (Fig. 7) was tested on two mice and two mock objects, where the tumor was built from modeling clay surrounded by soft paraffin simulating the brain tissue. An experiment is qualitatively rated following to the amount of the tumor which was trepanned from the brain. We introduce the labels *Complete*, *Partial* and *Off Target* tumor extraction.

Results. The two experiments with the mock objects resulted in *complete* tumor extractions. Both experiments with mice led to *partial* tumor samples (Fig. 8). This difference could be explained with the observation that the real brains slightly moved and got deformed at the moment the probe tool punctured the brain surface, whereas this was not the case with the mock objects. In general, it is important to notice that our navigation system is on the edge of meeting the required accuracy for a *complete* tumor extraction. Sampling a target with a 2 mm diameter using a sampling tool that has a diameter of 3 mm requires an accuracy ≤ 0.5 mm. The experiment above showed that we reach 0.48 mm $\pm$ 0.25 mm.

Fig. 7. Tumor extraction from a real mouse brain using the proposed navigation system. The experiment took place at the Animal Imaging Center of ETH Zurich.

Fig. 8. Reconstructed slice with 3 mm diameter using inline phase contrast SRμCT (pixel size 1.9 μm). The dark area represents the partially extracted tumor.

4 Conclusion

In this paper we proposed an AR navigation system applicable for guided brain tumor extraction in mice. The achieved accuracy of 0.48 mm combined with its relatively low cost opens up possibilities for using the system in other fields. However, for the presented task it would be useful to enhance the accuracy. The current system is operated with one camera and the tracked patterns are planar. A better accuracy can be achieved by using two cameras, which together form a stereo frame. The drawback with the latter approach is the reduced field of view, because both cameras need to spot the patterns. Another solution could be the usage of non-planar patterns. In theory, this enhances the 3D reconstruction accuracy [7]. The disadvantage is the complexity of constructing such a pattern. Our current research is focusing on this challenge.

Acknowledgments. We would like to thank Bert Müller for his initiative and helpful discussions, Therese Bormann for her help in the container design and the 3D printing at the FHNW Muttenz, Mathias Griessen and Alex Seiler for their support in the software implementation, Sandra Burgi for preparing the murine brain, and Marco Dominietto for his useful feedback and the MRT measurements at the Animal Imaging Center of ETH Zurich.

References

1. Arun, K.S., Huang, T.S., Blostein, S.D.: Least-squares fitting of two 3-d point sets. IEEE Trans. Pattern Anal. Mach. Intell. **5**, 698–700 (1987)
2. Broers, H., Jansing, N.: How precise is navigation for minimally invasive surgery? Int. Orthop. **31**(1), 39–42 (2007)

3. Gao, X.S., Hou, X.R., Tang, J., Cheng, H.F.: Complete solution classification for the perspective-three-point problem. IEEE Trans. Pattern Anal. Mach. Intell. **25**(8), 930–943 (2003)
4. Hartley, R., Zisserman, A.: Multiple view geometry in computer vision. Cambridge University Press, New York (2010)
5. Huynh, D.Q.: Metrics for 3D rotations: comparison and analysis. J. Math. Imag. Vis. **35**(2), 155–164 (2009)
6. Krucker, T., Lang, A., Meyer, E.P.: New polyurethane-based material for vascular corrosion casting with improved physical and imaging characteristics. Microsc. Res. Tech. **69**(2), 138–147 (2006). http://dx.doi.org/10.1002/jemt.20263
7. Luhmann, T.: Precision potential of photogrammetric 6DOF pose estimation with a single camera. ISPRS J. Photogrammetry Remote Sens. **64**(3), 275–284 (2009)
8. Müller, B., Lang, S., Dominietto, M., Rudin, M., Schulz, G., Deyhle, H., Germann, M., Pfeiffer, F., David, C., Weitkamp, T.: High-resolution tomographic imaging of microvessels. Proc. SPIE - Int. Soc. Opt. Eng. **7078**, 70780B-1–70780B-10 (2008). http://dx.doi.org/10.1117/12.794157
9. Onprasert, O., Suthakorn, J.: A novel method on tool tip calibration for biomedical application. In: Proceedings of the World Congress on Computer Science and Information Engineering, pp. 650–653 (2011)
10. Paganin, D., Mayo, S.C., Gureyev, T.E., Miller, P.R., Wilkins, S.W.: Simultaneous phase and amplitude extraction from a single defocused image of a homogeneous object. J. Microsc. **206**(1), 33–40 (2002). http://dx.doi.org/10.1046/j.1365-2818.2002.01010.x
11. Thalmann, P., Hieber, S.E., Schulz, G., Deyhle, H., Khimchenko, A., Kurtcuoglu, V., Olgac, U., Marmaras, A., Kuo, W., Meyer, E.P., Beckmann, F., Herzen, J., Ehrbar, S., Müller, B.: Three-dimensional registration of synchrotron radiation-based micro-computed tomography images with advanced laboratory micro-computed tomography data from murine kidney casts. Am. J. Physiol. Heart Circ. Physiol. **9212**, 92120Y-1–92120Y-9 (2014). http://dx.doi.org/10.1117/12.2060809
12. WHO: Research for patient safety (2008). http://www.who.int/patientsafety/information_centre/documents/ps_research_brochure_en.pdf
13. Zhang, Z.: A flexible new technique for camera calibration. IEEE Trans. Pattern Anal. Mach. Intell. **22**(11), 1330–1334 (2000)

Applications in Industry and Robotics

A Virtual Prototyping Platform to Improve CAE Analysis Workflow

Francesco Argese[1](✉), Andrea Martini[1], Lucio Colizzi[1], Marco Fina[2],
Giovanni Reo[2], Fiorenzo Ambrosino[3], Pasquale Bene[1], and Leonardo Cosma[1]

[1] Consorzio CETMA, C/o Cittadella Della Ricerca S.S. 7 - Km 706+030,
72100 Brindisi, Italy
francesco.argese@cetma.it
[2] SysMan Progetti and Servizi S.R.L., Via A. Montagna, 2,
72023 Mesagne (BR), Italy
[3] Enea, CR Portici (NA), Piazzale Enrico Fermi 1, 80055 Portici, Italy

Abstract. This paper describes an experimental software system that allows interfacing a virtual immersive environment with Computer Aided Engineering (CAE) open source software aiming for improving and simplifying design process and results evaluation. System includes a middleware to execute jobs on HPC architectures and to compare results of server-class processors with GPGPU hardware. The main innovation of the overall system is the possibility to setup the CAE job directly inside the virtual reality platform speeding-up the entire process. User evaluations on selected case studies show how the use of a virtual environment may enhance the perception of engineers ideas during the design process. In addition, the use of a system that allows reconfiguring and relaunching the job simplifies setup of job configuration. Results also show that HPC hardware based on GPGPU offers a perceivable speedup for problems with an high number of nodes.

Keywords: Virtual prototyping · Computer graphics · Virtual reality · Software engineering · Message oriented middleware · Computer aided engineering · High performance computing

1 Introduction

CAE analysis is a crucial aspect regarding to product development life-cycle, because it allows virtual prototyping [1]: it decreases manufacturing time, reduces prototyping costs and enhances re-usability of parts of product.

A study of Zeng and Horvt [2] envisions that the future CAD/E systems will hinge on two fundamental pillars: the first is designers mental model in the design process, particularly conceptual design process and the second includes technologies supporting activities underlying the entire design process. These premises suggest that modern CAE software design and development should require a multidisciplinary approach which involves Virtual Reality (VR), Software Engineering (SE), High performance computing (HPC) and Computer Aided Engineering (CAE). VR visualization and interaction are two points of the Scientific

© Springer International Publishing Switzerland 2015
L.T. De Paolis and A. Mongelli (Eds.): AVR 2015, LNCS 9254, pp. 267–286, 2015.
DOI: 10.1007/978-3-319-22888-4_20

Agenda proposed by Elmqvist and Niklas for Visualization Research [3]: it plays an important role to offer CAE engineers new tools which allow exploring analysis data through immersive systems [4]; HPC is very important to speedup time needed to execute a specific CAE analysis; Software Engineer is the glue that ties together all heterogeneous software modules. Even though these fields are very important for the future developments of CAE systems, great attention must be paid to the high budget required to obtain a minimal configuration working system.

During product development, Virtual Prototyping (VP) techniques are used to reduce production costs and consequently the time-to-market. In particular, CAE engineers usually need to launch many complex simulations to identify the best input parameters which guarantee the desired results. This approach might require many iterations (loop process) until an optimal result is reached. This procedure allows to overcome limitations of Rapid Prototyping techniques avoiding the realization of too many physical prototypes [5].

Over the last years the growth of cost-effective HPC architectures based on GPGPU (General Purpose Graphics Processing Unit), the lowering of workstations costs and the wide spread of immersive systems have occurred. All these aspects contribute to achieve CAE tools systems suitable for SMEs and not only for large enterprises, expanding the potential market to new customers [6].

For these reasons this paper presents an experimental work which investigates the entire process to build an overall virtual prototyping system including the following submodules:

1. CAE job analysis through multi-core architectures;
2. exploration of the results with immersive visualization;
3. middle-ware to tie the previous two items and to execute jobs directly from the VR environment.

Great effort on this experimental work has also been addressed to:

- evaluate parallelization strategies related to open source CAE software
- evaluate GPGPU architectures performances on CAE jobs comparing them with a server-class processor results.

Simulations described in this paper are related to CFD (Computational Fluid Dynamics) and FEM (Finite Element method).

2   Related Work

Many works have been proposed on virtual prototyping tools for CAE, each of them dealing with specific submodule previously introduced. In the following subsections there is a brief analysis related to each subsystem.

2.1 Software Brokers

With the increasing importance of event-based systems, the performance of underlying event transporting systems, such as message oriented middleware (MOM), becomes critical. [7]

Many works have been presented in this field. Dawar et al. [8] proposed an architecture including implementation and performance tests for a policy-based event processing system with a focus on performance of RabbitMQ. An approach to the integration of CAE Systems in a Grid Environment is described by Radchenko and Hudyakova [9], which proposed an approach to access remote distributed supercomputer resources, using the concept of distributed virtual test bed (DiVTB).

2.2 HPC

Many studies have been conducted on the parallelization of CAE jobs using GPGPU technologies to investigate the performance offered by these architectures. Jamshidi et al. [10] proposed the porting and the optimization of Open-FOAM on three different multi-core platforms. AlOnazi proposed optimizations aimed at accelerating simulations of OpenFOAM solvers using an hybrid MPI and GPGPU approach [11]. Tomczak proposed an implementation of PISO and SIMPLE solvers on GPUs showing that a Tesla C2070 video card can outperform a server-class 6-core CPU by up to 4.2 times [12].

2.3 Visualization

Major issues in visualization of CAE simulation results regards the following items:

1. Transformation of results to a format easily interpretable by a virtual reality application;
2. The computational problems related to visualization of a huge amount of continuous simulation data generated by such systems;
3. The user experience and the immersion level offered to the CAE engineers while evaluating the results.

Visualization problems have been faced in other works with different approaches. Maleshkov and Chotrov [13] proposed an algorithm for transforming the Ansys mesh, which includes steps to simplify geometry through the reduction of the number of nodes and triangles; Song and Yang proposed a visualization method based on a scene graph to represent continuous simulation data [14]; Rose and Ertl [15] proposed a new visualization technique which combines advantages of a specifically adapted mesh reduction algorithm with a texture-based rendering of surface details; this approach avoids reduction of triangles which should led to loose important details of simulation result.

2.4   Configurable CAE Simulation

Main issue in developing a CAE configurable job consists in modifying the mesh which is then used to calculate the simulation. A related work is described by the NTNU HPC Group in a tutorial [16], which is related to the calculation of the incompressible flow over 4-digit NACA airfoils (airfoil shapes for aircraft wings developed by the National Advisory Committee for Aeronautics).

2.5   Our Contributions

Many research studies have been conducted on the design and development of a virtual prototyping system for CAE simulations including a CAE middleware, and there are no doubts about its usefulness. To our knowledge, there is no previous work including:

- A virtual environment that allows re-launching a CAE analysis configuring job parameters directly inside the Virtual Reality environment;
- Interfaces to a middle-ware to launch jobs on GPGPU parallelization hardware using open source CAE software.

  Such system allows to investigate the following issues:

1. Identify for which types of CAE jobs an interactive evaluation of results could be possible;
2. Compare parallelization solutions on a GPGPU and on a server-class processor using open source CAE software;
3. Exploring the advantages of this approach comparing it with the VP traditional one.

3   System Description

The main aim of the system is to create an immersive system to respond to CAE engineers needs; such system requires integration of different hardware and software components. Being an experimental system, design and development of the software architecture focused mainly on modularity and expandability. In particular, as shown in Fig. 1, architecture has three main modules:

1. A set of HPC systems where CAE software are configured with parallelization modules;
2. A visualization system to display simulation results;
3. A middle-ware (or broker) which allows bi-directional communication among the previous two modules.

  Figure 1 represents the concept of the complete system. This paper describes only the interface with ENEA GPGPU and visualization through immersive and desktop platforms. In the following subsections there is a description of each module.

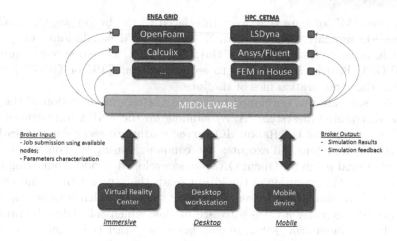

Fig. 1. Concept of complete system

3.1 CAE Software Integration

The Broker is a software module developed in C++ that allows the remote execution and monitoring of a job by sending messages over TCP/IP connections. The message handling was developed using the message-oriented middleware RabbitMQ, an implementation of the Advanced Message Queuing Protocol (AMQP) [17].

The AMQP Protocol makes use of acknowledgment signals to ensure that messages have been successfully delivered to the consumer.

The choice of RabbitMQ technology was carried out because its ease of use and reasonably good performance overcome the benefit of brute performance offered by other message oriented middlewares [18].

The system includes two main modules:

1. the RabbitMQ server, which handles the messages queues;
2. the RabbitMQ clients, which can interact with the server publishing messages on a queue and/or subscribing to an existing queue; they were developed using C++ RabbitMQ API.

The operating principle of the system is the following: when the immersive visualization system needs to execute a command with specific parameters, it creates a message containing these information and sends it on a specific queue of the job scheduler system; a client software running on the HPC ENEAGRID Cresco (based on a Linux environment) waits for the message and executes the commands in a shell.

The Broker can receive the messages both in synchronous (Get) and asynchronous (Consume) modes. When in synchronous mode, it reads the messages from the queue and, then, it closes the connection. In asynchronous mode it never detaches from the queue and loops waiting for messages.

The two CAE software that were interfaced to the broker are OpenFOAM [19] for CFD simulations and CalculiX [20] for FEM simulations. They were patched in order to be executed on the ENEA HPC Cresco servers equipped with GPGPU boards. It's possible to select between CPU or GPGPU usage modifying the configuration files of the jobs.

A C++ software was developed to permit the remote execution of the jobs from the distributed filesystem (AFS) running on the ENEA infrastructure. It attaches to a queue of the RabbitMQ server waiting to receive messages from the visualization system and executes the commands using the command line.

An additional patch for OpenFOAM was developed to add monitoring functionality during the execution of the job: it sends the "current time" data of the simulation to the RabbitMQ server. The client software which launches the jobs, simultaneously, executes a C++ software module which calculates the progress of the job. The monitoring software gets both the "start time" and "end time" values from the configuration file and the "current time" value available on the RabbitMQ queue; afterward, during each iteration performed by the software, it calculates the percentage of completion and posts the value on a new queue. The progress percentage value is then read by the software running on the visualization system and displayed on the screen.

During the visualization of the job output on the screen, some specific input parameters can be modified through a parser software module developed in C++ which performs the modification on the job's input file. The simulation can then be re-launched to observe the effects of the change on the previous job.

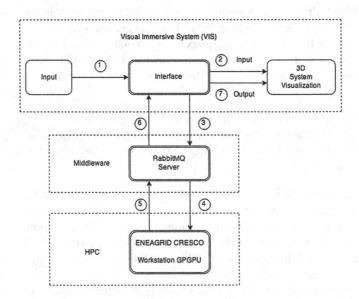

Fig. 2. Simulation of a job flow.

Fig. 3. Example of job's monitoring.

In Fig. 2 the entire workflow is shown; it includes the following steps:

1. Parameters of the job submitted by the user are handled by the client interface to the broker;
2. input parameters are displayed by the 3D system visualization;
3. the command to launch the job is sent to middle-ware RabbitMQ Server;
4. command is read by the software client on HPC hardware and job calculation starts;
5. the progress of the job is sent to the middleware RabbitMQ Server;
6. progress is read by the software module on the interface;
7. the progress is displayed on the 3D system untile completion.

When the job is complete, the results are copied to the local visualization hardware and displayed on 3D system.

In Fig. 3 an example of output printed by job's monitoring module.

3.2 Parallelization of Job Execution

Hardware. In Table 1 there are the specs of the hardware used for the parallelization.

Software. The parallelization of CAE jobs was performed using the Nvidia CUDA GPGPU architecture [21]. In order to solve linear systems and matrices, the version 0.4.0 of CUSP opensource library [22] was used; the library deals with

Table 1. HPC ENEA GPGPU hardware

CPU	Intel Xeon E5620 2.4 Ghz 4 Core
GPU	Nvidia Tesla S2050 (only 1 GPU 448 CUDA Core 3 GB GDDR5 was used)
RAM	24 GB

Table 2. HPC ENEA GPU libraries and software

CUDA version	5.5
Library for CUDA	cusp v. 0.4.0
OpenFOAM version	2.2.x
CUDA library for OpenFOAM	ofgpu v. 1.1
CalculiX Version	2.7
CUDA patch for CalculiX	v4 for ccx 2.7
Operating system	Red Hat 6.2
GCC Compiler version	4.8.2

memory allocation and handles computation on the GPGPU. For this reason the performance of the entire system is affected by this library. To parallelize the execution of OpenFOAM and CalculiX codes, the following open source libraries have been compiled: ofgpu v1.1 for OpenFOAM v 2.2.x [23] and CalculiX Extras Patch v4 for CalculiX v 2.7. [24]. In Table 2 there are the versions of the libraries used for CAE parallelization on GPGPU hardware.

The problem solution of a CAE work is composed by different phases: the stiffness of the matrix assembly, the solution of the linear equations system, the calculation of displacements, stress and strains, the output on the disk, the data transmission to and from the GPU. With the proposed approach, GPGPU calculations are useful in the linear system solution phase.

3.3 CAE Job Configurator

In the present work a configurable CFD simulation was chosen to evaluate configurator. The simulation was carried out with the OpenFOAM package and is, in principle, configurable and modifiable in a lot of ways. From a CAE perspective the geometry modifiability has a very important role; indeed a set of geometrical entities has been selected and used as parameters.

Geometrical parameters are used in a script which, in a batch job on the HPC system, prepares the proper geometry of the airfoil and the calculation mesh around it. The parameters are used to describe the following features:

- the geometric chord length of the airfoil;
- the angle of attack (in radians);
- the height of the channel surrounding the airfoil;
- the depth of airfoil (in the normal direction);
- the length of downstream section.

3.4 Visualization System

Hardware. The software was developed to be deployable on three main configurations: a desktop semi-immersive configuration, a 3D tv configuration and an

Fig. 4. Types of displays for 3D visualization

immersive configuration. First one configuration includes a professional workstation with NVidia Quadro 600 card and a 3D NVidia monitor using 3DVision technology; second one include a workstation with NVidia Quadro K4000 video card connected to a 3D tv; immersive configuration is composed of a complete Virtual Reality Center (VRC) with 3 workstations, each equipped with a NVidia FX480 video card connected to a projector for a WALL configuration. Total display size of the immersive configuration is 9,6 by 2,4 m. In Fig. 4 there are the three types of visualization displays used for the experiment.

Software. Virtual Reality environment related to the platform was developed starting from dune.review, an immersive design review software already described in [25]. The platform already included many features:

- 3D visualization of 3D objects using different types of stereoscopic technologies;
- exploration of 3D objects in an immersive manner;
- interaction with 3D objects using cost-effective tracking devices;
- 3D user interface allowing activation of functionalities and commands.

The effort in this CAE module was to allow integrating results calculated by CAE software through the broker described in Sect. 3.1.

The loading of CAE results was done in 2 main steps:

1. translation of results in .vtk format;
2. translation in a format compatible with existing platform.

The first step was included in OpenFOAM through use of foamToVtk while, for CalculiX, a converter was internally developed for translation. In the second step vtk file was converted in osg file format, adopted by OpenSceneGraph library [26]; this second step was required to allow integrating visualization results into the existing environment. In order to allow displaying continuous simulation, a particular scenegraph was built including a series of switch nodes that stores a different geometry for each time step; a specific command was added to allow running the specified simulation. The translation module includes some configuration options to reduce complexity of results with very big data; reduction regards time-steps and/or geometry triangles and can be configured before launching the job.

A 3D object was developed to display color map in the virtual environment and to launch commands through the broker. The 3D user interface follows the

Fig. 5. 3D visualization of CFD case study using tv configuration in mono configuration (left) and immersive configuration in stereo configuration (right).

same principles introduced in a previous paper [25]: it allows to select functionalities through a 3D pointer and consents to insert parameters through a wireless keyboard. Simulation exploration is allowed through a gamepad in all configurations and through head-tracking in immersive configuration.

Immersive visualization is based on different stereoscopic technologies (among which OpenGL quad buffer and Side by Side) to enable compatibility with many stereoscopic displays; it was tested on a multi channel virtual reality center and on a workstation with a stereoscopic monitor or 3D tv.

In Fig. 5 there is the 3D visualization platform of the CFD case study (described in Sect. 4.1) with 3D tv and immersive configurations including the color map and the 3D UI to interact; the figure on the left isn't in stereoscopic mode for printing purposes.

4   Case Studies

Two case studies were considered to cover both a CFD case study (developed with OpenFOAM) and a FEM study (developed with CalculiX). In the following subsections they are explained from a CAE technical point of view.

4.1   CFD Case Study

As anticipated in Subsect. 3.3 the case study is related to the airflow over a 4-digit NACA airfoil. This case is based on the wingMotion tutorial that uses two steps in the solution: in the first one it calculated the stationary solution, then it starts the transient solver. The advantage of this procedure is that, in the first step, the effects of non-physical initial conditions are simply discarded calculating quickly an averaged stationary flow field. This field is then used as the initial condition for a more computationally demanding transient solver. In Fig. 6 a sketch of the blockMesh topology taken from [16] is shown. Using this approach, the mesh is generated in a structured way allowing to easily parametrize several dimensions of the geometry and the mesh itself. In the case study the flow around the NACA 4412 airfoil has been simulated.

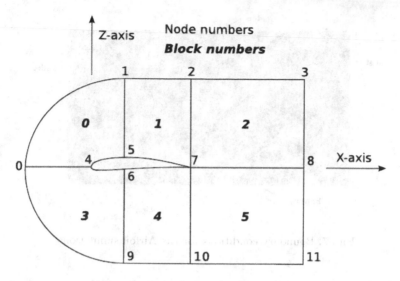

Fig. 6. Geometry and mesh topology for the CFD simulation [16]

Table 3. Airfoil geometric parameters adopted

c	chord length	1 m
α	angle of attack	0.05 rad
H	half heigth of the channel surrounding the airfoil	8 m
W	half depth of airfoil (in the normal direction)	5 m
D	length of downstream section	16 m

The geometrical parameters described in Subsect. 2.4 are chosen as shown in Table 3.

The generated mesh counts 620800 hexahedral cells and is suitable to parallel benchmarking on both CPU and GPGPU architectures.

Boundary conditions are chosen as shown in Fig. 7.

As mentioned before, the simulation is done in two steps: a stationary simulation has been carried out with the *simpleFoam* solver which is a steady-state solver for compressible, turbulent flow and it implements the SIMPLE algorithm; the second simulation is done on top of the previous one and is carried out by the *pimpleFoam* solver which is a large time-step transient solver for incompressible flow using the PIMPLE (merged PISO-SIMPLE) algorithm.

The flow field is air at environment conditions; at the inlet the flow field is a uniform velocity field of $2\,m/s$; the Reynolds number is about 500000; the turbulence model adopted is the standard $k - \omega SST$ model. In both stationary and transient simulations the Preconditioned Conjugate Gradient (PCG) linear solver has been used; it is available in both frameworks for CPU and GPGPU calculations. For CPU simulations the Diagonal incomplete-Cholesky

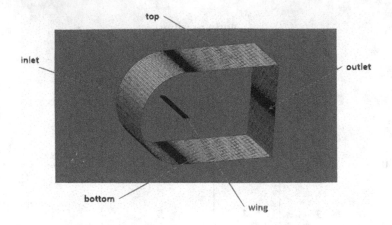

Fig. 7. Boundary conditions for the Airfoil simulations

preconditioner has been used. In both simulations first order schemes are used for discretization and interpolation.

4.2   FEM Case Study

Two non-linear structural case studies were considered as FEM case studies. The case study A concerned a metallic support plate subjected to a pressure load on its largest surface and fixed on the circular lateral surface.

The case study B concerned an aluminum sheet subjected to a plastic deformation process at room temperature (see Fig. 8). In both the models, material and geometric non-linearity were included; in addition, surface to surface contacts were modeled in the case study B. The main difference between the two case studies was the numerical complexity: the spatial discretization (mesh) of the case study A included about 280000 nodes, while nodes in the case study B were 4500. Furthermore, the case study A was a 3D problem, while the case study B was a 2D axisymmetric problem. In Fig. 9, the contour plot of the final equivalent stress is showed for both case studies.

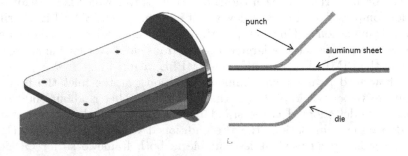

Fig. 8. FEM case study: Metallic support plate (left), aluminum sheet (right)

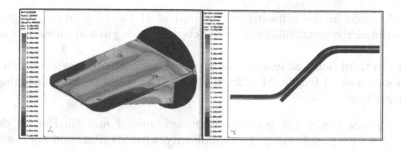

Fig. 9. Final equivalent stress for the case studies A (left) and B (right)

Calculations performed with different solvers (direct, traditional iterative and integrated CPU-GPU iterative) showed no differences in the numerical results.

5   Experiment Procedure and Design

5.1   Research Questions

Our primary goal was to determine to what extent a virtual prototyping platform, which allows configuring parameters directly from the virtual reality environment, can improve the CAE design workflow. We also wanted to determine the ability of the virtual system to simplify reviewing the results of a simulation and comparing performance among a server-class CPU and a GPGPU for selected case studies. Thus, our research questions are as follows:

1. How much time is needed to obtain a new updated visual result using the described approach?
2. What performance GPGPU architectures offer compared to high-end architectures when used for CAE analysis?
3. Can a Virtual Reality environment improve the review of a CAE simulation result integrating the possibility to investigate it in an immersive environment and allowing to apply modifications to the job?

5.2   Study Design

In order to evaluate the first two questions we used case studies described in Sect. 4 and we calculated the performance obtained comparing various measures for each case study and for each hardware platform available. For the third question we administered a questionnaire to CAE engineers, after giving them access to the use of the system.

5.3   Methodology

For the first two points of Subsect. 5.1 numeric measures were taken using the following approach: jobs were launched many times, each time taking the elapsed time calculated in the software; at the end of al the measures outliers were discarded and the mean value was considered for each job and for each configuration.

For the third point an experiment procedure was created involving ten participants (6 male, 4 female, M = 29,8, SD = 2,66). The procedure includes the following steps:

1. Participants would first read the informed consent and filled out a demographics survey, indicating their familiarity with 3D films and applications, with videogames and with 3D monoscopic applications; each question ranged on a scale from 1 (very little familiarity) to 7 (very high);
2. Participant was offered the possibility to choose CFD case study or FEM case study;
3. A brief overview of the chosen case study was given to each participant in order to allow understanding the problem and, eventually, the configurable parameters;
4. After using the system in three proposed visualization configuration another questionnaire was administered to each participant to collect statistics on the developed system.

5.4   Measures

Speedup. The speedup is the metric which was used to evaluate the relative performance improvement when executing tasks using different configurations. The speedup was calculated as the ratio of the running time of sequential execution (Ts) to the running time of the parallel execution (Tp).

$$S = Ts/Tp, \tag{1}$$

The speedup, in this case, provides information on how much faster is a parallel GPGPU calculation than a server-class sequential CPU one. The aim of the comparison is to assess the performance and, in particular, the running time of the calculation codes on CPU and GPGPU. The running time of the calculation codes which run on the CPU is represented by Ts (time serial) while the one on the GPU with Tp (time parallel).

The speedup for the case studies was calculated by running the job first on the CPU and then on GPGPU, comparing the execution time.

For CFD case study, a comparison of speedup between two algorithms is presented to estimate the speedup differences among computationally different algorithms.

Questionnaire. Questionnaire submitted to participants asked for the added value perceived, related to specific features of the proposed system. Further more it investigated on the advantages of this approach than the traditional one. It used answers ranging from 1 (very low) to 7 (very high), as shown in Table 4.

Table 4. Visualization system features of questionnaire.

Question	Desktop	3D tv	VRC
Stereoscopic perception	*from 1 (very low) to 7 (very high)*	*from 1 (very low) to 7 (very high)*	*from 1 (very low) to 7 (very high)*
3D CAE simulation exploration	*from 1 (very low) to 7 (very high)*	*from 1 (very low) to 7 (very high)*	*from 1 (very low) to 7 (very high)*
Interaction with CAE simulation	*from 1 (very low) to 7 (very high)*	*from 1 (very low) to 7 (very high)*	*from 1 (very low) to 7 (very high)*
CAE job configuration from VR environment	*from 1 (very low) to 7 (very high)*	*from 1 (very low) to 7 (very high)*	*from 1 (very low) to 7 (very high)*

The background information reported by the participants indicated that they had little familiarity with 3D stereoscopic films or tv (M: 2.7, SD: 1.16), more familiarity with videogames (M: 3.9, SD: 2.02), while they were more familiar with mono games and/or applications (M: 5.4, SD: 0.97).

6 Experimental Results and Discussion

In this section experimental results of various modules are presented.

6.1 Parallelization Results

CFD Case Study. The results of the parallelization tests for CFD case study using the GPGPU architecture are shown in Figs. 10 and 11: the former is related to simpleFoam solver, the latter is referred to the pimpleFoam solver.

In computational terms, this case study is fairly complex because it consists of 620800 cells and, therefore, it is suitable to be tested on the GPGPU architecture. The solver simpleFoam, being a stationary solver, is computationally significantly lighter than the transient solver pimpleFoam.

Results show that the speedup of the parallel GPGPU execution over the sequential CPU execution is twice with the simpleFoam solver and three times with the pimpleFoam solver.

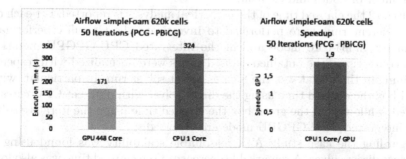

Fig. 10. SimpleFoam execution time CPU vs GPU and speedup

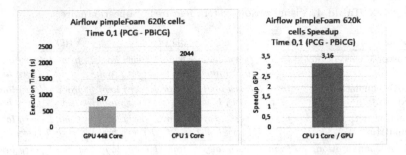

Fig. 11. PimpleFoam execution time CPU vs GPU and speedup

It's important to point out that the calculation is not entirely performed by the GPGPU because part of the work is done only by the CPU (sequential code) affecting the performance of the entire simulation.

The latency for the transfer of data on the GPGPU and between the GPGPU and the memory is a bottleneck and degrades the performance in a remarkable way when it's not negligible compared to the computational time. In particular, once the allocated space has been copied on the GPGPU, the resulting output must be transferred back to the CPU after the calculation.

Moreover, the calculation on a lot of core, when not needed, could lead to an increase of the computing time, due to decomposition and recomposition of the domain.

FEM Case Study. Three different solvers implemented in CalculiX were tested; one direct solver, based on Spooles 2.2 library, and two iterative solvers: the former is a traditional iterative solver with Cholesky pre-conditioning running on CPU, the latter is based on the Cuda-Cusp library implemented to run in the integrated CPU-GPGPU mode. In CalculiX, the direct solver can be used in multi-core mode, while the two iterative solvers use only one core. As a general rule, direct solvers are more robust and recommended for the non-linear problems solution. Instead, the iterative solvers are more efficient in terms of elapsed time and they are recommended for the complex linear problems solution, with huge number of nodes and elements.

In Fig. 12 the elapsed time of the numerical analyses is reported. For each case study, different runs were performed to investigate the CalculiX performance both in the multi-core mode and in the integrated CPU-GPGPU mode. For results comparison, the obtained elapsed times were normalized with respect to the minimum time, that was the 8 cores direct solver run. In particular, within the red box the elapsed time using the direct solver with different CPU cores are reported, while within the green box the elapsed time using the iterative solvers in the integrated CPU-GPGPU mode are reported.

Regarding the case study A, a reasonable scalability was found using the multi-core direct solver. A remarkable decrease of the elapsed time was also found using the integrated CPU-GPGPU iterative solver instead of the traditional one.

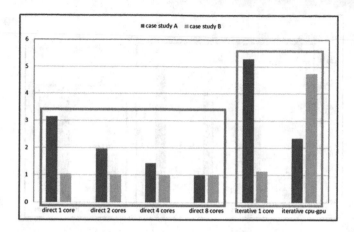

Fig. 12. Elapsed times normalized for the case studies "A" and "B"

In any case, the use of the multi-core direct solver is more convenient than the integrated CPU-GPGPU iterative solver, which uses only one CPU core.

Different results in terms of scalability were found in the case study B. The elapsed time obtained using the direct solver is unchanged by increasing the CPU cores, while it increases using the integrated CPU-GPGPU iterative solver. This unusual trend is due to the calculation procedures used by the FE (Finite Element) solver. As explained in Sect. 3.2 the problem solution of a CAE code is composed by different phases. Regarding CalculiX code, multi-core or GPGPU calculations are useful only in the linear system solution phase; as a consequence, real advantages are observed if this phase is prevailing on the others. This is the case when the complexity of the problem is sufficiently high in terms of nodes and elements number.

In Fig. 13 the speed up for the case studies A and B is also showed respectively for the direct and iterative solvers. As described above, the case study A has a numerical complexity (about 280000 nodes) that justifies the use of multi-core or the GPGPU solver; instead, the case study B has too low complexity (about 4500 nodes) to take advantages from these solutions. In the case study B the use of GPGPU is not recommended because of the latent time due to the data transmission to and from the GPGPU.

In conclusion, regarding the FE calculations results, the three different solvers implemented in CalculiX and tested during the benchmark tests are perfectly equivalent. In relation to the speed up, the use of multi-core or GPGPU is justified for complex models with a great number of nodes and elements. In these cases, the direct solver presents a reasonable scalability; similarly, the iterative CPU-GPGPU solver also allows a considerable increasing of the speed up.

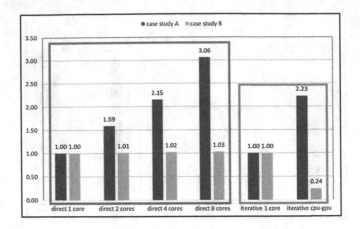

Fig. 13. Speed up for the case studies "A" and "B"

Table 5. Questionnaire results with mean and standard deviation of each feature.

Question	Desktop	3D tv	VRC
Stereoscopic perception	M: 3,4; SD: 1,07	M: 4,4; SD: 1,07	M: 6,2; SD: 0,63
3D CAE simulation exploration	M: 5,0; SD: 0,81	M: 6,2; SD: 0,78	M: 6,2; SD: 0,79
Interaction with CAE simulation	M: 3,9; SD: 0,99	M: 4.1; SD: 1.20	M: 4,5; SD: 1,08
CAE job configuration from VR environment	M: 4,2; SD: 1,03	M: 4,3; SD: 0,99	M: 5,1; SD: 0,99

6.2   Questionnaire Results

The information reported by the participants, reported in Table 5, show a poor stereoscopic visualization offered by low-end stereo devices, which sometimes are affected by ghosting and cross-talking problems, whereas a rich stereoscopic visualization is perceived with high-end stereo devices.

3D CAE simulation exploration feature perceived by participants seems to be particularly appreciated. It allows to navigate outside and inside the simulation data and, in this scenario, 3D visualization shows its added value in all three configurations.

Interaction with CAE simulation shows mid-level results, that should be justified with high familiarity using a mouse/keyboard configuration and little acquaintance using 3D devices declared by users.

Results in CAE job configurator from VR environment evidence how this system is evaluated useful by participants and how it should represent the new technology and methodology approach in the CAE analysis.

7   Conclusions and Future Work

An experimental virtual prototyping system for CAE engineers has been developed offering the possibility to setup job parameters directly inside the virtual environment and to visualize the simulation data in an immersive way. Following the main results got with the proposed system:

- a perceivable speedup is obtained on case studies which presents an high number of nodes;
- the middle-ware was proven to be extremely extensible to the integration of new interfaces;
- CAE engineers involved in the experiment, evaluated it as an useful tool to speed up their work, during parameters setup, and to explore results.

Further work is required to allow using multi-gpu configurations, doing more benchmarks on more complex data, automating the process to make a job configurable and completing interfaces to other CAE software and new visualization devices.

Acknowledgments. The research activities of this paper are partly funded by the research program PONREC VIS4Factory. Grant Cod. PON02_00634_3551288.

References

1. Wang, G.G.: Definition and review of virtual prototyping. J. Comput. Inf. Sci. Eng. **2**(3), 232–236 (2002)
2. Zeng, Y., HorváTh, I.: Editorial: fundamentals of next generation CAD/E systems. Comput. Aided Des. **44**(10), 875–878 (2012)
3. Elmqvist, N.: Visualization reloaded: redefining the scientific agenda for visualization research. In: Proceedings of HCI Korea. HCIK 2015, South Korea, Hanbit Media, Inc. 132–137 (2014)
4. Bryson, S.: Virtual environments in scientific visualization. In: Virtual Reality for Visualization, Course Notes of Tutorial 5 at Visualization 1995, Course (1995)
5. Chua, C., Teh, S., Gay, R.: Rapid prototyping versus virtual prototyping in product design and manufacturing. Int. J. Adv. Manuf. Technol. **15**(8), 597–603 (1999)
6. Zorriassatine, F., Wykes, C., Parkin, R., Gindy, N.: A survey of virtual prototyping techniques for mechanical product development. Proc. Inst. Mech. Eng. Part B: J. Eng. Manuf. **217**(4), 513–530 (2003)
7. Appel, S., Sachs, K., Buchmann, A.: Towards benchmarking of AMQP. In: Proceedings of the Fourth ACM International Conference on Distributed Event-Based Systems. DEBS 2010, pp. 99–100. ACM, New York (2010)
8. Dawar, S., van der Meer, S., Fallon, E., Keeney, J., Bennett, T.: Building a scalable event processing system with messaging and policies-test and evaluation of rabbitmq and drools expert (2013)
9. Radchenko, G., Hudyakova, E.: Distributed virtual test bed: an approach to integration of CAE systems in unicore grid environnement. In: 2013 36th International Convention on Information & Communication Technology Electronics & Microelectronics (MIPRO), 163–168. IEEE (2013)
10. Jamshidi, Z., Khunjush, F.: Optimization of openfoam's linear solvers on emerging multi-core platforms. In: 2011 IEEE Pacific Rim Conference on Communications, Computers and Signal Processing (PacRim), pp. 824–829. IEEE (2011)

11. AlOnazi, A.: Design and optimization of openfoam-based CFD applications for modern hybrid and heterogeneous HPC platforms. M.sc. thesis, University College Dublin, Dublin, December 2013
12. Tomczak, T., Zadarnowska, K., Koza, Z., Matyka, M., Mirosław, Ł.: Complete piso and simple solvers on graphics processing units. In: arXiv preprint (2012) arXiv:1207.1571
13. Maleshkov, S., Chotrov, D.: Post-processing of engineering analysis results for visualization in VR systems. In: CoRR abs/1308.5847 (2013)
14. Song, I., Yang, J.: A scene graph based visualization method for representing continuous simulation data. Comput. Ind. **62**(3), 301–310 (2011)
15. Frame, S.W., Rose, D., Ertl, T.: Interactive visualization of large finite element models. In: Workshop on Vision, Modelling, and Visualization VMV, vol. 3, pp. 585–592 (2003)
16. Wiki, H.: Openfoam - airfoil calculations (2013). https://www.hpc.ntnu.no/display/hpc/OpenFOAM+-+Airfoil+Calculations
17. Vinoski, S.: Advanced message queuing protocol. IEEE Internet Comput. **10**(6), 87–89 (2006)
18. Kamppuri, T., et al.: Message brokers and rabbitmq in action (2014)
19. Jasak, H., Jemcov, A., Tukovic, Z.: Openfoam: a C++ library for complex physics simulations. Int. Workshop Coupled Meth. Numer. Dyn. **1000**, 1–20 (2007)
20. Dhondt, G., Wittig, K.: Calculix: A Free Software Three-Dimensional Structural Finite Element Program. MTU Aero Engines GmbH, Munich (1998)
21. Nvidia, C.: Compute unified device architecture programming guide (2007)
22. Bell, N., Garland, M.: Cusp: generic parallel algorithms for sparse matrix and graph computations. Version 0.3. 0, 35 (2012)
23. Symscape: Gpu v1.1 linear solver library for openfoam. http://www.symscape.com/gpu-1-1-openfoam
24. Gustafson, P.A., Kapenga, J.A.: Implementation of the cuda cusp and cholmod solvers in calculix (2014)
25. Martini, A., Colizzi, L., Chionna, F., Argese, F., Bellone, M., Cirillo, P., Palmieri, V.: A novel 3d user interface for the immersive design review. In: IEEE Symposium on 3D User Interfaces 2015, ISBN: 978-1-4673-6886-5, pp. 175–176 (2015)
26. Burns, D., Osfield, R.: Open scene graph a: introduction, b: examples and applications (2004)

A Proposed Hardware-Software Architecture for Virtual Reality in Industrial Applications

Francesco Chionna[1], Piero Cirillo[1], Vito Palmieri[1], and Mauro Bellone[2](✉)

[1] Consorzio CETMA, c/o Cittadella Della Ricerca S.S. 7 - Km 706+030,
72100 Brindisi, Italy
[2] Department of Applied Mechanics, Chalmers University of Technology,
41296 Göteborg, Sweden
mauro.bellone@chalmers.se

Abstract. Increase the level of interaction with CAD engines constitutes a challenging problem for industries such as aerospace and automotive which require high degree of details inspection during the design
process. A high level of interaction can be provided using immersive
virtual environments. However, the use of virtual reality for industrial
applications introduces a number of problems since interaction requires
tracking systems but also the design of user-friendly 3D interfaces. Our
work aims to develop a cost-effective hardware/software VR platform
which increases the level of interaction, interfacing with the most common CAD engines. On one hand, the realization of such a complex platform requires high performance devices. On the other hand, industrial
applications require reliable and cost-effective solutions and, for this reason, the presented platform features a novel solution for the accurate
hand tracking which combines a depth camera and the WiiRemote in
this concern.

Keywords: Computer graphics · Virtual reality · Software engineering ·
Computer aided design

1 Introduction

Technologies in virtual reality and augmented reality keep continuously growing,
breaking up new boundaries in the design review process. From old 2D models to
modern 3D computer graphics, developers always look for new, and more communicative, ways for the creative expression of ideas. The natural consequence,
after 3D computer graphics, consists in the development of novel immersive systems which bring users into the ideas, using virtual environments. In this concern, researchers have been working since years on the investigation of VR and
computer graphics [1]. From their advent, the application of VR and immersive
systems has been investigated on several fields such as medical [2], entertainment [3], design review [4,5] and much more. Specifically, with design review
researchers generally refer to the specific process of digital examination and

© Springer International Publishing Switzerland 2015
L.T. De Paolis and A. Mongelli (Eds.): AVR 2015, LNCS 9254, pp. 287–300, 2015.
DOI: 10.1007/978-3-319-22888-4_21

inspection of products, mechanical parts or even construction projects, in order to take specific decisions before their physical realization.

Studying past researches in this field, it is evident that the development brought technologies from simple 3D visualization systems toward immersive VR systems, in which the user can interact with, and design review is revealed as a potential application attracting economic and industrial interests. Focusing on the latter, in [6] the authors have explored the problem of CAD models handling in virtual environments. Whereas, in [7] the impact that immersive VR technologies can have on the visualization of a design review scenario was studied. More specifically, the authors investigated the construction of a disabled bathroom in a block of flats in an immersive environment, helping in the contemplation of unexpected events during the design process. In support to recent developments of VR in the design review process for industrial application, in [8] the authors describe a method for virtual prototypes inspection through an immersive virtual environment. However, the method addressed in [8] requires the user to dress cyber gloves for hand localization and tracking.

Normally, to create immersive VR environments different techniques exist [9], classifiable by the screens types and number. Single surface display solution is widely used for its cost-effectiveness. In [10] the authors investigated the possibility of using a wide screen stereoscopic displays against a head mounted devices. Whereas, multiple screen solution is mostly used to provide to a group of users an immersive sensation, such as in [11] in which the authors studied interaction with graphical menus in virtual environments using a multi screen solution.

In spite of the great step forward that immersive technologies made in the last years, problems and open issues are countless resulting in a large number of research activities which involve worldwide universities. Among others, the development of simple and user-friendly 3D interactive user interfaces, referred to as 3dUIs, constitutes a crucial development line. A recent work in this issue cope with this problem using a smart-phone-based menu system interface for immersive virtual environments [12]. Although this research represents a step forward in the use of interaction interfaces in immersive reality, the use of a mobile device may result in a poor immersive sensation for the user due to possible distractions when the user looks at the mobile screen instead of large screen. Moreover, during a design review process often happens to discuss about different aspects of the same product. For instance, in the automotive field, the review process is related to mechanics, style and ergonomic issues, and the comparison of different models and solutions needs to run different instances of different software. In such a situation, the users may require to switch between visualizations or to discuss on different issues and even an interactive modification of 3D models [13].

In the light of all cited criticisms, it results evident that new contributions and further researches are required in order to increase the level of immersive sensation and usability for the user. As a contribution, our proposal includes an immersive system for CAD visualization in an immersive environment in which a 3dUI movable interface is projected onto the screen and it can be simply

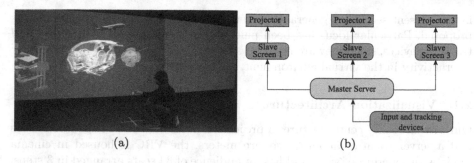

Fig. 1. Virtual Reality Center screens in stereographic rendering during a immersive session (a), and a general explanation of the master-slave configuration in the Virtual Reality Center (b).

controlled using a tracking system and a simple remote controller. Our software, referred to as Dune, aims to simplify the design review process through an immersive virtual reality system based on the combination of opensource platforms and cost effective tracking devices. Specifically, the Dune platform features a module which allows to load common 3D CAD models such as 'step', 'iges' or 'stl' files in order to provide the possibility to present, interact and manipulate them in the immersive environment through user movements.

In summary, the main strength of the proposed platform are:

- the interaction between user and virtual reality engine is mostly done using cost-effective tracking devices;
- the development of a software architecture that is simple to maintain and expand, thanks to its modularity;
- the implementation of a user friendly 3dUIs.

The rest of the paper is organized as follows. Section 2 discusses the system overview including a general hardware description. The software architecture is better detailed in Sect. 3, in which its single modules are thoroughly exposed, including our custom solutions to handle tracking devices. As further strength of our software architecture, Sect. 4 introduces the 3D user interfaces specifically conceived for this application. A discussion on users' opinions is given in Sect. 5. Finally, Sect. 6 gives some final conclusions.

2   System Overview

The aims of our custom platform is to create an immersive design environment that could answer to the designers requirements. It is evident that an immersive system requires the combination of hardware and software components. The main considerations about software concern reliability, modularity, maintainability and expandability, but also the implementation of a user friendly immersive interface, preserving the cost effectiveness of hardware components. Following in the present section, a general overview about the hardware of our system is proposed. Particular focus has been paid on the visualization architecture and trackers devices, since they are revealed as key issues to provide a high level user interactivity in the virtual environment.

2.1   Visualization Architecture

Our virtual reality center features a projection room of about 144 square meters and a server room of about 25 square meters, the VRC is housed in cinema mode with soundproof walls and has an audience of 34 seats arranged in 3 steps. Figure 1 shows our reality center screen during a design review session (a). The display system is characterized by the system MOVe of the BARCO and it features 3 movable screens. Each screen is characterized by a surface area of 3.3 m × 2.4 m for a total of 9.6 m long and 2.40 m height, the sides screens can be rotated from CADWALL configuration to a CAVE configuration, passing from intermediate configurations 0.0°, 22.5°, 45.0°, 90.0°. The choice of a multiple display is motivated by the necessity of increasing the user space mobility, this solution offers an high level of immersion [14]. Surfaces of the screens are made using a translucent material for projection and stereo rendering. Moreover, a rear projection system has been employed in order to ensure the maximization of user mobility and immersive experience avoiding any possible shadow in the scene. The set of the described features, as much as the use of a 3D stereo projection system, allow users to fully enjoy different scenarios and simulations into immersive environments.

Stereographic rendering requires two images to be generated and displayed at the same time, one computed for the right and one for the left eye. Our solution uses a high refresh rate CRT projector featuring up to 120 Hz as refresh rate. Using the inherent speed of DLP technology, the Optoma EX785 can output video and images at an astonishing rate of 120 Hz, allowing us to show full screen, full color, stereoscopic 3D scenes. The 3D effect is generated by splitting the signal into two standard video streams, one for each eye. As the visualization system requires high graphics performance, our computing system features 4 high-end workstations with Nvidia Quadro FX 4500. The workstations are interconnected in a master/slave architecture, better detailed in Fig. 1(b) Specifically, our architecture uses a single workstation as a master server and 3 slaves, one for each screen. The master has the task of visualization synchronization and sensors data acquisition, whereas the slaves are in charge of a single portion of the scene rendering. The connection between master and slave is made using a client-server structure.

2.2   Trackers and Input Devices

The difference between the implementation of a simple immersive environment and a design review immersive environment consists in the increasing level of interactivity which is required in the latter. Past immersive design review software could only visualize 3D parts, then a low level of interactive functions have been implemented. However, they generally include only basic functions of rotating and moving parts. Our challenge concerned the creation of a virtual environment dedicated to the visualization of CAD objects in which the user can interact with, in real-time using its own movements. In this concern, tracking systems provide an effective way to interpret users' movements in the real world and convert them into actions in the virtual world.

Nowadays, numerous technologies can achieve movements recognition, from visual skeleton tracking to electromagnetic motion tracking. The former provides high mobility and freedom for the user involving visual information, whereas electromagnetic sensors are much more accurate in position estimation but they may reduce user mobility since they are generally wearable devices. Bearing in mind the above considerations, Dune uses two different approaches to track the user position, a kinect device for visual skeletal information and a FASTRACK for accurate head and hand position. The kinect sensor is well-known and common in the computer graphics community. From RGB camera and depth information, the software is able to calculate a skeleton model of the user with the corresponding nodal points including their position with respect to the camera reference frame. The FASTRAK tracks the position (x, y, and z Cartesian coordinates) and orientation (ρ, θ, ϕ roll, pitch and yaw) of a small sensor as it moves in the space.

However, noise, vibration and the resulting jitter is sometimes unavoidable in the tracking applications. A numerical filter, the 1€filter [15], has been applied to all the joints position in order to minimize jitter and lag. The 1€ filter is an adaptive first-order low-pass filter: it adapts the cutoff frequency of a low-pass filter for each new sample according to an estimation of the signal speed.

Input devices aim to simplify the functionalities activation by designers. Gamepads or space navigators help designers to navigate into the scene and to control functionalities. However, if the user wants to be free to move using one hand to activate functionalities and to control objects, the use of a wireless remote control become mandatory. Our choice is the Nintendo Wii Remote device. The Wii Remote includes a set of buttons for the basic functions, an IR sensor for tracking up to four IR sources with a refresh rate of 100 Hz and a three axis linear accelerometer that provides motion sensor capabilities.

Dune uses Wii Remote capabilities as a pointer, for the wrist motion recognition and functionalities activation. In its original form, Wii Remote is used as a pointer in combination with an IR bar. While internal sensors, such as accelerometer and gyroscope, only allow to obtain the wrist orientation with a reasonable accuracy, the use of an IR bar is required to obtain wrist translation data [16]. However, in an immersive environment the use of an IR leds bar may be not effective due to the screen size and position. As the matter of fact, the IR sensor in the Wii Remote must be visible for the IR leds bar, and this can be a problem while pointing toward a high size screen.

Interaction in VR applications, using the Wii Remote accelerometer data, ranges from basic shake triggering, to tilt-and-balance control, till simple gesture recognition. Furthermore, the remote control is also used as a pointer. Using the

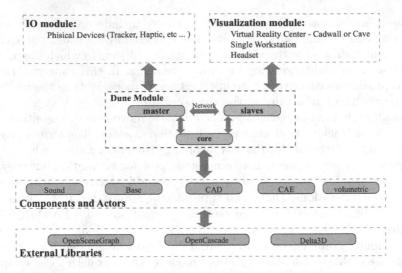

Fig. 2. Dune brief software architecture and its modules. Please refer to the Sect. 3 for further details.

Wii Remote, the Dune.Review immersive environment implements a large variety of functionalities, including mapping, selecting objects, moving the objects in the VE while the user moves in the real world, change and reset camera view, and much more.

3   Software Architecture

The complete Dune software architecture, schematically depicted in Fig. 2, is fully coded using C++, and it is based on popular open source libraries in 3D community, such as OpenSceneGraph, Delta3D and OpenCascade. At the current stage, our software is composed of several modules: Dune core, components, engines, IO and visualization.

Dune core: the core is in charge of messages parsing (among master and slaves), scene handling (light, virtual camera and viewpoint) and communication between modules. As mentioned in Sect. 3, a master workstation has the task of:

– system configuration (visualization, I/O devices, slaves, scene);
– I/O data and events handling;
– data communication;
– synchronization among clients;
– editing functionalities of the scene (among which animations and other simulation features).

The communication architecture is based on the Delta3D engine, which foresees that any module sends a message to the master which forwards the message to the appropriate module or device.

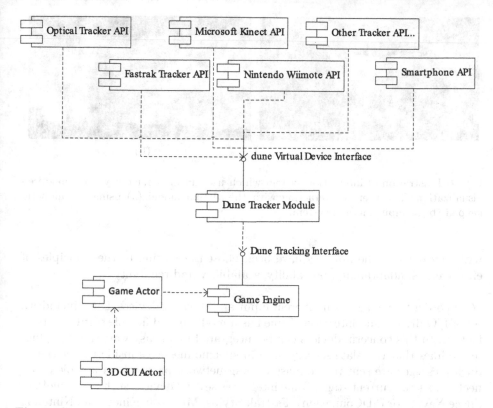

Fig. 3. Component diagram showing the tracking policy and communication with 3dUIs using virtual devices interfaces.

Components and actors: as derived from Delta3D, Dune objects in the immersive environment can be distinguished as *components* and *actors*. A component is a module handling 3D objects that must be always in the scene, such as lights or virtual camera, whereas all other objects dynamically loaded and projected into the scene are referred to as actors. Dune can handle several types of actors such as CAD models or UIs. As an actor can be any object, it becomes simple for programmers to implement a new module which simply adds a new actor into the scene, providing a high level of flexibility to the software. Moreover, this specific property of modularity allows to handle any actor using different manipulation functionalities, e.g. a CAD model can be modified in its shape, whereas the UIs can be used to select a new action, to change the viewpoint of the virtual camera or to modify lighting in the scene. In this way, the data logic functionalities are transferred to the actors. Using such approach, it is possible to populate the virtual world with multiple game actors simultaneously and to interact with each actor in an independent way, applying different functionalities.

External Libraries: the set of libraries at the base of Dune which allows the loading of any actor in the virtual environment, as much as the communication

(a)   (b)

Fig. 4. Illustration of interaction system which uses an immersive keyboard in stereo visualization. The user is interacting with the virtual model (a) using the numeric keypad (b) as input method system.

with any device. The libraries have been chosen according to the principles of effectiveness, adaptability, portability, scalability and reliability.

IO: in order to manage with different input and tracking devices, Dune includes a set of I/O drivers and interfaces. Dune has a modular and flexible software architecture. In this concern, devices can be integrated in an easy way, through plug-in modules that translate sensory data in specific messages inside the platform. Such messages are sent to the master using network protocols in a cabled connection. At the current stage, Dune integrates several devices such as: GamePad, Space Navigator (3DConnexion), Fastrak Stylus, Microsoft Kinect and Nintendo Wii Remote controller. As further strength of its modularity, the cited devices are integrated using open source libraries such as OpenNI and WiiYourself.

Visualization: this module is in charge of the visualization handling in Dune. This part is the most important in order to provide an effective immersive sensation during the design review sessions. The visualization on each screen is dedicated to one of the slaves which uses an Ethernet communication to be synchronized with the master. Following the principles of flexibility and portability, the visualization module allows the visualization on single channel, multichannel and even stereo visualization on portable devices (see Fig. 2).

As one of the key requirements of our software consists in the maximization of the immersion perception, the user has to interact with the virtual scene, moving in the real world. In this concern, Fig. 3 exposes how tracking devices data are handled in Dune.review. For the sake of preserving the modularity, all sensors APIs communicate with a so called *Virtual Device Interface*, which provides data for the tracking module. This gives much strength to our software allowing to simply add a new device by including a new API module (see Fig. 3). The tracking module is in charge of elaborating pose data (e.g. joints Cartesian coordinates and orientations) independently of which sensors they come from, forwarding them to the tracking interface. As last, pose data can be used to control scene components or they can be projected by the game engine as a

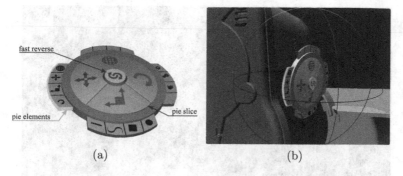

Fig. 5. Representation of our custom pie menú featuring different functions for the user. In (a) its 3D rendering is shown with emphasis to one of the slices, marked as blue, and a selected pie elements, labeled using green color. The fast reverse button is located in the center. Whereas the pie menú projected into a virtual environment is shown in (b) (Color figure online).

new actor (e.g. skeleton visualization). This functionality, achieved using the tracking sensor installed at the top of the center screen, provides a high sensation of immersion, since the user can change his viewpoint by interacting with the virtual camera, e.g. the user can see both sides of an object by moving his head on left or right.

4 3D Interaction

One of the main issues for a deep immersive experience is the simplicity of software functionalities selection. As designers are totally involved in the visualization system and require a total freedom of movements, an accurately designed graphics user interface must be embedded inside the virtual world. The 3D immersive GUI should be intuitive, immediate, and user-friendly [13]. In the proposed software for design review, two different immersive GUI have been implemented offering different levels of interaction. The former is an immersive keyboard, see Fig. 4, whereas the latter is a pie menú, shown in Fig. 5. Using immersive keyboards or numerical pads, designers are able to assign controlled values to geometrics, physics or mechanics magnitude. This feature is important when designers want to assign specific values to objects (e.g. position, scale, colors, material).

A pointing system helps the user to interact with the immersive UIs through his arms movements. In order to provide a realism during interaction [17], the virtual pointer in the virtual world must accurately follow the user's hand movements. Such pointing is realized using the Wii Remote device, hence the user points his hand toward the screen and a virtual ray is shown in the pointing direction, as shown in Fig. 4. In particular, specific algorithms for six Degree Of Freedom (a.k.a. 6DoF) wrist pose estimation through Inertial Measurement Unit (IMU) information have been used. It results evident that such measure must be

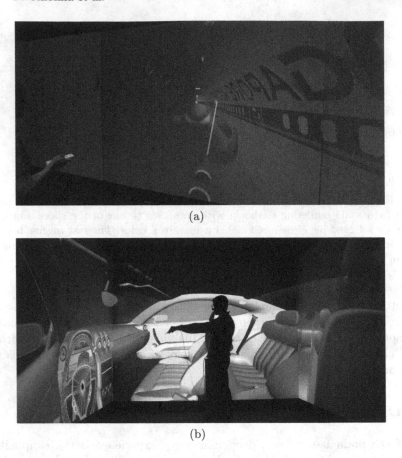

Fig. 6. Examples of Dune functionalities during a design review session in which the user regulates the shape of an airplane model (a), uses a torch function to navigate inside the virtual environment (b) and studies the car interior ergonomics (c).

done in real time to ensure the proper immersive sensation. The wrist orientation is calculated using three methods: (i) Simple Simpson integration with hard thresholding and weighted gravity update; (ii) Gradient descent; (iii) Mayhony's DCM (Direct Cosine Matrix). Methods (ii) and (iii) are based on Madgwick's implementation [18] with minor modifications. In order to use the Wii Remote as an orientation tracker for short-term and highly dynamic motions, researchers' choice focused on Madgwick's gradient descent approach, since it shows higher accuracy. As in this situation is not possible to use the IR bar (see Sect. 2 for more details), the Wii Remote can only provides information about wrist orientation through its inertial sensor. Hence, the problem of wrist position estimation with reference to the camera frame still remains. In this regards, a tracking system based on Kinect information has been also used. Our solution of combining Kinect and Wii Remote information was inspired by [19], in which an effective

Fig. 7. Example of design review session concerning a new mall, where the user can navigate inside the virtual environment.

approach that solves such problem has been thoroughly investigated. In such way, it is possible to obtain an effective pointing system, which is required to easily manipulate 3D objects through an immersive interface.

Classical design review software has a large number of functionalities, generally accessible through 2D interfaces which include windows, menus or tool boxes. On the contrary, during an interactive session, it is not possible to use common solutions. A pie menú was designed in this purpose, depicted in Fig. 5. Such 3D pie menú represents a starting point to define the guidelines for the implementation of richer 3dUIs.

Specifically, our pie menú has two reversible faces, each one including four widget and four handles. Each handle allows to change the visible widgets, which are binded to specific software actions, whereas the circle in the middle allows its fast reverse. The green color marks the selected pie-elements, see Fig. 5-(c). Using this approach, in a single pie space, it is possible to collect up to 32 software functionalities easily actionable by user interaction, e.g. translations, rotations, scaling or wireframe visualization of a specific object. Increasing the number of handles on a hypothetical concentric circle level around the pie menú, it is possible to increase the available functionalities. The user interacts with the menú using the virtual ray. Hence, the user simply points the ray toward a specific section of the 3D menú and push the Wii Remote button to activate the functionality.

5   Discussion

Along with the development, Dune.review has been intensively tested by developers in order to implement functionalities of increasing quality. Moreover, during our design review implementation two types of users have been involved: designers and unexperienced users[1]. Along with the tests, functionalities that have been perceived as a necessity by both have been implemented and tested. Specifically, while designers have pointed out the necessity of high level of interaction, unexperienced users have focused on navigation and visualization issues.

As first example, Fig. 6-(a) shows a designer while using the pie menú during a design review session. The designer is using CAD functionalities to regulate the shape of the plane while at the same time looking at its real shape in an immersive environment. The pie menú shows the CAD functionalities and, specifically, the user has selected the action to modify a NURBS (Non-Uniform Rationale B-Splines) through control points. It is worth to mention that this functionality allows to select a set of control points, or even a single point, and to manipulate them by freehand drag and drop. Moreover, the user can quickly display the result of the manipulation as soon as the control points are moved. One should note that, for this specific functionality, the accuracy of the pointing system must be enough high to ensure a simple manipulation. As further functionality, in Fig. 6-(b) an unexperienced user is looking inside the 3D model using a virtual torch function, which illuminates the portion of the model where the virtual ray is pointing on. This function has been detected as really helpful by users in order to focus on specific areas into a 3D model. The designers feel this functionality as helpful to thoroughly inspect the 3D models in order to detect possible unexpected defects. Lastly, Fig. 6-(c) shows an example of design review session in CAVE configuration, in which the user is interacting with a sportive car, studying its ergonomics in an immersive way. One of the important aspect of this analysis consists of the study of the car blind spots.

It is worth noting that, when the user navigates into the virtual environment, the pie menú may be located at the front of the virtual camera, occluding some parts of objects. On the contrary, it may be lost in a huge virtual environment, such as in Fig. 7.

In helping to solve these issues, the pie menú has two specific functions that allow to move it out of the viewpoint but also to bring it at the front of the user when it is necessary. This functionality can be activated pressing a shortcut available on the pointing device.

6   Conclusion

In this paper, a novel platform for design review was presented, with focus on 3D immersive interfaces. Specifically, the proposed 3dUIs are designed to be user-friendly while, at the same time, offering immersive CAD functionalities.

[1] Research activity conducted as part of the Italian research program – PONREC PROGIMM Cod. DM28904.

Extensive tests performed by both designers and unexperienced users revealed that the introduction of the pie menú into the virtual environment may enhance the access to immersive CAD functionalities. The pie menú was detected as helpful by designers for the high level of manipulation actions made available, as much as by unexperienced users for its navigation capabilities. However, more research is required to improve usability for beginners, since in literature it does not exist a cost effective solution to bind CAD functionalities and user-friendly interfaces in the immersive environments. To cite a future development line, the collaborative features will allow networked users to share the same CAD project in real time using an editing token policy. Further tracking or haptic devices could be also integrated to provide increasing level of interaction thanks to our modular architecture. Finally, the introduction of FEM analysis data, such as stress analysis or fluid dynamics, could bring these technologies toward new boundaries of the immersive design review.

Acknowledgments. The research activities of this paper are partly funded by the research program PONREC VIS4Factory. Grant Cod. PON02_00634_3551288.

References

1. Czernuszenko, M., Pape, D., Sandin, D., DeFanti, T., Dawe, G.L., Brown, M.D.: The immersadesk and infinity wall projection-based virtual reality displays. SIG-GRAPH Comput. Graph. **31**(2), 46–49 (1997)
2. Lim, D., Ibrahim, H., Ngah, U.: Development of virtual reality system for medical application using opengl. In: IEEE Conference on Innovative Technologies in Intelligent Systems and Industrial Applications, 2008. CITISIA 2008, pp. 44–48, July 2008
3. Zyda, M.: From visual simulation to virtual reality to games. Comput. **38**(9), 25–32 (2005)
4. Jayaram, S., Jayaram, U., Wang, Y., Tirumali, H., Lyons, K., Hart, P.: Vade: a virtual assembly design environment. IEEE Comput. Graph. Appl. **19**(6), 44–50 (1999)
5. Hughes, C.E., Zhang, L., Schulze, J.P., Edelstein, E., Macagno, E.: Cavecad: architectural design in the cave. In: 2013 IEEE Symposium on 3D User Interfaces (3DUI), pp. 193–194, March 2013
6. Weidlich, D., Cser, L., Polzin, T., Cristiano, D., Zickner, H.: Virtual reality approaches for immersive design. CIRP Ann. Manuf. Technol. **56**(1), 139–142 (2007)
7. Bassanino, M., Wu, K.C., Yao, J., Khosrowshahi, F., Fernando, T., Skjrbk, J.: The impact of immersive virtual reality on visualisation for a design review in construction. In: 2010 14th International Conference Information Visualisation (IV), pp. 585–589, July 2010
8. Fillatreau, P., Fourquet, J.Y., Bolloch, R.L., Cailhol, S., Datas, A., Puel, B.: Using virtual reality and 3D industrial numerical models for immersive interactive checklists. Comput. Ind. **64**(9), 1253–1262 (2013). Special Issue: 3D Imaging in Industry
9. Fuchs, P., Moreau, G., Guitton, P.: Virtual Reality: Concepts and Technologies, 1st edn. CRC Press Inc., Boca Raton (2011)

10. Naceri, A., Chellali, R., Dionnet, F., Toma, S.: Depth perception within virtual environments: a comparative study between wide screen stereoscopic displays and head mounted devices. In: Future Computing, Service Computation, Cognitive, Adaptive, Content, Patterns, 2009. COMPUTATIONWORLD 2009. Computation World, pp. 460–466, Nov 2009

11. Dang, N., Perrot, V., Mestre, D.: Effects of sensory feedback while interacting with graphical menus in virtual environments. In: IEEE Virtual Reality Conference, VR 2011, Singapore, 19–23 March 2011, pp. 199–200 (2011)

12. Gebhardt, S., Pick, S., Oster, T., Hentschel, B., Kuhlen, T.: An evaluation of a smart-phone-based menu system for immersive virtual environments. In: 2014 IEEE Symposium on 3D User Interfaces (3DUI), pp. 31–34, March 2014

13. Martini, A., Colizzi, L., Chionna, F., Argese, F., Bellone, M., Cirillo, P., Palmieri, V.: A novel 3D user interface for the immersive design review. In: IEEE Symposium on 3D User Interfaces 2015, pp. 175-176 (2015). ISBN: 978-1-4673-6886-5

14. Peternier, A., Cardin, S., Vexo, F., Thalmann, D.: Practical design and implementation of a CAVE environment. In: Proceedings 2nd International Conference on Computer Graphics Theory, pp. 129–136 (2007)

15. Casiez, G., Roussel, N., Vogel, D.: 1€ Filter: a simple speed-based low-pass filter for noisy input in interactive systems. In: CHI 2012, the 30th Conference on Human Factors in Computing Systems, pp. 2527–2530. Austin, ACM, May 2012

16. Lee, J.: Hacking the nintendo wii remote. IEEE Pervasive Comput. **7**(3), 39–45 (2008)

17. Ergonomics of human-system interaction: Human-centred design for interactive systems : ISO 9241–210. Number pt. 210 in DIN EN ISO. ISO (2010)

18. Madgwick, S.: An efficient orientation filter for inertial and inertial/magnetic sensor arrays. Report X-IO and University of Bristol (UK) (2010)

19. Hald, K.: Low-cost 3dUI using hand tracking and controllers. In: 2013 IEEE Symposium on 3D User Interfaces (3DUI), pp. 205–206, March 2013

Using Haptic Forces Feedback
for Immersive and Interactive Simulation
in Industrial Context

Marwene Kechiche[(✉)], Mohamed-Amine Abidi, Patrick Baert,
and Rosario Toscano

Ecole nationale d'ingénieurs de Saint-Etienne,
58, rue Jean Parot, 40023 Saint-Étienne, Cedex 2, France
{marwene.kechiche,mohamed-amine.abidi,patrick.baert,
rosario.toscano}@enise.fr

Abstract. In a world in continuous evolution of information technology and computer science, virtual reality (VR) is a very important technological tool in several areas such as industrial simulations. In this paper, we will present some cases of the uses of VR, mainly in the industrial area, and in ergonomic tests and evaluations. In this work, we will present our approach that allows the use of haptic force feedback using a subjective method. In the first part, we will start with the state of the art by presenting a new approach based on a set of acquisitions in the mobile rolling operation in the real world and in the industrial context. In addition to that, we will study operator muscular forces exercised over a rolling mobile operation (to displace it from one point to another). In particular, we will introduce how we can integrate a subjective method of calculating forces in a VR simulation for a realistic operator interaction and mobile behavior. We will also use certain techniques of virtual reality to immerse the operator, with the system of the relative forces exerted and other information.

This paper comprises three main parts: the first one is a general study of the haptic force feedback techniques in VR applications (haptic rendering). The second part presents the modules, the architecture and how we can integrate these techniques in our application. The final part is a discussion of the developed application and its results with some perspectives.

Keywords: Virtual reality · Haptic force feedback · 3D visualization · 3D interactions · Ergonomic evaluations

1 Introduction

The continuous evolution of computer science and 3D technologies (e.g. GPU, memories and graphic cards) has allowed VR to be more advanced and more useful. VR can be defined by the concept of dimension I^3 (Interaction-Immersion-Imagination) [1]. VR requires some human-machine interaction between the interactive virtual environment systems and the user. We can utilize different types of sensorimotor to interact with virtual environments (VE). Actually, several virtual reality applications are based on the visual rendering and the 3D display systems to immerse operators in

© Springer International Publishing Switzerland 2015
L.T. De Paolis and A. Mongelli (Eds.): AVR 2015, LNCS 9254, pp. 301–313, 2015.
DOI: 10.1007/978-3-319-22888-4_22

the virtual world. We can also use the auditory channels to hear the sounds in VR applications. Recently, we have become interested in another type of interaction and other sensorimotor channel: the haptic canal. Today, most VR simulations are based on the 3D visualization. Today, there are many standard approaches for using haptic feedback devices. VR applications are now used in many sectors such as: military, medical, education and industrial simulation. In this context, we will use some techniques of VR technology to solve our industrial issues. These issues are generally related to the ergonomic evaluation of workspace.

2   Industrial Context

The objective of this section consists on presenting the general context of our work which is, actually, an introduction to key concepts and terminology discussed in this paper.

In order to improve the industrial simulation of Renault Trucks operations (for caddy handling), we have developed a new framework of industrial simulation based on the haptic force feedback. In assembly operations of this company, they use caddy handling. The caddies are designed to carry tools that will be installed on the chassis. For this operation, the worker must exert considerable forces that can cause the Musculo-Skeletal Disorders (MSD). In our study we precisely identify the way we reproduce the actions performed by the worker to move the caddy from one area to another. Therefore, we will try to create a simulation that allows the ergonomist to evaluate the operation of pushing a rolling mobile and predicate the MSD. The aim of this work is to determine the feasibility of introducing the notion of haptic feedback techniques in driving simulation of a rolling mobile. This VR technique allows the operator to have a sensation of producing a realistic effort. This effort depends on the force and the trajectory imposed on the caddy by the operator. A characterization of the feedback force felt by the operator who manipulates the caddy is completed. The aim is to develop a new technique that allows us to have a force feedback on the haptic device directly correlated with the operator-device interactions.

This work enables the integration of a complex geometry from a detailed CAD design. The use of these types of meshes in simulation applications can be difficult in real time execution. Our purpose is to implement a standard approach that does not take into account the complexity of the geometry. Forces are not generally perceived objectively. However, the trajectory imposed by the operator and the response must be objective.

A set of acquisitions were performed on the forces exerted by the operator on the caddies in a real environment. To perform this operation we use force sensors that replace the wrists of caddies (see Fig. 1).

These sensors are used to read the forces on the real environment (X, Y, and Z). In our case the most important component is the Z-axis. It represents the axis that directs the movement of the carriage. The characteristic curve is computed after the acquisition of forces. This curve will be used later as a reference curve to find correlations between the virtual simulation and the real operation on the real environment.

Fig. 1. A 3D presentation of the virtual caddy in a simulation environment

The previous curve (see Fig. 2) presents the general behavior of forces on the two sensors, during the operation of pushing the caddies and putting the exhaust on the chassis. After analyzing the curve of Fig. 2, we deduce three phases:

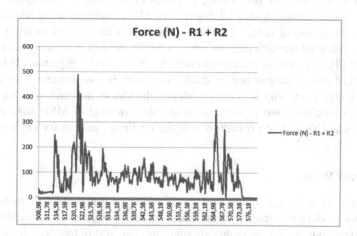

Fig. 2. Curve representing the operator forces during the rolling operation

- The first presents the startup phase. It is characterized by the maximum value of force to move the caddies.

The second phase presents the rolling of the caddy. In this phase, the force variations are practically null. As we have seen, the forces of the operator slightly vary.

- The last phase presents the incontrollable adjustment that depends on the position of the carriage relative to the chassis. In order to install the exhaust on the chassis, it is necessary for the operator to correct the position of the caddies. This operation requires a muscular strength.

3 Haptic Forces Feedback and Its Contribution to the Industrial Simulation

3.1 Ergonomic Evaluation

The ergonomic study in the industry was performed with a video camera recording the different motions and the different operations. The operator tasks were performed in a real workshop with real tools. The quality of ergonomic study results depends heavily on the ability of ergonomists for assessing the posture from the videos. With the development of virtual reality software and hardware, tools such as displays, tracking and motion capture systems can replace the video-recording. Ergonomists can now see in detail and manipulate the workshop by themselves, and hence they can evaluate postures and the accessibility problems. With the integration of numeric human or manikin we can conduct an ergonomic evaluation with specified tools like Rapid Upper Limb Assessment (RULA) [2]: a comparison of some methods in [3]. This numerical model provides an ergonomic assessment based solely on the postures and gestures of the operator without taking into consideration the muscular forces exerted to perform this task. For the workers performing physical effort using considerable forces to execute some tasks, musculoskeletal disorder (MSD) constitutes a big health problem for them in the industrial field. There are many studies and reports proving that over 50 % of the industrial workers have suffered of MSD, this has been analyzed mainly by Don Chaffin [4]. The overexertion of physical force or frequent high muscle load is the main reason of muscle fatigue and functional disability in muscles and other tissues of the human body; that is why we have developed the idea of integration of the forces in ergonomic evaluations. One of our aims is to find a method of MSD risks prediction and evaluation. This sort of problem is still the challenge subject for ergonomists.

3.2 Related Works

Several methods are used to develop applications of ergonomic simulations with sensor-motor devices to simulate an industrial process. Haptic force feedback began, then, to be known in the virtual reality simulations. This sort of feedback is mostly used in medical simulations, military applications and sculpture design. Recently, we have identified some utilization of haptic interactions in the industrial field. The haptic interfaces are basically used in training or ergonomic evaluations for certain tasks.

Hosseini et al. [5] describe a haptic virtual environment application for industrial training using haptic devices. Hence, sharing information through a collaborative application using textured avatars allows face-to face communication. This technique enables the check of accessibility of some buttons in workspace. In our case we need more than tactile forces feedback.

Jiang et al. [6] present the effectiveness of haptic feedback in a low cost virtual reality training environment for military and emergency purpose. This method can be used to transfer skills in a well-defined situation when the operator works under pressure, or in an emergency case, or even under less stressful conditions. We actually want to transfer skills in normal conditions. Bennis et al. [7] develop a framework that can evaluate MSD in a dynamic process. Within this system, virtual reality serves to generate a virtual working environment that can interact with haptic interfaces and optical motion capture systems. The prospects of this system will use the haptic force feedback to interact with the virtual objects.

De Winter et al. [8] use haptic feedback for driver simulations in their paper. They simulate some sort of dangerous situations and they test the demeanor of the operator in these dangerous situations. They can put the operator under pressure and stimulate dangerous situations. With this method we project the haptic force feedback in the tangible interface which is the wheel of control. In this paper only stressful situations are considered.

Dominjon *et al.* [9] present a comparative study between three main techniques (haptic rendering) to interact with large virtual environments using haptic devices with limited workspace. These cited methods are based on complex physics calculation. In training applications, we focus on an interaction aspect and especially the appearance of sensation which improves the transfer of skills. Applications demanding more assessment in terms of physical calculations require high precision. In our case the simulation is used to evaluate the efforts exerted by the operator. Our hypothesis in this situation is that we do not need physical simulation accuracy for prediction of problems. In this context we will develop a simulation based on a subjective non-complex calculation. Then we will compare the results obtained from the simulation with the results of acquisition on the operations of actual travel. Haptic rendering techniques used in the previous simulations are based on a physics calculation for each case. Indeed, our physics calculation will be simplified.

3.3 Haptic Forces Feedback

Haptic feedback is a recent technique that allows users to touch or manipulate the virtual objects present in the virtual environment. So we can enrich interactions in VR application using haptic rendering. Operator can see and feel (touch) the different objects of virtual environment using visual and haptic rendering. Haptic rendering is, most of the time, coupled with 3D rendering.

Actually, there are two haptic feedback interfaces:

- The force feedback: When we want to displace a virtual object, some forces oppose the movement of the virtual object in the virtual world. These forces can be the gravity forces or friction forces or others that are usually felt at the user's articulations. Force feedback rendering is projected in the haptic device.

- Tactile feedback: the tactile feedback presented by the sensation of surfaces. This kind of feedback interacts directly with captors resident in the human skin.

In this paper, we will restrict ourselves to force feedback interactions and haptic devices. Indeed, there are many devices for haptic feedback; Samur et al. [10] detail the technical properties of the most used haptic devices. Haptic devices are distinguished by two specific characteristics. The first one is the degree of freedom (Dof) and the second one is the maximum force value (translation or torque, continuous or discrete). With these characteristics we can define the best device for the simulation.

Thus, to use force feedback, we must have two modules, the first one is used to control the haptic devices, and here we can project our forces, and the second one is the software interface or algorithm that computes the different forces and sends it to the haptic device (haptic rendering). This software is based on a physics engine. This engine computes the response forces and the interactions between virtual entities. Glondu et al. [11] compares the four most used physics engines. There are many criteria to select one of the four physics engines. In our research work, we use Unity3D physics engine (PhysX). This will be used to compute only the collisions and the force responses (between virtual entities in a virtual environment). Another module will make the other calculations (haptic force feedback). The aim of this work consists of using a complex geometry in the virtual environment with the minimum calculus possible. In this context the precision of the task is not very important and we use a small haptic device that is limited in the feedback force and the workspace.

There are no standards for haptic rendering. Every device has its specific Application Programming Interface (API). But there is one architecture model for any virtual reality application containing haptic rendering [12].

4 Proposed Approach

There are many methods to compute force feedback and project it on the haptic device. In most cases we use a physic engine to compute force responses and to send it to the haptic devices. Martin et al. [13] cites the most used physic engines and compare them. In this paper we have another method used to compute forces feedback (introduced in the next section).

4.1 Subjective Compute

The subjective calculation means informally calculating force interaction between the operator and the 3D model (virtual entity) in the virtual environment. This calculation is based on the position and velocity of the haptic device. These values will be recovered in another module. This module requires forces that are independent of the 3D model or their physical characteristics, but these forces block the operator's actions with haptic force feedback. The blockading forces present the resistance of the rolling mobile. A curve profile allows us to decide when the caddy moves and the changing of phase.

4.2   Description of Our Method

Our method is based on a combination of an experimental study of the behavior of caddies in an industrial environment and a subjective utilization of the forces on the haptic device. The subjective projection (see previous section) is based on the principles of pseudo-haptic. We do not consider the real interaction and real force calculation, but we exert forces that hinder the forces exerted by the operator to give the sensation of pushing of the mobile in a definite direction. Then we deduct a curve profile.

This profile describes the repartition of force in the time to displace the caddy from one point to another. By analyzing this curve, we can identify three main phases; the first one is the start phase when the caddy switches from the static to the dynamic state, and starts rolling; the second phase is the rolling phase and here the caddy keeps rolling, and the final phase is the pose phase. The latter phase is more complex than the two others. Depending on the relativity of the caddy position to that of the chassis, the operator exercises the adjustment. To simulate this process and to use the curve data, we propose an architecture that allows using of the curve data. Our architecture is extensible, so we can add different modules and they can interact between us.

4.3   Architecture and Modules

Before describing the modules of the used architecture we will give the limitations of haptic device. The used haptic device is VIRTUOSE® 6D 35-45 with 30 N in discontinuous forces and 10 N in continuous forces. The used feedback force to displace the caddy is ten times greater than the forces supported by the haptic device. For this reason we use a scale of 10.

Thus we try to implement a subjective evaluation of force that allows the operator to feel the same difficulties of the exercise with less important forces. For simplification reasons, we start the development by implementing a basic approach that allows testing the communication protocols with all entities in the simulation program; then, in the simulator program, we are going to validate it and concretize the movement of the 3D objects with the movement of the haptic device.

Module of Position/Forces: In this module we get the 3D position of the haptic device. The program takes the position as input data and computes the feedback forces using speed data. In this module the feedback forces are computed subjectively. We calculate a force that blocks the movement of the operator and gives him enough resistance to fill the blocking in the device. If the operator feels hindered, he tries to exert more force to displace the caddy in the virtual scene. Actually, that is why we create a block coefficient. The latter allows the program to increase or decrease the illusion (pseudo-haptic) degrees; for instance, for the start phase the caddy is static, thus we need a larger force to displace it, and we need a big blocking coefficient as well. But, during the phase of rolling, this coefficient must be less important than that of the starting phase. The choice of the coefficient is empirical. We select 2 for the start phase, 1.5 for the rolling phase, and 2.5 for the putting phase. To calculate this block force we use the operator displacement speed. There are some constraints in the calculation of the force to protect the haptic device.

Force Interpreter: This module allows the analysis and the interpretation of the forces. In this module we try to simulate the experimental curve. This is the reason why we defined 3 key values; the first one is the threshold of the starting phase. This value depends of many parameters like the weight of the caddy, and the configuration of the wheels and their physical properties.

Phase Detector: This module detects the three phases of movement.

3D Display Module: This module represents the configuration of a visual rendering on a 3D display device. In our case the device used is a virtual reality head mounted display (Oculus Rift®). It increases both of the 3D visualization and the immersion level (Figs. 3 and 4).

```
Algorithm of haptic rendering:

phase = 'Start' ;
For each frame
{
Vector 3 p = Read_position_from_haptic_device();
Vector 3 v = Compute_velocity (old_pos, p);
Vector3 f = compute_forcehaptic_device_start(v);

switch (phase)
{
Case "start":
compute_forces_on_haptic_device_start(v);
Case "rolling":
compute_forces_on_haptic_device_rolling(v);
}
send_forces_haptic_device(f) ;
compare_forces_with_curve(f);
pahse = identify_phase(f,v)
old_pos = p
}
```

Fig. 3. Proposed algorithm

This architecture is extensible. We can exploit the different modules to generate other operations such as trajectory prediction and collision prediction. The prediction of the trajectory can influence the forces exerted by the operator in the last phase of the assembly operation (pose phase). The trajectory calculation allows us to suggest trajectories corrections in real time. This allows us to remove the forces exerted to adjust the position of the caddy vis-a-vis the chassis position.

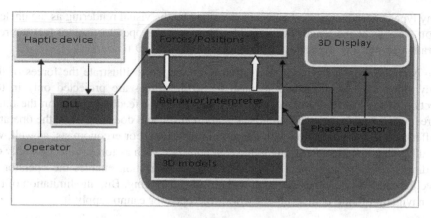

Fig. 4. Architecture of communication between the entities for the subjective computing

5 Virtual Reality Environment and Technics

In this section we will integrate our subjective method in a virtual reality application. This application will be based on the visual and haptic rendering. The coupling of the two types of rendering is done thanks to the proposed architecture.

For simplification reasons, we start the development by implementing a basic approach. It is used to test the communication protocols with all entities in the simulation program. Once the communication is invalidated, the movement of the 3D objects is concretized with the movement of the haptic device.

We used two types of navigation; the first one is a free navigation with feedback force only in motion direction.

In this mode of navigation the forces are only projected on the motion axis (1 DoF). The second type of navigation is the guided navigation; in this mode we use the three axes (3DoF) for translations and the Y-axis (1Dof) for rotations. The other degrees are directly blocked by the physical presentation of the caddy (tangible interface). At the end, we used also the information displays:

- Executed forces: the value of the forces executed by the operator on the motion axis (N)
- Speed of caddy: The instantaneous velocity of the caddy (cm/s).
- Distance caddy-chassis: The distance between the center of mass of the caddy and the chassis (cm).
- Traveled distance: The traveled distance by the caddy during the simulation (cm).

5.1 Experimental Result

For all types of navigation we kept the same hardware, the same virtual environment and the same scenario. Thanks to the visual rendering, the operator can see all the details and manipulate the caddy using the haptic device (without force feedback).

Many types of ergonomic problems are identified by the visual rendering as the unclear vision because of the length of the caddy. However, the operator cannot feel the real operation of pushing the caddy, if he is using only the 3D render.

Free Navigation. This type of navigation is developed to illustrate the forces of the caddy when the operator wants to push it. So the forces are projected only in the direction of the caddy movement and we have no haptic feedback force on the other degree of freedom (axes). This approach is not realistic and does not allow the operator to offer a complete interaction with the mobile sensation. For ergonomists, as well, we can affirm that it is less interesting to have an approach such as force projection only on the direction of the movement. This latter type of projection enables the operator to move the caddy in the other direction without force blocking. But, the limitation of the free navigation mode is that, in real world, the operator cannot apply it.

Guided Navigation. Unlike the free navigation where the forces are projected onto a single component; we block the entire degrees of freedom of the haptic device. The blocking forces are calculated by the program and are carried out on three translational axes haptic device (Fig. 5).

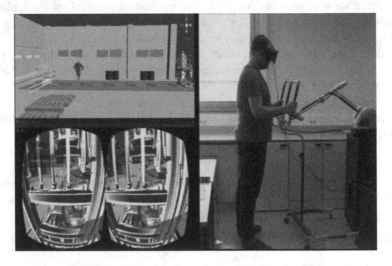

Fig. 5. Using haptic rendering with 3D visual.

The axes of rotation are locked by the fastening system designed for the tangible interface.

With this mode of navigation, the operator has more constraints. The haptic feedback is enabled in the 3 axes of motion, and the feedback forces are projected on the axes:

- Motion direction (Z-axis): this force is relative to the speed haptic device on the Z-axis.

F = 1.5 * velocity
- X-axis and Y-axis:
  F = 2 * velocity

For the guided navigation, we show the information relative to the motions and the displacements of the caddy. In order to see what kind of information is provided, some visual details can help the operator to understand the situation better. For example, when displaying the speed of the caddy, the operator can have an idea about the displacement of the caddy even if it is static (Figs. 6 and 7).

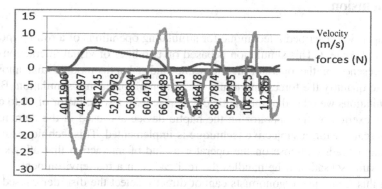

Fig. 6. Experiment curve 1

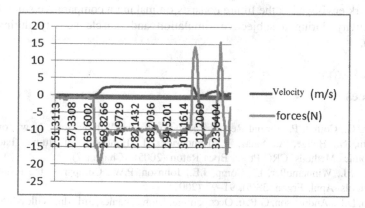

Fig. 7. Experiment curve 2

5.2 Comparison with Acquisitions

In this section we will make a comparison between the subjective method and the acquisitions part. The subjective part is based on the curves provided by the navigation without information and the navigation with information display. In the characteristic curve of a navigation with information display, we can notice that the startup first part is identical to that of the real curve (acquisitions made on the caddy). However, the rolling phase is not identical to the acquisition. This fallacy can be caused by the stability of the operator during the operation of the caddy displacement. The operator cannot determine the speed of the caddy. In a second step we added a display of information that indicates several factors, such as the distance caddy-chassis, the caddy speed, and the forces. With these configurations, we find that the curve presented in this method corresponds well to the real curve. So we can conclude that the simple display may deceive the brain. The operator, therefore, seeks to maintain the constancy of the caddy speed.

6 Conclusion

In this paper, we described a technique for simulating operations of a rolling mobile in an industrial context. This simulation is based on two lines of visual interactions made for the presence of the operator in the scene and a haptic module that allows the operator to quantify the forces and to use the notion of forces in a simulation. Because of the limitations we related to the haptic device, we used a scale factor of 10 to convert the forces exerted by the operator on the haptic device and used in the demonstrator. With this scale factor, a subjective technique is implemented. This technique allows us to calculate or rather impose on the operator a kind of interaction that allows him to have the same sensation if he handles the real caddy in a real environment.

With this technique, ergonomists cannot directly detect the disorder caused by the activity because the operator cannot feel the importance of the forces he has to exercise. But if we use the scaled values coupled with a force analyzer, we can predict the MSD.

The work envisaged in the future consists on making a comparative study between muscle activity during a subjective simulation and muscle activity during a real simulation.

References

1. Burdea, G., Coiffet, P.: Virtual Reality Technology. John Wily & Sons, New York (1994)
2. Stantom, N., Hedge, A., Salas, E., Henderick, H.: Handbook of Human Factors and Ergonomics Methods. CRC Press, Boca Raton (2005). (Chapter 7)
3. Russel, S.J., Winnemuller, L., Comp, J.E., Johnson, P.W.: Comparing the results of five lifting tools. Appl. Ergon. **38**(5), 91–97 (2007)
4. Chaffin, D.B., Andrersson, G.B.J.: Occupational Biomechanics, 3rd edn. Willey-Interscience, New York (1999)
5. Hosseini, M., Malaric, F., Georganas, N.D.: A haptic virtual environment for industrial training. IEEE International Workshop Haptic Virtual Environments and Their applications, pp. 25–30 (2002)
6. Jiang, L., Girotra, R., Cutkosky, M.R., Ulrich, C.: Reducing error rates with low cost haptic feedback in virtual reality-based training applications. In: Proceedings of WorldHAPTICS, Pisa, Italy, pp. 420–425
7. Ma, L., Bennis, F., Chabalet, D.: Framework for dynamic evaluation of muscle fatigue in manual handling work. In: IEEE International Conference on Industrial Technology, Chengdu, China, April 2008

8. De Winter, J., Dodou, D.: Preparing drivers for dangerous situations: a critical reflection on continuous shared control. In: Proceedings of IEEE International Conference on SMC, pp. 1050–1056 (2011)
9. Dominjon, L., Lécuyer, A., Burkhardt, J.-M., Richir, S.: A comparison of three techniques to interact in large virtual environments using haptic devices with limited workspace. In: Nishita, T., Peng, Q., Seidel, H.-P. (eds.) CGI 2006. LNCS, vol. 4035, pp. 288–299. Springer, Heidelberg (2006)
10. Samur, E.: Performance Metrics for Haptic Interfaces. Springer, London (2012)
11. Glondu, L., Marchal, M., Dumont, G.: Evaluation of physical simulation libraries for haptic rendering of contacts between rigid bodies. In: ASME, World Conference on Innovative Virtual Reality, July 2013
12. Salisbury, K., Conti, F., Barbgli, F.: Haptic rendering: introductory concepts. IEEE Comput. Graphics Appl. **24**(2), 24–32 (2004)
13. Martin, P., Féry, N., Clavel, C., Darses, F., Bourdot, P.: Sensorimotor Feedback for Interactive Realism: Evaluation of a Haptic Driving Paradigm for a Forklift Simulator, pp. 314–325. Springer, Heidelberg (2011)

A Flexible AR-based Training System for Industrial Maintenance

Andrea Sanna[1], Federico Manuri[1(✉)], Giovanni Piumatti[1], Gianluca Paravati[1], Fabrizio Lamberti[1], and Pietro Pezzolla[2]

[1] Politecnico di Torino, Dipartimento di Automatica e Informatica,
C.so Duca degli Abruzzi, 24, Turin, Italy
federico.manuri@polito.it
http://areeweb.polito.it/grains-group/
[2] Fidia S.p.A., C.so Lombardia, 11, San Mauro Torinese TO, Italy
p.pezzolla@fidia.it

Abstract. Augmented Reality (AR) has been proved to be an effective tool to improve and enhance the learning experience of students. On the other hand, issues regarding the inflexibility of AR contents can strongly limit the usability of AR applications in education. This paper presents results obtained by using the AR framework designed and developed for the EASE-R[3] European project and focused on the generation of maintenance procedures for machine tools. The high system flexibility allows instructors to easily make maintenance procedures suitable for the skill level of technicians to be trained. A case study is presented and results gathered so far analyzed and assessed.

Keywords: Augmented Reality · Maintenance · Training system

1 Introduction

Teachers, educators, instructors and trainers are always searching for new solutions to improve the learning experience of their students. New and emerging technologies can provide tools and opportunities to stimulate the students' interest in investigating and analyzing more in depth course materials.

Augmented Reality (AR) [36] provides researchers and developers new solutions to bridge the gap between real and virtual, thus allowing the implementation of engaging and exiting user interfaces. Computer generated hints (3D animations, text labels, 2D images, and so on) are overlapped and aligned to real objects. Computer generated hints (often named assets) are information that users cannot directly experience with their own senses. These *helps* can allow users to perform real-world tasks; moreover, despite of virtual reality environments, users never loose the contact with the real world around them using AR applications.

First AR applications can be dated back to 1960s [46] and AR technologies have been extensively using in fields such as: tourism, medical sciences, entertainment, manufacturing, and so on [3]. On the other hand, AR in education

© Springer International Publishing Switzerland 2015
L.T. De Paolis and A. Mongelli (Eds.): AVR 2015, LNCS 9254, pp. 314–331, 2015.
DOI: 10.1007/978-3-319-22888-4_23

has found a significative spread only in the last decade [22,23]. This can be explained by issues related to: technology acceptance [45], technological limitations [15] and pedagogical approaches [27,37]. On the other hand, AR provides educators great opportunities to enhance the learning experience of students (challenges and opportunities are well summarized in [50]). Moreover, AR helps to promote both collaborative and autonomous learning, thus changing the traditional education paradigm [34].

This paper presents preliminary results of an AR-based training for machine tools maintenance technicians. Maintenance procedures can be performed both by special purpose hardware (e.g., AR-glasses) and personal mobile devices (e.g. a tablet). The AR framework allows the instructor to easily make and change AR procedures, thus adapting the difficulty level of exercises to trainees' skill. Moreover, the instructor can also remotely assist a trainee, thus promoting autonomous learning. The proposed solution aims to tackle pedagogical issues mentioned above; in particular, this work attempts to assess the system flexibility in creating AR contents (the AR maintenance procedures), which is often a limiting factor for the spread of AR solutions in education.

The paper is organized as follows: the state of the art of AR in education (with a special focus on training for maintenance) is reviewed in Sect. 2, the system architecture is shown in Sect. 3, whereas the considered case study and gathered results are presented in Sects. 4 and 5, respectively.

2 Background

Augmented reality has been deeply investigated and used in order to improve traditional learning and training paths. The possibility to create enhanced user-machine and user-user interactions by AR technologies has been the basic motivation for a lot of researchers in designing and developing AR-based systems to support teaching and learning. Moreover, AR can be also an incentive for students, thus motivating them to analyze more in the detail course materials. AR can help instructors to simulate dangerous or destructive events as well as can help learners both in visualizing microspic/macrospic scale systems and in effectively collaborating with teachers and other students.

Several fields and disciplines benefited of AR for education purposes; the following list is not exhaustive (a survey is out of the scope of this manuscript) but it is aimed to provide readers a picture of the impact AR can have on everyday life. Several applications have been proposed for the education of: medicine (e.g., [1,32,43]), engineering (e.g., [30,31]), architecture and interior design (e.g., [6,10]), chemistry (e.g., [2,8]), mathematics and geometry (e.g., [24,25]), physics (e.g., [7,26]), geography and astronomy (e.g., [28,42]), history and archeology (e.g., [13,48]), art and music (e.g., [14,19]).

A lot of works have been also proposed in the more specific field of training for maintenance. The idea to train and support technicians by conveying computer-generated instructions can be dated back to early 1990s (the reader can refer to two surveys [38,39]). In particular, Feiner et al. [17] showed potentialities of AR-based applications for repair and assembly tasks by supporting maintenance procedures of a laser printer. AR technologies are now used for training and support technicians in a large number of application domains: aerospace [11,12], automotive [44,49], industrial plants [18,41] and so on. Benefits of AR to support maintenance, repair and assembly tasks are well investigated and presented in [20].

As AR technologies allow researchers to develop user interfaces able to reduce the gap between real and virtual objects, a lot of works are known in the literature about AR books (e.g., [5,21]). AR books allow to provide students interactive material and 3D visualizations, thus implementing the so called *blended education* (a term used to identify a hybrid approach that uses different types of training technologies). At the same way as AR books, AR games are a type of education that allows teachers to use a highly visual and interactive form of learning: Human Pacman [9], AR^2 Hockey [40] and ARQuake [47] are just the first examples of a new frontier of AR-based education. Despite of the last decade, when AR systems were mainly based on special purpose hardware, the evolution of mobile (personal) devices allow to replace the see-through AR-interfaces by means of hand-held AR-interfaces; as the best part of mobile devices (smartphones and tablets) is endowed with a GPS, the discovered-based learning [4] is growing up. Discovered-based learning is not only based on geo-localization (often used to teach history or geography) but also on face recognition (to provide information about a person) and, more in general, on object recognition.

All these examples show different forms of teaching/education by using augmented reality. On the other hand, an issue is shared by all the approaches: the difficulty for teachers to create AR contents [27]. For instance, in some AR systems the teaching sequence cannot be changed/adpated; in other words, instructors are not able to (efficiently and easily) accomplish students' needs. The proposed framework aims to address and mitigate this issue: a graphics and intuitive user interface allows the teacher to make training maintenance procedures as a sequence of states, at which a set of computer generated assets can be related to. Then, the teacher can generate the AR-based procedure both for special purpose AR-glasses and Android personal devices used by trainees. The level of complexity of each procedure can be easily "tuned" according the skill of students; moreover, the system allows the instructor to provide remote assistance to students: the teacher is able to see what the student's camera is framing and the state of the procedure the student is not able to perform. The teacher can dynamically make a new procedure to be sent the trainee. The framework developed for the EASE-R^3 project [16,29,33] has been used to support this new teaching methodology.

3   Framework Architecture

The proposed framework consists of a client-server architecture, as illustrated in Fig. 1. The interaction between the instructor and the student can be split in three steps:

1. providing the procedure to the student;

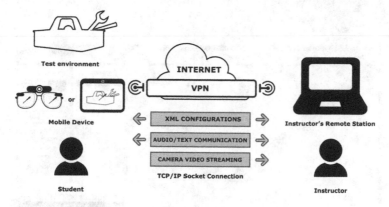

Fig. 1. The high-level architecture of the proposed framework.

2. executing the procedure and interacting with the instructor;
3. modifying the procedure and resubmitting it to the student.

This approach has been chosen to maximize the flexibility of the whole system: the instructor can easily produce a procedure for students, interact with them during the practice and update the procedure on the fly, on the basis of students' skills, feedbacks and real-time depending variables. Figure 2 shows the building layers of the two applications.

Server. The server side is represented by a Java-based application that runs on both Windows and Unix O.S.: the instructor's remote station. Figure 3 shows the interface of such application: the main section of the interface contains the state machine representation of the procedure. On the bottom-left corner a set of buttons allow the instructor to define procedures and modify them.

Each procedure consists of a series of edges and nodes. The nodes represent the steps of the procedure to perform and they contain all the virtual aids, or assets, chosen by the instructor. The edges represent the transitions from one state to another and are associated to a specific tracking configuration. A tracking configuration consists, in this case, of a CAD model, with a specific

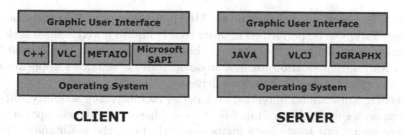

Fig. 2. Software layers of server and client applications.

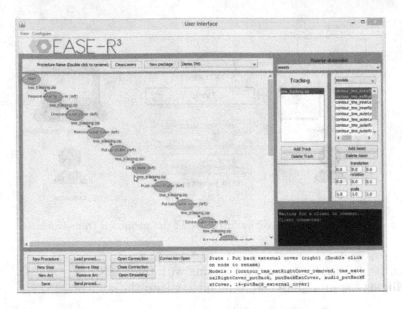

Fig. 3. The server application interface: states representing procedure steps are shown in the main area of the application, the right part allows instructor to select assets, whereas the bottom bar manages procedures and client connections.

viewpoint and real world dimensions: it represents the real object the student should interact with, e.g. a panel to open or a switch to turn on. For each step, the instructor chooses the tracking configuration that better represents the view the student should have of the real object to be managed.

On the right there are two columns: the rightmost has a widget that lists all the available assets to add at each step of the procedure and allows the instructor to adjust scale, rotation and location of 3D models and animations aids in the virtual scene. The other column contains a widget that lists the available tracking configurations and offers a preview of the corresponding CAD model. The server application is equipped with a communication module that allows the instructor to speak with a student and to see the video streamed from the client device camera.

Client. The client side consists of an AR application providing the student a sequence of steps to be performed in order to accomplish a well defined task. The application is available in two versions, both developed with the Metaio SDK [35]: an Android application for mobile devices and a Windows application for AR-glasses, which relies on Windows drivers.

This first application is intended for a better mobility, compatibility and costs as it runs on a generic Android mobile device, whereas the second option allows hand-free operations to students for better performing the maintenance procedure. The AR-glasses application comes with a speaking recognition module that maps all the commands available in the graphic interface for the Android application to vocal commands. The available commands are:

1. *start procedure* to start the practice;
2. *next* to move on to the following step of the procedure;
3. *previous* to go back to the previous step of the procedure;
4. *reload* or *restart* to repeat the tracking recognition of the real object;
5. *video* to play, if available, the video asset for the current step;
6. *instructions* to repeat the audio asset for the current step;
7. *assistance* to open the communication channel with the instructor.

Two vocal commands allow users to enable/disable the speech recognition interface in order to avoid false positive recognitions when they work in "noisy" environments or whey they communicate with the instructor.

Figure 4 shows the user interface of the Android application. The two arrow icons at the sides of the screen let the student go back and forth through the steps of the procedures. The circle arrow at the bottom forces the tracking engine to repeat the recognition phase, e.g. to better align the virtual aids to the real object. If a video asset is available for the current step, a movie frame icon at the bottom right of the user interface allows the student to display the current step performed by an expert, thus outlining any difficult or ambiguous operations. The receiver icon at the bottom right allows the student to request a communication with the instructor for remote assistance.

Workflow. When the student launches the client side application, a list of available procedures to train with is displayed. A remote assistance connections allows the student to request new procedures or update the current one. When a procedure is started, at each step, the real object has to be framed by the device camera: a silhouette representing the tracking configuration has to be aligned to the real object (the silhouette appears as a transparent 3D model on the user interface). When the tracking engine of the application recognizes the corresponding CAD model (e.g. the tracking configuration), visual and audio assets are provided to the user. When the current step is completed, the student can move on by the *next step* command. Then, the tracking engine looks for the new tracking configuration correspondence in the scene.

The choice to offer two explicit commands to freely move back and forth through procedure steps is for providing students more flexibility; for instance, the student can skip steps when computer-generated aids are not necessary or move back to check (and possibly fix) problems. Moreover, this choice limits the number of false positives in the tracking recognition process, as the student has to confirm to be ready to move on to the next step of the procedure. If the recognition of the next step does not work properly, it could be an operation that the student has forgotten to perform in a previous step.

If the student needs to interact with the instructor, the communication command allows to establish a communication channel. This function connects the AR-application to the instructor's remote station (usually over a Virtual Private

Fig. 4. The user interface of the Android mobile devices.

Network, VPN), opens a full duplex audio channel and sends the video framed by the student's device camera to the instructor. Data are sent over a TCP/IP socket and the procedure's format is an extension of the XML schema defined by Metaio, which contains all information about the tracking configurations and asset visualization, as they are necessary to describe the machine state diagram. When the instructor receives the state diagram of the procedure, the current step of the procedure is highlighted in the graphic interface, in this way, the instructor is informed about the step the student is actually performing.

Through the audio communication channel the student may request a specific help to the instructor, thus underlining inconsistency between the procedure and the real case or requesting an explanation about the operation to perform. Eventually, the instructor may need to fix/update the procedure and send it back to the student. The application at the server side allows the instructor to change assets, tracking configurations, remove/add nodes and edges in order to provide a new and better set of instructions to the student. When the reconfiguration is completed, the instructor can send it back to the student, which can move on with the procedure starting from the last performed step.

4   The Case Study

In order to evaluate the proposed framework, it has been used to support a real case proposed by Fidia, a company that designs and manufactures sophisticated machine tools (e.g., molding machines). The Fidia's training program depends both on specific knowledge and experience of technicians to be trained and on the machine tool of interest.

Fig. 5. The Fidia's TMS tool.

Usually, the first level of training, proposed to inexperienced technicians, starts with the study of available manuals. After this first phase, practical exercises are proposed both by training in laboratory and training on real case situations; exercises are performed both at the production factory and at customers' sites. The time required by this two training phases may vary considerably and the second one may last from one to three months, depending on the specific tasks requested to the technicians. The training is also different between installer technicians, who perform the initial setup of the machine, and assistance technicians, who interact with customers when problems show up and need a deeper focus on problem solving skills. In the past there were instructors that had the duty to teach the other technicians the procedures required for each available systems. As the number and complexity of available systems increased during the years, the choice for training was to support new technicians beside skilled ones for the same task/system.

Overall, the cost issues related to a specific procedure consist of three elements:

1. the time spent by the technician to learn the procedure;
2. the time spent by the technician to perform the procedure;
3. the number of errors that occurs performing the procedure, that could increase the time needed to perform the ongoing procedure or lead to further assistance requests.

These three elements also represents the performance indicators that should be used to evaluate the training system, as specified by the companies involved in the EASE-R^3 project.

For this case study the proposed procedure is the lenses cleaning of the Fidia's TMS (Fig. 5). A TMS is a tool that measures, through a laser beam,

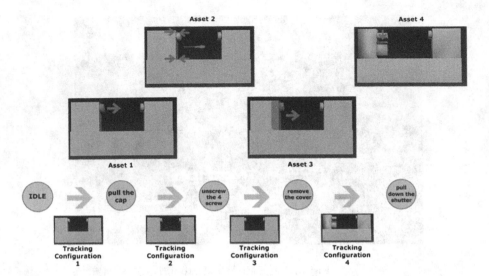

Fig. 6. A state machine diagram showing the short version of the procedure: for each state some assets and the tracking configuration to be recognized in order to move on to the next state are shown.

the condition of molding tools in order to evaluate their precision during the lifespan and eventually suggest their replacement. Usually, these tools are used in industrial context and dust, chippings and other scraps from the machinery processing can fill or cover the laser lenses. In this situation, a specific procedure to clean the lenses of the TMS is necessary to restore its working state. To evaluate the proposed framework, two procedures to perform the lenses cleaning of the TMS have been proposed: the first one is a shorter and easier version of the procedure, which aim is to evaluate if untrained, inexperienced people, which never practiced in such a field, could perform the proposed procedure in a meaningful way (Fig. 6). The second one is a longer, more difficult procedure proposed to former technicians untrained on the specific topic; in this case, the purpose is to evaluate if the framework could speed up the learning process necessary to train new technicians and other meaningful parameters such as its usability.

The first procedure consists of the following four steps:

1. remove the cap;
2. unscrew the four screw;
3. remove the external cover;
4. pull down the shutter to expose the lenses for cleaning.

When the lenses are reachable, in the real case, they should be cleaned using compressed air from an air can.

The second procedure, which is simply an extended version of the first one, adds the following ten steps, for a total of fourteen steps:

1. clean the lenses using compressed air from an air can;
2. pull up the shutter;
3. unscrew the shutter's crew and remove it;
4. remove the lens's cover;
5. clean the lens with a soft cloth;
6. put back the lens's cover;
7. put back the shutter in position and screw the crew that hold it;
8. put back the outer cover;
9. screw the four screw that hold in position the outer cover;
10. put back the cap.

To get the students ready to the practice test, the preliminary step was to briefly illustrate them the logic of the whole system. This step required no more than 10 min. All the students were instructed singularly, to be sure they did not forget anything before their turn to perform the practice test. Each student performed the test alone, therefore they do not acquired any experience from viewing other participants to the test. The training to the system consisted of the following steps:

1. a brief explanation of the generic task the student should perform;
2. tools available to perform the practice are shown;
3. kind of assets the AR system provides are presented;
4. the user interface of the Android client application is presented;
5. the user interface of the Windows client application is presented (the list of the vocal commands);
6. each vocal commands is singularly presented to the student;
7. the student are assisted in wearing the AR glasses in order to maximize the comfort, the field of view and the visibility;
8. the student performs a sample tracking step, thus experiencing computer-generated assets;
9. the communication with the instructor's remote station is tested.

Students started the practice with the AR glasses device (Fig. 7). During the practice a qualified instructor supervised the student operations without interfering, just to write down the execution time of the practice and the number of errors committed. Another instructor, placed in another room, monitored the operations through the remote station, thus waiting for help requests from the students. After completing the procedure with the AR glasses, students were also requested for repeating the procedure by using the tablet: this was necessary to evaluate advantages and drawbacks of a hand-free AR-solution, less comfortable in terms of wearing, with respect to a much handy device such a table, which instead slows down the practice when two hands are needed to perform the steps of the procedure.

5 Results

The framework was tested providing two groups of trainees by a pair of AR-glasses and an Android tablet with the client application, instructing them, one

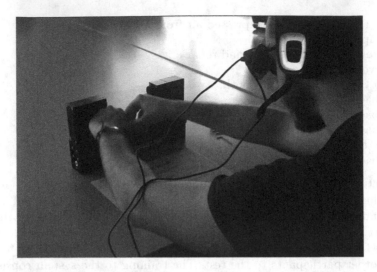

Fig. 7. A student technician performing the training procedure on the TMS tool by the AR-glasses client.

by one, as explained before. A first session of tests was performed with a group of 13 trainees (7 male and 6 female) enrolled in the BS degree in Visual Design. The aim was to check the overall framework functioning, evaluate the proposed system and verify if a group of people with no experience (and a completely different background) was able to complete the procedure (short version). A second group (8 males), selected among Fidia's technicians not previously trained for the specific task, performed the longer version of the procedure. Completion times and error rates were measured for both groups. After performing the test, trainees have been requested to compile a questionnaire to evaluate their experience.

Tables 1 and 2 show the answers gathered by the questionnaires proposed to the two groups of trainees. Although both groups of trainees have found hard (average values: group one = 3.31 and group two = 4.12) to perform the lenses cleaning task, every candidate of both groups was able to complete the assigned procedure. Even if most of the students had not previous experiences with AR applications (question 1), the overall evaluations of the framework and of the practice experience were over the average.

Figure 8 shows that while the first group of students, lacking of a technical background, was more prone to errors, most of the trainees of the second group performed the practice without any mistake. Evaluating the time spent by the first group of students (Fig. 9), what stands out is that there is a wider distribution from the average value of 08 min and 38 s, as some student had a better aptitude for the requested task or for the proposed framework and performed the practice very quickly; on the other hand, others did not adapt quickly to the system. In the second group of students the values of distribution are more close

Table 1. The table shows the results of a questionnaire proposed to all the participants (13) of the first test sessions; the values represent an average of the answers, where a higher value means a positive response to the question and a lower value a negative one in a range 1–5.

	Questions	Average	Max	Variance
1	Have you ever used augmented reality (AR) applications before?	1.15	3	0.13
2	How familiar are you with maintenance or assembly tasks (e.g. assembling IKEA furniture, repairing bicycles)?	3.31	5	1.75
3	Did you accomplish the required task?	2.23	3	0.17
4	How do you feel about the length of time required to complete the task?	3.62	5	0.24
5	How do you feel about the level of commitment needed to complete the task?	3.31	5	1.14
6	How difficult did you find the execution of the procedure?	3.31	5	0.82
7	How comfortable did you find the AR device?	3.15	5	1.51
8	How easy did you find catching the 3D model target (alignment for enabling the procedure execution)?	4.23	5	0.95
9	How did you find the alignment of the 3D model with the real object?	4.15	5	0.44
10	How effective did you find the interaction/navigation through the procedure?	3.31	5	0.98
11	How did you find the graphics of the AR device (e.g visualising 3D elements: contrast, brightness, clearness)?	3.15	5	0.90
12	Do you think the AR device would benefit from audio/video tools supporting the procedure?	4.84	5	0.28
13	How did you find the usability of the video support tools?	4.08	5	0.84
14	How did you find the usability of audio support tools?	4.23	5	0.95
15	Do you wear glasses?	0.15 (2)	13	0.13
16	If you wear glasses, did you feel your glasses interfered with the procedure?	3.5	5	0.25
17	How tired were you after completing the procedure?	3.61	4	0.24
18	Do you think you would now be able to complete the procedure without the AR support?	4.62	5	0.85

to the average value of 08 min and 06 s; in this case, the technical background of trainees smoothed over differences among trainee performances.

Moreover, all the students believed to have acquired enough experience to successfully repeat the procedure without neither the help of the AR application nor of the support of an expert technician. The possibility to open a video and audio channel with the instructor operating at the remote station helps students to overcome some problems, requesting assistance to the instructor when needed and allowing the instructor to overview the procedure's fulfilment.

The answers to the other questions provide useful indication about the usability of the system: higher values of variance in the evaluation of the assets and the user interface of the proposed framework (questions 8 to 14) point out which

Table 2. The table shows the results of a questionnaire proposed to all the participants (8) of the second test sessions; the values represent an average of the answers, where a higher value means a positive response to the question and a lower value a negative one in a range 1–5.

	Questions	Average	Max	Variance
1	Have you ever used augmented reality (AR) applications before?	1	3	0
2	How familiar are you with maintenance or assembly tasks (e.g. assembling IKEA furniture, repairing bicycles)?	4.12	5	0.61
3	Did you accomplish the required task?	2.62	3	0.23
4	How do you feel about the length of time required to complete the task?	3.87	5	1.11
5	How do you feel about the level of commitment needed to complete the task? 3.75	5	1.19	
6	How difficult did you find the execution of the procedure?	4.12	5	0.61
7	How comfortable did you find the AR device?	3	5	0.5
8	How easy did you find catching the 3D model target (alignment for enabling the procedure execution)?	3.87	5	0.36
9	How did you find the alignment of the 3D model with the real object?	3.87	5	0.36
10	How effective did you find the interaction/navigation through the procedure?	4.37	5	0.98
11	How did you find the graphics of the AR device (e.g visualising 3D elements: contrast, brightness, clearness)?	3.12	5	0.86
12	Do you think the AR device would benefit from audio/video tools supporting the procedure?	4.85	5	0.12
13	How did you find the usability of the video support tools?	3.87	5	0.86
14	How did you find the usability of audio support tools?	3.87	5	1.11
15	Do you wear glasses?	0.125 (1)	8	0.11
16	If you wear glasses, did you feel your glasses interfered with the procedure?	3	5	-
17	How tired were you after completing the procedure?	3.87	4	0.11
18	Do you think you would now be able to complete the procedure without the AR support?	4.12	5	1.11

aspects could be improved, even if this kind of results may depend on an excessive user expectation for a new technology not experienced before. Answers to questions 16 and 17 show that the proposed AR-glasses are not the best available option for user that wear glasses on their own. As we got only 3 results in the two test sessions, this issue should be further investigated in the future.

Finally, students believed that the two proposed devices, the AR glasses and the tablet, could offer the same experience in terms of effectiveness of the practice and task completing. The main point is that, considering advantages and

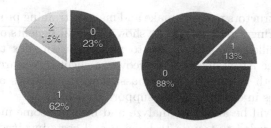

Fig. 8. The pie chart on the left shows the distribution of errors made by the participants of the first group, while the second one shows the distribution for the participants of the second one; the numbers over the percentage values represent the error occurrences.

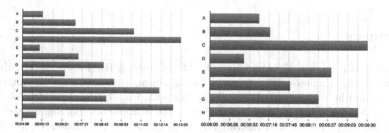

Fig. 9. The bar chart on the left shows the time spent by the participants of the first group performing the short procedure, while the second one shows the distribution for the participants of the second group performing the complete sequence of steps.

drawbacks between hand-free operability and wearing comfort, students believed that both devices could be useful depending on the task to be performed and the operational environment. Moreover, the technicians from Fidia proposed to build up a support for the tablet made of a magnetic hook and a mechanical arm to position the tablet near the focus point of the procedure, thus performing hand-free the steps of the procedure.

Overall, the most important result is that each student was able to complete the assigned procedure, without previous preparation. This fact is a substantial proof of the effectiveness of the system, as it fulfils the first performance indicator. Unfortunately, it was not possible to evaluate the other two performance indicators due to the lack of data for the standard training system. However, next year's main goal for the EASE-R[3] project is to evaluate the effectiveness of the proposed systems: as for AR systems the three performance indicators are time, costs and errors, so further evaluation of the system will occur in the near future.

6 Conclusion

This paper presents the usage of an innovative AR-framework for training purpose. The main goal is to overcome issues related to the AR content production, thus enabling instructors to easily make and manage training procedures. Results obtained considering a real case study show potential benefits of the considered framework. Unskilled people are able to perform a complex task on machine tools by means the AR application; moreover, a client-server architecture allows the instructor both to provide remote assistance to trainees and dynamically change procedures in order to better support students.

Future work will be aimed to analyze and measure some indicators such as effort and time needed to train a technician and costs involved in the training process. Moreover, this analysis will be also aimed to investigate different business models related to customer assistance: for some tasks, the augmented reality tool could also replace (or more likely complementary) the traditional assistance program, thus allowing customers to perform maintenance autonomously.

References

1. Abhari, K., Baxter, J.S.H., Chen, E.C.S., Khan, A.R., Peters, T.M., de Ribaupierre, S., Eagleson, R.: Training for planning tumour resection: augmented reality and human factors. IEEE Trans. Biomed. Eng. **62**(6), 1466–1477 (2014)
2. Amrit, M., Bansal, H., Yammiyavar, P.: Studies in application of augmented reality in E-learning courses. In: Chakrabarti, A. (ed.) ICoRD 2015 Research into Design Across Boundaries. Smart Innovation, Systems and Technologies, vol. 2, pp. 375–384. Springer, India (2015)
3. Azuma, R., Baillot, Y., Behringer, R., Feiner, S., Julier, S., MacIntyre, B.: Recent advances in augmented reality. IEEE Comput. Graph. Appl. **21**(6), 34–47 (2001)
4. Behzadana, A.H., Kamatb, V.R.: Enabling discovery-based learning in construction using telepresent augmented reality. Autom. Constr. **33**, 3–10 (2013)
5. Billinghurst, M., Kato, H., Poupyrev, I.: The MagicBook - moving seamlessly between reality and virtuality. IEEE Comput. Graph. Appl. **21**(3), 6–8 (2002)
6. Billinghurst, M., Anders, H.: Mobile architectural augmented reality. In: Wang, X., Schnabel, M.A. (eds.) Mixed Reality in Architecture, Design and Construction, pp. 93–104. Springer, Netherlands (2009)
7. Chae, C., Ko, K.: Introduction of physics simulation in augmented reality. In: International Symposium on Ubiquitous Virtual Reality, pp. 37–40 (2008)
8. Chen, T.C.: A study of comparing the use of augmented reality and physical models in chemistry education. In: Proceedings of the 2006 ACM International Conference on Virtual Reality Continuum and Its Applications, pp. 369–372 (2006)
9. Cheok, A.D., Fong, S.W., Goh, K.H., Yang, X., Liu, W., Farzbiz, F., Li, Y.: Human Pacman: a mobile entertainment system with ubiquitous computing and tangible interaction over a wide outdoor area. In: Chittaro, L. (ed.) Mobile HCI 2003. LNCS, vol. 2795, pp. 209–223. Springer, Heidelberg (2003)
10. Cook, J., Gibson, S., Howard, T., Hubbold, R.: Real-time photo-realistic augmented reality for interior design. In: ACM SIGGRAPH 2003 Sketches & Applications. ACM (2003)
11. Datcu, D., Cidota, M., Lukosch, S., Oliveira, D.M., Wolff, M.: Virtual co-location to support remote assistance for inflight maintenance in ground training for space missions. In: Proceedings of the 15th International Conference on Computer Systems and Technologies, pp. 134–141 2014

12. De Crescenzio, F., Fantini, M., Persiani, F., Di Stefano, L., Azzari, P., Salti, S.: Augmented reality for aircraft maintenance training and operations support. IEEE Comput. Graph. Appl. **31**(1), 96–101 (2011)
13. Deliyiannis, I., Papaioannou, G.: Augmented reality for aecheological environments on mobile devices: a novel open framework. Mediterr. Archaeol. Archaeometry **14**(4), 1–10 (2014)
14. Di Serio, A., Ibáñez, M.B., Kloos, C.D.: Impact of an augmented reality system on students' motivation for a visual art course. Comput. Educ. **68**, 586–596 (2013)
15. Dunleavy, M., Dede, C., Mitchell, R.: Affordances and limitations of immersive participatory augmented reality simulations for teaching and learning. J. Sci. Educ. Technol. **18**(1), 7–22 (2009)
16. EASE-R^3 project web site. http://www.easer3.eu/
17. Feiner, S., Blair, M., Dorée, S.: Knowledge-based augmented reality. Commun. ACM **36**(7), 52–62 (1993)
18. Goose, S., Sudarsky, S., Zhang, X., Navab, N.: Speech-enabled augmented reality supporting mobile industrial maintenance. IEEE Pervasive Comput. **2**(1), 65–70 (2003)
19. Gomes, L., Martins, V.F., Dias, D.C., de Paiva Guimara?s, M.: Music-AR: augmented reality in teaching the concept of sound loudness to children in pre-school. In: Proceedings of the XVI Symposium on Virtual and Augmented Reality, pp. 114–117 (2014)
20. Henderson, S., Feiner, S.: Exploring the benefits of augmented reality documentation for maintenance and repair. IEEE Trans. Vis. Comput. Graph. **17**(10), 1355–1368 (2011)
21. Ivanova, G., Aliev, Y., Ivanov, A.: Augmented reality textbook for future blended education. In: Proceedings of the International Conference on E-Learning, vol. 14, pp. 130–136 (2014)
22. Johnson, L.F., Levine, A., Smith, R.S., Haywood, K.: Key emerging technologies for elementary and secondary education. Educ. Digest **76**(1), 36–40 (2010)
23. Johnson, L.F., Levine, A., Smith, R.S., Haywood, K.: Key emerging technologies for postsecondary education. Educat. Digest **76**(2), 34–38 (2010)
24. Kaufmann, H.: Construct3D: an augmented reality application for mathematics and geometry education. In: Proceedings of the Tenth ACM International Conference on Multimedia, pp. 656–657 (2002)
25. Kaufmann, H., Schmalstieg, D.: Mathematics and geometry education with collaborative augmented reality. Comput. Graph. **27**(3), 339–345 (2003)
26. Kaufmann, H., Meyer, B.: Simulating educational physical experiments in augmented reality. In: ACM SIGGRAPH ASIA 2008 Educators Programme Article No. 3 (2008)
27. Kerawalla, L., Luckin, R., Seljeflot, S., Woolard, A.: Making it real: exploring the potential of augmented reality for teaching primary school science. Virtual Reality **10**(3), 163–174 (2006)
28. Kim, H., Yoon, O., Han, J., Nam, K.: Distributed cognition-applied smart learning environment: designa DN implementation. In: Porceedings of the 6th International Conference on Education and New Learning Technologies (2014)
29. Lamberti, F., Manuri, F., Sanna, A., Paravati, G., Pezzolla, P., Montuschi, P.: Challenges, opportunities and future trends of emerging techniques for augmented reality-based maintenance. IEEE Trans. Emerg. Top. Comput. **2**(4), 411–421 (2014). doi:10.1109/TETC.2014.2368833

30. Liarokapis, F., Petridis, P., Lister, P.F., White, M.: Multimedia augmented reality interface for e-learning (MARIE). World Trans. Eng. Technol. Educ. **1**, 173–176 (2002)
31. Liarokapis, F., Mourkoussis, N., White, M., Darcy, J., Sifniotis, M., Petridis, P., Basu, A., Lister, P.F.: Web3D and augmented reality to support engineering education. World Trans. Eng. Technol. Educ. **3**(1), 11–14 (2004)
32. Liu, D., Jenkins, S.A., Sanderson, P.M., Fabian, P., Russell, W.J.: Monitoring with head-mounted displays: performance and safety in a full-scale simulator and part-task trainer. Anesth Analg. **109**, 1135–46 (2009)
33. Manuri, F., Sanna, A., Lamberti, F., Paravati, G., Pezzolla, P.: A workflow analysis for implementing AR-based maintenance procedures. In: De Paolis, L.T., Mongelli, A. (eds.) AVR 2014. LNCS, vol. 8853, pp. 185–200. Springer, Heidelberg (2014)
34. Martin-Gutierrez, J., Fabiani, P., Benesova, W., Meneses-Fernandez, M.D., Mora, C.E.: Augmented reality to promote collaborative and autonomous learning in higher education. Computers in Human Behavior (2014). doi:10.1016/j.chb.2014.11.093
35. Metaio SDK web site. http://www.metaio.com/sdk/
36. Milgram, P., Kishino, F.: A taxonomy of mixed reality visual displays. IEICE Trans. Inf. Syst. **E77–D**(12), 1321–1329 (1994)
37. Mitchell, R.: Alien contact!: exploring teacher implementation of an augmented reality curricular unit. J. Comput. Math. Sci. Teach. **30**(3), 271–302 (2011)
38. Neea, A.Y.C., Onga, S.K., Chryssolourisb, G., Mourtzisb, D.: Augmented reality applications in design and manufacturing. CIRP Ann. Manufact. Technol. **61**, 657–679 (2012)
39. Ong, S.K., Yuan, M.L., Nee, A.Y.C.: Augmented reality applications in manufacturing: a survey. Intl J. Prod. Res. **46**, 2707–2742 (2008)
40. Ohshima, K.S., Yamamoto, H., Tamura, H.: AR^2 hockey system: a collaborative mixed reality system. Trans. VRSJ **3**(2), 55–60 (1998)
41. Pantoja, G., Garza, L.E., Mendivil, E.G.: Augmented reality in pneumatic conveying system: fuller pump dry material line charger. In: Proceedings of the 9th Iberian Conference on Information Systems and Technologies, pp. 1–5 (2014)
42. Shelton, B.E., Hedley, N.R.: Using augmented reality for teaching EarthSun relationships to Undergraduate Geography students. In: The First IEEE International Augmented Reality Toolkit Workshop (2002)
43. Sielhorst, T., Feuerstein, M., Navab, N.: Advanced medical displays: a literature review of augmented reality. J. Display Technol. **4**(4), 451–467 (2008)
44. Stanimirovic, D., Damasky, N., Webel, S., Koriath, D., Spillner, A., Kurz, D.: A mobile augmented reality system to assist auto mechanics. In: proceedings of the IEEE International Symposium on Mixed and Augmented Reality (2014)
45. Sumadio, D.D., Rambli, D.R.A.: Preliminary evaluation on user acceptance of the augmented reality use for education. In: Proceedings of the 2nd International Conference on Computer Engineering and Applications, vol. 2, pp. 461–465 (2010)
46. Sutherland, I.: A head-mounted three-dimensional display. In: Fall Joint Computer Conference on American Federation of Information Processing Societies (AFIPS) Conference Proceedings, vol. 33. Thompson Books, Washington, D.C., pp. 757–764 (1968)
47. Thomas, B., Close, B., Donoghue, J., Squires, J., De Bondi, P., Morris, M., Piekarski, W.: ARQuake: an outdoor/indoor augmented reality first person application. In: Proceedings of the 4th International Symposium on Wearable Computers, pp 139–146 (2000)

48. Tsai, C.H., Huang, J.Y.: A mobile augmented reality based scaffolding platform for outdoor fieldtrip learning. In: Proceedings of the 3rd International Conference on Advanced Applied Informatics, pp. 307–312 (2014)
49. Wang, J., Feng, Y., Zeng, C., Li, S.: An augmented reality based system for remote collaborative maintenance instruction of complex products. In: Proceedings of IEEE International Conference on the Automation Science and Engineering, pp. 309–314 (2014)
50. Wu, H.K., Lee, S.W.Y., Chang, H.Y., Liang, J.C.: Current status, opportunities and challenges of augmented reality in education. Comput. Educ. **62**, 41–49 (2013)

Training in VR: A Preliminary Study on Learning Assembly/Disassembly Sequences

Daniele Sportillo$^{(\boxtimes)}$, Giovanni Avveduto, Franco Tecchia,
and Marcello Carrozzino

Percro Lab, Scuola Superiore Sant'Anna, Pisa, Italy
{d.sportillo,g.avveduto,f.tecchia,m.carrozzino}@sssup.it
http://www.sssup.it

Abstract. This paper presents our ongoing work for operators training exploiting an immersive Mixed Reality system. Users, immersed in a Virtual Environment, can be trained in assembling or disassembling complex mechanical machineries. Taking input from current industry-level procedures, the training consists in guided step-by-step operations in order to teach the operators how to assemble, disassemble and maintain a certain machine. In our system the interaction is performed in a natural way: the user can see his own real hands, by means of a 3D camera placed on the HMD, and use them to grab and move the machine pieces in order to perform the training task. We believe that seeing your own hands during manipulative tasks present fundamental advantages over mediated techniques. In this paper we describe the system architecture and present our strategy as well as the results of a pilot test aiming at a preliminary evaluation of the system.

Keywords: Training · Immersive virtual environment · Natural interaction · Mixed Reality

1 Introduction

Global industrial manufacturing capacities constitute a large part of the world wealth and economy. A key component of any manufacturing business is training: training a specialized workforce as well as training the customers about the produced machineries requires huge amounts of time, resources and logistic facilities. Training has spill-over benefits for the industry (by providing a pool of skilled workers) and for the society (the improved employment outcomes and flow-on effects such as improved health and lower social welfare costs). Currently, in the field of industrial manufacturing training is a hugely expensive activity traditionally burdened by a number of issues such as the cost of realizing a training environment, the cost of using machineries beyond the working hours, security risks when a trainee uses an equipment and more. These considerations have in time lead to the suggestion that the use of Virtual Reality could introduce significant benefits in the training processes, by removing the need of physical

© Springer International Publishing Switzerland 2015
L.T. De Paolis and A. Mongelli (Eds.): AVR 2015, LNCS 9254, pp. 332–343, 2015.
DOI: 10.1007/978-3-319-22888-4_24

mock-ups in the training process or at least in some of the procedures. Virtual Environments provide, in fact, a 'sandbox' where certain operations can be performed and learnt safely, under full control, and with the possibility of replicating the experience multiple times, exactly in the same way or with any desired modification. In the industrial field training is important not only to optimize working skills but also to avoid incidents and fatalities. Real industrial environments can be dangerous or simply unavailable; training taking place outside the direct working environment can often produce only incomplete experiences and a limited impact. VR-based training can, instead, simulate real-life working conditions but in a safe playground. The training system presented in this paper is intended to be used by industrial companies who needs to train their operators on the tasks of assembly, disassembly or maintain large mechanical machines. What motivates the use of Virtual Reality is that a real copy of the machine could be cumbersome and expensive, and very likely it might result impossible to work together on the same machine at the same time. Moreover usually an expert assistant is required during the training phase in order to assist the operator. The proposed system provides the needed metaphors to interact and manipulate a 3D model of the machine in absolute autonomy with the purpose of following out a task. This system provides a controlled and safe training environment, in which damages to the real machine are reduced or avoided; hence, inexperienced users can take advantage of virtual training before actually facing the real machine.

2   Previous Work

The use of fully immersive Virtual Reality systems for training purposes has been extensively investigated in literature. A number of challenges have been highlighted, ranging from minimizing overall latency, interacting intuitively in the virtual environment, increasing users perceptual awareness of the virtual world and providing the user with a strong sense of immersion and embodiment [7]. Examples can be found in the mining industry [11], in the aerospace industry [3], in the automotive industry [5], in logistics [2] and, in general, in the sector of maintenance [6]. Opportunities provided by Mixed and Augmented Reality address issues similar to those addressed by VR, although with a slightly different perspective. In Mixed Reality, in fact, the real environment is not substituted by a virtual counterpart; rather it is integrated with virtual elements that enhance its information content. Therefore many safety issues effectively tackled by VR are commonly not addressed by MR systems which, in turn, may result more effective whenever the real context is fundamental.

In general, one of the most important consequences of living the training experience in a totally virtual context (as in VR), or keeping the vision on the real context (as in MR), is related to the body self visual perception. In VR, depending on the visualization device, users can still see their body (for instance in a CAVE) or not (if using a HMD; in this case a digital avatar must be shown in order to allow self perception). In MR the real context, including own body, is always present.

This has of course an impact in training, especially in tasks where manipulation operations, or other types of direct interaction with the body, take place. Avatar representations, in fact, might not correspond exactly to the dimensions or the current posture of the user and might, although slightly, mislead the self perception and limit the effectiveness of the virtual training. Last year we have presented an hybrid approach to the task of embodiment [10]. What made our approach novel, was that the users hands were video captured in 3D, reconstructed in real-time and graphically embedded in a synthetic Virtual Environment rendered in an HMD worn by the user. We have shown that the introduction of the photorealistic capture of users hands in a coherently rendered virtual scenario induces in the user a strong feeling of embodiment without the need of a virtual avatar as a proxy. Also the users ability to grasp and manipulate virtual objects using their own hands provides an intuitive user interaction experience and improves the users self perception and users perception of the environment. We used the same approach in the current work, so users are able to use their hands manipulating virtual objects in the scene and are able to navigate in the scene using their own body movements. The next section of this paper describes our training system, we then describe the pilot study we have conducted and present our initial results. Finally we present our concluding remarks.

3   Our VR-based Training System

In this section we describe the technical architecture of the system shown in the Fig. 1. The user wears an HMD and is free to walk around the scene as well as to use his own hands to manipulate virtual objects in the scene by means of a RGBD camera mounted on top of the HMD. This allows the system to get in real-time a textured geometric mesh of the visible parts of the hands and

Fig. 1. The system physical layout: OptiTrack cameras in red, finger thimbles in dark green, HMD with markers in blue and an example of what user sees in light green (Color figure online).

Fig. 2. The visualization system: Oculus Rift DK2 and PrimeSense Carmine 1.09

body (as seen from her/his own perspective) that can be rendered like any other polygonal model in the scene.

3.1 The Visualization System

The Fig. 2 shows the visualization system. It is composed by the following items: an optical marker, used for positional head tracking, an Oculus Rift DK2 HMD connected to an Intel workstation for visual feedback and a 3D camera mounted on top of the HMD support, and integral to it, which is used both for the real-time 3D capturing of the user hands correctly co-located in the virtual environment (and all the other parts of the body framed by the camera) and for the tracking of the hands. Hands position tracking takes place by means of coloured thimbles (blue and green) placed on the thumb and the index of the hand. We used the inside of our large CAVE installation to exploit our optical tracker.

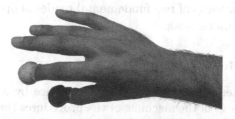

Fig. 3. The interaction system which consists of two colored markers (Color figure online)

3.2   The Interaction Interface

Finger tracking is performed by taking advantage of the RGBD data in order to detect the coloured markers placed on top of the user's fingers, as described in [10]. Simple color filtering is then used in order to identify which pixels of the RGB image match the marker colors. The algorithm also uses the depth map data in order to efficiently pre-cull away those pixels that are too far to be part of the user hands (Fig. 3).

A simple collision detection algorithm is applied to this data in order to enable grabbing and dragging interactive virtual objects. The implemented interaction is therefore almost completely natural, with the only added metaphor simulating a simplified grabbing. In fact, no actual physically-based contact is retrieved:when the two fingers (whose position is visually highlighted by making two spheres, with the same colours, appear on top of them - fingers are anyway visible as they are acquired in 3D and streamed by the 3Dcamera) touch each other within or in close proximity of an interactive object, the two spheres become one single red sphere, meaning that the object can be grasped and moved (the user can interact with just a single object at a time).

4   The Training Application

To handle most of the basic VR requirements (loading the 3D model of the environment, performing stereoscopic rendering, gather sensors data) we use the flexible and efficient XVR framework [8], that allows us to have a fine-grained control on the basic aspects of visualization and interaction. For the more specific tasks of real-time reconstruction and visualization of the data captured by the PrimeSense camera we have then developed a custom rendering XVR plugin based on the hardware-accelerated approach described in [4,9]. Another external module performs finger tracking from RGBD data. All the external modules have been developed in C++.

The application presents a scene consisting of a room, within which the user, wearing the visualization system described above, can walk around. At the center of the room is placed the 3D model of the machine, while on the wall are present the instruction tables that help the operator during the task (Fig. 4).

The application consists of two fundamental modes of operation: the authoring mode and the training mode.

4.1   Authoring Mode

This modality is intended to be performed only once by an expert who owns already deep-knowledge of the machine, of the procedures that can be performed on it, such as maintenance, and of each of the steps that needs to be followed to disassemble it. The expert can disassemble the machine, piece after piece. During this phase, the expert defines steps and sequences. In our mind a **sequence** consists of an ordered list of steps, and each **step** consists of an unordered

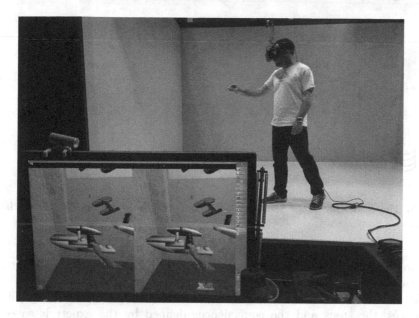

Fig. 4. A user performing a training session: in green, the group on which he is operating (Color figure online)

list of pieces to move. According to this *notation*, inside a step the pieces can be moved without a specific order, but inside a sequence the steps must be *sequentially* performed. The expert can also mark a step as a **group** of pieces: this implies that the step will consist only in the translation of the entire group into its target position. The expert thus disassembles the group piece-by-piece, with the possibility to further define nested groups. The concept of group is of primary importance especially in case of complex hierarchical machines: it allows to assemble/disassemble portions of the machine in a location different from the final one, helping the operator to have a more organized and schematic view of the entire machine. If during the disassembly the expert makes a mistake, he can navigate through the steps, undo the changes and start over.

While authoring, the expert places each item in a specific location. This location is marked as starting position for the specific piece during an assembly session: in other words, when the trainee will assemble the machine, at the beginning of each step he will find the pieces exactly in the position the expert left it. If inside a step, two or more pieces are left in the same position (and have the same dimensions) they are marked as **equivalent**. In this case, only one of the equivalent pieces is shown with a label indicating the number of equivalent pieces of which consists. This implies that in assembly mode, the operator can place an equivalent piece in the target position of any other equivalent (e.g. if the expert marks some screws as equivalent, the operator will be able to place screws in any well fitting location). During this phase the expert can also take snapshots of the state of the machine from its own point of view. These snapshots

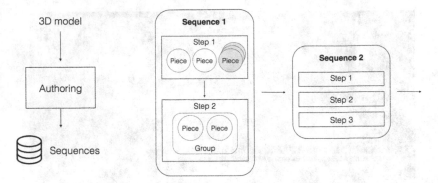

Fig. 5. The authoring stage produces the sequences structure starting from the 3d model

are stored and can be used and modified in order to define instructions tables that can be presented to the operators during the training phase.

At the end of the authoring session an ordered list containing all the sequences, the steps and the equivalences defined by the expert is saved on file, as shown in Fig. 5.

4.2 Training Mode

This mode is intended to be performed by operators for training. The trainee can either work on the machine in a "free" mode, or can perform a training session on the machine assembly or disassembly. In the first case the operator can interact with the machine model, without any constraint in terms of sequences and steps, in order to discover how it is made. When instead the operator performs a training session, he's constrained to the specific sequence previously executed by the expert in the authoring mode.

On the walls of the room, the operator can find the instruction tables relative to the step he's performing, and information about the progress of his task: number of remaining pieces, number of steps completed, number of sequences completed and time passed.

During the training several hints could be activated, depending on the difficult of the task, to help the operators: It is possible to define help layers that can be dynamically presented to the users that encounter difficulties in performing certain operations. Furthermore the operators can perform the same task several times - with a decreasing level of help - until they acquire the needed familiarity with the machine. The application's flow chart is shown in the Fig. 6.

Disassembly Mode. In this modality the instruction sequences are loaded from file in the same order they have been saved. At the beginning of the task, the machine is completely mounted and in order to move forward on the task, the operator must complete the needed steps by removing the right pieces from

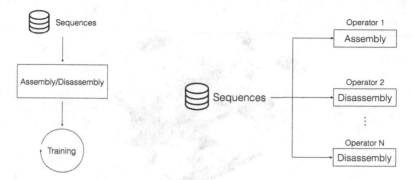

Fig. 6. The training system flow chart. Different operators can use the same sequences to perform different tasks on the same machine.

their starting position. Since it is a disassembly task, the operator is not required to put the items into a target position; in order to clean up the scene, at the end of each step, the moved pieces are translated into the position the expert left them. The operator is able to move only the pieces that must be actually moved inside that step. When the operator grabs a piece that can be moved it becomes green, while if the piece cannot be moved it becomes red. Each action results also in an acoustic feedback that alerts the users that the action has been actually performed by the system.

Assembly Mode. In this modality the instruction sequences are loaded from the file in a backward order. At the beginning, the first piece is already placed into its target position. The remaining pieces relative to the step/sequence are shown in their start position, namely where the expert left them during the authoring stage. Equivalent pieces are shown together with a label indicating the number of multiple items. The task of the operator is to put all the pieces into their right target position. If the operator leaves the pieces in a closest range of the target, they are automatically snapped to the correct position. Also in this case each action results in an acoustic feedback that alerts the users that the action has been actually performed by the system.

5 Pilot Study

In our pilot study, the aim of the subjects was to perform an assembly task of a 53-pieces model of the LEGO® Creator Sea Plane [1]. The final task has been preceded by a training phase on the same real model, or on an equivalent 3D model (Fig. 7).

The 3D model has been exported from 3ds MAX® using the specific XVR plugin. The authoring stage has been performed by one of the experimenter strictly following the original instructions provided with the model, dividing the model into 3 groups (the flying boat, the tail and the pontoons) and identifying 5 sequences (Fig. 8).

Fig. 7. The LEGO® Creator Sea Plane

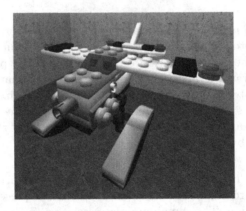

Fig. 8. The 3D model

5.1 Description

The test group consisted of 8 subjects, divided into two sub-groups. Both sub-groups have performed a 30-minutes training, the first one using the real model, and the second one using the virtual model with the presented system (Figs. 9 and 10).

During the training, the subjects were provided with the same instruction tables needed to accomplish the requested task and they could use the time at their disposal to perform the task several times, or just to study the model and the relative instruction tables.

After the training each subject has performed the actual task: an assembly of the real model of the Sea Plane without time constraints and instruction tables. The performing time has been registered and the results evaluated according to the number of pieces correctly placed.

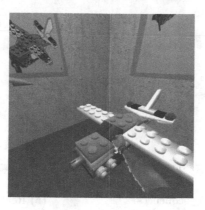

Fig. 9. Assembly of the virtual model

5.2   Results

The Figs. 11 and 12 show the results of the pilot study. In particular the Figs. 11a and 12a show the completion times of assembly sequences performed respectively during the real training and the virtual training. The Figs. 11b and 12b show the time needed to assemble the real model after the training (in yellow), and the percentage of completion of the model (in blue).

The charts show that the time needed to complete an assembly sequence significantly decreases in the virtual training with respect to the number of trials. The first trial in virtual training requires more time because of the needed familiarization with the environment. Even if the assembly of the real model after the virtual training has required longer time, all the subjects have been able to complete the assembly of the model for almost the 50 %, with a peak of 90 %.

Fig. 10. Assembly of the real model

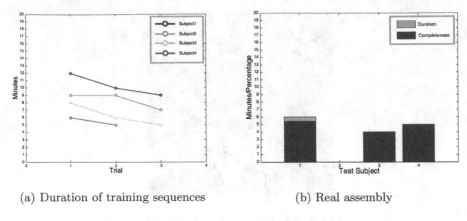

(a) Duration of training sequences   (b) Real assembly

Fig. 11. Training on the real model (Color figure online)

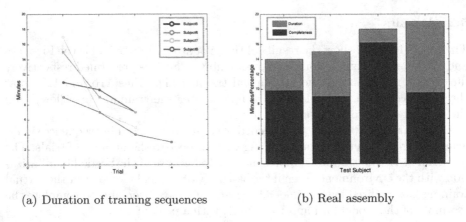

(a) Duration of training sequences   (b) Real assembly

Fig. 12. Training on the virtual model (Color figure online)

6   Conclusion and Future Work

In this paper we have presented an ongoing work about an application for operator training that exploits an immersive Mixed Reality system. The application allows to operate on a 3D model of a machine, defining the assembly/disassembly constraints that the operators will respect during the training. We have then presented the preliminary pilot study we conducted in order to confirm our original hypothesis that a training performed using the proposed system could be as helpful and effective as the training performed on the real model.

The results of this pilot study, although preliminary, are so promising to lead us to believe that this form of training has the potential to constitute a valid alternative to a more traditional training approach. A significant improvement to the proposed system could be brought with the introduction of a more enhanced interaction metaphor. To date, the interaction system allows only the translation of the virtual objects present in the scene. We deem important to allow also rotating and scaling the objects, providing users with a more direct and natural interaction. The addition of a multimodal feedback to the interaction system would also certainly lead to more convincing results.

Since we are encouraged by our findings, we are already planning to conduct a series of user studies with more subjects using the new interaction system to operate on several models, in order to further assess the benefits of our approach.

References

1. Lego$^{®}$ creator sea plane. http://shop.lego.com/en-US/Sea-Plane-31028. Accessed: 08 May 2015
2. Bergamasco, M., Perotti, S., Avizzano, C.A., Angerilli, M., Carrozzino, M., Ruffaldi, E.: Fork-lift truck simulator for training in industrial environment. In: 10th IEEE Conference on Emerging Technologies and Factory Automation, ETFA 2005, vol. 1, pp. 689–693. IEEE (2005)
3. De Sa, A.G., Zachmann, G.: Virtual reality as a tool for verification of assembly and maintenance processes. Comput. Graph. **23**(3), 389–403 (1999)
4. Huang, W., Alem, L., Tecchia, F.: HandsIn3D: supporting remote guidance with immersive virtual environments. In: Winckler, M. (ed.) INTERACT 2013, Part I. LNCS, vol. 8117, pp. 70–77. Springer, Heidelberg (2013)
5. Li, J.-R., Khoo, L.P., Tor, S.B.: Desktop virtual reality for maintenance training: an object oriented prototype system (v-realism). Comput. Ind. **52**(2), 109–125 (2003)
6. Magee, D., Zhu, Y., Ratnalingam, R., Gardner, P., Kessel, D.: An augmented reality simulator for ultrasound guided needle placement training. Med. Biol. Eng. Comput. **45**(10), 957–967 (2007)
7. Slater, M., Frisoli, A., Tecchia, F., Guger, C., Lotto, B., Steed, A., Pfurtscheller, G., Leeb, R., Reiner, M., Sanchez-Vives, M.V., Verschure, P., Bernardet, U.: Understanding and realizing presence in the presenccia project. IEEE Comput. Graph. Appl. **27**(4), 90–93 (2007)
8. Tecchia, F.: A flexible framework for wide-spectrum vr development. Presence **19**(4), 302–312 (2010)
9. Tecchia, F., Alem, L., Huang, W.: 3d helping hands: a gesture based mr system for remote collaboration. In: Proceedings of the 11th ACM SIGGRAPH International Conference on Virtual-Reality Continuum and its Applications in Industry, pp. 323–328. ACM (2012)
10. Tecchia, F., Avveduto, G., Brondi, R., Carrozzino, M., Bergamasco, M., Alem, L.:. I'm in vr!: using your own hands in a fully immersive mr system. In: Proceedings of the 20th ACM Symposium on Virtual Reality Software and Technology, pages 73–76. ACM (2014)
11. Van Wyk, E., De Villiers, R.: Virtual reality training applications for the mining industry. In: Proceedings of the 6th International Conference on Computer Graphics, Virtual Reality, Visualisation and Interaction in Africa, pp. 53–63. ACM (2009)

Applying Aesthetic Rules in Virtual Environments by Means of Semantic Web Technologies

Konstantinos Kontakis, Malvina Steiakaki, Michael Kalochrsitianakis[✉],
Kostas Kapetanakis, and Athanasios G. Malamos

Technological Educational Institution of Crete, Heraklion, Greece
kalohr@staff.teicrete.gr

Abstract. The recent vigorous advances in virtual reality during the last decade have led to the application of 3D technologies to divergent areas such as interior decoration. Our system aims to innovate by bringing automation capabilities such as the application of high level aesthetic rules to virtual worlds. The system takes advantage of three dimensional presentation technologies for the World Wide Web such as Web3D, appropriate vocabularies such as ontology languages, semantic rule definition languages and machine learning approaches in the area of case based reasoning. The system may thus store knowledge that allow its editing tool to customize virtual worlds according to high level rules that define moods or aesthetic styles.

Keywords: Virtual reality · Semantic web · Ontologies · Case based reasoning

1 Introduction

The evolution and spread of virtual environments has led to significant production of interior design artifacts for virtual reality during the last years. Such artifacts that are offered in groups, libraries or individually but there is only limited, if any, functionality for efficiently combining them for the purposes of decoration that is, though the application of high level rules that directly reflect decoration styles, or directives. Through systems such as the one presented in this paper vendors can describe their products in a standard way, suitable for use by interior design & decoration artifact vendors that take advantage of the internet. Such systems may lead to easier and more efficient design and decoration of virtual worlds, however implementing the general case inevitably has to address a number of technological issues. First, the basic type of information necessary to describe all objects and their aesthetic value within a virtual environment must be identified. That is, how the basic information about characteristics or value of objects/artifacts would be represented, where it can be stored, how or if such information can be acquired from the visualization or the virtualization technologies. Currently, there are very few, if any, attempts to organize the descriptive information of visual objects in terms of a specific ontology for interior design. There are scientific papers that cover the need for the existence of architectural ontology, without specifying specific ontological form; at the same time the need and benefits from the use of ontology in architecture, interior design, cultural services etc.

© Springer International Publishing Switzerland 2015
L.T. De Paolis and A. Mongelli (Eds.): AVR 2015, LNCS 9254, pp. 344–354, 2015.
DOI: 10.1007/978-3-319-22888-4_25

is clear, due to the capabilities such a representation would offer. Our system attempts to introduce a suitable schema for keeping the aesthetic qualities of objects that is, features such as multiple languages, information for the disabled, and more. Unlike CAD tools that take advantage of data about visual objects, as offered by the technology that implements them, and leave all types of decisions to users, our system has aimed to support all types of aesthetic qualitative characteristics and correlate them in order to infer decorative relations among them and thus facilitate the user in selecting matching components. It has been essential for such a system to review the existing standards for decorative information description and identify the ones capable to support its purpose. And then, pieces of this information or descriptions of artifact objects need to be shared through the World Wide Web and also need to be exploitable by visualization tools. Another issue has been how to correlate types of information attribute meaning to them within the same context and use them to an end in an optimal manner. Given a suitable content representation, this problem translates to the implementation of a rule production logic capable to combine the aforementioned information and produce rational results that will reflect non-trivial aesthetic differentiations on three dimensional scenes. Case based reasoning systems (CBR) or similar trainable artificial inference systems seem to be suitable for our problem; such solutions have been known to be capable to produce significant results especially for cases where solutions rely on previous cases using such as similarity criteria. Applications and APIs makes CBR development efficient through the use of general programming languages and also compatible due its relation with cutting-edge technologies and protocols for the internet. CBR techniques in combination with ontology structures has yielded satisfactory results as there are numerous valuable references in literature, please refer to related work, below. In this context, the use of Ontology Web Language (OWL) and Semantic Web Rule Language (SWRL) capabilities in CBR systems was used. SWRL combines elements from OWL and Report Markup Language (RML) and is supported by W3C. It is a rule creation language, based on RuleML capable to describe and execute rules against the content of an ontology for use with web applications. The application of such rules return semantic information that will refer to qualitative and quantitative characteristics of objects. Our system thus introduces rule-sets that may extent to any type of aesthetic/decorative priority such color combinations (complementarity, harmony, antithesis), material compatibility and room/furniture/spacing patterns, fabric combinations and space ergonomy besides others. The rest of the paper is organized as follows: Sect. 2 presents the related work as far as research and current practice in the relevant fields are concerned, Sect. 3 presents the our platform architecture, components and how it can be used. Section 4 presents our conclusions and future work.

2 Related Work

Web3D technologies have seen a significant rise during the last decade, especially as WebGL have become widely accepted. Other technologies such as X3D have existed for a long time however, recent advances in hardware and software now allow for significant progress in integrating interactive 3D graphics for the web. X3D in particular has drawn a lot of attention, largely due to the emergence of the X3D object model (OM) framework, which enables modern browsers to display fully interactive 3D content, written in X3D code, without the use of plug-ins or additional software. While WebGL allows powerful graphics manipulations in itself, X3D-OM offers a significant advantage; it relies on code written in XML and is thus easily accessible and modifiable, allowing information extraction, DOM manipulation and also integration of textual meta-data, all of which fit nicely with the content of services over the internet.

Semantic web technologies on the other hand, promise to transform information management by integrating high-level, human language concepts and their interrelationships with everyday information structures in order to facilitate organization and search. Various efforts to incorporate and organize real world facts into structured ontologies have been made over the recent years and, in the current state-of-the-art, domain-specific solutions can offer particularly helpful tools to handle and extract information in an intelligent and organized manner. There has been a number of cases where semantic technologies have been used for visualization purposes.

The AsIsKnown project [1] aimed at the collection of product data from European textile businesses, and their organization into ontological structures. The aim was to automate the design of spaces by appropriate selection of textile materials, colours and patterns. The system also proposed a virtual reality interface and a smart profiler in order to sample configurations and create demonstrations. There has also been further attempts to organize textile patterns into ontological structures [2].

A recent overview of the subject can be found in [3].

An interesting article [4] describes an integrated environment for architecture, engineering and construction where professionals from different disciplines can work over the same building plan document. The systems presents each user with the elements of their direct interest and hides objects of no interest. The system takes advantage of resource description framework (RDF) ontologies written in OWL, encompassing all aspects of the building process, conceptualizing elements, including engineering details to functional, design elements. The ontological descriptions are accompanied by X3D models for a potential authoring system to display in a virtual reality environment. The system displays significant similarities to our own, with respect to the merging of OWL ontology with X3D models for display.

However, on the one hand, their scope is different; our work focuses exclusively on interior design, and allow building the richest possible ontology that such a system could have. Our approach is not limited to showing or hiding particular 3D models with respect to the user; we aim to produce an integrated system where models are drawn from the ontology using decoration directives and thus produce differentiated visualizations.

Ontologies allow expedient administration of unstructured anthropocentric information [5] and have already been successfully established in IT industry via a variety of applications, such as, artificial intelligence and automated reasoning [6], biomedical informatics [7], agent systems [8], agricultural ontology service concept services [9], art [10], semantic digital libraries [11] and navigation systems [12]. Seremeti and Kameas also empower in their presentation [13] the need for introducing computer science technologies and ontologies in areas such as architecture, real estate, interior design; cultural services and digital libraries due to the difficulty of the administration and management manually of this information.

The standardization efforts, like ISO 10303-236, deal with constructional characteristics in the industry of furniture and accessories rather than the architecture and design as a genre application. Our systems needs an ontology focusing on the representation of interior design & decoration concepts and capable to support inter-operation with software and web services in order to enable knowledge distribution and exchange [14]. These characteristics can be achieved by relying on an annotation approach such as the one introduced in preferences of users. There has been significant work in the literature regarding visual, interactive interior design and semantically-aware assistive technologies.

One of the first systems can be found in [20]. It takes advantage knowledge base containing XML topic maps that describe physical relations and combinations between objects in a room. The system allows the construction of 2D room designs which in turn leads to a VRML representation. Modifications can then be applied such as moving objects, modifying them or adding new ones. The platform uses SOAP messages for the communication among its components including a module for authors to demonstrate the assembly procedure using haptics.

Another attempt in the direction of incorporating high level design concepts for interior design is a language-based attempt, described in [21]. The pro-system accepts natural language commands for the placement of objects in a room. Commands such as "place an armchair on the right side of the sofa" can be interpreted and applied in scenes; queries such as "where is the green chair?" can also be used to retrieve information. Lexicons and natural language processing and a set of rules and constraints are implemented through the CLIPS framework for expert systems. Besides querying for properties accessible by the 2D design technology the system supports aesthetic recommendations and it is capable of including general rules interior design rules.

The XML annotation will be hierarchical and its graph form result will be a tree. Hence every annotated space will be represented as a tree, where the root is the room and the leafs represent the objects contained in it. The position of an object on the tree depicts its hierarchical position in the interior space.

For example, in a graph of a room, a vase, will be a child of the object table on which it is placed. The table itself will be a child of the floor object on which it rests. And, in turn, the floor object will be a child of the room it belongs to. Every matching problem of two spaces, becomes now a tree matching problem. The correspondence of leafs and trees is a thoroughly studied issue and there are a lot of efficient solutions [22].

3   Overview of the System

Our system aims to provide an integrated framework capable to offer the application of aesthetic rules for end-users. The system also has the potential to appeal to content providers, designers besides potential end-users. The first step in the process of setting the system up start with populating the knowledge base with items to be used in rooms. Content providers, such as a furniture or textile retailers may use the web-based interface to assign individuals to classes and define their properties.

The object's characteristics such as material, colour and design style can be selected from the ontology; our ontology may also store X3D models for each object. After the initial setup it is straightforward to use an editor for building virtual worlds. Room objects, their intended styles and use are defined first, and then the floor, the walls and ceiling are added. Each such scene can be accompanied by an SVG plan that will define the spatial structure of the room, and of course the various individual object corresponding to structures, furniture and items that are to be placed in the room. To the extent that these items are also accompanied by X3D models, a 3D reconstruction of the room can then be built. Users are capable to design their own room space and place its objects through a convenient and flexible SVG design environment, which comes with a predefined set of geometrical shapes, furniture, accessories and floor colors in the form of HTML option elements.

The designer can then visualize the room they have created, using an SVG-to-X3D converter included in the system that exploits XSLT transformation, the X3D information stored in the ontology and last but not least the basic concepts implemented in the ontology, such as its classes, properties and individuals. Using the drag sensor interface incorporated in the system, users can manually customize the positioning of items within the room down to a high level of precision.

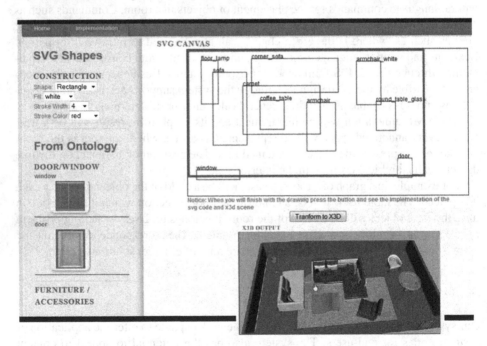

Fig. 1. The X3D output of the system presents the final scene where interior design rules have been applied

Figure 1 illustrates the X3D interface of the system and more specifically how it uses the SVG design and the selected objects to present a complete room. Far from simply allowing designers to make any choice they like on a room, out of a very large list of possibilities, we have integrated an SWRL/SPARQL recommender system in our project. The designer begins by setting up the basic aspects of a room, such as the shape/area, the basic room components and a small number of aspects.

The SWRL/SPARQL system is then enabled, which proceeds to determine other aspects by applying the decoration priorities known to the system. For instance if a modern style with limited contrast is to be applied, the system would detect the floor colour and propose matching carpet colours and styles.

For instance, for terracotta coloured floors the proposed carpets could be ginger with Persian motifs. The 3D visualization subsystem will operate in parallel with the decoration, offering visual representations of the room that are the result of the application of aesthetic rules fill the room with additional items and alter the colouring and materials of the existing ones in real time. Thus, users may play with the mood and the decorative style of their room and when the result is satisfactory they can store it in the knowledge base for future use.

Having populated a platform with items and integrated room designs, potential customers can then visit it and look for ready-made solutions for their needs. By filling out a questionnaire giving as many specifications about the room as they need, the closest match is returned to them, and, again, displayed in X3D and open to small modifications. We have thus a proof-of-concept end-to-end platform for content providers, designers and users to promote, organize and experience the interior design procedure, using an ontological structure that offers full access to content and incorporate automatic design recommendations. The core of the system is an ontological framework that aims to organize all relevant aspects of an interior space into a coherent and usable structure. The framework relies on previous work in interior design ontological design [18] implemented OWL-DL, a sublanguage of OWL intended to convey maximum expressiveness while retaining computational completeness and decidability.

Table 1. Spatial properties and axioms PROPERTY NAME PROPERTY CHARACTERISTIC

PROPERTY NAME	PROPERTY CHARACTERISTIC
is_Over_the	owl:TransitiveProperty
Intersects	owl:TransitiveProperty, owl:SymmetricProperty
Is_Across_The	owl:TransitiveProperty, owl:SymmetricProperty
Is_In_Front_Of	owl:TransitiveProperty, owl:inverseOf: Is_Behind_Of
Is_Behind_Of	owl:TransitiveProperty, owl:inverseOf: Is_In_Front_Of
Is_Lower_Than	owl:TransitiveProperty, owl:inverseOf: Is_Upper_Than
Is_Upper_Than	owl:TransitiveProperty, owl:inverseOf: Is_Lower_Than
Is_On_the_Left_Side	owl:TransitiveProperty, owl:inverseOf: Is_On_the_Right_Side
Is_On_the_Right_Side	owl:TransitiveProperty, owl:inverseOf: Is_On_the_Left_Side

The design of the ontology follows the object oriented design starting from the abstract room at the top of the hierarchy. Our system has defined all necessary elements for the description of two major room object types, that is bedroom and living room. The following paragraphs present the fuse of SWRL and SPARQL technologies under our ontological framework.

This framework is heavily depending on the utilization of an OWL-DL ontology which defines a set of classes and properties for the sufficient annotation of objects that represent interior spaces, mainly living-rooms and bedrooms. The ontology of the system was developed according to the OWL-DL standard in order to support expressiveness in the terms of meaning and semantics. In order to enhance the overall reasoning capabilities of the framework, the properties of spatial objects have been enriched with additional characteristics.

The original set of OWL constructs have thus been limited to suit the needs of our system. Below, these characteristics are described in the form of property axioms along with their corresponding limitations, skipping the default set of property constructs which are self-evident during the definition of each OWL property:

- the adoption of a simplified 3D model, without shadows, without radiosity and with low texture resolution would provide a poor integration. An unacceptable quality of the final result, not to say about the meaningful problem of the items located at various depths, which partially obliterate the reconstruction and are partially obliterated by the reconstruction in turn. In one AR scene, a 3D object should solve all these problems, plus the problems related to the real time restitution. In the solution shown in these pages, the reconstructed three-dimensional model is integrated into the urban fabric by means of a simple masking that considers various objects placed in depth, the global illumination and, last but not least, the point of view of the observer.
- owl:inverseOf, a relation property characteristic capable of inferring that if A, B are individuals, and A is related to B through a property X, then B is also related to A through an opposite property Y. This automatically implies that every inverse property is also a symmetric property
- owl:SymmetricProperty, a logical property characteristic capable of inferring that if A, B are individuals that belong to the same class, and A is related to B, then B is also related to A. This property also implies that the domain and range fields of any symmetric property are the same
- owl:TransitiveProperty, a logical property characteristic capable of inferring that if A, B, C are individuals which belong to the same class, A is related to B, and B is related to C, then A is also related to C. It is worth mentioning that none type of cardinality constraint has been used on transitive properties, since such a thing would violate the OWL-DL sublanguage constraint

Even though that our datatype properties do not contain any spatial annotation capabilities, their usage in such property axioms would be rendered useless, since in the OWL-DL specification defines that the aforementioned characteristics cannot be defined for datatype properties. Table 1 presents the object properties of our ontology which have been attributed with at least one kind of property characteristic. After the desired room space is drawn and filled with objects, its 3D projection is feasible with the employment of the X3DOM framework and an XSLT algorithm capable of transforming SVG elements to their corresponding X3D elements.

The decorative procedure is backed by Apache Jena, a semantic web framework capable to support a wide number of internal and external reasoners for inference procedures. A lot of internal reasoners are capable to deal with our ontology and to successfully infer the statements stemming from the above mentioned property constructs. Specific external reasoners could also be deployed, but their use at this point leads to performance penalty since these constructs either are not OWL complex types nor complete reasoning of the loaded ontology is necessary.

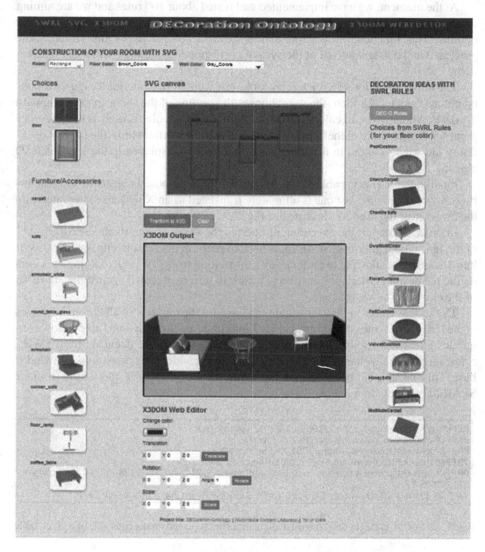

Fig. 2. The final room output in X3D and compatible objects after the application of SWRL reasoning

We implemented a finite set of SWRL rules that apply to interior decoration. The rules were authored using the Protégé-OWL editor and its corresponding entailments can be accessed through specific rule engines. The SWRL rules were integrated into the ontological framework and their entailments were made available with the assistance of an external description logic reasoner, the Pellet reasoner. This reasoner is able to infer the additional OWL concepts described into our SWRL rules, where the latter ones incorporate knowledge related to color theory and decoration priorities.

At the moment, we have implemented and tested about 100 rules and we are aiming to support much more along with extending our virtual knowledge base with further options. This functionality is expressed as aesthetic proposals for the virtual scene presented at the user interface of the system corresponding mainly to floor color selections.

The implementation of SWRL rules took into account two interior design textbooks on colour theory [22]. First, the user chooses the outline of the room space along with the desired floor and wall colors. Amongst them, the floor color is used as the reference point for the matching of the corresponding SWRL rules. Afterwards, the interior decoration knowledge stored in these rules is deducted and displayed in the form of X3D objects.

Finally, the user is capable of placing any of these proposed objects to decorate his room space, where the last one is ultimately translated as an X3D scene integrated into the browser of the user, as illustrated in Fig. 2.

In order to support the execution of queries the system supports the SPARQL API of the Jena model interface. SPARQL is used to perform queries directly upon the OWL knowledge base, allowing to retrieve any information from OWL-DL ontologies. Users define the desired criteria for the query, which in turn is executed against the entire set of the existing knowledge base.

The code segment in Fig. 3 illustrates a query for the retrieval of all the chairs placed in the left side of a the table shown in Fig. 2 identified as "RoundGlassTable". However, queries like the previous are incapable to return the knowledge deducted from SWRL rules, since such statements are not contained into the underlying ontology's knowledge base. This obstacle has been surpassed by using the CONSTRUCT query form from the SPARQL specification.

```
REFIX rdf: <http://www.w3.org/1999/02/22-rdf-syntax-ns#>
PREFIX owl: <http://www.w3.org/2002/07/owl#>
PREFIX xsd: <http://www.w3.org/2001/XMLSchema#>
PREFIX rdfs: <http://www.w3.org/2000/01/rdf-schema#>
PREFIX ont:<http://www.semanticweb.org/ontologies/2009/5/Ontology1244033197062.owl#>
SELECT ?x ?y
WHERE {?x a ont:Chairs; ont:is_On_the_Right_Side ?y. ?y ont:has_code_name ?z.
```

Fig. 3. SPARQL code for the retrieval of all chair objects placed on the right side of a given table

The execution of such queries are able to deduct entailments that do not physically exist in the form of triples in the OWL knowledge base, but are authored from other rule-systems, such as JENA rules or SWRL, and inferred through special external reasoning mechanisms, such as the Jess rule engine or the Pellet reasoner we use. In that way, the interoperability of our proposed interior decoration solutions is guaranteed across distinct platforms, and at the same time, rules are quite durable in the passage of time.

4   Conclusions and Future Work

This paper presented a web based application that takes advantage of semantic technologies to produce automations in the area of interior design. The proposed ontology is capable of describing indoor areas by supporting the involved objects and immovable structures.

Furthermore the ontology is designed to be capable of maintaining aesthetic interrelations by storing qualitative information about each object. The implementation of proper SWRL rules allows the automation of the design process that is, the application of the corresponding aesthetic principles. The system takes advantage of SPARQL to query the ontology for instances matching particular wishes or needs.

The implementation poses as a proof of concept that includes all the aspects of a possible system; it implements a technique for creating 3D scenes from SVG designs that is, by exploiting spatial information about the structure and size of the various objects and also the room walls. The resulting scene is presented in a X3D browser, allowing users to graphically modify their content in terms of object placing, size and orientation. The viewer is capable to explore any ontology on the fly and utilize the graphical information contained in it that is, the SVG plans for walls, floor, ceilings and also X3D objects.

Future work will focus on the evaluation of the output of the system that is, assess how good it is and also compare it with results produced by interior designer professionals. This procedure will provide feedback for the elaboration of our platform that is, the improvement of the interior design rules and the reasoning. From the technical perspective, future work will focus on improving the interaction characteristics of the system in order to make it more modern and friendly.

Acknowledgements. This work has been funded by the European Union and the Hellenic Ministry of Education under the "Archimedes III" research framework. Project Title: "DECO - Ontology and semantic search applications for the support in interior architecture and decoration design", Project Code 32.

References

1. Valintinat, T., Backhaus, W., Enning, K.H.: Non invasive, cross-sector development and management of trends. In: Proceedings of the 13th ISPE International Conference on Concurrent Engineering, Frontiers of Artificial Intelligence and Applications, vol. 143, p. 393 (2006)
2. Arnold, D.Y., Helmer, S., Velásquez Arando, R.: Towards building a knowledge base for research on andean weaving. In: Sexton, A.P. (ed.) BNCOD 26. LNCS, vol. 5588, pp. 180–188. Springer, Heidelberg (2009)
3. Nasir, S., Ooor, N.: Automating the mapping process of traditional malay textile knowledge model with the core ontology. Am. J. Econ. Bus. Adm. 3(1)
4. Lee, J., Jeong, Y.: User-centric knowledge representations based on ontology for AEC design collaboration. Comput. Aided Des. 44(8), 735–748 (2012)

5. Kondylakis, H., Doerr, M., Plexousakis, D.: Empowering provenance in data integration. In: Grundspenkis, J., Morzy, T., Vossen, G. (eds.) ADBIS 2009. LNCS, vol. 5739, pp. 270–285. Springer, Heidelberg (2009)

6. Nakai, T., Bagarinao, E., Tanaka, Y., Matsuo, K., Racoceanu, D.: Ontology for fMRI as a biomedical informatics method. Magn. Reson. Med. Sci. **7**(3), 141 (2008)

7. Moeller, M., Mukherjee, S.: Context – Driven ontological annotations in DICOM images towards semantics PACS. In: International Conference on Health Informatics, pp. 294–299 (2009)

8. Kemke, C.: An Action Ontology Framework for Natural Language Interfaces to Agent Systems, Artificial Intelligence Review. Springer, Dordrecht (2007)

9. Liang, A., Lauser, B., Sini, M., Keizer, J., Katz, S.: From AGROVOC to the agricultural ontology service/concept server. An OWL model for managing ontologies in the agricultural domain, Atlanta. In: Proceedings of OWL: Experiences and Directions Workshop, pp. 76–78 (2006)

10. Thomasso, A.L.: The Ontology of Art. The Blackwell Guide to Aesthetics (Chapter 4). Blackwell Publishing Ltd, Oxford (2008)

11. Shum, S.B., Motta, E., Domingue, J.: ScholOnto: an ontology-based digital library server for research documents and discourse. Int. J. Digit. Libr. **3**, 237 (2000)

12. Kritsotakis, M., Michou, M., Nikoloudakis, E., Bikakis, A., Patkos, T., Antoniou, G., Plexousakis, D.: C-NGINE: a contextual navigation guide for indoor environments. In: Aarts, E., Crowley, J.L., de Ruyter, B., Gerhäuser, H., Pflaum, A., Schmidt, J., Wichert, R. (eds.) AmI 2008. LNCS, vol. 5355, pp. 258–275. Springer, Heidelberg (2008)

13. Seremeti, L., Kameas, A.: Multimedia ontologies, on text awareness in ubiquitous environment. In: Proceedings of the 3rd International Conference on Mobile Multimedia Communications (2007)

14. Patkos, T., et al.: Design and challenges of a semantics-based framework for context-aware services. Int. J. Reasoning-Based Intell. Syst (IJRIS) **1**(1), 18 (2009)

15. Malamos, A.G., Sympa, P.V., Mamakis, G.S.: Xml annotation of conceptual characteristics. In: Proceedings of 6th NHIBE International Conference on Interior Decoration (2009)

16. Art and Architecture Thesaurus Online. http://www.getty.edu/research/conducting_research/vocabularies/aat/. Accessed 20 April 2015

17. O'Connor, M.F., Knublauch, H., Tu, S., Grosof, B.N., Dean, M., Grosso, W., Musen, M.A.: Supporting rule system interoperability on the semantic web with SWRL. In: Gil, Y., Motta, E., Benjamins, V., Musen, M.A. (eds.) ISWC 2005. LNCS, vol. 3729, pp. 974–986. Springer, Heidelberg (2005)

18. Frederick, M.: 101 Things I Learned in Architecture School. MIT Press, Cambridge (2007)

19. Chinn, A.: The Home Decorator's Colour and Texture Sourcebook. Quarto Publishing plc, London (2007)

20. Tsampoulatidis, I., Nikolakis, G., Tzovaras, D., Strintzis, M.: Ontology based interactive graphic environment for product presentation. In: International Conference on Computer Graphics, p. 664 (2004)

21. Kemke, C., Galka, R., Hasan, M.: Towards an intelligent interior design system. In: Proceedings of the Intelligent Virtual Design Environments conference, pp. 2139–2142 (2006)

22. Suters, W.H., Abu-Khzam, F.N., Zhang, Y., Symons, C.T., Samatova, N.F., Langston, M.A.: A new approach and faster exact methods for the maximum common subgraph problem. In: Wang, L. (ed.) COCOON 2005. LNCS, vol. 3595, pp. 717–727. Springer, Heidelberg (2005)

Bilateral Control of a Robotic Arm
Through Brain Signals

Víctor H. Andaluz[1(⊠)], Jessica S. Ortiz[2], and Jorge S. Sanchéz[1]

[1] Universida de las Fuerzas Armadas ESPE, Sangolquí, Ecuador
vhandaluz1@espe.edu.ec
[2] Iniversidad Tecnológica Indoamérica, Ambato, Ecuador
jsortiz@uti.edu.ec

Abstract. This work presents the design of a bilateral teleoperation system for a robotic arm, allowing people with upper limb impairments to move and manipulate objects through brain signals. The person receives visual feedback from the remote site, and it sends position commands and movement velocity to the slave. The desired velocity of the end-effector is considered as a function of the disregard of the person to move the robotic arm. Additionally, the singular configuration prevention through the system's manipulability control is considered. Finally, the simulation results are reported to verify the performance of the proposed system.

Keywords: Robotic arm · Path following · Electromyogram signals

1 Introduction

In recent years, robotics research has experienced a significant change. Research interests are moving from the development of robots for structured industrial environments to the development of autonomous mobile robots operating in unstructured and natural environments [1–8]. The integration of robotic issues into the medical field has become of great interest in recent years. Service, assistance, rehabilitation and surgery are the more benefited human health-care areas by the recent advances in robotics. Specifically, prosthesis for people with physical disabilities to enable them to move or manipulate an object are one of the important goals in robotics assistance [1–4, 9, 10].

Hence, a trajectory will be automatically generated and a trajectory tracking control will guide the robotic arm to the desired target. As indicated, the fundamental problems of motion control of robotic arm can be roughly classified in three groups [11]: (1) *point stabilization*: the goal is to stabilize the arm at a given target point, with a desired orientation; (2) *trajectory tracking*: the arm is required to track a time parameterized reference; and (3) *path following*: the arm is required to converge to a path and follow it, without any time specifications; this work is focused to resolve the path following problem. The path following problem has been well studied and many solutions have been proposed and applied in a wide range of applications. Let $P_d(s) \in \Re^2$ be a desired geometric path parameterized by the curvilinear abscissa $s \in \Re$. In the literature is common to find different control algorithms for path following where is consider $s(t)$ as an additional control input.

© Springer International Publishing Switzerland 2015
L.T. De Paolis and A. Mongelli (Eds.): AVR 2015, LNCS 9254, pp. 355–368, 2015.
DOI: 10.1007/978-3-319-22888-4_26

Inside the different architectures of control already proposed in the literature there is described the teleoperation which allows to govern the robot (slave) by means of the algorithms sent by the operator the same ones that will have to interact with the environment [12]. The disabled people have difficulty in moving his body freely, but his brain there issue signs electroencephalography (EEG), the same ones that can be expressed so freely as they want with the suitable equipment (Emotiv), the major possible degree can obtain of telepresence, that is to say, that allows to the operator to realize tasks with so many skill as if it was manipulating directly the environment [13, 14].

The operator issues signs measured as mental commands, facial expressions or brain performance metrics known as EEG, is a non-invasive method to record electrical activity of the brain along the scalp. EEG measures voltage fluctuations resulting from ionic current flows within the neurons of the brain, this information combined with a good feedback of efforts allows him to realize his task of a more skillful way [15, 16].

In such context, this work proposes a bilateral teleoperation system in order to allow people with upper extremity impairments or severe motor dysfunctions to overcome the difficulties in manipulability of objects. It comprises a robotic arm (slave) so that it can move and manipulate objects. The human operator receives visual and force signals and sends velocity and position commands generated by electromyogram signals through Emotiv EPOC haptic device (master) to the remote site. The desired velocity of the end-effector is considered as a function of the disregard of the person to move the robotic arm. On the other hand, the design of the teleoperation system structure is mainly composed by two parts, each one being a controller itself. The first one is a minimum norm controller to solve the path following problem which considered the disregard of the person to move of the arm; additionally, the maximum manipulability during task execution is included in the kinematic controller design for the handling of the system's redundancy. The second one is a dynamic compensation controller, which receives as inputs the velocity references calculated by the kinematic controller. In addition, both stability and robustness properties to parametric uncertainties in the dynamic model are proven through Lyapunov's method. To validate the proposed teleoperation system, results are included and discussed.

The work is organized as follows: in Sect. 2 the problem formulation and the control strategy for robotic arm are presented. Section 3 describes the teleoperation system, while that the kinematic and dynamic modeling of the robotic arm are shown in Sect. 4. Next in Sect. 5 the controllers design and the analysis of the system's stability is developed, and finally the results are presented and discussed in Sect. 6.

2   Formulation Problem

People who have lost their upper extremities have problems moving and manipulating objects, therefore, various solutions have been proposed from the field of robotics; these solutions are mainly based on the electromyography signals of surface EMG; however, it is not always possible to obtain these signals, because the muscle cells of the upper extremities are dead (muscular atrophy), among other reasons. This problem motivates proposing a new scheme of bilateral tele-operation in which a human operator who lacks an upper extremity is considered, for which it is proposed to perform the closed loop control of a robotic arm through brain signals. In this context the human operator controls the robotic arm through brain signals; these signals are transformed into position commands to be sent to the remote site, which will be executed by the robotic arm.

On other hand, from the viewpoint of control theory, the end-effector of the robotic arm must follow the path desired by a person and generated through brain signals, as shown in Fig. 1.

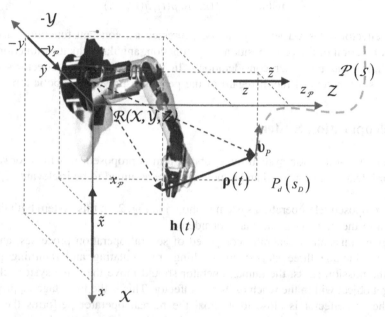

Fig. 1. The orthogonal projection of the point of interest over the path

As represented in Fig. 1, the path to be followed is denoted as $P(s)$, where $P(s) = (x_P(s), y_P(s), z_P(s))$; the actual desired location $P_d(s_D) = (x_P(s_D), y_P(s_D), z_P(s_D))$ is defined as desired point of the person, *i.e.*, the closest point on $P(s)$, with s_D being the curvilinear abscissa defining the point P_d; $\tilde{x} = x_P(s_D) - x\psi$ is the position error in the X direction; $\tilde{y} = y_P(s_D) - y\psi$ is the position error in the Y direction; $\tilde{z} = z_P(s_D) - z\psi$ is the position error in the Z direction; ρ represents the distance between the end-effector position of the robotic arm $h(x, y, z)$ and the desired point for the person P_d, where the position error in the ρ direction is $\tilde{\rho} = 0 - \rho = -\rho$, *i.e.*, the desired distance between the end-effector position $h(x, y, z)$ and the desired point P_d must be zero.

Hence, the path following problem is to find the control law for the robotic arm as a function of the control errors (position and orientation of the end-effector) and the desired velocities of the end-effector

$$\dot{\mathbf{q}}_{\mathbf{ref}}(s_D, h) = f(\rho(t, s), \upsilon_P(s_D, h)) \tag{1}$$

such that $\tilde{x} = 0$, $\tilde{y} = 0$ and $\tilde{z} = 0$. Therefore, if $\lim_{t\to\infty} \tilde{x}(t) = 0$, $\lim_{t\to\infty} \tilde{y}(t) = 0$ and $\lim_{t\to\infty} \tilde{z}(t) = 0$ then $\lim_{t\to\infty} \rho(t) = 0$.

Worth noting that the reference desired velocity $\upsilon_P(s_D, h)$ of the end-effector during the tracking path needs not be constant, which is common in the literature [1, 3, 13–16],

$$\upsilon_P(s_D, h) = f(k, s_D, \rho(t), \dot{q}(t), \dots) \tag{2}$$

the end-effector's desired velocity can be expressed as: constant function, curvilinear abscissa function of the path, position error function, angular velocities function of the robotic arm; and the other considerations. In this paper the end-effector's desired velocity is a function of the disregard of the person to move the robotic arm.

3   Teleoperation System

A bilateral tele-operation system for a robotic arm is proposed, in which forward and backward delay between local and remote sites are assumed to be irrelevant ($\zeta_1(t) = 0$ and $\zeta_2(t) = 0$).

The proposed tele-operation system is shown in Fig. 2. In this system both the force back-fed to the human operator are considered.

A given mission is generally composed of several operation processes, and these commonly include three stages: approaching, manipulating and returning process. When the mission starts, the human operator should move the slave system closed to the target object within the reach of its end-effector. This is the first stage: approaching. Once the end-effector is close to its goal the human operator performs the task of grasp. When the grasp mission is completed, the human operator changes again the mode from manipulation to locomotion and the slave would go back to a safe area.

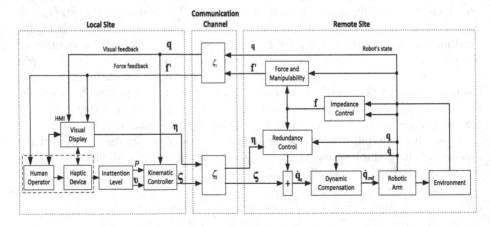

Fig. 2. Block diagram of the bilateral tele-operation system

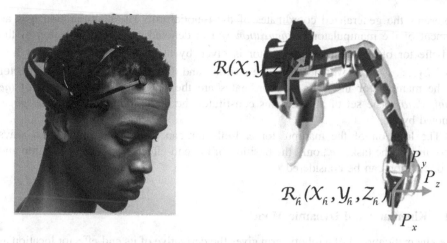

Fig. 3. Emotiv EPOC haptic device [13]

In this context the human operator controls the robotic arm by sending position commands to the end-effector of the robot: h_l, h_m, and h_n, one for each axis in respect to the inertial frame $R(X, Y, Z)$, using a haptic device.

$$\mathbf{h_d} = \begin{bmatrix} h_l & h_m & h_n \end{bmatrix}^T$$

The human operator commands are generated with the use of the Emotiv EPOC haptic device from Emotiv Systems Electronics Company [12] as indicated in Fig. 3. Its positions P_x, P_y, and P_z are translated into position commands h_l, h_m and h_n for the manipulation mode, through the following rotation matrix,

$$\begin{bmatrix} h_l \\ h_m \\ h_n \end{bmatrix} = \begin{bmatrix} \cos(q_1) & -\sin(q_1) & 0 \\ \sin(q_1) & \cos(q_1) & 0 \\ 0 & 0 & 1 \end{bmatrix} \begin{bmatrix} P_x \\ P_y \\ P_z \end{bmatrix} \tag{3}$$

where q_1 represents the first joint of the robotic arm that rotates about the axis Z.

In the case of robotic manipulators, the force feedback is the result of a physical interaction with the environment.

On the other hand, the human operator has the possibility of changing the desired internal configuration of the robotic arm at any time during the execution of a mission, through the visual display (HMI), i.e., $\boldsymbol{\eta} = \begin{bmatrix} q_{1d} & q_{2d} & \cdots & q_{nd} \end{bmatrix}^T$. This desired configuration vector may or may not have the values that maximize manipulability of the robotic arm.

4 Robotic Arm

The manipulator configuration is defined by a vector $\mathbf{q}(t)$ of n independent coordinates, called *generalized coordinates of the manipulator*, where $\mathbf{q} = \begin{bmatrix} q_1 & q_2 & \cdots & q_n \end{bmatrix}^T$

represents the generalized coordinates of the robotic arm. The configuration $\mathbf{q}$ is an element of the manipulator *configuration space*; denoted by N. The location of the end-effector of the mobile manipulator is given by the m –dimensional vector $\mathbf{h} = [h_1 \quad h_2 \quad \ldots \quad h_m]^T$ which defines the position and the orientation of the end-effector of the manipulator in R. Its m coordinates are the *operational coordinates of the manipulator*. The set of all locations constitutes the *manipulator operational space*, denoted by M.

The location of the manipulator end-effector can be defined in different ways according to the task, *i.e.*, only the position of the end-effector or both its position and its orientation can be considered.

4.1 Kinematic and Dynamic Model

The kinematic model of a robotic arm gives the derivative of its end-effector location as a function of the derivatives of both the robotic arm configuration and the location of the mobile platform,

$$\dot{\mathbf{h}}(t) = \mathbf{J}(\mathbf{q})\dot{\mathbf{q}}(t) \tag{4}$$

where $\mathbf{J}(\mathbf{q})$ is the Jacobian matrix that defines a linear mapping between the vector of the robotic arm velocities $\dot{\mathbf{q}}(t)$ and the vector of the end-effector velocity $\dot{\mathbf{h}}(t)$.

On the other hand, the mathematic model that represents the dynamics of a robotic arm can be obtained from Lagrange's dynamic equations, which are based on the difference between the kinetic and potential energy of each of the joints of the robot (energy balance) [17, 18].

The mathematic model that represents the dynamics of a robotic arm can be obtained from Lagrange's dynamic equations, which are based on the difference between the kinetic and potential energy of each of the joints of the robot (energy balance) [19]. The dynamic equation of the robotic arm can be represented as follows,

$$\bar{\mathbf{M}}(\mathbf{q})\ddot{\mathbf{q}} + \bar{\mathbf{C}}(\mathbf{q},\dot{\mathbf{q}})\dot{\mathbf{q}} + \bar{\mathbf{g}}(\mathbf{q}) = \tau$$

where, $\bar{\mathbf{M}}(\mathbf{q}) \in \Re^{\delta_n \times \delta_n}$ is a symmetrical positive definite matrix that represents the system's inertia, $\bar{\mathbf{C}}(\mathbf{q},\dot{\mathbf{q}})\dot{\mathbf{q}} \in \Re^{\delta_n}$ represents the components of the centripetal and Coriolis forces, $\bar{\mathbf{g}}(\mathbf{q}) \in \Re^{\delta_n}$ represents the gravitational forces and $\tau \in \Re^{\delta_n}$ is the torque input vector. For more details on the model see [19].

Most of the commercially available robots have low level PID controllers in order to follow the reference velocity inputs, thus not allowing controlling the voltages of the motors directly. Therefore, it becomes useful to express the dynamic model of the robotic arm in a more appropriate way, taking the rotational and longitudinal reference velocities as the control signals. To do so, the velocity controllers are included in the model. The dynamic model of the robotic arm, having as control signals the reference velocities of the system, can be represented as follows,

$$\mathbf{M}(\mathbf{q})\ddot{\mathbf{q}} + \mathbf{C}(\mathbf{q}, \dot{\mathbf{q}})\dot{\mathbf{q}} + \mathbf{g}(\mathbf{q}) = \dot{\mathbf{q}}_{ref} \qquad (5)$$

where, $\mathbf{M}(\mathbf{q}) = \mathbf{H}^{-1}(\bar{\mathbf{M}} + \mathbf{D}), \mathbf{C}(\mathbf{q},\dot{\mathbf{q}}) = \mathbf{H}^{-1}(\bar{\mathbf{C}} + \mathbf{P}), \mathbf{g}(\mathbf{q}) = \mathbf{H}^{-1}\bar{\mathbf{g}}(\mathbf{q})$. Thus, $\bar{\mathbf{M}}(\mathbf{q}) \in \mathfrak{R}^{\delta_n \times \delta_n}$ is a positive definite matrix, $\bar{\mathbf{C}}(\mathbf{q}, \mathbf{v})\mathbf{v} \in \mathfrak{R}^{\delta_n}, \bar{\mathbf{G}}(\mathbf{q}) \in \mathfrak{R}^{\delta_n}$ and $\dot{\mathbf{q}}_{ref} \in \mathfrak{R}^{\delta_n}$ is the vector of velocity control signals, $\mathbf{H} \in \mathfrak{R}^{\delta_n \times \delta_n}, \mathbf{D} \in \mathfrak{R}^{\delta_n \times \delta_n}$, and $\mathbf{P} \in \mathfrak{R}^{\delta_n \times \delta_n}$ are constant symmetrical diagonal matrices, positive definite, that contain the physical parameters of the robotic arm, e.g., motors, velocity controllers.

The full mathematic model of the robotic arm is represented by: (4) the kinematic model and (5) the dynamic model, taking the reference velocities of the system as control signals.

5 Control Design

The design of the kinematic controllers for the robotic arm is based on a minimal norm solution, which means that, at any time, the mobile manipulator or robotic arm will attain its navigation target with the smallest number of possible movements.

5.1 Kinematic Controller

The design of the kinematic controller of the robotic arm is based on the kinematic model of the arm (4). The following control law is proposed

$$\begin{aligned}
\dot{\mathbf{q}}_c = \mathbf{J}^{\#}\left(\upsilon_d + \mathbf{L_K}\tanh\left(\mathbf{L_K^{-1}}\mathbf{K}\,\tilde{\mathbf{h}}\right)\right)+ \\
+ (\mathbf{I} - \mathbf{J}^{\#}\mathbf{J})\mathbf{L_B}\tanh\left(\mathbf{L_B^{-1}}\mathbf{B}\,\Lambda\right)
\end{aligned} \qquad (6)$$

where $\mathbf{J}^{\#} = \mathbf{W}^{-1}\mathbf{J}^T\left(\mathbf{J}\mathbf{W}^{-1}\mathbf{J}^T\right)^{-1}$, being $\mathbf{W}$ a definite positive matrix that weighs the control actions of the system, υ_d is the desired velocities vector of the end-effector $\mathbf{h}$, $\tilde{\mathbf{h}}$ is the vector of control errors, defined as $\tilde{\mathbf{h}} = \mathbf{h_d} - \mathbf{h}$, $\mathbf{B}$ and $\mathbf{L_B}$ are definite positive diagonal matrices that weigh the vector Λ. In order to include an analytical saturation of velocities in the robotic arm the use of the **tanh** (.) function is proposed, which limits the error in $\tilde{\mathbf{h}}$ and the magnitude of the vector Λ.

The second term of (6) represents the projection on the null space of $\mathbf{J}$, where Λ is an arbitrary vector which contains the velocities associated to the robotic arm. Therefore, any value given to Λ will have effects only on the internal structure of the arm, and will not affect the final control of the end-effector at all. By using this term, different secondary control objectives can be achieved effectively.

A robotic arm is defined as a redundant system because it has more degrees of freedom than the required to achieve the desired end-effector motion. The redundancy of such system can be effectively used for the achievement of additional performances such as: avoiding obstacles in the workspace and singular configuration, or to optimize various performance criterions. In this work the singular configuration prevention through the system's manipulability control is considered.

The *manipulability measure* w_a of the robotic arm can be defined as [20],

$$w = \sqrt{\det\left(\mathbf{J(q)J}^T\mathbf{(q)}\right)} \tag{7}$$

The behaviour of the control error of the end-effector $\mathbf{h}$ is now analysed assuming - momentarily - perfect velocity tracking $\dot{\mathbf{q}}(t) \equiv \dot{\mathbf{q}}_c(t)$, $\dot{\mathbf{q}}_c = [\dot{q}_{1c} \quad \dot{q}_{2c} \quad \cdots \quad \dot{q}_{nc}]^T$. By substituting (6) in (4) the close loop equation is obtained,

$$\left(\boldsymbol{\upsilon}_d - \dot{\mathbf{h}}\right) + \mathbf{L_K}\tanh\left(\mathbf{L_K^{-1}K\,\tilde{h}}\right) = \mathbf{0} \tag{8}$$

Remember that, the desired velocity vector $\boldsymbol{\upsilon}_d$ is different from the time derivative of the desired location $\dot{\mathbf{h}}_d$. Now, defining a difference signal $\Upsilon = \dot{\mathbf{h}}_d - \boldsymbol{\upsilon}_d$ and remembering that $\dot{\tilde{\mathbf{h}}} = \dot{\mathbf{h}}_d - \dot{\mathbf{h}}$, (8) can be written as

$$\dot{\tilde{\mathbf{h}}} + \mathbf{L_K}\tanh\left(\mathbf{L_K^{-1}K\,\tilde{h}}\right) = \Upsilon. \tag{9}$$

Remark 1: $\boldsymbol{\upsilon}_d$ is collinear to $\dot{\mathbf{h}}_d$ (tangent to the path), then Υ is also a collinear vector to $\boldsymbol{\upsilon}_d$ and $\dot{\mathbf{h}}_d$.

For the stability analysis the following Lyapunov's candidate function is considered $V(\tilde{\mathbf{h}}) = \frac{1}{2}\tilde{\mathbf{h}}^T\tilde{\mathbf{h}}$. Its time derivative on the trajectories of the system is,

$$\dot{V}(\tilde{\mathbf{h}}) = \tilde{\mathbf{h}}^T\Upsilon - \tilde{\mathbf{h}}^T\mathbf{L_K}\tanh\left(\mathbf{L_K^{-1}K\,\tilde{h}}\right) \tag{10}$$

A sufficient condition for $\dot{V}(\tilde{\mathbf{h}})$ to be negative definite is,

$$\left|\tilde{\mathbf{h}}^T\mathbf{L_K}\tanh\left(\mathbf{L_K^{-1}K\,\tilde{h}}\right)\right| > \left|\tilde{\mathbf{h}}^T\Upsilon\right| \tag{11}$$

For large values of $\tilde{\mathbf{h}}$, the condition in (11) can be reinforced as,

$$\left\|\tilde{\mathbf{h}}^T\mathbf{L_K'}\right\| > \|\tilde{\mathbf{h}}\|\|\Upsilon\|$$

with $\mathbf{L_K'} = \mathbf{L_K}\tanh\left(k_{aux}\mathbf{i}\right)$, where k_{aux} is a suitable positive constant and $\mathbf{i} \in \Re^m$ is the vector of unity components. Then, $\dot{V}(\tilde{\mathbf{h}})$ will be negative definite only if

$$\|\mathbf{L_K}\| > \frac{\|\Upsilon\|}{\tanh\left(k_{aux}\right)} \tag{12}$$

Hence, (11) establishes a design condition to make the errors $\tilde{\mathbf{h}}$ to decrease. Now, for small values of $\tilde{\mathbf{h}}$, condition (11) will be fulfilled if

$$\left\| \tilde{\mathbf{h}}^T \mathbf{K} \frac{\tanh{(k_{aux})}}{k_{aux}} \tilde{\mathbf{h}} \right\| > \|\tilde{\mathbf{h}}\| \|\Upsilon\|$$

Which means that a sufficient condition for $\dot{V}$ to be negative definite is,

$$\|\tilde{\mathbf{h}}\| > \frac{k_{aux} \|\Upsilon\|}{\lambda_{min}(\mathbf{K}) \tanh{(k_{aux})}}$$

Thus implying that the error $\tilde{\mathbf{h}}$ is ultimately bounded by,

$$\|\tilde{\mathbf{h}}\| \leq \frac{k_{aux} \|\Upsilon\|}{\varsigma \lambda_{min}(\mathbf{K}) \tanh{(k_{aux})}}; \text{ with } 0 < \varsigma < 1 \tag{13}$$

Once the control error is inside the bound (13), that is with small values of $\tilde{\mathbf{h}}$, $\mathbf{L_K} \tanh{(\mathbf{L_K^{-1} K} \tilde{\mathbf{h}})} \approx \mathbf{K}\tilde{\mathbf{h}}$. Now, we prove by contradiction that this control error tends to zero. The closed loop Eq. (9) can be written as, $\dot{\tilde{\mathbf{h}}} + \mathbf{K}\tilde{\mathbf{h}} = \Upsilon$ or after the transient, in Laplace transform,

$$\tilde{\mathbf{h}}(s) = \frac{1}{s\mathbf{I} + \mathbf{K}} \Upsilon(s). \tag{14}$$

According to (14) and recalling that $\mathbf{K}$ is diagonal positive definite, the control error vector $\tilde{\mathbf{h}}$ and the velocity vector Υ cannot be orthogonal. Nevertheless both vectors are orthogonal by definition (see *Remark 3.1* and remember the minimum distance criteria for $\mathbf{h_d}$ on P). Therefore the only solution for steady state is that $\lim_{t \to \infty} \tilde{\mathbf{h}}(t) = 0$ asymptotically.

5.2   Controller with Dynamic Compensation

The proposed kinematic controllers presented in Subsect. 5.1 assume perfect velocity tracking; nevertheless this is not true in real contexts, *i.e.*, $\dot{\mathbf{q}}(t) \neq \dot{\mathbf{q}}_c(t)$, mainly when high-speed movements or heavy load transportation are required. Therefore, it becomes essential to consider the robot's dynamics, in addition to its kinematics. Then, the objective of the dynamic compensation controller is to compensate the dynamics of the system, thus reducing the velocity tracking error. This controller receives as inputs the desired velocities calculated by the kinematic controllers, and generates velocity references for the mobile platform and robotic arm. Hence, relaxing the perfect velocity tracking assumption, there will be a velocity error defined as,

$$\tilde{\dot{\mathbf{q}}}(t) = \dot{\mathbf{q}}_c(t) - \dot{\mathbf{q}}(t) \tag{15}$$

This velocity error motivates the dynamic compensation process, which will be performed based on the inverse dynamics of the system. With this aim, the exact model of the system without disturbances is considered, thus the following control is proposed,

$$\dot{\mathbf{q}}_{ref} = \mathbf{M}(\mathbf{q})\sigma + \mathbf{C}(\mathbf{q}, \dot{\mathbf{q}})\dot{\mathbf{q}} + \mathbf{g}(\mathbf{q}) \tag{16}$$

where $\sigma = \ddot{\tilde{\mathbf{q}}}_c + \mathbf{L_v}\tanh\left(\mathbf{L_v}^{-1}\mathbf{K_v}\dot{\tilde{\mathbf{q}}}\right)$. Now, Replacing (16) in (5) it results

$$\ddot{\tilde{\mathbf{q}}} + \mathbf{L_v}\tanh\left(\mathbf{L_v}^{-1}\mathbf{K_v}\dot{\tilde{\mathbf{q}}}\right) = \mathbf{0} \tag{17}$$

For the stability analysis the following Lyapunov's candidate function is considered $V\left(\dot{\tilde{\mathbf{q}}}\right) = \frac{1}{2}\dot{\tilde{\mathbf{q}}}^{\mathrm{T}}\dot{\tilde{\mathbf{q}}}$, its time derivative is $\dot{V}\left(\dot{\tilde{\mathbf{q}}}\right) = -\dot{\tilde{\mathbf{q}}}^{\mathrm{T}}\mathbf{L_v}\tanh\left(\mathbf{L_v}^{-1}\mathbf{K_v}\dot{\tilde{\mathbf{q}}}\right) < 0$. Thus it can be immediately concluded that the error vector $\lim_{t\to\infty}\dot{\tilde{\mathbf{q}}}(t) = 0$ asymptotically, provided that $\mathbf{K_v}$ and $\mathbf{L_v}$ are symmetrical positive definite matrices.

6   Simulation Results

In order to illustrate the performance of the proposed tele-operation structure, several simulation experiments were carried out for path following control of a robotic arm through brain signals; the most representative results are presented in this section. The experiments were carried with the kinematic and dynamic models of a robotic arm 5 DOF which was developed at the University of the Armed Forces ESPE (only 3 DOF of the 5 available DOFs are used in the experiments, see Fig. 4). The robotic arm is built with a structure of Acrylonitrile Butadiene Styrene, ABS, and the links are controlled by a network of servomotors Dinamixel communicated via a RS-485 interface; the servomotors back-fed the position and velocity of each servomotor. On the other hand, the local station consists of a PC Pentium 4 (3.0 GHz) and the haptic device. Communication between the robotic arm and the remote station is performed through Bluetooth.

The simulated task consists on moving and manipulating objects. The robotic arm is guided from an initial position to the object that will be manipulated. The desired

Fig. 4. 6 DOF robotic arm

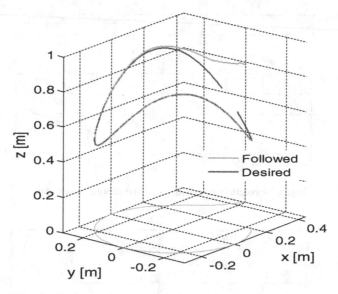

Fig. 5. Stroboscopic movement of the robotic arm experiment

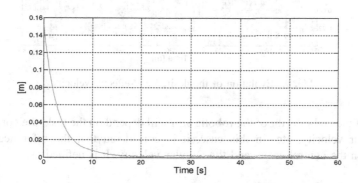

Fig. 6. Distance between the robotic arm and the closest point on the desired path

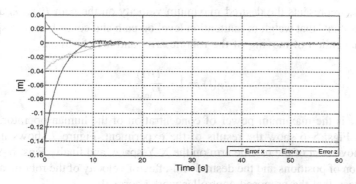

Fig. 7. Evolution of the control errors of the robotic arm

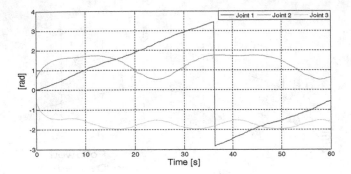

Fig. 8. Evolution of positions of the robotic arm joints

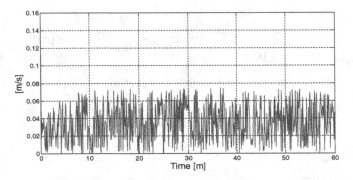

Fig. 9. Evolution of the desired end-effector velocity.

velocity of the end-effector of the robotic arm will depend on the task, the control error, the angular velocity, etc. In this case, it is considered that the reference velocity depends on the control errors and the angular velocity. It is defined as,

$$|\boldsymbol{v}_P(s_D, h)| = v_{P\max} \frac{1}{1 + k_i i_P + k_\rho \|\rho\|}$$

where, $v_{P\max}$ represents the desired maximum velocity on the path $P(s)$; k_i and k_ρ are positive constants that weigh of inattention level on path and control error, respectively; i_P is the inattention of moving of the robotic arm, and is defined as:

$$i_P(t) = 1 - \frac{U(t)}{U_{\max}}$$

where $U_{\max}$ is the maximum power of concentration of the human operator.

Hence, Figs. 5–6 show the results of the experiment. Figure 7 shows the control errors in movement of the robotic arm on the X-Y space, and finally Figs. 8–9 presents the evolution of positions and the desired end-effector velocity of the robotic arm joints. It can be seen that the proposed controller works correctly.

References

1. Ison, M., Vujaklija, I., Whitsell, B., Farina, D.: High-density electromyography and motor skill learning for robust long-term control of a 7-DoF robot arm. IEEE Trans. Neural Syst. Rehab. Eng. (2015)
2. Faidallah, E.M., Hossameldin, Y.H., Abd Rabbo, S.M., El-Mashad, Y.A.: Control and modeling a robot arm via EMG and flex signals. In: International Workshop on Research and Education in Mechatronics (REM), pp. 1–8 (2014)
3. Kiguchi, K., Hayashi, Y.: Estimation of joint torque for a myoelectric arm by genetic programming based on EMG signals. In: World Automation Congress (WAC), pp. 1–4 (2012)
4. Ranky, G.N., Adamovich, S.: Analysis of a commercial EEG device for the control of a robot arm. In: IEEE Annual Northeast Bioengineering Conference (2010)
5. Gauthaam, M., Kumar, S.S.: EMG controlled bionic arm. In: Innovations in Emerging Technology (NCOIET), pp. 111–114 (2011)
6. López, N.M., Orosco, E., di Sciascio, F.: Multichannel surface electromyography classification based on muscular synergy. In: International Conference of the Engineering in Medicine and Biology Society, pp. 1658–1661 (2010)
7. Shekhar, H., Guha, R., Juliet A.V., Kumar, J.: Mathematical modeling of neuro-controlled bionic arm. In: International Conference on Advances in Recent Technologies in Communication and Computing, pp. 576–578 (2009)
8. Bastos-Filho, T., et al.: Towards a new modality-independent interface for a robotic wheelchair. IEEE Trans. Neural Syst. Rehab. Eng. 22(3), 603–612 (2014)
9. Arroyo, C.: Cirugía robótica. Elementos: Ciencia y Cultura 12(58), 13–17 (2005)
10. Artemiadis, P.K., Kyriakopoulos, K.J.: EMG-based teleoperation of a robot arm using low-dimensional representation. In: International Conference on Intelligent Robots and Systems, pp. 489–495 (2007)
11. Soeanto, D., Lapierre, L., Pascoal, A.: Adaptive non-singular path-following, control of dynamic wheeled robots. In: Proceedings of 42nd IEEE Conference on Decision and Control, Hawaii, USA, 9–12 December, pp. 1765–1770 (2003)
12. Hirche, S., Buss, M.: Human-oriented control for haptic teleoperation. Proc. IEEE 100(3), 623–647 (2012)
13. Emotiv Systems Electronics Company. http://emotiv.com/
14. Jang, W.A., Lee, S.M., Lee, D.H.: Development BCI for individuals with severely disability using EMOTIV EEG headset and robot. In: 2014 International Winter Workshop Brain-Computer Interface (BCI) (2014)
15. Enache, A., Cepisca, C., Paraschiv, M., Banica, C.: Virtual instrument for electroencephalography data acquisition. In: 7th International Symposium on Advanced Topics in Electrical Engineering (ATEE), pp. 1–4 (2011)
16. Huang, D., Qian, K., Fei, D.-Y., Jia, W.: Electroencephalography (EEG)-based Brain-Computer Interface (BCI): A 2-D virtual wheelchair control based on event-related desynchronization/synchronization and state control. IEEE Trans. Neural Syst. Rehab. Eng. 20(3), 379–388 (2011)
17. Sciavicco, L., Siciliano, B.: Modeling and Control of Robot Manipulators. Springer, London Limited, Great Britain (2000)

18. Hui, Z., Yingmin, J., Junping, D., Jun, Z.: New kinematic notation and automatic generation of symbolic dynamics equations for space robots. In: 33rd Chinese Control Conference (CCC), pp. 8341–8346 (2014)
19. Siciliano, B., Sciavicco, L., Villani, L., Oriolo, G.: Robotics: Modeling, Planning, and Control. Springer, London (2009). ISBN: 978-1-84628-641-4
20. Tanaka, Y., Nishikawa, K.,Yamada, N., Tsuji, T.: Analysis of operational comfort in manual tasks using human force manipulability measure. IEEE Trans. Haptics 8–19 (2015)

Interfaces

Natural User Interfaces for Virtual Character Full Body and Facial Animation in Immersive Virtual Worlds

Konstantinos Cornelis Apostolakis[✉] and Petros Daras

Information Technologies Institute, Centre for Research and Technology Hellas,
Thessaloniki, Greece
{kapostol,daras}@iti.gr

Abstract. In recent years, networked virtual environments have steadily grown to become a frontier in social computing. Such virtual cyberspaces are usually accessed by multiple users through their 3D avatars. Recent scientific activity has resulted in the release of both hardware and software components that enable users at home to interact with their virtual persona through natural body and facial activity performance. Based on 3D computer graphics methods and vision-based motion tracking algorithms, these techniques aspire to reinforce the sense of autonomy and telepresence within the virtual world. In this paper we present two distinct frameworks for avatar animation through user natural motion input. We specifically target the full body avatar control case using a Kinect sensor via a simple, networked skeletal joint retargeting pipeline, as well as an intuitive user facial animation 3D reconstruction pipeline for rendering highly realistic user facial puppets. Furthermore, we present a common networked architecture to enable multiple remote clients to capture and render any number of 3D animated characters within a shared virtual environment.

Keywords: Virtual character animation · Markerless performance capture · Face animation · Kinect-based interfaces

1 Introduction

In recent years, the introduction of the Microsoft Kinect ignited the avatar full body motion control paradigm based on the concept of avateering. *Avateering* or *puppetting* a virtual 3D avatar refers to the process of mapping a user's natural motoring activity and live performance to a virtual human's deforming control elements in order to faithfully reproduce the user's activity during rendering cycles. Already, a multitude of different schemes for full body avatar control exist in the scientific literature based on the skeleton tracking capabilities offered by software development kits and application programming interfaces plugging into the Kinect sensor [2, 11–13]. Similarly, avatar facial animation through vision-based methods has been explored following a similar approach in which facial features on the user's face are tracked via a Kinect [15]

© Springer International Publishing Switzerland 2015
L.T. De Paolis and A. Mongelli (Eds.): AVR 2015, LNCS 9254, pp. 371–383, 2015.
DOI: 10.1007/978-3-319-22888-4_27

or single image acquisition methods [3, 4, 10] to generate animation via detailed face rigs or pre-defined blendshapes. In this paper we present two distinct, real-time user avatar control interfaces specifically tailored for use in tele-immersive virtual worlds connecting remote users within a shared virtual environment. We present two similarly built frameworks for remote avatar full body and facial animation through the use of consumer-grade hardware such as the Microsoft Kinect sensor and standard HD webcams. Our Natural User Interface (NUI) frameworks have been developed for use in real-time, tele-immersive shared virtual environments and are designed to enable both user direct and responsive mapping of body movements to avatar characters in the virtual world as well as a means of reconstructing and animating user lookalike, highly realistic 3D virtual facial avatars.

The remainder of this paper is organized as follows: Sect. 2 presents a brief overview of the common networked architecture of each NUI framework. Sections 3 and 4 better elaborate on each framework individually, outlining the methods used to obtain avatar animation data from raw Kinect, and standard webcam output respectively. Section 5 then concludes with a discussion on the authors' final thoughts and future work.

2   Common Framework Architecture

Each framework described in this paper, is comprised of both a remote capturing and a rendering component. These are responsible for the acquisition of the proper user motion estimated data originating from the module's targeted hardware input, processing of the latter raw form into sensible avatar animation data and updating of the rendering pipelines in order to output the 3D character in a user motion-mimicking posture. Both frameworks' capturing component is deployed whenever a user is connecting to the shared virtual world via an *application layer multicast* (ALM) server/

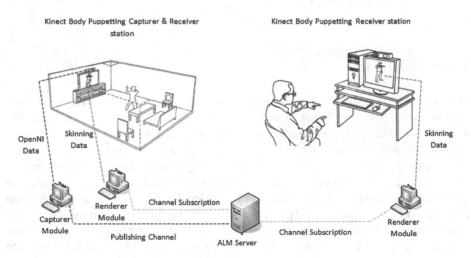

Fig. 1. Kinect full body avateering framework component architecture network.

client network architecture [16]. Each capturing component (one per user) is respon-sible for creating a single, new ALM channel and publishing data to it. The rendering component of each framework is similarly setup to serve a three-fold purpose: (a) it generates a number of ALM channel subscribers which receive and reconstruct the user animation data published by any number of respective capturers; (b) it loads the appro-priate avatar assets; and (c) it handles the real-time rendering and animation of all avatars in the system.

Through this scheme, multiple users can connect to a shared virtual environment and view any number of 3D animated avatars by simply subscribing to each users' capturing component publishing channel. In the case of the Kinect full body avateering framework, the ALM capturer channel is publishing user skeleton data, which the subscribing rendering components turn into avatar skinning data, as is demonstrated in the frame-work architecture diagram shown in Fig. 1. Elaborate details on the depicted data flow are presented in the following Section. Similarly, the webcam facial animation frame-work features a tracking pipeline for turning raw camera input into user facial landmark animation data at the capturing site, which is posted on the capturer's publishing channel. The latter is in turn translated to 3D vertex buffer information at the receiving rendering components. The process is described in more detail in Sect. 4. A diagram of the archi-tecture is depicted in Fig. 2.

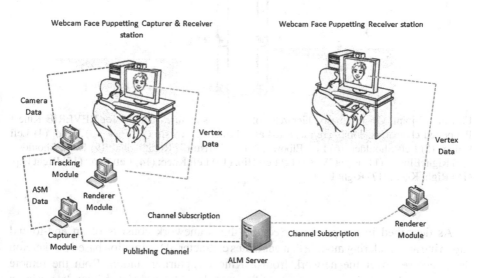

Fig. 2. Webcam avatar facial animation framework component architecture network.

3   Full Body Avatar Control Using Kinect-based Interface

Our Kinect full-body avateering framework enables users to transfer their physical body motion into a shared virtual environment through the use of markerless capturing via the skeleton tracking algorithms implemented for the Microsoft Kinect sensor. The process requires that the avatar 3D mesh is parented to an articulated structure of control elements called *bones*. Bones can be viewed as oriented 3D line segments that connect transformable *joints* (such as a knee or a shoulder). These joints usually offer a three-to-six Degrees-Of-Freedom deformation control of the avatar's mesh geometry, with respect to translation and rotation transformations. In order to provide a 1-by-1 mapping of Kinect trackable joints to avatar control elements, the avatars are required to be rigged with a pre-defined 17-joints hierarchy defined by the OpenNI and NiTe joint tracking structure depicted in Fig. 3[1].

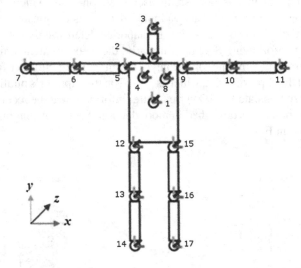

Fig. 3. 17-joint, OpenNI-based hierarchy of control structures defined for REVERIE Kinect Puppetted characters. Joints are identified as follows: (1) Torso; (2) Neck; (3) Head; (4) Left Collar; (5) Left Shoulder; (6) Left Elbow; (7) Left Wrist; (8) Right Collar; (9) Right Shoulder; (10) Right Elbow; (11) Right Wrist; (12) Left Hip; (13) Left Knee; (14) Left Foot; (15) Right Hip; (16) Right Knee; (17) Right Foot.

As described in the previous Section, the framework consists of an end-to-end capturing and rendering module that generates character 3D animation based on skeleton data, received over the network from a Kinect capturing station. Both the remote capturing and rendering components of the module address skeleton joint data using a pre-defined path traversing all joints starting at the root of the hierarchy (the torso) and moving towards the end effectors (head, wrists and feet) in a left-to-right manner. This

---

[1] PrimeSense, who was founding member of the OpenNI, shutdown the original OpenNI project on which our modules are linking to when it was acquired by Apple on November 24, 2013. The module retains its operability through the latest legacy version of the library (1.5.4.0 as of May 7, 2012).

way, a 1-to-1 correspondence of Kinect user tracked joint data to avatar virtual joint information is ensured.

For each animation frame, the remote *capturing* component of the full-body avateering framework generates joint position and rotation data with respect to the Kinect camera's world coordinate system. This data is represented by two sequences of floating point numbers, one referring to the XYZ-positions of the 17 joints while the other accumulates all 3×3 orientation matrices describing the rotation of each joint in camera world space. However, avatar mesh assets loaded and rendered by the remote *rendering* component of the framework, are usually stored with skinning information that constitutes a hierarchical bone structure requiring any affine transformations to be applied to each joint in its local axis space, in additional relation to its parent. Furthermore, avatar bones are defined with a static length, which should remain constant throughout the animating session regardless of varying user anthropometric measurements acquired by the skeleton tracking module, as multiple users of different ethnic backgrounds and physical attributes should be able to control avatars that share a common skeleton animation template basis. Therefore, a one-by-one direct copying of the tracked skeleton data to the avatar's joints would result in unrealistic rendered characters, as the remote capturing component would, in all, neglect any constraints applied to the animated 3D model skeleton during the characters' design in the 3D modelers' workshop. To achieve a plausible and constraint-bound 3D animation flow, the data obtained by the remote capturing component of the module is received and translated to joint-specific local-coordinate orientation quaternions in the remote rendering component before the joint matrices are updated and applied in the skinning calculations taking place in the hardware-accelerated avatar rendering pipeline. The process is described in detail in Algorithm 1 [2]. The root joint's quaternion can safely be obtained by the 3×3 global orientation matrix sent by the capturer.

After all local joint coordinate rotation quaternions are computed, avatar animation applies to standard skinning equations, with calculations being shared between the CPU and the GPU through dedicated skinning GLSL shaders loaded by the remote rendering module for the sake of real-time performance. The 3D mesh geometry is calculated per vertex by passing appropriate skinning matrices and per-vertex joint indices and weights along with the standard 3D vertex, normal and texture coordinates attributes to the vertex shader. The process requires the calculation of these skinning matrices by *posing* the virtual skeleton in the CPU according to the following scheme:

Algorithm 1. *Kinect Avatar Animation Data*

Input: User's tracked joint positions P_i
Output: Avatar joint rotation quaternions q_i

1. (off-line step) For each avatar rig joint $J_i, i = 1, 2, \dots, 17$, the bone lengths $L_i^c, c \in CH\{i\}$ to its first-level child joints $CH\{i\}$ are calculated in the avatar rig hierarchy along with the corresponding unit-vector directions $d_i^c = \frac{(J_c - J_i)}{\|J_c - J_i\|}$. For notational simplicity, the c superscript referring to a child joint of J_i is dropped, wherever it's implied.

2. For each tracking frame, the user's tracked joint positions P_i with respect to the camera's world coordinate system are retrieved by the OpenNI and NiTe skeleton tracking libraries.

3. The direction of each user-tracked bone is determined by the normalized unit vector $s_i = \frac{P_c - P_i}{\|P_c - P_i\|}$, similar to the calculation made in step (1). The result is then multiplied by its corresponding length L_i, to ensure that all tracked joints are within the predefined avatar bone length distances from each other.

4. The axis of rotation m_i is determined by calculating the cross product $d_i \times s_i$, while the angle of rotation is calculated by $\theta_i = \cos^{-1}(d_i \cdot s_i)$, i.e. from the inner product of d_i and s_i.

5. The avatar's new joint position is set by traversing the joint hierarchy from the parent joint and adding the offset $L_i \cdot s_i$. The local rotation quaternion q_i^{lo}, is calculated from the axis m_i and the eigen-angle θ_i.

6. The final rotation quaternion q_i is calculated by multiplying the inverse rotation quaternion of the parent q_i^{pa} with q_i^{lo}, i.e. $q_i = (q_i^{pa})^{-1} \cdot q_i^{lo}$.

---

1. Setup the avatar skeleton. Traverse the avatar joint hierarchy from the root and calculate final 4×4 joint skinning matrix M_i by first calculating local rotation matrix M_i' from previous rotation quaternion q_i and multiplying with the joint's parent skinning matrix M_i^{pa}, i.e. $M_i = M_i^{pa} \cdot M_i'$. For the root joint, $M_i = M_i'$.
2. Flatten bone matrices to an array of floating point numbers for passing to the GPU via uniform bindings.
3. Normalize skinning weights using Manhattan distance metric and pass the appropriate buffers to the shader as vertex attributes.

Afterwards, the final vertex transformations are applied in the GPU by applying the following calculations:

1. Retrieve bone matrices M_x^v and M_y^v, corresponding to the bone matrices of joints x, y influencing vertex v according to the latter *skin indices* attribute.
2. Calculate skinned vertex position by applying the appropriate skinning weights w_x^v, w_y^v, retrieved from the vertex' attributes, to the transformation calculation:

$$v^{skin} = M_x^v \cdot v \cdot w_x^v + M_y^v \cdot v \cdot w_y^v \tag{1}$$

3. Apply model-view-projection transformations MVP to the skinned vertex:

$$v^{out} = MVP \cdot v^{skin} \tag{2}$$

An example of the module output is shown in Fig. 4. All rendering components are based on plain OpenGL and GLSL shading languages, and are easily portable to both in-house as well as third-party 3D rendering engines providing integrated support for externally written shaders (e.g. Unity).

Fig. 4. Screenshot of an animated 3D avatar rendered by our Kinect full body avateering framework inside a virtual environment.

4   Avatar Facial Animation Control Using a Webcam Interface

Our webcam-based facial avatar animation framework enables users to display their natural facial activity and expressions through their 3D avatars in the virtual environment, using a marker-less facial landmark tracking scheme based on Active Shape Models (ASMs) [5], applied to frames obtained from a standard HD web camera. Unlike the full body animation framework described in the previous Section, which requires control elements (bones) to re-target animation of the user onto the character's bone structure, and unlike the scientific literature which uses either facial animation controls (rigs) [4, 10] or predefined blendshapes [3, 15] for animating the various 3D facial expressions, our framework works by directly applying changes to the mesh geometry through a one-by-one correspondence of the 3D mesh vertex data to the 2D tracked facial landmarks of the ASM shape fitted onto an instance of the user's face at each consecutive camera frame. In other words, the 3D shape geometry is reconstructed anew in each frame based on the 2D ASM geometry resulting from the fitting process. This 1-on-1 mapping is achieved by using the avatar's face mesh as a template for training an ASM on a large database of hand-annotated images. This way, for each tracked frame, the vertex/landmark index remains constant. The mesh geometry manipulation is achieved by projecting the 2D shape model to the 3D world, keeping the depth coordinate constant and aligned to the template's original size. As the 2D landmarks and camera frame also provide a means to obtain a live texture map and corresponding coordinates per frame, the avateering effect can be further enhanced in terms of realism by continuously updating the 3D model's texture information. This enhanced 3D animated mesh can otherwise be viewed as a time-constant, template-based 3D reconstruction of the user's face: each capturing frame generates a new set of 3D vertex position and texture coordinate attributes which result in a new 3D mesh object, which retains the original structure of the hand-modelled template. The live texturing features can also be dropped without further affecting the process of character animation in order to allow users to avateer characters who share little to no resemblance to their actual users. Furthermore, standard deformation techniques, like blend-shape morph targets can be applied to generate a multitude of 3D geometries based on a single person's avatar face mesh. This allows our framework to easily create user 3D caricatures in real time. Examples of different animated avatars created from a single input camera frame are shown in Fig. 5.

Obtaining a shape model of considerable detail (i.e. modern, real-time virtual character face meshes consist of over 500 vertices for enhanced visual detail) requires training on a large dataset of human face images. Such training is done by annotating

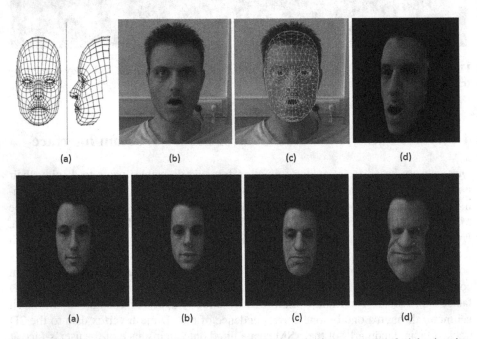

(a)   (b)   (c)   (d)

(a)   (b)   (c)   (d)

Fig. 5. Example of enhanced functionality possible through the webcam avatar facial animation framework, with both vertex and texture coordinate deform options active. Top row: (a) Template 3D face mesh; (b) webcam input frame; (c) corresponding real-time ASM fit; and (d) 3D reconstructed face with high amount of realism. Second row: original reconstructed face mesh (a) and three examples (b, c, d) of caricature avatars obtained by applying morphs in real time.

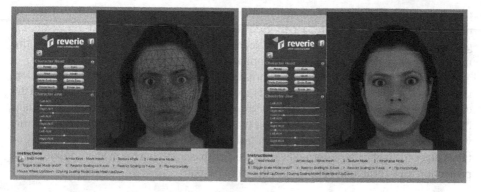

Fig. 6. Screenshots of the *RAAT*-powered web-based annotation tool developed and used for quickly annotating images with high resolution (>500) ASM landmarking schemes such as the one depicted in this image, featuring 511 vertices. The *left* image showcases the ASM model in wireframe mode which greatly helps placing groups of landmarks in their correct positions. The *right* image showcases the ASM model in generic textured view, which helps define facial features such as the eyebrows, lip lining, nostril outline etc.

(usually by hand) each image, keeping landmark annotation continuity consistent throughout the entire database. This process is almost inconceivable for a human annotator, given the amount of detail required and the close proximity of a large number of landmarks due to the geometry structure of the 3D model meshes. In order to address this problem, an intuitive web-based visual annotation application was created using the *Reverie Avatar Authoring Tool* [1]. The annotation tool was developed specifically for generating ASM files targeted by this framework. The application was designed to accelerate the annotation procedure, by allowing annotators to superimpose an instance of the entire face mesh over the image and make appropriate adjustments to the face 3D pose, its anthropometric features (eye/nose/mouth size, position, rotation etc.) as well as the facial expression visual cues (such as individual Action Units [8] and FAPs [9]) by selecting between a large set of pre-defined blendshapes modelled for the generic template mesh in an external 3D modeling application[2]. Once the annotator has approximated the overlaid face image landmark geometry, an automatic process that projects the superimposed 3D model vertices to the 2D image plane generates an annotation file for the image. For rapidly acquiring twice the amount of data, an automatic, index-invariant flipping algorithm ensures a consistent annotation file is automatically generated for the x-plane flipped image, by keeping the model's vertex indices consistent (i.e., not flipping them) throughout the set. Using this intuitive tool, the annotation of a single image with over 500 landmarks is possible in less than 5 min. This efficiency measurement is of considerable note to the authors, seeing how traditional annotation schemes [7] are known take up at least as much time for 10 times less landmarks per model, while the procedure is done by placing each landmark individually on top of the desired image-plane coordinates, making the process delicate to human errors. The eventual ASM files are built using a third-party, pre-compiled C++ OpenCV library *asmlibrary* [14]. Since

---

[2] Blender, free, open source 3D Computer Graphics Software http://www.blender.org/.

the landmarks recorded onto the annotation files are merely 2D projections of the 3D model's geometrical structure, a 1-to-1 correspondence of landmarks-to-3D vertices is guaranteed as an added bonus. Two screenshots of the annotation tool used for this module are shown in Fig. 6, to better emphasize on the scheme's efficiency.

After loading the appropriate ASM build model, each frame retrieved by the camera is processed to obtain a reconstructed 3D face model according to the Algorithm 2. After calculating the new 3D vertex coordinates, the model's vertex and texture coordinate buffers are appropriately updated at each drawing frame, along with the diffuse texture which is updated with the current camera frame. At GPU level, no additional calculation takes place to display the deformed vertices other than applying the avatar's model-view projection transformation *MVP* to get the final output:

$$v^{out} = MVP \cdot v \qquad (3)$$

An example of the rendered output of this framework is depicted in Fig. 7.

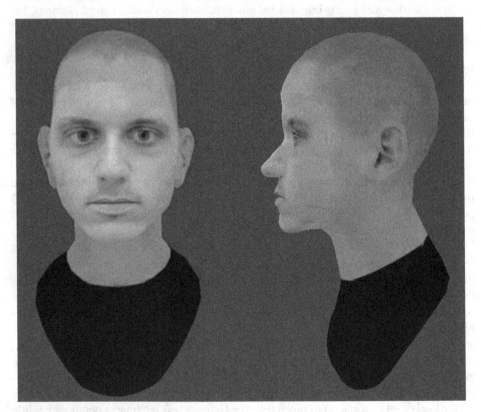

Fig. 7. Front and side view of real-time 3D facial animation avatar anchored at chin with body mesh. Post processing rendering effects are applied to ensure a smooth color transition between the face mesh and the body mesh diffuse textures.

Algorithm 2. *3D vertex reconstruction from ASM tracking data*

Input: set of 2D landmarks χ_i corresponding to the ASM vertices.
Output: Avatar 3D vertex data v_i and (optionally) texture coordinates data c_i

1. (Optional) The current landmarks $\chi_i(x_i^\chi, y_i^\chi)$ coordinates are normalized to retrieve texture coordinates $c_i = (\frac{x_i^\chi}{width}, 1.0 - \frac{y_i^\chi}{height})$, where $width$ and $height$ correspond to the camera frame XY-resolution.

2. The current shape model is aligned to an orthogonal posture of the same model to nullify the effects of any roll-pitch-yaw rotation of the user's head. This is achieved by minimizing the following weighted sum of squares:

$$E = \sum_{i=1}^{n} \left(\chi'_i - T_t(\chi_i)\right)^T W_i(\chi'_i - T_t(\chi_i))$$

where χ_i, χ'_i are the two sets of n points corresponding to the original and aligned shape respectively, and $T_t(\chi)$ is a transformation with parameters t [6].

3. The 2D landmark coordinates for each point $\chi'_i(x_i'^\chi, y_i'^\chi)$ in the aligned shape are projected to a pseudo-3D space centered at (0, 0, 0) (with the z-coordinate being kept constant all through the algorithm and retrieved by the 3D mesh model file loaded by the module) through the following equation:

$$v_i'(x,y,z) = (x_i', y_i', z_i) = ((\frac{x_i'^\chi}{width}) - 0.5, 0.5 - (\frac{y_i'^\chi}{height}), z_i)$$

where z_i is the z-coordinate of the 3D model vertex at the same index i.

4. The XY coordinates of each vertex obtained in step 2 are multiplied by an appropriate scaling factor for each dimension dim calculated using the ASM model scale s_{dim}^{asm} in comparison to the 3D mesh model scale s_{dim}^{model} loaded onto the module:

$$v_i''(x,y,z) = (x_i'', y_i'', z_i) = (x_i' \cdot \frac{s_x^{model}}{s_x^{asm}}, y_i' \cdot \frac{s_y^{model}}{s_y^{asm}}, z_i)$$

5. Finally the coordinates are translated to an offline designated anchor point $v^{anchor}(x^{anchor}, y^{anchor}, z^{anchor})$ (in our implementation, we use the 3D model's chin vertex as the anchor point) to obtain the final coordinates:

$$v_i(x,y,z) = (x_i'' + x^{anchor}, y_i'' + y^{anchor}, z_i)$$

---

5   Conclusions

In this paper, we presented two NUI frameworks for remote avateering of 3D characters in shared virtual environments using ALM network architecture. We elaborated on our data flow pipelines and demonstrated how raw sensory input can be translated into sensible animation data for controlling both avatar full body movements, as well as a capturing and reconstruction pipeline of the user's current facial image into a highly realistic representation of the user in a shared 3D space to enhance the element of tele-presence. Towards this latter approach we demonstrated how a simple ASM face fitting process can be expanded to train and build high resolution (>500 landmarks) shape models which in turn correspond to the 3D vertices of the avatar face model. This enables the acquisition of both 3D vertex as well as 2D texture coordinates data per tracked landmark, to generate a highly realistic virtual 3D representation of the user using a single image, standard HD camera capturing framework. By supplementing additional 3D mesh deformation and texturing techniques, we demonstrated how our framework further enhancement of the rendered output by generating identifiable virtual 3D user caricatures. We expect our results to be particularly useful for future tele-immersive systems, video games, low-cost actor performance capturing, virtual mirror applications and more.

Acknowledgement.   The research leading to this work has received funding from the European Community's Horizon 2020 Framework Programme under grant agreement no. 644204 (ProsocialLearn project).

References

1. Apostolakis, K.C., Daras, P.: RAAT-the reverie avatar authoring tool. In: 2013 18th International Conference on Digital Signal Processing (DSP). IEEE (2013)
2. Apostolakis, K.C., et al.: Blending real with virtual in 3DLife. In: 2013 14th International Workshop on Image Analysis for Multimedia Interactive Services (WIAMIS). IEEE (2013)
3. Cao, C., et al.: 3D shape regression for real-time facial animation. ACM Trans. Graph. **32**(4), 41 (2013)
4. Cho, T., et al.: Emotional avatars: appearance augmentation and animation based on facial expression analysis. Appl. Math. **9**(2L), 461–469 (2015)
5. Cootes, T.F., et al.: Active shape models-their training and application. Comput. Vis. Image Underst. **61**(1), 38–59 (1995)
6. Cootes, T.F., Taylor, C.J.: Statistical models of appearance for computer vision (2004)
7. Cootes, T.F.: Modeling and Search software. http://personalpages.manchester.ac.uk/staff/timothy.f.cootes/software/am_tools_doc/index.html
8. Ekman, P., Friesen, W.V.: Manual for the Facial Action Coding System. Consulting Psychologists Press, Palo Alto (1978)
9. Ostermann, J.: Face animation in MPEG-4. In: Pandzic, I., Forchheimer, R. (eds.) MPEG-4 Facial Animation: The Standard, Implementation and Applications, pp. 17–55. Wiley, Chichester (2002)
10. Rhee, T., et al.: Real-time facial animation from live video tracking. In: Proceedings of the 2011 ACM SIGGRAPH/Eurographics Symposium on Computer Animation. ACM (2011)
11. Sanna, A., et al.: A kinect-based interface to animate virtual characters. J. Multimodal User Interfaces **7**(4), 269–279 (2013)
12. Shapiro, A., et al.: Automatic acquisition and animation of virtual avatars. In: VR (2014)
13. Spanlang, B., et al.: Real time whole body motion mapping for avatars and robots. In: Proceedings of the 19th ACM Symposium on Virtual Reality Software and Technology. ACM (2013)
14. Wei, Y.: Research on facial expression recognition and synthesis. Master Thesis, Department of Computer Science and Technology, Nanjing (2009)

15. Weise, T., et al.: Realtime performance-based facial animation. ACM Trans. Graph. (TOG) **30**(4), 77:1-77:10 (2011). ACM
16. Zahariadis, T., et al.: Utilizing social interaction information for efficient 3D immersive overlay communications. In: Kondoz, A., Dagiuklas, T. (eds.) Novel 3D Media Technologies, pp. 225–240. Springer, New York (2015)

ARTworks: An Augmented Reality Interface as an Aid for Restoration Professionals

Raffaello Brondi$^{(\boxtimes)}$ and Marcello Carrozzino

PERCRO Laboratory, Scuola Superiore Sant'Anna,
Via Alamanni, 13b, 56010 Pisa, Italy
r.brondi@sssup.it
http://www.percro.org/

Abstract. Augmented Reality (AR) has proven to provide effective tools to assist the human work in a wide range of sectors. Many examples can be found in literature of innovative AR tools used in medicine, industry and the military fields. Recently AR has been successfully applied also to cultural heritage, mainly for communication and educational purposes. Nevertheless, we argue that also the activity of professional operators dealing with cultural heritage, such as conservators and restorers, can benefit from the use of AR-systems. The restoration process commonly builds on the analysis and study of prior interventions and, very often, on the results of pre-operative diagnoses performed on the artwork. All the information gathered during these stages is necessary during the restoration and, using AR, it can be directly overlaid on top of the artwork avoiding the necessity of a continuous visual switch between the artwork and the documentation. Moreover, through an AR-system, new digital information can be produced directly while working, fostering also new forms of documentation.

We hereby present ARTworks, an AR-system intended to assist the restorer both during the operating phases, providing contextualized information, and during documentation, allowing the insertion of new registered digital information. The system, composed by a mechanical interface and an Android tablet, has been purposely designed taking into account the particular application field of restoration.

Keywords: Augmented Reality · Cultural heritage · Augmented reality information system · Cultural Heritage Information System · Restoration · Conservation

1 Introduction

Augmented Reality is a branch of the bigger research field of Mixed Reality (MR), which also includes Virtual Reality (VR) [11]. It is distinguished by the blending of the virtual and the real world with the aim of augmenting the human perception of the surrounding environment and enable novel metaphors of interaction.

AR has been successfully applied also to Cultural Heritage (CH), mainly for communication and educational purposes [12]. Among the first AR applications developed in the CH field is ARCHEOGUIDE [21]. Using a Head Mounted

© Springer International Publishing Switzerland 2015
L.T. De Paolis and A. Mongelli (Eds.): AVR 2015, LNCS 9254, pp. 384–398, 2015.
DOI: 10.1007/978-3-319-22888-4_28

Display (HMD) visitors of archaeological sites can see virtual reconstructions of temples and other monuments directly on the real ruins. Nowadays thanks to the ubiquitous networking availability and the technological progresses in mobile computing the ARCHEOGUIDE concept has been further developed. New researches are focusing on mobile devices as a gateway to provide augmented cultural content everywhere [1,5].

Other AR applications developed in the same field aim at providing new ways of interaction between visitors and artworks inside museums. This "augmentation" of the real-world environment can lead to an intuitive access to museum information and enhance the impact of the museum exhibition on virtual visitors [17]. Wojciechowski et al. [24] developed an AR-system composed by an authoring tool and an AR-browser. Using the former instrument, museum superintendents can design Virtual and Augmented Reality exhibitions. Through the AR-browser, installed for example in a kiosk, visitors can see the representations of cultural objects overlaid on the video captured by a camera. Similarly Chen et al. [7] proposed a new AR guidance system for museums based on markers. ARCube [10] exploits a 3D marker to enable 360 interaction with fully reconstructed three-dimensional archaeological artefacts in real-world contexts. Debenham et al. [9] developed an AR-system used inside the Natural History Museum in London which provides visitors with augmented contents through hand-held displays in order to enable an exciting new way to present the evolutionary history of our planet.

Far from being only an entertainment technology, given its unique features Augmented Reality has proven to be also an ideal tool to assist the human work in a wide range of sectors [2,6,20]. In literature many examples can be found of innovative AR tools adopted in the military, industrial and medical fields as an aid for workers. Nowadays the application of AR technologies to the cultural heritage field is mostly limited to education and dissemination purposes. The potential benefits of the introduction of AR-systems for a professional use in Cultural Heritage are still unexplored. Nevertheless the restoration activity would arguably get a valuable help from the adoption of AR-systems, as already happens in other sectors. Art restorers require access to digital information during the restoration process and, at the same time, they have to document the activities carried out. This documentation is typically managed and used in an unstructured way, or using software tools often presenting unfriendly interfaces for people not necessarily possessing high ICT skills. Augmented Reality provides a natural interface to access and visualize digital information directly on the workspace of the operator. Moreover AR make easier documenting the ongoing activity allowing new digital registered documentation to be created directly while working.

ARTworks (Augmented Reality Trackhold for artworks restoration), a new Augmented Reality system composed by a mechanical interface and an Android tablet, is hereby presented. ARTworks is intended to assist the restorer both during the operating phases, providing contextualized information in place without the needs of a continuous switch of the visual context between the artwork and the documentation, and during the documentation, allowing the insertion of new digital information registered on the asset. It has been designed to address the particular application field of restoration and to be cost effective. In the following the peculiarities of the restoration field are discussed in order to identify the main issues to be considered while designing an AR-system dedicated to artwork restoration. Then a description of a first prototype is given. A discussion and the identification of possible future directions for an effective use of these technologies in the cultural sector is finally given.

2   Field of Application

As highlighted by a previous investigation [4], the work of restorers can be compared to that of surgeons: just as each surgical operation is different because each patient is different, so each restoration project has its own peculiarities due to the type and history of the artwork. Just as surgeons require a series of analysis and reports that make perceptible information invisible to the naked eye before operating a patient, so restorers require a whole series of analyses on the artwork before carrying out a conservation-restoration (C-R) treatment (see Fig. 1). In both cases, during the execution phases, it is of primary importance to be able to efficiently access the information collected before the operation. While examples exist of AR-systems used during surgery operations to ease the access to valuable information, facilitating surgical planning and increasing precision [14,22], nothing has been done in the C-R field.

Although a great deal of documentation related to artworks is already available in the digital domain (text, vectorial graphics, photos or diagnostic images), it is typically managed and used in an unstructured way. Attempts exist to structure the use of this data using paradigms typical of Geographical Information Systems (GISs), but to date these attempts have met a limited success. Cultural Heritage Information Systems (CHISs) are adaptations of GISs specially devoted to CH applications. An example is SICAR [3], a Web-based GIS for the documentation of ongoing C-R works. The system allows to store information day by day and to easily retrieve relevant documents (such as diagnoses, chemical analyses, maps, etc.), linked to a specific area in the digitalized ortho-image of the object under treatment. CHISs are extremely powerful compared to other solutions because they allow to manage various data types in a structured way. Nevertheless they are not yet widely adopted in C-R. They are mainly designed for bi-dimensional data manipulation/visualization and they often miss important functionalities useful in restoration. Some recent projects try to address also 3D artworks [13,18]; extending methodologies and procedures from 2D to 3D is not trivial not only because user interfaces are commonly designed for 2D contexts (and hardly suitable to manage 3D data without a considerable additional effort both on the developer and on the user side) but also because of the peculiarities of 3D artworks and related C-R procedures (sculptures, for instance, are designed to be seen from all sites, so its unlimited mobility is required during conservation process; structures of sculptures are often complex, having usually a number of original layers and several additional layers inserted in later periods - such as overpaintings and re-carving - causing some investigations, like stratigraphy, to be usually complicated; conservation of polychrome sculptures requires

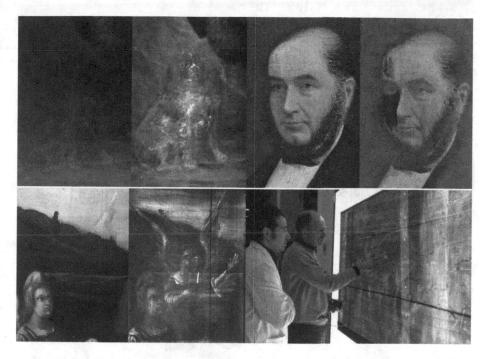

Fig. 1. Example of different preoperative documentation: infrared (top-left), UV ray (top-right) and radiography (bottom-left) images of paintings (from http://fineartconservation.ie/). On the bottom right corner, restorers looking at a radiography at Opificio delle Pietre Dure in Florence.

both pictorial and sculptural skills, etc.). Other types of software applications (e.g. Meshlab [8]) offers extremely powerful tools and allows many different elaboration of raw three-dimensional data. Anyway they are not conceived to be used as documentation systems and they do not provide a way to structure data.

Even if all these applications represent valid and established solutions for some of the C-R issues addressable by ICT technologies, none of them offers an integrated approach and, moreover, they are designed as classical desktop computer programs and are not suitable to be interactively used during the restoration process. The main concern raised by conservator-restorers is that these tools commonly require a demanding training in order to be mastered. Due to their unfamiliarity with ICT tools many professionals of the restoration sector prefer simpler software tools, such as word and image processors, in order to produce non-structured documentation easily exchanged among professionals [4].

3   AR-based Information System for Art Restoration

Restorers commonly alternate operational and documentary phases. During operation, they actively work on the assets exploiting the collected documentation.

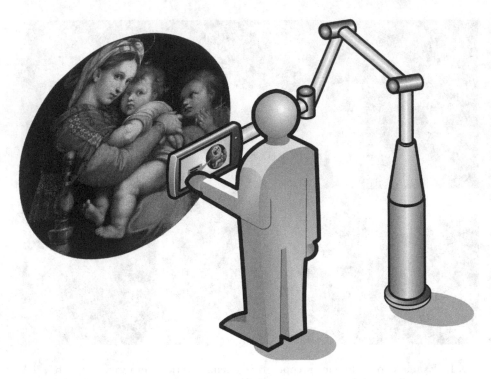

Fig. 2. Conceptual design of an AR-system as an aid for restorers

During the documentary phase, new material is produced and attached to the existing one. The newly created information will be available during the next operational phase for consulting.

Simple documents (e.g. images, videos, text document) can be very difficult to manage after some time if not well structured. CHISs offer a way to organize these materials in order to enable an easier and localized access. Nevertheless, as above highlighted, these tools are currently not entirely suitable to be used during the operational phase; whenever it is necessary to access the needed information, conservator-restorers have to stop and leave their work. Similarly new documentation cannot be created while working. In the same way as it happens with the old logbook method, conservator-restorers have to choose between frequently suspending their work in order to create a more punctual documentation, or try to recall and document all the performed operations at the end of a session.

The main limitations of the existing solutions can therefore be summarized in:

- use of standard user interfaces, not conceived to allow an effective real-time access to and modification of data;
- complex interaction with slow learning curves, requiring an aimed training to operators.

These issues can be overcome using a different approach, such as the one offered by AR. Augmented Reality has the ability to bring digital information into the real space where the user actually operates, allowing the development of new and more natural metaphors of interaction (see Fig. 2). Through AR-based interaction, information will be available in real-time directly in the field of view of the human operator and visually co-located on the artwork they are related to. Restorers will not have to leave their workspace in order to seek the needed information as it will be available directly on the asset. Any type of documentation (e.g. stratigraphy data, ultraviolet photographs, contextual descriptions, etc.) can be structured in layers like CHISs do and through AR layers can be overlaid and registered on the artwork.

AR-based systems can also provide an extremely powerful way to create new documentation. Conservators and restorers commonly provide at the end of the intervention an exhaustive documentation of each operation performed. This will be part of the a priori knowledge linked to the asset and used during future interventions. Documentation can be therefore considered as the basis for collaboration among professionals. AR-systems can enable real-time documentation spatially and temporally registered on the artwork. They allow restorers to record new data without leaving the work (see Fig. 2). Furthermore the documentation process can take advantage of the new media (like video, audio, or real-time 3D reconstructions) enabled by this technology. This richer documentation represents also new important material that can be used inside museums (or on the web) to show the restoration activities carried out for education and dissemination purposes.

As the real and the digital world coexist within the same interface, AR offers also new, powerful and more natural way of interaction to users. Conservator-restorers do not have to practice with complex interfaces just to understand how to access and visualize information. They just need to move the AR-device where the information needs to be displayed. To create new localized documentation, they just need to move the AR-device where the new information have to be placed and insert it.

4   Prototype Design

A new prototype AR-system has been developed to assist restorers during their work addressing the aforementioned issues. Artwork restoration is a really huge and diversified application field. It spans from architectonic restoration of big buildings to micro interventions on paintings, from wooden to metal to stonework artefacts. We decided to start focusing on restoration of bidimensional surfaces (e.g. paintings, frescos, paper, etc.) which still represents an important part of the whole C-R activity but reduces the design complexity of the AR-system.

In an Augmented Reality application it is necessary to localize the user or the device with respect to the environment to be augmented. This information is required in order to align virtual and real contents. Several methods exist based on different types of technology (inertial, acoustical, magnetic, optical,

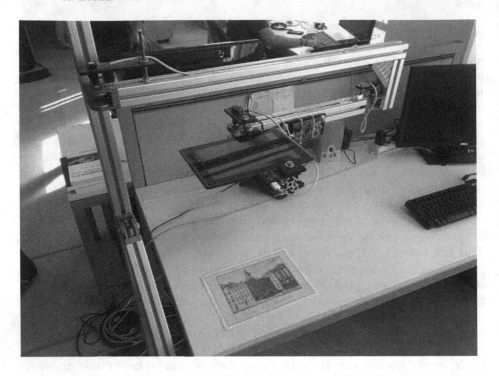

Fig. 3. First ARTworks prototype used to augment bidimensional surfaces

mechanical etc.), each presenting specific pros and cons in terms of precision, accuracy, workspace, etc. [25]. The current state of the art of mobile technologies enables feature-based tracking algorithm on mobiles [19,23], but this remains one of the more challenging aspects of mobile AR-systems. According to the survey results [4], the interface should provide a self sustained structure to leave restorer's hands free and allow free movements on top of the artwork.

The first ARTworks prototype (see Fig. 3) is therefore composed by a sensorized mechanical interface sustaining an Android tablet placed on the end effector. Given the availability of this structure, the registration of the augmented content exploits both kinematic and computer vision techniques in order to estimate the position of the tablet with respect to the asset. In the following the prototype structure, the tracking system and the user interface are presented.

4.1   Prototype Structure

The mechanical interface consists of a structure made by commercial components (http://www.boschrexroth.com) and providing 3DOF. Each revolute joint is sensorized with a single turn linear $4.7\,k\Omega$ potentiometer. The result is a 3R planar manipulator as depicted in Fig. 4.

An STM32F4-discovery board featuring 32-bit ARM Cortex-M4F core is used to gather the signals coming from the potentiometers. Readings from the potentiometers are sampled with a frequency of $\sim 5\,\mathrm{MHz}$. The values are averaged by the board and sent over a serial communication channel at a frequency of $\sim 60\,\mathrm{Hz}$.

The mechanical interface is described using the Denavit Hartenberg (DH) [16] convention by the parameters in Table 1. The interface is completely passive. The user is free to drag the end effector over the surface to be augmented. The position is obtained in realtime applying the direct kinematics of the mechanical interface to the angles read by the potentiometers.

The mechanical arm terminates with a slot that accommodates an Android tablet. The current prototype configuration uses an Asus Transformer tf101 equipped with Android 4.0.3 Ice Cream Sandwich (ICS). The software application has been written to run on any Android mobile devices running ICS or greater versions of the Operating System, so that it can be easily replaced with newer and more powerful devices.

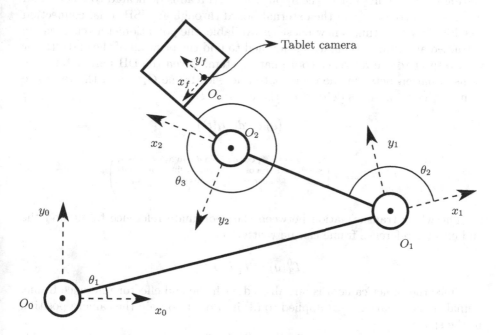

Fig. 4. Top view schema of the prototyped mechanical interface

Table 1. Denavit-Hartenberg link parameters. Values given in meters

Link	a_i	α_i	d_i	ϑ_i
1	0.815	0.0	−0.155	θ_1
2	0.473	0.0	0.0	θ_2
3	0.0825	0.0	−0.0292	θ_3

This component is in charge of powering up the mechanical interface, and processing/managing the data coming from the board. The tablet screen is used as a video-through display, and it is in charge to provide the augmented view of the artwork placed under it. The data arriving from the board is used to evaluate the position of the end effector while computer vision techniques are used to estimate the position of the artwork with respect to the tablet camera. The registration process is accomplished merging the information coming from the mechanical interface with those resulting from a feature matching algorithm implemented with OpenCV. The software application has been written partly in Java and partly in C++ in order to exploit the maximum capability of the device.

4.2   Calibration and Tracking

During the entire lifetime of the application a thread is dedicated to receive and process data coming from the external board through an USB serial connection (see Fig. 5). Every time a new packet is available, the potentiometer readings are extracted and direct kinematics is applied to find the position of the end effector with respect to the reference coordinate system. Given the DH parameters, the transformation between the coordinate reference frame O_{i-1} and the reference frame O_i (see Fig. 4), is defined by the matrix (2)

$$q_i = \begin{pmatrix} a_i & \alpha_i & d_i & \vartheta_i(t) \end{pmatrix} \tag{1}$$

$$T_i^{i-1}(q_i(t)) = \begin{pmatrix} \cos\vartheta_i & -\sin\vartheta_i\cos\alpha_i & \sin\vartheta_i\sin\alpha_i & a_i\cos\vartheta_i \\ \sin\vartheta_i & \cos\vartheta_i\cos\alpha_i & -\cos\vartheta_i\sin\alpha_i & a_i\sin\vartheta_i \\ 0 & \sin\alpha_i & \cos\alpha_i & d_i \\ 0 & 0 & 0 & 1 \end{pmatrix} \tag{2}$$

The whole transformation between the coordinate reference frame and the end effector reference frame can be written as

$$T_3^0(q) = T_1^0 T_2^1 T_3^2 \tag{3}$$

Since the tablet camera is not aligned with the end effector reference frame, a final transformation T_f is applied to (3) in order to obtain the camera position in the space.

$$T_c(t) = T_3^0(q(t))T_f \tag{4}$$

Using (4) the position of the camera can be obtained with respect to the mechanical interface over the time.

The main application process is executed in another thread. The process work-flow can be summarized in a first calibration step followed by the main application process during which the augmentation of the asset is provided as described in Fig. 5.

Before being able to augment the artwork, a calibration step is required in order to know the position of the asset with respect to the mechanical interface. A scan

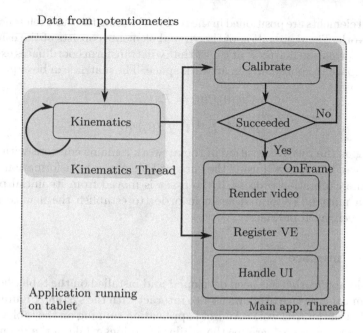

Fig. 5. Flow diagram of the application

of the artwork must be previously acquired and loaded on the device. The features of this sample image are statically extracted using the ORB feature detector [15].

During the calibration procedure, the application acquires a set of frames from the camera. On each frame acquired, features are detected using the same ORB feature detector. Found features are matched against the ones extracted from the scanned image using the OpenCV library. If enough matches are found, the position and pose of the tablet camera is estimated relative to the artwork, otherwise the process continues until enough good matches are found. A transformation matrix that transform a point in the camera coordinate frame to the artwork reference frame $P(0)$ is composed.

While looking for matches in frames, the calibration process receives also (4) which describes the position of the camera over the time with respect to the mechanical interface reference frame. As a result of the calibration process, the position of the artwork with respect to the camera is then obtained as

$$R_0 = T_c(0)P(0) \tag{5}$$

where $T_c(0)$ is the kinematics matrix at calibration time.

Once (5) has been estimated, the application proceeds to the augmented phase. For each frame the application renders the video coming from the tablet camera, registers and renders virtual elements loaded on the scene (for instance new digital information layers created by the user) and finally processes any user interactions that may happen (see Fig. 5).

Virtual elements are positioned in the real world using the same reference frame of the artwork. The registration of the virtual elements consists of the evaluation of the transformation matrix P at time t that will transform coordinates expressed in camera space to coordinates in artwork space. The matrix can be expressed

$$T_c(0)P(0) = T_c(t)P_t \tag{6}$$

$$P(t) = T_c^{-1}(t) \, T_c(0)P(0) \tag{7}$$

As long as the relative position of the artwork remains constant with respect to O_0, (7) can be evaluated using the current kinematics transformation and the result of the calibration process. If the asset is moved from its initial position, the system must be calibrated again in order to establish the new correlation with the mechanical interface.

4.3   User Interface

An Android application has been developed and installed on the tablet hosted on the mechanical interface to allows user to interact with the system. Figure 6 shows a screen shot of the ARTworks Android application running on the tablet. On the left side a command dock groups the available options while in the main central area the video acquired by the camera and the augmented content are displayed.

Fig. 6. Screen shot of the ARTworks Android application running on the tablet. Five layers, one punctual, three polygonal and one image, are loaded in the command dock and shown overlaid on the video captured by the tablet camera

Information inside ARTworks is organized in Virtual Layers(VLs). A Virtual Layer represents a combination of uniform data registered on the asset, coded in a JSON[1] file. Currently three different type of data can be encoded and understood by the application:

- punctual elements
- polygonal elements
- images

Punctual elements are defined by a set of points to which a color is assigned. Poligonal elements are defined by a sequence of points connected by a line. The surface enclosed by the line represents the polygon area. Both the line and the surface of the polygon have a color linked to them. Images are parallelogram surfaces to which an image is associated. A caption can be optionally linked to each element of a VL.

Virtual Layers can be preloaded on the tablet, or created by the user during a working session. New layers can be loaded by simply copying them inside a public folder on the tablet sd-card. When the application starts, it looks for available VLs in the sd-card. The name of each available layer is shown in a list on the command dock placed on the left edge of the display (see Fig. 6). A VL can be enabled or disabled using the switch button associated. When a layer is enabled its virtual content is drawn in the scene, overlaid on the video stream of the camera. The order in which the VLs are listed in the command dock represents the z-order used to draw them. User can change the position of each layer by dragging each element of the list in a different position.

The "Create layer" button in the command dock allows the user to create new registered VLs. First the user has to chose the type of layer (punctual, polygonal or image) he/she wants to create. Then the new VL is created by simply tapping on the screen. When the layer has been composed, it can be saved to be successively loaded.

When a layer is enabled, if the user taps on a part of it, the caption linked to the entity is displayed in the command dock.

5   Results

Calibration and tracking capabilities has been tested with three different paintings. On the current prototype set-up, the error settles among 3 mm to 5 mm (3.98 ± 0.87 mm) depending on the distance between the artwork and the tablet camera, and the number and the quality of features detected. During the interviews it was asked to restorers: *"Which level of precision the augmentation must reach for your intended use in restoration?"*. Four categories have been given:

---

[1] JSON (JavaScript Object Notation) is a lightweight data-interchange format. It is easy for humans to read and write. It is easy for machines to parse and generate. See http://www.json.org/.

- up to 2 mm (35.7 %)
- from 2 to 5 mm (26.3 %)
- from 5 mm to 1 cm (19 %)
- more than 1 cm (19 %)

Given the average error, ARTworks prototype is therefore able to satisfy more than the 60 % of the restoration professionals.

The calibration procedure needs at least 10 inliers feature matches in order to assess the artwork position and orientation respect to the camera. The average time required to perform the calibration is about ~ 4 (4.47 ± 1.02) seconds on the image suit used to evaluate the system.

The tracking performed using the mechanical interface kinematics correctly estimate the endeffector position. The result is stable. More of the noise coming from the sensor readings is cut off by a low pass filter done by on the external board. The mechanical structure is affected by some torsions that degrades the registration of the virtual environments especially at the margin of the mechanical interface workspace.

The kinematics thread provides new evaluation of the end effector position with a frequency of about ~ 60 Hz which is absolutely fine for the needs of an AR application. The graphic thread runs at a frequency of about ~ 20 (18.3 ± 1.8) fps.

As pointed out by all the interviewed restorer [4], probably one of the main problems in adopting this new technological instruments is related to the limited budget commonly available. For these reasons ARTwork has been designed in order to be as cheap as possible. The overall structure that composes the ARTworks prototype costs less than 600 €.

6   Conclusions and Future Works

In this paper we have presented ARTworks, a prototype of a novel interface specifically designed to assist restoration professionals. The system is able to provide digital information spatially referenced on the artworks using the paradigm of Augmented Reality. It also provides an easy and powerful tool for restoration professionals to create and manage new digital information fostering a structured documentation process. Moreover, it can enhance the collaboration between restorers, enabling new forms of communication between the operators.

The ARTworks design has been based on the results of interviews conduced among several professionals. Thanks to this information it has been possible to identify the main aspects and issues typical of this application field. The interface design and development has been therefore lead by these guidelines in order to respond to restorers needs. The main mechanical structure is solid and easily portable. The Android tablet used as augmented display can be easily replaced with any other similar common device.

ARTworks currently exists as a working prototype. The final user interface has been tailored on the restorer needs to make it simple and easy to use. New digital input will be introduced such as audio, video and three-dimensional meshes to enrich the information that restorers can use and share using this interface. We plan to explore different tracking technologies based on pure computer vision techniques, like SLAM, or on hybrid approaches. The possible integration with existing GISs will be evaluated in order to load and store digital information directly from/to this software applications. The kinematics of the mechanical interface will be expanded to reach the required degrees of freedom in order to achieve a three-dimensional workspace.

ARTworks will be tested in real scenarios in order to evaluate the effectiveness of the developed interface in assisting restorer professionals during their work. We will ask all the interviewed restorers to test the interface; a second survey will be then conduced in order to assess the effectiveness of the interface. Furthermore, the digital documentation produced through the system will be used to verify if this kind of system can be proficiently used to train apprentices.

Subsequently, the adoption of the information produced during the intervention as educational material inside museums will be evaluated.

References

1. Armanno, G., Bottino, A., Martina, A.: Skylinedroid: an outdoor mobile augmented reality application for virtual heritage. In: Proceedings of the International Conference on Cultural Heritage and Tourism (CUHT 2012), Cambridge, England, pp. 25–27 (2012)
2. Azuma, R., Baillot, Y., Behringer, R., Feiner, S., Julier, S., MacIntyre, B.: Recent advances in augmented reality. IEEE Comput. Graph. Appl. 21(6), 34–47 (2001)
3. Baracchini, C., Lanari, P., Scopigno, R., Tecchia, F., Vecchi, A.: SICAR: geographic information system for the documentation of restoration analyses and intervention. In: Optical Metrology, pp. 149–160. International Society for Optics and Photonics, October 2003
4. Brondi, R., Carrozzino, M.: Fostering collaboration among restoration professionals using augmented reality. In: 2014 IEEE 23rd International WETICE Conference (WETICE), pp. 243–248. IEEE (2014)
5. Brondi, R., Carrozzino, M., Tecchia, F., Bergamasco, M.: Mobile augmented reality for cultural dissemination. In: ECLAP 2012 Conference on Information Technologies for Performing Arts, Media Access and Entertainment, p. 113 (2012)
6. Carmigniani, J., Furht, B., Anisetti, M., Ceravolo, P., Damiani, E., Ivkovic, M.: Augmented reality technologies, systems and applications. Multimedia Tools Appl. 51(1), 341–377 (2011)
7. Chen, C.Y., Chang, B.R., Huang, P.S.: Multimedia augmented reality information system for museum guidance. Pers. Ubiquit. Comput. 18(2), 315–322 (2014)
8. Cignoni, P., Corsini, M., Ranzuglia, G.: Meshlab: an open-source 3d mesh processing system. Ercim News 73, 45–46 (2008)
9. Debenham, P., Thomas, G., Trout, J.: Evolutionary augmented reality at the natural history museum. In: 2011 10th IEEE International Symposium on Mixed and Augmented Reality (ISMAR), pp. 249–250. IEEE (2011)
10. Jiménez Fernández-Palacios, B., Nex, F., Rizzi, A., Remondino, F.: Arcubethe augmented reality cube for archaeology. Archaeometry (2014)
11. Milgram, P., Kishino, F.: A taxonomy of mixed reality visual displays. IEICE Trans. Inf. Syst. 77(12), 1321–1329 (1994)

12. Noh, Z., Sunar, M.S., Pan, Z.: A review on augmented reality for virtual heritage system. In: Chang, M., et al. (eds.) Learning by Playing. LNCS, vol. 5670, pp. 50–61. Springer, Heidelberg (2009)
13. Pecchioli, L., Carrozzino, M., Mohamed, F., Bergamasco, M., Kolbe, T.H.: ISEE: information access through the navigation of a 3d interactive environment. J. Cult. Heritage 12(3), 287–294 (2011)
14. Pratt, P., Mayer, E., Vale, J., Cohen, D., Edwards, E., Darzi, A., Yang, G.Z.: An effective visualisation and registration system for image-guided robotic partial nephrectomy. J. Robot. Surg. 6(1), 23–31 (2012)
15. Rublee, E., Rabaud, V., Konolige, K., Bradski, G.: Orb: an efficient alternative to sift or surf. In: 2011 IEEE International Conference on Computer Vision (ICCV), pp. 2564–2571. IEEE (2011)
16. Siciliano, B.: Robotica: modellistica, pianificazione e controllo. McGraw-Hill libri Italia, Milano (2008)
17. Styliani, S., Fotis, L., Kostas, K., Petros, P.: Virtual museums, a survey and some issues for consideration. J. Cult. Heritage 10(4), 520–528 (2009)
18. Torres, J., Lopez, L., Romo, C., Arroyo, G., Cano, P., Lamolda, F., Villafranca, M.: Using a cultural heritage information system for the documentation of the restoration process. In: Digital Heritage International Congress (DigitalHeritage), vol. 2, pp. 249–256. IEEE (2013)
19. Ufkes, A., Fiala, M.: A markerless augmented reality system for mobile devices. In: 2013 International Conference on Computer and Robot Vision (CRV), pp. 226–233. IEEE (2013)
20. Van Krevelen, D., Poelman, R.: A survey of augmented reality technologies, applications and limitations. Int. J. Virtual Reality 9(2), 1 (2010)
21. Vlahakis, V., Karigiannis, J., Tsotros, M., Gounaris, M., Almeida, L., Stricker, D., Gleue, T., Christou, I.T., Carlucci, R., Ioannidis, N.: Archeoguide: first results of an augmented reality, mobile computing system in cultural heritage sites. In: Virtual Reality, Archeology, and Cultural Heritage, pp. 131–140 (2001)
22. Volonté, F., Pugin, F., Bucher, P., Sugimoto, M., Ratib, O., Morel, P.: Augmented reality and image overlay navigation with osirix in laparoscopic and robotic surgery: not only a matter of fashion. J. Hepato-Biliary-Pancreatic Sci. 18(4), 506–509 (2011)
23. Wagner, D., Reitmayr, G., Mulloni, A., Drummond, T., Schmalstieg, D.: Real-time detection and tracking for augmented reality on mobile phones. IEEE Trans. Vis. Comput. Graph. 16(3), 355–368 (2010)
24. Wojciechowski, R., Walczak, K., White, M., Cellary, W.: Building virtual and augmented reality museum exhibitions. In: Proceedings of the Ninth International Conference on 3D Web Technology, pp. 135–144. ACM (2004)
25. Zhou, F., Duh, H.B.L., Billinghurst, M.: Trends in augmented reality tracking, interaction and display: A review of ten years of ismar. In: Proceedings of the 7th IEEE/ACM International Symposium on Mixed and Augmented Reality, pp. 193–202. IEEE Computer Society (2008)

Design and Preliminary Evaluation of Free-Hand Travel Techniques for Wearable Immersive Virtual Reality Systems with Egocentric Sensing

Giuseppe Caggianese$^{(\boxtimes)}$, Luigi Gallo, and Pietro Neroni

National Research Council of Italy (ICAR-CNR),
Institute of High Performance Computing and Networking, Naples, Italy
{giuseppe.caggianese,luigi.gallo,pietro.neroni}@na.icar.cnr.it

Abstract. The recent availability of low cost wearable displays coupled with contactless motion sensing devices is leveraging the design of immersive and highly interactive virtual environments. In such virtual worlds, the human-computer interface, and particularly the navigation technique, plays a crucial role. This paper presents a preliminary evaluation of traveling constraints in egocentric vision. In more detail, we describe and compare in an ego-vision scenario two travel techniques, both based on a combination of visual controls and hand gestures but proving to be different in terms of the number of travel directions allowed to the user and of the travel velocity control. The experimental results indicate that, despite the users appreciating the possibility of controlling the travel direction with both head and arrows, not all the directions are considered useful in the same way. However, direct control of the velocity proves to affect positively the navigation experience in all the considered scenarios.

Keywords: 3D navigation · Traveling techniques · Ego-vision · Leap motion · Comparative evaluation

1 Introduction

In recent years, the rapid spread of low cost Virtual Reality (VR) head-mounted displays (HMDs) and even better low cost VR headset kits, such as the Google Cardboard [1], which exploits the user's smartphone display, have been opening up new opportunities for intense and engaging immersive user experiences. In particular, these devices allow users to immerse themselves in virtual environments (VEs) anywhere, and at any time without having to wear cumbersome equipment. Consequently, these systems have started to be profitably used in many different application areas, such as entertainment, marketing, education, training and tourism.

A generic issue in immersive VEs is that the user can not see anything of the real world around her/him while wearing the VR headset; for this reason, most common input devices such as the keyboard, mouse, joystick or touch surface

© Springer International Publishing Switzerland 2015
L.T. De Paolis and A. Mongelli (Eds.): AVR 2015, LNCS 9254, pp. 399–408, 2015.
DOI: 10.1007/978-3-319-22888-4_29

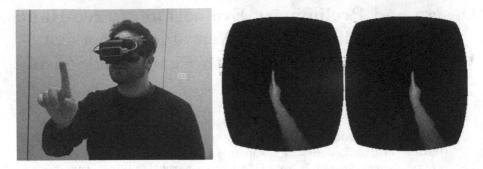

Fig. 1. On the left, the interactive VR headset worn by a user. On the right, the user's hand as seen from the sensor viewpoint.

are not suitable for use with this device. Moreover, the possibility of diving into an immersive virtual environment by simply using a smartphone, adds more constraints in the design of the human-machine interface in order to preserve the user's mobility and comfort. An interesting possibility is that of using sensing devices small enough to be worn together with the VR headset. Such devices allow the system to track the user's actions by exploiting the egocentric vision. The benefits of this solution are twofold: the user can interact with the VE by using her/his hands without the need to manipulate any specific device; and, her/his hands, which are tracked by the sensor, can be reproduced in the VE, so overcoming the aforementioned interaction limitations (see Fig. 1).

Immersed users need to interact naturally with virtual objects in the scene but, at the same time, they need to navigate the surrounding environment. In this paper, we deal with the traveling problem, the non-cognitive subset of navigation that controls the user's viewpoint motion through a VE [5]. Traveling is a common and universal interaction task which needs to be as simple as possible in order to maximize the users' comfort and productivity. We have designed two gaze direction steering techniques, "Head direction steering" and "Four head direction steering". They are both based on a combination of hand movements and visual controls but present different constraints related to the movements allowed to the user. In fact, when using the first technique, the user is allowed to move only straight ahead, whereas the second technique allows the user to move also in cardinal directions. In this paper, we detail the design of the techniques, describing the problems encountered and discussing the results of a preliminary evaluation study.

The rest of the paper is structured as follows. In Sect. 2, we review related work in the design of travel techniques for VEs. In Sect. 3, we describe and explain the design of the two proposed travel techniques. Afterward that, Sect. 4 focuses on the qualitative evaluation test performed, also providing a discussion of the experimental results. Finally, in Sect. 5, we present our conclusions.

2 Related Work

Bowman et al. [6] classified travel techniques into: physical techniques, where the user translates and rotates her/his viewpoint by using eye, head or body movements; and virtual techniques, in which the user's body remains stationary even though the virtual viewpoint moves.

The most direct approach among the physical techniques is that of real walking, which maps physical walking with a corresponding motion through the virtual environment in order to replicate the effective energy and motion of walking. As shown in [9], real walking provides better spatial orientation and movement understanding. However, usually the physical techniques require a complete 6 degrees of freedom (DOF) tracking system to track the user's position and orientation. In addition, the range of the user's motion through the virtual world is constrained by the size of the available tracking area. To overcome this limitation, Razzaque et al. [19] attempt to keep the user within the tracking area by imposing undetectable rotations of the virtual scene. Other studies in the same field focus on providing a lower subjective sense of presence than real walking [21,23]. Moreover, hardware solutions such as treadmills and foot platforms have also been proposed [3,15], but their weight and cost make them unsuitable for use in an "always on" scenario.

On the other hand, virtual techniques have the advantage of allowing arbitrarily large virtual environments using a small physical workspace. Virtual techniques in immersive VEs commonly use a combination of head tracking integrated into head-mounted displays and 3D spatial input devices for interaction. In [4], the authors define a taxonomy that splits the virtual travel design into three components: Direction/Target Selection, Velocity/Acceleration Selection, and Input Condition. Examples of these techniques are: gaze-directed steering [6], which allows to travel in the direction in which the user is looking; and, the pointing steering technique [16], in which the user's view and traveling direction are decoupled and hand pointing is considered instead of gaze direction. In [4], the authors have shown that pointing steering reveals an advantage over gaze-directed steering in scenarios with relative motion tasks, whereas that advantage vanishes in scenarios with absolute motion tasks.

In recent years, the release of new motion sensors, particularly in the entertainment field (e.g., the Wii Remote) has enabled a more intuitive interaction based on body movements [24]. Researchers have been motivated to exploit these technologies to perform omnifarious interaction tasks, navigation included. As an example, in [12] yaw, pitch and roll angles of a Wii Remote controller were used to navigate within a large virtual environment. However, these devices require the user to hold or wear an additional device to track hand gestures and therefore they are unsuitable for all types of applications.

Nowadays, the rise of contactless motion sensing devices (e.g., Microsoft Kinect [2]) offers the possibility of designing body movement-based interaction techniques that do not require the user to physically touch the input device. Many different free-hand 3D navigation techniques by using contactless motion sensing devices have been proposed. Most of them use fixed camera systems to allow users to navigate within a virtual environment visualized on large displays [10,11,18,20]. However, VE navigation in egocentric vision has been much less frequently explored. For this reason, we have focused on the opportunity of exploring the ego-vision for traveling, taking our inspiration from the Augmented Reality (AR) field, in which wearable sensors have already widely used to realize gesture-based interfaces [8,13,17].

3 Egocentric Traveling Techniques

In the design of the travel techniques, we have only considered first-person travel tasks, in which the user's view corresponds to the camera viewpoint in order to study situations in which the user needs to explore a VE in the first person.

The interaction commands to manipulate the viewpoint are mapped to the user's head and hand movements. For this reason, we have integrated a depth sensing device, Leap Motion, into a commercial VR headset, in order to track both head and hand movements (see Fig. 2). Head movements are tracked by using a magnetometer and a gyroscope embedded in the 4.95 inches smartphone used as the display for the VR headset. The hand segmentation and tracking are executed by using depth information returned by Leap Motion, since it is one of the lightest off-the-shelf sensors (only 45 grams) that strongly facilitates the segmentation of the hands, even in gloves or with cluttered backgrounds. The headset used is the Durovis Dive 5. Combined with the smartphone and the lens, it allows a field of view (FOV) of about 90°, while Leap Motion provides a horizontal FOV of 135°, a vertical FOV of 120°, and a maximum operating distance of 0.60 m.

Choosing a method from each of the three branches of the taxonomy proposed by Bowman et al. [4], we have designed two travel techniques that prove to be different from each other in the traveling directions allowed to the user. The first branch of the taxonomy refers to the method by which the user steers the view point and so the traveling direction; the proposed techniques are all based on gaze direction steering. We have chosen this method because, since the sensor is assembled on the VR headset, the interaction area of the sensor always matches the user's gaze direction. This condition allows a tracking of the user's hands only when these are placed in front of the user, in the gaze direction and so in the

Fig. 2. The hardware components used for the design and evaluation.

interaction area of the sensor. Although a well known limitation of gaze selection is that the user cannot look around while traveling [16], the steering technique exploiting gaze is probably the most common 3D travel technique. However, the term "gaze" proves to be really misleading. In fact, when eye tracking is not performed, the direction of the gaze is inferred from the head tracker orientation and, for this reason, we prefer to use the terminology head direction steering.

In order to specify the start and end time of the travel, we have chosen to apply a combination of visual interface and hand gestures, which allow a satisfaction of the user's need to have full control of the duration of the travel. In fact, the user visualizes in her/his viewpoint a control interface with which the user interacts by using spatial hand gestures. The interfaces for the two proposed techniques prove to be different in terms of the number of travel directions allowed to the user. The left side of Fig. 3 shows the interface presented to the user for the head direction steering technique. Visual control traveling proves to be limited to a single movement. Indeed, interacting with that control, the user is allowed to travel only in the head direction. In contrast, the second proposed technique, four head direction steering, relaxes the previous constraints introducing three more visual widgets (as shown in the right side of Fig. 3) and consequently the same number of travel directions. In this case, the user is allowed to move in the four cardinal directions related to the viewpoint orientation. Therefore, although both techniques exploit the head direction to choose the travel direction, they prove to be different in terms of the travel constraints.

For instance, using the first technique, a user who want to slide the viewpoint to her/his side has to rotate the view by 45°, perform the needed forward movement, and then finally rotate by 45° in the opposite direction, so as to reorient the view in the initial direction. On the contrary, the second technique allows the user to directly move to her/his side with respect to her/his head direction. Therefore, in the second case, the user, to slightly move to her/his side, does not need to rotate two times her/his viewpoint. Moreover, the second technique allows the user not to lose a visual contact with the target to reach.

To interact with the controls of the interface the user needs to use her/his hand. By introducing her/his hand in the interaction area of the sensor, the system will start to track the hand waiting for a starting gestures. To start to travel the user has to press on the widget (see Fig. 3). To stop, she/he has to

Fig. 3. On the left, the single control visualized in the head direction steering technique. On the right, the four controls visualized in the four head direction steering technique.

release the control. However, there are also two implicit stop conditions: first, when the user, during the travel, move her/his hand out of the interaction area of the control, unintentionally releasing it; and, secondly, when she/he completely moves her/his hand out of the interaction area of the sensor.

The designed interaction interface for both the techniques requires a head-hand coordination. For this reason, the widgets are visualized at the center of the user's viewpoint to be always easily reachable. Every time the user rotates her/his head, the widget will follow the viewpoint, to avoid that if the user was interacting with the widget, that interaction is not lost.

The last branch of the taxonomy we have considered is related to the selection of the travel velocity. By activating a different pressure on the widget, like with the accelerator pedal in a car, the user can control the travel velocity. In order to simulate a pedestrian traveling, when the user starts the interaction the velocity has been set equal to a standard human walk, 67 meters per minute; by increasing the velocity, the user can achieve a maximum speed of 330 meters per minute, which is equivalent to a human running slowly.

Finally, considering the aforementioned problem of interacting with a widget in an egocentric vision, the user sees in the VE a corresponding 3D model of her/his hands. Moreover, since the FOV of the VR headset is smaller than the interaction area of the sensor, we have mapped opportunely the hand movements captured by the sensor in the user's view, allowing the possibility that each time the hand is tracked it is also visible in the VE. In this way, we can avoid unintentional user interactions that can happen when the hands are still in the interaction area of the sensor but not in the FOV of the visor. With this solution the user also immediately realizes when her/his hand is not tracked, a fact which is important in an interaction that involves both head and hand movements.

4   User Study

4.1   Goal

The object of this study was to evaluate the perceived usability of the two proposed techniques and to understand if the travel velocity control was considered useful by the user. Our aim was to assess the preferred combination of technique and velocity controls in order to perform, in a future work, a quantitative test on that specific combination.

4.2   Design

We conducted a within-subject evaluation, in which all the subjects tested both the presented traveling techniques using the velocity control as a factor with two possible levels, present and absent. Each subject performed four different trials, one for each condition. Finally, the combinations were counter-balanced to reduce carry over effects.

4.3   Participants

We recruited 12 unpaid volunteers, a multiple of the number of conditions, to perform the study. The participants' ages ranged from 25 to 45 years old, with an average age of 34.2. Three of the participants were female and all of them were right-handed.

4.4   Procedure

The experiment was performed using a single VR headset and the same simulated scenario for all the users, guaranteeing the same set-up and conditions for each tester. The simulated scenario of a metropolitan city, was designed to dive the subject into a dense VE containing multiple distractors.

Initially, a facilitator showed, to each volunteer, a brief video to introduce the system and the elements of the user interface. Specifically, the video was used to explain the head-hand movements necessary to control the travel, the functions of the widgets, the velocity control and the task to perform.

After the demonstration video, in a practice session designed to make the participants feel more comfortable and relaxed, the subjects were left free to familiarize themselves with the interface without any limitations, also being allowed to switch between the proposed techniques. The practice session serves to improve the subject's confidence in wearing the VR headset and especially in dealing with the hand movements necessary to interact with the widgets. In this phase, the facilitator was only allowed to switch between the approaches on the participants' request.

Next, the test session started with the users receiving precise instructions from the facilitator about the tasks to perform. The subjects were immersed in a dense VE reproducing a metropolitan city with multiple distractors. In the experimental trials we asked the subjects to perform three consecutive travels with an equivalent number of start-target position pairs in the environment. Each start-target pair was carefully selected in order to avoid straight line trajectories. We placed many obstacles (city buildings) between the two positions in order to force the user to look around constantly and consequently to use a head-hand coordination to move. The start and target positions, as shown in Fig. 4, were represented respectively as a green and a red cylinder higher than all the city buildings in order to be always visible from all places in the city. The test session was organized with the repetition of two different and consecutive moments for each trial. In fact, each tester was allowed first to use a technique and then, systematically, was asked to evaluate it by using a questionnaire. No time limit was imposed on the participant when using the technique; each user's interaction was observed to collect all the possible impressions of their experience. The participants were also asked to think aloud, describing their intentions and possible difficulties. In the same way, no time limit was imposed on the completion of the proposed questionnaire. However, the users were asked to record the answer to each item as quickly as possible, rather than thinking about the questions for a long time.

To measure both the usability and the user's experience, we used five point Likert-scale questionnaires [14] structured to fulfill all of the criteria listed by

Fig. 4. View from the top of the dense environment used in the experiment. Green and Read cylinders indicate respectively the start viewpoint position and target position to reach.

Uebersax [22]. The participants answered the questions using a scale from 1 (very low) to 5 (very high). In detail, the users were asked to complete the System Usability Scale (SUS) [7], which allows you to obtain a rapid evaluation of the techniques expressed as a single number which ranges from 0 to 100.

4.5   Results and Discussion

Almost all subjects complained of an initial difficulty in coordinating their head and hand movements during the travel where even a small rotation of the head causes a loss of the contact between the synthetic finger and the widget. However, these problems were quickly solved after the initial training before the trials. In the same way, two of the subjects reported, after a few minutes of use, a light dizziness that also disappeared during the initial training.

In relation to the techniques, the first consideration we received was related to the visual controls of the four head direction steering techniques. In fact, most of the subjects considered the four arrows visualized in their FOV a disturbing factor, revealing, at the same time, a preference for the simpler control (a single arrow allowing only forward movements) proposed in the head direction steering techniques. In more details, the four head direction steering was considering only partially useful to complete the proposed trial. Considering the three further directions offered, the subjects gave different evaluations; only the backward direction was considered an improvement for the traveling in order to reach the goal position while the left and right directions were evaluated as unnecessary or easily replaceable with a sequence of other movements.

In contrast, the opportunity of controlling the travel velocity was accepted with enthusiasm by almost all subjects. In fact, despite some initial difficulties in coordinating the steering and velocity, the subjects significantly exploited this opportunity to rapidly move among the city streets in order to first find and then reach the target position.

Finally, the evaluation showed that the head direction steering technique was the most appreciated by all the users, because of its ease of use and the reduced occlusion of the view. The presence of a single arrow with which to interact, according to the subjects, simplifies the interface and allows you to see the surrounding environment without occlusions. However, the backward traveling present in the four head direction steering technique was frequently mentioned in the subjects' comments during the trials because it was considered very useful in achieving the objective.

These observations were also confirmed by the results of the SUS questionnaire. The average SUS score, whose values can range from 0 to 100, was 67.51 for the head direction steering without velocity control, 70.62 for the head direction steering with velocity control, 62.33 for the four head direction steering without velocity control, and 63.12 for the four head direction steering with velocity control.

5   Conclusion

Wearable VR technologies are rapidly evolving. Many start-up companies are going to release low-cost, wearable VR technologies that have the potential to enter into everyday life. However, a challenge still open is the design of 3D navigation techniques that do not force the user to wear or handle any device. In this paper, we have detailed the design of two traveling techniques for wearable VR systems, which are based on an interaction that mixes widgets with free-hand gestures. We have also described the results of a preliminary usability evaluation, which showed that users prefer simple techniques rather than more powerful, but complex techniques. The results also indicated the velocity control is an important feature in performing navigation tasks. Our work will focus on improving the travel techniques in ego vision by following the user's preferences and then on carrying out a quantitative evaluation of these techniques with a larger group of users.

References

1. Google cardboard. https://www.google.com/get/cardboard/
2. Microsoft kinect. https://www.microsoft.com/en-us/kinectforwindows/
3. Virtuix omni. http://www.virtuix.com/
4. Bowman, D.A., Koller, D., Hodges, L.: Travel in immersive virtual environments: an evaluation of viewpoint motion control techniques. In: Virtual Reality Annual International Symposium, 1997, 1997, vol. 215, pp. 45–52. IEEE March 1997
5. Bowman, D.A., Kruijff, E., LaViola, J.J., Poupyrev, I.: An introduction to 3-d user interface design. Presence: Teleoper. Virtual Environ. **10**(1), 96–108 (2001)
6. Bowman, D.A., Kruijff, E., LaViola Jr., J.J., Poupyrev, I.: 3D user interfaces: theory and practice. Addison-Wesley, Boston (2004)
7. Brooke, J.: Sus: a quick and dirty usability scale. In: Jordan, P.W., Weerdmeester, B., Thomas, A., Mclelland, I.L. (eds.) Usability evaluation in industry. Taylor and Francis, London (1996)

8. Caggianese, G., Neroni, P., Gallo, L.: Natural interaction and wearable augment-edreality for the enjoyment of the cultural heritage in outdoor conditions. In: De Paolis, L.T., Mongelli, A. (eds.) AVR 2014. LNCS, vol. 8853, pp. 267–282. Springer, Heidelberg (2014)

9. Chance, S.S., Gaunet, F., Beall, A.C., Loomis, J.M.: Locomotion mode affects the updating of objects encountered during travel: the contribution of vestibular and proprioceptive inputs to path integration. Presence: Teleoper. Virtual Environ. **7**(2), 168–178 (1998)

10. Dam, P., Braz, P., Raposo, A.: A study of navigation and selection techniques in virtual environments using microsoft kinect®. In: Shumaker, R. (ed.) VAMR 2013. LNCS, vol. 8021, pp. 139–148. Springer, Berlin, Heidelberg (2013)

11. Dam, P.F., Carvalho, F.G., Braz, P., Raposo, A.B., Haas, A.: Hands-free inter-action techniques for virtual environments. In: Symposium on Virtual and Aug-mented Reality, pp. 100–108 (2013)

12. Deligiannidis, L., Larkin, J.: Navigating inexpensively and wirelessly. In: 2008 Con-ference on Human System Interactions, pp. 165–169, May 2008

13. Lee, M., Billinghurst, M., Baek, W., Green, R., Woo, W.: A usability study of multimodal input in an augmented reality environment. Virtual Reality **17**(4), 293–305 (2013)

14. Likert, R.: A technique for the measurement of attitudes. Archives Psychol. **22**, 1–55 (1932)

15. Medina, E., Fruland, R., Weghorst, S.: Virtusphere: Walking in a human size VR hamster ball. In: Proceedings of the Human Factors and Ergonomics Soci-ety Annual Meeting, vol. 52(27), pp. 2102–2106 (2008)

16. Mine, M.R.: Virtual environment interaction techniques. Technical report (1995)

17. Park, G., Ha, T., Woo, W.: Hand tracking with a near-range depth camera for virtual object manipulation in an wearable augmented reality. In: Shumaker, R., Lackey, S. (eds.) VAMR 2014, Part I. LNCS, vol. 8525, pp. 396–405. Springer, Heidelberg (2014)

18. Pietroni, E., Ray, C., Rufa, C., Pletinckx, D., Van Kampen, I.: Natural interaction in VR environments for cultural heritage and its impact inside museums: the etr-uscanning project. In: 2012 18th International Conference on Virtual Systems and Multimedia (VSMM), pp. 339–346, September 2012

19. Razzaque, S., Swapp, D., Slater, M., Whitton, M.C., Steed, A.: Redirected walking in place. In: Proceedings of the Workshop on Virtual Environments 2002, EGVE 2002, pp. 123–130. Eurographics Association (2002)

20. Ren, G., Li, C., O'Neill, E., Willis, P.: 3D freehand gestural navigation for inter-active public displays. IEEE Comput. Graph. Appl. **33**(2), 47–55 (2013)

21. Templeman, J.N., Denbrook, P.S., Sibert, L.E.: Virtual locomotion: walking in place through virtual environments. Presence: Teleoper. Virtual Environ. **8**(6), 598–617 (1999)

22. Uebersax, J.S.: Likert scales: dispelling the confusion. http://www.john-uebersax.com/stat/likert.htm

23. Usoh, M., Arthur, K., Whitton, M.C., Bastos, R., Steed, A., Slater, M., Brooks Jr., F.P.: Walking > walking-in-place > flying, in virtual environments. In: Proceedings of the 26th Annual Conference on Computer Graphics and Interactive Techniques, SIGGRAPH 1999, pp. 359–364. ACM Press/Addison-Wesley Publishing Co. (1999)

24. Vaughan-Nichols, S.: Game-console makers battle over motion-sensitive controllers. Computer **42**(8), 13–15 (2009)

Perception of Basic Emotions from Facial Expressions of Dynamic Virtual Avatars

Claudia Faita(✉), Federico Vanni, Cristian Lorenzini, Marcello Carrozzino, Camilla Tanca, and Massimo Bergamasco

PERCRO Perceptual Robotics Laboratory, Institute of Communication Information and Perception Technologies, Scuola Superiore Sant'Anna, Pisa, Italy
{c.faita,f.vanni,c.lorenzini,m.carrozzino,c.tanca,m.bergamasco}@sssup.it

Abstract. Virtual Reality experiences featuring realistic Virtual Humans with convincing facial expressions are a useful tool to improve social skill in humans. For this reason several investigations have been carried out on the recognition of virtual avatar emotions, based on dynamic and static facial cues originated by basic emotions developed by Ekman. Dynamism and realism of facial expressions are both important aspects of the process of face-to-face interaction in everyday life. In this paper we present the results of a research aiming at investigating the impact of the combination of dynamic facial expressions corresponding to particular emotions with a high level of realism of virtual faces. A study where we have measured the level of intensity in the correspondence between facial expressions of virtual avatars and emotional stimuli perceived by an observer was carried out on two groups of participants with different expertise in Virtual Reality. Results show a high level of intensity in this correspondence in both groups through the evaluation of two variables: time response and the score assigned to each emotion. We suggest that the use of dynamic virtual avatars offers advantages for studying emotion recognition in a face in that they recreate a realistic stimuli in emotion research.

Keywords: Avatar · Dynamic virtual avatar · Virtual Reality · Facial expression · 3d character · Emotion perception · Face perception · Dynamic emotion · Basic emotion

1 Introduction

Facial expressions are one of the most important form of nonverbal communication, being one of the more immediate channels of social interaction between humans. Many previous investigations suggest that human faces, through the activation of certain muscle movements, convey specific emotions in a universal way. According to this theory, the psychologist Paul Ekman developed the idea that there is a universal connection between facial expressions of emotion and the corresponding emotional states [1]. Ekman opposed the idea that culture and learning processes shape the way in which emotions are perceived in the

© Springer International Publishing Switzerland 2015
L.T. De Paolis and A. Mongelli (Eds.): AVR 2015, LNCS 9254, pp. 409–419, 2015.
DOI: 10.1007/978-3-319-22888-4_30

facial expressions [2], rather arguing the existence of six universal basic emotions (happiness, sadness, anger, fear, disgust and surprise) [3]. This theory has been supported by several experiments based on the use of static and isolated pictures of faces, proving that humans are able to distinguish the different features of expressions characterizing emotions [4,5]. Based on this approach in 1978 a system to taxonomize facial movements, called Facial Action Coding System (FACS) [6], was developed.

However, the use of fixed photographs was a limitation in the ecological validity of such research line, because they did not reproduce the vividness and the true shape of the faces that humans encounter in everyday life. In fact, in face-to-face interactions the observer does not simply decode the emotional message, but needs also to understand the way in which emotions are processed. In [7] it is showed that emotions in moving faces were significantly better recognized than in still faces.

In the latest few years the interest in reproducing the inherent dynamism of natural face expressions by animating 3d virtual avatars has grown. Several studies focused on the similarity between the recognition of emotions in virtual and real faces and found significant correlations [8]. The use of virtual faces constitutes a major advantage over movie clips since the former can be adapted and tuned, even in real-time, according to different purposes. Moreover, Virtual Reality (VR) systems featuring animated realistic avatars conveying emotions are useful tools to improve interpersonal communication in people suffering from emotional and behavioral disorders [9].

Starting from the characteristics of the muscular activity identified in FACS, 3d animated virtual faces have been evaluated in many experiments [8,10,11]. However, these studies did not pay attention to the level of realism of virtual faces and to its combination with the dynamism of the delivered facial stimuli. In order to take this factor into account, we have conducted a study in which highly realistic virtual avatars were dynamically animated by triggering the real facial emotional expressions of an actor who imitates the basic emotions developed by Ekman. The aim of this research was to create Dynamic Virtual Avatars (DVAs) reproducing vividness and intensity of facial emotions in a life-like way. For this purpose, an experiment aimed at investigating the accuracy of the correspondence between facial expressions of DVAs and basic emotional stimuli perceived by an observer was carried out. Five out of the six basic emotional expressions identified by Ekman were used: Anger, Disgust, Fear, Happiness and Sadness, to which we added the Neutral expression (Fig. 1). We will refer from now on to this set of emotions as {EKMAN+N}. Surprise was excluded following previous studies which did not always consider surprise among the basic emotions [12], and because surprise can often be confused with the expression of fear, as explained in [1,12].

Based on the results of this experiment DVAs will be integrated in different immersive Virtual Environments (VEs), in order to create a strong face-to-face interaction between the human and the avatar for investigating emotion recognition in controlled experimental environments which keep similarity to daily life conditions.

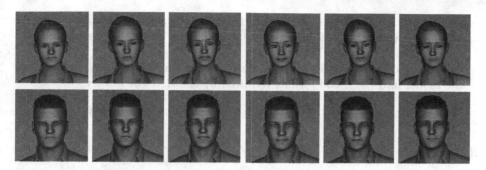

Fig. 1. Basic facial emotions of DVAs plus the neutral one to the experiment participants during their trials. From left to right the facial expressions were labeled as anger,
disgust, fear, happiness, neutral and sadness.

2   Apparatus for Facial Stimuli

The experiment is based on a VR application developed by using the XVR technology [13], a framework internally developed, able to allow an easy deployment
of VR applications to a range of VR devices such as screens, CAVE-like environments and Head-Mounted Displays (HMDs). The XVR application in our
experiment shows a VE with an avatar featuring a sequence of facial expressions. The sequences of avatars and their facial expressions are randomly generated at startup, granting the correct number of repetitions for each avatar and
each expression. These animations exploit an hardware accelerated library for
real-time character animation (HALCA) [14]. HALCA uses the Cal3D^{TM} file format to describe skeleton-weighted meshes, animations and materials. The core
of HALCA consists of a motion mixer and an avatar visualization engine and
allows to animate and visualize realistic characters on different platforms, including XVR. HALCA was selected because it extends Cal3D^{TM} abstract mixer class
by adding functionality to play, morph and blend animations, and in addition to
directly access and modify the state of the whole or parts of the avatars skeleton
efficiently. The combination XVR+HALCA has been already used to generate
immersive VEs with animated avatars [15] which, however, lacked convincing
facial features. The two 3D models of virtual humans (one male, one female)
have been selected within the Rocketbox library (www.rocketbox-libraries.com).
These avatars have been animated using Faceshift studio (www.faceshift.com), a
tool for high quality markerless motion capture which uses Microsoft Kinect sensor [16,17]. The software also provides a plugin to bind the animations recorded
to a custom model, both using morphtarget or, as in our case, facial bones.

   The pipeline of our acquisition consists in:

- recording the desired animations starting from a neutral expression, miming
  Ekman expressions [6], and exporting them in the binary Faceshift format
  (FSB);

- using Autodesk Maya and its Faceshift plugin to import FSB motion capture data, and export the model animated into the FBX format to be subsequently imported in Autodesk 3d Studio Max;
- using Autodesk 3d Studio Max to clean animation noise, if any, and export the model into the Cal3d format required by the HALCA library.

In Fig. 1 it is shown the result of the procedure described above.

3   Materials and Methods

The aim of the present study is to investigate the correspondence between DVAs facial expressions related to a set of basic emotions and perception of such emotions by an observer. This correspondence has been evaluated in terms of the intensity of the perceived emotion. For this purpose, we set up an experiment in which participants must associate a score from 1 to 5 to each of the {EKMAN+N} emotions after seeing a particular expression rendered on the avatar face. In this section the selection of participants and the experimental procedure are explained; then, measures, data analysis and results are described.

3.1   Participants

16 subjects were recruited for this study (7 females and 9 males), aged $29.75 \pm 5.51 y.o.$ with a level of education equal or higher than the bachelor degree. Participants read and signed an informed consent in which the experiment was briefly explained, and took a questionnaire used to collect their self-evaluated experience on a 5-point Likert scale in the use of computer (average 4.87 ± 0.34), video-games (average 2.56 ± 1.03) and VR (average 2.5 ± 1.55). Based on this information the sample was divided in two groups which differed in the experience in the use of VR: Expert Group (Exp) scoring a medium-to-high self-assessed experience (average 3.75 ± 1.16) and a Lay Group (Lay) scoring a low-to-very-low level of experience (average 1.25 ± 0.46).

3.2   Procedure

Prior to the experiment, the experimenter provided each subject with a detailed outline of the experimental session. At the beginning of the experiment, in order to assess their momentary affect state, participants also compiled the Italian version of the Positive and Negative Affect Schedule (PANAS) validated by Terraciano et al. [18]. It is a 20-item self-report questionnaire that measures positive and negative affective state at the present moment yielding two separate scores [19]. Then, participants were located in front of a 17-inch computer laptop, at a distance of 60 cm from its screen, and when they felt ready the experimenter started the application as shown in Fig. 2.

Participants viewed 24 facial animations extracted from the {EKMAN+N} set, as shown in Fig. 1. Such animations were randomly displayed in two cycles of

Fig. 2. Experimental setup. A participant is performing the task in the experimental room.

12, shown on a male avatar and on a female avatar. Each emotion-laden animation lasted 5 second, starting with a 1-second neutral expression and following with a 4-second target emotional expression. The Neutral expression remained stationary for the entire 5-second period. After each animation ended, a screen showing a list of six labels corresponding to the names of the emotions in the {EKMAN+N} set appeared, associated with a scale from 1-No correspondence to 5-Maximum correspondence was displayed as shown in Fig. 3. Participants' task was to assign a score rating the correspondence between each emotion in the {EKMAN+N} set and the emotion they perceived in the facial expression just displayed. The six labels were randomly rearranged on the screen by the system at each trial.

3.3 Measures

PANAS was used as a self-report questionnaire to assess the momentary positive and negative affect state of participants when undertaking the experiment.

The main question we have investigated is whether the animated virtual faces displayed in the experiment were capable of conveying the basic emotions that are recognised by adult human observers. For this purpose, we analysed observations of two variables. First, the time T_{resp} taken for rating on the 5-point scale the accordance of each basic emotion and neutrality with the displayed expression. This is a measure of how difficult it was for participants to perceive basic emotions from the virtual faces. Second, we studied the scores S_{expr} assigned to rate how much the displayed emotion was concordant with the intended basic emotion or with no emotion. This measure was meant as an indicator of the intensity of the emotion perceived by participants.

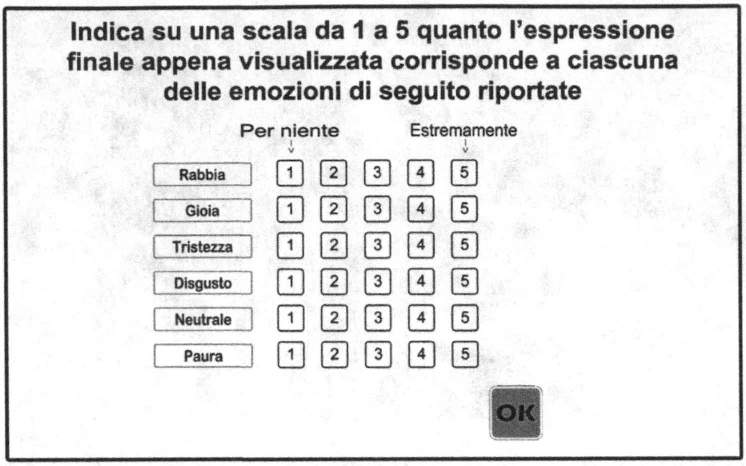

Fig. 3. Screen visualized after each animation. Participants should assign a score to each emotion plus the neutral one, rating the level of correspondence between the emotion perceived in the DVA facial expression just visualized and the emotions labeled in the {EKMAN+N} set. The options on the screen are in Italian because all participants were Italian native speakers.

3.4 Data Analysis

Data collected were organized by considering two experimental factors: Group and Expression. Group had two levels – Expert and Lay – and was a between-subject factor. Expression represented the facial expression displayed on the avatar face and had the six levels of the {EKMAN+N} set. Expression was a within-subject factor.

The two dependent variables extracted from the data were the means of T_{resp} and S_{expr} for each participant and for each displayed emotion across animation trials. The effects of Group and Expression on such variables were investigated. In the light of the comparatively small number of observations, randomization tests [20] with 1000 permutations and F-statistic computations were carried out. *Post-hoc* tests for multiple comparisons between the levels of Expression were carried out using the t-test and adjusting p-values by controlling the false discovery rate according to [21].

3.5 Results

The two groups, Exp and Lay, did not differ for their momentary affective state as measured by the PANAS, and their scores were similar to those found in the general population [19]. The Exp group showed a Positive Affect score of 32.88 ± 5.96 and a Negative Affect score of 14.38 ± 3.16, while the Lay group showed 33.88 ± 3.36 and 15.88 ± 5.84 respectively.

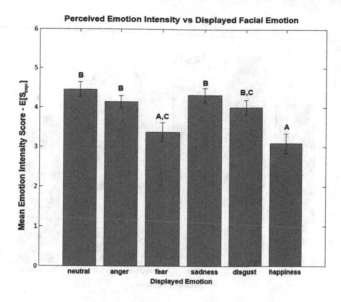

Fig. 4. Mean score $E[S_{resp}]$ computed as the average of the mean scores assigned by each participant to rate the correspondence between the dynamic facial expression shown by the avatars and the intended basic emotion or neutral expression. The standard deviation is shown over the bars. Capital letters (A, B and C) are used to summarise statistical outcomes of multiple comparisons: letters shared in common between conditions denote no significant difference.

Permutation tests yielded no significant effect of Group and no significant interaction between Group and Expression on both T_{resp} and S_{expr}. Rather, a significant main effect of Expression emerged on both T_{resp} ($p < 0.05$) and S_{expr} ($p < 10^{-3}$). Observed means with indication of the significantly different conditions are reported in Figs. 4 and 5. The *post-hoc* tests on T_{resp} yielded a significant difference ($p(FDR) = 0.015$) only between the Anger and Happiness conditions, with the mean response time for rating Anger (19.23 ± 2.084 s) higher than the mean response time taken to rate Happiness (13.55 ± 1.148 s). This seems to suggest that Happiness was easier than Anger to be recognised on the virtual faces shown in he experiment. *Post-hoc* multiple comparisons applied to the mean of S_{expr} returned several statistically significant differences between expressions (Fig. 4). Again, Happiness appears outstanding, as its correspondence to the virtual facial expression is scored 3.094 ± 0.246, which is significantly lower than for all other basic emotions except Fear and lower than the score for the Neutral expression ($p(FDR) \leq 0.01$). Other statistically significant differences in scores were found between Fear and all other expressions, but Disgust and Happiness. The mean score observed for Fear was 3.375 ± 0.238, which was significantly lower ($p(FDR) \leq 0.05$) than the mean scores for Neutral, Anger and Sadness.

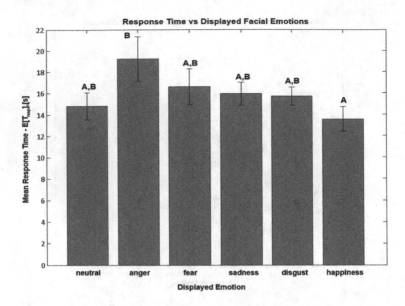

Fig. 5. Mean time $E[T_{resp}]$ computed as the average of the mean time taken by each participant to rate the correspondence between the dynamic facial expressions and all the emotions in the {EKMAN+N} set. The standard deviation is shown over the bars. Capital letters (A and B) are used to summarise statistical outcomes of multiple comparisons: letters shared in common between conditions denote no significant difference.

4   Discussion

In this research we have evaluated the ability of DVAs to induce the perception of basic emotions in an observer. Based on the correspondence between the intended emotion expressed by avatars faces and the score assigned by participants to a set of basic emotions, the level of intensity for each emotion was evaluated. To this goal, two variables were considered: T_{resp}, i.e. the time taken by participants to rate each facial expression concordance with the chosen basic emotions and the neutral expression, and S_{expr}, i.e. the score assigned by participants as a rate of correspondence between the intended basic emotion and the facial expression displayed in each animation visualized.

As for T_{resp} one would assume that the familiarity with VR could facilitate the ability to recognize basic emotions in avatars faces because of the experience with the appearance of the virtual characters. Rather, the results showed no statistical difference between Lay and Expert groups in time performance. This finding suggests that the perception of basic emotions in the DVAs faces is not affected by observers familiarity with VR.

Instead, the results showed a significant difference in the response time for each facial emotion visualized. In particular, participants labeled the expression of anger after the longest time, mean of $T_{resp} = 19.23\,\mathrm{s} \pm 2.084\,\mathrm{s}$, while the expression of happiness obtained the best time performance, $T_{resp} = 13.54\,\text{s} \pm$ 1.148 s. The *Post-hoc* test indicated a relevant difference between the above-mentioned emotions. However, based on the second variable analyzed S_{expr}, the rate assigned to the happy face was the lowest as it can be seen in Fig. 5. This may be not completely in line with previous research which showed that happiness is usually recognized with a high level of accuracy and intensity [8]. Moreover, the result showed that the score assigned to the happy face is lower than the score assigned to each of the other emotions, and this difference was statistically significant. It might seem surprising that happy face obtained the best time performance and the lowest rate in perceptual performance. However, we assume that the presence of four out of five negative emotion expressions (anger, disgust, fear and sadness Versus happiness) may have a negative impact on the mood of the participants. Accordingly, the observers perceived a lower level of intensity in the single positive emotion visualized. To further examine this relationship both balance and a displacement between positive and negative facial emotions should be evaluated in future studies.

The higher score was obtained by the neutral face with a mean of $S_{expr} = 4.453 \pm 0.187$. The tendency to give a high rate to a neutral face may depend on the fact that participants were clearly instructed about the chance to meet a face showing no emotional expression. Previous research [10] showed a high pattern of errors in the recognition of neutral expressions in avatar faces, but did not detect confusion between the neutral and completely different emotions; they explained this result inferring the tendency to rate a face as neutral when people are unsure about the emotion expressed. In the experimental procedure, in order to avoid this behavior users were invited to choose neutrality only when they actually detected no emotional expression in DVAs.

A surprising result is the high mean in the score assigned to disgust $S_{expr} = 4 \pm 0.19$. Almost all studies on the perception of basic emotions in virtual avatar faces have showed a certain difficulty in conveying disgust expressions with avatars, because of a wrinkling at the base of the nose that is mechanically difficult to recreate [8, 10, 22, 23]. [8, 10] showed that disgust was the only emotion that could not achieve a satisfying recognition rate in virtual faces. All these studies created facial expressions by modeling the animation of the different muscular units of the virtual character, starting from a static expression extracted from FACS. In our research DVAs were animated through the direct acquisition of a hyper-realistic imitation performed by an actor who has amplified the emotional value of the emotions through his face expressions. We suggest that this methodology may have increased the emotional salience of disgusting facial stimuli as shown in the score assigned to disgust. For the other facial expressions the scores obtained were high and in line with the rate evaluated in previous studies [8, 10].

5   Conclusions and Future Work

The findings of data analysis showed a high level of intensity assigned to each emotion in correspondence with the same facial emotion displayed in DVAs. We suggest that these results depend on two characteristics of DVAs:

– the dynamism of the animation,
– the high level of avatar realism.

This reflects previous studies which explained that the dynamism of facial expressions increases the performance in the recognition of basic emotions [9,10]. The positive impact of the realism of human-like faces on user experiences in interfaces has been also previously shown [24]. The importance of combination of these findings is reflected in the usefulness of the virtual avatars to investigate the process of emotion recognition in faces. We suggest that the level of intensity of facial emotions can be more naturally calibrated by using dynamic facial expressions acquired from real ones. Thus DVAs with different emotional salience can be used for assessing the ability of emotion recognition also in patients with a lack or absence of cognitive skills in social relation, as with schizophrenia or autism.

In the future the present research will be improved as follows: - in order to strengthen the statistical findings of this study, the experiment will be evaluated with a greater number of participants; - we will investigate different levels of intensity in the basic emotional expressions in order to create a library of facial emotions for social interaction research. Moreover, DVAs will be integrated in an immersive virtual scenario. In this condition it will be extremely interesting to measure how convincing DVAs impact on the perceived presence [25] and, conversely, the impact of highly immersive VEs on the emotion recognition.

References

1. Ekman, P., Friesen, W.V.: Constants across cultures in the face and emotion. J. Pers. Soc. Psychol. **17**(2), 124 (1971)
2. Mead, M.: Visual anthropology in a discipline of words. Principles of Vis. Anthropol. **3**, 3–12 (1975)
3. Ekman, P.: Are there basic emotions? Psychol. Rev. **99**, 550–553 (1992)
4. Adolphs, R.: Recognizing emotion from facial expressions: psychological and neurological mechanisms. Behav. Cogn. Neurosci. Rev. **1**(1), 21–62 (2002)
5. Leppänen, J.M., Hietanen, J.K.: Positive facial expressions are recognized faster than negative facial expressions, but why? Psychol. Res. **69**(1–2), 22–29 (2004)
6. Ekman, P., Friesen, W.V.: Facial Action Coding System: A Technique for the Measurement of Facial Movement. Consulting Psychologists Press, Palo Alto (1978)
7. Knight, B., Johnston, A.: The role of movement in face recognition. Vis. Cogn. **4**(3), 265–273 (1997)
8. Spencer-Smith, J., Wild, H., Innes-Ker, Å.H., Townsend, J., Duffy, C., Edwards, C., Ervin, K., Merritt, N., Pair, J.W.: Making faces: creating three-dimensional parameterized models of facial expression. Behav. Res. Meth., Instrum. Comput. **33**(2), 115–123 (2001)
9. Gutiérrez-Maldonado, J., Rus-Calafell, M., González-Conde, J.: Creation of a new set of dynamic virtual reality faces for the assessment and training of facial emotion recognition ability. Virtual Reality **18**(1), 61–71 (2014)
10. Dyck, M., Winbeck, M., Leiberg, S., Chen, Y., Gur, R.C., Mathiak, K.: Recognition profile of emotions in natural and virtual faces. PLoS One **3**(11), e3628 (2008)

11. Fabri, M., Moore, D., Hobbs, D.: Mediating the expression of emotion in educational collaborative virtual environments: an experimental study. Virtual Reality **7**(2), 66–81 (2004)
12. Ekman, P.: Facial expressions. Handb. Cogn. Emot. **53**, 226–232 (1999)
13. Carrozzino, M., Tecchia, F., Bacinelli, S., Cappelletti, C., Bergamasco, M.: Lowering the development time of multimodal interactive application: the real-life experience of the xvr project. In: Proceedings of the 2005 ACM SIGCHI International Conference on Advances in Computer Entertainment Technology, pp. 270–273. ACM (2005)
14. Gillies, M., Spanlang, B.: Comparing and evaluating real time character engines for virtual environments. Presence: Teleoperators Virtual Environ. **19**(2), 95–117 (2010)
15. Normand, J.-M., Spanlang, B., Tecchia, F., Carrozzino, M., Swapp, D., Slater, M.: Full body acting rehearsal in a networked virtual environmenta case study. Presence: Teleoperators Virtual Environ. **21**(2), 229–243 (2012)
16. Weise, T., Bouaziz, S., Li, H., Pauly, M.: Realtime performance-based facial animation. ACM Trans. Graph. (TOG) **30**(4), 77 (2011). ACM
17. Bouaziz, S., Wang, Y., Pauly, M.: Online modeling for realtime facial animation. ACM Trans. Graph. (TOG) **32**(4), 40 (2013)
18. Terraciano, A., McCrae, R.R., Costa Jr., P.T.: Factorial and construct validity of the italian positive and negative affect schedule (panas). Eur. J. Psychol. Assess. **19**(2), 131 (2003)
19. Watson, D., Clark, L.A., Tellegen, A.: Development and validation of brief measures of positive and negative affect: the panas scales. J. Pers. Soc. Psychol. **54**(6), 1063 (1988)
20. Manly, B.F.: Randomization, Bootstrap and Monte Carlo Methods in Biology, vol. 70. CRC Press, Boca Raton (2006)
21. Benjamini, Y., Hochberg, Y.: Controlling the false discovery rate: a practical and powerful approach to multiple testing. J. Roy. Stat. Soc. Ser. B (Methodol.) **57**(1), 289–300 (1995)
22. Kohler, C.G., Turner, T.H., Bilker, W.B., Brensinger, C.M., Siegel, S.J., Kanes, S.J., Gur, R.E., Gur, R.C.: Facial emotion recognition in schizophrenia: intensity effects and error pattern. Am. J. Psychiatry **160**(10), 1768–1774 (2003)
23. Moser, E., Derntl, B., Robinson, S., Fink, B., Gur, R.C., Grammer, K.: Amygdala activation at 3t in response to human and avatar facial expressions of emotions. J. Neurosci. Meth. **161**(1), 126–133 (2007)
24. Yee, N., Bailenson, J.N., Rickertsen, K.: A meta-analysis of the impact of the inclusion and realism of human-like faces on user experiences in interfaces. In: Proceedings of the SIGCHI Conference on Human Factors in Computing Systems, pp. 1–10. ACM (2007)
25. Slater, M., Frisoli, A., Tecchia, F., Guger, C., Lotto, B., Steed, A., Pfurtscheller, G., Leeb, R., Reiner, M., Sanchez-Vives, M.V., et al.: Understanding and realizing presence in the presenccia project. IEEE Comput. Graph. Appl. **27**(4), 90–93 (2007)

Bridging Offline and Online World Through Augmentable Smart Glass Interfaces

Zulqarnain Rashid[1]([✉]), Joan Melià-Seguí[2], and Rafael Pous[1]

[1] Department of Information and Communication Technologies,
Universitat Pompeu Fabra, Barcelona, Spain
{zulqarnain,rafael.pous}@upf.edu
[2] Estudis d'Informàtica, Multimèdia i Telecomunicació Internet Interdisciplinary Institute (IN3),
Universitat Oberta de Catalunya, Barcelona, Spain
melia@uoc.edu

Abstract. Online shopping is gaining momentum over offline shopping. Online shopping offers more features and engaging experience as compared to offline one. Bridging online features to brick-and-mortar shopping would benefit user experience. We propose Augmented Reality interfaces developed for smart glass, linked to a physical Smart Space to bridge offline and online world. Empirical testing in the laboratory demonstrates that the user is able to interact with the products in the physical spaces while having access to all the online shopping features. System is tested and validated with 150 tagged products at Radio Frequency based smart shelf, achieving 99 % accuracy in product identification.

Keywords: Augmented reality · Smart glass · RFID · Intelligent interfaces · Human computer interaction · Ubiquitous computing

1 Introduction

Nowadays online sales are growing rapidly over brick and mortar sales [6, 7]. Moreover, retailers and overall companies are experiencing difficulties to engage and support customers at physical locations. Users report online shopping to be more engaging and provide more satisfaction [7], compared with brick-and-mortar shopping which is traditionally disconnected from the online world. However, there is an ongoing trend among companies to distribute products and services using Omni -channel strategy, including brick-and-mortar (physical) stores and online portals. Multi-channel retailing has currently experienced a significant growth [16]. Hence, there is the need for convergence between online shopping and offline retail stores [1], making shopping connected, social, engaging and fun.

Nevertheless, the physical point of sale will remain focal and strategic, as it is the main point of contact between brands and customers. Many individuals visit the store or commercial spaces without really purchasing any item. The purpose of visiting the store can be to entertain, enjoy, spend time, socialize or simply because they like the ability to see and touch items before purchasing them [16]. Future generation shopping will happen at physical locations like store or super markets, but with complete connectivity to online services as well [6].

© Springer International Publishing Switzerland 2015
L.T. De Paolis and A. Mongelli (Eds.): AVR 2015, LNCS 9254, pp. 420–431, 2015.
DOI: 10.1007/978-3-319-22888-4_31

For instance, industry is experiencing the generalization of Heads-Up Display (HUD), commonly referred as Smart Glass. These devices can provide a valid approach to bridging offline and online world together thanks to Augmented Reality (AR), enhancing user perception in the real world by overlaying computer generated objects or information. Another ubiquitous technology example in retail is Radio Frequency Identification (RFID), which allows unassisted and automated objects identification, including inventory and product localization. RFID is usually implemented in stores in Smart Shelves, intelligent mirrors or point-of-sales [1]. RFID turns the shelves into a Smart Space by which all the items present on the shelf can be inventoried, localized, also measuring interactions with customers.

In order to improve online and offline convergence we propose to combine Smart Glass and RFID technologies. The main goal is to let users browse products in a brick-and-mortar store while obtaining the same in-depth information about them one would expect from browsing about the same products in an online store. Instead of clicking on a screen, users select the objects by means of cricking [1], which seeks to provide a user experience similar to that of clicking, but on the brick-and-mortar physical space.

We present in this paper a practical implementation of our proposed system, achieving the following objectives:

- Development of a novel system comprised of HUD /Smart Glass, and smart shelf, enabling the user to browse and interact with the physical space.
- Dynamic contextualization of the items present in the physical space.
- Laboratory empirical experimentation.

After a certain period of time focusing on a specific shelf area, information is displayed on the Smart Glass as an AR interface. We have used AR markers to map the physical space coordinates, distance and orientation between users and shelf. Once items information is presented at Smart Glass, users are bridged from offline world to online. From the Smart Glass interface user can access online information about the items including price, size, user comments, etc. Item detection, localization, contextualization and presentation on the real environment through AR and RFID are performed on the smart glasses and smart spaces.

The remaining part of this paper is organized as follows: Sect. 2 introduces related work. Methodology is detailed in Sects. 3 and 4 describes a setup of system and pilot application while Results and Discussion is provided in Sect. 5. Finally, Sect. 6 closes the paper.

2 Related Work

Browsing physical space [3, 4] in context with retrieving online information related to physical objects is underway. Some of the major research contributions that enable browsing physical spaces with different technologies like augmented reality, wearable devices and RFID are proposed in [2]. The concept of *cricking* [1] allows clicking the physical spaces using pervasive technologies. Ishii and Ullmer [14] proposed the concept of Tangible Bits, pointing the way to the concept of using physical objects as an interface to access the digital world. Jun Rekimoto et al. [15] coined the term

Augmentable Reality and discussed the possibilities of using object IDs and locations to enrich an augmented reality application. Välkkyenn et al. [11] introduced the concept of Physical Browsing using a mobile terminal and RFID technology, but RFID was on the terminal, not on the physical space. Merrill and Maes [3] used specially designed electronic devices to turn everyday gestures such as looking, pointing or reaching into browsing mechanisms. Chen et al. [10] presented a similar system but using computer vision instead of RFID. Kahl et al. [12] presented an implementation of Dual Reality in a retail store using RFID among other technologies, but more oriented to measuring and managing than to provide an interface for shoppers. Kleiner and Schäfer [13] implemented an Augmented Shelf, based only on augmented reality and computer vision techniques. Recently B. Zhang et al. [18] presented a nice system that allows interacting with smart objects in physical space through Google Glass and IR controller but it has a limitation of infrared (IR) as an extra device and IR is not so common in retail industry.

Previously we have presented [19] an application for bridging online and offline scenario through Smart Glass tethered with Smart Phone and head beam light without AR interfaces.

In this paper we are presenting a standalone system based on Smart Glass AR interfaces. We propose to use AR Markers in shelves, in combination with RFID labels for object identification, since it is usually impossible to distinguish items with little or no apparent difference with feature tracking or computer graphics. Items that are hidden or not visible to the camera are also detectable by RFID, since RFID does not require direct line of sight.

3   Methodology and System Setup

Augmented Reality and RFID technologies are used to link offline objects to online features. Both technologies complement each other, RFID is becoming essential for retail because of numerous properties it offers, and AR allows enriching the user view by providing information about the environment. RFID inventories and localizes the products, and AR captures user position, orientation, and interaction, showing information on top of a real shelf. Next, we detail the building blocks of our proposed system.

3.1   Methodology

System overview is shown in Fig. 1. We divide the system into two main parts i.e. physical space that can also be called offline space, and AR interfaces that can be referred to as online world. In the physical world we have items equipped with RFID. The RFID system contains antennas connected through a multiplexer to the reader. The reader is then connected to the host controlling the RFID system. It inventories all the items present on the shelf and makes this shelf a Smart Space. In the Smart Space we have the information about the items present with their precise location. All the information about the items is then passed to the server through the RFID host. The second part referred to as online part that captures the user interaction. User interactions are being converted to the physical coordinates with the help of AR application.

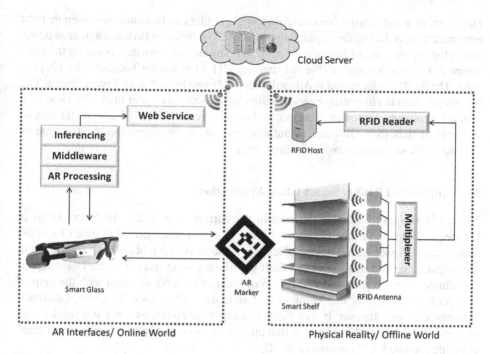

Cloud Server

Web Service

Inferencing

Middleware

AR Processing

Smart Glass

AR Marker

AR Interfaces/ Online World

RFID Reader

RFID Host

Multiplexer

RFID Antenna

Smart Shelf

Physical Reality/ Offline World

Fig. 1. System overview: In offline world RFID system inventories and localizes all the items present on the shelf and sends those to the server through RFID host, while in online world smart Glass application dynamically contextualize all the items by accessing the server and construct AR interfaces at user click location with the help of AR marker. Both offline world and online world are interconnected and synchronize in a real time.

After processing, these coordinates are passed to the server. AR application translates digital world coordinates obtained through user interaction to physical world coordinates. Both online world and offline world are interconnected through server and constantly being synchronized.

3.2 Physical Smart Space

Radio Frequency Identification (RFID) is becoming an essential part of retail industry because of properties it offers such as stock count, localization anti theft, etc. The tags contain electronically stored information. Unlike a bar code, the tag does not necessarily need to be within the line of sight of the reader, and may be embedded in the tracked object. RFID (location estimation) is a wireless technology used for automated identification, tracking and object localization by means of electronic labels. The tags contain electronically stored information acting as identifier. To turn a physical space into Smart Space an RFID system is used. RFID is getting an essential part of retailing due to the properties it offers i.e. inventorying, localization and theft prevention of products. Our target space is a group of shelves with number of products. Since there is no "a priori" information on where the products will be placed, the whole surface must be covered.

However, by using multiplexers only one single reader can be connected to up to 1024 antennas, thus, reducing the implementation cost. The distance between antennas determines the accuracy of the location information. The antennas are dependent on the shelf material. For wooden shelves the Advantenna-P11 from Keonn Technologies [20] are used. The RFID reader model is AdvanReader-100 also from Keonn Technologies. The system provides the inventory every minute with an accuracy better than 99 % (less than 1 in a 100 objects missed in average), and a space resolution of 25 cm. RFID tags of different models from different manufacturers were used, depending on the type of product, with an average cost of 5 Euro cents.

3.3 Augmented Reality Smart Glass Application

Vuzix M100 Smart Glass [17] is used in the current case. When the Smart Glass is focused or aimed to the shelf at particular location for certain period of time (3 s in the current case), it uses an AR marker placed on a known position of the shelf to determine the origin, scale and rotation of the shelf coordinates with respect to the Glass screen coordinates. The position and orientation of the user is also calculated with the help of AR marker. AR marker can be of variant size, depending upon the desired distance between shelf and the user. If user wants to keep more distance bigger size marker can be used. We are using 12 cm maker that allows user to stand up to 3.5 m far from shelf covering the 100 * 120 cm area of shelf.

When a user clicks, the coordinates of the corresponding shelf position are calculated by the AR system. Click is considered when user focuses or aims the same area for a certain period of time. A web service obtains a list of all the Electronic Product Code (EPC) codes that the RFID system has reported as located within a certain distance of such shelf position. A further web service call obtains the information and images of those objects, which are shown by the AR application on the screen. An area of interest referred as red square superimposed on the shelf live image indicates at all times the area about which the information is being shown.

Interactive images of the items are shown at the bottom of the screen, where the user can select the image of the product with a Smart Glass gesture, or voice interface to further explore the related information. The user can go to online stores with the particular product selection (i.e. Amazon, eBay, etc.) and can analyze product ratings and compare prices.

Augmented Reality Handheld Application. Smart Glass app is built on Android platform, so it can be run on any handheld device that supports Android operating system. The application is tested on an Android-enabled tablet, additionally giving user the option to click (touch) on the screen of handheld device as handheld devices has clickable screen and touch events to know the user click area. The user aims the camera of handheld device at the shelf so that the marker is visible on the screen. Then the user can click on any point on the live image of the shelf on the screen. Green square is placed at the click point, and interactive images of the items are shown at the bottom of the screen. As the user moves the screen, the green square continues to point at the same shelf locations, even though this shelf location moves around the screen (as long as the marker continues to be visible). If the user clicks on an item image, the available item information is shown on the screen. Figure 2 shows the screen shots of user interacting with the shelf through handheld device. This paper discusses Smart Glass Application in detail only.

Fig. 2. A: Handheld device pointing at the smart shelf, where the AR marker is visible. B: Close up view of the handheld screen, showing the superimposed item information, and the green square indicating the active area i.e. the user clicked location.

3.4   Internal System Implementation

The RFID system produces a list of the Electronic Product Codes (EPC) of every object on the shelf, and its approximate location, and stores it in a local computer. The EPC is the common standard used to identify objects with RFID. In its most common format it's a 96 bit number. Ultra High Frequency (UHF) RFID, defined in the Electronic Product Code Class 1 Gen2 (EPC Gen2), is de facto standard in retail. A database stores information about every possible product class (a.k.a. Stock-Keeping Unit - SKU), including their images. Every time a new object is added to the system, the EPC code of its RFID tag is added to the database, linking it to the particular product class. This way product information is normalized, stored only once per product class, even though many objects (product instances) of such product class are present. An inventory list, consisting of all the EPCs of the objects present on the shelf, together with their approximate locations is periodically uploaded to the database from the local computer of the RFID system. The cloud database is built using a Postgres DBMS.

We have divided the shelf into segments based on the RFID accuracy, each shelf segment is 25 * 25 cm. All the items present within one segment will be regarded as one location. The identification of different segments of shelf is done through transformation matrix and Metaio SDK [5] build on android operating system. Vuzix Smart Glass supports both Metaio SDK and Android SDK.

A red square is drawn in the center of the Smart Glass screen in order to give user the focus area, once the user keep the specific area of shelf under red square it is considered as user area of interest and click location, Always the center of the screen pixels i.e. mid of screen are passed to the AR SDK in order to calculate the X, Y and Z coordinates on the real plane i.e. shelf. Once user's areas of interest coordinates are calculated, a number of products that are present at that X, Y and Z coordinates are inquired by the RFID system. The RFID system inventories and localizes the products in terms of their X, Y and Z coordinates in a cyclic manner. In this way both AR system and RFID are collaborating with each other by synchronizing and sharing the coordinates of the products through a server in a real time.

A web service returns the list of all objects which are reported by the RFID system to be within 25 cm of the calculated coordinates. Another web service call obtains all the information available about the objects, including the images. Since the products used are DVDs and CDs, the images of the set of products are presented with "Interact able Cover Flow" interface at the bottom of the Smart Glass screen. User can interact and scroll the products images in the horizontal and vertical direction with the help of gesture control provided by Vuzix Glasses. The information can be seen by interacting the images are category, price, comments and ratings etc.

4   Pilot Application: Virtual Shop

As a pilot application for testing the system, we have implemented a Virtual Shop in a university department. The Virtual Shop simulates the real shop or super market environment with shelves full of products.

Figure 3 shows overall working system at Virtual Shop. The overall height of the shelves is 200 cm and width is 240 cm. We regard these groups of shelves as one shelf. In order to cover the whole surface a RFID antenna is placed at every 25 cm distance both in horizontal and vertical direction, so 16 rows of 8 antennas were used. Since the reader only has 4 antenna ports, 8 1-to-8 multiplexers AdvanMux-8 are used. 4 AR Markers of 12 cm are used to map the whole physical surface of shelf to the smart glass screen coordinates. These markers are detectable up to 3.5 m distance from the shelf. 150 RFID tagged products i.e. CD's and DVD's are placed at the different locations of the shelf with different placement, some are stacked and cover is visible to the user and some with cover not visible to the user as RFID detects all the item without being in line of sight. User is given Glasses to aim or focus at any point or location on the shelf for at least 3 s (click time- adjustable). When the user aims at particular point on the shelf for three continuous seconds, the information about the products present at that specific location is shown as AR interfaces on the smart glass. User is able to interact with these items through AR interfaces.

System has shown an accuracy of more than 99 % in detecting and showing all the products on the smart glass screen correctly at the right location. If the product is removed or location is updated it will be reflected to the interfaces in real time.

Fig. 3. A: User is aiming at particular point highlighted with red arrow on the shelves with smart glass AR app for a certain period of time. B: The items present at user clicked location are shown on the smart glass as superimposed images with product information (Color figure online).

5   System Evaluation

The qualitative and quantitative evaluation of the system has been done through 5 frequent online shoppers (volunteer university students), 3 of them were female and 2 of them were male with an average age of 29. The user recruitment process involves the shoppers who prefer purchasing online rather than offline and have purchased at least 2 products online in last 6 weeks. This section describes the evaluation in detail.

5.1   Usability Study

An initial questionnaire was prepared in order to conduct the usability study. Furthermore users were observed closely and interviewed in an informal way in order to figure out the easiness and satisfaction. Every user was given 30 min to interact with the shelf, select products and see the AR information. After using the system, questionnaire that were asked are

1. Do you like to have such a system while shopping?
2. Will it enrich your shopping experience?
3. How easy was it to see AR information?
4. Did you enjoy using the application?
5. Current level of options is sufficient?

For questionnaire responses a 5 point Likert scale was employed from strongly disagree option to strongly agree option. Moreover they were given the opportunity to write any additional comments about the system.

5.2   Results

After using the system users were very excited to know and use the system, when asked about having such a system for them at shops or being owned by them, 4 out of them wanted to have this system at shops with strongly agree option and one wants to have it with agree option. When asked about enriching offline shopping experience with this system, 1 respondent remains neutral while 1 chose agree and 3 chose strongly agree. The response of how easy was it see the AR information that includes images and text i.e. category, price, comments and ratings etc., 2 of them opted for agree, 2 selected strongly agree while one remained neutral. About the question of enjoying the application all five marked strongly agree. About the current levels of options 4 chose agree and one strongly agrees. Over all questionnaire responses are shown in Fig. 4. The vertical axis represents the questions and horizontal axis shows users response as strongly disagree = 1 and strongly agree = 5.

In the additional comments most of the users wanted to have this system connected to the social networks so they can post or get their friends comments in a real time.

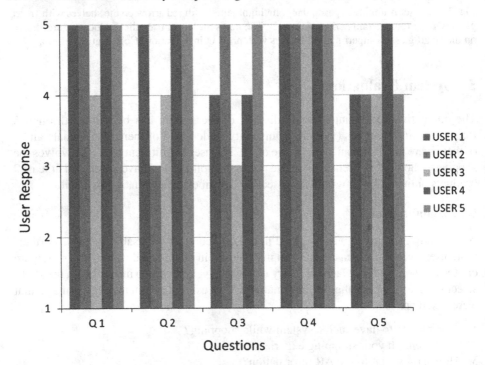

Fig. 4. Evaluation results

The overall results are highly encouraging and positive that shows the usability of such a system in an offline. System shows user satisfaction and interesting dimension for retailers and digitally savvy shoppers by providing them online connectivity at offline shops. Access to feedback, reviews, price comparisons at offline shops mean shoppers now have more information and choice at their fingertips that until recently wasn't possible through Smart Glass.

5.3 Discussion

During the study one user was wearing eye sight glasses, for her it was little difficult to adjust the Smart Glass on top of her eye sight glasses and that makes it difficult to see the AR information. In general users find the system easy to use, intuitive and alternative to online shopping. The rapid development of sensing technologies has created many opportunities for new ways to interact with smart objects. In our system, we carefully selected sensing techniques that are readily available, easy to deploy and becoming part of retail at a fast pace and our system is simple and easy to use.

A more thorough evaluation of the system is planned with the participants from diverse background including retail and frequent online shoppers in a real store. Detail questionnaire will be made and interfaces will be more enriched based on the user's evaluation.

6   Conclusion and Future Works

Retailers and overall companies are having a difficulty to engage and support customers at physical locations while the online sales are increasing because of user satisfaction and increased options for consumer at online sale facilities. The proposed system allows the traditional stores to provide shoppers with a user experience close to that of online commerce, but in a physical store. Shoppers are able to browse the shelves, looking at the products on them and obtaining, if so desired, in-depth or comparative information about them. It enables shoppers to use the system for quickly locating products on a store. The system proves to be a nexus between traditional and online commerce. For instance if a shopper finds a garment he or she likes but the correct size is unavailable, an option will be given to order the correct size online for home delivery. The system has shown an accuracy of more than 99 % in detecting and showing all the products on the smart glass screen correctly at the right location. All these products are envisioned to be connected to online information i.e. comments, ratings, related produces and social networks. As future work, we are in a process of deploying the system at a real store in order to get the feedback by the real shoppers and retailers. We plan to allow users to publish content about the physical products on their favorite social networks. Also the comparison of different AR interfaces based on Smart Glass and handheld devices is envisioned from scalability, usability and user satisfaction point of view.

Acknowledgements. This paper was partially supported by the ICT PhD program of Universitat Pompeu Fabra through a travel grant.

References

1. Pous, R., Melià-Seguí, J., Carrerasc, A., Morenza, M., Rashid, Z.: Cricking: customer-product interaction in retail using pervasive technologies. In: Proceedings of the 2013 ACM Conference on Pervasive and Ubiquitous Computing Adjunct Publication, UbiComp 2013 Adjunct, pp. 1023–1028. ACM, New York (2013)
2. Rashid, Z., Pous, R., Melià-Seguí, J., Morenza, M.: Mobile augmented reality for browsing physical spaces. In: Proceedings of the 2014 ACM International Joint Conference on Pervasive and Ubiquitous Computing: Adjunct Publication, UbiComp 2014 Adjunct, pp. 155–158. ACM, New York (2014)
3. Merrill, M., Maes, P.: Augmenting looking, pointing and reaching gestures to enhance the searching and browsing of physical objects. In: LaMarca, A., Langheinrich, M., Truong, K.N. (eds.) Pervasive 2007. LNCS, vol. 4480, pp. 1–18. Springer, Heidelberg (2007)
4. Lupiana, D., O'Driscoll, C., Mtenzi, F.: Taxonomy for ubiquitous computing environments. In: First International Conference on Networked Digital Technologies, NDT 2009, pp. 469–475 (2009)
5. Metaio. http://www.metaio.com
6. Next Generation Shopping. http://www.ccrrc.org/2011/02/19/attracting-the-next-generation-of-asian-shoppers
7. K-Pin, C., Dholakia, R.: Factors driving consumer intention to shop online: an empirical investigation. J. Consum. Psychol. 13(1), 177–183 (2003)
8. Online Shopping. http://www.goldminenetwork.com/_did_you_know_online_shopping.pdf
9. Shopping Behavior. www.ebeltoftgroup.com
10. Chen, D., Tsai. S., Hsu, C.-H., Jatinder, S., Boris, G.: Mobile augmented reality for books on a shelf. In: Proceedings of the 2011 IEEE International Conference on Multimedia and Expo, ICME 2011, pp. 1–6. IEEE Computer Society, Washington (2011)
11. Valkkynen, P., Niemela, M., Tuomisto, T.: Evaluating touching and pointing with a mobile terminal for physical browsing. In: Proceedings of the 4th Nordic conference on Human-computer interaction: changing roles, NordiCHI 2006, pp. 28–37. ACM (2006)
12. Gerrit, K., Stefan, W., Pascal, L., Spassova, L., Boris, B.: Management dashboard in a retail scenario. In: Kahl, G., Schwartz, T., Nurmi, P., Dim, E., Forsblom, A. (eds.) Workshop on Location Awareness in Dual and Mixed Reality, pp. 22–25. Online-Proceedings (2011)
13. Kleiner, E., SchAd'fer, B.: Augmented shelf: digital enrichment of library shelves. In: M ~ Aijnchen. Oldenbourg Verlag, pp. 541–544 (2012)
14. Ishii, H., Ullmer, B.: Tangible bits: towards seamless interfaces between people, bits and atoms. In: Proceedings of the ACM SIGCHI Conference on Human Factors in Computing Systems, CHI 1997. ACM, pp. 234–241 (1997)
15. Rekimoto, J., Ayatsuka, Y., Hayashi, K.: Augment-able reality: situated communication through physical and digital spaces. In: Second International Symposium on Wearable Computers. Digest of Papers, pp. 68–75 (1998)
16. Faria, S., Assunçao, J., Carvalho, V., Silva A., Ferreira, P., Reinares, E.: Consumer behavior in retail: online and offline – what is the future? In: International Conference on Marketing and Consumer Behavior, ICMC 2013 (2013)
17. Vuzix M100 Glass. http://www.vuzix.com/consumer/products_m100/
18. Zhang, B., Chen Y., Tuna C., Dave, A., Y. Li, Lee E., Hartmann, B.: HOBS: head orientation-based selection in physical spaces. In: ACM Symposium on Spatial User Interaction, SUI 2014 (2014)

19. Rashid, Z., Pous, R., Melià-Seguí, J., Morenza, M.: Cricking: browsing physical spaces with smart glass. In: Proceedings of the 2014 ACM International Joint Conference on Pervasive and Ubiquitous Computing: Adjunct Publication, UbiComp 2014 Adjunct. ACM, New York, pp. 155–158 (2014)
20. Keonn Technologies International. www.keonn.com

Touchless Interaction for Command and Control in Military Operations

Alessandro Zocco[1]([⊠]), Matteo D. Zocco[2], Antonella Greco[3],
Salvatore Livatino[4], and Lucio Tommaso De Paolis[2]

[1] Product Innovation and Advanced EW Solutions, Elettronica S.p.A., Rome, Italy
alessandro.zocco@elt.it
[2] Department of Engineering for Innovation, University of Salento, Lecce, Italy
matteodamiano.zocco@studenti.unisalento.it, lucio.depaolis@unisalento.it
[3] High Tech Unit, Capgemini Italia S.p.A, Rome, Italy
antonella.greco@capgemini.com
[4] School of Engineering and Technology, University of Hertfordshire, Hatfield, UK
s.livatino@herts.ac.uk

Abstract. The military strategy to obtain information superiority is enshrined in the concept of Network Centric Warfare: a modern doctrine based on the interconnection of knowledgeable entities. By increasing the number of commanded platforms, the volume of the data that can be accessed grows exponentially with a high risk to get a state of information overload. This paper proposes an augmented environment for efficient command and control in net-centric operations. Touchless interaction by means of Leap Motion has been explored in order to provide a faster and more natural way to issue commands and increase situational awareness. The proposed approach was evaluated by twelve users who performed different tasks on Loki, a command and control system for electronic warfare developed by Elettronica S.p.A. The results show a strong improvement in users' performance (i.e., completion time, number of failures, failure rate) and experience (i.e., control simplicity, level of immersion and situational awareness).

Keywords: Touchless Interaction · Leap Motion · Human computer interaction · Network Centric Warfare · Command and control system · Augmented Reality

1 Introduction

The transition from industrial to information age and the resulting globalization have brought deep changes in the society and in the political-strategic field. The end of the bipolar conflict, that has been replaced by asymmetric conflict, and the terrorism have decisively affected the defence sector that has undergone a continuous reformulation of its operating model to adapt to changing technology needs.

The military's response in the development of strategies for managing the critical issues, arising from the intrinsic characteristics of the contemporary

© Springer International Publishing Switzerland 2015
L.T. De Paolis and A. Mongelli (Eds.): AVR 2015, LNCS 9254, pp. 432–445, 2015.
DOI: 10.1007/978-3-319-22888-4_32

threats, is enshrined in the concept of Network Centric Warfare (NCW) [2,3]: a modern military doctrine based on the interconnection of knowledgeable entities (sensors, decisors and actuators) that are geographically or hierarchically distributed.

In this context the Command and Control (C2) system holds an important role: it performs the data fusion process by correlating data from all available sources and provides a single identical view of relevant information concerning friendly, enemy and neutral forces. The current DoD term for this shared view is Common Operational Picture (COP).

Commanders operate C2 systems by means of an interaction environment to get access to the COP and manifest decisions such as plans and orders.

Being the visualized information the result of several inputs conveyed to the same displayed area, a state of *information overload* [21,22] is likely to occur when increasing the number of commanded platforms and then of sensors. Most people in the scientific community accept the general definition that information overload is the feeling of too much information to be processed for the cognitive capacity of a person.

Several research groups have developed new display technologies for improving COP reading, presenting, and understanding. Stereoscopic 3D (S3D) vision improves depth impression since it allows a correct estimation of spatial relations, also in cases of minor discrepancies such as occurring with military icons representing platforms or threats [24,25]. The Augmented Reality (AR) provides a digitally enhanced view of the real world that assures advantages in terms of understanding perception and situational awareness [26,27]. This leads to a significant reduction of the reaction time and of the number of errors made during the execution of complex tasks.

However, traditional devices (i.e., keyboard and trackpad) are not suitable for immersive environments, since are not ergonomically designed for it. Therefore, it is necessary to introduce and validate novel technologies in order to effectively interact within S3D AR environments reducing the time required to accurately manifest decisions and orders.

This paper proposes the use of touchless interaction by means of Leap Motion for C2 during net-centric operations. The purpose is to replace keyboard and trackpad with hand gesture and motion control. The solution proposed is assessed on realistic NCW scenarios. The performed study is quite unique as nothing similar has been found in the literature works.

Next sections introduce to touchless interaction (Sect. 2) and related works (Sect. 3). The proposed solution is then presented (Sect. 4) followed by a description of our experiments (Sect. 5). Conclusions are finally drawn (Sect. 6).

2   Hand Gesture and Motion Control

Gesture control might be the most natural and intuitive way to communicate between people and machines, since it closely emulates the mode humans operate and interact in the real world [19].

Among different human body parts, the hand is the most effective general-purpose interaction tool, due to its dexterity. The adoption of hand gesture not only allows the deployment of a wide range of applications in sophisticated computing environments but also benefits our daily life such as maintaining absolute sterility in health care environment by means of touchless interfaces [20].

Currently, the most used tools for capturing hand gesture are electromechanical or magnetic sensing devices (i.e., data gloves) [7,8]. These technologies employ sensors attached to a glove that transduces finger flexions into electrical signals to determine the hand gesture. However, they have several drawbacks: the naturalness of hand gesture is hindered and complex calibration and setup procedures are required to obtain precise measurements. These usability limits preclude their use in military applications.

Vision-based hand gesture recognition is a promising alternative to data gloves because of its potential to provide more natural, unencumbered, and contactless interaction. Microsoft Kinect is one of low-cost devices used for this purpose. It infers body position in a two-stage process: first computes a depth map using structured light, then infers body position using machine learning. It does not require wearable devices (e.g., gloves, physical markers) and recognize the users' actions through cameras and sensors contained in the main unit [14]. Vision-based control is still far from satisfactory for mission-critical applications because of the limitations of the optical sensors: the quality of the captured images is sensitive to lighting conditions and cluttered backgrounds, thus it is usually not able to detect and track the hands robustly.

Leap Motion [12] is a new device that determines the location of fingers, the angle of the hand, the existence and position of any tools (e.g., pens, pencils), and an approximation of the curvature of the palm by means of two cameras and three IR sources. Its sensory space is in the shape of an inverted pyramid with the apex at the center of the device. Compared to depth cameras like the Kinect and similar devices, it produces a more limited amount of information (only a few keypoints instead of the complete depth map) and its interaction zone is rather limited but the extracted data is more accurate (the accuracy is of about $200\,\mu m$ [23]) and it is not necessary to perform image processing tasks to extract the relevant points [15]. Moreover, Leap Motion is characterized by a great robustness because no calibration is required. A drawback of this technology is the difficulty in maintaining accuracy and fidelity of detection when the hands do not have direct line of sight with the controller. This means that during detection, if a hand is rotated from a position of palm parallel to the flat surface of the controller to a position of palm perpendicular to the flat surface of the controller, the detection can often deteriorate entirely [18].

3   Related Works

Several research groups have focused their activities on the design and development of new interaction paradigms and technologies for advanced C2 in mission critical operations.

Hodicky and Frantis [9] have conducted a research program to investigate ways to increase the level and quality of battlefield visualization and interaction. A 3D model of the mission area is projected into a high resolution Head Mounted Display (HMD) and is explored by head and body movements: left head rotation moves the current scene into the left area of interest (the right head rotation works on the contrary); the movement of the whole body creates effect of flying over the virtual terrain. Moreover, a data glove is used to communicate with new presentation layers: predefined gestures manipulate the Virtual Reality (VR) battlefield in order to get more detailed information about selected unit. The HMD and data glove are detected by tracking sensors to get the information about head and hand position. The proposed interaction system suffers from well known data glove limitations (i.e., poor robustness, poor durability, need for calibration); furthermore, unwanted actions occur by unintentional movements.

The same authors have conducted a research activity that brought a new natural way for C2 in military operations [10]: body movements and gestures are tracked by a Kinect and are used to control the COP visualization process. At the beginning of each session, commander must calibrate the sensor system by standing with arms raising forward. The application saves his position, body height and length of his arms. Movements in the virtual environment are controlled by real movements in the sensory space. Step forward means the virtual camera movement in the same direction proportionally; it works similar with movements in other directions. Distance between the commander and the saved calibrated position controls the velocity of the virtual camera movements. The left hand controls the altitude of the camera over the terrain, while the right hand movements replace the mouse operation. However, some lighting conditions (e.g., users or sensors in direct sunlight) can make it difficult for Kinect to identify or track movements. Moreover, the hand tracking fails when the hands are close to the body or are moving fast.

Alexander et al. [4] proposed a stereoscopic 3D system for the visualization of relevant data at higher command level. The presentation is interactive, so that the point-of-view can be adjusted and modified. A standard mouse allows a desktop-like interaction for navigation or activation of drop-down command menus. Moreover, speech recognition was integrated into the system: the operator controls the system through a set of command words. A drawback of this study is that the use of traditional devices (i.e., mouse and keyboard) reduces the level of immersion. Moreover, speech recognition in adverse conditions (such as within a C2 center) is still a difficult task and its accuracy in environments with reverberation and background noise is still staying at low levels. For applications in-the-field, the authors have proposed an AR sandbox. This system provides a bird's-eye view of the situation of own and opponents units and is very useful for illustrating strategies and tactics. Like with a real sandbox, team members can sit or stand around the 3D map and work with the synthetic terrain. The selection and manipulation of 3D content is achieved by mapping a portable 2D input device into a virtual 3D scene. The cursor that is projected into the 3D scene is displayed as a virtual 3D pointer. This type of interaction does not require extra training for a potential user because nowadays almost everyone uses to work with a standard PC mouse. However the 2D device cursor does not provide any information about the depth of the selected objects. The user has to rely only on the depth cues provided by the virtual environment, such as perspective deformation, shading and shadows. Moreover, conflicts between the 2D space in which the 2D cursor lays and the 3D content occur.

Adithya et al. [1] have developed a novel AR system for paper map data visualization and interaction. Military forces typically make use of paper maps to visualize terrain features and other geographical information during operations in-the-field. The interaction with a flat paper map is natural and intuitive. However, these maps are static, so the user cannot zoom-in or zoom-out to fully comprehend the finer or broader details of terrain structure. The authors have explored the possibility to extend the dimensions of a paper map to more than two by using computer-vision. Specifically, the AR technology has been used to enhance paper maps with digital information. The entire map is split into a grid of sub-regions and a database of 3D terrain information in VRML format is associated to each cell. Whenever the user selects a sub-region, the VRML data relative to it are used to build the 3D model. A fixed marker, representing the reference system for terrain generation, is used to calibrate the boundary corners of the map. When user places a second marker on the map, the system calculates the location and loads the appropriate virtual terrain model. Once the model pops up, the marker can be picked up and examined closely. The main limitation of using marker-based tracking is the control of lighting: changing levels of light and limited contrasts disable correct registration and produce an inaccurate pose estimation and a noticeable jittering. Another problem is the occlusion: markers need to be fully within camera view to be detected, even partial occlusions can dramatically increase the risk of tracking failure. Finally, the physical marker occludes the real map and affects its legibility.

Generally, it is difficult to quantify the operational effectiveness of the proposed solutions due to the lack of usability testing.

4   Proposed Investigation

This paper proposes an augmented environment for efficient C2 in net-centric operations. Touchless interaction by means of Leap Motion has been explored in order to provide a faster and more natural way to issue commands and increase the level of immersion. The final goal is to reduce the time required to obtain high-level situational awareness and to take command decisions (e.g., plans, orders). This leads to better and faster decision-making.

The system proposed is part of Loki, an advanced C2 system for Electronic Warfare (EW) that coordinates a set of heterogeneous platforms (air, surface, subsurface) having on board sensors and actuators in the domain of electronic defence.

4.1   High-Level Architecture of Loki

Figure 1 shows the high-level architectural view of the Loki system.

The core component continuously executes an advanced multi-sensor data fusion process on the data retrieved from cooperating systems. Once these data are properly fused, the system is capable to infer new important information such as a better localization of emitters and countermeasures strategy. These information are transferred to the presentation layer using a communication middleware based on Data Distribution Service (DDS) paradigm [6].

The AR User Interface (UI) provides a digitally enhanced view of a real C2 table configuring the visual appearance of the COP and accepting and validating user input. Moreover, it provides a persistence mechanism to decouple the data-access logic from the core logic.

4.2   AR Visualization

The mission area is visualized in a new way that allows to increase the situational awareness. The operator, looking through the lens of an optical see-through HMD (NVIS nVisor ST50), sees the virtual world superimposed on the real world.

The precise alignment between real and virtual world is obtained through the use of an electromagnetic tracker (Polhemus's Patriot). It includes a system electronic unit, one source and two sensors. The source, that is also the system's reference frame for sensors measurements, is fixed under the real table. The virtual world coordinate system was matched with the source and shifted up by the table top thickness (Fig. 2). This configuration has several advantages: it is not subject to flickering of rendered model and it allows to have the source near the user without cluttering the table top.

The virtual environment consists of a geo-referenced 3D map of the mission area on which the EW scenario is positioned. The localized platforms (characterized by latitude, longitude and altitude) are placed on the scene faithfully reflecting their geographic coordinates and are represented according to MIL-STD-2525C [16]. If the Direction of Arrival (DOA) of a threat is known with

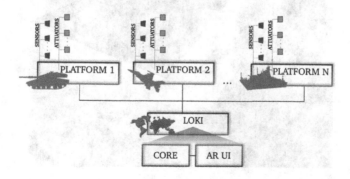

Fig. 1. Loki architecture in the large.

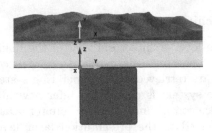

Fig. 2. Tracker's source fixed under the table top.

a margin of error, the uncertainty volume is shown as a pyramid with vertex in the platform that has performed the detection.

Different kinds of views are provided through the activation of layers normal to the C2 table. A small viewport, placed in the upper left corner of the display, provides critical information (e.g., warning emitters detection) to the operator. This type of visualization permits to visualize in a correct way the different elements of the scene and to delete any form of information overload.

Users around the C2 table can collaborate face-to-face maintaining the ability to use real-world objects.

4.3 Interaction

The Leap Motion allows to control a 3D cursor directly by moving the index finger in the sensory space (Fig. 3).

The selection of EW elements (i.e., platforms, threats) is achieved by *tap* gesture. In order to visualize portions of the 3D map that are not included in the

Fig. 3. User interacts within the augmented environment through Leap Motion.

Fig. 4. Leap Motion gestures.

actual view frustum, the *circle clockwise and anticlockwise* gestures are used respectively to zoom-in and zoom-out while the *swipe* gesture provides panning. Correlation and triangulation are two basic actions performed by commander during the analysis of complex EW scenarios. The former, performed by means of *keytap* gesture, results in the fusion of data related to the same threat coming from different sensors. The latter, achieved by *fist* gesture, provides threat position at the intersection of the uncertainty volumes of several detections.

Figure 4 depicts the gestures discussed above.

In a mutually exclusive manner, traditional interaction by means of trackpad and keyboard is provided to commander.

4.4 SW Design and Implementation

An extensible SW architecture that consists of reusable components for key sub-problems of AR has been designed according to MIL-STD-498 [17]. The Layers architectural pattern has been used to structure the system into three layers. The first layer includes low-level services (e.g., tracking systems, display and input devices). These are completely abstracted by the second layer that provides high-level functionality needed by most AR systems. The application is itself the third layer. This approach allows to implement different issues separately and supports incremental coding and testing. Another advantage is that different technologies can be dynamically added or removed.

The SW has been developed in C++ using OGRE, an open-source 3D engine that abstracts the details of the underlying system libraries (e.g., OpenGL, DirectX) and provides an interface based on high-level classes. In addition, the Qt framework has been integrated for its powerful mechanism for object communication called Signals&Slots and for its platform-independent thread support. The Leap Motion API provides motion tracking data as a series of snapshots called frames. Each frame contains information about the hand detected (e.g., fingers position, gestures).

The high-definition map of the mission area has been generated through several steps. First, the 3D model has been generated starting from Digital Terrain Elevation Data (DTED), using Autodesk infrastructure design suite. After that, Autodesk 3DS Max has been used to add textures, details and colours. Finally, the resultant model has been converted in a format supported by OGRE. An important thing that must be considered is that in this process the geo-referencing information is lost and a mapping algorithm [5] to associate a specific point inside the map to each pair of longitude and latitude value has been implemented.

To avoid a different spatial perception of the virtual context through the HMD in contrast to the real world, the camera view frustum has been calibrated to the display view frustum. The calibration method adopted [11] requires that user aligns tracked real world markers with virtual target positions and can be completed in approximately one minute for both eyes.

5   Experimental Design and Test Procedure

The evaluation study took place at the ELT facilities in Rome and was designed according to the recommendations given in [13].

Subjects were selected to be as representative as possible of the intended users of the system: 12 members of the armed forces of different countries expert in the field of EW with no experience in using AR and Leap Motion, and an age between 32 and 45 (average 35.5).

Two realistic EW scenarios were simulated in order to evaluate effectiveness of touchless interaction under different situations of information load:

– *Scenario A*: 100 threats detected by 3 cooperating platforms;
– *Scenario B*: 512 threats detected by 5 cooperating platforms.

On each scenario the users had to work out a solution to the tasks described in Table 1 within the indicated time intervals.

The evaluation study was a within-subject evaluation: all participants executed all tasks on scenario A and B using both touch and touchless interaction within the augmented environment. The assigned task and interaction mode (touch or touchless) was scheduled according to a pre-determined order to counterbalance learning and fatigue effects.

In mathematical terms, considering *factors*:

$$S = \{Scenario\ A,\ Scenario\ B\}$$
$$I = \{Touch\ Interaction, Touchless\ Interaction\}$$

(1)

we define a *session* as a couple:

$$(s,i) : s \in S \land i \in I.$$

(2)

Table 1. Scheduled tasks timeout

Task	Timeout for Scenario A [seconds]	Timeout for Scenario B [seconds]
Selection	30	60
Correlation	90	120
Triangulation	90	120

The set of all sessions performed from each user during the evaluation is given by the cartesian product:

$$S \times I := \{(s, i) : s \in S \land i \in I\}. \tag{3}$$

In order to measure operational behaviors, the following quantitative measurements were automatically acquired during the usability study:

- *Completion Time*: the time employed to complete all tasks in a session;
- *Number of Failures*: the number of failed tasks in the number of failed tasks in a session;
- *Failure Rate*: the number of errors per second in a session.

In addition the following qualitative data, referring to the users' experience, were collected using questionnaires and interviews at the end of the test:

- *Control Accuracy*: the degree of correspondence between the desired and actual action;

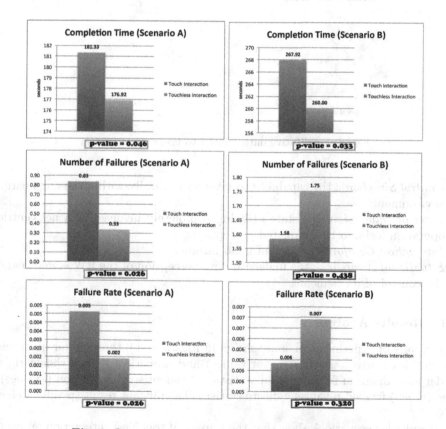

Fig. 5. Quantitative data related to users' performance.

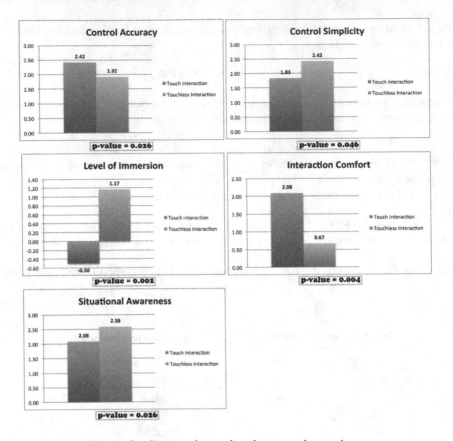

Fig. 6. Qualitative data related to users' experience.

- *Control Simplicity*: the capability to interact naturally within the augmented environment;
- *Level of Immersion*: the state of being completely involved in a net-centric operation losing other unrelated perceptions;
- *Interaction Comfort*: the level of hand fatigue;
- *Situational Awareness*: the understanding perception of the EW scenario and the control of its elements.

5.1 Results Analysis

The results of experimentation are shown in Figs. 5 and 6 through bar diagrams for the descriptive statistics (mean values) and numerical figures shown right under each diagram for inferential statistics (Student's t-distribution p-values). The (green) framed p-values indicate statistical significant result (p-value below 0.05).

Results for scenario A show that the impact of touchless interaction on *completion time*, *number of failures* and *failure rate* is significant (all p-values are below 0.05). This means that using Leap Motion users successfully completed more tasks in less time than using trackpad.

The effect of touchless interaction becomes less evident with increasing the level of task difficulty (scenario B). The reduction of *completion time* remains significant (268 seconds employed with touch interaction versus 260 with touchless interaction) while the differences in *number of failures* and *failure rate* are not significant. Therefore, in complex situations Leap Motion interaction, although more natural and immediate (it is possible to issue commands without the need to open contextual menu), is less accurate than trackpad.

This outcome is consistent with the following qualitative results: a higher *control accuracy* is perceived by the majority of participants using touch interaction (p = 0.026) while *control simplicity* is significantly better using touchless interaction (p = 0.046).

Level of immersion significantly increases using touchless interaction (p = 0.002). According to many users, the availability of a 3D sensory space reduces distraction resulting from trackpad localization.

Many users commented that the use of Leap Motion causes hand-fatigue in fact, the *interaction comfort* is significantly higher using trackpad (p = 0.004).

A higher *situational awareness* is perceived by the majority of participants with touchless interaction. The improvement is significant (p = 0.026). Users claimed that control of the mission is better and faster using Leap Motion. This is a fundamental aspect for the success of military operations.

6   Conclusions and Future Work

In the design and development of C2 systems for net-centric operations, a key element is the interaction system. Wrong assumptions may lead the operator to an information overload state.

This paper proposes the use of touchless interaction by means of Leap Motion within an immersive environment that leverages the AR technology to provide a digitally enhanced view of a real C2 table.

The results of the evaluation showed very clear trends with our users performing significantly better using hand gesture control in terms of *control simplicity*, *level of immersion* and *situational awareness*.

Leap Motion interaction is still sometimes criticized because of hand fatigue and inadequate level of accuracy during the analysis of complex EW scenarios.

The results presented represent the initial experimentation phase of continuing research into user interaction for military purposes. The lack of comparative evaluation with respect to other works specifically addressing NCW is due to the actual complexity of this domain.

In the next future an investigation into improving Leap Motion accuracy will be conducted and gesture and motion control by means of wearable devices (e.g., Myo) will be explored.

References

1. Adithya, C., Kowsik, K., Namrata, D., Nageli, V.S., Shrivastava, S., and Rakshit, S.: Augmented Reality Approach for Paper Map Visualization. In: International Conference Communication and Computational Intelligence, pp. 352–356, Erode (2010)
2. Alberts, D.S., Garstka, J.J., Stein, F.P.: Network Centric Warfare: Developing and Leveraging Information Superiority. CCRP Publication Series, Washington DC (1999)
3. Alberts, D.S., Hayes, R.E.: Power to the Edge: Command.. Control.. in the Information Age. CCRP Publication Series, Washington DC (2003)
4. Alexander, T., Renkewitz, H., Conradi, J.: Applicability of Virtual Environments as C4ISR Displays. In: Virtual Media for Military Applications Workshop, pp. 1–12, West Point (2006)
5. Bowditch, N.: The American Practical Navigator. National Imagery and Mapping Agency, Reston (2012)
6. Data Distribution Service. http://portals.omg.org/dds/
7. Gallotti, P., Raposo, A., Soares L.: V-glove: A 3D virtual touch interface. In: 13th Symposium on Virtual Reality, pp. 242–251, Uberlandia (2011)
8. Hoang, T.N., Smith, R.T., Thomas, B.H.: Passive deformable haptic glove to support 3D interactions in mobile augmented reality environments. In: 2th IEEE and ACM International Symposium on Mixed and Augmented Reality, pp. 257–258, Adelaide (2013)
9. Hodicky, J., Frantis, P.: Decision support system for a commander at the operational level. In: 1st International Conference on Knowledge Engineering and Ontology Development, pp. 359–362, Madeira (2009)
10. Hodicky, J., Frantis, P.: Gesture and body movement recognition in the military decision support system. In: 9th International Conference on Informatics in Control Automation and Robotics, pp. 301–304, Rome (2012)
11. Kellner, F., Bolte, F., Bruder, G., Rautenberg, U., Steinicke, F., Lappe, M., Koch, R.: Geometric calibration of head-mounted displays and its effects on distance estimation. IEEE Trans. Visual Comput. Graphics $18(4)$, 589–596 (2012)
12. Leap Motion. https://www.leapmotion.com/
13. Livatino, S., Koeffel C.: Handbook for Evaluation Studies in Virtual Reality. In: IEEE International Conference on Virtual Environments, Human Computer Interface and Measurement Systems, Ostuni (2007)
14. Lun, R., Zhao W.: A survey of applications and human motion recognition with microsoft kinect. International Journal of Pattern Recognition and Artificial Intelligence, Accepted for publication (to appear 2015)
15. Marin, G., Dominio, F., Zanuttigh, P.: Hand gesture recognition with jointly calibrated Leap Motion and depth sensor. Multimedia Tools and Applications, Accepted for publication (to appear 2015)
16. MIL-STD-2525C. http://www.mapsymbs.com/ms2525c.pdf
17. MIL-STD-498. http://en.wikipedia.org/wiki/MIL-STD-498
18. Potter, L.E., Araullo, J., Carter, L.: The leap motion controller: a view on sign language. In: 25th Australian Computer-Human Interaction Conference: Augmentation, Application, Innovation, Collaboration, pp. 175–178, Adelaide (2013)
19. Ren, Z., Meng, J., Yuan, J.: Depth camera based hand gesture recognition and its applications in Human-Computer-Interaction. In: 8th International Conference on Information, Communications and Signal Processing, pp. 1–5, Singapore (2011)

20. Rosa, G.M., Elizondo, M.L.: Use of a gesture user interface as a touchless image navigation system in dental surgery: Case series report. Imaging Sci. Dent. **44**(2), 155–160 (2014)
21. Shanker, T., Richtel, M.: In New Military: Data Overload can be Deadly. The New York Times, New York (2011). http://www.nytimes.com
22. Strother, J.B., Ulijn, J.M.: The challenge of information overload. In: IEEE International Professional Communication Conference, pp. 1–3, Orlando (2012)
23. Weichert, F., Bachmann, D., Rudak, B., Fisseler, D.: Analysis of the accuracy and robustness of the leap motion controller. Sensors **13**(5), 6380–6393 (2013)
24. Zocco, A., Cannone, D., De Paolis, L.T.: Effects of stereoscopy on a human-computer interface for network centric operations. In: 9th International Conference on Computer Vision Theory and Applications, pp. 249–260, Lisbon (2014)
25. Zocco, Alessandro, Livatino, Salvatore, Tommaso De Paolis, Lucio: Stereoscopic-3D vision to improve situational awareness in military operations. In: De Paolis, Lucio Tommaso, Mongelli, Antonio (eds.) AVR 2014. LNCS, vol. 8853, pp. 351–362. Springer, Heidelberg (2014)
26. Zocco, A., De Paolis, L.T.: Augmented command and control table to support network-centric operations. Defence Sci. J. **65**(1), 39–45 (2015)
27. Zocco, A., De Paolis, L.T., Greco, L., Manes, C.L.: An Augmented Environment for Command and Control Systems. In: 10th International Conference on Computer Vision Theory and Applications, pp. 209–214, Berlin (2015)

Short Papers

Development of a Framework to Support Virtual Review Within Complex-Product Lifecycle Management

Giorgio Bernabei[1](✉), Angelo Corallo[2], Roberto Lombardo[2],
Simone Maci[3], Valerio Galli[4], Danilo Cannoletta[5],
and Antonio Notaro[5]

[1] Dhitech Scarl, Lecce, Italy
giorgio.bernabei@dhitech.it
[2] Università del Salento, Lecce, Italy
{angelo.corallo,roberto.lombardo}@unisalento.it
[3] EKA, Lecce, Italy
simone.maci@eka-systems.com
[4] ESI Italia, Bologna, Italy
valerio.galli@esi-group.com
[5] Alenia Aermacchi, Pomigliano d'Arco, Italy
{danilo.cannoletta,antonio.notaro}@alenia.it

Abstract. New Product Development process requires increasing innovation in order to reduce time-to-market and cost and to improve product quality. Products are realized by following a lifecycle made of phases and activities, related to each other, managed by many actors inside and outside the company and characterized by moments of verification and review of the work performed. In this scenario, a critical activity is the Review of the work performed. One of the most critical aspects is the retrieving of the right data, at the right moment and as quickly as possible, in order to avoid wrong decisions.

The paper proposes a methodological framework and a technological environment to support the integration of the different information sources of a company. The objective of the project is the development of an innovative Virtual Review process for companies that develops complex products. The specific objectives of the project can be summarized with three concepts: conceptualization, comparison and collaboration. An integrated and modular solution, named VIEW VIrtual Environment Workbench, has been designed and implemented adopting IC.IDO as DMU software and Exalead for dashboarding. The results is a workbench where users can retrieve all desired information by easily selecting the 3D ITEMs under review (components, assemblies, systems) and can require the visualization of information in the form of dashboards.

The aggregation of all the product-related information, in a single environment, facilitates decision-making so that the fulfilment of the project requirements is reached; in this way it is possible to operate at the right time and in the most appropriate manner, with considerable reduction of the time and cost of development and industrialization.

Keywords: Virtual reality · Virtual review · Dashboarding · Product lifecycle management · New product development

© Springer International Publishing Switzerland 2015
L.T. De Paolis and A. Mongelli (Eds.): AVR 2015, LNCS 9254, pp. 449–457, 2015.
DOI: 10.1007/978-3-319-22888-4_33

1 Introduction

Nowadays, industrial competition is based on several aspects; one of the most interesting is the New Product Development process that requires increasing innovation in order to reduce the time-to-market, the cost and to improve product quality. Products are realized by following a lifecycle made of phases and activities related to each other, managed by many actors inside and outside the company and characterized by moments of verification and review of the work performed. In this scenario, it is necessary to spend less time in data retrieving in order to focus on value-adding activities. In addition, it is necessary to collaborate with all the actors involved in this process (Fig. 1).

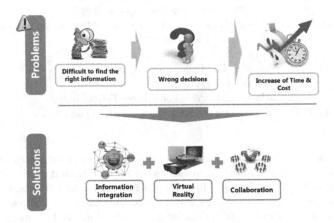

Fig. 1 Problems and solutions

In this scenario, a critical activity is the Review of the work performed. It is obvious that one of the most critical aspects is the retrieving of the right data, at the right moment and as quickly as possible, in order to avoid wrong decisions that result in increasing time and cost during product development.

The paper proposes a methodological framework and a technological environment to support the integration of the different information sources of a company, accessible in virtual and collaborative environment. Virtual Reality will enable the interaction with the digital mock-up of a product in a virtual and immersive environment, before its physical realization [1], while Dashboarding tools will support the retrieving of required information.

The study is part of a research project among cPDM Lab – Università del Salento, EKA, ESI Italia and the living lab KLIO Lab. The project is in collaboration with leading national industries aimed at innovating methodologies and technologies for an integrated management of data and information along the product lifecycle. Furthermore, this study deals with the implementation of a software prototype within ESI IC. ICO environment.

The next sections of the paper are a background section describing the main relevant issues on Virtual Reality, Dashboarding and Product Lifecycle Management.

A further section describes the proposed Architectural Framework, in terms of objective, functional and physical architecture. After the discussion of results, a final section of conclusions ends the paper.

2 Background

The realization of complex products, typical of Automotive and Aerospace industry, presupposes that information about the product and the process should be easily accessible, both inside the company and throughout the supply chain (partner, suppliers and customers), with needs of information integration and collaboration between the actors involved. In this scenario, the adoption of an approach oriented to the management of the product life cycle is necessary, as it allows companies to build channels within the entire value chain, through which the knowledge can go beyond the traditional exchange of specifications, drawings and contracts. Product lifecycle management is a wide concept [4] that represents both a business approach and a software solution, evolved in recent years from a series of engineering tools to fully integrated solution at the enterprise level [2]. The approach is based on the access to a shared data repository, containing product/process related information; the aim is the connection between the different organizational units, with the main benefit to centrally manage all the technological resources of the company [3].

In this vision, different disciplines are integrated; some are already relatively mature, but certain features can be extended to provide new tools to support the product lifecycle management. Virtual Reality is the set of technologies that allows the creation of the digital prototypes of a product, in order to visualize the final appearance, to simulate the operational behaviour, to evaluate aspects of ergonomics for the operator and to provide a valuable support for the decision-making. The automotive and aerospace industries, and more in general the sector of transports, in recent years have demonstrated a considerable interest in the adoption of these technologies, facing huge investment; this is due to the advantages that the technology ensures when companies are involved in the design of complex systems [1]. Most of the engineering projects are realized by following the cycle of new product development, consisting of phases and activities connected together and controlled by actors belonging to different departments. Often, these actors are located in different geographical areas and cooperate by sharing information, data and results. Within this heterogeneous environment, it is necessary the implementation of a process of knowledge management, which makes use of technologies and approaches typical of Product Lifecycle Management (PLM), also with the support of tools for virtual prototyping [5]. With Virtual Reality (VR) it is possible to have a three-dimensional visualization of the product and of its components, allowing the users to immerse themselves in a Virtual Room, interacting with stereoscopic display, greatly improving the overall impact of visualization [6]. The technological advances have made possible to apply the technology of virtual reality in different areas of engineering (design, modelling, process simulation, production planning, training, testing) allowing designers to highlight any problems or errors before starting the production phase. The introduction of Digital MockUp (DMU) provides a virtual view of the product before it is realized, giving the opportunity to understand if parts can be manufactured and properly installed. The use of Digital Mockup enables, through dedicated graphical tools, the visualization of the product structure in its various stages of maturity.

The DMU contributes to the construction of the Virtual Product Model, which is an extension of the 3D visualization including manufacturing data and various documents that contribute to the definition of the product in the context of the "Extended Enterprise". The interactions between the different actors within the extended enterprise generate high volumes of data that can be used as input for dashboarding and analytics tools. Users can collect, synthesize and provide information to support the monitoring of activities for new product development. The applications of dashboarding and analytics can be different: program management and supply-chain monitoring, process data analysis, operational intelligence, definition of predictive models based on historical data. The benefit is a better fruition of the information in a more simple, fast and effective way.

3 VIEW – Virtual Environment Workbench

The objective of the project is the development of an innovative process of Virtual Review for companies that develops complex products, supported by technologies of Virtual Reality.

The process of Virtual Review involves all stages of the product life cycle. It enhances the exchange of information to foster concurrent and collaborative engineering. Its application enables the ability to collect and integrate heterogeneous information in the various business information systems and to display them in a 3D interactive and user-friendly environment, making them available even to users not involved in the technical activities of the product development. The process facilitates the interaction between individuals with diverse skills, maybe located in different sites, according to a collaborative logic.

The Virtual Review, with support for stereoscopic view in three dimensions and through interactive tools for pointing and manipulation, permits a quick and easy access to information. The actors involved in the business logic of collaborative-review, have a clearer view of the information they need to make optimal decisions in order to reduce errors and reworks. This may have implications in terms of increased productivity and better matching of products to the initial requirements.

More specifically, the aim of this project is the development of a functional model of the processes for a virtual environment dedicated to virtual reviews; this will be integrated with technologies dedicated to virtual prototyping, to enrich the user experience by retrieving information associated with different items of a product, at different stages of the life cycle.

In the above framework, business information systems will act as data sources for the acquisition, management and organization of information and knowledge.

The framework is expected to integrate information from corporate informative systems, such as: product lifecycle management system, dashboarding systems, simulation software, legacy databases, documental and requirements management systems.

The integration of information generated in the whole product life cycle and the correlation between information and the geometry of product will enable:

- geometric trouble analysis;
- measure of distance, surfaces and volumes;
- simulations of component installation sequence;
- simulations for ergonomics;
- information exchange between actors;
- visualization of product-related information (simulations, dashboarding, engineering, documentation).

The specific objectives of the project can be summarized with three concept, that prof. Michael Grieves identifies with the Human Knowledge Toolkit [7]: conceptualization, comparison and collaboration (Fig. 2).

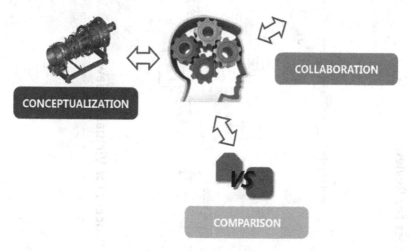

Fig. 2 Human knowledge toolkit

The first refers to the possibility to conceptualize and visualize contents, in a form as close as possible to our perception with natural three-dimensional vision. The second is the possibility to compare different design solution and to obtain information related to product lifecycle. Last, but not least, is the possibility to collaborate with remote users located in different sites.

Architectural Framework

In Fig. 3, it can be seen that the adoption of virtual technologies within the review process causes two main differences with respect to the as is situation:

- the introduction of collaboration with remote users
- the capability to obtain information about product lifecycle in an automatized way, as information are integrated and stored in a shared repository

An integrated and modular solution, named VIEW – VIrtual Environment Workbench, has been designed. In particular, to enable Virtual Review a software for Digital

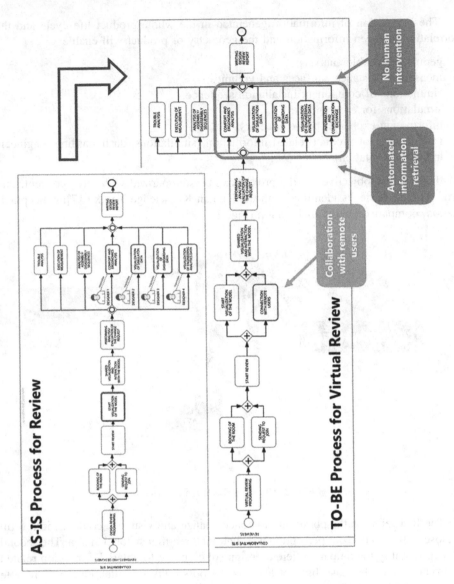

Fig. 3 Virtual review process

Mock-up is proposed as access-point to all the review features. This software is able to interface with the dashboarding module, with the PDM system and with all other enterprise information systems. In addition, the DMU can be used both on desktop and in a Virtual Room for collaborative reviews.

In this implementation of the VIEW concepts, IC.IDO has been chosen as DMU software while Exalead implements the dashboarding layer.

IC.IDO is the most powerful solution for Virtual Reality, combining high-end visualization and real-time simulation of product behavior in its actual size. Exalead is an advanced research engine that indexes structured and unstructured data sources (such as database, enterprise informative systems, documentation), elaborates information and presents dashboards in the form of dynamic jsp pages (Fig. 4).

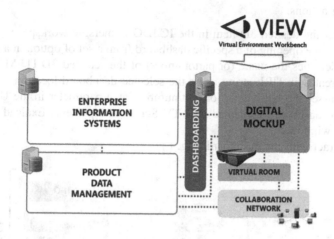

Fig. 4 Virtual environment workbench

The solution for Virtual Review allows the users to use the content in digital form, and to interact directly with the geometric model. It is moreover possible to interact with remote users, even if they are not present in the same place. Depending on privileges, users have instantaneous access to data. The integration between software for design, simulation and PDM allows taking the right decision with time and cost savings and with a greater product quality.

Technological Results

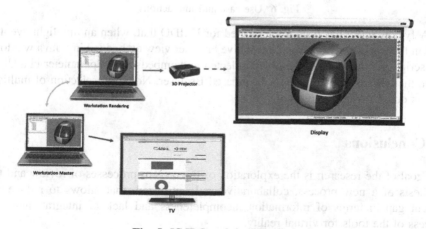

Fig. 5 IC.IDO and dashboarding

The results is a customization of IC.IDO, where users can retrieve all desired information by easily selecting the 3D ITEMs under review (components, assemblies, systems) and require the visualization of dashboards (Fig. 5).

Starting from the 3D interface in IC.IDO, dashboards are visualized by executing the following actions:

1. users select the desired 3D item in the IC.IDO immersive workspace
2. users select the opening of a specific dashboard from a set of option in a Ring Menu
3. IC.IDO identifies the name (or part/number) of the selected 3D ITEM
4. IC.IDO creates an URL string using the selected dashboard location
5. IC.IDO passes the item name (or part/number) as a parameter in the URL
6. the desired dashboard is opened on a TV Screen and presents Exalead results in a browsing windows
7. users interact with the dashboard (Fig. 6)

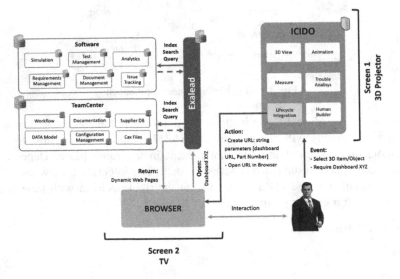

Fig. 6 Use case and interactions

A Jython Script has been implemented for IC.IDO that, when an highlight event is fired in the workspace, opens an interactive browser view embedded in a Java window. The script gets the name of the object selected and embeds it as a parameter in a URL. Then, the URL is opened using a Java-based Browser. Note that selection of multiple objects doesn't trigger the event.

4   Conclusions

The goal of the research is the exploration of the current processes of review and the synthesis of a new process, collaborative and optimized, that allows to reduce the current gap in terms of information incompleteness and lack of integration in the process of the tools for virtual reality.

The new solution aims to solve the problems that characterize the processes of development of a new complex product, reducing errors during planning, design and production.

It introduces innovation, as currently the technology of virtual reality is used only for displaying the geometry, but remain disconnected from all over the corporate world that surrounds the product.

The aggregation, in a single environment, of all the product-related information facilitates decision making so that the fulfilment of the requirements of the project is reached. Conducting periodic checks during the various stages of the life cycle of the product make possible to intervene at the right time and in the most appropriate manner, with considerable reduction of the time and cost of development and industrialization.

References

1. Caputo, F., Di Gironimo, G.: La realtà virtuale nella progettazione industriale (2007)
2. Garetti, T.: Product lifecycle management definizione, caratteristiche e questioni aperte. Technical report (2003). http://coenv.it/bo/allegati/Files/23_definizione_plm.pdf
3. Grieves, M.: Product Lifecycle Management: Driving the Next Generation of Lean Thinking. McGraw-Hill, New York (2005)
4. T, Lee, Verstraeten, J.: Product lifecycle management in aviation maintenance, repair and overhaul. Comput. Ind. **59**, 296–303 (2008). (Elsevier)
5. Mahdjoub, M., Monticolo, D., Gomes, S., Sagot, J.C.: A collaborative design for usability approach supported by virtual reality and a multi-agent system embedded in a PLM environment. Comput. Aided Des. (Adv. Emerg. Virtual Augmented Reality Technol. Product Des.) **42**, 402–413 (2009)
6. Mujber, T.S., Szecsi, T., Hashami, M.S.J.: Virtual reality applications in manufacturing process simulation. In: Proceedings of the International Conference on Advances in Materials and Processing Technologies: Part 2, vol. 155–156, pp. 1834-1838 (2004)
7. Grieves, M.: Digital twin: manufacturing excellence through virtual factory replication (2014)

3D Physics Virtual Laboratory as a Teaching Platform

Yevgeniya Daineko[1]([✉]), Madina Ipalakova[1], Viktor Dmitriyev[1,2],
Andrey Giyenko[1], and Nazgul Rakhimzhanova[1]

[1] Department of Computer Science and Software Engineering,
International IT University, 050040 Almaty, Kazakhstan
{yevgeniya2001,m.ipalakova,andrey.giyenko,nazgul.rakhimzhanova}@gmail.com
[2] Department of Computing Science, Carl von Ossietzky University of Oldenburg,
26129 Oldenburg, Germany
viktor.dmitriyev@uni-oldenburg.de

Abstract. Current work demonstrates an usage of the 3D Physics Virtual Laboratory within the teaching process of the students who are getting their bachelor degrees at a technical universities. The main advantages of presented software package is an utilization of the complete simulation of the real world physics in an virtual environment. Additional advantage of work is that it's flexibility-by-design. The flexibility of the 3D Physics Virtual Laboratory software package is achieved through the completed development loop adapted under agile methodology. The work also shows the overall structure of the components within the software package, technological foundation and description of the laboratory. The Microsoft .NET with it's framework .NET XNA were used as an software foundation for building core elements of the current 3D Physics Virtual Laboratory.

Keywords: Physics Virtual Laboratory · Higher education · Teaching · 3D · Physics · University

1 Introduction

For the Kazakhstan market, the new teaching techniques, that use information technologies, software systems and tools, that implement those techniques, become highly demanded [1]. Moreover, this issue is extremely important both for courses, that normally use computers and multimedia content in the education process, as well as for the subjects, that did not require use of information technologies initially.

One such example is the use of virtual laboratories. The Virtual Laboratory (VL) is a computer program or set of related programs carried out the computer simulations of certain processes [2]. The use of VL is particularly important in cases when it's impossible to conduct a real experiment and such conditions are happening very often in case of teaching physics. By with means of virtual laboratory almost everything can be simulated with a very good accuracy. For

L.T. De Paolis and A. Mongelli (Eds.): AVR 2015, LNCS 9254, pp. 458–466, 2015.
DOI: 10.1007/978-3-319-22888-4_34

example, the motion of material points and bodies in gravitational, electric and magnetic fields, the processes occurring in the different states of matter - solid, liquid, gas, plasma, and etc.

Besides Kazahstan, the virtual laboratories are rising a lot of attention around the globe. Most of the virtual laboratories are started as an in-house developments with particular functionality within the virtual environment. To list a few recently done work [3–6]. Each implementation has it's own main ideas behind to use particular developed tool in the teaching processes. Some of the virtual laboratories target the ability of bringing real work experience to the virtual world. Whether other virtual laboratories try to go beyond the border of the physical laboratory and enhance the understanding and acceptance rate from the students side.

The current work targets a creation of a balanced mixture of the various goals, which are related to the virtual laboratories in comparisons with real world laboratories:

– Bring real work experience to the virtual environment;
– Avoid usage of the 2D models as a projections (except the cases when it's unavoidable);
– Give the ability to take deeper look at the ongoing physical process;
– Create unique experiment data for each student for further interpretation;
– Automate routines and trivial experimental actions and making experiment more attractive;
– Provide safeness for the student while working on experiment;

As it was listed above, there are several advantages of a real virtual laboratories in comparison with real world laboratories.

First of all, in order to study in detail different physical processes it is not necessarily to buy quite expensive equipment and dangerous radioactive materials. Thus, for instance, specially equipped laboratories are required to conduct the laboratory works on quantum, atomic or nuclear physics.

Secondly, using the virtual physical laboratory it is possible to simulate the processes, which are impossible to reproduce in the lab. In particular, the majority of the classical laboratory works on molecular physics and thermodynamics are the close systems. At their output a set of electrical quantities is measured; then they are used to calculate unknown quantities, applying electrodynamics and thermodynamics equations. And all the molecular-kinetic and thermodynamic processes, which take place during the experiment, are inaccessible to observation.

While conducting the virtual laboratory works on these branches of physics, students can observe dynamical simulations of studied physical phenomena and processes, which cannot be seen during a real experiment. Moreover, it is possible at the time of the virtual experiment to observe graphical construction of the corresponding dependencies of physical quantities.

Thirdly, the virtual laboratory works can provide more descriptive visualization of physical and chemical processes, than it can be seen during the usual laboratory works. For example, with the virtual laboratory it is possible to examine the physical processes, such as motion of charged particles, or p-n-transition principle, in more detail and clearly. Besides, computer modeling of physical phenomena allows penetrating insight the processes, which last fractions of a second or several years, for instance, planetary motion.

Another important factor is safety. Applying the virtual laboratory to study physical processes is undoubtedly much safer way of studying rather than using the real laboratory equipment. In particular, the virtual laboratory works are more than justified in the cases of operations with high voltage or hazardous chemical substances.

The total amount of physics experiments that were implemented within the work is 6. The whole set of experiments is reflecting experiments that are typically given as a laboratory works during the Physics I course in the high educational schools (such as universities) in the Kazakhstan for non-physical technical degrees such as Computer Science.

2   The Use of the Agile Methodology for the Project Development

For many years software development system has been improved. The best practices have been accumulated and turned into the robust knowledge for some specific project types. At the developing of the 3D Physics the Virtual Laboratory, Agile methodology [7] was employed, since it is the most promising way of software development and engineering. Agile methodology corresponds to a new flexible style of software development. All its methods are based on iterative and incremental development, where requirements and solutions are accepted through team collaboration.

The main things that differ Agile from the traditional view of software process are adaptive planning and people-centered approach.

The main quotes that are associated with Agile methodology were accepted by agile founders and described within the "Manifesto for Agile Software Development" [8]:

- Individuals and interactions over processes and tools;
- Working software over comprehensive documentation;
- Customer collaboration over contract negotiation;
- Creating uniques experiment data for each student for interpretation;
- Responding to change over following a plan.

Scrum is the most spread software development methodology that supports the principles of Agile Manifesto. It is an incremental and iterative agile software development framework used for managing software projects development [9].

Key principle of Scrum is that the customers can change their views about what they want and need and those unpredictable changes in requirements can be easily ad-dressed using Scrum in opposite a traditional model of development.

Scrum is a set of principles which are the base for the development process. It al-lows within fixed short time intervals (sprints from 2 to 4 weeks) to provide working software with added functions to an end user. The functionality that needs to be implemented within a particular sprint is determined before the beginning at the planning stage and cannot be modified during the entire sprint. The fact that the length of any sprint is strictly fixed and short makes the development process predictable and flexible. Monitoring and control of the process are done by daily scrum meetings [9]. A classical Scrum consists of the following components [7,9]:

1. Roles: (a) product owner is a person responsible for the development of the product; (b) scrum-master is the main role usually performed by a project manager, provide an interface between a team and management, and in general is responsible for the project success; (c) team is a group of professionals (7 ± 2) that assumes obligations to fulfil the tasks with a sprint; team is self-organizing, self-managing and cross-functional.
2. Artefacts: (a) product backlog is a prioritized list of requirements with evaluation effort; (b) sprint backlog is a part product backlog with the highest overall importance ratings; (c) product increment is a new product functionality created during a sprint.
3. Processes (are characterized by Scrum meetings, as this methodology based on communications): (a) sprint planning; (b) sprint review; (c) scrum meeting; (d) sprint.

After describing the fundamental principles of Agile methodology and Scrum, it is possible to summarize that Agile means flexibility, adaptability, reduction of risks and scalability; orientation to the efficient team work and more probable and predictable deadlines.

3   Structure, Description and Technological Base of the 3D Physics Virtual Laboratory

In the process of developing a prototype of 3D scene of the Physics Virtual Laboratory the principle of economy of computer resources were addressed, ensuring the minimum system requirements, as well as realistic physical models and simulated processes. Another important factor is that the possibility of program code revision and edition. As well as ensuring the mutual independence of software modules for more efficient computations on the commodity hardware. In this context, it is appropriate to use integrated development environment that supports basic object-oriented programming paradigms together with robust and well supported by industry and community frameworks [10,11]. This is an advantageous difference of this project from existing analogues, which are difficult to modify and improve.

A virtual reality is an imitation of the real word that surrounds us to some extend. Usually, the imitation is done on very high level of quality, that means that virtual reality tries to copy the properties of an real world and reflect them to the virtual world. A virtual reality provides user of it with an ability to interact with objects and receive an feedback from the interaction. There are a multiple types of virtual reality exists. The main idea in differentiating between various types of virtual reality is how deep the user of a virtual reality immersed into particular virtual world. The most simplest way to achieve an virtual reality feeling at users side is to use a special type of software tools that are able to create 3D scenes on the screens of commodity computers. Usually, in 3D animation approach, the users play a role of an external observer. However, there is also a possibility to provide end user with manipulations facilities of the ongoing 3D simulated activities to give him or her "real feelings".

In order to facilitates highest possible involvement of the learner (e.g., students, pupils, etc.) in the learning process, the Physics Virtual Laboratory was designed in a way that it transfers a feeling of the real world interactions with particular laboratory equipment to the virtual world. In particular, the room, which is typical for physical experiments laboratory, was created and also equipped with tables, wardrobes, shelfs, lightning, etc. Additionally, for each specific laboratory task (Atwood machine, Maxwell's pendulum, Clèment-Desormes method for identification of adiabatic constant, as well as constant of Stefan-Boltzmann and investigations of photo conductivity properties of semiconductors), their own required equipments and it's parts were introduced. Besides having a demonstrative view on the equipment (animating the particular physical experiment), the laboratory is also able to generate new datasets for each particular measurement in order to make the students analyze his own, generated by him self, data. The generating data process is taking into consideration all physical properties of particular experiment and conditions it was placed into.

The overall structure of the 3D Physics Virtual Laboratory is shown on the Fig. 1. As it's shown on the Fig. 1, 6 physical experiments were ported to the virtual environments: (1) Atwood Machine; (2) Maxwell Pendulum; (3) Clèment-Desormes Method; (4) Magnetic Induction; (5) Stefan-Boltzmann Constant; (6) Photoconductivity Properties of Semiconductors. The figure represents the Component Diagram of the software package depicted in terms of Unified Modelling Language (UML) and adapted from [12].

From the software point of view, the virtual laboratory work is a project implemented in the C# language [13,14]. The entry point component of the 3D Physics Virtual Laboratory is implemented as a single screen with buttons which indicate six laboratory works, as it shown on the Fig. 2. By clicking on one of them particular laboratory work can be chosen. Also, Central Component Module contains instructions and a description of the physical experiment itself. All experiments were created using a template that reduces the time needed to work with the new software modules while adding new virtual experiments in the future.

When choosing a particular laboratory work from the main menu, the appropriate executable file of the laboratory work is executed. The bases of the laboratory works project is a "scenes". The scene consists out of a background components and particular physical experiment elements. The background scene

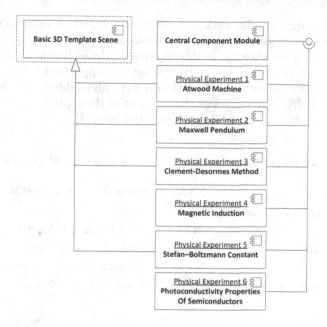

Fig. 1. Component diagram of the 3D Physics Virtual Laboratory

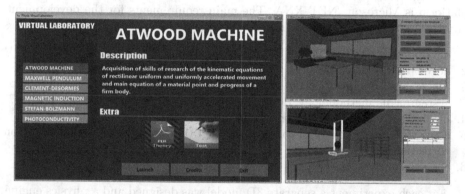

Fig. 2. General view of the 3D Physics Virtual Laboratory

components are common between almost all virtual experiments, whether the elements of the experiment are showing the only experiment related facilities. For example, in the "Physical Experiment 1: Atwood Machine", the experiment is consists of two weights of different mass connected by a light in extensible cord of particular length, which are passed over a pulley of predefined radius.

The software module 3D Physics Virtual Laboratory is developed in English, and includes instructions and guidelines for the completion of tasks, consistently built on the following form: the purpose of the task, the theoretical material, the experimental setup, instructions for writing of the task report. In addition, each lab contains a quiz that includes an assessment of the basic knowledge needed to successfully carry out the work and the final quiz, which aims to control the residual knowledge of the results of the laboratory work.

While choosing software for the development of three-dimensional scenes with the possibility of providing interactivity and the opportunity to emulate the physical world more accurately, 3 platforms were highlighted such as OpenGL, Direct3D and XNA. The results of the analysis of these platforms by the minimum criteria are shown on the Table 1 adapted from [1].

Table 1. Results of the virtual laboratories development platform analysis

Criteria	XNA	OpenGL	Direct3D
(a) Complexity of mastering	Low	High	High
(b) Supported Languages	.NET	Most languages	Most languages
(c) Popularity	Middle	High	High
(d) Support	Microsoft	Community	Community
(e) Future potential	High	Good	Normal

On the basis of this analysis, it was concluded that the most appropriate platform is Microsoft .NET XNA. The main requirements for the development of virtual physics laboratories are the following:

1. development quality;
2. development speed;
3. use of best practices in the field of software development (version control system, agile methodology, design, bug-tracking, automatic testing, etc.);
4. flexibility to address changing requirements;
5. convenient maintenance of the final product (updates, adding new labs, error correction);
6. the continuity of generations

For each experiment a separate 3D model was designed and a physics engine that calculates the interaction of the model objects was implemented. The models were created using Blender [15, 16] and Maya 3D [17], and the basic functionality has been implemented on the .NET platform, in particular C# programming language and Microsoft XNA 4.0 framework were used.

4   Conclusion

Thus, the current global trend in higher education is the widespread use of information and communications technology. The developed 3D Physics Virtual Laboratory is one of the examples of a teaching platform. The given application has a simple and effective design and authors strongly believe that the usage of such platforms is going to be one of the motivation factors to study physics subject for students. The further work will be done in two directions. The first direction is the usage of the web technologies and porting existing virtual laboratories to be acceptable via browser over web. The second direction is the process of adding new virtual laboratories in order to cover more aspects of the physic subject.

Acknowledgment. The work was done under the funding of the Ministry of Education and Science of the Republic of Kazakhstan 2015 Scientific Program (No. 2622/GF4).

References

1. Daineko, Y., Dmitriyev, V., Ipalakova, M., Chaiko, Y., Zhumakhmet, A.: Use of information and communication technologies (ict) in higher education. In: 7th The International Conference on New Trends in Information and Communication Technologies (ICTT), Almaty, Kazakhstan, February 2014
2. Trukhin, A.: Vidy virtualnykh kompyuternukh laboratoriy. Otkrytoe I distancionnoe obrazovanie **3**(11), 12–21 (2003)
3. Ali, N., Ullah, S., Rabbi, I., Alam, A.: The effect of multimodal virtual chemistry laboratory on students' learning improvement. In: De Paolis, L.T., Mongelli, A. (eds.) AVR 2014. LNCS, vol. 8853, pp. 65–76. Springer, Heidelberg (2014)
4. Saravanan, R.: Creating a browser-based virtual computer lab for classroom instruction. In: van der Walt, S., Bergstra, J. (eds.) Proceedings of the 13th Python in Science Conference, pp. 76–83. Austin, Texas (2014)
5. Ur Rehman, I., Ullah, S., Rabbi, I.: Measuring the student's success rate using a constraint based multi-modal virtual assembly environment. In: De Paolis, L.T., Mongelli, A. (eds.) AVR 2014. LNCS, vol. 8853, pp. 53–64. Springer, Heidelberg (2014)
6. Wu, B., Wang, A.I., Strom, J.E., Kvamme, T.B.: An evaluation of using a game development framework in higher education. In: 22nd Conference on Software Engineering Education and Training, 2009, CSEET 2009, pp.41–44. IEEE (2009)
7. Dingsøyr, T., Nerur, S., Balijepally, V., Moe, N.B.: A decade of agile methodologies: towards explaining agile software development. J. Syst. software **85**(6), 1213–1221 (2012)
8. Agile Manifesto Founders, A.: Manifesto for agile software development, May 2015. http://agilemanifesto.org/
9. Schwaber, K.: Agile project management with Scrum. Microsoft Press (2004)
10. Sung, K., Panitz, M., Wallace, S., Anderson, R., Nordlinger, J.: Game-themed programming assignments: the faculty perspective. In: ACM SIGCSE Bulletin, vol. 40, pp. 300–304. ACM (2008)
11. Furtado, A.W.B., Santos, A.L., Ramalho, G.L.: Computer games software factory and edutainment platform for Microsoft.NET. Software IET **1**(6), 280–293 (2007)
12. Daineko, Y., Dmitriyev, V.: Software module "virtual physics laboratory" in higher education. In: 8th International Conference on Application of Information and Communication Technologies, Astana, Kazakhstan, October 2014
13. Microsoft: C# language specification, May 2015. https://msdn.microsoft.com/en-us/library/ms228593(v=vs.100).aspx
14. Hejlsberg, A., Torgersen, M., Wiltamuth, S., Golde, P.: The C# Programming Language (Covering C# 4.0). Addison-Wesley Professional (2010)

15. Blender: blender.org - free and open 3D creation software, May 2015. http://www.blender.org/
16. Hess, R.: The essential Blender: guide to 3D creation with the open source suite Blender. No Starch Press (2007)
17. AutoDesk: Comprehensive 3D animation software, May 2015. http://www.autodesk.com/products/maya/overview

Experiences in the Development of an Augmented Reality Dressing Room

Ugo Erra$^{(\boxtimes)}$ and Valerio Colonnese

Dipartimento di Matematica, Informatica ed Economia,
Università Degli Studi Della Basilicata, Campus di Macchia Romana,
85100 Potenza, Italy
{ugo.erra,valerio.colonnese}@unibas.it

Abstract. Augmenting reality technology is changing the face of retail and altering consumer purchasing decisions wherever it is used, whether on home computers, mobile devices, or in kiosks in stores. This is because the technologies behind these applications are becoming increasingly affordable and sufficiently cheap that developers are exploiting their greatest potential to bring about a revolution in the way purchases are made. In this paper, we describe our experiences of designing an augmented reality dressing room where 3D models of the clothing are overlaid with a camera-captured color image to achieve the function of a virtual mirror. In this way, customers can move around to decide whether the clothing suits and fits them well. The project is implemented in Unity 4 Pro in combination with Microsoft Kinect 2 for the tracking process. In this paper, we discuss design issues and technical implementation and prospects for further development of the techniques.

Keywords: Augmented reality · Human body tracking · Dressing room

1 Introduction

Today, shopping has become a highly popular and time-consuming activity. For some people, clothes shopping is a leisure activity, whereas for others it is a stressful and tedious activity because of the guesswork involved in deciding whether a set of clothing suits and fits them well. Experiments with so-called augmented reality dressing room technology have been around for years. In these experiments, customers can try on clothing to check the fit or the style virtually rather than physically and make their purchases quickly and easily. These approaches implemented with augmented reality reflect the current state of the art in human body tracking technologies.

Recent developments in sensor technologies allow accurate and robust human body tracking, enabling a new set of possibilities. In particular, entertainment technologies such as Microsoft Kinect [1] and other related devices have lowered the barrier to entry to these possibilities in terms of both cost and development complexity. However, the technology behind Microsoft Kinect has gone much further than gaming and has been used in many contexts in very creative ways,

© Springer International Publishing Switzerland 2015
L.T. De Paolis and A. Mongelli (Eds.): AVR 2015, LNCS 9254, pp. 467–474, 2015.
DOI: 10.1007/978-3-319-22888-4_35

ranging from advanced user interfaces to high-quality 3D scans, and even as a tool for stroke recovery.

Therefore, the goal of the present study was to develop an augmented virtual dressing room application that can run on a common desktop personal computer equipped with an off-the-shelf Microsoft Kinect 2 device. This application can enhance the way customers shop and help them to choose the correct type of item of clothing. The proposed approach is designed to be computationally efficient, and it can be used with cheap hardware. The major benefits from this type of application are expected to be: (1) an improved ability to make a correct buying decision, reducing the time required; (2) increasing opportunities for fashion designers to experiment creatively; and (3) parallel use for other goods and accessories such as jewelry, spectacles, handbags, and shoes.

This paper describes our experiences during the design, with a discussion of the technical solutions that we chose for our approach. A sample application with a user interface was developed to test practicality and performance. The user interface allows the user to choose an item of clothing by making a hand movement toward it. Preliminary results indicate that this is a promising approach, and further design experiments are needed.

2   Related Works

In the past, several approaches have been implemented for augmented reality dressing rooms. These reflect the current state of the art in human body tracking technologies. Three lines of research are briefly discussed in this section: image processing, fiducial marker, and hardware-based tracking.

Martin and Erdal [2] present an image-processing design flow for visualizing an augmented dressing room and that is designed to be compatible with a common webcam. The software is implemented by a three-stage algorithm: detection and sizing of the user's body, identification of reference points based on face detection and augmented reality markers, and superimposition of the clothing over the user's image. The limitations of this tracking method means that clothes can be superimposed only as 2D images. A similar approach is described in [3].

Fiducial marker-based tracking involves the automatic detection of patterns in digital images that are taken with a camera. Kjrside et al. [4] propose a tag-based approach that requires the manual labeling of body parts with one or more markers. The video frames received from the camera are analyzed in real time using image-processing techniques to determine the 3D position and orientation of the markers and then to create an augmented reality of the customer wearing the clothing. A similar approach is presented in Araki and Muraoka [5]. The capturing of a person is accomplished by positioning small colored markers on the user's joints. The markers have different colors according to the placement on the body. A negative point of this approach is that the user cannot be captured from the side. In addition, more generally, the printed marker pattern must be placed on the user's body, which may be time-consuming and cumbersome from the consumer's point of view. The manual labeling of body parts with tags may also be a source of error.

Tracking hardware allows for a more accurate and robust solution that enables the investigation of various augmented reality dressing approaches. The solution proposed by Furkan and Gokcehan [6] is based on a 2D model that is scaled based on the distance between the user and the Microsoft Kinect sensor and then overlaid with the video image. However, this technique is designed specifically for t-shirts, and the researchers do not show the treatment in use for other items of clothing. A similar approach based on depth data from the Microsoft Kinect is presented in Presle [7]. Recently, several commercial applications have appeared based on the Microsoft Kinect. Such virtual dressing rooms are available from, for example, FaceCake [8] or Fitnect [9].

Our work also attempts to exploit body tracking technologies based on Microsoft Kinect. However, a key aspect of our solution that differs from other approaches is the use of 3D clothing with skeleton animation. This aspect allows the user complete freedom of the room and adds movement flexibility by utilizing smooth continuous tracking.

3 Fundamentals

This section provides a basic outline of the fundamentals of our approach, in particular for the two technologies used in our approach: Microsoft Kinect 2 (also known as Kinect for Xbox One) and Unity 3D.

Microsoft Kinect 2 [10] is a device for the Xbox One game console that allows users to control and interact with games through a natural user interface by using gestures and spoken commands. Microsoft Kinect 2 has a cone-shaped tracking area of 70°. The user comes into full view of the Microsoft Kinect 2 camera at approximately 1.4 m. At distances closer to the camera, only partial skeleton tracking is possible, and the end of the Microsoft Kinect 2 tracking range is 4.2 m from the camera. At its closest full body tracking range, the user can move up to 1 m to each side of the camera. At its furthest range, the user can move up to 2.9 m from each side of the camera. This results in a total tracking range of just over 10 m² [11]. The tracking process of the Microsoft Kinect 2 is based on retrieval of the particular body joint positions [12]. This algorithm allows real-time detection and tracking of the user's skeleton in a stable and efficient way. Moreover, the algorithm allows a full rotation of the body and a robust distinction between the left and right side of the user's body.

Unity 3D [13] is a feature-rich, fully integrated development engine that provides out-of-the-box functionality for the creation of interactive 3D content. With Unity, this content can be published on multiple platforms such as personal computer, Web, iOS, Android, and Xbox, and allows the augmented reality dressing room in combination with the Microsoft Kinect to be executed on several operating systems. Unity's complete toolset, intuitive workspace, and on-the-fly play testing and editing feature can save developers time and effort. Unity enables developers to extend its functionality by using platform-specific native code libraries called native plugins. These allow access to features such as OS calls and third-party code libraries that would otherwise not be available in Unity. Through these plugins, the Microsoft Kinect API set can be made available in Unity Pro (the commercial full version), giving developers full access to the Microsoft Kinect core functionality. In particular, the plugins enable vision detection and tracking functionality within Unity and allow developers to create augmenting applications and games relatively easily [1].

Fig. 1. A proposed basic setup of the dressing room. It consists of the Microsoft Kinect 2 device, a vertical display, and a computer. The person in front of the Microsoft Kinect is interacting at a certain distance and inside a limited area. The green line indicates the appropriate height placement of the Microsoft Kinect.

4 Design

The idea behind our augmented reality dressing room is to allow users to try on clothes virtually in front of a vertical large screen, which acts as an augmented mirror, so that the users can quickly decide whether the clothing fits them physically and aesthetically. In this way, customers can try on more clothes in less time. This may improve the mood of customers and help to affect their decision to buy the clothing or try it on for real.

Most approaches based on body tracking involve mapping a 2D texture as cloth to the user's body. When the user moves around, the clothing does not accurately capture the user's position and movement, therefore causing several unaesthetic effects. To achieve a more realistic simulation of the process of dressing, we based our approach on the adoption of 3D clothing models. This approach has several advantages. First, it does not make any assumption of the user's dimensions (body shape, height, width, length of limbs, etc.) from the data captured by Microsoft Kinect and therefore does not require a prior 3D scan. Second, the full 3D clothing model will always follow the motion of the user captured by the Microsoft Kinect. As the user moves around, the Microsoft Kinect will capture the skeleton tracking information, which will be mapped onto the 3D clothing model. In this way, the clothes will match the movements of the user. Therefore, a realistic simulation of dressing is achieved by the interaction between the skeleton of the user and the virtual skeleton of the 3D clothing model.

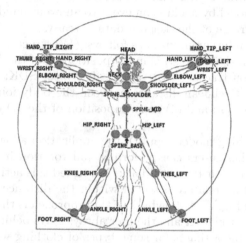

Fig. 2. The 20 joints that make up a Microsoft Kinect skeleton [14].

To use this approach, we require the editing of a skeleton animation in the 3D clothing model. Skeleton animation is a well-known technique used in computer animation in which a character is represented in two parts: a surface representation called a mesh used to render the character, and a hierarchical set of interconnected bones called the skeleton. Each bone in the skeleton is associated with some portion of the mesh's visual representation. In this way, the movement of a portion of the skin is influenced by one or more associated bones [15]. The rigging is the process of constructing the series of bones used to animate the mesh. Usually, a 3D computer graphics program is used to provide a default skeleton to animate humans, for example, 3D Studio Max, which is the program we used for our implementation. The modeler must place the joints exactly where they would be in a real-world skeleton and associate the bones with the mesh (Fig. 3). Although this technique is often used to animate human characters, it can be used to control the deformation of any object. In our case, the rigging is easy because we can use the default skeleton provided for human characters, but we only need to associate the bones that are bound to the mesh of the 3D clothing model (left and right foot bones are never used). For example, in the case of a long skirt, we require only the spine base and right and left knees.

The Microsoft Kinect SDK 2.0 provides information about the location of users standing in front of the Microsoft Kinect sensor array with detailed position and orientation data. These data are input into the application code as a set of 20 body joints (Fig. 2), namely skeleton position. These joints are used to locate the parts of the 3D clothing model and therefore represent the user's current position and pose. The application can therefore use the skeleton data to measure various dimensions of users' parts and control. In particular, we can use the Euclidean distance from the head to one of the ankles to estimate the user height and the distance between the left and right shoulders to estimate user width. The skeleton data are retrieved with the abovementioned image retrieval method—calling a frame retrieval method and passing a buffer—while our application can then use an event model by hooking an event to an event handler to capture the frame when a new frame of the skeleton data is ready.

Our approach can be summarized as follows: (1) extraction of the user tracking information from the video stream; (2) positioning of the 3D clothing model by using the skeleton tracker of the Microsoft Kinect SDK; (3) scaling of the model by using the Euclidean distance between the body joints and the user's distance from the sensor; and (4) superimposition of the 3D clothing model on the user.

Because the clothing model is in 3D, the application allows horizontal rotation of the user. Thus, users can perform a full rotation in front of the augmented mirror to see their front and back. We tested this action and found that the body joints are adequately detected within the distance range of approximately 2–3.2 m (see Fig. 1). A drawback of this approach is that the 3D model is superimposed on the top layer and the user always stays behind the model. This causes some inevitable artifacts for some types of clothing when users perform certain actions such as folding their arms.

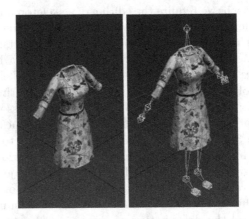

Fig. 3. A 3D item of clothing without (left) and with (right) the virtual skeleton.

Figure 4 shows the user interface elements in our application with some examples of clothing. The button on the upper right side can be used to force the application to re-acquire the user's dimensions. The buttons on right and left

Fig. 4. The user interface of the application and some examples of clothing.

central sides are functions for the selection of previous and next item of clothing. A hand position indicator shows the current coordinates of the hand on
the screen, similar to a mouse. This facilitates user interaction because it allows
users to switch easily from one item of clothing to another by simply holding
their hand above the elements for two seconds.

5 Conclusions

In this paper, we have described our experiences during the design of an augmented reality dressing room. We introduced our approach, which combines the
visualization capabilities of the game development tool Unity Pro with the position and body tracking capabilities of Microsoft Kinect 2. The overall system
software does not require calibration, is inexpensive, and is easy to use. The low
cost and ease of use makes it accessible to a wider group of vendors who do not
normally have access to a professional augmenting reality facility.

Compared with other approaches to augmenting reality dressing rooms, our
approach offers good visualization results in terms of appearance. Moreover,
our approach allows customers to move around relatively freely with an item of
clothing because the user's position and movement are captured with skeleton
mapping. At the same time, the initial setup in terms of the design of the 3D
clothing model is relatively inexpensive. Although it would mean that every piece
of clothing in a vendor's inventory would have to be modeled and textured and
added to the 3D repository in advance, several ad-hoc applications are available
for designing clothing, for example, Marvelous Designer [16].

In future work, our augmented reality dressing room may be enhanced in
some areas. First, we will conduct an empirical evaluation of the proposed system to investigate customer satisfaction in relation to service quality. The illumination of clothes by the lighting conditions of the real-world captured camera

images could be used to enhance the realism of the rendering. Another possible improvement is the implementation of a complete 3D scanning procedure of the clothing to enable a new item to be added into a 3D repository more quickly and easily.

Acknowledgements. Work in this paper has been funded by Basiliata Innovazione under the agreement "Studio di fattibilità finalizzato allo Sviluppo di una Vetrina 3D basata sulla Realtà Aumentata" in 2014.

References

1. Kinect SDK 2.0. https://www.microsoft.com/en-us/kinectforwindows/develop/
2. Martin, G.C., Oruklu, E.: Human friendly interface design for virtual fitting room applications on android based mobile devices. J. Sig Inf. Process. **3**(4), 481–490 (2012)
3. Shaikh, A.A., Shinde, P.S., Singh, S.R., Chandra, S., Khan, R.A.: A review on virtual dressing room for e-shopping using augmented reality. Int. J. Soft Comput. Eng. (IJSCE) **4**(5), 98–102 (2014)
4. Kjrside, K., Kortbek, K.J., Hedegaard, H., Grnbk, K.: ARDressCode: augmented dressing room with tag-based motion tracking and real-time clothes simulation. In: Central European Multimedia and Virtual Reality Conference (2005)
5. Araki, N., Muraoka, Y.: Follow-the-trial-fitter: real-time dressing without undressing. In: Third International Conference on Digital Information Management, 2008. ICDIM 2008, pp. 33–38, November 2008
6. Isikdogan, F., Kara, G.: A real time virtual dressing room application using kinect. In: Computer Vision Course Project (2012)
7. Presle, P.: A virtual dressing room based on depth data. Master's thesis, Institut für Softwaretechnik und Interaktive Systeme (2012)
8. Facecake marketing technologies, inc. http://www.facecake.com/
9. Fitnect. http://www.fitnect.hu/
10. Kinect for Windows features. https://www.microsoft.com/en-us/kinectforwindows/meetkinect/features.aspx
11. Greuter, S., Roberts, D.J.: Spacewalk: movement and interaction in virtual space with commodity hardware. In: Proceedings of the 2014 Conference on Interactive Entertainment, IE2014, pp. 1:1–1:7. ACM, New York (2014)
12. Shotton, J., Fitzgibbon, A., Cook, M., Sharp, T., Finocchio, M., Moore, R., Kipman, A., Blake, A.: Real-time human pose recognition in parts from a single depth image. In: CVPR. IEEE, June 2011
13. Unity Game Engine. https://unity3d.com/
14. Tracking Users with Kinect Skeletal Tracking. https://msdn.microsoft.com/en-us/library/jj131025.aspx
15. Parent, R.: Computer Animation: Algorithms and Techniques, 3rd edn. Morgan Kaufmann Publishers Inc., San Francisco, CA, USA (2012)
16. Marvelous designer. http://www.marvelousdesigner.com/

Development of a Virtual Laboratory for Investigating the Interaction of Materials with Plasma

Anuar M. Zhukeshov, Asylgul T. Gabdullina[✉], Assem Amrenova,
Zhandos M. Moldabekov, Anar Kusyman, Mira Amirkozhanova,
Tannur Bakytkazy, Kuantay Fermakhan, Argynbek Kaibar,
and Kaster Serik

Scientific – Research Institute of Experimental and Theoretical Physics,
Nanotechnology Laboratory of Kazakh National University Named After
al-Farabi, Almaty, Kazakhstan
azhukezhov@gmail.com,
{a_gabdullina, kusiman_anar}@mail.ru

Abstract. It was investigated the obtaining of the surfaces on the metal alloys with the help of treatments of the pulsed plasma accelerators. It was created the virtual laboratories and e-books for visualization of the physical processes appearing through the plasma treatment. After pulsed processing of the metal materials surface by plasma, the subsurface layers with new properties, consisting of modified structure, were formed. The virtual model of plasma effects on materials was developed in the present work.

Keywords: Pulsed plasma treatment · Vacuum-plasma method · Spraying · Visualization

1 Introduction

In the last decades, concentrated energy flows are actively used for modification and doping of the surface layers of metallic and semiconductor materials. High-current electron beams, powerful ion beams, continuous and pulsed laser beams, high-temperature pulsed plasma flows are widely used [1, 2]. Results of recent studies of pulsed plasma accelerators [3, 4] have shown, that materials processing by high-energy fluxes leads to significant changes of the microstructure and phase composition (selection of small dispersion secondary phase, the formation of metastable phases, etc.).

The main effects of the pulsed plasma on the material surface are heating to a high temperature, melting and fast cooling, which lead to the hardening of subsurface layers. Theoretical and practical significance of the study is closely related to the use of plasma treatment: plasma cleaning and surface activation and processing, as well as the surface of the semiconductor products in a vacuum, quartz, glass and other dielectric materials introduction. Methods of pulsed plasma treatment based on the ultrafast energy impact of plasma flows in the surface layers of the material were studied. This methods are the

L.T. De Paolis and A. Mongelli (Eds.): AVR 2015, LNCS 9254, pp. 475–481, 2015.
DOI: 10.1007/978-3-319-22888-4_36

part of vacuum-plasma methods of surface modification, mainly based on magnetron and vacuum arc technology [5, 6]. However, the pulsed plasma processing showed the active development, which expects more effective results [7]. And for the visualization of such processes the use of the modern electronics resources is important.

2 The Experimental Data and the Stages of Development of a Virtual Laboratory

It was used two different devices to study the process of spraying and processing of materials with plasma treatment. Coaxial plasma accelerator-30 (CPA-30) is a simplified version of the Marshall accelerator and can be used with the gas content. The scheme and working principle of the Vacuum arc accelerator (VAA-1) are similar to CPA but there is the difference in the construction and output parameters [8, 9] (Table 1).

Table 1. CPA-30 and VAA-1 technical parameters

Devices		CPA-30	VAA-1
Discharge voltage		7–30 кV	300–1000 V
Discharge current		100–350 кА	5–35 A
Capacity of system memory		to 70 мcF	to 300 мcF
Electrode material		Copper	Copper
Electrode diameter	External	0,09 m	0,09 m
	Internal	0,03 m	0,03 m
The length of the electrode	External	0,6 m	0,09 m
	Internal	0,55 m	0,05 m
Gas		Constant pressure air	Constant pressure air
Energy flux density		$0,1$–$1,5 \times 10^5$ J/m^2	$1,4 \times 10^3$ J/m^2
Pulse duration		10–20 μs	10–20 μs
The temperature of the plasma		10^4–10^5 K	10^4–10^5 K
Plasma particle velocity		$(1$–$15) \times 10^5$ m/s	10^3 m/s

In the experiment with using of the two different devices the plasma temperature of the CPA-30 was 10^4–10^5 K at which the melting of the subsurface layer material and the change in structure and properties occur. On the VAA-1 device the temperature of the plasma flows are much lower and plasma treatment leads to the sputtering of the surface layer and at the exposure of which the surface of the materials was formed.

In the experiment the samples of the construction materials as steel (2 mm thick) and aluminum (2 mm thick) were used. Aluminum and steel samples undergone the preliminary treatment (grinded and polished). Then the metal samples were exposed by plasma modification on CPA-30 and VAA-1 devices.

To study the changes of the structure and physical-mechanical properties of the tested materials were used the known methods of analysis: scanning electron (Quanta 200i 3D on the microscope investigated) and atomic force microscopy, X-ray spectral and X-ray structure development (D8 ADVANCE studied on the diffractometer), metallography etc. [10].

For the investigation of the pulse-plasma interaction with the surface of the material the virtual laboratory and e-books were created. (Figs. 1a, b, 2a, b).

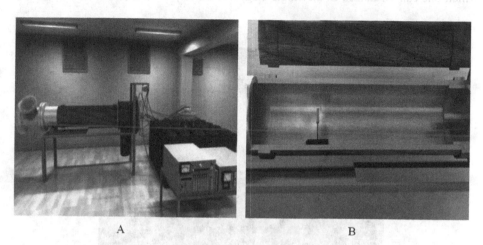

A   B

Fig. 1. Virtual laboratory screenshot a) The appearance of the accelerator CPA-30, b) the surface of the material under the influence of the plasma processing

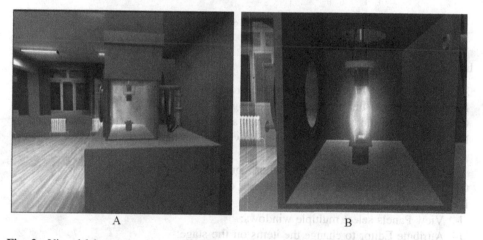

A   B

Fig. 2. Virtual laboratory screenshot a) The appearance of the accelerator VAA-1, b) plasma pollinated under the influence of the surface of the material to be processed

The Virtual laboratory was created with the help of the Autodesk Maya packages. The Autodesk Maya packages allow to create the computer graphics, visualization, 3D models and animation environment with dynamic effects (Fig. 3) [7]. Then with the help of this program the data for pulsed plasma processing of materials on two experimental laboratory devices obtained on several years were issued in the electronic form. The given electronic page was developed such way that the experiment data can be filled any time. The created Virtual laboratories and electron pages on the plasma treatment of the surface materials were combined into a single interface with the help of which one can visualized as the single stages of the experiment as a whole one.

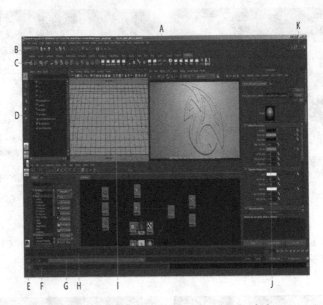

Fig. 3. For Autodesk Maya 2015 Service Pack 3 users

In Fig. 3 are shown:

A- Menu bar and the main roads of the program;
B- Status Line visual processes on the stage;
C- Shelf - with the help of Maya - quick and large selection of used equipment;
D- QWERT Toll Box and transformacïlaw establishment of a unit;
E- Help Line on auxiliary data;
F- Command Line via MEL or Python commands in writing;
G- Range Slider staff to change the range of right-to-left;
H- Time Slider object animation;
 I- View Panels select multiple windows;
 J- Attribute Editor to change the items on the stage;
K- Modeling Toolkit, Channel Box, Attribute Editor, Tool Box-editing geometry.

To make the model of the VAA - 1 and the CPU – 30 devices the Autodesk Maya software was used.

Modeling of the pump tube of VAA - 1 installation's external camera is presented on the Fig. 4.

Modeling for animation of the work of VAA - 1 installation is presented on Fig. 5.

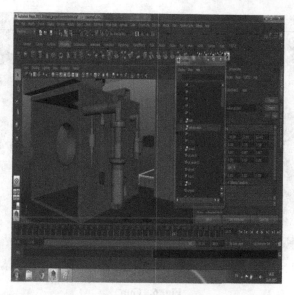

Fig. 4. Pump tube of VAA - 1 installation's external camera

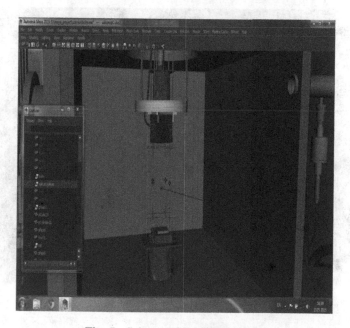

Fig. 5. Scheme of VAA installation

At the development of the gun which was necessary for CPU – 30 installation it was used the UV texture editor command (Fig. 6).

The general external imagion of CPU – 30 installation is presented on Fig. 7.

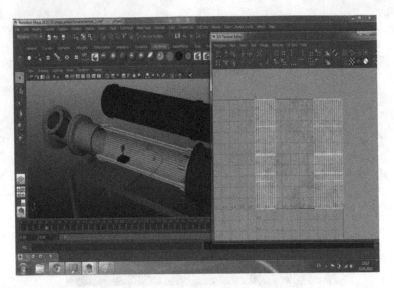

Fig. 6. Gun

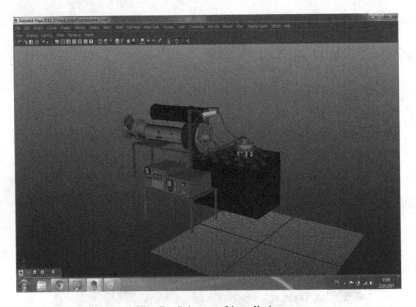

Fig. 7. Scheme of installation

3 Conclusions

Thus, the using of plasma accelerators in plasma treatment of the materials is the unique method of the modification of the surfaces of the various materials and the presented Virtual laboratory can allow to investigate the processes occurring at the pulsed plasma treatment by different treatment technologies. In addition, this Virtual laboratory can be used in the education and scientific aims.

Acknowledgements. The work is funded by grants №3058, 3111 GF4/2015 for basic research in the natural sciences of the MES RK Science Committee.

References

1. Richter, E., et al.: Modification of titanium surface by its alloying with silicon using intense pulsed plasma beams. Surf. Coat. Technol. **158–159**, 324–327 (2002)
2. Peng, Z., Miao, H., Wang, W., Yang, S., Liu, C., Qi, L.: Hard and wear-resistant titanium nitride films for ceramic cutting tools by pulsed high energy density plasma. Surf. Coat. Technol. **166**(2), 183–188 (2003)
3. Chebotarev, V.V., Garkusha, I.E., Langner, J., Sadowski, M., Starosta, W., Tereshin, V.I., Derepovski, N.T.: Surface structure changes induced by pulsed plasma streams processing. Plasma Phys. **3**(3), 273–275 (1999)
4. Chebotarev, V.V., Garkusha, I.E., Langner, J., et al.: Surface structure changes induced by pulsed plasma streams processing. Probl. At. Sci. Technol.: Plasma Phys. **3**(3), 273–275 (1999)
5. Lieberman, M.A., Lichtenberg, A.G.: Principles of Plasma Discharges and Materials Processing, p. 450. Wiley, New York (1994)
6. Grigoriev, S.V., Koval, N.N., Devjatkov, V.N., Teresov, A.D.: In: Proceedings of the 9th International Conference on Modification of Materials with Particle Beams and Plasma Flows, Tomsk, pp. 19–22 (2008)
7. Chebotarev, V.V., Garkusha, I.E., Bovda, A.M., Tereshin, V.I.: Application of pulsed plasma accelerators for surface modification. Nukleonika **46**, 27–30 (2001)
8. Morozov, A.I.: Physics and Application of Plasma Accelerators, vol. 268. Tekhnika, Minsk (1974)
9. Artsimovich, L.A. (ed.): Plasma Accelerators, vol. 268, p. 416. Mashinostroenie, Moscow (1973)
10. Zhukeshov, A.M.: Status and prospects of research on modification of materials by pulsed plasma flows. In: Proceedings of National Academy of Sciences of Kazakhstan, vol. 6, pp. 35–38 (2006)
11. Ganeev, R.M.: 3D-modeling characters in Maya. - M. Hotline - Telecom, p. 284 (2012)

Aspects Concerning Algorithms of VRML Surfaces' Generation

Lucian Ilea[1], Catalin Boanta[1], Cornel Brisan[1(✉)],
and Veturia Chiroiu[2]

[1] Department of Mechatronics and System Dynamics,
Technical University of Cluj-Napoca, Cluj-Napoca, Romania
{ylucian, boanta_catalin}@yahoo.com,
Cornel.Brisan@mdm.utcluj.ro
[2] Institute of Solid Mechanics of the Romanian Academy, Bucharest, Romania
veturiachiroiu@yahoo.com

Abstract. 3D objects and generation of surfaces are important issues in several areas, such as simulators and games. There are different methods of approach to this subject: methods based on interpolation, using Voronoi diagrams and even unusual ones, based on Fractal Theory. This article presents and explores a method, which combines basic Geometry and probabilistic changes in both the shape and position of a given 2D curve.

Keywords: Surface · Tetragon · 2D curve · 3 × 3 matrix of probabilities · VRML scene

1 Introduction

The problem of generating surfaces in a realistic way is an obvious issue that arises within a large group of applications: simulators, games, modelling and the display of maps. The questions that arise are connected to the method of representation of the surfaces and to the the method used to combine both randomness and uniformity. Several ways to represent surfaces can be considered, each with its own benefits: surfaces represented as a collection of spatial triangles, surfaces represented as a matrix of given heights over a rectangular grid, surfaces represented as quadtrees.

There are several ways that have been considered and investigated, in order to describe the surfaces mathematically. In the early 1960s, parametric curves and surfaces were introduced by Ferguson at the Boeing Company and later discussed and enhanced in [1, 2]. Independently, in the late 1960s, another method that uses four boundary conditions was introduced by Coons. These aspects have also been presented in [3, 4]. Therefore, even if controlling the design of surfaces is laborious and unintuitive, the parametrization concept has been universally adopted and has become a standard method for describing curves and surfaces.

Some other methods of generating surfaces [5] considered that the generation of 3D surfaces is a process that consists of two important steps, the first step being used to create a random surface and the second step being used to smoothen the rough surface resulted from the first step. In [6] the authors investigated the ways to apply the

© Springer International Publishing Switzerland 2015
L.T. De Paolis and A. Mongelli (Eds.): AVR 2015, LNCS 9254, pp. 482–489, 2015.
DOI: 10.1007/978-3-319-22888-4_37

Douglas-Peucker algorithm [7] to reduce the number of points that are used to represent a 3D surface, introducing an extension of the so called "onion-peeling" algorithm [8].

This research proposes a coherent way to apply two known techniques: independent jumps and Coons patching over a set of 2D curves belonging to the same family, investigating the results which can be obtained.

The considered surfaces lie inside a transparent cuboid of a given size. Without restricting the generality, the height is taken into account only at the end of the process and is obtained by applying a simple vertical scaling of the surface. Figure 1 contains an example of a surface that can be obtained.

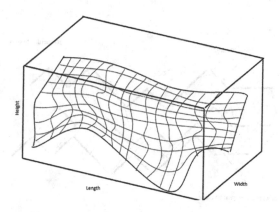

Fig. 1. Example of desired surface

2 Generating the Surfaces

The 3D surface generating process can be split in two parts: the rough part and the adjusting one.

2.1 Rough Surface Generating Technique

The process starts with a 2D curve made exclusively out of pairs of segments with equal lengths, in one of the following possible configurations: ∧ (peaks), – (horizontal areas), ∨ (valleys). Figure 2 contains an example of a starting 2D curve.

The initial curve is copied and then modified in two ways:

1. In terms of location, in the coordinate system, the copy is placed right beside its original position and then moved to a nearby new vertical 2D plan. This process is repeated for an established number of times. Different settings may be added, for instance: the copy always gets a smaller height than its previous state. Figure 3 shows two copies of the same original 2D curve.

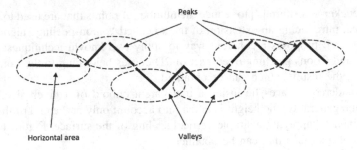

Fig. 2. Initial 2D curve example

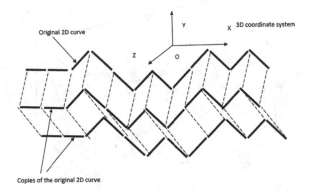

Fig. 3. Two copies of the initial 2D curve

2. In terms of shape, each pair of consecutive segments may change its configuration into a different one (for instance from peaks to horizontal areas or valleys). Figure 4 shows how the configurations can change.

These changes take place according to a 3 × 3 matrix of probabilities for one configuration to turn into another. This matrix is shown in Table 1. For instance, P[0][1] is the probability for a peak to transform into a horizontal area in the next generated copy of the 2D curve. The sum of the values in the P table for each line equals 1.

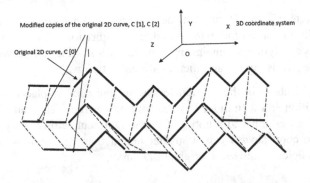

Fig. 4. Two modified copies of the initial 2D curve

Table 1. The P matrix which contains the probabilities for configurations to transform

P	∧	–	V
∧	P[0] [0]	P[0] [1]	P[0] [2]
–	P[1] [0]	P[1] [1]	P[1] [2]
V	P[2] [0]	P[2] [1]	P[2] [2]

The values from this table can seriously affect the final shape of the surface, its influence thus becoming a field of interest in this research.

2.2 Adjusting the Surface

At this point, the rough surface can be considered a collection of adjacent torsioned tetragons, as seen in Fig. 5. Because of the random changes added in the values of coordinates, it is a reliable assumption that no two different vertices of the tetragons have the same y (height) value.

The surface's aspect can now be improved, as each tetragon that initially appeared

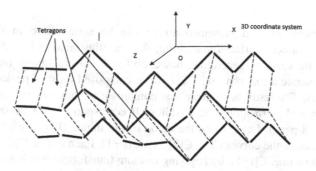

Fig. 5. Tetragons formed by corresponding segments in successive modified 2D curves

in the rough surface is then divided into smaller pieces that reflect differences better. This step can be performed algorithmically by either using an extension of the recursive dividing technique on which quadtrees are built or by a method that divides pairs of opposite edges of the tetragons and subsequently connects corresponding points. The second method, which uses the division in the same number of segments for each two opposite edges of one tetragon is based on the fact that all the lines which connect corresponding points from opposite edges intersect all the lines constructed for the other pair of opposite segments of the tetragon. Actually, this is a particular case of the general method named "Coons patch" [4], used to smoothly join surfaces together.

The number of segments on each pair of opposite edges can be arbitrarily chosen. In Fig. 6 a number of four segments was chosen.

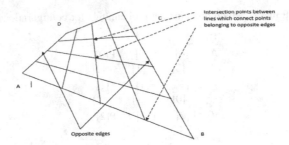

Fig. 6. The ABCD tetragon is divided into smaller pieces by connecting corresponding points situated on opposite edges

Fig. 7. VRML scene. Surface obtained after the adjusting step

The generating method presented above can be summarised in the following algorithm and produces surfaces resembling the one illustrated in Fig. 7.

Algorithm for surfaces generating, based on the 3×3 probability matrix:

Step 1. Generate a random initial 2D curve composed only of peaks, valleys and horizontal areas. The result is an array that contains n integer values belonging to the $\{-1, 0, 1\}$ set (-1 corresponds to a valley, 0 corresponds to a horizontal area, 1 corresponds to a peak). Let C[0] be the name of the initial 2D curve.

Step 2. Generate the curves C[1], C[2], ..., C[n−1]. Each curve, C[i], is determined from the previous one, C[i−1], by applying random transformations based on the 3×3 P matrix.

Step 3. For each curve, C[i], i = 0, ..., n−1, determine the coordinates of the points situated at the ends of its segments and apply random displacements.

Step 4. For each tetragon determined by two corresponding segments apply the adjustment method.

3   Numerical Results

A C++ program was obtained based on the ideas presented above. This program allows the user to choose different values in the initial 3×3 P matrix. The program creates a VRML file (these files have the extension.wrl) that can be opened by common browsers like Google Chrome or Internet Explorer.

Table 2 contains the results obtained for some predefined values in the P matrix.

Table 2. Surfaces obtained for different values in the 3×3 P matrix

P matrix	Surfaces
P /\ – – \/ /\ 0.0 1.0 0.0 – – 0.0 1.0 0.0 \/ 0.0 1.0 0.0	 Particular case: a smooth surface is obtained. The probability of transformation into horizontal area equals 1.
P /\ – – \/ /\ 0.8 0.1 0.1 – – 0.1 0.8 0.1 \/ 0.1 0.1 0.8	 The probabilities of preserving the same shape between consecutive steps are high, the main diagonal having a value of 0.8.
P /\ – – \/ /\ 1.0 0.0 0.0 – – 0.0 1.0 0.0 \/ 0.0 0.0 1.0	 Particular case: the surface follows the shape of the initial 2D curve. The probability matrix has 1 on its main diagonal.
P /\ – – \/ /\ 0.0 1.0 0.0 – – 0.0 0.0 1.0 \/ 1.0 0.0 0.0	 Particular case: the surface is composed of a succession of peaks, valleys and horizontal areas.

P	$\wedge$	$--$	$\vee$
$\wedge$	0.2	0.6	0.2
$--$	0.2	0.6	0.2
$\vee$	0.2	0.2	0.6

Due to random values in the P matrix, a realistic surface may be obtained.

P	$\wedge$	$--$	$\vee$
$\wedge$	0.4	0.1	0.5
$--$	0.5	0.1	0.4
$\vee$	0.4	0.5	0.1

Random values in the 3x3 P matrix.

P	$\wedge$	$--$	$\vee$
$\wedge$	0.0	0.0	1.0
$--$	0.0	1.0	0.0
$\vee$	1.0	0.0	0.0

Particular case: each peak is followed by a valley and vice-versa. The horizontal areas remain unchanged.

4   Conclusions

The presented algorithm, which is based on the 3×3 matrix of probabilities and independent jumps, may very well lead to the creation of diverse surfaces. The shape of the surfaces is created in a non-parametric manner requiring minimal mathematical computation. This way, a user friendly and straightforward approach is developed.

The variation of the probability matrix leads to the generation of different types of surfaces. The shift between peaks, valleys and horizontal areas starts from a particular case and evolves randomly due to the probability matrix, this being the tool for the user to improve or obtain any desired types of surfaces (e.g. predominant peaks/valleys, smooth surfaces or realistic surfaces).

Future research will study the possibility of developing an adaptative algorithm, which would process the randomly generated rough surfaces by creating new lines according to different rules and step by step updating of the table of probabilities, P.

Acknowledgements. This research was elaborated through the PN-II-PT-PCCA-2011-3.1-0190 Project nr. 149/2012 of the National Authority for Scientific Research (ANCS, UEFISCDI), Romania. Research supported by the grant 149/2012.

References

1. Ailisto, H., Pietkainen, M.: Ferguson patch based method for representation of 3-D scenes. In: Conference. Robotics and Automation. Proceedings (1987). doi:10.1109/ROBOT.1987. 1087764
2. Yamaguchi, F.: Curves and Surfaces. In: Computer Aided Geometric Design, pp. 87–134. Springer, Heidelberg (1998)
3. Farin, G.: Curves and Surfaces for Computer Aided Geometric Design, 4th edn. Academic Press, San Diego (1997)
4. Nielson, G.M., Holliday, D., Roxborough, T.: Cracking the cracking problem with Coons patches. In: Proceedings of the Visualization 1999, pp. 285–290. IEEE Computer Society Press, Los Alamitos (1999)
5. Saupe, D.: Algorithms for random fractals. In: Peitgen, H.-O., Saupe, D. (eds.) The Science of Fractal Images, pp. 71–136. Springer-Verlag New York Inc., New-York (1988)
6. Ilea, L., Munteanu, L., Dumitriu, D., Dudescu, M., Brişan, C., Chiroiu, V.: Aspects of generating 3D surfaces with applications to 3D normal tire/off road contact. The publishing house of the Romanian Academy (2015)
7. Douglas, D.H., Peucker, T.K.: Algorithms for the reduction of the number of points required to represent a digitized line or its caricature. Cartographica. Int. J. Geogr. Inf. Geovisualization 10, 112–122 (1973)
8. Fadili, M.-J., Mahmoud, M., Abderrahim, E.: Non-convex onion-peeling using a shape hull algorithm. Pattern Recogn. Lett. 25, 1577–1585 (2004)

Towards a Framework for Information Presentation in Augmented Reality for the Support of Procedural Tasks

Tobias Müller[(✉)]

Robert Bosch GmbH, Robert-Bosch-Campus 1, 71272 Renningen, Germany
Tobias.Mueller8@de.bosch.com

Abstract. The support of procedural tasks is a very promising application of augmented reality and is already used in practice, e.g. in VW's MARTA app. The design of user interfaces for this purpose still poses a problem to date and is only partly covered by guidelines. In this paper a framework to model information presentation in such user interfaces is proposed. It consists of five conceptual layers which are (i) the physical world, (ii) the mediated physical world (e.g. by some video device), (iii) virtual objects which are spatially referenced and are of spatial nature (e.g. 3D models of physical parts), (iv) virtual objects that are spatially referenced but not of spatial nature (e.g. annotations) and (v) objects that don't have any connection to the physical world (e.g. information on the current progress of the task). Additionally the six design criteria "clarity", "consistency", "visibility", "information linking", "position preservation" and "orientation" are given that define how these layers must be presented and how a connection between them must be made. Where possible, measures how to implement these criteria are suggested.

Keywords: Augmented reality · Mixed reality · User interface

1 Introduction

In recent years augmented reality has become a promising technology for supporting procedural tasks, which are common in many work domains like manufacturing or maintenance. This is due to the ability to show information concerning the work steps spatially registered and in situ at the work place. Even though first systems like VW's MARTA app are already in practical use, it is not yet known how to structure and display information in augmented reality applications and instead naive approaches are used. Examples are CAD models that are laid directly over their corresponding physical objects or labels which are placed arbitrarily in the view area. Obviously these approaches will not lead to optimal work results because the user will most likely miss out important information about the physical world, will have to deal with a big cognitive overload etc.

These problems need to be addressed and measures must be defined to help designers to create improved user interfaces. Thus currently a conceptual framework is in development that consists of five conceptual layers, which represent different types of information and includes rules on how to present and how to connect these layers. The current

© Springer International Publishing Switzerland 2015
L.T. De Paolis and A. Mongelli (Eds.): AVR 2015, LNCS 9254, pp. 490–497, 2015.
DOI: 10.1007/978-3-319-22888-4_38

state will be presented in the following. Please note that due to its prevalence currently only visual augmented reality is addressed. Also the framework is fully focused on the support of procedural tasks and guidelines for other areas, e.g. quality control, may and probably will widely differ.

2   Related Work

For user interfaces of classical desktop systems a lot of extensive guidelines exist. A very well known standard is ISO 9241 with parts like 110 with guidelines on dialogue principles or 151 with guidelines on World Wide Web user interfaces [11]. Besides that also much literature on guidelines for user interfaces has been published (e.g. [10, 25]). Though some parts are transferable to augmented reality [5], the problem still is that these guidelines do not address the combination of a physical environment and virtual data, which is the core of augmented reality. Also they are optimized for a limited 2D screen space, which does not exist in an augmented reality setting.

For virtual reality, which is closer to augmented reality in many aspects than traditional desktop systems, guidelines have been created as well (e.g. [2, 4]). Though they can give relevant input, they are not addressing the combination of physical world and virtual data and the limited manipulability of the physical environment.

For augmented reality several design recommendations have already been proposed and their development is still subject of current research and scientific discussion. One approach, presented in [5], is to transfer known rules for desktop user interfaces to augmented reality user interfaces. This leads to a set of rules, which are rather general. Other authors concentrated on collecting the available knowledge on human perception in augmented reality environments, e.g. how colors are perceived with changing backgrounds or what kind of text drawing styles are most legible and infer implications for the design of augmented reality applications [17, 19]. As part of the SKILLS research project a guideline has been created on how to support learning of procedural skills with the help of virtual and augmented reality [28, 29]. The authors propose several features that an augmented reality based training system should include. Besides these more general approaches a lot of research has been done on specific problems like text legibility (e.g. [7, 8]) or depth perception (e.g. [6, 20]), which needs to be taken into account for optimal support of procedural tasks.

One approach to describe augmented reality user interfaces, which is also based on layers that are called spaces by the authors, was made by Vincent et al. [26, 27]. They divide the augmented space into the subspaces physical world, the representation of the physical world, the augmentation and the control space. In their model the four spaces are connected by spatial mappings that are affected by inaccuracies, e.g. tracking errors or imprecise gestures. To mitigate problems that arise from the inaccuracies they suggest interaction techniques that relax the spatial relations or work on different spaces. Even though their model includes layers as well, these are used to address interaction and not information presentation.

3   Five Layers of Information

The basis of the proposed framework is formed by five conceptual layers each representing a different graduation of the spatial connection information can have. The two lowest layers originate in the physical world. The first one, called direct physical layer, contains the information the user perceives from the physical world and thus has the highest spatial connection of all of them. The next one, called indirect physical layer, contains the information from the physical world the user perceives in a mediated way, e.g. via a video see-through HMD or a mobile device. The upper three layers originate from virtual data. The third layer, called spatial virtual layer, contains all the virtual objects which are spatially referenced and are of spatial nature, e.g. 3D models of physical parts. The fourth, called spatially referenced virtual layer, contains the virtual objects that are spatially referenced but not of spatial nature, e.g. annotations. The fifth, called symbolic virtual layer, contains the objects that don't have any spatial connection to the physical world, e.g. information on the current progress of the task.

It is important to understand that the spatial connection does not stand for proximity to the viewpoint of the user or implies an order of overlapping. It is easily possible that virtual objects are placed behind physical objects or may not even be visible. Also not all the layers have to exist in every application, e.g. when an HMD with optical see-through is used, no indirect physical layer is present. The only constraint is that at least one of the two physical and one of the three virtual layers have to exist.

From a user's standpoint the various layers are combined into one overall perception, which can be highly volatile. Depending on the environment and the virtual data a slight change, e.g. caused by a change of the view point or a change in one of the layers, can cause a very different perception. Also the intensification of one layer diminishes the other layers. An example for this are combinations of one color and different backgrounds, which can significantly influence the way the color is perceived by the viewer [19]. This changing perception creates a cognitive overhead for the user that diverts mental resources from executing a work task and thus slowing her or him down and making the work more error prone. This can even lead to rendering an augmented reality application useless [17]. Thus the sensory and mental effort to perceive the information from the layers must be minimized.

The layers do not only overlay each other but are also connected with each other. Objects from one layer, e.g. a screw in the direct physical layer, correspond with objects from other layers, e.g. the model of a screw in the spatial virtual layer. Usually the connection is made by spatial mapping, i.e. by overlaying the virtual objects on the physical world in close proximity or directly over the corresponding physical object. Again, the mental effort for the user to make the connections must be minimized (in most cases, there may be situations during learning that require it [28]).

Also the mapping of the five layers to each other can be affected by errors and imprecision [26, 27]. The connection of the virtual with the physical layers may be affected by tracking errors. The connection of the virtual layers and the indirect physical layer to the direct physical layer may be affected by delay caused by slow hard- or software. Again, the mental effort to compensate these effects must be minimized.

4 Design Criteria

In the following six criteria are presented that define how these layers must be presented and how a connection between them must be made. Where possible, measures how to implement these criteria are suggested. Depending on the application scenario, the environment, the used combiner etc. some of these measures may not be applicable or new ones must be added and thus the given list can only be a starting point. While some criteria could be applied to an augmented reality user interface without the concept of the layers, e.g. clarity, especially visibility and information linking rely on it.

- **Clarity.** The presentation of single objects must be optimized with consideration that the different layers are combined into one view. Independently from the current superposition of the layers the user must be able to perceive all the visible relevant information with minimal sensory or mental effort. This criterion especially includes measures to improve color selection, text representation and distinguishability of objects. However, the actual measures depend on the application scenario, the environment and the combiner.

  Colors play an important role and must be easily seen and distinguished by the user. Thus measures to select appropriate colors and luminescence and to handle the combination of colors are important. In case of optical see-through systems or semi-transparent objects, the shine through of colors is also relevant. Overviews over color perception in augmented reality environments and recommendation on color usage can be found in [17, 19].

  Text must be easily legible for the user. Measures to ensure this are the selection of the right font size [23], the text color and the drawing style [7, 8, 18]. Anyway, it has not been finally clarified how to predict legibility in augmented reality applications depending on the environment.

  To help the user to differentiate virtual objects, these should be spatially separated. This can be either done via a vertical or horizontal distance [1, 21] or by a stereoscopic separation [22].

- **Visibility.** All the information that is needed to complete the current work step must be fully visible to the user. Besides the virtual objects this also includes the visibility of the relevant parts of the physical world. These must not be covered or cluttered. Especially when important physical parts are not or only hardly visible behind virtual objects, the augmented reality application hinders the user more than it provides support.

  From existing research on overlapping virtual objects in augmented reality, e.g. [20], it becomes clear that understanding the presented information in such a case puts at least a mental strain on the user or may even keep her or him from seeing the relevant information. To the best of the author's knowledge so far no solution to this problem has been brought up for the case of procedural task support. One idea to solve this is to view the five layers as overlays on each other that pass the relevant information of the underlying layers through without obstructing it while adding more information. For example in a setup with an optical see-through HMD the spatial virtual layer needs to pass all the information that the user must perceive from the direct physical layer and may not cover it.

For the combination of the direct physical layer and the indirect physical layer this means that the latter may not obstruct any information that is needed by the user from the physical environment and has to pass this information through. For the virtual objects this can be done by positioning the objects from the spatial virtual layer around the areas of the physical layers that transport relevant information. The objects from the spatially referenced virtual layer must be arranged around the relevant parts of the physical layers and the spatial virtual layer. Finally the objects from the symbolic virtual layer need to be arranged around all the other layers.

The proposed order is defined by the decreasing spatial connection of the layers to the physical world. This way as much as possible spatial information is preserved and is easily perceptible by the user. Also the physical and virtual objects from the various layers are presented to the user without losing important parts of the view or causing unnecessary mental strain. The decision which information has to be passed through cannot be made in general but is defined by the task an augmented reality system supports. Though first ad hoc tests in a car door repair scenario showed promising results, a scientific evaluation is still to be made.

- **Consistency.** The layers must be in a consistent state as much as possible, i.e. it must be avoided to show conflicting information to the user. This means that for every manipulation or every change in one layer there must be either an automatism to update all the other layers or a simple function for the user to restore consistency. An automatism is preferred to keep the effort for the user low. This means for example that a delay may not be bigger than a certain amount of time, that only virtual objects may be shown which belong to the current work step or that only correct virtual representations of physical objects may be shown.

  One important factor is a consistent provision of depth cues. These allow the users to integrate the virtual objects into the physical world. While some cues are monocular, i.e. can be perceived with one eye, others are stereoscopic and need a different image for each eye. In [6, 9] one can find more information on the various depth cues and how to include them into augmented reality applications.

  Another factor is delay. When it becomes too large, each change in a layer or a viewpoint causes the user to perceive inconsistent information until all the layers and mappings of the layers are updated again. This creates a mental strain that heavily decreases the benefit of an augmented reality application [17]. For some users inconsistent sensory perceptions even leads to nausea that makes an augmented reality system unusable.

  Also the representation of objects in different layers must be consistent, e.g. a CAD model must actually match the corresponding physical part and a descriptive label may not give a non fitting description of a physical object. If this is not the case, it's likely that the application will be rejected by users [14].

- **Information Linking.** The user must be easily able to connect objects from each of the layers with their counterparts in other layers. When e.g. labels are assigned to physical parts, the user must easily be able to infer which label belongs to which part. This includes the correct visualization of depth, as previously described, connections of objects to each other and visual compensation of tracking errors.

One way to connect objects from different layers is to create an optical connection, e.g. via a direct line or a color coding. Among the virtual layers this is easily possible but from a virtual layer to a physical layer the mapping errors must be taken into account. Another way is to use context visualization, which means that parts of objects from other layers are also included in the graphical presentation of an object to create a context for the user [13]. Congruency is also possible as a means of information linking because humans perceive similarly looking objects as belonging together [15]. Also objects which are displayed close together are perceived as belonging together [15].

When it comes to tracking errors, strategies like context visualization [24] or the visualizations of error margins can be applied to ameliorate the negative effect that physical and virtual layers are randomly displaced with respect to one another. When the expected tracking errors get too large it can also help to decouple physical and virtual layers [24].

- **Position Preservation.** The positions of objects should be stable, i.e. a change of one layer or a changed superposition of the layers should only have a minimal impact on the position of the virtual objects. This is due to the reason that moved objects have to be found again by the user, which takes time and needs mental effort [1, 16]. Also when the scene changes, e.g. through a change of the current work step, the positions of the objects should change as little as possible for the same reasons as mentioned before. This is dependent on the reference system used for positioning the objects, which e.g. may be the user's head or the work place.
- **Orientation.** The user must be able to orient her- or himself at any time and easily infer where she or he is located relatively to the different layers. This means that she or he must see (i) the own position in the physical world, (ii) how the indirect physical layer is placed relatively to the physical world and (iii) where the relevant virtual and physical objects are located.

One important factor is the correct depth perception as already discussed for the criteria consistency. Also the user must be able see the surroundings, which is trivial in the case of hand held devices but must also be maintained for HMDs. In case of hand held devices the user must be able to relate the content of the device to the environment, which is not possible if the display gets too cluttered [12].

Also the user must be able to locate virtual objects outside of the viewing area. Techniques like an attention funnel can support this [3].

5 Conclusion and Next Steps

Augmented reality becomes a more and more important tool to provide information for procedural tasks but still it is not clear what an appropriate user interface of such a system must look like. In the previous sections the current state of an ongoing development of a novel framework to support information presentation in such user interfaces has been presented. Especially that it addresses the spatial properties of different types of information distinguishes it from existing approaches. However, many of the given criteria, especially visibility, need further research to clarify measures to implement them. Thus as a next step the criterion visibility will be further investigated and a user study will be conducted in which it will be tested with a real life task.

Under certain conditions some criteria need opposing measures to implement them. These so called design conflicts will be collected and it will be examined how conflicting requirements can be balanced. Also direct or indirect input methods are not yet considered in the framework while they are an integral part of any augmented reality user interface. Thus it will be further examined how they can be integrated and how this influences the presented layers and criteria.

References

1. Azuma, R., Furmanski, C.: Evaluating label placement for augmented reality view management. In: Proceedings of the 2nd International Symposium on Mixed and Augmented Reality (ISMAR 2003), pp. 66–75 (2003)
2. Bach, C., Scapin, D.: Ergonomic criteria adapted to human virtual environment interaction. In: Proceedings of the 15th French-speaking conference on human-computer interaction (IHM 2003), pp. 24–31 (2003)
3. Biocca, F., Tang, A., Owen, C., Xiao, F.: Attention funnel: omnidirectional 3D cursor for mobile augmented reality platforms. In: Proceedings of the SIGCHI Conference on Human Factors in Computing Systems (CHI 2006), pp. 1115–1122 (2006)
4. Bowman, D., Kruijff, E., LaViola, J., Poupyrev, I.: An introduction to 3-D user interface design. Presence: Teleoperators Virtual Environ. 10(1), 96–108 (2001)
5. Dünser, A., Grasset, R., Seichter, H., Billinghurst, M.: Applying HCI principles to AR systems design. In: Proceedings of the 2nd International Workshop on Mixed Reality User Interfaces: Specification, Authoring, Adaptation, pp. 37–42 (2007)
6. Furmanski, C., Azuma, R. Daily, M.: Augmented-reality visualizations guided by cognition: perceptual heuristics for combining visible and obscured information. In: Proceedings of the 1st International Symposium on Mixed and Augmented Reality (ISMAR 2002) (2002)
7. Gabbard, J., Swan, J.E., Hix, D., Kim, S., Fitch, G.: Active text drawing styles for outdoor augmented reality: a user-based study and design implications. In: Proceedings of the Virtual Reality Conference (VR 2007), pp. 35–42 (2007)
8. Gabbard, J., Swan, J.E., Hix, D.: The effects of text drawing styles, background textures, and natural lighting on text legibility in outdoor augmented reality. Teleoperators Virtual Environ. 15(1), 16–32 (2006)
9. Gabbard, J.: A taxonomy of usability characteristics in virtual environments. Master's thesis, Department of Computer Science, University of Western Australia (1997)
10. Galitz, W.: The Essential Guide to User Interface Design: An Introduction to GUI Design Principles and Techniques. Wiley, New York (1997)
11. International Organization for Standardization: ISO 9241 - Ergonomics of Human System Interaction (2015)
12. Julier, S., Baillot, Y., Brown, D., Lanzagorta, M.: Information filtering for mobile augmented reality. Comput. Graph. Appl. 22, 12–15 (2002)
13. Kalkofen, D., Mendez, E., Schmalstieg, D.: Interactive focus and context visualization for augmented reality. In: Proceedings of the 6th International Symposium on Mixed and Augmented Reality (ISMAR 2007), pp. 1–10 (2007)
14. Knöpfle, C., Weidenhausen, J., Chauvigné, L., Stock, I.: Template based authoring for augmented reality based service scenarios. In: Proceedings of the IEEE Virtual Reality Conference 2005, pp. 249–252. IEEE Computer Society, Los Alamitos, CA, USA (2005)

15. Koffka, K.: Principles of Gestalt Psychology. Lund Humphries, London (1935)
16. Kolers, P.A., Duchnicky, R.L., Ferguson, D.C.: Eye movement measurement of readability of crt displays. Hum. Factors 23, 517–527 (1981)
17. Kruijff, E., Swan, J., Feiner, S.: Perceptual issues in augmented reality revisited. In: Proceedings of the 9th International Symposium on Mixed and Augmented Reality (ISMAR 2010), pp. 3–12 (2010)
18. Leykin, A., Tuceryan, M.: Automatic determination of text readability over textured backgrounds for augmented reality systems. In: Proceedings of the 3rd International Symposoim on Mixed and Augmented Reality (ISMAR 2004), pp. 224–230 (2004)
19. Livingston, M.A., Gabbard, J.L., Swan II, J.E., Sibley, C.M., Barrow, J.H.: Basic perception in head-worn augmented reality displays. In: Huang, W., Alem, L., Livingston, M.A. (eds.) Human Factors in Augmented Reality Environments, pp. 35–65. Springer, Heidelberg (2013)
20. Livingston, M., Swan J.E., Gabbard, J., Höllerer, T., Hix, D., Julier, S., Baillot, Y., Brown, D.: Resolving multiple occluded layers in augmented reality. In: Proceedings of the 2nd International Symposium on Mixed and Augmented Reality (ISMAR 2003) (2003)
21. Peterson, S., Axholt, M., Ellis, S.: Label segregation by remapping stereoscopic depth in far-field augmented reality. In: Proceedings of the 7th International Symposium on Mixed and Augmented Reality (ISMAR 2008), pp. 143–152 (2008)
22. Peterson, S., Axholt, M., Ellis, S.: Technical section: objective and subjective assessment of stereoscopically separated labels in augmented reality. Comput. Graph. 33(1), 23–33 (2009)
23. Renkewitz, H., Kinder, V., Brandt, M., Alexander T.: Optimal font size for head-mounted-displays in outdoor applications. In: Proceedings of the 12th International Conference Information Visualisation (IV 2008), pp. 503–508 (2008)
24. Robertson, C., MacIntyre, B.: An evaluation of graphical context as a means for ameliorating the effects of registration error. In: Proceedings of the 6th International Symposium on Mixed and Augmented Reality (ISMAR 2007), pp. 99–108 (2007)
25. Shneiderman, B.: Designing the User Interface: Strategies for Effective Human-Computer Interaction, 3rd edn. Addison-Wesley Longman Publishing, Boston (1997)
26. Vincent, T., Nigay, L., Kurata, T.: Classifying handheld augmented reality: three categories linked by spatial mappings. In: Workshop on Classifying the Augmented Reality Presentation Space at ISMAR 2012 (2012)
27. Vincent, T., Nigay, L., Kurata, T.: Handheld augmented reality: spatial relationships and frames of reference. In: Workshop Designing Mobile Augmented Reality at MobileHCI 2013 (2013)
28. Webel, S., Bockholt, U., Engelke, T., Gavish, N., Olbrich, M., Preusche, C.: An augmented reality training platform for assembly and maintenance skills. Robot. Auton. Syst. 61(4), 398–403 (2013)
29. Webel, S., Bockholt, U., Keil, J.: Design criteria for AR-based training of maintenance and assembly tasks. In: Shumaker, R. (ed.) HCII 2011. LNCS, vol. 6773, pp. 123–132. Springer, Heidelberg (2011)

A Dynamic-Oriented Decision Support System for Group Interview Knapsack Problem

Sihem Ben Jouida$^{(\boxtimes)}$ and Saoussen Krichen

LARODEC Laboratory, Institut Supérieur de Gestion,
University of Tunis, Tunis, Tunisia
benjouida_sihem@hotmail.fr, saoussen.krichen@isg.rnu.tn

Abstract. We address in this paper a dynamic platform for knapsack selection that handles sequential arriving items looking for an optimized investment in terms of values and risk aversion. Investment items, specified by their costs and their values (e.g. stochastic modelling of the possible rewards that can be generated), arrive sequentially, by groups, over time to be later scheduled for an eventual investment. It is worth mentioning that items arrive over time to be firstly evaluated, then accepted or discarded, based on partial previous information about already observed items and no information about forthcoming ones. Such decision depends solely on the decision makers ranking of the arriving items. The decision support system (DSS) inputs the calibration of the decision makers preference levels and the whole set of problem parameters followed by their probability distributions. From a theoretical point of view, this problem can be viewed as an online knapsack problem, an NP-hard optimization problem solved using a dynamic programming algorithm. The proposed platform is experienced on numerous problem instances to show its effectiveness in generating profitable decisions.

Keywords: Online knapsack problem · Decision support system · Dynamic programming · Optimal stopping

1 Introduction

Modeling real world decision processes for resource allocation problems, in dynamic environments, is becoming a challenging research topic because of the uncertain feature when resource opportunities arrive over time. As a large panoply of decision problems are naturally dynamic, and the best decision depends upon the quality and the timing of the selected decision, we try in this paper, to study the online knapsack problem, in which case, a set of items' opportunities arrive sequentially over time and have to be evaluated whether to be accepted or discarded [1]. Online knapsack problem is of the most challenging optimization problems in combinatorial optimization [1–3], as it models a wide variety of real-world applications especially in the area of logistics where the decision is constructed concurrently with the arrival of new options [4]. Furthermore,

© Springer International Publishing Switzerland 2015
L.T. De Paolis and A. Mongelli (Eds.): AVR 2015, LNCS 9254, pp. 498–506, 2015.
DOI: 10.1007/978-3-319-22888-4_39

the online knapsack problem has already been considered with the optimal stopping problem (OSP) [3]. The OSP is a design of a large class of decision processes that involve items (or decision alternatives) to be presented one by one over time while ignoring the features of the upcoming items. Numerous problems can be modelled as an OSP namely the problem of hiring an employee among a large set of candidates, the problem of selecting an investment project, and purchasing assets in stock exchanges. This problem has been addressed for the first time by Wald in 1945 in the theory of sequential analysis, and investigated later in [5,6]. In its basic version, the problem requires a DM observing a sequence of items to select the best one where no recall of the previously inspected items is allowed. In fact, the DM decides immediately about the currently inspected item. If he beliefs that the current item is not interesting or expect to receive better items in next periods, he will reject the item and observe the next one. Otherwise if he is satisfied by the current one, the item will be selected and the DM stops receiving new items. The problem is then to maximise the probability of selecting the best item of the whole sequence and to stop at it. Within this context, [7] and [3] proposed the so-called *group selection problem(GSP)*, in which a DM is required to select a single item among a stream of items dispatched in groups. Each period of time, a group of items is observed to determine whether to retain its best item or to abandon it to observe the next group. Motivated by such ability, we propose, in this paper, to study a new generalization of the GSP where multiple items are to be selected and loading in knapsack with a limited capacity. The group of items is received each time step. No prior information is available about the potential items until they are received, except of their total number. Each new stage, a new group of items is received and the already inspected groups are recalled and reconsidered in the selection. However, we allow the recall of foregoing groups in next stages: items discarded in earlier stages are reconsidered in their groups in next stages. Items differ by their profit and weight and their values, while important for determining the items desirability. Once a group of items is received, the DM disposes of two options. Either to select the best item of the current group or refuse it. The DM's decision strategy on a given item is based on its expected utility when stopping (when selecting it), and its expected utility when continuing (when delaying it). Such situation allows the DM to select among a set of items the most rewarding subset in terms of expected values. Selected items are packed sequentially in the knapsack under its capacity constraint. The selection process is stopped when the amount to be invested (e.g. knapsack's capacity) is exhausted. Therefore, a decision rule is required to help decision makers (DMs) identify the best investment alternatives that maximize his total profit, dynamically, and without exceeding his investment amount. We propose a dynamic programming approach to solve the group interview knapsack problem problem using an online approach. We develop dynamic recursive equations that will allow us to compute the expected utilities of each item and then to decide whether to load a given item or to reject it. A Decision Support System, for the selection problem, is also developed. The DSS starts by the extraction of the items' features that correspond to the data entry for weights, values and the repartition of items in groups. Such data and packing information constitute the inputs for the resolution step. We illustrate the proposed approach by a numerical experimentation and analyze the obtained results.

The remainder of this article is organized as follows: the knapsack problem is described in Sect. 2. Section 3 develops the dynamic formulation of the problem and Sect. 4 states the DSS. An experimental study and an illustrative example are studied and analyzed in Sect. 5.

2   Problem Description

We consider a situation where a DM is involved in the selection, among a set of n items, the most rewarding subset in terms of expected value. Each time step, the DM receives a number of items simultaneously and evaluate them to determine the best item of the current group. Hence, a ranking of the items is required. An ultimate decision about that item should be taken without knowing anything about the upcoming groups of items. If the DM decides to select a current item, it will load it in a knapsack under the capacity constraint. Otherwise, it will be discarded and next group will be inspected. Already observed items can be re-examined, in later stages, before observing the next ones. This problem requires a dynamic decision strategy, as decisions should be made in real-time. Such dynamic decision, to accept or not an item, is based on an utility function defined by the DM. Following are the main features of the group interview knapsack problem:

- A DM with a fixed utility is involved in the selection process
- The DM is looking for the best subset to be packed in a knapsack
- A budget/knapsack of limited capacity
- n items are receiving sequentially by groups
- Groups of items arrive in a random order: all orders are equally likely
- Items' features (weight and value) are unknown a priori
- The DM evaluates the current group and ranks its items
- Each group of items is evaluated once arrived
- The recall of items is not allowed
- The process ends if knapsack capacity is over.

The searching process aims to select the fittest items of the whole sequence. To do so, the DM starts by evaluating a group of items and ranking its available items. Items' ranking indicates their desirability among the so far received items. Once items in the current group are ranked, the DM can select its best item. A decision stategy, based on utility function, is then used by the DM's to either accept or discard a given item. That is, if the expected utility when stopping exceeds the expected utility when continuing, the current item will be considered as an accepted, otherwise it is delayed to next stages and updating the problem parameters. The process is over, if the knapsack capacity is in its maximum, the number of items is zero or if the weight of all remaining items exceeds the remaining capacity.

3   Notation and Problem Formulation

This section starts with the enumeration of the relevant notations that are being used in this work. Then, we define and investigate the utility function of the DM.

Notation	Explanation
k	absolute rank of the current item
r	relative rank of the current item
$U(k)$	the utility of DM
$Ev(i, r)$	the expected utility of DM at group i
$Ev_s(i, r)$	the expected utility when stopping at group i
$Ev_c(i)$	the expected utility when continuing of DM
n	the total number of items
g	the number of groups
M_i	the number of items inspected until group i
m_i	the number of items contained in group i
w_{li}	the weight of item l in group i
v_{li}	the value of item l in group i

The concept of utility is fundamental when making decisions as it measures the DM's satisfaction of a given item. Consequently, the *utility function* is the numerical representation of the satisfaction experienced by having that item. For more insight into the utility function concept, we provide a brief overview of the potential utility function.

The Nothing but the Best (1-0). This utility function reflects the attitude of a DM that nothing but the best item satisfies him [5,6,8]. Accordingly, his utility function can be stated as:

$$U(k) = \begin{cases} 1 & \text{if } k = 1 \\ 0 & \text{otherwise} \end{cases} \tag{1}$$

where k is the absolute rank according to DM. The DM wins 1 if he selects the best item and 0 otherwise. As DM seeks to determine the appropriate time to stop a selection process, two terms deserve consideration: the expected utility when stopping and the expected utility when continuing.

The Individual Expected Utility When Stopping. This expected utility implies that the DM decided to accept the best item of the current group and is convinced that there will be no better items in the subsequent stages (or groups).

$Ev_s^p(i, r_p)$ is expressed in terms of the *relative rank* of the selected item in the ith group and the number of observed items M_i and it is expressed as:

$$Ev_s(i, r) = \sum_{a=r}^{M_g - M_i + r} U(a) \frac{\binom{a-1}{r-1}\binom{M_g - a}{M_i - r}}{\binom{M_g}{M_i}} \qquad (2)$$

The Individual Expected Utility When Continuing. It reports the expected reward of the DM if he chooses to discard the best item of the current group and to continue the selection process. When the current group is declined, the DMs observe the next group $i + 1$ where m_{i+1} item are to be evaluated. When the *nothing but the best* utility function is considered, the expected utility when continuing is:

$$Ev_c(i) = \frac{m_{i+1}}{M_{i+1}} \times Ev(i+1, 1) + \frac{M_i}{M_{i+1}} \times Ev_c(i+1) \qquad (3)$$

with m_i denotes the number of items in group i, and M_i is the number of items inspected until group i.

The Individual Expected Utility. The expected utility of each DM at stage i with a relative rank r is expressed in terms of his expected utility of stopping and the expected utility of continuing:

$$Ev(i, r) = \begin{cases} Ev_s(i, r)\chi_E + Ev_c(i)(1 - \chi_E) & \text{if } i < g \\ U(r) & \text{if } i = g, (r = k) \end{cases} \qquad (4)$$

where

- Each DM wishes to select the best item of the sequence.
- The indicator function χ_E is denoted by:

$$\chi_E = \begin{cases} 1 & \text{if } Ev_s(i, r) \geq Ev_c(i) \\ 0 & \text{otherwise} \end{cases} \qquad (5)$$

4   The DSS Design for Knapsack Problem with Dynamic Computations

We develop in the subsequent of the present section a DSS for solving the knapsack problem. The DSS starts by the extraction of the data from the stock market database that provides available items followed by their weights and expected values. Figure 2 shows the first screenshot of the DSS that corresponds to the data entry for the knapsack decision making problem. The input data correspond to the budget announced by the DM (e.g. knapsack capacity) and the set of available group of items. A thorough investigation of the generated solutions in terms of the expected utilities and the processing time illustrates how well the computational algorithm operates. The DSS outputs the solution to be later evaluated by the DM and visualised in a statistical format.

- *INTERFACE 1:* The first screenshot of the DSS, displayed in Fig. 1, inputs the groups of items followed by their weights and expected values
- *INTERFACE 2:* After fixing all problem and algorithmic parameters, the DSS proceeds by computing the accept/decline decision for each arriving items. Such dynamic decisions are based on expected rewards generated step by step along the sequential process Fig. 2.

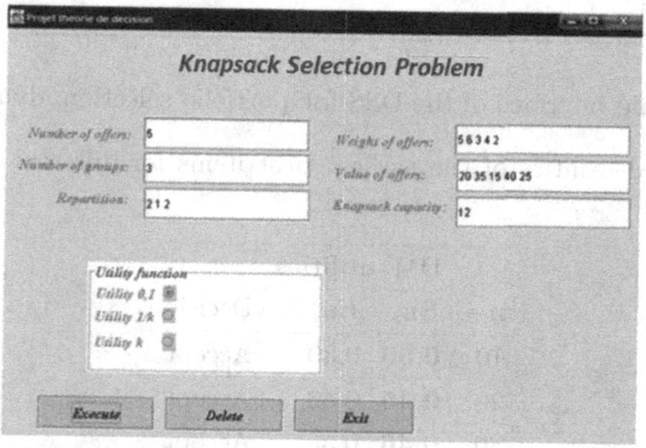

Fig. 1. The first interface of the DSS for knapsack selection: input data

5 Experimental Results

The experiments were conducted with different instances ranging in size from 10 to 150-item. For each problem, we generate randomly five repartitions of the items over a varying number of groups. Results provided here are the average of the number of runs of each problem size.

In our experiments, we assume that DM adopts the nothing but the best utility function. We report in Table 1 the expected utilities that allowed the first possible item to be reached and loaded in the knapsack, for each size of the problem. In other words, it contains the expected utilities of the best item at the earliest possible group. Both DM's expected utilities appear in the table as well as the corresponding individual decision. For instance, with $n = 30$ the expected utility of the DM to accpect item is greater than its expected utility to doscard it. Then the individual decision will be to accept the item (so it is a best compromise to be loaded in the knapsack.

The items to be invested are selected based on an expected rewards defined by the decision maker. For each problem, items arrive randomly in a dynamic way.

Fig. 2. The second interface of the DSS for portfolio selection: dynamic resolution

Table 1. Expected utilities of the earliest best items for different sizes of knapsack selection

	DM' utilities		
n	Eu_s	Eu_c	Decision
10	**0.50**	0.39	Accept
20	**0.45**	0.43	Accept
30	**0.46**	0.36)	Accept
40	**0.50**	0.38	Accept
50	0.40	**0.41**	Reject
60	**0.66**	0.30	Accept
70	0.42	**0.43**	Reject
80	**0.50**	0.40	Accept
90	**0.50**	0.30	Accept
100	**0.42**	0.42	Accept

A permutation is a sequence of absolute ranks of the arriving investment items. Table displays results for each problem size: we give the capacity of the knapsack, the values and the weights of the packed offers, the number of iterations until the end of the process and in the last column we have the remaining capacity of the knapsack when the process is over. We also notice from Table 2 that the knapsack capacity and the value of the packed items are in there maximums, when the items are dispatched in groups with different sizes and the execution time of the charging process are less that the problem when the items are given one by one (see the instances where $n = 10$ and $n = 20$). Furthermore, we can conclude that the cumulative values of the accepted offers is proportional to the

Table 2. Expected results for different sizes of the final knapsack selection

n	Knapsak capacity	Values	Weights	Number of iteration	Remaning capaity
10	25	125	25	6	0%
20	50	257	50	11	0%
30	70	265	68	13	2.85%
40	90	345	88	15	3.22%
50	110	361	92	18	3.42%
60	130	386	98	19	3.57%
70	150	405	124	21	3.94%
80	170	425	146	24	3.85%
90	190	460	168	27	4.11%
100	210	500	189	30	4.72%
Avg					3.64%

values of the best items inside the first groups. Something that is explained by the fact that the offers of the first groups are accepted, under the stopping rule and the knapsack capacity, in the first position. We can also read from Table 2 that our approach yields to load the knapsack in an optimal way and that the remaining capacity which assumed to be in average 3.64 % for all considered instances.

6   Conclusion

We proposed, in this paper, a DSS for the knapsack selection problem where a DM is about choosing a set of investment alternatives. Items arrive by groups in a random order, all orders are equally likely. We have written the dynamic equations and performed a dynamic interactive approach to solve the online problem that incorporates a stopping rule at each stage of the loading process. Once an item is selected by the two DMs under the stopping rule and the knapsack capacity, the sequence is updated by decrementing the problem size. The DSS displays the optimal strategy to be followed for each problem instance. Experimental results show that the optimal policy is strongly influenced by the problem inputs and the dynamic approach can operate only on small-sized instances. Thats why a future research can address the embedment of a heuristic approach that generates a near optimal policy in a concurrencial running time.

References

1. Bazgan, C., Hugot, H., Vanderpooten, D.: Solving efficiently the 0–1 multi-objective knapsack problem. Comput. Oper. Res. **36**(1), 260–279 (2009)
2. Babaioff, M., Immorlica, N., Kempe, D.: A knapsack secretary problem with applications. In: APPROX 2007 (2007)
3. Chun, Y.H., Moskowitz, H., Plante, R.D.: Dynamic programming formulation of the group interview problem with a general utility function. Eur. J. Oper. Res. **78**(1), 81–92 (1994)

4. Kleywegt, A.J., Papastavrou, J.D.: The dynamic and stochastic knapsack problem. Oper. Res. **46**, 17–35 (1998)
5. Dynkin, E.B.: Optimal choice of the stopping moment of a markov process. Dokl. Akad. Nauk. SSSR **150**, 238–240 (1963)
6. Lindley, D.V.: Dynamic programming and decision theory. Appl. Stat. **10**, 39–51 (1961)
7. Chun, Y.H.: Optimal partitioning of groups in selecting the best choice. Comput. Oper. Res. **28**, 1367–1386 (2001)
8. Gilbert, J.P., Mosteller, F.: Recognizing the maximum of a sequence. J. Am. Stat. Assoc. **61**(313), 35–73 (1966)

Virtual Reality as a Cross-Domain Language in Collaborative Environments

Carlo Vizzi[✉]

ALTEC S.p.A., Turin, Italy
carlo.vizzi@altecspace.it

Abstract. Working in the space domain means working in a complex and challenging domain, but also dealing with huge amount of datasets and several actors (engineers, scientists, discipline experts, etc.). To fully exploit people's know-how and all the available data, it is necessary to find a way to ease the communication and collaboration among the actors involved.

Virtual Reality is the solution. It enables new methods and techniques to create a collaborative environment where all the experts can join their effort for a common objective: the analysis, visualization and dissemination of data and information.

ALTEC strongly believes in this vision and it is developing its own Virtual Reality Laboratory in order to support programs and activities already ongoing in the company, but also to enable new researches, collaborations, projects and a better dissemination of achievements and results.

ALTEC is also participating to the EU FP7 CROSS DRIVE project which aims at creating innovative tools and techniques for the visualization and sharing of exploration data to strength collaborative science data analysis and real-time operations. The Mission Control Center (MCC) of the CROSS DRIVE Collaborative Environment will be hosted in ALTEC exploiting the functionalities of ALTEC VR-Lab.

ALTEC VR-Lab and the work done within CROSS DRIVE project are described in this paper.

Keywords: Virtual reality · Collaborative environment · Space data analysis · Cross-Domain collaboration

1 Introduction

ALTEC – Advanced Logistics Technology Engineering Center – is the Italian center of excellence for the provision of engineering and logistics services to support operations and utilization of the International Space Station (ISS) and the development and implementation of planetary exploration missions. ALTEC services range from engineering and logistics support, training of astronauts, to support experiments in biomedicine in particular, the processing of scientific data, the development and management of the ground segment of space programs and the promotion of space culture.

© Springer International Publishing Switzerland 2015
L.T. De Paolis and A. Mongelli (Eds.): AVR 2015, LNCS 9254, pp. 507–514, 2015.
DOI: 10.1007/978-3-319-22888-4_40

This variety of activities leads not only to the production of huge amount of space exploration data, but also to the simultaneous involvement of several actors such as engineers, scientists, discipline experts and developers. Sometimes, this diversity in types of data and experts' background makes difficult the communication and collaboration and this lead to the not fully exploitation of the collected data. This situation triggers questions like: How to exploit data? How to analyze and merge different kind of data? How to make data understandable for non-expert people?

ALTEC strongly believes that Virtual Reality is the right means to improve data analysis and the exploitation of space-based observations data providing new methods and systems for enabling a better collaborative environment.

2   Virtual Reality in ALTEC

Virtual Reality is a very effective tool in scientific and educational field since it eases the access to complex data and information making the experience more entertaining and understandable. The benefits of Collaborative Virtual Environments have been implemented in various industrial fields allowing Real-Time multi-user collaborative work among people from different disciplines and with different backgrounds.

Exploiting the benefits of advanced Immersive Virtual Environments (IVE) has been recognized as an important interaction paradigm to facilitate future space exploration. For this reason, ALTEC is working on the creation of its own Virtual Reality Laboratory (VR-Lab) in order to not only support the activities ongoing in the company (programs and research projects), but also to enables new collaborations, projects, researches and a better dissemination of data and results.

ALTEC VR-Lab foresees two different set-ups:

- Fixed Configuration: it is a Virtual Reality Room where 3D scenes and simulations are displayed to the audience projecting the images that are elaborated by a cluster of PCs on a PowerWall by means of a stereoscopic projector. The tracking system allows the interaction with the scenes. The layout of the VR-Lab fixed configuration is showed in Fig. 1.
- Mobile Configuration: it is a simplified version of the fixed configuration. It is composed by a 4 K 3D-TV, a Workstation and mobile tracking system. Such a configuration allows moving the 3D environment wherever it is needed (Control Rooms, meeting rooms, expositions, etc.).

To enhance and open the exploitation of space data, and also data from different domains, to a broader audience, it is necessary to increase the number of experts involved in a project or mission since the early phases, providing them a new approach for collaborating. The success of this phase shall lead to open new markets, find new possible customers and new partners for processing, analyzing or exploiting data.

This vision led ALTEC to initiate and then actively take part in the CROSS DRIVE project.

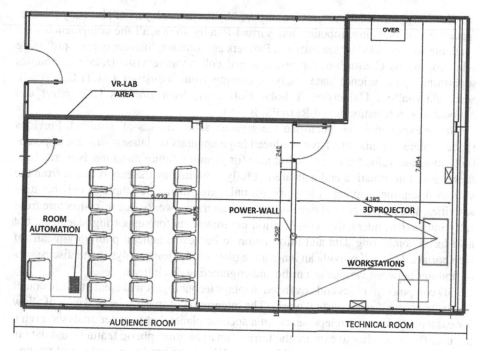

Fig. 1. VR-LAB fixed configuration layout

3 Cross Drive

3.1 Objectives

CROSS DRIVE[1]– Collaborative Rover Operations and Planetary Science Analysis System based on Distributed Remote and Interactive Virtual Environments - is an EU FP7 project started in January 2014. The project aims at creating innovative tools and techniques for the visualization and sharing of exploration data to strength collaborative science data analysis and real-time operations. CROSS DRIVE main objectives are:

- Mobilize the best expertise in the field of science data collection and analysis to study and propose synergic combinations and benchmarking of selected data set.
- Deploy a core team of 3D visualization experts, computing and Virtual Reality Collaborative systems to prepare an innovative Framework for data analysis and sharing.
- Test and exercise the proposed system by using actual data set.

[1] The research depicted in this presentation has received funding from the European Union Seventh Framework Programme (FP7/2007-2013) under grant agreement n° 607177.

The Consortium of the project is composed by the main players of planetary science, space mission planning, robotics and Virtual Reality so that all the competencies are available and provided by the partners. Partners are from six different nations providing a heterogeneous Consortium for research and collaborative visualization techniques supporting space science data analysis coming from industries (ALTEC, TAS-I), academia (Salford University, Tohoku University, John Hopkins University) and national research institutes (DLR, IAPS, BISA).

Space exploration has been one the greatest achievements of mankind. Previous space exploration missions have produced huge amounts of datasets that are of potentially immense value for research, but also for planning future missions. Nevertheless, these valued information and data are not fully exploited by the expert teams from the various disciplines leaving little scope for unlocking their value through collaborative activities. The project aims at developing a collaborative workspace infrastructure from fully immersive, interactive visualization environments for supporting scientists, but also for disseminating data and information to interested general public by means of web portals. This will provide an innovative platform for joint analyses and discussions of findings between various scientific and engineering disciplines.

3D computer graphics and advanced displays technologies will create the illusion of being "teleported" into a virtual world. The integration of space science data will allow for example to simulate telepresence on a specific planet that is under analysis, giving the user the possibility to explore the terrain, analyze atmospheric features and data in the dimensions of space and time. Moreover, VR can be used as a medium of telepresence simulating the "sense of being there" increasing awareness, vividness, interactivity and media richness.

3.2 Collaborative Workspace

The creation of a collaborative workspace platform is the key idea of the CROSS DRIVE project. It will provide access to remote scientists and engineers, from different domains, to collaborate in analyzing and exploring space data. Space exploration is a very complex and challenging domain, so CROSS DRIVE can be considered a project that addresses collaboration under extremely challenging conditions requiring a high degree of collaboration among remote experts to interpret and analyze extremely large complex data sources (atmospheric, terrain, engineering, etc.), but also to make real-time critical decisions involving real-time data.

The purpose of the platform proposed in the project is to enable the collaboration in a shared 3D environment among scientific and engineering teams distributed across the world in order to interact simultaneously with the displayed data.

CROSS DRIVE aims at investigating three different workspaces in order to enable different forms of collaboration in different contexts:

- Core Collaboration Workspace: for the core mission team
- External Public Workspace: for engaging selected scientists
- Web Portal: for a broader dissemination and engagement of scientific community.

This paper is focused on the Core Collaboration Workspace, so the External Public Workspace and the Web Portal Workspace will not be discussed in further details.

The platform integrates various distributed data sources, displays systems, simulations systems and HW components. The **Core Collaboration Workspace**, represented in Fig. 2, is made up by three remote sites connected via a private network to a central premise called Mission Control Center (MCC). The MCC is the core of the platform and it is responsible for the coordination and supervision of the collaborative sessions. The remote sites represent the facilities of two science teams (Science Home Bases, SHB1, 2) responsible for specific science analysis and computations, and the Engineering Support Centre (ESC) responsible for monitoring and verification of the spacecraft subsystems' performance. Each premise has its own Virtual Reality environment in order to allow the interactive data sharing, computing and simultaneous multi-users visualization. The four sites, during their joined activities, are supported by dedicated software and tools for: 3D interactive visualization; Telepresence and collaborative workspace to allow immersive and interactive teleconferences and data sharing; real-time computing and comparison tools to provide partial updates of the science data-sets and simulations; data archiving and sharing of both real-time and off-line computations.

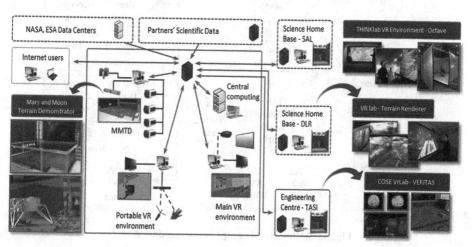

Fig. 2. CROSS DRIVE core collaboration workspace

Within the CROSS DRIVE project, two 3D visualization systems, developed by two partners of the Consortium, will be used in order to support the space missions: the Terrain Render (from DLR-SST) and the rover spacecraft simulator (from TAS-I).

The terrain visualization Framework is an advanced rendering and data management system that allows to interactively exploring massive terrain datasets. It enables geological studies and mapping of planetary surface in a spatial and intuitive manner.

The rover spacecraft simulator is an application contained in TAS-I VR Framework called VERITAS (Virtual Environment Research in Thales Alenia Space). VERITAS is a platform containing various applications focused on the space domain, such as the trajectory visualization of celestial bodies and spacecraft; visualization of radiation on a spacecraft and around Earth; the physics simulation of a rover moving on planetary surface and the simulation of environmental features (wind, dust, atmosphere scattering, and gravity).

The features of these two systems will be combined in order to get a unified visualization environment at the same time in order to get a 3D scene containing rover/spacecraft, location/status/payload and terrain cartography and atmosphere.

The system is also composed by three local computing and archiving systems connected to a central one, located at the MCC in order to store local user data (raw data and pre-computed results) and results of local real-time computations. The architecture of the platform and the data flow are represented in Fig. 3.

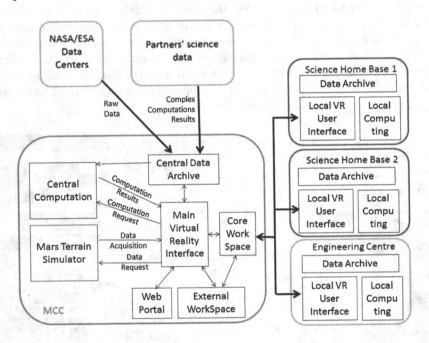

Fig. 3. Architectural components and data flow

The MCC will be located at ALTEC and it exploits the functionalities of ALTEC VR-Lab facilities. The fixed set-up will be used for hosting collaborative sessions, visualization and review of the results, while the mobile set-up will be used for the emulation of the rover operation and can be moved into the ALTEC Mars Terrain Simulator facility: a 20x20 m testing area and control room used for rover's localization, mobility and control test.

The MCC will host different teams of experts that will collaborate in a complex and stressful environment never experienced before in European missions. Three main types of events will be expected in the VR-Lab:

- Virtual meetings: when users present to the entire team the results of previous analysis and operative sessions, interacting with already archived datasets and discussing the outcomes with other users.
- Science Sessions: when users visualize data, execute real-time computations and interact with results and previously archived datasets.
- Operative Sessions: when users visualize data, execute computations, interact with datasets, provide commands to the spacecraft and monitor their correct connection.

At the moment of the submission of this paper, the CROSS-DRIVE project is still half way and the first tests on the scenarios will be implemented in the next months.

4   Conclusions

The complexity of data coming from exploration space missions and the variety of teams involved made, up to now, these kinds of activities very difficult leaving little scope for unlocking knowledge and dissemination of data and information. The usage of Virtual Reality as a Cross-Domain Language will facilitate the communication among the actors involved and the understanding of the datasets under analysis.

VR provides a realistic sensory experience of the Virtual Environment by means of 3D environments and applications. VR can adapt to different styles and needs in learning and understanding processes since people take information differently, according to their backgrounds, their knowledge of the specific topic and their degree of interests. In such a way, experts from a specific domain can access and understand complex data and information coming from others domains, as well as students and public audience can understand concepts and topics through a more involving and appealing experience. Presenting information in 3D allows viewing a certain topic from an immersed viewpoint with the possibility to interact with the information itself. The process of learning and understanding abstract concept data or other kinds of information is dramatically reduced using VR.

ALTEC experience in CROSS DRIVE and other Virtual Reality researches will be essential to increase the internal know-how on VR and to establish the basis for new project and collaboration not only in the space domain, but also enabling new business and activities in different domains.

References

1. www.altecspace.it
2. www.cross-drive.eu
3. Millar, R.: Why is science hard to learn. J. Comput. Assist. Learn. 7(2), 66–74 (2008)
4. Donalek, C., Djorgovsky, S.G., Cioc, A., Wang, A., Zhang, J., Lawler, E., Yeh, S., Mahabal, A., Graham, M., Drake, A., Davidoff, S., Norri, J.S., Longo, G.: Immersive and collaborative data visualization using virtual reality platforms. In: IEEE International Conference on Big Data (2014)

5. Thronson, H., Valinia, A., Garvin, J., Lester, D., Schmidt, G., Fong, T., Wilcox, B.: Space exploration via telepresence: the case for synergy between science and human exploration. In: Exploration Telerobotics Symposium, NASA Goddard Space Flight Center, 2–3 May 2012
6. Matsukura, R., et al.: VizGrid: collaborative visualization grid environment for natural interaction between remote researchers. FUJITSU Sci. Tech. J. **40**(2), 205–216 (2004)
7. Wong, G., Wong, V.: Virtual reality in space exploration. Surprise 96 J. 4, http://www.doc.ic.ac.uk/~nd/surprise_96/journal/vol4/kcgw/report.html
8. Merchant, J.: Telepresence for the human exploration and development of space. http://theinstitute.ieee.org/technology-focus/technology-topic/telepresence-for-the-human-exploration-and-development-of-space484
9. http://futurehumanevolution.com/visualizing-the-universe-virtual-reality
10. https://www.youtube.com/watch?v=DXT-ynvI3Lg

Author Index

Abidi, Mohamed-Amine   301
Aloisio, Giovanni   51
Ambrosino, Fiorenzo   267
Amirkozhanova, Mira   475
Amrenova, Assem   475
Andaluz, Víctor H.   355
Apostolakis, Konstantinos Cornelis   371
Argese, Francesco   267
Arthana, Ketut Resika   71
Avveduto, Giovanni   332
Baert, Patrick   301
Bakytkazy, Tannur   475
Baldiris, Silvia   17
Bellone, Mauro   287
Beltramello, Olga   188
Bene, Pasquale   267
Bergamasco, Massimo   220, 409
Bernabei, Giorgio   449
Boanta, Catalin   482
Brisan, Cornel   482
Brondi, Raffaello   384

Caggianese, Giuseppe   399
Cannoletta, Danilo   449
Carrozzino, Marcello   220, 332, 384, 409
Castro, Silvia   89
Cattin, Philippe C.   255
Charrotton, Yannick   199
Chionna, Francesco   287
Chiroiu, Veturia   482
Cirillo, Piero   287
Clini, Paolo   38
Colizzi, Lucio   267
Colonnese, Valerio   467
Colosi, Francesca   25
Copelli, Chiara   244
Corallo, Angelo   449
Cosma, Leonardo   267
Côté, Stéphane   63
Crisnapati, Padma Nyoman   71

Daineko, Yevgeniya   458
Daras, Petros   371
Darmawiguna, I. Gede Mahendra   71
De Amicis, Raffaele   168

De Paolis, Lucio Tommaso   51, 125, 233, 244, 432
Degache, Francis   199
Derstroff, Adrian   135
Dilberovic, Milan   135
Dmitriyev, Viktor   458

Epicoco, Italo   51
Erdt, Marius   109
Erra, Ugo   467

Fabregat, Ramon   17
Faita, Claudia   220, 409
Fauquex, Aurélien   199
Fermakhan, Kuantay   475
Fina, Marco   267
Franke, Andre   135
Frischknecht, Rolf   199
Frontoni, Emanuele   25, 38

Gabdullina, Asylgul T.   475
Gabellone, Francesco   3
Galli, Valerio   449
Gallo, Luigi   399
Garrido, Raynel Mendoza   17
Gazcón, Nicolás   89
Girard-Vallée, Antoine   63
Giyenko, Andrey   458
Gobron, Stéphane Claude   199
Greco, Antonella   432

Hebborn, Anna Katharina   109, 135
Herrmann, Heiko   233
Hieber, Simone E.   255
Höhner, Nils   135

Ilea, Lucian   482
Invitto, Sara   125
Ipalakova, Madina   458

Jiménez, Danilo Vargas   17
Jouida, Sihem Ben   498

Kaibar, Argynbek   475
Kalochrsitianakis, Michael   344
Kapetanakis, Kostas   344

Kechiche, Marwene   301
Kesiman, Made Windu Antara   71
Kontakis, Konstantinos   344
Krechel, Patrick   135
Krichen, Saoussen   498
Kusyman, Anar   475

Lamberti, Fabrizio   314
Lauria, Michel   199
Livatino, Salvatore   432
Lombardo, Roberto   449
Lorenzini, Cristian   220, 409

Maci, Simone   449
Malamos, Athanasios G.   344
Malinverni, Eva Savina   25
Mancini, Marco   51
Manuri, Federico   314
Martini, Andrea   267
Mele, Francesca   51
Melià-Seguí, Joan   420
Moldabekov, Zhandos M.   475
Müller, Stefan   109, 135
Müller, Tobias   490

Nattamai Sekar, Lakshmi Prabha   188
Neroni, Pietro   399
Notaro, Antonio   449

Orazi, Roberto   25
Ortiz, Jessica S.   355

Palmerius, Karljohan Lundin   151
Palmieri, Vito   287
Paolis, Lucio Tommaso De   233
Paravati, Gianluca   314
Pastorelli, Emiliano   233
Pezold, Simon   255
Pezzolla, Pietro   314
Pierdicca, Roberto   25, 38
Piumatti, Giovanni   314
Pous, Rafael   420

Prandi, Federico   168
Prinz, Lisa   135

Quattrini, Ramona   38

Rakhimzhanova, Nazgul   458
Rashid, Zulqarnain   420
Reo, Giovanni   267
Ricciardi, Francesco   233, 244

Samini, Ali   151
Sanchéz, Jorge S.   355
Sanna, Andrea   314
Santos, Alexander   188
Schmitt, Carl   199
Schneider, Adrian   255
Serik, Kaster   475
Simões, Bruno   168
Spada, Italo   125
Sportillo, Daniele   332
Steiakaki, Malvina   344
Sturari, Mirco   38
Sunarya, I. Made Gede   71
Szirmai, Astrid   135

Tanca, Camilla   409
Tecchia, Franco   220, 332
Thalmann, Peter   255
Toscano, Rosario   301

Vanni, Federico   409
Vecchio, Pietro   51
Vizzi, Carlo   507

Weigend, Fabian   135
Wenk, Nicolas   199

Zannini, Nicolas   199
Zhukeshov, Anuar M.   475
Zingaretti, Primo   25, 38
Zocco, Alessandro   432
Zocco, Matteo D.   432

Printed in the United States
By Bookmasters